collections

Houghton
Mifflin
Harcourt

collections

GRADE 10

Program Consultants:

Kylene Beers

Martha Hougen

Carol Jago

William L. McBride

Erik Palmer

Lydia Stack

Kylene Beers Nationally known lecturer and author on reading and literacy; 2011 recipient of the Conference on English Leadership Exemplary Leader Award; coauthor of *Notice and Note: Strategies for Close Reading*; former president of the National Council of Teachers of English. Dr. Beers is the nationally known author of *When Kids Can't Read: What Teachers Can Do* and coeditor of *Adolescent Literacy: Turning Promise into Practice*, as well as articles in the *Journal of Adolescent and Adult Literacy*. Former editor of *Voices from the Middle*, she is the 2001 recipient of NCTE's Richard W. Halley Award, given for outstanding contributions to middle-school literacy. She recently served as Senior Reading Researcher at the Comer School Development Program at Yale University as well as Senior Reading Advisor to Secondary Schools for the Reading and Writing Project at Teachers College.

Martha Hougen National consultant, presenter, researcher, and author. Areas of expertise include differentiating instruction for students with learning difficulties, including those with learning disabilities and dyslexia; and teacher and leader preparation improvement. Dr. Hougen has taught at the middle school through graduate levels. Recently her focus has been on working with teacher educators to enhance teacher and leader preparation to better meet the needs of all students. Currently she is working with the University of Florida at the Collaboration for Effective Educator Development, Accountability, and Reform Center (CEEDAR Center) to improve the achievement of students with disabilities by reforming teacher and leader licensure, evaluation, and preparation. She has led similar efforts in Texas with the Higher Education Collaborative and the College & Career Readiness Initiative Faculty Collaboratives. In addition to peer-reviewed articles, curricular documents, and presentations, Dr. Hougen has published two college textbooks: *The Fundamentals of Literacy Assessment and Instruction Pre-K–6* (2012) and *The Fundamentals of Literacy Assessment and Instruction 6–12* (2014).

Carol Jago Teacher of English with 32 years of experience at Santa Monica High School in California; author and nationally known lecturer; and former president of the National Council of Teachers of English. Currently serves as Associate Director of the California Reading and Literature Project at UCLA. With expertise in standards assessment and secondary education, Ms. Jago is the author of numerous books on education, including *With Rigor for All* and *Papers, Papers, Papers*, and is active with the California Association of Teachers of English, editing its scholarly journal *California English* since 1996. Ms. Jago also served on the planning committee for the 2009 NAEP Framework and the 2011 NAEP Writing Framework.

William L. McBride Curriculum specialist. Dr. McBride is a nationally known speaker, educator, and author who now trains teachers in instructional methodologies. He is coauthor of *What's Happening?*, an innovative, high-interest text for middle-grade readers, and author of *If They Can Argue Well, They Can Write Well*. A former reading specialist, English teacher, and social studies teacher, he holds a master's degree in reading and a doctorate in curriculum and instruction from the University of North Carolina at Chapel Hill. Dr. McBride has contributed to the development of textbook series in language arts, social studies, science, and vocabulary. He is also known for his novel *Entertaining an Elephant*, which tells the story of a veteran teacher who becomes reinspired with both his profession and his life.

Erik Palmer Veteran teacher and education consultant based in Denver, Colorado. Author of *Well Spoken: Teaching Speaking to All Students* and *Digitally Speaking: How to Improve Student Presentations*. His areas of focus include improving oral communication, promoting technology in classroom presentations, and updating instruction through the use of digital tools. He holds a bachelor's degree from Oberlin College and a master's degree in curriculum and instruction from the University of Colorado.

Lydia Stack Internationally known teacher educator and author. She is involved in a Stanford University project to support English Language Learners, *Understanding Language*. The goal of this project is to enrich academic content and language instruction for English Language Learners (ELLs) in grades K-12 by making explicit the language and literacy skills necessary to meet the Common Core State Standards (CCSS) and Next Generation Science Standards. Her teaching experience includes twenty-five years as an elementary and high school ESL teacher, and she is a past president of Teachers of English to Speakers of Other Languages (TESOL). Her awards include the TESOL James E. Alatis Award and the San Francisco STAR Teacher Award. Her publications include *On Our Way to English, Visions: Language, Literature, Content*, and *American Themes*, a literature anthology for high school students in the ACCESS program of the U.S. State Department's Office of English Language Programs.

Additional thanks to the following Program Reviewers

Rosemary Asquino

Sylvia B. Bennett

Yvonne Bradley

Leslie Brown

Haley Carroll

Caitlin Chalmers

Emily Colley-King

Stacy Collins

Denise DeBonis

Courtney Dickerson

Sarah Easley

Phyllis J. Everette

Peter J. Foy Sr.

Carol M. Gibby

Angie Gill

Mary K. Goff

Saira Haas

Lisa M. Janeway

Robert V. Kidd Jr.

Kim Lilley

John C. Lowe

Taryn Curtis MacGee

Meredith S. Maddox

Cynthia Martin

Kelli M. McDonough

Megan Pankiewicz

Linda Beck Pieplow

Molly Pieplow

Mary-Sarah Proctor

Jessica A. Stith

Peter Swartley

Pamela Thomas

Linda A. Tobias

Rachel Ukleja

Lauren Vint

Heather Lynn York

Leigh Ann Zerr

COLLECTION 1
Ourselves and Others

KEY LEARNING OBJECTIVES

Support inferences about theme.
Analyze character motivations.
Analyze impact of word choice on tone.
Analyze how author creates tension
  through pacing.
Analyze impact of cultural background
  on point of view.

Cite text evidence to support inferences.
Analyze order of ideas.
Determine purpose and point of view.
Analyze seminal U.S. documents.

Close Reader

eBook *Explore It!*

 Video Links   **Visit hmhfyi.com**
for current articles and
informational texts.

COLLECTION **2**
The Natural World

KEY LEARNING OBJECTIVES	Support inferences about theme.	Determine figurative, connotative, and technical meanings.
	Determine theme through objective summary.	Analyze author's claim.
	Determine figurative meanings.	Determine author's purpose.
	Analyze text structure.	
	Determine a central idea.	

Close Reader

Image Credits: ©Carlos Sanchez Pereyra/JAI/Corbis

eBook *Explore It!*

▶ **Video Links**   **Visit hmhfyi.com** for current articles and informational texts.

Responses to Change

KEY LEARNING OBJECTIVES	Cite text evidence to support inferences.	Analyze cause-and-effect order.
	Support inferences about theme.	Determine technical meanings.
	Analyze representations in different mediums.	Analyze development of ideas.

Close Reader

Image Credits: ©Dennis Novak/Photographer's Choice/Getty Images

eBook *Explore It!*

 Video Links   **Visit hmhfyi.com** for current articles and informational texts.

COLLECTION 4

How We See Things

KEY LEARNING OBJECTIVES

Paraphrase and summarize ideas.
Analyze poetic structure.
Analyze representations in different mediums.
Cite text evidence to support analysis.

Analyze development of ideas.
Understand scientific words and ideas.
Analyze effects of author's choices about structure.

Close Reader

eBook *Explore It!*

▶ **Video
Links**

 Visit hmhfyi.com
for current articles and
informational texts.

COLLECTION 5

Absolute Power

KEY LEARNING OBJECTIVES

Analyze interactions between character and theme.
Support inferences about how word choice affects tone.

Analyze representations of a scene.
Analyze how an author draws on Shakespeare.
Analyze historical text.
Analyze use of rhetoric in an argument.

Close Reader

DRAMA
from The Tragedy of Macbeth, Act I   William Shakespeare

Image Credits: ©Ruthven Carstairs/Alamy Images

eBook *Explore It!*

▶ **Video Links**   **Visit hmhfyi.com**
for current articles and
informational texts.

Hard-Won Liberty

KEY LEARNING OBJECTIVES		
Analyze how tone contributes to theme.		Analyze use of rhetoric in an argument.
Analyze interactions between character and theme.		Analyze accounts of a subject in different mediums.
Analyze evidence and ideas in a functional document.		Analyze argument in a seminal document.

Image Credits: Calle II, 2008 (oil on canvas) ©Bill Jacklin/Private Collection/The Bridgeman Art Library

Close Reader

eBook *Explore It!*

 Video Links   **Visit hmhfyi.com** for current articles and informational texts.

Student Resources

Connecting to Your World

Every time you read something, view something, write to someone, or react to what you've read or seen, you're participating in a world of ideas. You do this every day, inside the classroom and out. These skills will serve you not only at home and at school, but eventually in your career.

The digital tools in this program will tap into the skills you already use and help you sharpen those skills for the future.

Start your exploration at my.hrw.com

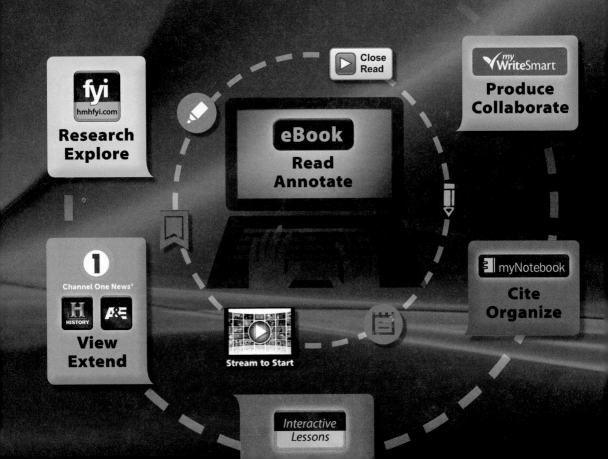

fyi
hmhfyi.com
Research Explore

Close Read

eBook
Read Annotate

✓ my WriteSmart
Produce Collaborate

❶ Channel One News®
HISTORY   A&E
View Extend

Stream to Start

myNotebook
Cite Organize

Interactive Lessons

INTERACTIVE LESSONS

Writing and Speaking & Listening

Communication in today's world requires quite a variety of skills. To express yourself and win people over, you have to be able to write for print, for online media, and for spoken presentations. To collaborate, you have to work with people who might be sitting right next to you or at the other end of an Internet connection.

Available Only in Your eBook

Interactive Lessons

These interactive lessons will help you master the skills needed to become an expert communicator.

What Does a Strong Argument Look Like?

Read this argument and answer the questions about how the writer states and supports his position.

Tip

Pitching Perfect Pitch
by José Alvarez

Did you know that when you are listening to your favorite vocalist, you might be hearing a computer-generated pitch? Many record companies use pitch-correction software to ensure that their performers are pitch-perfect. While perfectionism is an admirable goal, there is a fine line between using technology to enhance music and using it to make performers into something they're not. Whether recording in the studio or playing a live performance, musicians should not use pitch-correction software. ●

Music production has become a digital experience. Producers use software to cut and paste pieces of music together, just like you cut and paste words together in your word-processing software. ○ When editing these different things together digitally, slight imperfections can occur where the pieces are joined. Enter the correction software. What began as a method to streamline the digital editing process has turned into an almost industry-wide standard of altering a musician"s work. "Think of it like plastic surgery," says a Grammy-winning recording engineer.

What is the writer's position, or **claim,** on the use of pitch-correction software?

- Musicians should learn to live with their imperfections.
- ✓ Musicians should never use the software.
- Musicians should use the software to enhance live performances only.

Writing Arguments
Master the art of proving your point.

W 1, W 10

Interactive Lessons

1. Introduction
2. What Is a Claim?
3. Support: Reasons and Evidence
4. Building Effective Support
5. Creating a Coherent Argument
6. Persuasive Techniques
7. Formal Style
8. Concluding Your Argument

Writing Informative Texts
Shed light on complex ideas and topics.

W 2, W 10

Interactive Lessons

1. Introduction
2. Developing a Topic
3. Organizing Ideas
4. Introductions and Conclusions
5. Elaboration
6. Using Graphics and Multimedia
7. Precise Language and Vocabulary
8. Formal Style

Writing Narratives
A good storyteller can always capture an audience.

W 3, W 10

Interactive Lessons

1. Introduction
2. Narrative Context
3. Point of View and Characters
4. Narrative Structure
5. Narrative Techniques
6. The Language of Narrative

Writing as a Process

Get from the first twinkle of an idea to a sparkling final draft.

Interactive Lessons	
1. Introduction	4. Revising and Editing
2. Task, Purpose, and Audience	5. Trying a New Approach
3. Planning and Drafting	

Producing and Publishing with Technology

Learn how to write for an online audience.

Interactive Lessons	
1. Introduction	3. Interacting with Your Online Audience
2. Writing for the Internet	4. Using Technology to Collaborate

Conducting Research

There's a world of information out there. How do you find it?

Interactive Lessons	
1. Introduction	5. Conducting Field Research
2. Starting Your Research	6. Using the Internet for Research
3. Types of Sources	7. Taking Notes
4. Using the Library for Research	8. Refocusing Your Inquiry

Evaluating Sources

Approach all sources with a critical eye.

W 8

Interactive Lessons	1. Introduction 2. Evaluating Sources for Usefulness	3. Evaluating Sources for Reliability

Using Textual Evidence

Put your research into writing.

W 7, W 8, W 9

Interactive Lessons	1. Introduction 2. Synthesizing Information 3. Writing an Outline	4. Summarizing, Paraphrasing, and Quoting 5. Attribution

Participating in Collaborative Discussions

SL 1

There's power in putting your heads together.

Interactive Lessons	1. Introduction 2. Preparing for Discussion 3. Establishing and Following Procedure	4. Speaking Constructively 5. Listening and Responding 6. Wrapping Up Your Discussion

Analyzing and Evaluating Presentations

Is there substance behind the style?

Interactive Lessons	
1. Introduction	4. Tracing a Speaker's Argument
2. Analyzing a Presentation	5. Rhetoric and Delivery
3. Evaluating a Speaker's Reliability	6. Synthesizing Media Sources

Giving a Presentation

Learn how to talk to a roomful of people.

Interactive Lessons	
1. Introduction	4. Style in Presentation
2. Knowing Your Audience	5. Delivering Your Presentation
3. The Content of Your Presentation	6. Presenting a Recitation

Using Media in a Presentation

If a picture is worth a thousand words, just think what you can do with a video.

Interactive Lessons	
1. Introduction	3. Using Presentation Software
2. Types of Media: Audio, Video, and Images	4. Practicing Your Presentation

eBook | myNotebook | **fyi** hmhfyi.com | ✔ my WriteSmart

Supporting 21st-Century Skills

The amount of information people encounter each day keeps increasing. Whether you're working alone or collaborating with others, it takes effort to analyze the complex texts and competing ideas that bombard us in this fast-paced world. What can allow you to succeed? Staying engaged and organized. The digital tools in this program will help you to think critically and take charge of your learning.

Stream to Start

Ignite your Investigation

You learn best when you're engaged. The **Stream to Start** video at the beginning of each collection is designed to inspire interest in the topics being explored. Watch it and then let your curiosity lead your investigations.

and how do we cope?

Learn How to Do a Close Read

An effective close read is all about the details; you have to examine the language and ideas a writer includes. See how it's done by accessing the **Close Read Screencasts** in your eBook. Hear modeled conversations about anchor texts.

Who, almost dead for breath, had scarcely more
Than would make up his message.

Lady Macbeth.   Give him tending.
35   He brings great news.

[Messenger *exits.*]

              The raven himself is hoarse
That croaks the fatal entrance of Duncan
Under my battlements. Come, you spirits
That tend on mortal thoughts, unsex me here,

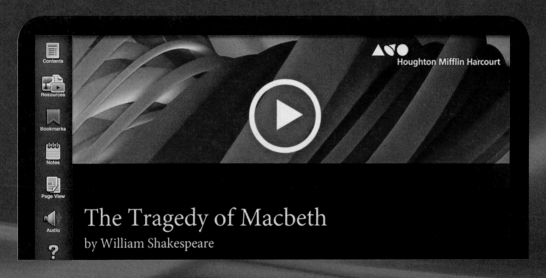

The Tragedy of Macbeth
by William Shakespeare

Houghton Mifflin Harcourt

The raven himself is hoarse

That croaksthe fatal entrance of Duncan

Under my battlements. Come, you spirits

Thattend on mortalthoughts, unsex me here,

And fill me from the crown to the toe top-full

Of direst cruelty. Make thick my blood.

Stop up th' access and passage to remorse,

That no compunctious visitings of nature

> The raven is a symbol of death and evil.

Annotate the Texts

Practice close reading by utilizing the powerful annotation tools in your eBook. Mark up key ideas and observations using highlighters and sticky notes. Tag unfamiliar words to create a personal word list in *my*Notebook.

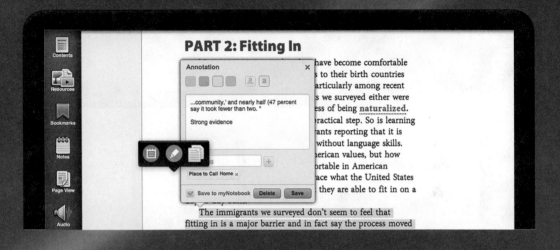

Find More Text Evidence on the Web

Tap into the *FYI* website for links to high-interest informational texts about collection topics. Synthesize information and connect notes and text evidence from any Web source by including it in *my*Notebook.

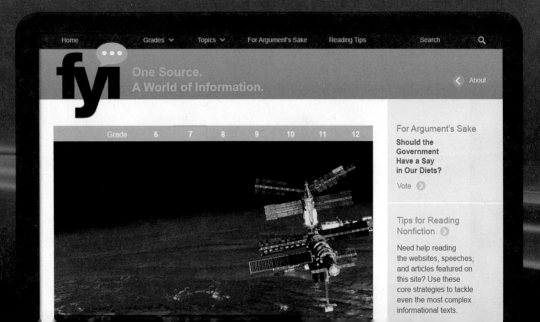

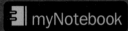

Save and Organize Your Notes

Save your annotations to *my*Notebook, where you can organize them to use as text evidence in performance tasks and other writing assignments. You can also organize the unfamiliar words you tagged by creating word lists, which will help you grow your vocabulary.

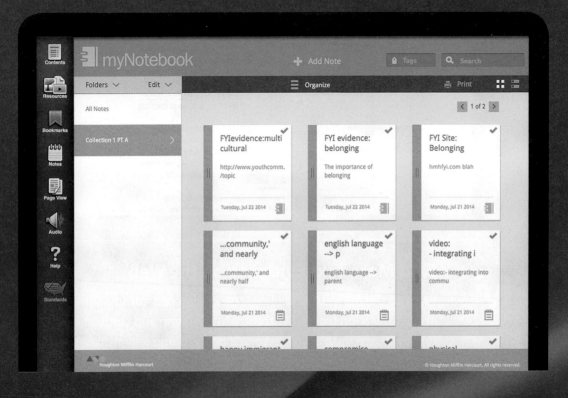

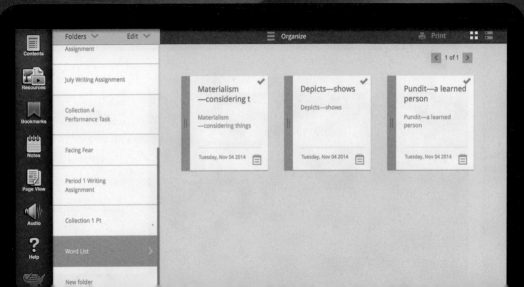

Create, Communicate, and Collaborate

Use the technology provided by the **myWriteSmart** tool to keep track of your writing assignments, create drafts, and collaborate and communicate with peers and your teacher. Use the evidence you've gathered in *my*Notebook to support your ideas.

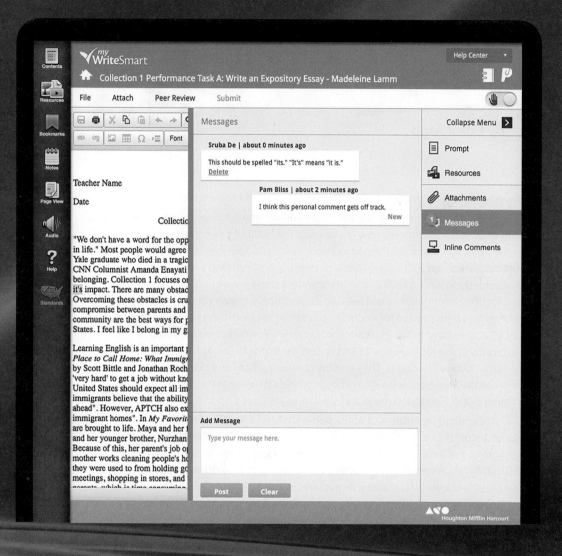

Navigating Complex Texts in the 21st Century

By Carol Jago

Reading complex literature and nonfiction doesn't need to be painful.

But to enjoy great poetry and prose you are going to have to do more than skim and scan. You will need to develop the habit of paying attention to the particular words on the page closely, systematically, even lovingly. Just because a text isn't easy doesn't mean there is something wrong with it or something wrong with you. Understanding complex text takes effort and focused attention. You will need to think critically at every turn. Problem solving isn't only needed for math. Do you sometimes wish writers would just say what they have to say more simply or with fewer words? I assure you that writers don't use long sentences and unfamiliar words to annoy their readers or make readers feel dumb. They employ complex syntax and rich language because they have complex ideas about complex issues that they want to communicate. Simple language and structures just aren't up to the task.

Excellent literature and nonfiction—the kind you will be reading over the course of the year—challenge readers in many ways. Sometimes the background of a story or the content of an essay is so unfamiliar that it can be difficult to understand why characters are behaving as they do or to follow the argument a writer is making. By persevering—reading like a detective and following clues in the text—you will find that your store of background knowledge grows. As a result, the next time you read about global issues, financial matters, political events, environmental news (like the California drought), or health research, the text won't seem nearly as hard. Navigating a terrain you have been over once before never seems quite as rugged the second time through. The more you read, the better reader you become.

Good readers aren't scared off by challenging text. When the going gets rough, they know what to do. Let's take vocabulary, a common measure of text complexity, as an example. Learning new words is the business of a lifetime. Rather than shutting down when you meet a word you don't know, take a moment to think about the word. Is any part of the word familiar to you? Is there something in the context of the sentence or paragraph that can help you figure out its meaning? Is there someone or something that can provide you with a definition? When we read literature or nonfiction from a time period other than our own, the text is often full of words we don't know. Each time you meet those words in succeeding readings you will be adding to your understanding of the word and its use. Your brain is a natural word-learning machine. The more you feed it complex text, the larger vocabulary you'll have and as a result, the easier navigating the next book will be.

Have you ever been reading a long, complicated sentence and discovered that by the time you reached the end you had forgotten the beginning? Unlike the sentences we speak or dash off in a note to a friend, complex text is often full of sentences that are not only lengthy but also constructed in intricate ways. Such sentences require readers to slow down and figure out how phrases relate to one another as well as who is doing what to whom. Remember, rereading isn't cheating. It is exactly what experienced readers know to do when they meet dense text on the page. On the pages that follow you will find stories and articles that challenge you at a sentence level. Don't be intimidated. By paying careful attention to how those sentences are constructed, you will see their meanings unfold before your eyes.

> "Your brain is a natural word-learning machine. The more you feed it complex text, the larger a vocabulary you'll have."

That same kind of attention is required for reading the media. Every day you are bombarded with messages—online, offline, everywhere you look. These, too, are complex texts that you want to be able to see through; that is, to be able to recognize the message's source, purpose, context, intended audience, and appeals. This is what it takes to be a 21st-century reader.

Another way text can be complex is in terms of the density of ideas. Sometimes a writer piles on so much information that you find even if your eyes continue to move down the page, your brain has stopped taking in anything. At times like this, turning to a peer and discussing particular lines or concepts can help you pay closer attention and begin to unpack the text. Sharing questions and ideas, exploring a difficult passage together, makes it possible to tease out the meaning of even the most difficult text.

Poetry is by its nature particularly dense and for that reason poses particular challenges for casual readers. Don't ever assume that once through a poem is enough. Often, a seemingly simple poem in terms of word choice and length—for example an Emily Dickinson, Mary Oliver, or W.H. Auden poem—expresses extremely complex feelings and insights. Poets also often make reference to mythological and Biblical allusions which contemporary readers are not always familiar with. Skipping over such references robs your reading of the richness the poet intended. Look up that bird. Check out the note on the page. Ask your teacher.

You will notice a range of complexity within each collection of readings. This spectrum reflects the range of texts that surround us: some easy, some hard, some seemingly easy but hard, some seemingly hard but easy. Navigating this sea of texts should stretch you as a reader and a thinker. How could it be otherwise when your journey is in the realms of gold? Please accept this invitation to an intellectual voyage I think you will enjoy.

Understanding the Common Core State Standards

What are the English Language Arts Common Core State Standards?

The Common Core State Standards for English Language Arts indicate what you should know and be able to do by the end of your grade level. These understandings and skills will help you be better prepared for future classes, college courses, and a career. For this reason, the standards for each strand in English Language Arts (such as Reading Informational Text or Writing) directly relate to the College and Career Readiness Anchor Standards for each strand. The Anchor Standards broadly outline the understandings and skills you should master by the end of high school so that you are well prepared for college or for a career.

How do I learn the English Language Arts Common Core State Standards?

Your textbook is closely aligned to the English Language Arts Common Core State Standards. Every time you learn a concept or practice a skill, you are working on mastery of one of the standards. Each collection, each selection, and each performance task in your textbook connects to one or more of the standards for English Language Arts listed on the following pages.

The English Language Arts Common Core State Standards are divided into five strands: Reading Literature, Reading Informational Text, Writing, Speaking and Listening, and Language.

Strand	What It Means to You
Reading Literature (RL)	This strand concerns the literary texts you will read at this grade level: stories, drama, and poetry. The Common Core State Standards stress that you should read a range of texts of increasing complexity as you progress through high school.
Reading Informational Text (RI)	Informational text includes a broad range of literary nonfiction, including exposition, argument, and functional text, in such genres as personal essays, speeches, opinion pieces, memoirs, and historical and scientific accounts. The Common Core State Standards stress that you will read a range of informational texts of increasing complexity as you progress from grade to grade.
Writing (W)	The Writing strand focuses on your generating three types of texts—arguments, informative or explanatory texts, and narratives—while using the writing process and technology to develop and share your writing. The Common Core State Standards also emphasize research and specify that you should write routinely for both short and extended time frames.
Speaking and Listening (SL)	The Common Core State Standards focus on comprehending information presented in a variety of media and formats, on participating in collaborative discussions, and on presenting knowledge and ideas clearly.
Language (L)	The standards in the Language strand address the conventions of standard English grammar, usage, and mechanics; knowledge of language; and vocabulary acquisition and use.

Common Core Code Decoder

The codes you find on the pages of your textbook identify the specific knowledge or skill for the standard addressed in the text.

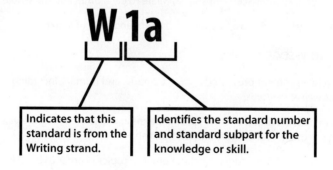

| Indicates that this standard is from the Writing strand. | Identifies the standard number and standard subpart for the knowledge or skill. |

English Language Arts Common Core State Standards

Listed below are the English Language Arts Common Core State Standards that you are required to master by the end of grade 10. We have provided a summary of the concepts you will learn on your way to mastering each standard. The CCR anchor standards and high school grade-specific standards for each strand work together to define college and career readiness expectations—the former providing broad standards, the latter providing additional specificity.

College and Career Readiness Anchor Standards for Reading

Common Core State Standards

KEY IDEAS AND DETAILS

1. Read closely to determine what the text says explicitly and to make logical inferences from it; cite specific textual evidence when writing or speaking to support conclusions drawn from the text.

2. Determine central ideas or themes of a text and analyze their development; summarize the key supporting details and ideas.

3. Analyze how and why individuals, events, and ideas develop and interact over the course of a text.

CRAFT AND STRUCTURE

4. Interpret words and phrases as they are used in a text, including determining technical, connotative, and figurative meanings, and analyze how specific word choices shape meaning or tone.

5. Analyze the structure of texts, including how specific sentences, paragraphs, and larger portions of the text (e.g., a section, chapter, scene, or stanza) relate to each other and the whole.

6. Assess how point of view or purpose shapes the content and style of a text.

INTEGRATION OF KNOWLEDGE AND IDEAS

7. Integrate and evaluate content presented in diverse media and formats, including visually and quantitatively, as well as in words.

8. Delineate and evaluate the argument and specific claims in a text, including the validity of the reasoning as well as the relevance and sufficiency of the evidence.

9. Analyze how two or more texts address similar themes or topics in order to build knowledge or to compare the approaches the authors take.

RANGE OF READING AND LEVEL OF TEXT COMPLEXITY

10. Read and comprehend complex literary and informational texts independently and proficiently.

Reading Standards for Literature, Grades 9–10 Students

The College and Career Readiness Anchor Standards for Reading apply to both literature and informational text.

Common Core State Standards	What it Means to You
KEY IDEAS AND DETAILS	
1. Cite strong and thorough textual evidence to support analysis of what the text says explicitly as well as inferences drawn from the text.	You will use details and information from the text to support your understanding of its main ideas—both those that are stated directly and those that are suggested.
2. Determine a theme or central idea of a text and analyze in detail its development over the course of the text, including how it emerges and is shaped and refined by specific details; provide an objective summary of the text.	You will analyze the development of a text's main ideas and themes by showing how they progress throughout the text. You will also summarize the main idea of the text as a whole without adding your own ideas or opinions.
3. Analyze how complex characters (e.g., those with multiple or conflicting motivations) develop over the course of a text, interact with other characters, and advance the plot or develop the theme.	You will analyze the development of a text's characters and how their actions, thoughts, and words contribute to the story's plot or themes.
CRAFT AND STRUCTURE	
4. Determine the meaning of words and phrases as they are used in the text, including figurative and connotative meanings; analyze the cumulative impact of specific word choices on meaning and tone (e.g., how the language evokes a sense of time and place; how it sets a formal or informal tone).	You will analyze specific words and phrases in the text to determine both what they mean individually as well as how they contribute to the text's tone and meaning as a whole.
5. Analyze how an author's choices concerning how to structure a text, order events within it (e.g., parallel plots), and manipulate time (e.g., pacing, flashbacks) create such effects as mystery, tension, or surprise.	You will analyze the ways in which the author has chosen to structure and order the text and determine how those choices affect the text's mood or tone.
6. Analyze a particular point of view or cultural experience reflected in a work of literature from outside the United States, drawing on a wide reading of world literature.	You will analyze the point of view or cultural experience of a work of literature from outside the United States.

Common Core State Standards	What it Means to You
INTEGRATION OF KNOWLEDGE AND IDEAS	
7. Analyze the representation of a subject or a key scene in two different artistic mediums, including what is emphasized or absent in each treatment (e.g., Auden's "Musée des Beaux Arts" and Breughel's *Landscape with the Fall of Icarus*).	You will compare and contrast how events and information are presented in visual and non-visual texts.
8. (Not applicable to literature)	
9. Analyze how an author draws on and transforms source material in a specific work (e.g., how Shakespeare treats a theme or topic from Ovid or the Bible or how a later author draws on a play by Shakespeare).	You will recognize and analyze how an author draws from and uses source material from other texts or other types of sources.
RANGE OF READING AND LEVEL OF TEXT COMPLEXITY	
10. By the end of grade 10, read and comprehend literature, including stories, dramas, and poems, at the high end of the grades 9–10 text complexity band independently and proficiently.	You will demonstrate the ability to read and understand grade-level appropriate literary texts by the end of grade 10.

Reading Standards for Informational Text, Grades 9–10 Students

Common Core State Standards	What it Means to You
KEY IDEAS AND DETAILS	
1. Cite strong and thorough textual evidence to support analysis of what the text says explicitly as well as inferences drawn from the text.	You will use details and information from the text to support your understanding of its main ideas—both those that are stated directly and those that are suggested.
2. Determine a central idea of a text and analyze its development over the course of the text, including how it emerges and is shaped and refined by specific details; provide an objective summary of the text.	You will analyze the development of a text's main ideas and themes by showing how they progress throughout the text. You will also summarize the main idea of the text as a whole without adding your own ideas or opinions.

Common Core State Standards	What it Means to You
3. Analyze how the author unfolds an analysis or series of ideas or events, including the order in which the points are made, how they are introduced and developed, and the connections that are drawn between them.	You will analyze the ways in which the author has chosen to structure and order the text and determine how those choices affect the text's central ideas.

CRAFT AND STRUCTURE

Common Core State Standards	What it Means to You
4. Determine the meaning of words and phrases as they are used in a text, including figurative, connotative, and technical meanings; analyze the cumulative impact of specific word choices on meaning and tone (e.g., how the language of a court opinion differs from that of a newspaper).	You will analyze specific words and phrases in the text to determine both what they mean individually as well as how they contribute to the text's tone and meaning as a whole.
5. Analyze in detail how an author's ideas or claims are developed and refined by particular sentences, paragraphs, or larger portions of a text (e.g., a section or chapter).	You will examine specific portions of the text (sentences, paragraphs, or larger sections) to understand how they develop the author's ideas and claims.
6. Determine an author's point of view or purpose in a text and analyze how an author uses rhetoric to advance that point of view or purpose.	You will understand the author's purpose and analyze how the author uses language to effectively communicate that purpose.

INTEGRATION OF KNOWLEDGE AND IDEAS

Common Core State Standards	What it Means to You
7. Analyze various accounts of a subject told in different mediums (e.g., a person's life story in both print and multimedia), determining which details are emphasized in each account.	You will compare and contrast the ways in which various media, such as newspapers, television, documentaries, blogs, and the Internet, portray the same events.
8. Delineate and evaluate the argument and specific claims in a text, assessing whether the reasoning is valid and the evidence is relevant and sufficient; identify false statements and fallacious reasoning.	You will evaluate the strength of the author's claims by examining the supporting details and reasoning and identifying any faults or weaknesses in them.
9. Analyze seminal U.S. documents of historical and literary significance (e.g., Washington's Farewell Address, the Gettysburg Address, Roosevelt's Four Freedoms speech, King's "Letter from Birmingham Jail"), including how they address related themes and concepts.	You will read and analyze influential documents and explain how they address important themes related to United States history and culture.

Common Core State Standards	What it Means to You
RANGE OF READING AND LEVEL OF TEXT COMPLEXITY	
10. By the end of grade 10, read and comprehend literary nonfiction at the high end of the grades 9–10 text complexity band independently and proficiently.	You will demonstrate the ability to read and understand grade-level appropriate literary nonfiction texts by the end of grade 10.

College and Career Readiness Anchor Standards for Writing

Common Core State Standards
TEXT TYPES AND PURPOSES
1. Write arguments to support claims in an analysis of substantive topics or texts, using valid reasoning and relevant and sufficient evidence.
2. Write informative/explanatory texts to examine and convey complex ideas and information clearly and accurately through the effective selection, organization, and analysis of content.
3. Write narratives to develop real or imagined experiences or events using effective technique, well-chosen details, and well-structured event sequences.
PRODUCTION AND DISTRIBUTION OF WRITING
4. Produce clear and coherent writing in which the development, organization, and style are appropriate to task, purpose, and audience.
5. Develop and strengthen writing as needed by planning, revising, editing, rewriting, or trying a new approach.
6. Use technology, including the Internet, to produce and publish writing and to interact and collaborate with others.
RESEARCH TO BUILD AND PRESENT KNOWLEDGE
7. Conduct short as well as more sustained research projects based on focused questions, demonstrating understanding of the subject under investigation.
8. Gather relevant information from multiple print and digital sources, assess the credibility and accuracy of each source, and integrate the information while avoiding plagiarism.
9. Draw evidence from literary and/or informational texts to support analysis, reflection, and research.
RANGE OF WRITING
10. Write routinely over extended time frames (time for research, reflection, and revision) and shorter time frames (a single sitting or a day or two) for a range of tasks, purposes, and audiences.

Writing Standards, Grades 9–10 Students

Common Core State Standards	What it Means to You
TEXT TYPES AND PURPOSES	
1. Write arguments to support claims in an analysis of substantive topics or texts, using valid reasoning and relevant and sufficient evidence.	You will write and develop arguments with strong evidence and valid reasoning that include
a. Introduce precise claim(s), distinguish the claim(s) from alternate or opposing claims, and create an organization that establishes clear relationships among claim(s), counterclaims, reasons, and evidence.	**a.** a clear organization of precise claims and counterclaims
b. Develop claim(s) and counterclaims fairly, supplying evidence for each while pointing out the strengths and limitations of both in a manner that anticipates the audience's knowledge level and concerns.	**b.** relevant and unbiased support for claims
c. Use words, phrases, and clauses to link the major sections of the text, create cohesion, and clarify the relationships between claim(s) and reasons, between reasons and evidence, and between claim(s) and counterclaims.	**c.** use of transitional words, phrases, and clauses to link information
d. Establish and maintain a formal style and objective tone while attending to the norms and conventions of the discipline in which they are writing.	**d.** a tone and style appropriate to the task
e. Provide a concluding statement or section that follows from and supports the argument presented.	**e.** a strong concluding statement or section that summarizes the evidence presented
2. Write informative/explanatory texts to examine and convey complex ideas, concepts, and information clearly and accurately through the effective selection, organization, and analysis of content.	You will write clear, well-organized, and thoughtful informative and explanatory texts with
a. Introduce a topic; organize complex ideas, concepts, and information to make important connections and distinctions; include formatting (e.g., headings), graphics (e.g., figures, tables), and multimedia when useful to aiding comprehension.	**a.** a clear introduction and organization, including headings and graphic organizers (when appropriate)

Common Core State Standards	What it Means to You
b. Develop the topic with well-chosen, relevant, and sufficient facts, extended definitions, concrete details, quotations, or other information and examples appropriate to the audience's knowledge of the topic.	**b.** sufficient supporting details and background information
c. Use appropriate and varied transitions to link the major sections of the text, create cohesion, and clarify the relationships among complex ideas and concepts.	**c.** appropriate transitions
d. Use precise language and domain-specific vocabulary to manage the complexity of the topic.	**d.** precise language and relevant vocabulary
e. Establish and maintain a formal style and objective tone while attending to the norms and conventions of the discipline in which they are writing.	**e.** a tone and style appropriate to the task
f. Provide a concluding statement or section that follows from and supports the information or explanation presented (e.g., articulating implications or the significance of the topic).	**f.** a strong concluding statement or section that restates the importance or relevance of the topic
3. Write narratives to develop real or imagined experiences or events using effective technique, well-chosen details, and well-structured event sequences.	You will write clear, well-structured, detailed narrative texts that
a. Engage and orient the reader by setting out a problem, situation, or observation, establishing one or multiple point(s) of view, and introducing a narrator and/or characters; create a smooth progression of experiences or events.	**a.** draw your readers in with a clear topic and an interesting progression of events or ideas
b. Use narrative techniques, such as dialogue, pacing, description, reflection, and multiple plot lines, to develop experiences, events, and/or characters.	**b.** use literary techniques to develop and expand on events and/or characters
c. Use a variety of techniques to sequence events so that they build on one another to create a coherent whole.	**c.** have a coherent sequence and structure
d. Use precise words and phrases, telling details, and sensory language to convey a vivid picture of the experiences, events, setting, and/or characters.	**d.** use precise words and sensory details that keep readers interested
e. Provide a conclusion that follows from and reflects on what is experienced, observed, or resolved over the course of the narrative.	**e.** have a strong conclusion that reflects on the topic

Common Core State Standards	What it Means to You

PRODUCTION AND DISTRIBUTION OF WRITING

4. Produce clear and coherent writing in which the development, organization, and style are appropriate to task, purpose, and audience. (Grade-specific expectations for writing types are defined in standards 1–3 above.)	You will produce writing that is appropriate to the task, purpose, and audience for whom you are writing.
5. Develop and strengthen writing as needed by planning, revising, editing, rewriting, or trying a new approach, focusing on addressing what is most significant for a specific purpose and audience. (Editing for conventions should demonstrate command of Language standards 1–3 up to and including grades 9–10.)	You will revise and refine your writing to address what is most important for your purpose and audience.
6. Use technology, including the Internet, to produce, publish, and update individual or shared writing products, taking advantage of technology's capacity to link to other information and to display information flexibly and dynamically.	You will use technology to share your writing and to provide links to other relevant information.

RESEARCH TO BUILD AND PRESENT KNOWLEDGE

7. Conduct short as well as more sustained research projects to answer a question (including a self-generated question) or solve a problem; narrow or broaden the inquiry when appropriate; synthesize multiple sources on the subject, demonstrating understanding of the subject under investigation.	You will engage in short and more complex research tasks that include answering a question or solving a problem by using multiple sources. The product of your research will demonstrate your understanding of the subject.
8. Gather relevant information from multiple authoritative print and digital sources, using advanced searches effectively; assess the usefulness of each source in answering the research question; integrate information into the text selectively to maintain the flow of ideas, avoiding plagiarism and following a standard format for citation.	You will effectively conduct searches to gather information from different sources and assess the relevance of each source, following a standard format for citation.
9. Draw evidence from literary or informational texts to support analysis, reflection, and research. a. Apply grades 9–10 Reading standards to literature (e.g., "Analyze how an author draws on and transforms source material in a specific work [e.g., how Shakespeare treats a theme or topic from Ovid or the Bible or how a later author draws on a play by Shakespeare]").	You will paraphrase, summarize, quote, and cite primary and secondary sources, using both literary and informational texts, to support your analysis, reflection, and research.

Common Core State Standards	What it Means to You
b. Apply grades 9–10 Reading standards to literary nonfiction (e.g., "Delineate and evaluate the argument and specific claims in a text, assessing whether the reasoning is valid and the evidence is relevant and sufficient; identify false statements and fallacious reasoning").	

RANGE OF WRITING

Common Core State Standards	What it Means to You
10. Write routinely over extended time frames (time for research, reflection, and revision) and shorter time frames (a single sitting or a day or two) for a range of tasks, purposes, and audiences.	You will write for many different purposes and audiences both over short and extended periods of time.

College and Career Readiness Anchor Standards for Speaking and Listening

Common Core State Standards

COMPREHENSION AND COLLABORATION

1. Prepare for and participate effectively in a range of conversations and collaborations with diverse partners, building on others' ideas and expressing their own clearly and persuasively.

2. Integrate and evaluate information presented in diverse media and formats, including visually, quantitatively, and orally.

3. Evaluate a speaker's point of view, reasoning, and use of evidence and rhetoric.

PRESENTATION OF KNOWLEDGE AND IDEAS

4. Present information, findings, and supporting evidence such that listeners can follow the line of reasoning and the organization, development, and style are appropriate to task, purpose, and audience.

5. Make strategic use of digital media and visual displays of data to express information and enhance understanding of presentations.

6. Adapt speech to a variety of contexts and communicative tasks, demonstrating command of formal English when indicated or appropriate.

Speaking and Listening Standards, Grades 9–10 Students

Common Core State Standards	What it Means to You
COMPREHENSION AND COLLABORATION	
1. Initiate and participate effectively in a range of collaborative discussions (one-on-one, in groups, and teacher-led) with diverse partners on grades 9–10 topics, texts, and issues, building on others' ideas and expressing their own clearly and persuasively.	You will actively participate in a variety of discussions in which you
a. Come to discussions prepared, having read and researched material under study; explicitly draw on that preparation by referring to evidence from texts and other research on the topic or issue to stimulate a thoughtful, well-reasoned exchange of ideas.	a. have read any relevant material beforehand and have come to the discussion prepared
b. Work with peers to set rules for collegial discussions and decision-making (e.g., informal consensus, taking votes on key issues, presentation of alternate views), clear goals and deadlines, and individual roles as needed.	b. work with others to establish goals and processes within the group
c. Propel conversations by posing and responding to questions that relate the current discussion to broader themes or larger ideas; actively incorporate others into the discussion; and clarify, verify, or challenge ideas and conclusions.	c. initiate dialogue by asking and responding to questions and by relating the current topic to other relevant information
d. Respond thoughtfully to diverse perspectives, summarize points of agreement and disagreement, and, when warranted, qualify or justify their own views and understanding and make new connections in light of the evidence and reasoning presented.	d. respond to different perspectives and summarize points of agreement or disagreement when needed
2. Integrate multiple sources of information presented in diverse media or formats (e.g., visually, quantitatively, orally) evaluating the credibility and accuracy of each source.	You will integrate multiple sources of information, assessing the credibility and accuracy of each source.
3. Evaluate a speaker's point of view, reasoning, and use of evidence and rhetoric, identifying any fallacious reasoning or exaggerated or distorted evidence.	You will evaluate a speaker's argument and identify any false reasoning or evidence.

Common Core State Standards	What it Means to You
PRESENTATION OF KNOWLEDGE AND IDEAS	
4. Present information, findings, and supporting evidence clearly, concisely, and logically such that listeners can follow the line of reasoning and the organization, development, substance, and style are appropriate to purpose, audience, and task.	You will organize and present information to your listeners in a logical sequence and style that are appropriate to your task and audience.
5. Make strategic use of digital media (e.g., textual, graphical, audio, visual, and interactive elements) in presentations to enhance understanding of findings, reasoning, and evidence and to add interest.	You will use digital media to enhance and add interest to presentations.
6. Adapt speech to a variety of contexts and tasks, demonstrating command of formal English when indicated or appropriate. (See grades 9–10 Language standards 1 and 3 for specific expectations.)	You will adapt the formality of your speech appropriately, depending on its context and purpose.

College and Career Readiness Anchor Standards for Language

Common Core State Standards
CONVENTIONS OF STANDARD ENGLISH
1. Demonstrate command of the conventions of standard English grammar and usage when writing or speaking.
2. Demonstrate command of the conventions of standard English capitalization, punctuation, and spelling when writing.
KNOWLEDGE OF LANGUAGE
3. Apply knowledge of language to understand how language functions in different contexts, to make effective choices for meaning or style, and to comprehend more fully when reading or listening.
VOCABULARY ACQUISITION AND USE
4. Determine or clarify the meaning of unknown and multiple-meaning words and phrases by using context clues, analyzing meaningful word parts, and consulting general and specialized reference materials, as appropriate.
5. Demonstrate understanding of figurative language, word relationships, and nuances in word meanings.
6. Acquire and use accurately a range of general academic and domain-specific words and phrases sufficient for reading, writing, speaking, and listening at the college- and career-readiness level; demonstrate independence in gathering vocabulary knowledge when encountering an unknown term important to comprehension or expression.

Language Standards, Grades 9–10 Students

Common Core State Standards	What it Means to You
CONVENTIONS OF STANDARD ENGLISH	
1. Demonstrate command of the conventions of standard English grammar and usage when writing or speaking.	You will correctly use the conventions of English grammar and usage, including
a. Use parallel structure.	a. parallel structure
b. Use various types of phrases (noun, verb, adjectival, adverbial, participial, prepositional, absolute) and clauses (independent, dependent; noun, relative, adverbial) to convey specific meanings and add variety and interest to writing or presentations.	b. phrases and clauses
2. Demonstrate command of the conventions of standard English capitalization, punctuation, and spelling when writing.	You will correctly use the conventions of English capitalization, punctuation, and spelling, including
a. Use a semicolon (and perhaps a conjunctive adverb) to link two or more closely related independent clauses.	a. semicolons
b. Use a colon to introduce a list or quotation.	b. colons
c. Spell correctly.	c. spelling
KNOWLEDGE OF LANGUAGE	
3. Apply knowledge of language to understand how language functions in different contexts, to make effective choices for meaning or style, and to comprehend more fully when reading or listening.	You will apply your knowledge of language in different contexts, including
a. Write and edit work so that it conforms to the guidelines in a style manual (e.g., *MLA Handbook*, Turabian's *Manual for Writers*) appropriate for the discipline and writing type.	a. conforming to a style manual when writing and editing

Common Core State Standards	What it Means to You
VOCABULARY ACQUISITION AND USE	
4. Determine or clarify the meaning of unknown and multiple-meaning words and phrases based on grades 9–10 reading and content, choosing flexibly from a range of strategies.	You will understand the meaning of grade-level appropriate words and phrases by
a. Use context (e.g., the overall meaning of a sentence, paragraph, or text; a word's position or function in a sentence) as a clue to the meaning of a word or phrase.	a. using context clues
b. Identify and correctly use patterns of word changes that indicate different meanings or parts of speech (e.g., *analyze, analysis, analytical; advocate, advocacy*).	b. recognizing and adapting root words according to meaning or part of speech
c. Consult general and specialized reference materials (e.g., dictionaries, glossaries, thesauruses), both print and digital, to find the pronunciation of a word or determine or clarify its precise meaning, its part of speech, or its etymology.	c. using reference materials
d. Verify the preliminary determination of the meaning of a word or phrase (e.g., by checking the inferred meaning in context or in a dictionary).	d. inferring and verifying the meanings of words in context
5. Demonstrate understanding of figurative language, word relationships, and nuances in word meanings.	You will understand figurative language, word relationships, and slight differences in word meanings by
a. Interpret figures of speech (e.g., euphemism, oxymoron) in context and analyze their role in the text.	a. interpreting figures of speech in context
b. Analyze nuances in the meaning of words with similar denotations.	b. analyzing slight differences in the meanings of similar words
6. Acquire and use accurately general academic and domain-specific words and phrases, sufficient for reading, writing, speaking, and listening at the college and career readiness level; demonstrate independence in gathering vocabulary knowledge when considering a word or phrase important to comprehension or expression.	You will develop vocabulary knowledge at the college and career readiness level and demonstrate confidence in using it appropriately.

Ourselves and Others

❝ We, as human beings, must be willing to accept people who are different from ourselves ❞

This collection explores how we interact with other people—family, enemies, neighbors, strangers, and those with whom we disagree.

Stream to Start

hmhfyi.com

Channel One News®

COLLECTION

PERFORMANCE TASK Preview

At the end of this collection, you will have the opportunity to complete two tasks:

• Deliver a speech about how people's relationships with others shape who they are.

• Write an essay about how the texts in this collection do or do not support the idea that people must accept others who are different from themselves.

ACADEMIC VOCABULARY

Study the words and their definitions in the chart below. You will use these words as you discuss and write about the texts in this collection.

Word	Definition	Related Forms
discriminate (dĭ-skrĭm´ə-nāt´) v.	to note clear differences; to separate into categories	discrimination, discriminatory
diverse (dĭ-vûrs´) adj.	made up of elements that are different from each other	diversify, diversity
inhibit (ĭn-hĭb´ĭt) v.	to hold back or prevent from acting	inhibition
intervene (ĭn´tər-vēn´) v.	to come between two things, persons, or events	intervention
rational (răsh´ə-nəl) adj.	based on logic or sound reasoning	rationale, rationalize, irrational

Background *The Jewish people were expelled from their homeland, Israel, in the first century CE. In the late 1800s, Jews from Europe, Asia, Africa, and the Americas began returning to the region; World War II and the Holocaust drastically increased this immigration. Israel became an independent nation in 1948, but tensions with its Arab neighbors and its Arab citizens have led to conflict. With the collapse of the Soviet Union in 1991, many Russian Jews were finally able to move to Israel and make their own mark on the nation's culture. In this story, Israeli writer* **Etgar Keret** *(b. 1967) explores the hopes and dreams of people in this diverse society.*

What, of This Goldfish, Would You Wish?

Short Story by Etgar Keret   Translated by Nathan Englander

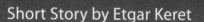

AS YOU READ Think about the kinds of things people wish for to make their lives happier. In particular, look for clues to what Sergei Goralick wants from life. Note any questions you have as you read.

Yonatan had a brilliant idea for a documentary. He'd knock on doors. Just him. No camera crew, no nonsense. Just Yonatan, on his own, a small camera in hand, asking, "If you found a talking goldfish that granted you three wishes, what would you wish for?"

Folks would give their answers, and Yoni would edit them down and make clips of the more surprising responses. Before every set of answers, you'd see the person standing stock-still in the entrance to his house. Onto this shot he'd superimpose[1] the subject's name, family situation, monthly income, and maybe even
10 the party he'd voted for in the last election. All that, combined with the three wishes, and maybe he'd end up with a **poignant** piece of social commentary, a testament to the massive rift between our dreams and the often compromised reality in which we live.

poignant
(poin´yənt) *adj.*
emotionally moving or stimulating.

---

[1] **superimpose:** place one thing on top of another so that both remain visible.

Image Credits: (t) ©Marco Secchi/Corbis; (c) ©Mike Kemp/Rubberball/Alamy Images; (c) ©Eddie Gerald/Alamy Images

It was genius, Yoni was sure. And, if not, at least it was cheap. All he needed was a door to knock on and a heart beating on the other side. With a little decent footage, he was sure he'd be able to sell it to Channel 8 or Discovery in a flash, either as a film or as a bunch of vignettes,[2] little cinematic corners, each with that singular soul standing in a doorway, followed by three killer wishes,

20 precious, every one.

Even better, maybe he'd cash out, package it with a slogan and sell it to a bank or cellular phone company. Maybe tag it with something like "Different dreams, different wishes, one bank." Or "The bank that makes dreams come true."

No prep, no plotting, natural as can be, Yoni grabbed his camera and went out knocking on doors. In the first neighborhood he went to, the kindly folk that took part generally requested the foreseeable things: health, money, bigger apartments, either to shave off a couple of years or a couple of pounds. But there were

30 also powerful moments. One drawn, **wizened** old lady asked simply for a child. A Holocaust survivor with a number on his arm asked very slowly, in a quiet voice—as if he'd been waiting for Yoni to come, as if it wasn't an exercise at all—he'd been wondering (if this fish didn't mind), would it be possible for all the Nazis left living in the world to be held accountable for their crimes? A cocky, broad-shouldered lady-killer put out his cigarette and, as if the camera wasn't there, wished he were a girl. "Just for a night," he added, holding a single finger right up to the lens.

And these were wishes from just one short block in one

40 small, sleepy suburb of Tel Aviv. Yonatan could hardly imagine what people were dreaming of in the development towns and the collectives[3] along the northern border, in the West Bank settlements and Arab villages, the immigrant absorption centers full of broken trailers and tired people left to broil out in the desert sun.

Yonatan knew that if the project was going to have any weight, he'd have to get to everyone, to the unemployed, to the ultrareligious, to the Arabs and Ethiopians and American expats.[4] He began to plan a shooting schedule for the coming days: Jaffa, Dimona, Ashdod, Sderot, Taibe, Talpiot. Maybe Hebron, even.

50 If he could sneak past the wall, Hebron would be great. Maybe somewhere in that city some **beleaguered** Arab man would stand in his doorway and, looking through Yonatan and his camera, looking out into nothingness, just pause for a minute, nod his head, and wish for peace—that would be something to see.

wizened
(wĭz′ənd) *adj.*
shrunken and wrinkled.

beleaguered
(bĭ-lē′gərd) *adj.*
troubled with many problems.

---

[2] **vignettes:** small scenes or images.
[3] **collectives:** here, communal settlements.
[4] **expats:** expatriates, people living in a foreign country.

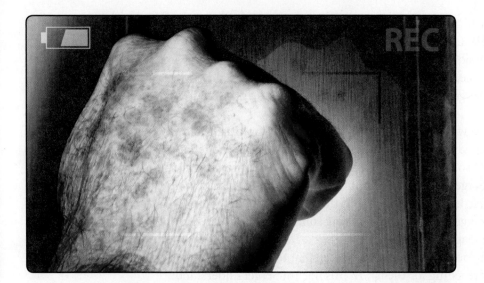

Sergei Goralick doesn't much like strangers banging on his door. Especially when those strangers are asking him questions. In Russia, when Sergei was young, it happened plenty. The KGB felt right at home knocking on his door. His father had been a Zionist,[5] which was pretty much an invitation for them to drop by any old time.

60 When Sergei got to Israel and then moved to Jaffa, his family couldn't wrap their heads around it. They'd ask him, What are you looking to find in a place like that? There's no one there but addicts and Arabs and pensioners.[6] But what is most excellent about addicts and Arabs and pensioners is that they don't come around knocking on Sergei's door. That way Sergei can get his sleep, and get up when it's still dark. He can take his little boat out into the sea and fish until he's done fishing. By himself. In silence. The way it should be. The way it was.

Until one day some kid with a ring in his ear . . . comes
70 knocking. Hard like that—rapping at his door. Just the way Sergei doesn't like. And he says, this kid, that he has some questions he wants to put on the TV.

Sergei tells the boy, tells him in what he thinks is a straightforward manner, that he doesn't want it. Not interested. Sergei gives the camera a shove, to help make it clear. But the earring boy is stubborn. He says all kinds of things, fast things. And it's hard for Sergei to follow; his Hebrew isn't so good.

The boy slows down, tells Sergei he has a strong face, a nice face, and that he simply has to have him for this movie picture.
80 Sergei can also slow down, he can also make clear. He tells the kid to shove off. But the kid is slippery, and somehow between saying

---

[5] **Zionist:** supporter of a separate state for Jewish people.
[6] **pensioners:** people living on modest retirement payments.

no and pushing the door closed, Sergei finds that the kid is in his house. He's already making his movie, running his camera without any permission, and from behind the camera he's still telling Sergei about his face, that it's full of feeling, that it's tender. Suddenly the kid spots Sergei's goldfish flitting around in its big glass jar in his kitchen.

The kid with the earring starts screaming, "Goldfish, goldfish," he's so excited. And this, this really pressures Sergei, who tells
90 the kid, it's nothing, just a regular goldfish, stop filming it. Just a goldfish, Sergei tells him, just something he found flapping around in the net, a deep-sea goldfish. But the boy isn't listening. He's still filming and getting closer and saying something about talking and fish and a magic wish.

Sergei doesn't like this, doesn't like that the boy is almost at it, already reaching for the jar. In this instant Sergei understands the boy didn't come for television, what he came for, specifically, is to snatch Sergei's fish, to steal it away. Before the mind of Sergei Goralick really understands what it is his body has done, he seems
100 to have taken the burner off the stove and hit the boy in the head. The boy falls. The camera falls with him. The camera breaks open on the floor, along with the boy's skull. There's a lot of blood coming out of the head, and Sergei really doesn't know what to do.

That is, he knows exactly what to do, but it really would complicate things. Because if he takes this kid to the hospital, people are going to ask what happened, and it would take things in a direction Sergei doesn't want to go.

"No reason to take him to the hospital anyway," says the goldfish, in Russian. "That one's already dead."
110 "He can't be dead," Sergei says, with a moan. "I barely touched him. It's only a burner. Only a little thing." Sergei holds it up to the fish, taps it against his own skull to prove it. "It's not even that hard."

"Maybe not," says the fish. "But, apparently, it's harder than that kid's head."

"He wanted to take you from me," Sergei says, almost crying.

"Nonsense," the fish says. "He was only here to make a little something for TV."

"But he said . . . "
120 "He said," says the fish, interrupting, "exactly what he was doing. But you didn't get it. Honestly, your Hebrew, it's terrible."

"Yours is better?" Sergei says. "Yours is so great?"

"Yes. Mine's supergreat," the goldfish says, sounding impatient. "I'm a magic fish. I'm **fluent** in everything." All the while the puddle of blood from the earring kid's head is getting bigger

fluent
(flo͞o´ənt) *adj.*
able to express
oneself clearly and
easily.

and bigger and Sergei is on his toes, up against the kitchen wall, desperate not to step in it, not to get blood on his feet.

"You do have one wish left," the fish reminds Sergei. He says it easy like that, as if Sergei doesn't know—as if either of them ever
130 loses count.

"No," Sergei says. He's shaking his head from side to side. "I can't," he says. "I've been saving it. Saving it for something."

"For what?" the fish says.

But Sergei won't answer.

"You do have one wish left."

That first wish, Sergei used up when they discovered a cancer in his sister. A lung cancer, the kind you don't get better from. The fish undid it in an instant—the words barely out of Sergei's mouth. The second wish Sergei used up five years ago, on Sveta's boy. The kid was still small then, barely three, but the doctors already knew
140 something in her son's head wasn't right. He was going to grow big but not in the brain. Three was about as smart as he'd get. Sveta cried to Sergei in bed all night. Sergei walked home along the beach when the sun came up, and he called to the fish, asked the goldfish to fix it as soon as he'd crossed through the door. He never told Sveta. And a few months later she left him for some cop, a Moroccan with a shiny Honda. In his heart, Sergei kept telling himself it wasn't for Sveta that he'd done it, that he'd wished his wish purely for the boy. In his mind, he was less sure, and all kinds of thoughts about other things he could have done with that wish
150 continued to gnaw at him, half driving him mad. The third wish, Sergei hadn't yet wished for.

"I can restore him," says the goldfish. "I can bring him back to life."

"No one's asking," Sergei says.

"I can bring him back to the moment before," the goldfish says. "To before he knocks on your door. I can put him back to right there. I can do it. All you need to do is ask."

"To wish my wish," Sergei says. "My last."

The fish swishes his fish tail back and forth in the water, the way he does, Sergei knows, when he's truly excited. The goldfish can already taste freedom. Sergei can see it on him.

After the last wish, Sergei won't have a choice. He'll have to let the goldfish go. His magic goldfish. His friend.

"Fixable," Sergei says. "I'll just mop up the blood. A good sponge and it'll be like it never was."

That tail just goes back and forth, the fish's head steady.

Sergei takes a deep breath. He steps out into the middle of the kitchen, out into the puddle. "When I'm fishing, while it's dark and the world's asleep," he says, half to himself and half to the fish, "I'll tie the kid to a rock and dump him in the sea. Not a chance, not in a million years, will anyone ever find him."

"You killed him, Sergei," the goldfish says. "You murdered someone—but you're not a murderer." The goldfish stops swishing his tail. "If, on this, you won't waste a wish, then tell me, Sergei, what is it good for?"

It was in Bethlehem, actually, that Yonatan found his Arab, a handsome man who used his first wish for peace. His name was Munir; he was fat with a big white mustache. Superphotogenic.[7] It was moving, the way he said it. Perfect, the way in which Munir wished his wish. Yoni knew even as he was filming that this guy would be his promo for sure.

Either him or that Russian. The one with the faded tattoos that Yoni had met in Jaffa. The one that looked straight into the camera and said, if he ever found a talking goldfish he wouldn't ask of it a single thing. He'd just stick it on a shelf in a big glass jar and talk to him all day, it didn't matter about what. Maybe sports, maybe politics, whatever a goldfish was interested in chatting about.

Anything, the Russian said, not to be alone.

COLLABORATIVE DISCUSSION Why does Sergei save his third wish for so long? With a partner, discuss the reasons for his behavior. Cite specific evidence from the text to support your answer.

---

[7] **superphotogenic:** looking extremely good in photos or on film.

Analyze Character: Motivations

A good fictional character is complex, just like a real person. A character develops over the course of a story as his or her unique personality is revealed by the author. To analyze the complex character of Sergei Goralick, find clues about his traits and consider his **motivations,** the reasons behind his actions.

Character Traits	Character Motivations
Authors provide numerous clues about character traits: • **What does the character say?** A character's words can reveal whether he or she is polite or rude, shy or bold, caring or cruel. Dialogue can also reveal a character's relationships with other characters. • **How does the character act?** The actions of characters move a story's plot forward. They also show what the characters want and how they respond to the world around them. • **What does the character think?** A character's thoughts, if revealed, provide deeper insight into what he or she is truly like. • **How does he or she interact with other characters?** Observe how well—or badly—the character gets along with others. Both personality and life history will affect relationships.	You understand a character when you can explain the motivations behind his or her actions. A character might even have two conflicting motivations for the same action. For example, Yoni makes his video thinking of commercial gain. But at the same time, he hopes to create a serious documentary. Consider these questions: • What does the character value? • What does the character want? Does he or she want conflicting things? • What does the character believe? • What does the character fear?

Analyze Point of View: Cultural Background

This story is set in Tel Aviv, Israel. Each character's experience in Israel's complex society shapes his or her point of view. The majority of Israelis are Jews, but their backgrounds are diverse. Immigrants brought with them the cultures of the many countries in which they had lived. Russian Jews were among the last to arrive, but they now make up about 15 percent of the population. They have tended to settle in neighborhoods with other Russians and to speak Russian, not Hebrew. The experiences of Israel's Arab population add another dimension to this story's cultural context. Arabs are full citizens, but ethnic and religious differences—as well as disputes over territory—have often led to conflict with their Jewish neighbors.

Analyzing the Text

RL 1, RL 2, RL 3,
RL 5, RL 6,
SL 1a

Cite Text Evidence   Support your responses with evidence from the selection.

1. **Analyze** Consider how Sergei reacts when Yoni comes to his door. Does his response seem rational (reasonable) or not? How does Sergei's cultural experience help explain his reaction?

2. **Analyze** What does the dialogue between Sergei and the goldfish reveal about their relationship?

3. **Infer** When you **infer**, you use details in a text to draw a conclusion about something that the author does not state directly. What can you infer about Sergei's character based on the way he uses his first two wishes?

4. **Draw Conclusions** Sergei considers the goldfish to be his friend. What details in the story reveal their conflict with each other? Can their relationship truly be called a friendship? Explain.

5. **Analyze** When Sergei realizes that Yoni is dead, he must make a decision. What conflicting motivations must he sort out before he can decide whether or not to use his last wish?

6. **Evaluate** The last section of the story is a flash forward. Readers must infer what happens in the intervening time between Sergei's conversation with the fish and Yoni's final report on his video. Is this structure effective, or would it have been better to know the details about Sergei's decision? Explain.

7. **Analyze** A **theme** is an important idea about life or human nature expressed through a story's characters and events. What theme about happiness does this story convey through Sergei's situation and actions and the outcome of events?

PERFORMANCE TASK

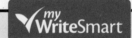

Speaking Activity: Response to Literature "What, of This Goldfish, Would You Wish?" provides a modern twist on the "three wishes" structure used in many folk tales. Explore this aspect of the story with a small group.

- Each group member should research one folk tale involving three wishes. Retell your folk tale to the rest of the group. Discuss similarities and differences between the tales. What happens to the characters, and why?

- Then, discuss how Etgar Keret's story fits in with the others. What elements are similar? What makes it unique?
- Write a summary of your group's conclusions about Keret's story and other tales of three wishes.

Critical Vocabulary

poignant   **wizened**   **beleaguered**   **fluent**

Practice and Apply Answer these questions to demonstrate your understanding of each Critical Vocabulary word.

1. You have just read a **poignant** blog post. Will you still be thinking about it tomorrow, or will you forget it immediately? Explain.

2. The flowers you received last week appear **wizened.** What will you do with them? Why?

3. Maria feels **beleaguered** on the first day of school. Does her facial expression show confidence or panic? Why?

4. Doug is **fluent** in French. Does he need to pack a French dictionary when he travels to France? Explain.

Vocabulary Strategy: Context Clues

If you come across an unfamiliar word while reading, you can use **context clues,** or information in the surrounding text, to figure out the word's meaning. For example, the word *fluent* appears in the context of a conversation about Sergei's poor understanding of the Hebrew language. The goldfish says, "Mine's supergreat. . . . I'm fluent in everything." The contrast between Sergei's poor Hebrew and the fish's fluent Hebrew helps you guess that *fluent* means "able to express oneself clearly and easily."

Practice and Apply Find these words in the story: *testament* (line 12), *foreseeable* (line 28), *accountable* (line 35), *promo* (line 181). Working with a partner, use context clues to determine each word's meaning as it is used in the story.

1. Determine the word's function in the sentence. Does it function as a noun, adjective, verb, or adverb? How might the word fit into the overall meaning of the sentence?

2. If the sentence does not provide enough information, read the paragraph in which the word appears and consider the larger context of the story. How might the word fit with what you know about the characters or the plot?

3. Write down your definition and the clues you used to determine the meaning of each word.

Language and Style:
Formal Versus Informal Tone

An author's word choices and sentence structures express a particular **tone**, or attitude, toward characters and events. The tone may also reflect the personality of one or more characters. Etgar Keret's writing uses techniques such as slang and incomplete sentences to create an informal tone. Read this passage from the story.

> Yonatan had a brilliant idea for a documentary. He'd knock on doors. Just him. No camera crew, no nonsense. Just Yonatan, on his own, a small camera in hand, asking, "If you found a talking goldfish that granted you three wishes, what would you wish for?"

The author could have used more formal language, like this:

> Yonatan had a brilliantly simple idea for a documentary. He would do all the filming himself, without a camera crew. Knocking on people's doors with a small hand-held camera, he would inquire of each person, "If you found a talking goldfish that granted you three wishes, what would you wish for?"

The informal language sets a tone that is better suited to Yoni's youthful enthusiasm and his spirit of adventure.

Here are some other examples of language from the story and how they contribute to the informal tone:

Example	How It Affects Tone
"three killer wishes"	*Killer* is slang for "excellent." Slang is the language of casual, everyday speech.
"When Sergei got to Israel and then moved to Jaffa, his family couldn't wrap their heads around it."	The expression *wrap their heads around* ("understand") is an idiom that people use in conversation but not in formal writing or speech.
"But the earring boy is stubborn."	Calling Yoni "the earring boy" reflects Sergei's private thoughts. The humor in this mild insult fits the informal tone of the story.

Practice and Apply Write two versions of a paragraph describing an experience you have had. Choose words, phrases, and sentence structures that create a formal tone in the first version and an informal tone in the second. Identify which version best fits the event your writing describes.

Background *Conflict between Israeli Jews and Palestinians dates back to even before 1948, when the state of Israel was established to give Jews a homeland following the horrors of the Holocaust. The decades since have been marked by numerous outbreaks of violence interspersed with attempts to broker peace agreements. The documentary film My So-Called Enemy, by Emmy-award winning director Lisa Gossels, follows a group of teenagers from the two sides of the conflict for seven years. These teens were first brought together in the United States by a leadership group called Building Bridges for Peace in an attempt to sow peace one friendship at a time.*

MEDIA ANALYSIS

Trailer for
My So-Called Enemy

Film directed by Lisa Gossels

AS YOU VIEW Consider the choices the director makes about arranging shots and including media features such as music and on-screen text. Note any questions you generate during viewing.

COLLABORATIVE DISCUSSION With a partner, discuss the overall feeling or impression you take from the trailer. Identify how the director created this overall impression, citing specific shots or media techniques to support your ideas.

Analyze Order: Structure and Juxtaposition

RI 3

Both writers and film directors craft their work to increase the impact of their ideas and messages. They make choices such as these about how to **structure** or arrange the interviews, facts, and other diverse sources of material:

Order of events or ideas, including how to set the scene and where to place the most important points	How ideas are introduced and developed, moving from basic information to deeper or more significant points about the ideas	How to show connections among events and ideas and add meaning through **juxtaposition**, placing key elements close to each other in the piece

Determine Purpose and Point of View

RI 6

Even when documenting a factual subject, writers and filmmakers have a point of view or purpose. Directors choose events, music, voiceovers, and on-screen text to advance a particular point of view. Note what you feel while reading or viewing a factual work, and identify how that effect was achieved. Understanding the choices a writer or director makes can help you identify his or her purpose.

Analyzing the Media

RI 1, RI 3, RI 6, W 1, SL 4

Cite Text Evidence Support your responses with evidence from the selection.

1. **Interpret** Identify the ways the conflict and people are introduced and developed in the trailer. Which shots or scenes most help you understand the situation the girls face? Why?

2. **Evaluate** List examples of media techniques used in the trailer, including news reports, music, and on-screen text. Which technique or example do you find most effective in achieving the director's purpose? Why?

3. **Analyze** Describe the shots that immediately follow Inas explaining her conflicted feelings about Jews. What is the effect of these shots, and how does this juxtaposition serve the director's purpose?

PERFORMANCE TASK

Speaking Activity: Argument Do you think that face-to-face interactions can help resolve conflicts? Express your view in a short speech.

- Review the trailer, noting evidence that supports your ideas. Add ideas from your experiences to your notes.

- Write a one-page argument expressing and supporting your ideas. Then, deliver the argument as a speech.

Background *At the 1984 Republican National Convention in Dallas, Texas, protesters march, held signs, and chanted slogans opposing the policies of then-President Ronald Reagan. One of the protesters, Gregory Lee Johnson, set an American flag on fire. He was punished with a fine and a jail term for breaking a state law banning flag desecration. He appealed, and the case was sent to the Supreme Court to decide whether flag burning is a form of expression protected by the Constitution. The Court delivered its ruling in 1989.*

William J. Brennan *(1906–1997), who served on the Supreme Court from 1956 to 1990, wrote the majority opinion in the case. His staunch defense of First Amendment rights influenced many significant Court decisions.*

from

Texas v. Johnson Majority Opinion

Court Opinion by William J. Brennan

American Flag Stands for Tolerance

Newspaper Editorial by Ronald J. Allen

from

Texas v. Johnson Majority Opinion

Court Opinion by William J. Brennan

AS YOU READ Pay attention to the details that explain the Court's reasons for its decision. Note any questions you have as you read.

We decline, therefore, to create for the flag an exception to the joust[1] of principles protected by the First Amendment. . . . [2]

To say that the government has an interest in encouraging proper treatment of the flag, however, is not to say that it may criminally punish a person for burning a flag as a means of political protest.

---

[1] **joust:** competition.

[2] **First Amendment:** the part of the Bill of Rights added to the U.S. Constitution that deals with freedom of speech, among other freedoms.

Image Credits: ©Guy Jarvis/Houghton Mifflin Harcourt

National unity as an end which officials may foster by persuasion and example is not in question. The problem is whether, under our Constitution, **compulsion** as here employed is a permissible means for its achievement.

[Barnette, 319 U.S. at 640.]

We are fortified in today's conclusion by our conviction that forbidding criminal punishment for conduct such as Johnson's will not endanger the special role played by our flag or the feelings it inspires. To paraphrase Justice Holmes, we submit that nobody can suppose that this one gesture of an unknown man will change our Nation's attitude towards its flag [*Abrams* v. *United States*]. Indeed, Texas' argument that the burning of an American flag "is an act having a high likelihood to cause a breach of the peace," and its statute's **implicit** assumption that physical mistreatment of the flag will lead to "serious offense," tend to confirm that the flag's special role is not in danger; if it were, no one would riot or take offense because a flag had been burned.

We are tempted to say, in fact, that the flag's deservedly cherished place in our community will be strengthened, not weakened, by our holding today. Our decision is a **reaffirmation** of the principles of freedom and inclusiveness that the flag best reflects, and of the conviction that our toleration of criticism such as Johnson's is a sign and source of our strength. Indeed, one of the proudest images of our flag, the one immortalized in our own national anthem, is of the bombardment it survived at Fort McHenry.[3] It is the Nation's **resilience**, not its rigidity, that Texas sees reflected in the flag—and it is that resilience that we reassert today.

The way to preserve the flag's special role is not to punish those who feel differently about these matters. It is to persuade them that they are wrong.

compulsion
(kəm-pŭl´shən) *n.*
forced obligation.

implicit
(ĭm-plĭs´ĭt) *adj.*
understood, but not expressed.

reaffirmation
(rē´ăf-ər-mā´shən) *n.*
the act of verifying or endorsing again.

resilience
(rĭ-zĭl´yəns) *n.*
ability to return to a normal state after a change or an injury.

COLLABORATIVE DISCUSSION With a partner, discuss what the Court decided and why. Cite specific textual evidence from the opinion to support your ideas.

---

[3] **Fort McHenry:** War of 1812 battle site in Baltimore. In 1814, poet Francis Scott Key, being held prisoner on a ship nearby, was elated to see the American flag flying there and wrote the poem that became "The Star-Spangled Banner" to celebrate this American victory over the British.

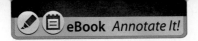
RI 9

Analyze Seminal U.S. Documents

Seminal means "creative, original, and having great influence on what follows." A **seminal document**, then, is one that establishes or defines principles that shape the way others think or act. The *Texas* v. *Johnson* opinion is a seminal document. It sets forth a rational interpretation of the First Amendment that includes protection of "symbolic speech," such as flag burning. This decision set a precedent for rulings in later cases, and it increased understanding of how First Amendment principles apply to contemporary situations.

Analyzing the Text

RI 1, RI 3, RI 4, RI 5, RI 9, W 2b

Cite Text Evidence   Support your responses with evidence from the selection.

1. **Connect** What earlier points of law does Justice Brennan use to support the Court's opinion in this case?

2. **Compare** In its argument to make flag burning a criminal offense, what events did Texas predict might happen? How does the Court interpret the significance of these possible events?

3. **Cite Evidence** How does Justice Brennan support the idea that "the flag's deservedly cherished place in our community will be strengthened, not weakened" by the ruling?

4. **Analyze** How is the image of the flag flying over Fort McHenry related to the central idea of the opinion?

5. **Analyze** What does Justice Brennan's repetition of the word *resilience* to refer to the nation suggest about his view of the Constitution?

PERFORMANCE TASK

Writing Activity: Comparison The Supreme Court determines whether official actions follow the Constitution. In *Texas* v. *Johnson*, the Court's ruling centered on the First Amendment. Compare ideas in the decision and the amendment:

> ***First Amendment*** *Congress shall make no law respecting an establishment of religion, or prohibiting the free exercise thereof; or abridging the freedom of speech, or of the press; or the right of the people peaceably to assemble, and to petition the Government for a redress of grievances.*

- Identify concepts that are discussed in both documents. How does each document address them?

- In a paragraph, compare the two documents. Support your points with examples from both texts.

American Flag Stands for Tolerance

Newspaper Editorial by Ronald J. Allen

AS YOU READ Pay attention to words and details that communicate the author's opinion on his topic.

In a controversial decision, the Supreme Court, by the closest possible margin of a 5-to-4 vote, held that a person has a right to express disagreement with governmental policies by burning the American flag. In a decision at least as controversial, the leadership of the People's Republic of China decided that citizens who peacefully express disagreement with government policies may be slaughtered.[1] On the surface, these two events may seem to bear little relationship to one another, but deep and fundamental lessons can be drawn from their comparison.

10   The American flag is a cherished symbol of our national aspirations. It is the closest object to a national icon,[2] rivaled only by the Constitution and the Declaration of Independence. Given the widespread and deeply felt reverence for this symbol of what we perceive to be the best of our civilization, what is the harm in insisting upon a modicum[3] of respect for it? After all, no one can seriously equate a prohibition on flag burning with the imposition of governmental **orthodoxy** in political speech. Any messages that burning the flag might convey easily can be communicated in other ways. Those are powerful points, deserving the greatest respect. If

20 not rebutted,[4] they compel the conclusion that the Supreme Court was wrong in its decision.

The Supreme Court was not wrong. Indeed, a decision contrary to the one reached would have been a definitive step away from our national aspirations. A commitment to the intertwined freedoms of conscience and expression is at the core of those aspirations. What most distinguishes our civilization from both its predecessors and its contemporary competitors is a belief in the **sanctity** of the human conscience. Each individual is to have the freedom to develop by his or her own lights, and not by the command of

orthodoxy
(ôr´thə-dŏk´sē) *n.*
traditionally accepted codes and customs.

sanctity
(săngk´tĭ-tē) *n.*
sacredness or ultimate importance.

---

[1] **People's Republic of China . . . slaughtered:** In June 1989, government tanks fired on citizens who had gathered in Beijing's Tiananmen Square to demand democratic reforms. Hundreds were killed.

[2] **icon:** symbol of deeply held values.

[3] **modicum:** small amount offered as a symbol or gesture.

[4] **rebutted:** opposed using reasons and evidence.

Dallas police arrest Gregory Lee Johnson for burning an
American flag outside the 1984 Republican National Convention.

30 officialdom. That requires not just the right to be let alone, but
also the right to communicate with, to learn from and test views in
conversations.

It is, thus, no surprise that the First Amendment is where it is
in the Bill of Rights, for it is first in importance. A concomitant of
the commitment to freedom of conscience, in a sense its mirror
image, is that no one has better access to truth than anyone else.
Official **dogma** is not better (perhaps no worse) than the beliefs of
private citizens.

The **dissenters** in the flag-burning case and their supporters
40 might at this juncture note an irony in my argument. My point
is that freedom of conscience and expression is at the core of our
self-conception and that commitment to it requires the rejection of
official dogma. But how is that admittedly dogmatic belief different
from any other dogma, such as the one inferring that freedom of
expression stops at the border of the flag?

The crucial distinction is that the commitment to freedom
of conscience and expression states the simplest and least self-
contradictory principle that seems to capture our aspirations.
Any other principle is hopelessly at odds with our commitment
50 to freedom of conscience. The controversy surrounding the flag-
burning case makes the case well.

The controversy will rage precisely because burning the flag
is such a powerful form of communication. Were it not, who

dogma
(dôg′mə) *n.*
principles or beliefs
that an authority
insists are true.

dissenter
(dĭ-sĕn′tər) *n.*
one who disagrees or
refuses to accept.

American Flag Stands for Tolerance **19**

would care? Thus were we to embrace a prohibition on such communication, we would be saying that the First Amendment protects expression only when no one is offended. That would mean that this aspect of the First Amendment would be of virtually no consequence. It would protect a person only when no protection was needed. Thus, we do have one official dogma—each

60 American may think and express anything he wants. The exception is expression that involves the risk of injury to others and the destruction of someone else`s property. Neither was present in this case.

At the core of what the flag symbolizes, then, is tolerance. More than anything else, the flag stands for free expression of ideas, no matter how distasteful. The ultimate irony would have been to punish views expressed by burning the flag that stands for the right to those expressions.

. . . Perhaps, though, there is another way to look at it—to

70 acknowledge that not even such a fundamental value as the commitment to freedom of conscience should be free from controversy. With controversy comes debate, enlightenment and renewed commitment. Perhaps, then, we are in the court's debt for not treating the flag-burning case like the simple case it is. Let the controversy rage. After all, it is in robust debate that we are most true to ourselves.

COLLABORATIVE DISCUSSION Does the author agree or disagree with the Court's ruling? With a partner, discuss the author's opinion and attitude toward the decision. Cite specific textual evidence to support your ideas.

Cite Evidence

Editorial writers express opinions on current issues and events, supporting their ideas with reasons and evidence, including facts, examples, and expert views. To decide whether you agree with the writer's argument, you must be sure you understand both the **explicit meaning**—the ideas stated directly in the text—and the ideas that are implied. To make **inferences**, or logical assumptions, about the writer's implied meaning you must identify text evidence as well as consider what you already know.

Analyze Impact of Word Choice: Compare Tone

Tone reflects a writer's attitude toward the subject, audience, and context for writing. The **context,** or situation for which a piece of writing is created, often determines both its form and its tone.

A Supreme Court ruling is written in a serious and thoughtful context; it must use precise language and reasoning because it represents the law of the land and may be cited in future decisions as a **precedent**—the legal basis of other rulings with far-reaching effects. A newspaper editorial, on the other hand, is written in a more immediate and emotional context; it expresses the writer's current thinking about a controversial topic.

Compare the tone and meaning expressed in the following passages from Brennan's and Allen's writing:

Brennan	Allen
To say that the government has an interest in encouraging proper treatment of the flag, however, is not to say that it may criminally punish a person for burning a flag as a means of political protest.	The ultimate irony would have been to punish views expressed by burning the flag that stands for the right to those expressions.

When you compare the language the two writers use, consider the cumulative impact of their word choices. In this example, Brennan's precise word choices and careful sentence construction add up to a deliberate, careful, painstaking tone. In contrast, Allen's word choices are more evocative and his sentence structure more free. His tone is more that of a fiery speech than of the law of the land.

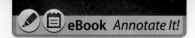
Analyzing the Text

RI 1, RI 3,
RI 4, RI 8,
W 2

Cite Text Evidence   Support your responses with evidence from the selection.

1. **Infer** What words in the second paragraph convey Allen's feelings toward the flag? Does understanding his attitude make you feel that his argument is stronger or weaker? Why?

2. **Analyze** In his editorial, Allen talks about the "sanctity of the human conscience" and the "enlightenment" that comes from debate. Explain how the connotations of these words convey his tone.

3. **Compare** What ideas are expressed in both the editorial and the court opinion? Which argument do you find more convincing? Why?

4. **Evaluate** A **fallacy** is an error in reasoning. Suppose Allen had included this sentence in his editorial: *Anyone who wants to throw flag burners in jail is obviously not a supporter of the Constitution*. In what way is this statement a fallacy? What would have been the effect of this sentence on Allen's argument?

5. **Analyze** Allen discriminates, or distinguishes, between what people *should* do and what they *should be allowed* to do. How does he reconcile this apparent contradiction in his argument?

PERFORMANCE TASK

Writing Activity: Analysis Beginning with the examples on the previous page, analyze the differences in meaning and tone between the *Texas* v. *Johnson* court opinion and the newspaper editorial discussing the decision.

- Using photocopies or sticky notes, identify word choices and sentences in both texts that strongly contribute to the overall tone of each.

- Write a one-page analysis of the differences in tone between the two texts. Conclude your analysis by explaining how the tone of each text fits the context for which it was written.

Critical Vocabulary

compulsion	implicit	reaffirmation	resilience
orthodoxy	sanctity	dogma	dissenter

Practice and Apply Answer each question by incorporating the meanings of both Critical Vocabulary words.

1. Which is more flexible, **orthodoxy** or **dogma?**

2. When might a **dissenter** show **resilience?**

3. What is a situation in which a **compulsion** might be **implicit?**

4. How might the **sanctity** of something need **reaffirmation?**

Vocabulary Strategy: Words from Latin

The Critical Vocabulary words *compulsion, implicit, reaffirmation, resilience, sanctity,* and *dissenter* all have Latin roots. Knowing the meaning of a root helps you define the various words derived from it. This chart defines several Latin roots and shows English words that derive from them:

Latin Root and Its Meaning	Related Words
sanctus means "sacred"	sanctity, sanctuary
firmus means "strong"	reaffirmation, firmament
resilire means "to leap back"	resilience, resilient
sentire means "to feel"	dissenter, sentiment

Practice and Apply For each row of the chart, identify one new word that belongs to the word family. (You may use a dictionary if needed.) For each word you choose, follow these steps:

1. Write a definition that incorporates the meaning of the Latin root.

2. Identify the part of speech.

3. Use the word in a sentence that reflects its meaning.

Language and Style: Noun Clauses

An **independent clause** is a group of words with a subject and a verb that can stand alone as a complete sentence. By contrast, a **dependent** or **subordinate clause** also contains a subject and a verb, but it cannot stand alone as a sentence.

> **Independent clause:** I ran

> **Dependent or subordinate clause:** While I was running

Subordinate clauses help writers express complex and specific ideas while also adding variety and interest to their writing style. A **noun clause** is a type of subordinate clause that takes the place of a noun in a sentence.

The author of "American Flag Stands for Tolerance" uses noun clauses frequently to convey important information. Read this sentence from the editorial:

> **In a controversial decision, the Supreme Court, by the closest possible margin of a 5-to-4 vote, held <u>that a person has a right to express disagreement with governmental policies by burning the American flag</u>.**

In this sentence, the noun clause acts as the direct object of the verb *held*. It states an idea that could not be summed up in one or two words without sacrificing clarity and meaning. It is introduced by the pronoun *that* and contains its own subject (*person*) and verb (*has*).

Many words besides *that* can introduce noun clauses. In this chart, note the various introductory words and the way each noun clause functions in the example sentence.

Uses of Noun Clauses	
Function	**Example**
subject	**Why he wakes so early in the morning** is a mystery to his parents.
indirect object	I gave **whoever asked first** the prize.
predicate nominative	The fair is **what we wait for all year.**
object of a preposition	I wrote about **how we conducted the experiment.**

Practice and Apply Work with a partner to write a paragraph expressing your own thoughts about the ruling on flag burning. Include noun clauses that serve each of the four functions listed in the chart.

Shirley Jackson (1919–1965) *said about her writing, "It's great fun and I love it." Although some of her works humorously chronicle her life with her husband and four children, she is best known for exploring the darker side of human nature. Her story "The Lottery" ignited controversy when it was published in* The New Yorker *in 1948. Readers canceled their subscriptions and sent hundreds of letters expressing their outrage over the tale. Her novel* The Haunting of Hill House, *considered by many to be the "greatest haunted house story ever written," and the gothic horror tale* We Have Always Lived in the Castle *have been adapted for film and stage and are still widely read.*

The Lottery

Short Story by Shirley Jackson

AS YOU READ Pay attention to details that reveal the purpose of the lottery and the villagers' reactions to it. Note any questions you have.

The morning of June 27th was clear and sunny, with the fresh warmth of a full-summer day; the flowers were blossoming **profusely** and the grass was richly green. The people of the village began to gather in the square, between the post office and the bank, around ten o'clock; in some towns there were so many people that the lottery took two days and had to be started on June 26th, but in this village, where there were only about three hundred people, the whole lottery look less than two hours, so it could begin at ten o'clock in the morning and still be through in time to allow the
10 villagers to get home for noon dinner.

The children assembled first, of course. School was recently over for the summer, and the feeling of liberty sat uneasily on most of them; they tended to gather together quietly for a while before they broke into boisterous play, and their talk was still of the classroom and the teacher, of books and reprimands. Bobby Martin had already stuffed his pockets full of stones, and the other boys soon followed his example, selecting the smoothest and roundest stones; Bobby and Harry Jones and Dickie Delacroix—the villagers

profusely
(prə-fyo͞os´lē) *adv.* plentifully, in a freely available way.

pronounced this name "Dellacroy"—eventually made a great
20 pile of stones in one corner of the square and guarded it against
the raids of the other boys. The girls stood aside, talking among
themselves, looking over their shoulders at the boys, and the very
small children rolled in the dust or clung to the hands of their older
brothers or sisters.

Soon the men began to gather, surveying their own children,
speaking of planting and rain, tractors and taxes. They stood
together, away from the pile of stones in the corner, and their jokes
were quiet and they smiled rather than laughed. The women,
wearing faded house dresses and sweaters, came shortly after
30 their menfolk. They greeted one another and exchanged bits
of gossip as they went to join their husbands. Soon the women,
standing by their husbands, began to call to their children, and the
children came reluctantly, having to be called four or five times.
Bobby Martin ducked under his mother's grasping hand and ran,
laughing, back to the pile of stones. His father spoke up sharply,
and Bobby came quickly and took his place between his father and
his oldest brother.

The lottery was conducted—as were the square dances, the
teenage club, the Halloween program—by Mr. Summers, who had
40 time and energy to devote to civic activities. He was a round-faced,
jovial man and he ran the coal business, and people were sorry for
him, because he had no children and his wife was a scold. When
he arrived in the square, carrying the black wooden box, there
was a murmur of conversation among the villagers, and he waved
and called, "Little late today, folks." The postmaster, Mr. Graves,
followed him, carrying a three-legged stool, and the stool was put in
the center of the square and Mr. Summers set the black box down
on it. The villagers kept their distance, leaving a space between
themselves and the stool, and when Mr. Summers said, "Some of
50 you fellows want to give me a hand?" there was a hesitation before
two men, Mr. Martin and his oldest son, Baxter, came forward to
hold the box steady on the stool while Mr. Summers stirred up the
papers inside it.

The original paraphernalia[1] for the lottery had been lost long
ago, and the black box now resting on the stool had been put into
use even before Old Man Warner, the oldest man in town, was
born. Mr. Summers spoke frequently to the villagers about making
a new box, but no one liked to upset even as much tradition as was
represented by the black box. There was a story that the present box
60 had been made with some pieces of the box that had preceded it, the
one that had been constructed when the first people settled down

---

[1] **paraphernalia:** necessary items and equipment for a particular activity.

to make a village here. Every year, after the lottery, Mr. Summers began talking again about a new box, but every year the subject was allowed to fade off without anything's being done. The black box grew shabbier each year; by now it was no longer completely black but splintered badly along one side to show the original wood color, and in some places faded or stained.

Mr. Martin and his oldest son, Baxter, held the black box securely on the stool until Mr. Summers had stirred the papers
70 thoroughly with his hand. Because so much of the ritual had been forgotten or discarded, Mr. Summers had been successful in having slips of paper substituted for the chips of wood that had been used for generations. Chips of wood, Mr. Summers had argued, had been all very well when the village was tiny, but now that the population was more than three hundred and likely to keep on growing, it was necessary to use something that would fit more easily into the black box. The night before the lottery, Mr. Summers and Mr. Graves made up the slips of paper and put them in the box, and it was then taken to the safe of Mr. Summers' coal company and locked up

until Mr. Summers was ready to take it to the square next morning. The rest of the year, the box was put away, sometimes one place, sometimes another; it had spent one year in Mr. Graves's barn and another year underfoot in the post office, and sometimes it was set on a shelf in the Martin grocery and left there.

There was a great deal of fussing to be done before Mr. Summers declared the lottery open. There were the lists to make up—of heads of families, heads of households in each family, members of each household in each family. There was the proper swearing-in of Mr. Summers by the postmaster, as the official of the lottery; at one time, some people remembered, there had been a recital of some sort, performed by the official of the lottery, a **perfunctory**, tuneless chant that had been rattled off duly each year; some people believed that the official of the lottery used to stand just so when he said or sang it, others believed that he was supposed to walk among the people, but years and years ago this part of the ritual had been allowed to lapse. There had been, also, a ritual salute, which the official of the lottery had had to use in addressing each person who came up to draw from the box, but this also had changed with time, until now it was felt necessary only for the official to speak to each person approaching. Mr. Summers was very good at all this; in his clean white shirt and blue jeans, with one hand resting carelessly on the black box, he seemed very proper and important as he talked interminably to Mr. Graves and the Martins.

Just as Mr. Summers finally left off talking and turned to the assembled villagers, Mrs. Hutchinson came hurriedly along the path to the square, her sweater thrown over her shoulders, and slid into place in the back of the crowd. "Clean forgot what day it was," she said to Mrs. Delacroix, who stood next to her, and they both laughed softly. "Thought my old man was out back stacking wood," Mrs. Hutchinson went on, "and then I looked out the window and the kids was gone, and then I remembered it was the twenty-seventh and came a-running." She dried her hands on her apron, and Mrs. Delacroix said, "You're in time, though. They're still talking away up there."

Mrs. Hutchinson craned her neck to see through the crowd and found her husband and children standing near the front. She tapped Mrs. Delacroix on the arm as a farewell and began to make her way through the crowd. The people separated good-humoredly to let her through; two or three people said, in voices just loud enough to be heard across the crowd, "Here comes your Missus, Hutchinson," and "Bill, she made it after all." Mrs. Hutchinson reached her husband, and Mr. Summers, who had been waiting, said cheerfully, "Thought we were going to have to get on without

perfunctory
(pər-fŭngk´tə-rē)
adj. done mechanically and without enthusiasm.

you, Tessie." Mrs. Hutchinson said, grinning, "Wouldn't have me leave m'dishes in the sink, now, would you, Joe?," and soft laughter ran through the crowd as the people stirred back into position after Mrs. Hutchinson's arrival.

130 "Well, now," Mr. Summers said soberly, "guess we better get started, get this over with, so's we can go back to work. Anybody ain't here?"

"Dunbar," several people said. "Dunbar, Dunbar."

Mr. Summers consulted his list. "Clyde Dunbar," he said. "That's right. He's broke his leg, hasn't he? Who's drawing for him?"

"Me, I guess," a woman said, and Mr. Summers turned to look at her. "Wife draws for her husband," Mr. Summers said. "Don't you have a grown boy to do it for you, Janey?" Although Mr. Summers and everyone else in the village knew the answer perfectly well, it was the business of the official of the lottery to ask such questions

140 formally. Mr. Summers waited with an expression of polite interest while Mrs. Dunbar answered.

"Horace's not but sixteen yet," Mrs. Dunbar said regretfully. "Guess I gotta fill in for the old man this year."

"Right," Mr. Summers said. He made a note on the list he was holding. Then he asked, "Watson boy drawing this year?"

A tall boy in the crowd raised his hand. "Here," he said. "I'm drawing for m'mother and me." He blinked his eyes nervously and ducked his head as several voices in the crowd said things like "Good fellow, Jack," and "Glad to see your mother's got a man to

150 do it."

"Well," Mr. Summers said, "guess that's everyone. Old Man Warner make it?"

"Here," a voice said, and Mr. Summers nodded.

A sudden hush fell on the crowd as Mr. Summers cleared his throat and looked at the list. "All ready?" he called. "Now, I'll read the names—heads of families first—and the men come up and take a paper out of the box. Keep the paper folded in your hand without looking at it until everyone has had a turn. Everything clear?"

The people had done it so many times that they only half

160 listened to the directions; most of them were quiet, wetting their lips, not looking around. Then Mr. Summers raised one hand high and said, "Adams." A man disengaged himself from the crowd and came forward. "Hi, Steve," Mr. Summers said, and Mr. Adams said, "Hi, Joe." They grinned at one another humorlessly and nervously. Then Mr. Adams reached into the black box and took out a folded paper. He held it firmly by one corner as he turned and went hastily back to his place in the crowd, where he stood a little apart from his family, not looking down at his hand.

"Allen," Mr. Summers said. "Anderson. . . . Bentham."

170   "Seems like there's no time at all between lotteries any more," Mrs. Delacroix said to Mrs. Graves in the back row. "Seems like we got through with the last one only last week."

"Time sure goes fast," Mrs. Graves said.

"Clark. . . . Delacroix."

"There goes my old man," Mrs. Delacroix said. She held her breath while her husband went forward.

"Dunbar," Mr. Summers said, and Mrs. Dunbar went steadily to the box while one of the women said, "Go on, Janey," and another said, "There she goes."

180   "We're next," Mrs. Graves said. She watched while Mr. Graves came around from the side of the box, greeted Mr. Summers gravely, and selected a slip of paper from the box. By now, all through the crowd there were men holding the small folded papers in their large hands, turning them over and over nervously. Mrs. Dunbar and her two sons stood together, Mrs. Dunbar holding the slip of paper.

"Harburt. . . . Hutchinson."

"Get up there, Bill," Mrs. Hutchinson said, and the people near her laughed.

190   "Jones."

"They do say," Mr. Adams said to Old Man Warner, who stood next to him, "that over in the north village they're talking of giving up the lottery."

Old Man Warner snorted. "Pack of crazy fools," he said. "Listening to the young folks, nothing's good enough for *them*. Next thing you know, they'll be wanting to go back to living in caves, nobody work any more, live *that* way for a while. Used to be a saying about 'Lottery in June, corn be heavy soon.' First thing you know, we'd all be eating stewed chickweed and acorns.

200   There's *always* been a lottery," he added **petulantly**. "Bad enough to see young Joe Summers up there joking with everybody."

"Some places have already quit lotteries," Mrs. Adams said.

"Nothing but trouble in *that*," Old Man Warner said stoutly. "Pack of young fools."

"Martin." And Bobby Martin watched his father go forward. "Overdyke. . . . Percy."

"I wish they'd hurry," Mrs. Dunbar said to her older son. "I wish they'd hurry."

"They're almost through," her son said.

210   "You get ready to run tell Dad," Mrs. Dunbar said.

Mr. Summers called his own name and then stepped forward precisely and selected a slip from the box. Then he called, "Warner."

"Seventy-seventh year I been in the lottery," Old Man Warner said as he went through the crowd. "Seventy-seventh time."

"Watson." The tall boy came awkwardly through the crowd. Someone said, "Don't be nervous, Jack," and Mr. Summers said, "Take your time, son."

"Zanini."

After that, there was a long pause, a breathless pause, until
220   Mr. Summers, holding his slip of paper in the air, said, "All right, fellows." For a minute, no one moved, and then all the slips of paper were opened. Suddenly, all the women began to speak at once, saying, "Who is it?," "Who's got it?," "Is it the Dunbars?," "Is it the Watsons?" Then the voices began to say, "It's Hutchinson. It's Bill," "Bill Hutchinson's got it."

"Go tell your father," Mrs. Dunbar said to her older son. People began to look around to see the Hutchinsons. Bill Hutchinson was standing quiet, staring down at the paper in his hand. Suddenly, Tessie Hutchinson shouted to Mr. Summers, "You didn't give him
230   time enough to take any paper he wanted. I saw you. It wasn't fair!"

"Be a good sport, Tessie," Mrs. Delacroix called, and Mrs. Graves said, "All of us took the same chance."

"Shut up, Tessie," Bill Hutchinson said.

"Well, everyone," Mr. Summers said, "that was done pretty fast, and now we've got to be hurrying a little more to get done in time." He consulted his next list. "Bill," he said, "you draw

petulantly
(pĕch´ə-lənt-lē) *adv.*
in a grouchy or bad-tempered way.

for the Hutchinson family. You got any other households in the Hutchinsons?"

"There's Don and Eva," Mrs. Hutchinson yelled. "Make *them* take their chance!"

"Daughters draw with their husbands' families, Tessie," Mr. Summers said gently. "You know that as well as anyone else."

"It wasn't *fair*," Tessie said.

"I guess not, Joe," Bill Hutchinson said regretfully. "My daughter draws with her husband's family, that's only fair. And I've got no other family except the kids."

"Then, as far as drawing for families is concerned, it's you," Mr. Summers said in explanation, "and as far as drawing for households is concerned, that's you, too. Right?"

"Right," Bill Hutchinson said.

"How many kids, Bill?" Mr. Summers asked formally.

"Three," Bill Hutchinson said. "There's Bill, Jr., and Nancy, and little Dave. And Tessie and me."

"All right, then," Mr. Summers said. "Harry, you got their tickets back?"

Mr. Graves nodded and held up the slips of paper. "Put them in the box, then," Mr. Summers directed. "Take Bill's and put it in."

"I think we ought to start over," Mrs. Hutchinson said, as quietly as she could. "I tell you it wasn't *fair*. You didn't give him time enough to choose. *Every*body saw that."

Mr. Graves had selected the five slips and put them in the box, and he dropped all the papers but those onto the ground, where the breeze caught them and lifted them off.

"Listen, everybody," Mrs. Hutchinson was saying to the people around her.

"Ready, Bill?" Mr. Summers asked, and Bill Hutchinson, with one quick glance around at his wife and children, nodded.

"Remember," Mr. Summers said, "take the slips and keep them folded until each person has taken one. Harry, you help little Dave." Mr. Graves took the hand of the little boy, who came willingly with him up to the box. "Take a paper out of the box, Davy," Mr. Summers said. Davy put his hand into the box and laughed. "Take just *one* paper," Mr. Summers said. "Harry, you hold it for him." Mr. Graves took the child's hand and removed the folded paper from the tight fist and held it while little Dave stood next to him and looked up at him wonderingly.

"Nancy next," Mr. Summers said. Nancy was twelve and her school friends breathed heavily as she went forward, switching her skirt, and took a slip daintily from the box. "Bill, Jr.," Mr. Summers said, and Billy, his face red and his feet overlarge, nearly knocked the box over as he got a paper out. "Tessie," Mr. Summers said. She

> # I tell you it wasn't *fair.*

hesitated for a minute, looking around **defiantly,** and then set her lips and went up to the box. She snatched a paper out and held it behind her.

"Bill," Mr. Summers said, and Bill Hutchinson reached into the box and felt around, bringing his hand out at last with the slip of paper in it.

The crowd was quiet. A girl whispered, "I hope it's not Nancy," and the sound of the whisper reached the edges of the crowd.

290   "It's not the way it used to be," Old Man Warner said clearly. "People ain't the way they used to be."

"All right," Mr. Summers said. "Open the papers. Harry, you open little Dave's."

Mr. Graves opened the slip of paper and there was a general sigh through the crowd as he held it up and everyone could see that it was blank. Nancy and Bill, Jr., opened theirs at the same time, and both beamed and laughed, turning around to the crowd and holding their slips of paper above their heads.

"Tessie," Mr. Summers said. There was a pause, and then Mr. 300 Summers looked at Bill Hutchinson, and Bill unfolded his paper and showed it. It was blank.

"It's Tessie," Mr. Summers said, and his voice was hushed. "Show us her paper, Bill."

Bill Hutchinson went over to his wife and forced the slip of paper out of her hand. It had a black spot on it, the black spot Mr. Summers had made the night before with the heavy pencil in the

defiantly
(dĭ-fī′ənt-lē) *adv.*
boldly, rebelliously.

coal-company office. Bill Hutchinson held it up, and there was a stir in the crowd.

"All right, folks," Mr. Summers said. "Let's finish quickly."

310 Although the villagers had forgotten the ritual and lost the original black box, they still remembered to use stones. The pile of stones the boys had made earlier was ready; there were stones on the ground with the blowing scraps of paper that had come out of the box. Mrs. Delacroix selected a stone so large she had to pick it up with both hands and turned to Mrs. Dunbar. "Come on," she said. "Hurry up."

Mrs. Dunbar had small stones in both hands, and she said, gasping for breath, "I can't run at all. You'll have to go ahead and I'll catch up with you."

320 The children had stones already, and someone gave little Davy Hutchinson a few pebbles.

Tessie Hutchinson was in the center of a cleared space by now, and she held her hands out desperately as the villagers moved in on her. "It isn't fair," she said. A stone hit her on the side of the head.

Old Man Warner was saying, "Come on, come on, everyone." Steve Adams was in the front of the crowd of villagers, with Mrs. Graves beside him.

"It isn't fair, it isn't right," Mrs. Hutchinson screamed, and then they were upon her.

COLLABORATIVE DISCUSSION At what point did you realize the purpose of the lottery? With a partner, discuss how the villagers' reactions affected your own response. Cite specific textual evidence from the story to support your ideas.

Analyze Impact of Word Choice: Tone

In a fictional story such as "The Lottery," the narrator's **tone** or attitude influences how readers see and understand the setting, characters, and events. Over the course of a story, the specific words an author chooses to use work together to create a tone. The tone of a story may evoke a sense of time and place to help readers more fully experience the setting. It may also point toward the underlying theme, or message, of the story.

Shirley Jackson evokes a timeless, small-town setting with her word choices. In these examples, note how the tone would change if Jackson had chosen a different word.

Jackson's words	Synonyms
village	town, community
noon dinner	lunch, the midday meal
gossip	news, information

Analyze Author's Choices: Tension and Surprise

An author uses the structure of a story as well as narrative and literary devices to create a certain **mood** or feeling in readers. Jackson relies on the following elements to generate a mood of horror and surprise.

Irony	Foreshadowing	Pacing
Situational irony is the contrast between what is expected and what actually happens. This type of irony can be used to surprise readers. For example, "The Lottery" takes place on a beautiful June day. The peaceful setting lulls readers into thinking that nothing bad will happen, making later events more startling.	**Foreshadowing** is a writer's use of clues to hint at events that will occur later in the story. Jackson uses foreshadowing to add **suspense,** or tension, and to hold readers' interest as they wonder what the characters are doing and why.	**Pacing** is the way in which the writer moves the action along. Pacing helps to create mood. For example, a deceptively peaceful mood is developed by the slow pace of the narrator's detailed descriptions in the first part of the story. By speeding up the pacing in the second part of the story, the author also changes the mood.

Analyzing the Text

RL 1, RL 2,
RL 4, RL 5, W 1

Cite Text Evidence   Support your responses with evidence from the selection.

1. **Cite Evidence** How does the author use foreshadowing to increase suspense in the first four paragraphs of the story? Provide specific examples and explain their connection to the story's outcome.

2. **Infer** The author does not include the year in which the story takes place or the name of the village. Why are these details of setting omitted?

3. **Infer** The word *ritual* is used four times to describe the lottery. Why might viewing the lottery as a ritual inhibit the villagers' possible objections to it?

4. **Evaluate** Explain why Jackson waits until the end of the story to reveal the **conflict** —the purpose of the lottery. How would the story be less effective if the conflict were revealed earlier?

5. **Analyze** At the end of the story, Mrs. Delacroix selects a huge stone and urges Mrs. Dunbar to hurry. Explain why this is **ironic** or unexpected. What important idea is brought out by this instance of irony?

6. **Analyze** In the first part of the story, readers learn about characters, setting, and plot through the narrator's exposition. The second part of the story depends mostly on dialogue to advance the plot. How does this change affect the pacing and mood of this part of the story?

7. **Infer** How would you describe the narrator's tone throughout the story? Identify words that convey this tone to readers.

8. **Evaluate** Do you find the narrator's tone strange, or even shocking? Why? What theme about cruelty or injustice does this tone help communicate?

PERFORMANCE TASK

Writing Activity: Letter The publication of "The Lottery" in *The New Yorker* prompted many readers to write letters expressing their feelings about it. What would you say to the magazine's editors about the story's events and its overall meaning? Write your own letter, following these steps.

1. Support your explanation of your reaction and interpretation with specific evidence from the story.

2. Conclude by relating what you have discussed to the broader issue of whether the story should have been published.

Critical Vocabulary

profusely   **perfunctory**   **petulantly**   **defiantly**

Practice and Apply Write the Critical Vocabulary word that most accurately answers each question. Explain the reason for your choice.

1. Which word is associated with a challenge? Why?

2. Which word goes with daily routines? Why?

3. Which word goes with an unhappy child? Why?

4. Which word is associated with excessive growth? Why?

Vocabulary Strategy: Denotation and Connotation

The **denotation** of a word is the meaning found in a dictionary. The **connotation** of a word refers to the feelings or ideas associated with it. In writing "The Lottery," Shirley Jackson chose words for both their denotations and their connotations. In this sentence, she describes Old Man Warner as speaking petulantly: "'There's *always* been a lottery,' he added petulantly." The denotation of *petulantly* is "irritably." But by choosing *petulantly*, Jackson suggests that Old Man Warner is whiny, unreasonable, and childish as well. This chart shows the connotations and denotations of the remaining Critical Vocabulary words:

Word	Denotation	Connotation
profusely	plentifully	over the top; overly generous
perfunctory	done with little interest	done carelessly
defiantly	resistantly	rebelliously or angrily

Practice and Apply Work with a partner to brainstorm at least two synonyms for these words from the story. Note the connotation of each original word, and discuss how the connotation of each synonym changes the meaning of the original sentence.

1. assembled (line 11)

2. stained (line 67)

3. thrown (line 107)

Language and Style: Colloquialisms

Colloquialisms are words or expressions used in everyday speech in a particular region. In "The Lottery," although the narrator uses formal English, the villagers speak colloquially to each other. This use of colloquial language results in dialogue that flows naturally and sounds authentic for the characters.

> Read this line of dialogue from the story.

"Horace's not but sixteen yet . . . Guess I gotta fill in for the old man this year."

Jackson captures a small-town feel through informal grammatical structures ("Horace's"; "not but"; "Guess I") and slang expressions ("gotta"; "fill in"; "old man"). Now look at how the replacement of colloquial language with more standard wording changes the flow of the dialogue as well as your impression of the character:

"Horace is only sixteen. I suppose I'll have to take my husband's place this year."

With standard English dialogue, readers lose the sense of character and setting so crucial to Jackson's story.

This chart includes some of the characteristics of the colloquial language used in the story.

Characteristic	Example
implied subject rather than stated	"Seems like there's no time at all . . ."
nonstandard verb forms	"The kids was gone . . . I . . . came a-running"
use of idioms and slang	"Some of you fellows want to give me a hand?" "People ain't the way they used to be."

Practice and Apply List additional examples of the colloquial language in "The Lottery." Then, incorporate your examples into a three- or four-sentence dialogue. Share your conversation with a partner and evaluate each other's use of colloquialisms. In particular, note how the colloquialisms create a mood or sense of setting in each dialogue.

Without Title

for my Father who lived without ceremony

Poem by Diane Glancy

AS YOU READ Think about how Diane Glancy, a poet of Native American descent, portrays the life of the speaker's father. In what ways is it different from the traditional life of his people?

It's hard you know without the buffalo,
the shaman,[1] the arrow,
but my father went out each day to hunt
as though he had them.
5   He worked in the stockyards.
All his life he brought us meat.
No one marked his first kill,
no one sang his buffalo song.
Without a vision[2] he had migrated to the city
10   and went to work in the packing house.
When he brought home his horns and hides
my mother said
get rid of them.
I remember the animal tracks of his car
15   backing out the drive in snow and mud,
the aerial[3] on his old car waving
like a bow string.
I remember the silence of his lost power,
the red buffalo painted on his chest.
20   Oh, I couldn't see it
but it was there, and in the night I heard
his buffalo grunts like a snore.

COLLABORATIVE DISCUSSION What is the meaning of the subtitle, "for my Father who lived without ceremony"? With a partner, discuss what is missing from the father's life, citing evidence from the poem.

---

[1] **shaman:** a person who interacts with the spiritual world.
[2] **vision:** a guiding experience that often comes in a dream or a trance.
[3] **aerial:** a thin, metal antenna.

Support Inferences About Theme

RL 1, RL 2

The **theme** of a poem is a message about life or about human nature that the poet wishes to communicate to readers. Usually, the theme is not stated directly. Readers must **infer** the theme, or draw a conclusion based on details in the text. A theme can be stated in a sentence, such as "Honesty is the sign of a true friendship."

Follow these steps to determine theme in a poem:

- Develop an objective summary of the poem. In a sentence or two, state the most important ideas and details that the poet presents.
- Ask yourself what message about life or about people the poem conveys. A poem may have more than one theme, but all themes must be supported by textual evidence.
- Write a sentence that states the theme. Check to make sure there are enough details in the poem to support your theme. The evidence must be both strong and thorough.

Analyzing the Text

RL 1, RL 2, RL 3,
W 3a–b, e, SL 6

Cite Text Evidence   Support your responses with evidence from the selection.

1. **Identify** What details does the speaker use to contrast life in her father's original culture and life in the city?

2. **Infer** What can you infer about the speaker's feelings toward her father? Why doesn't she try to intervene in the conflict between her parents? Cite evidence from the text to support your answer.

3. **Analyze** What theme about tradition and community does this poem convey? Draft an objective summary, and then cite key details that help develop the theme over the course of the poem.

PERFORMANCE TASK

Speaking Activity: Narrative Presentation Plan and present a spoken narrative about one day in the life of the speaker's family.

- Decide who will be the narrator: the speaker, the speaker's father or mother, or a third-person narrator outside the poem.
- Write a draft describing the events of one day through your narrator's voice, incorporating details from the poem.

- Make sure your narrative builds to a logical conclusion that reflects what the characters experience in the poem.
- Speak using conventions of English that are appropriate to the narrator and context.

Present a Speech

This collection explores the significance of our relationships with others, as individuals and in groups. Look back at the texts you have read, including the anchor text "What, of This Goldfish, Would You Wish?," and make a generalization about how our relationships help define who we are. Share your ideas in a speech that incorporates media elements.

SL 4 Present information, findings, and supporting evidence clearly, concisely, and logically.
SL 5 Make strategic use of digital media in presentations.
SL 6 Adapt speech to a variety of contexts and tasks.

An effective speech

- presents a clear, logical thesis statement
- provides evidence from the texts to illustrate the thesis
- incorporates appropriate images, music, and other media to enhance meaning and maintain audience interest
- engages listeners with appropriate and clear use of language, emphasis, volume, and gestures

Visit hmhfyi.com to explore your topic and enhance your research.

PLAN

Analyze the Texts Choose two texts from this collection, including "What, of This Goldfish, Would You Wish?" In addition, choose one secondary source from the hmhfyi.com site. Identify the key relationship represented in each text.

- Make notes about each relationship, including how the relationships define who the people or characters are.
- Pay attention to specific examples from the texts that provide insights into the relationships.

Gather Evidence Save each piece of evidence to *my*Notebook, in a folder titled *Collection 1 Performance Task A*.

ACADEMIC VOCABULARY

As you share your ideas about relationships, be sure to use these words.

discriminate
diverse
inhibit
intervene
rational

myNotebook

"What, of This Goldfish, Would You Wish?"

"'He wanted to take you from me,' Sergei says, almost crying.

'Nonsense,' the fish says. 'He was only here to make a little something for TV.'"

Sergei's relationship with the fish shows us a side of Sergei we haven't seen before—a lonely man desperate for companionship.

Evaluate Your Own Experience Think about how your own relationships help to define who you are.

- Make notes about the role of relationships in your life.
- Support your view with evidence from your own experience.
- Explain why you agree or disagree with the authors of your three chosen texts.

Write a Thesis Statement Use your evidence to write a thesis statement about how our relationships help define us. Make sure you can support your statement with evidence from both primary and secondary sources.

Get Organized Organize your notes in an outline to make the connections among your ideas clear. In a logical sequence, list

- your thesis statement
- your key ideas about how our relationships define who we are
- text support for each key idea
- places where media elements might enhance or clarify an idea

PRODUCE

my WriteSmart

Write Your Speech Use your notes to write a clearly organized speech with an introduction, body, and conclusion. Include

- quotations and examples from the texts and from your own experience that support your thesis statement
- media elements, such as photos, music, and video clips, that enhance or illustrate your ideas and appeal to your audience
- language that is appropriately formal for an oral presentation

Write your rough draft in *my*WriteSmart. Focus on getting your ideas down, rather than perfecting your choice of language.

Interactive Lessons

For help incorporating media elements into your speech, use:
- Giving a Presentation: Types of Media; Audio, Video, and Images

Language and Style: Modal Expressions

A **modal expression** is a helping verb or an adverb that sets a particular mood in your writing or speaking. Modal expressions such as *possibly* or *could* communicate ideas about what is not yet the case, but might be in the future. See the following examples:

expressing an attitude or opinion We would be saying that the First Amendment protects expression only when no one is offended.

tempering or qualifying a statement Perhaps, though, there is another way to look at it.

Review your speech and insert modal expressions to express your attitude or to temper your statements.

Fine Tune Use the following chart to revise your draft.

Questions	Tips	Revision Techniques
Does the introduction grab the audience's attention?	**Underline** the questions or statements that would interest the audience.	If needed, **add** an attention-grabber to your introduction.
Is a generalization about how others help shape who we are clearly stated?	**Highlight** the statement of your central generalization.	**Add** a statement of your generalization or clarify it if needed.
Are ideas presented in a clear and logical way with precise word choices?	**Underline** precise word choices, and **note** the key idea or topic of each section of the speech.	**Replace** vague word choices with precise ones, and **reorder** ideas to explore one key idea at a time.
Do examples or quotations from at least two texts illustrate ideas?	**Highlight** quotations, paraphrases, or summaries of text evidence.	**Add** text evidence to support or contrast with your ideas.
Do media choices enhance the presentation's ideas or impact?	Next to each relevant media feature you plan to include, **note** the idea it enhances.	**Add** relevant images, video, music, or other media to enhance your message.

Have your partner or a group of peers review your draft in *my*WriteSmart. Ask your reviewers to note any details that do not support the generalization.

Interactive Lessons
For help in revising your draft, use
· Giving a Presentation: Style in Presentation

Practice Before presenting to the class, practice with a partner.

- Mark your text to show where you will use your voice or a gesture to emphasize a point. Think about when you might want to stress a particular word or pause for effect.

- Speak at an appropriate volume and pace so that your audience can hear you clearly.

- Set up and practice using any media elements in your speech. Make sure that the equipment you need will be available and working, and practice several times while incorporating media elements into your speech.

- Ask your partner to give you feedback so that you can improve your speech before presenting it to the whole class.

Deliver Your Speech As you present your speech, keep your audience in mind and remember to speak loudly and clearly at an appropriate pace.

Interactive Lessons
For help in rehearsing your speech, use
· Giving a Presentation: Delivering Your Presentation

PERFORMANCE TASK RUBRIC
SPEECH

	Ideas and Evidence	Organization	Language
4	• The speaker presents relevant examples from all of the chosen texts and media sources to support a logical generalization. • The speech effectively synthesizes analysis of the texts and personal experience to strengthen the generalization. • Media choices effectively illustrate and expand on ideas. • The conclusion reinforces the generalization and summarizes key ideas.	• The speech's organization helps listeners identify the generalization and the supporting ideas and evidence. • Ideas are presented in a logical order with clear connections between ideas.	• The speaker uses appropriately formal English to discuss the texts and ideas. • The speaker consistently quotes accurately from the texts to support ideas. • The speaker is easy to understand and adapts volume and pacing to audience needs. • The speaker effectively uses nuanced modal expressions.
3	• The speaker states a generalization and supports it with relevant ideas and evidence from the texts and media sources. • The speech synthesizes ideas from texts and experience. • Media choices are clearly linked to the speaker's ideas. • The speaker concludes with a statement that reinforces the generalization.	• The organization makes clear the generalization, supporting ideas, and evidence. • Ideas are presented in a logical order.	• The speaker mostly uses formal English to discuss the texts and ideas. • The speaker mostly quotes accurately from the texts to support ideas. • The speaker is generally easy to understand and uses appropriate volume and pacing. • The speaker uses a variety of familiar modal expressions.
2	• The speaker states a generalization but may support it with only limited evidence. • Common themes or connections among texts may not be clear to listeners. • Media choices lack a clear connection to the speaker's ideas. • The conclusion does little to reinforce the generalization.	• The organization may make it difficult to identify the speaker's generalization, supporting ideas, or evidence. • Ideas may seem somewhat disorganized.	• The speaker inconsistently uses formal English to discuss the texts and ideas. • The speaker may misquote one or more examples. • The speaker is occasionally difficult to understand. • The speaker uses at least one modal expression.
1	• The speaker's generalization is unclear; ideas and evidence are not coherent. • No attempt is made to synthesize ideas from multiple texts. • Media choices are absent or distracting. • The speech lacks any kind of conclusion or summary.	• The organization fails to distinguish among a generalization, support, and evidence. • Ideas are presented in a disorganized way.	• The speaker uses informal English and/or slang, resulting in ideas that are not clearly expressed. • The speaker frequently misquotes the texts. • The speaker is often difficult to understand. • Modal expressions are absent or cause confusion.

Write an Analytical Essay

This collection focuses on the way we relate to and interact with others. Look back at the texts you have read—particularly the anchor selections on burning the American flag—in the context of the collection-opening quotation from Barbara Jordan. Synthesize your ideas in an analytical essay.

An effective analytical essay

- makes logical connections between the quotation and texts
- clearly and accurately analyzes the texts' content and themes
- provides quotations or examples from the texts that support and elaborate on the analysis
- has an introduction, a logically structured body including transitions, and a conclusion
- uses appropriately formal style and sentence structures

W 2a–f Write informative/explanatory texts to examine and convey complex ideas, concepts, and information.

W 9a–b Draw evidence from literary or informational texts to support analysis, reflection, and research.

Visit hmhfyi.com to explore your topic and enhance your research.

> **PLAN**

Analyze the Texts Think back to the quotation from Barbara Jordan that opened this collection: "We, as human beings, must be willing to accept people who are different from ourselves." How does the quotation play out in the selections you have read?

- Choose three texts from this collection, including either "*Texas* v. *Johnson* Majority Opinion" or "American Flag Stands for Tolerance."
- Note relationships among people or groups explored in each text.
- Make notes about how people accept others in each text. If they discriminate against others, what are their reasons?
- Compare and contrast the authors' views. Do the authors present a common view about acceptance, or do they differ? Explain.

Mentor Text In this excerpt, columnist Ronald J. Allen analyzes the Supreme Court ruling on flag burning and what it says about people with opposing views.

> " At the core of what the flag symbolizes, then, is tolerance. More than anything else, the flag stands for free expression of ideas, no matter how distasteful. The ultimate irony would have been to punish views expressed by burning the flag that stands for the right to those expressions. "

myNotebook

Use the annotation tools in your eBook to find evidence that supports your ideas. Save each piece of evidence to your notebook.

ACADEMIC VOCABULARY

As you share your ideas about the role of individuals in society, be sure to use these words.

discriminate
diverse
inhibit
intervene
rational

Get Organized Outline your essay, including these elements:

Introduction

- attention-getting opener
- thesis statement about accepting those different from us

Body

- analysis of the two (or more) sides presented in each text
- supporting quotations or examples from each text
- connection between each text's themes and the quotation

Conclusion

- restatement of your thesis in light of the evidence presented
- general idea about people's acceptance of others

PRODUCE

Write your rough draft in *my*WriteSmart.

Write a Draft Use your outline to write an essay that explores how each text embraces or refutes the central idea of the quotation.

Remember to

- provide a clear and cohesive introduction, body, and conclusion
- support your main points with evidence from the text
- use language that is appropriate for your audience
- include transitions to link the major sections of the text

As you draft your analytical essay, remember that this kind of writing requires formal language and a respectful tone. Essays that analyze texts are expected to be appropriate for an academic context.

Interactive Lessons
For help in using appropriate language and tone, use
- <u>Writing Informative Texts: Formal Style</u>

Language and Style: Connect Ideas

You can show readers how your ideas are connected by combining clauses. A **clause** is a group of words with a subject and verb; you can combine two or more clauses to create compound or complex sentences that give your ideas more context and expressiveness. Notice how the highlighted clauses in the following sentences are linked.

compound sentence: On the surface, these two events may seem to bear little relationship to one another, but deep and fundamental lessons can be drawn from their comparison.

complex sentence: The controversy will rage precisely because burning the flag is such a powerful form of communication.

Review your draft, strengthening the connections among ideas by combining clauses where appropriate.

Have your partner or a group of peers review your draft in *my*WriteSmart.

Improve Your Draft You should now have a rough draft that analyzes the concept of acceptance in each of your chosen texts. Use the questions, tips, and revision techniques in the following chart to revise your draft.

Questions	Tips	Revision Techniques
Does the introduction clearly state a thesis?	**Underline** the thesis about accepting those who are different.	**If** needed, **add** a thesis statement to your introduction.
Is the analysis of relationships in each text accurate and supported by evidence?	**Note** the evidence that supports the analysis of each of the three chosen texts.	**Add** evidence to support each analysis, and **revise** your analysis if warranted by the text evidence.
Are the themes or ideas in each text clearly linked to the collection quotation?	**Highlight** references to the quotation.	**Add** statements relating ideas in the texts to the quotation as needed.
Does a general conclusion wrap up the analysis?	**Underline** the concluding statement about acceptance of others.	**Add** a concluding statement if needed.
Is an appropriately formal tone used throughout the essay?	**Highlight** each word or phrase that contributes to a formal tone.	**Replace** informal word choices and sentence structures as needed.

Interactive Lessons
To help you revise your draft, complete these lessons in Writing Informative Texts:
- Introductions and Conclusions
- Elaboration

PRESENT

Exchange Essays When your final draft is completed, exchange essays with a partner. Read your partner's essay and provide feedback. Reread the criteria for an effective analytical essay on the next page, and answer the following questions:

- What did your partner do well in the essay?
- How could your partner's essay be improved?

PERFORMANCE TASK RUBRIC
ANALYTICAL ESSAY

	Ideas and Evidence	Organization	Language
4	• The introduction is intriguing and informative. • The topic is strongly developed with relevant facts, concrete details, interesting quotations, and examples from the texts. • The writer makes logical assertions about the texts and synthesizes ideas from the texts with the quotation in an insightful way. • The concluding section capably follows from and supports the ideas presented.	• The organization of body paragraphs is effective and logical throughout the essay. • Clauses are combined in a variety of ways to successfully connect related ideas.	• The writing reflects a formal style and an objective, knowledgeable tone. • The writing demonstrates strong command of the conventions of standard English writing, including spelling, capitalization, punctuation, grammar, and usage. If handwritten, the analysis is legible.
3	• The introduction clearly states the topic of the essay. • One or two key points could use additional support in the form of relevant facts, details, quotations, and examples from the texts. • The writer accurately identifies ways in which the chosen texts relate to the quotation. • The concluding section mostly follows from and supports the ideas presented.	• The organization of body paragraphs is generally clear. • The writer clearly links ideas by combining clauses in compound or complex sentences.	• The style is generally formal, though the tone is subjective at times. • Minor errors in spelling, capitalization, punctuation, grammar, or usage occur but do not hinder communication. If handwritten, the analysis is mostly legible.
2	• A brief introduction may identify the topic. • Most key points need additional support in the form of relevant facts, details, quotations, and examples from the texts. • The writer identifies how only one text relates to the quotation, or makes illogical connections. • The concluding section may simply restate the topic or fail to follow from the ideas presented.	• The organization of body paragraphs is confusing. • Clauses are combined in one or two compound sentences to join ideas.	• The style is too informal; the tone is subjective. • Spelling, capitalization, and punctuation are often incorrect and in some cases cause confusion. If handwritten, the analysis may be partially illegible. • Grammar and usage are incorrect in many places, making some of the writer's ideas unclear.
1	• Facts, details, quotations, and examples from the texts are missing. • The writer fails to identify connections between the chosen texts and the quotation. • Introduction and/or conclusion may be absent.	• A logical organization is not used; information is presented randomly. • Related ideas are not joined by combining clauses.	• The style and tone are inappropriate for the essay. • Spelling, capitalization, and punctuation are incorrect throughout. If handwritten, the analysis may be partially or mostly illegible. • Many grammatical and usage errors hinder the meaning of the writer's ideas.

The Natural World

“Wildness reminds us what it means to be human, what we
are connected to rather than what we are separate from.”

—Terry Tempest Williams

The Natural World

We are intertwined with nature:
We affect it as much as it
affects us.

Stream to Start

hmhfyi.com

Channel One News®

Image Credits: ©Carlos Sanchez Pereyra/AWCorbis

COLLECTION

PERFORMANCE TASK Preview

At the end of this collection, you will have the opportunity to complete two tasks:

• Write a research report about an interaction between humans and nature.

• Present an oral narrative about a meaningful experience with nature.

ACADEMIC VOCABULARY

Study the words and their definitions in the chart below. You will use these words as you discuss and write about the texts in this collection.

Word	Definition	Related Forms
advocate (ăd´və-kāt´) *v.*	to argue for or plead in favor of	advocacy, advocator
discrete (dĭ-skrēt´) *adj.*	made up of separate or distinct things or parts	discretely, discreteness
domain (dō-mān´) *n.*	a sphere of activity	dominion
enhance (ĕn-hăns´) *tr.v.*	to make better, or add to the value or effectiveness	enhancement, enhancer
scope (skōp) *n.*	the size or extent of the activity or subject that is involved	scope out

Background *Desert plants have both beauty and clever mechanisms for survival. Despite extreme temperatures and scarce rain, they have thrived and adapted, ensuring that the desert will continue to bloom far into the future.*

Barbara Kingsolver (b. 1955) *was awarded the National Humanities Medal in 2000 for service to the United States through her writing.* Writer's Digest *named Kingsolver one of the 20th century's most influential writers. Much of her writing focuses on humans' relationship with the natural world.*

Called Out

Science Essay by Barbara Kingsolver   Written with Steven Hopp

AS YOU READ Pay attention to how the author describes a series of events to show how desert plants adapt, survive, and thrive in the harsh desert environment. Note any questions you have as you read.

As you read, save new words to ***myWordList***.

The spring of 1998 was the Halley's Comet[1] of desert wildflower years. While nearly everyone else on the planet was cursing the soggy consequences of El Niño's[2] downpours, here in southern Arizona we were cheering for the show: Our desert hills and valleys were colorized in wild schemes of maroon, indigo, tangerine, and some hues that Crayola hasn't named yet. Our mountains wore mantles of yellow brittlebush on their rocky shoulders, as fully transformed as eastern forests in their colorful autumn foliage. Abandoned cotton fields—flat, salinized ground long since left for
10 dead—rose again, wearing brocade. Even highway medians were so crowded with lupines and poppies that they looked like the seed-packet promises come true: that every one came up. For weeks, each

---

[1] **Halley's Comet:** an orbiting comet that is only visible from Earth once every 76 years.

[2] **El Niño (ĕl nēn´ yō):** a temporary change in climate caused by currents in the eastern Pacific Ocean.

day's walk to the mailbox became a **botanical** treasure hunt, as our attention caught first on new colors, then on whole new species in this terrain we thought we had already cataloged.

The first warm days of March appear to call out a kind of miracle here: the explosion of nearly half our desert's flowering species, all stirred suddenly into a brief cycle of bloom and death. Actually, though, the call begins subtly, much earlier, with winter rains and gradually climbing temperatures. The intensity of the floral outcome varies a great deal from one spring to another; that much is obvious to anyone who ventures outdoors at the right time of year and pays attention. But even couch potatoes could not have missed the fact that 1998 was special: Full-color wildflower photos made the front page of every major newspaper in the Southwest.

Our friends from other **climes** couldn't quite make out what the fuss was about. Many people aren't aware that the desert blooms at all, even in a normal year, and few would guess how much effort we devote to waiting and **prognosticating**. "Is this something like Punxsutawney Phil on Groundhog Day?"[3] asked a friend from the East.

"Something like that. Or the fall color in New England. All winter the experts take measurements and make forecasts. This year they predicted gold, but it's already gone platinum. In a spot where you'd expect a hundred flowers, we've got a thousand. More kinds than anybody alive has ever seen at once."

"But these are annual flowers?"

"Right."

"Well, then. . . ." Our nonbiologist friend struggled to frame her question: "If they weren't there *last* year, and this year they *are*, then who planted them?"

One of us blurted, "*God* planted them!"

We glanced at each other nervously: A picturesque response indeed, from scientifically trained types like ourselves. Yet it seemed more compelling than any pedestrian lecture on life cycles and latency periods.[4] Where *had* they all come from? Had these seeds just been lying around in the dirt for decades? And how was it that, at the behest of some higher power than the calendar, all at once there came a crowd?

The answers to these questions tell a tale as complex as a Beethoven symphony. Before a concert, you could look at a lot of sheet music and try to prepare yourself mentally for the piece it inscribed, but you'd still be knocked out when you heard it performed. With wildflowers, as in a concert, the magic is in the

botanical
(bə-tăn´ĭ-kəl) *adj.*
related to plants.

clime
(klīm) *n.*
climate area.

prognosticate
(prŏg-nŏs´tĭ-kāt´) *v.*
to forecast or predict.

---

[3] **Punxsutawney Phil on Groundhog Day:** the "official" Pennsylvania animal whose shadow or lack thereof on February 2 forecasts the duration of winter.

[4] **latency periods:** times when growth stops or pauses.

timing, the subtle combinations—and, most important, the extent
of the preparations.

For a species, the bloom is just the means to an end. The flower
show is really about making seeds, and the object of the game is
persistence through hell or high water, both of which are features
60 of the Sonoran Desert. In winter, when snow is falling on much
of North America, we get slow, drizzly rains that can last for days
and soak the whole region to its core. The Navajo call these female
rains, as opposed to the "male rains" of late summer—those rowdy
thunderstorms that briefly disrupt the hot afternoons, drenching
one small plot of ground while the next hill over remains parched.
It's the female rains that affect spring flowering, and in some years,
such as 1998, the **benefaction** trails steadily from winter on into
spring. In others, after a lick and a promise, the weather dries up
for good.

70   Challenging conditions for an **ephemeral**, these are. If a little
seed begins to grow at the first promise of rain, and that promise
gets broken, that right there is the end of its little life. If the same
thing happened to every seed in the bank, it would mean the end
of the species. But it *doesn't* happen that way. Desert wildflowers
have had millennia in which to come to terms with their incon-
stant mother. Once the plant has rushed through growth and
flowering, its seeds wait in the soil—and not just until the next
time conditions permit germination,[5] but often longer. In any given
year, a subset of a species's seeds don't germinate, because they're
80 programmed for a longer dormancy. This seed bank is the plant's

benefaction
(bĕn´ə-făk´shən) *n.*
a gift or assistance.

ephemeral
(ĭ-fĕm´ər-əl) *n.*
a short-lived plant.

---

[5] **germination:** the process in which plants emerge from seeds.

protection against a beckoning rain followed by drought. If any kind of wildflower ever existed whose seeds all sprouted and died before following through to seed-set, then that species perished long ago. This is what natural selection is about. The species that have made it this far have encoded genetic smarts enough to out-wit every peril. They produce seeds with different latency periods: Some germinate quickly, and some lie in wait, not just loitering there but loading the soil with many separate futures.

90 Scientists at the University of Arizona have spent years exam-ining the intricacies of seed banks. Desert ephemerals, they've learned, use a surprising variety of strategies to fine-tune their own cycles to a climate whose cycles are not predictable—or at least, not predictable given the relatively short span of human observation. Even in a year as wet as 1998, when photo-ops and seed production exploded, the natives were not just seizing the moment; they were stashing away future seasons of success by varying, among and within species, their genetic schedules for germination, flowering, and seed-set. This variation reduces the intense competition that would result if every seed germinated at once. Some species 100 even vary seed size: Larger seeds make more resilient sprouts, and smaller ones are less costly to produce; either morph may be programmed for delayed germination, depending on the particular strategy of the species. As a consequence of these sophisticated adaptations, desert natives can often hold their own against potential invasion by annual plants introduced from greener, more predictable pastures. You have to get up awfully early in the morning to outwit a native on its home turf.

The scientific term for these remarkable plants, "ephemeral annuals," suggests something that's as fragile as a poppy petal, a 110 captive to the calendar. That is our misapprehension, along with our notion of this floral magic show—now you see it, now you don't—as a thing we can predict and possess like a garden. In spite of our determination to contain what we see in neat, annual packages, the blazing field of blues and golds is neither a beginning nor an end. It's just a blink, or maybe a smile, in the long life of a species whose blueprint for perseverance must outdistance all our record books. The flowers will go on mystifying us, answering to a clock that ticks so slowly we won't live long enough to hear it.

COLLABORATIVE DISCUSSION In what way is the desert bloom even more impressive when viewed with an awareness of the underlying science? With a partner, discuss the complex ways desert plants ensure their survival. Cite specific textual evidence to support your ideas.

Determine Central Idea

Barbara Kingsolver uses many specific details to shape her **central idea** in "Called Out." By analyzing these details, you can better understand how Kingsolver develops her central idea over the course of the essay. A graphic organizer can help you analyze details and determine a central idea. You can then use this information to write an **objective summary** of the text, one that captures the main ideas and most important details but does not express your opinions.

Detail: Some seeds are "programmed for a longer dormancy." (lines 79–80)

Detail: Seeds have different latency periods: "some germinate quickly" while others "lie in wait." (lines 86–87)

Central Idea: _____
_____
_____

Detail: Desert plant species vary their "genetic schedules for germination" to reduce competition. (lines 96–99)

Detail: "Some species even vary seed size: Larger seeds make more resilient sprouts. . . ." (lines 99–100)

Determine Word Meanings

An author chooses words carefully to enhance the overall meaning and **tone**, or attitude, of a text. Kingsolver skillfully integrates figurative, connotative, and technical language to help convey her sense of wonder at the adaptability of desert plants.

Figurative	Connotative	Technical
Figurative meanings go beyond the literal to make a striking comparison. If a word doesn't make sense at first, consider its figurative meanings. For example, when Kingsolver describes fields as "wearing brocade," you can determine that the fields are not covered in elaborate fabric; this figurative use creates a vivid picture of how the fields look.	**Connotative language** is a writer's use of the feelings suggested by words to prompt an emotional response. Kingsolver uses connotative language to suggest awe at the ability of plants to survive in the desert. For example, describing the plants as "fragile" not only expresses their physical state but may make readers appreciate and want to protect them.	**Technical words and phrases** precisely describe complicated ideas or processes. Particularly in science writing, you may encounter unfamiliar words or technical meanings of familiar words, such as "bank" in line 90. Use footnotes or a dictionary as you read to be sure you understand technical meanings.

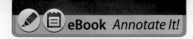

Analyzing the Text

RI 1, RI 2, RI 4,
RI 5, SL 1, L 5a,
L 5b

Cite Text Evidence   Support your responses with evidence from the selection.

1. **Cite Evidence** How does the author use figurative language to establish a tone of wonder in the first two paragraphs of the essay? Provide specific examples and explain how they provide the reader with a unique sense of the desert.

2. **Summarize** Reread lines 26–49. How does this passage help develop a central idea of Kingsolver's essay? Explain that central idea in an objective summary.

3. **Cite Evidence** Throughout the essay, the author uses connotative words and phrases such as "treasure hunt" (line 13) that suggest a contest or competition is taking place in the desert. Find several other examples of language that suggests competition. Explain how these discrete, or separate, word choices work together to shape the overall meaning and tone of the essay.

4. **Compare** What is the difference between the "female rains" and the "male rains"? What are the effects of each type of rain on the desert, and why is this difference significant?

5. **Analyze** In the second half of the essay, the author uses technical words and phrases to provide a more scientific description of how plant seeds survive in the desert. Find some examples, and explain how this technical language helps refine, or sharpen, her ideas about desert seeds.

6. **Draw Conclusions** Reread the last paragraph of the essay. Why does the author conclude by stating that the "flowers will go on mystifying us"?

PERFORMANCE TASK

Speaking Activity: Response to Literature Kingsolver's essay uses figurative, connotative, and technical language to give readers new perspectives on the desert ecosystem. Which kind of language is most effective in communicating scientific information to a general audience? Discuss this topic with a small group of classmates.

1. Working with a partner, review the text to find especially good examples of figurative, connotative, and technical language.

2. Form a small group to discuss the examples you have identified. Why is each one effective?

3. When you have discussed all the examples, take a vote on which kind of language best communicates information.

4. Write a summary of your group's discussion that includes your conclusion, the reasons for it, and some examples from the text.

Critical Vocabulary

| botanical | clime | prognosticate | benefaction | ephemeral |

Practice and Apply Complete each sentence stem so that your addition reflects the meaning of the Critical Vocabulary word.

1. To **prognosticate** the next big desert bloom is difficult because . . .

2. In the desert, rain is considered a **benefaction** because . . .

3. Kingsolver's essay could be called a **botanical** essay because . . .

4. It would be hard to plan a trip to see a particular desert **ephemeral** in bloom because . . .

5. People in a different **clime** might be surprised that the desert spring is so colorful because . . .

Vocabulary Strategy: Scientific Terms

Knowing the meanings of the scientific words and phrases used in Kingsolver's essay is essential for understanding her central ideas. For instance, Kingsolver uses the Critical Vocabulary word *ephemeral* several times in the second half of her essay. This word is more commonly used as an adjective meaning "lasting a short time." However, readers need to understand its scientific meaning as a very specific kind of desert plant to appreciate her discussion of these plants' survival mechanisms. The chart shows another example.

Word	Example of Usage from Text	Significance
botanical	"For weeks, each day's walk to the mailbox became a *botanical* treasure hunt, as our attention caught first on new colors, then on whole new species in this terrain we thought we had already cataloged."	The meaning of *botanical* ("relating to plants") clarifies that the new colors and species are those of plants that have bloomed in the yard.

Practice and Apply With a partner, review the text and identify three other scientific terms in Kingsolver's essay. With each word you choose, follow these steps:

1. Define each term. You may consult a glossary, college-level dictionary, or specialized reference source, but write the definition in your own words.

2. Provide an example of how the term is used in the essay and explain its significance to Kingsolver's central ideas and her purpose for writing.

3. Use each word you chose in a sentence.

Language and Style: Participial Phrases

A **participle** is a verb form that functions like an adjective, modifying nouns and pronouns. Typically, a participle uses a present-tense verb form ending in *-ing* or a past-tense verb form ending in *-ed* or *-en*. Kingsolver uses participles to add vibrancy and specificity to her descriptions, as in "*flowering* species" (lines 17–18).

Participial phrases are made up of participles and their modifiers and complements. An example from Kingsolver's essay is "ground *long since left for dead*" (lines 9–10). In this example, the participle is *left*, and words that modify it are *long since* and *for dead*. The entire participial phrase modifies the noun *ground*.

Read the following sentence from the essay:

Some germinate quickly, and some lie in wait, not just loitering there but loading the soil with many separate futures.

Kingsolver could have expressed this idea using two separate sentences:

Some germinate quickly, and some lie in wait. These seeds do not just loiter there but load the soil with many separate futures.

While this version communicates the same idea, the wording is less engaging and creates a pause between linked ideas. The use of the participial phrase, *not just loitering there but loading the soil with many separate futures,* in the original version conveys a relationship more quickly and holds the reader's interest.

Practice and Apply Understand and use participial phrases by following these steps:

1. Working with a partner, identify three additional participial phrases in "Called Out" and discuss how these phrases add to your understanding of the topic.

2. Then on your own, write a short paragraph on a topic of your choice. In your paragraph, include two sentences that contain participial phrases. Trade your paragraph with your partner. Identify the participial phrases in your partner's paragraph while your partner identifies the participial phrases in your paragraph.

Walt Whitman (1819–1892) *ended his formal schooling and went to work at age 11. Apprenticing for a local newspaper, he discovered that he loved putting words to paper. In the 1840s he began writing poems for his masterpiece,* Leaves of Grass. *Because no publisher would accept his unorthodox poems, Whitman self-published his collection in 1855. He continued to revise and add to it for the rest of his life. Many modern critics view Whitman's poems as distinctly American, marked by democratic values, a love of nature, and optimism for the future.*

When I Heard the Learn'd Astronomer

Poem by Walt Whitman

AS YOU READ Pay attention to contrasts in the poem. Jot down specific images that you find striking or interesting. Also, write down any questions you generate during reading.

When I heard the learn'd astronomer,
When the proofs,[1] the figures, were ranged in columns before me,
When I was shown the charts and diagrams, to add, divide, and
    measure them,
When I sitting heard the astronomer where he lectured with much
    applause in the lecture-room,
5 How soon unaccountable I became tired and sick,
Till rising and gliding out I wander'd off by myself,
In the mystical moist night air, and from time to time,
Look'd up in perfect silence at the stars.

COLLABORATIVE DISCUSSION With a partner, discuss the images you jotted down. Which images contrast with each other?

---

[1] **proofs:** formal scientific statements of evidence.

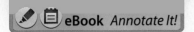

Determine Theme Through Objective Summary

RL 2

The **theme** of a literary work is a message about life that the writer wants readers to understand. Because Whitman, like most poets, does not directly state his theme, readers must infer it from details in the poem. The poem's images, structure, symbolism, and other poetic devices can serve as clues. Sometimes, writing an **objective summary**—a brief statement of the most important events or ideas in the poem—can be a good starting point in determining the poem's theme. Once you have identified the key events and ideas, you can consider what deeper meaning the poet may be trying to convey. As you analyze Whitman's poem, consider how the speaker responds to the lecture and what changes occur by the end of the poem.

Analyzing the Text

RL 1, RL 2, RL 4, RL 5, W 4

Cite Text Evidence Support your responses with evidence from the poem.

1. **Analyze** Whitman uses **parallelism**, the repetition of a grammatical structure, in lines 1–4. Describe what is parallel in these lines. What impression of the astronomer's lecture does the parallelism create?

2. **Summarize** Write a two-sentence objective summary of the poem. Summarize what happens or what is stated directly, without including any of your own opinions or interpretations.

3. **Contrast** How does Whitman's language describing the domain of science in lines 1–4 contrast with his language in lines 5–8? How does this contrast express a theme in the poem?

4. **Draw Conclusions** The speaker notes that the astronomer's lecture is greeted "with much applause in the lecture-room." What **tone**, or attitude, does the speaker have toward the other people in the room?

PERFORMANCE TASK

Writing Activity: Comparison Whitman's poem contrasts two different ways of viewing the natural world. Write a paragraph that similarly contrasts two ways of looking at something in your world.

1. Think of a place, event, or idea that people view in different ways. Create a T-chart to brainstorm details about the opposing views of your subject.

2. Write a paragraph that explores contrasting views of your subject, describing your own view last.

3. Share your paragraph with the class, and explain how it does or does not mirror Whitman's theme.

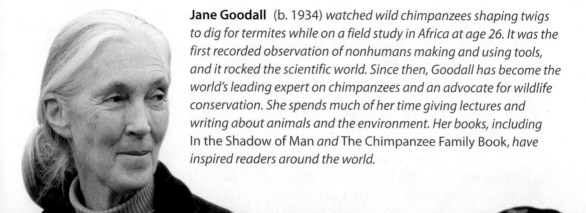

Jane Goodall (b. 1934) *watched wild chimpanzees shaping twigs to dig for termites while on a field study in Africa at age 26. It was the first recorded observation of nonhumans making and using tools, and it rocked the scientific world. Since then, Goodall has become the world's leading expert on chimpanzees and an advocate for wildlife conservation. She spends much of her time giving lectures and writing about animals and the environment. Her books, including* In the Shadow of Man *and* The Chimpanzee Family Book, *have inspired readers around the world.*

from

Hope for Animals and Their World

Argument by Jane Goodall

AS YOU READ Look for examples that show the role of the burying beetle and other insects in the environment.

American Burying Beetle
(Nicrophorus americanus)

The American burying beetle is but one of the millions of insects and other invertebrates[1] that play such a major, though seldom acknowledged, role in the maintenance of habitats and ecosystems. Most people simply lump them all into the category "creepy-crawlies" or "bugs." Some, such as butterflies, are admired and loved for their beauty (though people tend to be less interested in or even repelled by their caterpillars). Others, such as spiders, are the inadvertent cause of fear—even terror. Cockroaches are **loathed**. Hundreds of species are persecuted for the role they play in damaging our food—such as the desert locust, which ravages crops across huge areas. And there are countless species such as

10

loathe
(lōth) *v.*
to hate or despise.

---

[1] **invertebrates:** animals without backbones or spinal columns.

mosquitoes, tsetse flies, fleas, and ticks that carry diseases that can devastate other creatures, including ourselves.

It is for these reasons that they have been attacked by farmers, gardeners, and governments. Unfortunately the weapons of choice have been chemical pesticides—and this has led to horrific damage of all too many ecosystems, either through directly killing countless life-forms in addition to the intended targets, or when poisoned insects are eaten by creatures higher up the food chain.

Yet for every species that harms us or our food, there are countless others that work away, sometimes unseen, for the good of the environment where they live. I first became aware of this when I was a small child, picking up every earthworm I found stranded on the road (as did Dr. Albert Schweitzer,[2] by the way), and then learning about the valuable contribution they make to soil health. Millions of invertebrates provide food for species—including our own—higher up the food chain.

In many places people feast on termites, locusts, and beetle larvae—even I have tasted these things! Bees **pollinate** the vast majority of our food crops, and the current devastation of hives in North America and Europe is causing real anxiety.

pollinate
(pŏl´ə-nāt´) v.
to fertilize.

And what about the American burying beetle? What role, if any, does it play in our environment? This is what I learned about when, on March 18, 2007, I met with Lou Perrotti and Jack Mulvena of the Roger Williams Park Zoo in Providence, Rhode Island. Back in 1989, they told me, biologists had realized that the American burying beetle was fast declining, and it became one of just a few insect species to be listed under the Endangered Species Act. Then in 1993, the Roger Williams Park Zoo started a breeding program for the US Fish and Wildlife Service; in 2006, this beetle became the first insect species to be assigned a Species Survival Plan. Lou is currently the coordinator for the American burying beetle for the Association of Zoos and Aquariums.

As he began talking about the beetles, it was immediately apparent that they had the perfect spokesman! He is a man passionately interested in insects and, he told me, has "loved all things creepy-crawly" since he was a child. Like so many of the other people I have talked to while gathering information for this book, Lou had parents who were understanding and supportive of his fascination with invertebrates. (And other creatures, too—they allowed him to breed boa constrictors when he was nine years old!)

While we talked, Lou became increasingly animated. "Somebody needs to be out there saving these critters [the burying beetles]," he said. And that is just what he is doing. Let me share some of what I

---

[2] **Dr. Albert Schweitzer:** (1875–1965) Noted physician and writer who operated a hospital in Africa.

" Would the loss of the American burying beetle matter? "

learned from him about these remarkable beetles. Most people have no idea how fascinating they are. Certainly I hadn't.

The American burying beetle is the largest member of its genus[3] in North America—it is sometimes called the "giant carrion beetle." Once these beetles lived in forest and scrub grassland
60   habitats—anyplace where there was carrion of a suitable size and soil suitable for burying it—in thirty-five states throughout temperate eastern North America. But by 1920, populations in the East had largely disappeared. By 1970 populations had also disappeared from Ontario, Kentucky, Ohio, and Missouri. And during the 1980s, the beetle declined rapidly throughout the American Midwest.

Today there are only seven places where they are known to exist—Block Island (Rhode Island), a single county in eastern Oklahoma, scattered populations in Arkansas, Nebraska, South Dakota, Kansas,
70   and a recently discovered population on a military installation in Texas. One reason for the species' **precipitous** decline across its historical range, in addition to habitat loss and fragmentation, is possibly connected with the extinction of the passenger pigeon and the greatly reduced number of black-footed ferrets and prairie chickens, all of which provided carrion of ideal size.

precipitous
(prĭ-sĭp´ĭ-təs) *adj.*
sudden and rapid.

Why We Need the Burying Beetle

Let me return to the question I asked earlier—would the loss of the American burying beetle matter? The answer, stressed by Lou and Jack, is an emphatic *yes*. They feed on carrion—the flesh of dead animals. Lou calls them "nature's most efficient recyclers"
80   because they are responsible for recycling decaying animals back into the ecosystem. This returns nutrients to the earth, which stimulates the growth of plants. And by burying carcasses underground, this industrious beetle helps keep flies and ants from reaching epidemic proportions.

Lou explained how these beetles find their meals. They can "smell" carrion from as far away as two miles, by means of sensors

---

[3] **genus:** a category or group of species.

on their antennae. Flying noisily through the dusk, a male usually
reaches the carcass he has located soon after dark. Then he—
and any other males who have also discovered the feast—emits
90 pheromones that are irresistible to females of the species. Thus,
you'll likely find a number of beetles gathered around any one
corpse. It seems they form pairs, and there may be a good deal of
fighting until one couple claims the prize. They then cooperate to
bury it. This can be hard work: A carcass the size of a blue jay will
take about twelve hours to bury.

Beetle Co-Parenting

Once the carcass is safely underground, the beetles strip it of
feathers or hair and then coat it with . . . secretions, which help to
preserve the flesh that will serve as food for their young. Next, the
couple consummates their pairing, and within a day the female
100 lays the fertilized eggs in a small chamber that they have dug out
close to the carcass. Here both parents wait for their eggs to hatch,
which will be in two or three days. Both mother and father carry
the larvae to their "larder." And then—and this really blew my
mind away—the young beetles will stroke the mandibles of their
parents to entice feeding, and the adults will regurgitate food for
their young. How absolutely amazing—an insect species in which
mother and father care for their young together!

Usually, by the time the carcass is safely underground, flies
have already laid their eggs on it. These hatch quickly into hungry
110 competitors for the young beetles. But help is close by: Riding on
the bodies of the adult beetles are tiny orange mites that quickly
climb onto the carcass, where they feed on fly eggs and maggots.
In about two weeks, the **sated** beetle larvae burrow into the soil to
pupate,[4] and the parents move on. As they do so, the orange mites
hop back on board. The young beetles will emerge about forty-five
days later.

sate (sāt) *v.* to fully feed or satisfy an appetite.

Lou and his team have been very successful with their captive
breeding program—by the end of 2006, more than three thousand
beetles had been reared and released into the wild on Nantucket
120 Island. The captive-bred females (each paired with a genetically
suitable mate) are transported to the release site in plastic
containers. These are placed in an Igloo cooler, since the beetles
cannot survive undue heat. A second cooler is used to transport
dead quail, which the beetles will use as the carrion for their young.
With a chuckle, Lou told us, "I can be traveling on a ferry during
the height of tourist season and will still have room around me due
to the terrible smell coming from the coolers."

---

[4] **pupate:** grow from a larva to the next development stage.

Image Credits: Gary Chancey/U.S. Dept of Agriculture/Forest Service

At the release site, holes have been pre-dug for the beetles. The dead quail are placed into the holes with floss tied to their feet and
130 attached to a small orange flag to assist the recovery team with finding the buried carcasses at a later date. The beetles are then released into the hole, where ideally they will realize that they have a jump start on the reproduction process! Lou said that Nantucket was chosen as a release site because, as with Block Island, there are no mammalian competitors present. After a while, though, birds such as crows and seagulls began to recognize that an orange flag represented a food source, and began to dig up the beetles' carrion, so the recovery team is now also placing a mesh screen over each brood to protect it.

140 Lou told me that he really enjoys teaching children about insects. We agreed that it does not take much to trigger their interest—children are naturally curious. And "creepy-crawlies," although they may elicit fear and horror, hold a real fascination for them. I told Lou I had spent hours as a child watching spiders, dragonflies, bumblebees, and the like. My son was fascinated as a little boy to watch ants as they set out in an orderly column to raid a termite nest, and returned each bearing an unfortunate victim in its mandibles. And my sister's three-year-old grandson, after

watching a snail crawling over the ground, suddenly placed it on
150 the windowpane and rushed indoors to look through the glass,
clearly fascinated and curious about the mechanism that enabled
the creature to glide forward, as if by magic.

Unfortunately, Lou finds it much harder to interest adults in
the efforts being made to save the American burying beetle. "So
often the first question," he told me, "is 'Will it eat my garden?'"
If only people would take the time to listen, retain the curiosity
and wonder of childhood, how much richer their lives would be.
Certainly during my short early-morning meeting with Lou and
Jack, I had been transported to a different and utterly fascinating
160 world, where giant insects nurture their young and tiny mites,
in exchange for a free meal and a ride to the restaurant, rid their
benefactors of their competitors.

After our visit, Lou sent me a beautiful print of an American
burying beetle, its orange and black colors vivid and glowing. It is
propped against the wall as I write, reminding me of all the magic
of the natural world.

COLLABORATIVE DISCUSSION What have you learned about the
burying beetle and other insects? With a partner, discuss how the author
makes a case for the burying beetle's importance to the environment.
Cite specific evidence from the text to support your ideas.

Analyze Author's Claim and Determine Purpose

In any kind of text, the author's **purpose** is his or her reason for writing. An **argument** is a particular kind of writing in which the author states a **claim**, or a position on an issue, and then supports it with reasons and evidence. If the argument is well reasoned and provides sufficient evidence, readers are likely to accept the claim made by the author.

Some arguments begin with a clear statement of the author's claim. Others develop a claim over the course of the argument through the presentation of information and through **rhetoric**, the art of using language effectively to appeal to an audience. When you read or listen to an argument, consider these two ways of developing a claim:

Information in each section that contributes to an overall picture of the issue
Consider:
• In what order does Goodall present information about the beetles? How does this order build reader empathy for them?
• How does each section or subheading of the text contribute to Goodall's larger claim about the beetles' importance?

Rhetoric that advances the author's point of view on the issue
Consider:
• What words does Goodall choose when writing about the work done by the American burying beetle? Do her words suggest a positive or negative perspective on the beetles?
• Why do you think Goodall emphasizes the beetles as parents? What words link beetle parents to human parents?

The author of any argument bases his or her claim on a specific **point of view**, or perspective. If that point of view isn't clear from the start, you will need to watch for clues as you read.

Keep in mind that the writer's point of view drives both the information provided and the rhetoric used. For example, Jane Goodall has been concerned about animals and the environment throughout her life. Her passion for these issues gives her a particular point of view on every topic she writes about. However, what kinds of information and rhetoric would you expect in an argument about endangered beetles written from the point of view of a real-estate developer? Read with an awareness that the scope and substance of any argument depends on the writer's perspective; this strategy will help you carefully evaluate the argument.

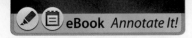

Analyzing the Text

RI 1, RI 2, RI 3,
RI 4, RI 5, RI 6,
RI 10, W 2

> *Cite Text Evidence*   Support your responses with evidence from the selection.

1. **Analyze** Why does Goodall begin her argument by acknowledging that many people dislike insects? How does this order of ideas help her develop her claim?

2. **Cite Evidence** Identifying persuasive rhetoric can help readers understand an author's point of view. In the second paragraph, how does the author use word choice to show her point of view on the use of pesticides against insects? Provide specific examples of word choice from the text to support your answer.

3. **Identify** In line 32, the discussion of insects returns to a focus on the American burying beetle. What rhetorical device does Goodall use to shift the discussion? How does this device help engage readers in her argument?

4. **Evaluate** Describe the importance of using Lou Perrotti and Jack Mulvena to tell the story of the American burying beetle. How does Goodall invite the reader to share her enthusiasm for the beetle? Describe the rhetoric she uses to persuade the reader.

5. **Draw Conclusions** What is Goodall's point of view on insects generally and on the American burying beetle in particular? Given the way she expresses this point of view, what is her purpose for writing the selection? Give specific textual evidence to support your answer.

6. **Infer** Summarize the life cycle of the American burying beetle. Why does the author offer so much detail about the beetle's life cycle? How does the information cited about the beetle support the author's purpose?

7. **Analyze** Reread the first sentence of the selection and think of it as the "rough draft" of Goodall's claim. What facts and reasons does she use to develop this claim throughout the text? After reading the entire selection, how would you state her claim in your own words?

PERFORMANCE TASK

Writing Activity: Analysis A key aspect of Goodall's writing style is her enthusiastic tone. In two paragraphs, analyze how she creates this tone and what effect it has on her argument.

1. Review the text, noting word choices, punctuation, and other examples that contribute to Goodall's tone. Summarize these techniques in your first paragraph.

2. Reflect on your response to Goodall's tone as you read. Did her tone make you more or less receptive to her claim about the importance of the American burying beetle? Discuss this effect in your second paragraph.

Critical Vocabulary

loathe	pollinate	precipitous	sate

Practice and Apply Answer each question with the appropriate Critical Vocabulary word and an explanation of why you chose the word you did.

1. Which Critical Vocabulary word goes with a cliff? Why?

2. Which Critical Vocabulary word goes with flowering plants? Why?

3. Which Critical Vocabulary word goes with a big meal? Why?

4. Which Critical Vocabulary word goes with something disgusting? Why?

Vocabulary Strategy: Patterns of Word Changes

Identifying patterns in the way a root word changes meaning when various word parts are added to it will help you clarify the meaning of unknown words. The Critical Vocabulary word *precipitous,* for example, is an adjective formed by adding the suffix -*ous*, meaning "full of," to the Latin root *praecipit*, meaning "headlong or extremely steep." Various suffixes indicate different meanings or parts of speech when paired with the same root. Note the underlined suffixes in the chart and how they affect the meaning and part of speech.

Noun Suffix + Meaning	Verb Suffix + Meaning	Adjective Suffix + Meaning
precipitousness, precipitation, precipitator -*ness:* state, quality -*ation:* state, condition; action, process -*ator:* one that performs a specified action	precipitate -*ate:* to act upon or become	precipitous -*ous:* possessing, full of

Practice and Apply Refer to both the chart above and a dictionary as needed to complete the following steps:

1. Choose two other words from the text that include suffixes. Identify and define the root—that is, the main word part without the suffix—for each word.

2. Combine each root word with a noun, verb, or adjective suffix to produce a new word. Write definitions for the words you produce.

3. Identify the parts of speech for the original words you selected from the text and the new words you created. Then, write an original sentence for each of the words, the two original words and the new words.

Language and Style: Relative Clauses

A **relative clause** is sometimes called an adjective clause because it can be used to describe a noun or pronoun. A writer's use of relative clauses can help readers better understand complex ideas. Relative clauses convey specific meanings and add variety and interest to writing. They are a type of **subordinate clause** because they cannot stand alone as sentences even though they include a subject and verb. In "Hope for Animals and Their World," Jane Goodall frequently links ideas by using relative clauses.

Read the following sentence from the selection. The relative clause is underlined.

> **Then he . . . emits pheromones <u>that are irresistible to females of the species.</u>**

The author could instead have expressed the same ideas this way:

> **Then he emits pheromones. The pheromones are irresistible to females of the species.**

Notice how the first example expresses the idea more clearly. Use of the relative clause allows the reader to more easily connect the noun, *pheromones*, with its modifying information: the fact that these pheromones are irresistible to female beetles.

Relative clauses can be signaled by **relative pronouns**, most often *who, which, that, whose,* or *whom,* and by **relative adverbs,** such as *where, when,* and *why.* The following chart shows examples of relative clauses from the selection:

	Identifying Relative Clauses	
Signal Word	**Relative Clause (underlined)**	**Word Modified**
who	Lou had parents <u>who were understanding and supportive of his fascination with invertebrates.</u>	parents
where	Today there are only seven places <u>where they are known to exist</u> . . .	places
that	. . . within a day the female lays the fertilized eggs in a small chamber <u>that they have dug out close to the carcass.</u>	chamber

Practice and Apply Look back at the paragraphs you wrote for this selection's Performance Task. Find two places to add relative clauses to more clearly express your ideas. Trade papers with a partner and evaluate the clarity of each other's sentences before and after revision.

Margaret Atwood (b. 1939) *has published more than fifty works of fiction, poetry, and nonfiction. This Canadian author uses her keen intellect and sharp wit to explore ideas about nature, science, the search for identity, social criticism, and human rights. Her award-winning novels include* The Handmaid's Tale, *which was made into a movie,* Cat's Eye, Alias Grace, *and* Oryx and Crake.

My Life as a Bat

Short Story by Margaret Atwood

AS YOU READ Think about the narrator's attitudes toward bats and toward humans. Pay attention to clues that show which species the narrator thinks is superior. Note any questions you have as you read.

1. Reincarnation

In my previous life I was a bat.

If you find previous lives amusing or unlikely, you are not a serious person. Consider: a great many people believe in them, and if sanity is a general **consensus** about the content of reality, who are you to disagree?

Consider also: previous lives have entered the world of commerce. Money can be made from them. *You were Cleopatra,*[1] *you were a Flemish duke, you were a Druid priestess,* and money changes hands. If the stock market exists, so must previous lives.

In the previous-life market, there is not such a great demand for Peruvian ditch-diggers as there is for Cleopatra; or for Indian latrine-cleaners, or for 1952 housewives living in California split-levels. Similarly, not many of us choose to remember our lives as vultures, spiders, or rodents, but some of us do. The fortunate few. Conventional wisdom has it that reincarnation as an animal is a

consensus
(kən-sĕn′səs) *n.*
agreement.

---

[1] **Cleopatra:** Queen of Egypt in the first century B.C.

punishment for past sins, but perhaps it is a reward instead. At least a resting place. An interlude[2] of grace.

Bats have a few things to put up with, but they do not inflict. When they kill, they kill without mercy, but without hate. They are immune from the curse of pity. They never gloat.

2. Nightmares

I have recurring nightmares.

In one of them, I am clinging to the ceiling of a summer cottage while a red-faced man in white shorts and a white V-necked T-shirt jumps up and down, hitting at me with a tennis racket. There are cedar rafters up here, and sticky flypapers attached with tacks, dangling like toxic seaweeds. I look down at the man's face, foreshortened and sweating, the eyes bulging and blue, the mouth emitting furious noise, rising up like a marine float, sinking again, rising as if on a swell of air.

The air itself is muggy, the sun is sinking; there will be a thunderstorm. A woman is shrieking, "My hair! My hair!" and someone else is calling, "Anthea! Bring the stepladder!" All I want is to get out through the hole in the screen, but that will take some concentration and it's hard in this din of voices, they interfere with my sonar.[3] There is a smell of dirty bathmats—it's his breath, the breath that comes out from every pore, the breath of the monster. I will be lucky to get out of this alive.

In another nightmare I am winging my way—flittering, I suppose you'd call it—through the clean-washed demilight before dawn. This is a desert. The yuccas are in bloom, and I have been gorging myself on their juices and pollen. I'm heading to my home, to my home cave, where it will be cool during the burnout of day and there will be the sound of water trickling through limestone, coating the rock with a glistening hush, with the moistness of new mushrooms, and the other bats will chirp and rustle and doze until night unfurls again and makes the hot sky tender for us.

But when I reach the entrance to the cave, it is sealed over. It's blocked in. Who can have done this?

I vibrate my wings, sniffing blind as a dazzled moth over the hard surface. In a short time the sun will rise like a balloon on fire and I will be blasted with its glare, shriveled to a few small bones.

Whoever said that light was life and darkness nothing?

For some of us, the mythologies are different.

---

[2] **interlude:** an intermission or time of rest.
[3] **sonar:** a system for identifying objects with reflected sound.

3. Vampire Films

I became aware of the nature of my previous life gradually, not only through dreams but through scraps of memory, through hints, through odd moments of recognition.

There was my preference for the **subtleties** of dawn and dusk, as opposed to the vulgar blaring hour of high noon. There was my déjà vu[4] experience in the Carlsbad Caverns—surely I had been
60 there before, long before, before they put in the pastel spotlights and the cute names for stalactites and the underground restaurant where you can combine claustrophobia and indigestion and then take the elevator to get back out.

There was also my dislike for headfuls of human hair, so like nets or the tendrils of poisonous jellyfish: I feared entanglements. No real bat would ever suck the blood of necks. The neck is too near the hair. Even the vampire bat will target a hairless extremity—by choice a toe, resembling as it does the teat of a cow.

Vampire films have always seemed ludicrous to me, for this
70 reason but also for the idiocy of their bats—huge rubbery bats, with red Christmas-light eyes and fangs like a sabertoothed tiger's, flown in on strings, their puppet wings flapped sluggishly like those of an overweight and degenerate bird. I screamed at these filmic moments, but not with fear; rather with outraged laughter, at the insult to bats.

O Dracula, unlikely hero! . . . Why was it given to you by whoever stole your soul to transform yourself into bat and wolf, and only those? Why not a vampire chipmunk, a duck, a gerbil? Why not a vampire turtle? Now that would be a plot.

4. The Bat as Deadly Weapon

80 During the Second World War they did experiments with bats. Thousands of bats were to be released over German cities, at the hour of noon. Each was to have a small **incendiary** device strapped onto it, with a timer. The bats would have headed for darkness, as is their habit. They would have crawled into holes in walls, or secreted themselves under the eaves of houses, relieved to have found safety. At a preordained moment they would have exploded, and the cities would have gone up in flames.

That was the plan. Death by flaming bat. The bats too would have died, of course. Acceptable megadeaths.
90 The cities went up in flames anyway, but not with the aid of bats. The atom bomb had been invented, and the fiery bat was no longer thought necessary.

subtleties
(sŭt´l-tēz) *n.* fine details or nuances.

incendiary
(ĭn-sĕn´dē-ĕr´ē) *adj.* intended to cause fire; flammable.

---

[4] **déjà vu:** a sense of having already experienced a present condition or event.

If the bats had been used after all, would there have been a war memorial to them? It isn't likely.

If you ask a human being what makes his flesh creep more, a bat or a bomb, he will say the bat. It is difficult to experience loathing for something merely metal, however ominous. We save these sensations for those with skin and flesh: a skin, a flesh, unlike our own.

5. Beauty

100 Perhaps it isn't my life as a bat that was the interlude. Perhaps it is this life. Perhaps I have been sent into human form as if on a dangerous mission, to save and redeem my own folk. When I have gained a small success, or died in the attempt—for failure, in such a task and against such odds, is more likely—I will be born again, back into that other form, that other world where I truly belong.

More and more, I think of this event with longing. The quickness of heartbeat, the vivid plunge into the nectars of crepuscular flowers, hovering in the infrared of night; the dank lazy half-sleep of daytime, with bodies rounded and soft as furred
110 plums clustering around me, the mothers licking the tiny amazed faces of the newborn; the swift love of what will come next, the anticipations of the tongue and of the infurled, corrugated and scrolled nose, nose like a dead leaf, nose like a radiator grille, nose of a **denizen** of Pluto.

And in the evening, the supersonic hymn of praise to our Creator, the Creator of bats, who appears to us in the form of a bat and who gave us all things: water and the liquid stone of caves, the woody refuge of attics, petals and fruit and juicy insects, and the beauty of slippery wings and sharp white canines and shining eyes.
120 What do we pray for? We pray for food as all do, and for health and for the increase of our kind; and for deliverance from evil, which cannot be explained by us, which is hair-headed and walks in the night with a single white unseeing eye, and stinks of half-digested meat, and has two legs.

Goddess of caves and grottoes: bless your children.

denizen
(děn´ĭ-zən) *n.* a resident.

COLLABORATIVE DISCUSSION With a partner, discuss whether you do or do not agree with the narrator's views of bats and humans. Cite specific evidence from the text to support your answer.

Determine Figurative Meanings

Writers often make imaginative comparisons between two dissimilar things to create vivid images and to convey specific meanings. **Similes** are comparisons that use the words *like* or *as*; **metaphors** are comparisons that are implied rather than stated. To analyze the figurative meanings of the comparisons that Margaret Atwood uses in "My Life as a Bat," form a mental image of the two things that are being compared. Then, ask yourself questions such as the ones in the following examples.

- **Simile:** "flypapers . . . dangling like toxic seaweeds." In what way are the items being compared similar? What feeling does the word *toxic* convey?
- **Metaphor:** "his breath, . . . the breath of the monster." Is the man really a monster? What does this comparison suggest about him or his likely actions? What is the narrator's **tone**, or attitude, toward him?

Analyze Author's Choices: Text Structure

Most stories follow a structure of exposition, rising action, climax, falling action, and resolution.

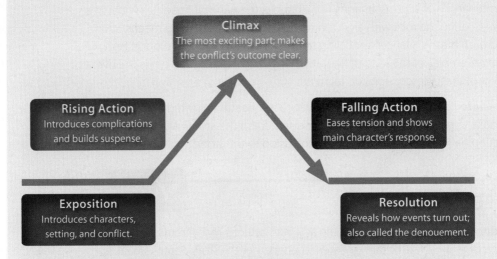

Climax
The most exciting part; makes the conflict's outcome clear.

Rising Action
Introduces complications and builds suspense.

Falling Action
Eases tension and shows main character's response.

Exposition
Introduces characters, setting, and conflict.

Resolution
Reveals how events turn out; also called the denouement.

    In this story, Atwood dispenses with traditional narrative structure. Instead, she arranges events, conflicts, and reflections using an informative essay format, with numbered heads. Readers must piece together the narrative to determine the order and significance of events. As you read a story such as this one that uses an unusual narrative structure, consider the effect of the author's choices: How does the structure work to maintain reader interest and communicate theme?

Analyzing the Text

Cite Text Evidence   Support your responses with evidence from the selection.

1. **Cite Evidence** What evidence does the narrator offer for believing in a past life as a bat? What device or method does the author use to provide this evidence?

2. **Analyze** Throughout the story, the author uses wry humor in the form of exaggeration and irony. Give an example of humor from the text. How does the humor develop the character of the narrator?

3. **Interpret** The narrator, as a bat, describes the sun rising "like a balloon on fire" (line 50). What meaning is conveyed by this simile in the context of the flashback?

4. **Compare** What are some of the main contrasts the narrator makes between humans and bats? Cite specific statements as well as stories that imply the differences. What theme about people is developed through these contrasts?

5. **Evaluate** Details that appeal to the senses can create positive or negative feelings. What sensory details does the narrator use to describe the bat's domain and tell what it feels like to be a bat? What tone toward bats do the sensory details create?

6. **Analyze** Some of Atwood's figurative language involves unexpected combinations of sensory images. For example, the narrator imagines water in a cave "coating the rock with a glistening hush" (line 44). *Glistening* means "shiny" and *hush* means "silence," appealing to both sight and hearing at once. Find other examples of this kind of figurative language in the text. What is the overall effect of these descriptions on readers?

7. **Evaluate** The last section of the story is called "Beauty." Why did the author choose to place this section last in the structure of the story? Would any other section have worked as well as the conclusion to the story? ·

PERFORMANCE TASK

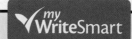

Speaking Activity: Research "My Life as a Bat" includes many details about how bats live. Examine these details to determine whether the story details are factually accurate.

1. With a partner, list details about bats from the story, such as where they live, how they behave, what they eat, what they look like.

2. Research facts about these aspects of bats.

3. Create a chart or a Venn diagram to compare the story details and facts.

4. Write and present your findings in a brief informative presentation in which you evaluate the author's use of factual material.

Critical Vocabulary

consensus   subtleties   incendiary   denizen

Practice and Apply Answer the questions to demonstrate your understanding of each Critical Vocabulary word.

1. What **consensus** do humans hold about bats?

2. What are some of the **subtleties** of life inside a bat colony?

3. Why might military strategists choose to use bats as **incendiary** weapons?

4. What environments can a bat be considered a **denizen** of?

Vocabulary Strategy: Using Reference Sources

If you come across an unfamiliar word while reading, look first for a footnote on the page. If one is not provided, you can use the context—the words and sentences around the unfamiliar word—to help you determine the meaning. If context is not helpful, turn to a reference source, such as a glossary, dictionary, or thesaurus. For advanced or foreign terms, you may need to consult a college-level or bilingual dictionary.

Glossary	Dictionary	Thesaurus
• **Where it is found:** at the back of the book in which the word is used	• **Where it is found:** library; Internet; print and digital versions	• **Where it is found:** library; Internet; print and digital versions
• **What it includes:** pronunciation; definition as it is used in the text	• **What it includes:** part of speech; syllable division; pronunciation; definitions; synonyms; etymology	• **What it includes:** synonyms; shades of meaning

Practice and Apply Use reference sources to find the specified information about each of the Critical Vocabulary words. Write your answers and explain which reference source you used and why.

1. Write three synonyms for **consensus**.

2. Write the pronunciation for **subtleties.**

3. Write the etymology, or origin, of the word **incendiary.**

4. Write the part of speech and syllable division for **denizen.**

Language and Style: Colons and Dashes

A writer's use of punctuation helps clarify meaning for the reader by showing places of emphasis or change of tone. In "My Life as a Bat," Margaret Atwood uses colons and dashes not only for meaning but also to create an engaging style.

Colons are used to introduce lists, as in the following passage from the story:

And in the evening, the supersonic hymn of praise to our Creator, the Creator of bats, who appears to us in the form of a bat and who gave us all things: water and the liquid stone of caves, the woody refuge of attics, petals and fruit and juicy insects, and the beauty of slippery wings and sharp white canines and shining eyes.

Colons can also be used to introduce direct quotations, as in this example:

Atwood suggests that humans could learn from animals' lives: "When they kill, they kill without mercy, but without hate. They are immune from the curse of pity. They never gloat."

Just as readers naturally pause at a colon to prepare for what comes after it, they also pause at a dash. A dash or pair of dashes is used to set off or emphasize ideas. Here are some common uses of dashes:

Uses of Dashes	
Purpose	**Example from the Text**
set off a definition or explanation	In another nightmare I am winging my way—flittering, I suppose you'd call it—through the clean-washed demilight before dawn.
show a sudden break in thought in a sentence	When I have gained a small success, or died in the attempt—for failure, in such a task and against such odds, is more likely—I will be born again, back into that other form, that other world where I truly belong.
emphasize a word, a series of words, a phrase, or a clause	There is a smell of dirty bathmats—it's his breath, the breath that comes out from every pore, the breath of the monster.

Practice and Apply Look back at the presentation you created for this selection's Performance Task. Revise your written presentation to include at least one colon and one dash or set of dashes. Then, discuss with a partner how each punctuation mark you added clarifies or enhances the meaning of your ideas.

Linda Hogan (b. 1947) *grew up in Oklahoma and Colorado. A member of the Chickasaw Nation, Hogan has received many awards and honors for her writing. She is a strong advocate for preserving endangered species, and her work reflects her deep interest in environmental issues, native cultures, and spirituality. Hogan says of her writing: "It takes perseverance. I will do it over and over again until I get it right." Her poetry collections include* The Book of Medicines *and* Rounding the Human Corners. *Her first novel,* Mean Spirit, *was a finalist for the Pulitzer Prize.*

Carry

Poem by Linda Hogan

AS YOU READ Think about what the images in the poem reveal about the cycle of nature. Write down any questions you generate during reading.

From water's broken mirror
we pulled it,
alive and shining,
gasping the painful other element of air.
5   It was not just fish.
There was more.
It was hawk, once wild with
hunger, sharp talons
locked into the dying twist
10 and scale of fish,
its long bones
trailing like a ghost
behind fins
through the dark, cold water.

15   It was beautiful, that water,
      like a silver coin stretched thin
      enough to feed us all,
      smooth as skin before anyone knew
      the undertow's[1] rough hands
20   lived inside it, working everything down
      to its absence,
      and water is never lonely,
      it holds so many.
      It says, come close, you who want to swallow me;
25   already I am part of you.
      Come near. I will shape myself around you
      so soft, so calm
      I will carry you
      down to a world you never knew or dreamed,
30   I will gather you
      into the hands of something stronger,
      older, deeper.

COLLABORATIVE DISCUSSION What does the hawk's fate reflect
about nature, if anything? Discuss your ideas with a partner. Cite
specific evidence from the text to support your ideas.

---

[1] **undertow:** a strong current below the surface of water.

Support Inferences About Theme

The **theme** of a work is the message about life that the writer wants to communicate. Because readers make inferences to discover theme, a work may reveal different meanings to different readers. Your interpretation of theme will be valid if you base it on evidence from the text.

To determine themes in "Carry," look for clues in the poem's images and descriptive details, and think about the writer's use of symbols and repetition. Pay attention to how the writer uses details to shape and refine particular themes throughout the poem. This chart can help guide your analysis.

Text Evidence to Consider	Examples	Analysis and Questions
metaphors that create strong images	"water's broken mirror"	• This image is attractive but somewhat unsettling. • Is water used as a symbol throughout the poem? If so, what might it represent?
similes that create strong images	"its long bones / trailing like a ghost / behind fins"	• This striking image depicts the opposite of the expected predator/prey outcome. • What message is intended here? Do other images of death appear in the poem?
descriptive details that create a mood or feeling	"like a silver coin stretched thin / enough to feed us all"	• This simile creates an image of water as nourishing force, counterbalancing the image of water as an agent of death. • What broad idea does the water represent?
personification that conveys feelings or emotions	"and water is never lonely"	• Here, certain character traits are associated with water. • What does this depiction of water add to its symbolic meaning within the context of the entire poem?
title	"Carry"	• The title is a clue to the writer's broader message about the force of nature.

To make sure you understand what the poet is saying explicitly, draft an objective summary that provides the basic facts of the poem. Your final step in determining theme will be to synthesize your summary and your analysis of text evidence into a theme statement that expresses the poet's message.

Analyzing the Text

RL 1, RL 2, RL 3,
RL 4, RL 5,
SL 1a, W 4, L 5a

Cite Text Evidence   Support your responses with evidence from the selection.

1. **Summarize** Review what is stated explicitly in lines 1–14 and write a brief summary of what the speaker describes. How does the image created in these lines affect the **mood,** or emotion, of the poem?

2. **Infer** Use clues from the text to infer what happened to the hawk. Why is this unexpected?

3. **Analyze** Words and phrases that describe how things look, feel, sound, taste, or smell are called **sensory details.** Write down sensory details from lines 15–23. How do these details help engage readers in the poem?

4. **Interpret** Explain what is meant by lines 22–23: "and water is never lonely, / it holds so many." Support your interpretation with evidence from other lines.

5. **Analyze** Review the water's plea and promise at the end of the poem (lines 24–32). What does the water want? What does it offer?

6. **Interpret** A **symbol** is something that stands for or represents something beyond itself. Review the descriptions of water in the poem. What does the water symbolize?

7. **Cite Evidence** What theme about our connection with nature does this poem convey? Support your theme statement with evidence from the poem.

PERFORMANCE TASK

Speaking Activity: Response to Literature In "Carry," descriptions of water are central to the poem's meaning. Discuss the choices the poet made in her use of water imagery.

- Form a small group of three or four students to analyze the descriptions of water throughout the poem.

- For each image of water in the poem, ask questions about what feelings or ideas the author wanted to convey. For example, why did the poet choose to use a "broken mirror" as an image?

- Consider how the images of water develop throughout the poem, from an inanimate object to a powerful living force.

- Write a brief summary that includes the most important insights from the discussion.

Write a Research Report

The texts in this collection present various viewpoints on nature. Choose three texts, including "Called Out." Identify an element of the interaction between humans and nature reflected in the texts, and conduct research about it. Synthesize your findings in a report that develops your thesis.

W 2a–f Write informative/ explanatory texts.
W 4 Produce clear and coherent writing.
W 7 Conduct research projects.
W 8 Gather relevant information from multiple sources.
W 9a–b Draw evidence from texts.

Your research report should include

- a clear thesis, supported by text evidence and additional research

- an introduction, a logically structured body, and a conclusion

- smoothly integrated source information that avoids plagiarism and cites sources correctly

- precise use of language with appropriately formal tone and style

Visit hmhfyi.com to explore your topic and enhance your research.

PLAN

Analyze the Texts Reread "Called Out," and identify an interaction between humans and nature. Review your other chosen texts, and formulate a question you have about the relationship between humans and nature. This question will guide your research.

Research Next, gather additional evidence about your topic from other print or online resources.

- Locate information on your topic in books, magazines, or online.

- Make note of any important details or quotations on index cards. Include reference information on your cards. You will need this later when you cite the text.

- You can also save evidence to *my*Notebook, in a folder titled *Collection 2 Performance Task A*.

Interactive Lessons
To help you research effectively, complete these lessons from Conducting Research.
· Using the Internet for Research
· Taking Notes

ACADEMIC VOCABULARY

As you write your research report, be sure to use these words.

advocate
discrete
domain
enhance
scope

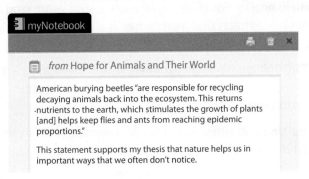

Get Organized Organize your details and evidence in an outline.

- Decide what organizational pattern you will use for your report. Will you support your central idea by presenting the evidence text by text?

- Decide which textual and research evidence most effectively supports the key points in your thesis.

- Use your organizational pattern to sort your textual evidence and research information into a logical order.

Interactive Lessons
Use the following
lesson for more help:
- Writing Informative
  Texts: Organizing
  Ideas

PRODUCE

my WriteSmart

Draft Your Report Write a draft of your report, using your outline as a guide. Be sure to do the following:

Write your rough draft in *my*WriteSmart. Focus on getting your ideas down rather than perfecting your choice of language.

- Use your introduction to grab your readers' attention and clearly state your thesis.

- Cite sources for facts, quotations, and examples from your chosen collection texts and your research. Use introductory phrases to provide context for quotations.

- Any time you discuss a new text or a new key point, include transitions to help guide your readers.

- End your report with a universal closing statement about the relationship between humans and nature.

- Create a reference page or Works Cited list. Include each author's last and first name; the title of the source; the year of publication; the publisher; and other details as required by your teacher.

Language and Style: Citing Sources

Use footnotes or endnotes to credit your sources. Footnotes appear at the bottom of the same page as the information they document; endnotes are grouped together at the end of the report. Each note is numbered in sequence. Use the following example as a model:

Report text Nature can also help heal us: For example, researchers in the Amazon rain forest have discovered over 70 plant extracts that treat cancer and over 50 that treat infections caused by bacteria.[1]

Footnote/Endnote text 1. Tom Phillips, "Brazilian explorers search 'medicine factory' to save lives and rainforest," The Guardian, http://www.theguardian.com/environment/2009/apr/27/amazon-rainforest-medicine

Look carefully through your draft, adding either footnotes or endnotes (whichever your teacher prefers) to document the source of every quotation and every fact that isn't common knowledge.

Have a partner or a group of peers review your draft in *my*WriteSmart.

Improve Your Draft Revise your draft to make sure it is clear, coherent, and engaging. Use the chart below as a guide.

Questions	Tips	Revision Techniques
Is a clear and logical thesis stated in the introduction?	**Underline** the thesis statement.	**If** needed, **add** a thesis statement to your introduction.
Is the thesis supported by text evidence?	**Note** each source of evidence.	**Add** supporting evidence from a variety of sources.
Are quotations smoothly integrated into sentences that provide context?	**Underline** sentence parts that provide context for quotations from sources.	**Revise** sentences containing quotations to add context.
Are sources correctly cited for quotations and facts that are not common knowledge?	**Highlight** quotations and facts. **Highlight** their citations in footnotes or endnotes.	**Add** footnotes or endnotes to cite the sources of facts or quotations as needed.
Does a conclusion sum up ideas?	**Underline** the summary of ideas in the conclusion.	**Add** a concluding statement if needed.

Present Your Report Share your final draft, either by printing it or by posting it on a class web page. If you do the latter, consider embedding links to footnotes or endnotes in the citation numbers to help readers locate your sources more easily.

PERFORMANCE TASK RUBRIC
RESEARCH REPORT

	Ideas and Evidence	Organization	Language
4	• The introduction is compelling and informative; the thesis statement clearly identifies a research question. • Sufficient, well-chosen evidence from the texts and from reliable sources provides strong support. • The writer cites information from multiple authoritative sources. • The concluding section effectively summarizes the answer to the research question and makes a thoughtful observation.	• The organization of key points and supporting evidence is effective; ideas are arranged logically. • Varied, well-crafted transitions effectively connect ideas.	• The writing has a formal style and a knowledgeable, objective tone. • Precise language is skillfully used. • Sentence beginnings, lengths, and structures vary and have a rhythmic flow. • Spelling, capitalization, and punctuation are correct. • Grammar and usage are correct. • All sources are completely and correctly identified in footnotes or endnotes or a Works Cited list.
3	• The introduction is adequate; the thesis statement identifies a research question. • Evidence from the texts and reliable sources supports key points. • Additional authoritative sources would strengthen the key ideas. • The concluding section summarizes the answer to the research question.	• The organization of key points and supporting evidence is generally clear. • Transitions usually connect ideas.	• The style is generally formal, though the tone is sometimes opinionated. • Most language is precise. • Sentence beginnings, lengths, and structures vary somewhat. • Minor spelling, capitalization, and punctuation mistakes occur. • Some grammatical and usage errors occur but do not hinder understanding. • A few formatting errors appear in footnotes, endnotes, or the Works Cited list.
2	• The introduction is partially informative; the thesis statement does not clearly identify the research question. • Evidence from the texts and from sources supports some key points but is often too general. • Many cited sources are not authoritative or reliable. • The concluding section gives an incomplete summary of the answer to the research question.	• The organization of key points and supporting evidence is logical in some places, but some noticeable gaps in logic occur. • More transitions are needed throughout to connect ideas.	• The style is often informal, and the tone communicates a superficial understanding of the topic. • Language is vague or general at times. • Sentence structures barely vary; some fragments or run-on sentences occur. • Many spelling, capitalization, and punctuation mistakes occur. • Grammar and usage are incorrect in many places, but ideas are mostly clear. • One or two sources are missing from footnotes, endnotes, or the Works Cited list.
1	• The appropriate elements of an introduction are missing. • Evidence from the texts and sources is irrelevant or missing. • Sources are unreliable or not cited. • The paper lacks an identifiable concluding section.	• An organizational strategy is not used; information is presented randomly. • Transitions are not used, making the paper difficult to understand.	• The style and tone are inappropriate for a research paper. • Language is vague and repetitive. • Repetitive sentence structure, fragments, and run-on sentences occur. • Spelling and capitalization are often incorrect, and punctuation is missing. • Many grammatical and usage errors hinder the writer's ideas. • Footnotes, endnotes, or the Works Cited list is missing.

COLLECTION **2**
PERFORMANCE TASK B

To help you complete this
task, use
• *Giving a Presentation*
• *Writing Narratives*

Present an Oral Narrative

Every text in this collection was inspired by its author's experience with nature. Consider the kinds of experiences related in three of these texts, including the anchor text "My Life as a Bat." What experience of your own do one or more of these texts bring to mind? Explore that experience more deeply, and share it in an oral narrative.

W 7 Conduct short research projects.

SL 1a–d Initiate and participate effectively in a range of collaborative discussions with diverse partners, building on others' ideas and expressing their own clearly and persuasively.

SL 4 Present information clearly.

SL 5 Use digital media in presentations to enhance understanding and add interest.

Your oral narrative should

- incorporate ideas from texts in this collection and other sources
- use effective narrative techniques
- explore the significance of the experience
- use logical transitions to link events and ideas
- include media elements that enhance or clarify your ideas

PLAN

myNotebook

Use the annotation tools in your eBook to find examples of vivid sensory language. Save each example to your notebook.

Analyze the Texts Review the texts in this collection. What kind of experience with nature does each text describe, and why is it meaningful? List narrative techniques each author uses to bring events to life. Narrative techniques can include

- dialogue ("If they weren't there *last* year, and this year they *are*, then who planted them?")
- pacing and tone (Goodall's quick, upbeat writing)
- description, including sensory details ("bodies rounded and soft as furred plums")

Choose an Experience Think back to a meaningful experience you had that involved something in nature. Make notes about

- key events and sensory impressions
- why this event has stuck with you or changed you

Research Find out more about what natural processes went into your experience. Gather facts about a plant, animal, or natural phenomenon that was central to the event. Your notes should include

- key findings about the natural element you have chosen
- information about your sources, including title and author
- quotations from experts and media elements you might use

ACADEMIC VOCABULARY

As you plan your speech, be sure to use these words.

advocate
discrete
domain
enhance
scope

Draft Your Narrative As you draft what you plan to say in your oral narrative, be sure to do the following:

- Make a clear connection between one of your chosen texts and the event you describe. Choose a logical organization to communicate key events and ideas.
- Incorporate evidence from your research into your explanation of what happened.
- Use narrative techniques to bring the event to life for your audience.
- Include media elements to clarify or enhance your ideas.
- Conclude with a reflection on why the experience was important to you.

Write your rough draft in *my*WriteSmart. Focus on getting your ideas down rather than perfecting your choice of language.

Interactive Lessons
To help you draft your narrative, complete this lesson:
- Writing Narratives: Narrative Techniques

Mentor Text See how Goodall reflects on her experience in this excerpt from the conclusion of *Hope for Animals and Their World*:

" After our visit, Lou sent me a beautiful print of an American burying beetle, its orange and black colors vivid and glowing. It is propped against the wall as I write, reminding me of all the magic of the natural world. "

Language and Style: Transitions

Transitions are words, phrases, clauses, and even whole sentences that show the relationships among the events and ideas you are communicating. Connecting ideas by using logical transitions throughout your speech will help make your experience clear for your listeners. Here are some ways you can use transitions:

Purpose	Sample connecting words	Examples
to show a contrast	*however, on the other hand, but, except, although, yet*	"I'm heading to my home, to my home cave. . . . But when I reach the entrance to the cave, it is sealed over."
to show causes and effects	*therefore, as a result, because of*	"If a little seed begins to grow at the first promise of rain, and that promise gets broken, that right there is the end of its little life."
to provide context for sequence, time, or location	*once, before, after, next, above, below, beyond, where, when, as, while*	"As he began talking about the beetles, it was immediately apparent that they had the perfect spokesman!"

Review the draft of your speech and add words, phrases, clauses, or sentences that clearly and logically link ideas and events.

Fine-Tune Your Speech

Your listeners can't go back and reread your narrative if they get confused. They're counting on you to clearly explain what happened and why it matters. Use these questions, tips, and revision techniques to make your narrative memorable.

Questions	Tips	Revision Techniques
Does the introduction grab listener interest and make a connection to one or more collection texts?	**Underline** any attention-grabbing statements and references to collection texts.	**Add** an attention-grabbing idea or quotation to your introduction. **Add** a reference to a collection text.
Do narrative techniques bring the events and ideas to life?	**Highlight** each example of dialogue or sensory description.	**Add** dialogue if appropriate, and **add** details that appeal to the senses.
Are ideas and events clearly linked with transitions?	**Underline** words, phrases, clauses, or sentences that show a relationship among ideas or events.	**Add** transitions as needed to clearly connect the ideas and events in the narrative.
Do media elements clarify or enhance descriptions of events or ideas?	**Note** which idea or event each media element supports.	**Add** or **replace** media elements to support ideas in the narrative.
Does the conclusion express why the experience was meaningful?	**Highlight** the reflection on the event's importance.	**Add** one or more sentences reflecting on the significance of the experience.

Ask your reviewers to note any parts of the story that are confusing or that could benefit from more descriptive details.

Interactive Lessons
To help you rehearse your speech, complete this lesson:
• Giving a Presentation: Delivering Your Presentation

PRESENT

Deliver Your Narrative

Bring your experience to life for listeners by delivering it clearly and expressively. Here are some tips:

- Write key ideas, events, details, and facts on notecards. Referring to notecards while you speak instead of reading your draft will make your speech lively and natural.

- Practice incorporating media elements during rehearsals to make sure you can smoothly deliver your narrative without distractions or technical problems.

- Use appropriate eye contact, adequate volume, and clear pronunciation to communicate your ideas to your audience.

- Use your voice, gestures, and brief pauses for emphasis at appropriate points during the narrative.

PERFORMANCE TASK RUBRIC
ORAL NARRATIVE

	Ideas and Evidence	Organization	Language
4	• The speaker effectively communicates an event and its significance. • Media choices effectively illustrate and expand on ideas. • Research findings are smoothly incorporated into the narrative.	• The speaker makes an insightful link between a collection text and the experience described. • Ideas and events progress in a logical order and are linked with effective transitions.	• Narrative techniques effectively bring the experience to life. • The speaker is easy to understand and adapts volume and pacing to audience needs.
3	• The event and its significance are clear to listeners. • Media choices are clearly linked to the speaker's ideas. • The speaker includes some facts from research in the narrative.	• A link or comparison is made between a collection text and the speaker's experience. • The order of ideas and events is logical, and transitions are generally used.	• The speaker describes events and ideas using some narrative techniques. • The speaker is generally easy to understand and uses appropriate volume and pacing.
2	• What happened or why it mattered to the speaker may be vague at times. • Media choices lack a clear connection to the speaker's ideas. • One or two ideas from research are weakly connected to the event.	• A collection text is mentioned, but the connection between it and the speaker's experience may be weak. • Ideas and events may seem disorganized, and the narrative may lack some needed transitions.	• The speaker may include a sensory detail or brief dialogue in the narrative. • The speaker is occasionally difficult to understand.
1	• The speaker fails to communicate the event clearly or identify its significance. • Media choices are absent or distracting. • Research findings are absent from the narrative.	• The speaker makes no link to a text from the collection. • Ideas and events are presented in a disorganized way with no transitions.	• Descriptions of events and ideas are vague and fail to create an impression of what the experience was like. • The speaker is often difficult to understand.

Responses to Change

❝When the wind of change blows, some build walls
while others build windmills.❞

—Chinese proverb

Responses to Change

Change is inevitable; how we respond to it reveals who we are.

Stream to Start

hmhfyi.com

Channel One News®

COLLECTION

PERFORMANCE TASK Preview

At the end of this collection, you will have the opportunity to complete two tasks:

- Participate in a panel discussion about the ways in which people either do or do not adapt to change.

- Write an argument about the positive and negative aspects of change.

ACADEMIC VOCABULARY

Study the words and their definitions in the chart below. You will use these words as you discuss and write about the texts in this collection.

Word	Definition	Related Forms
abstract (ăb-străkt´) *adj.*	apart from physical existence; theoretical rather than concrete	abstraction, abstractly
evolve (ĭ-vŏlv´) *v.*	to change or develop gradually over time	evolution
explicit (ĭk-splĭs´ĭt) *adj.*	clearly stated or expressed	explicitly, explicitness
facilitate (fə-sĭl´ĭ-tāt´) *v.*	to make something easier	facility, facilitator
infer (ĭn-fûr´) *v.*	to deduce from evidence or reason	inference, inferential

Franz Kafka (1883–1924) *was born in Prague and overcame emotional, physical, and financial struggles to become a leading twentieth-century writer. His innovative fiction has been compared to Shakespeare's works for its literary importance. Kafka even has a literary term named after him—* Kafkaesque, *which means "a twisted reality that is foreboding and oppressive." After a long illness, Kafka died before many of his works were published. His influence spread with the wide translation of his works.*

from
The Metamorphosis

Novella by Franz Kafka   Graphic Novel by Peter Kuper

from **The Metamorphosis**

Novella by Franz Kafka
Translated by David Wyllie

AS YOU READ Pay attention to how details and pacing help the story evolve. Write down any questions you generate during reading.

One morning, when Gregor Samsa woke from troubled dreams, he found himself transformed in his bed into a horrible **vermin**. He lay on his armor-like back, and if he lifted his head a little he could see his brown belly, slightly domed and divided by arches into stiff sections. The bedding was hardly able to cover it and seemed ready to slide off any moment. His many legs, pitifully thin compared with the size of the rest of him, waved about helplessly as he looked.

   "What's happened to me?" he thought. It wasn't a dream.
10 His room, a proper human room although a little too small, lay peacefully between its four familiar walls. A collection of textile

vermin
(vûr´mĭn) *n.* creatures that are considered destructive, annoying, or repulsive; pests.

samples lay spread out on the table—Samsa was a traveling salesman—and above it there hung a picture that he had recently cut out of an illustrated magazine and housed in a nice, gilded frame. It showed a lady fitted out with a fur hat and fur boa who sat upright, raising a heavy fur muff[1] that covered the whole of her lower arm towards the viewer.

Gregor then turned to look out the window at the dull weather. Drops of rain could be heard hitting the pane, which made him feel quite sad. "How about if I sleep a little bit longer and forget all this nonsense," he thought, but that was something he was unable to do because he was used to sleeping on his right, and in his present state couldn't get into that position. However hard he threw himself onto his right, he always rolled back to where he was. He must have tried it a hundred times, shut his eyes so that he wouldn't have to look at the floundering legs, and only stopped when he began to feel a mild, dull pain there that he had never felt before.

"Oh, God," he thought, "what a strenuous career it is that I've chosen! Traveling day in and day out. Doing business like this takes much more effort than doing your own business at home, and on top of that there's the curse of traveling, worries about making train connections, bad and irregular food, contact with different people all the time so that you can never get to know anyone or become friendly with them. It can all go to Hell!" He felt a slight itch up on his belly; pushed himself slowly up on his back towards the headboard so that he could lift his head better; found where the itch was, and saw that it was covered with lots of little white spots which he didn't know what to make of; and when he tried to feel the place with one of his legs he drew it quickly back because as soon as he touched it he was overcome by a cold shudder.

He slid back into his former position. "Getting up early all the time," he thought, "it makes you stupid. You've got to get enough sleep. Other traveling salesmen live a life of luxury. For instance, whenever I go back to the guest house during the morning to copy out the contract, these gentlemen are always still sitting there eating their breakfasts. I ought to just try that with my boss; I'd get kicked out on the spot. But who knows, maybe that would be the best thing for me. If I didn't have my parents to think about I'd have given in my notice a long time ago, I'd have gone up to the boss and told him just what I think, tell him everything I would, let him know just what I feel. He'd fall right off his desk! And it's a funny sort of business to be sitting up there at your desk, talking down at your **subordinates** from up there, especially when you have to go right

subordinate
(sə-bôrʹdn-ĭt) *n.* a person of a lesser rank or under another's authority.

---

[1] **boa . . . muff:** A boa is a long, thin piece of women's clothing that is worn around the neck. A muff is a short, soft tube into which people put their hands for warmth.

"I've got to get up,
my train leaves
at five."

up close because the boss is hard of hearing. Well, there's still some hope; once I've got the money together to pay off my parents' debt to him—another five or six years I suppose—that's definitely what I'll do. That's when I'll make the big change. First of all though, I've got to get up, my train leaves at five."

    And he looked over at the alarm clock, ticking on the chest of
60 drawers. "God in Heaven!" he thought. It was half past six and the hands were quietly moving forwards, it was even later than half past, more like quarter to seven. Had the alarm clock not rung? He could see from the bed that it had been set for four o'clock as it should have been; it certainly must have rung. Yes, but was it possible to quietly sleep through that furniture-rattling noise? True, he had not slept peacefully, but probably all the more deeply because of that. What should he do now? The next train went at seven; if he were to catch that he would have to rush like mad and the collection of samples was still not packed, and he did not at all
70 feel particularly fresh and lively. And even if he did catch the train he would not avoid his boss's anger as the office assistant would have been there to see the five o'clock train go, he would have put in his report about Gregor's not being there a long time ago. The office assistant was the boss's man, spineless, and with no understanding. What about if he reported sick? But that would be extremely strained and suspicious as in fifteen years of service Gregor had never once yet been ill. His boss would certainly come round with

the doctor from the medical insurance company, accuse his parents of having a lazy son, and accept the doctor's recommendation not to make any claim as the doctor believed that no one was ever ill but that many were workshy.[2] And what's more, would he have been entirely wrong in this case? Gregor did in fact, apart from excessive sleepiness after sleeping for so long, feel completely well and even felt much hungrier than usual.

He was still hurriedly thinking all this through, unable to decide to get out of the bed, when the clock struck quarter to seven. There was a cautious knock at the door near his head. "Gregor," somebody called—it was his mother—"it's quarter to seven. Didn't you want to go somewhere?" That gentle voice! Gregor was shocked when he heard his own voice answering, it could hardly be recognized as the voice he had had before. As if from deep inside him, there was a painful and uncontrollable squeaking mixed in with it, the words could be made out at first but then there was a sort of echo which made them unclear, leaving the hearer unsure whether he had heard properly or not. Gregor had wanted to give a full answer and explain everything, but in the circumstances contented himself with saying: "Yes, mother, yes, thank you, I'm getting up now." The change in Gregor's voice probably could not be noticed outside through the wooden door, as his mother was satisfied with this explanation and shuffled away. But this short conversation made the other members of the family aware that Gregor, against their expectations, was still at home, and soon his father came knocking at one of the side doors, gently, but with his fist. "Gregor, Gregor," he called, "what's wrong?" And after a short while he called again with a warning deepness in his voice: "Gregor! Gregor!" At the other side door his sister came **plaintively**: "Gregor? Aren't you well? Do you need anything?" Gregor answered to both sides: "I'm ready, now," making an effort to remove all the strangeness from his voice by **enunciating** very carefully and putting long pauses between each individual word. His father went back to his breakfast, but his sister whispered: "Gregor, open the door, I beg of you." Gregor, however, had no thought of opening the door, and instead congratulated himself for his cautious habit, acquired from his traveling, of locking all doors at night even when he was at home.

The first thing he wanted to do was to get up in peace without being disturbed, to get dressed, and most of all to have his breakfast. Only then would he consider what to do next, as he was well aware that he would not bring his thoughts to any sensible conclusions by lying in bed. He remembered that he had often felt a

plaintively
(plān´tĭv-lē) adv.
sadly or wistfully.

enunciate
(ĭ-nŭn´sē-āt´) v.
to articulate or
pronounce clearly.

---

[2] **workshy:** lazy; unwilling to perform labor.

slight pain in bed, perhaps caused by lying awkwardly, but that had always turned out to be pure imagination and he wondered how his imaginings would slowly resolve themselves today. He did not have the slightest doubt that the change in his voice was nothing more than the first sign of a serious cold, which was an occupational hazard for traveling salesmen.

It was a simple matter to throw off the covers; he only had to blow himself up a little and they fell off by themselves. But it became difficult after that, especially as he was so exceptionally broad. He would have used his arms and his hands to push himself up; but instead of them he only had all those little legs continuously moving in different directions, and which he was moreover unable to control. If he wanted to bend one of them, then that was the first one that would stretch itself out; and if he finally managed to do what he wanted with that leg, all the others seemed to be set free

and would move about painfully. "This is something that can't be done in bed," Gregor said to himself, "so don't keep trying to do it."

The first thing he wanted to do was get the lower part of his body out of the bed, but he had never seen this lower part, and could not imagine what it looked like; it turned out to be too hard to move; it went so slowly; and finally, almost in a frenzy, when he carelessly shoved himself forwards with all the force he could gather, he chose the wrong direction, hit hard against the lower bedpost, and learned from the burning pain he felt that the lower part of his body might well, at present, be the most sensitive.

So then he tried to get the top part of his body out of the bed first, carefully turning his head to the side. This he managed quite easily, and despite its breadth and its weight, the bulk of his body eventually followed slowly in the direction of the head. But when he had at last got his head out of the bed and into the fresh air it occurred to him that if he let himself fall it would be a miracle if his head were not injured, so he became afraid to carry on pushing himself forward the same way. And he could not knock himself out now at any price; better to stay in bed than lose consciousness.

It took just as much effort to get back to where he had been earlier, but when he lay there sighing, and was once more watching his legs as they struggled against each other even harder than before, if that was possible, he could think of no way of bringing peace and order to this chaos. He told himself once more that it was not possible for him to stay in bed and that the most sensible thing to do would be to get free of it in whatever way he could at whatever sacrifice. At the same time, though, he did not forget to remind himself that calm consideration was much better than rushing to desperate conclusions. At times like this he would direct his eyes to the window and look out as clearly as he could, but unfortunately, even the other side of the narrow street was enveloped in morning fog and the view had little confidence or cheer to offer him. "Seven o'clock, already," he said to himself when the clock struck again, "seven o'clock, and there's still a fog like this." And he lay there quietly a while longer, breathing lightly as if he perhaps expected the total stillness to bring things back to their real and natural state.

But then he said to himself: "Before it strikes quarter past seven I'll definitely have to have got properly out of bed. And by then somebody will have come round from work to ask what's happened to me as well, as they open up at work before seven o'clock." And so he set himself to the task of swinging the entire length of his body out of the bed all at the same time. If he succeeded in falling out of bed in this way and kept his head raised as he did so he could probably avoid injuring it. His back seemed to be quite hard, and probably nothing would happen to it falling onto the carpet. His main concern was for the loud noise he was bound to make, and which even through all the doors would probably raise concern if not alarm. But it was something that had to be risked.

When Gregor was already sticking half way out of the bed—the new method was more of a game than an effort, all he had to do was rock back and forth—it occurred to him how simple everything would be if somebody came to help him. Two strong people—he had his father and the maid in mind—would have been more than enough; they would only have to push their arms under the dome of his back, peel him away from the bed, bend down with the load and then be patient and careful as he swang over onto the floor, where, hopefully, the little legs would find a use. Should he really call for help though, even apart from the fact that all the doors were locked? Despite all the difficulty he was in, he could not suppress a smile at this thought.

After a while he had already moved so far across that it would have been hard for him to keep his balance if he rocked too hard. The time was now ten past seven and he would have to make a final decision very soon. Then there was a ring at the door of the flat. "That'll be someone from work," he said to himself, and froze very still, although his little legs only became all the more lively as they danced around. For a moment everything remained quiet. "They're not opening the door," Gregor said to himself, caught in some nonsensical hope. But then of course, the maid's firm steps went to the door as ever and opened it. Gregor only needed to hear the visitor's first words of greeting and he knew who it was—the chief clerk himself. Why did Gregor have to be the only one condemned to work for a company where they immediately became highly suspicious at the slightest shortcoming? Were all employees, every one of them, louts, was there not one of them who was faithful and devoted who would go so mad with pangs of conscience that he couldn't get out of bed if he didn't spend at least a couple of hours in the morning on company business? Was it really not enough to let one of the trainees make enquiries—assuming enquiries were even necessary—did the chief clerk have to come himself, and did they have to show the whole, innocent family that this was so suspicious that only the chief clerk could be trusted to have the wisdom to investigate it? And more because these thoughts had made him upset than through any proper decision, he swang himself with all his force out of the bed. There was a loud thump, but it wasn't really a loud noise. His fall was softened a little by the carpet, and Gregor's back was also more elastic than he had thought, which made the sound muffled and not too noticeable. He had not held his head carefully enough, though, and hit it as he fell; annoyed and in pain, he turned it and rubbed it against the carpet.

"Something's fallen down in there," said the chief clerk in the room on the left. Gregor tried to imagine whether something of the sort that had happened to him today could ever happen to the chief clerk too; you had to concede that it was possible. But as if in gruff reply to this question, the chief clerk's firm footsteps in his highly polished boots could now be heard in the adjoining room. From the room on his right, Gregor's sister whispered to him to let him know: "Gregor, the chief clerk is here." "Yes, I know," said Gregor to himself; but without daring to raise his voice loud enough for his sister to hear him.

"He isn't well, he said this morning that he is, but he isn't."

"Gregor," said his father now from the room to his left, "the chief clerk has come round and wants to know why you didn't leave on the early train. We don't know what to say to him. And anyway, he wants to speak to you personally. So please open up this door. I'm sure he'll be good enough to forgive the untidiness of your room." Then the chief clerk called, "Good morning, Mr. Samsa." "He isn't well," said his mother to the chief clerk, while his father continued to speak through the door. "He isn't well, please believe me. Why else would Gregor have missed a train! The lad only ever thinks about the business. It nearly makes me cross the way he never goes out in the evenings; he's been in town for a week now but stayed home every evening. He sits with us in the kitchen and just reads the paper or studies train timetables. His idea of relaxation is working with his fretsaw.[3] He's made a little frame, for instance, it only took him two

---

[3] **fretsaw:** a saw used to cut delicate curves in wood.

Image Credits: Louis C. Kramer/Library of Congress Prints & Photographs Division

250 or three evenings, you'll be amazed how nice it is; it's hanging up in
his room; you'll see it as soon as Gregor opens the door. Anyway, I'm
glad you're here; we wouldn't have been able to get Gregor to open
the door by ourselves; he's so stubborn; and I'm sure he isn't well, he
said this morning that he is, but he isn't." "I'll be there in a moment,"
said Gregor slowly and thoughtfully, but without moving so that he
would not miss any word of the conversation. "Well I can't think of
any other way of explaining it, Mrs. Samsa," said the chief clerk, "I
hope it's nothing serious. But on the other hand, I must say that if we
people in commerce ever become slightly unwell then, fortunately
260 or unfortunately as you like, we simply have to overcome it because
of business considerations." "Can the chief clerk come in to see you
now then?" asked his father impatiently, knocking at the door again.
"No," said Gregor. In the room on his right there followed a painful
silence; in the room on his left his sister began to cry.

So why did his sister not go and join the others? She had
probably only just got up and had not even begun to get dressed.
And why was she crying? Was it because he had not got up, and had
not let the chief clerk in, because he was in danger of losing his job
and if that happened his boss would once more pursue their parents
270 with the same demands as before? There was no need to worry
about things like that yet. Gregor was still there and had not the
slightest intention of abandoning his family. For the time being he
just lay there on the carpet, and no one who knew the condition he
was in would seriously have expected him to let the chief clerk in. It
was only a minor discourtesy, and a suitable excuse could easily be
found for it later on, it was not something for which Gregor could
be sacked on the spot. And it seemed to Gregor much more sensible
to leave him now in peace instead of disturbing him with talking at
him and crying. But the others didn't know what was happening,
280 they were worried, that would excuse their behavior.

The chief clerk now raised his voice, "Mr. Samsa," he called to
him, "what is wrong? You barricade yourself in your room, give us
no more than yes or no for an answer, you are causing serious and
unnecessary concern to your parents and you fail—and I mention
this just by the way—you fail to carry out your business duties
in a way that is quite unheard of. I'm speaking here on behalf of
your parents and of your employer, and really must request a clear
and immediate explanation. I am astonished, quite astonished.
I thought I knew you as a calm and sensible person, and now
290 you suddenly seem to be showing off with peculiar whims. This
morning, your employer did suggest a possible reason for your
failure to appear, it's true—it had to do with the money that was
recently entrusted to you—but I came near to giving him my word
of honor that that could not be the right explanation. But now that

I see your incomprehensible stubbornness I no longer feel any wish whatsoever to intercede on your behalf. And nor is your position all that secure. I had originally intended to say all this to you in private, but since you cause me to waste my time here for no good reason I don't see why your parents should not also learn of it. Your turnover has been very unsatisfactory of late; I grant you that it's not the time of year to do especially good business, we recognize that; but there simply is no time of year to do no business at all, Mr. Samsa, we cannot allow there to be."

"But Sir," called Gregor, beside himself and forgetting all else in the excitement, "I'll open up immediately, just a moment. I'm slightly unwell, an attack of dizziness, I haven't been able to get up. I'm still in bed now. I'm quite fresh again now, though. I'm just getting out of bed. Just a moment. Be patient! It's not quite as easy as I'd thought. I'm quite all right now, though. It's shocking, what can suddenly happen to a person! I was quite all right last night, my parents know about it, perhaps better than me, I had a small symptom of it last night already. They must have noticed it. I don't know why I didn't let you know at work! But you always think you can get over an illness without staying at home. Please, don't make my parents suffer! There's no basis for any of the accusations you're making; nobody's ever said a word to me about any of these things. Maybe you haven't read the latest contracts I sent in. I'll set off with the eight o'clock train, as well, these few hours of rest have given me strength. You don't need to wait, sir; I'll be in the office soon after you, and please be so good as to tell that to the boss and recommend me to him!"

And while Gregor gushed out these words, hardly knowing what he was saying, he made his way over to the chest of drawers—this was easily done, probably because of the practice he had already had in bed—where he now tried to get himself upright. He really did want to open the door, really did want to let them see him and to speak with the chief clerk; the others were being so insistent, and he was curious to learn what they would say when they caught sight of him. If they were shocked then it would no longer be Gregor's responsibility and he could rest. If, however, they took everything calmly he would still have no reason to be upset, and if he hurried he really could be at the station for eight o'clock. The first few times he tried to climb up on the smooth chest of drawers he just slid down again, but he finally gave himself one last swing and stood there upright; the lower part of his body was in serious pain but he no longer gave any attention to it. Now he let himself fall against the back of a nearby chair and held tightly to the edges of it with his little legs. By now he had also calmed down, and kept quiet so that he could listen to what the chief clerk was saying.

340 "Did you understand a word of all that?" the chief clerk asked his parents, "surely he's not trying to make fools of us." "Oh, God!" called his mother, who was already in tears, "he could be seriously ill and we're making him suffer. Grete! Grete!" she then cried. "Mother?" his sister called from the other side. They communicated across Gregor's room. "You'll have to go for the doctor straight away. Gregor is ill. Quick, get the doctor. Did you hear the way Gregor spoke just now?" "That was the voice of an animal," said the chief clerk, with a calmness that was in contrast with his mother's screams. "Anna! Anna!" his father called into the kitchen through
350 the entrance hall, clapping his hands, "get a locksmith here, now!" And the two girls, their skirts swishing, immediately ran out through the hall, wrenching open the front door of the flat as they went. How had his sister managed to get dressed so quickly? There was no sound of the door banging shut again; they must have left it open; people often do in homes where something awful has happened.

Gregor, in contrast, had become much calmer. So they couldn't understand his words any more, although they seemed clear enough to him, clearer than before—perhaps his ears had become used to
360 the sound. They had realized, though, that there was something wrong with him, and were ready to help. The first response to his situation had been confident and wise, and that made him feel better. He felt that he had been drawn back in among people, and from the doctor and the locksmith he expected great and surprising achievements—although he did not really distinguish one from the other. Whatever was said next would be crucial, so, in order to make his voice as clear as possible, he coughed a little, but taking care to do this not too loudly as even this might well sound different from the way that a human coughs and he was no longer sure he could
370 judge this for himself. Meanwhile, it had become very quiet in the next room. Perhaps his parents were sat at the table whispering with the chief clerk, or perhaps they were all pressed against the door and listening.

Gregor slowly pushed his way over to the door with the chair. Once there he let go of it and threw himself onto the door, holding himself upright against it using the adhesive on the tips of his legs. He rested there a little while to recover from the effort involved and then set himself to the task of turning the key in the lock with his mouth. He seemed, unfortunately, to have no proper teeth—how was he, then, to grasp the key?—but the lack of teeth was, of course,
380 made up for with a very strong jaw; using the jaw, he really was able to start the key turning, ignoring the fact that he must have been causing some kind of damage as a brown fluid came from his mouth, flowed over the key and dripped onto the floor. "Listen,"

said the chief clerk in the next room, "he's turning the key." Gregor was greatly encouraged by this; but they all should have been calling to him, his father and his mother too: "Well done, Gregor," they should have cried, "keep at it, keep hold of the lock!" And with the idea that they were all excitedly following his efforts, he bit on the key with all his strength, paying no attention to the pain he was causing himself. As the key turned round he turned around the lock with it, only holding himself upright with his mouth, and hung onto the key or pushed it down again with the whole weight of his body as needed. The clear sound of the lock as it snapped back was Gregor's sign that he could break his concentration, and as he regained his breath he said to himself: "So, I didn't need the locksmith after all." Then he lay his head on the handle of the door to open it completely.

Because he had to open the door in this way, it was already wide open before he could be seen. He had first to slowly turn himself around one of the double doors, and he had to do it very carefully if he did not want to fall flat on his back before entering the room.

He was still occupied with this difficult movement, unable to pay attention to anything else, when he heard the chief clerk exclaim a loud "Oh!" which sounded like the soughing[4] of the wind. Now he also saw him—he was the nearest to the door—his hand pressed against his open mouth and slowly retreating as if driven by a steady and invisible force. Gregor's mother, her hair still disheveled from bed despite the chief clerk's being there, looked at his father.

410 Then she unfolded her arms, took two steps forward towards Gregor and sank down onto the floor into her skirts that spread themselves out around her as her head disappeared down onto her breast. His father looked hostile, and clenched his fists as if wanting to knock Gregor back into his room. Then he looked uncertainly round the living room, covered his eyes with his hands and wept so that his powerful chest shook.

COLLABORATIVE DISCUSSION What elements of this novella distort the reader's sense of reality, while at the same time make Gregor Samsa's situation feel very real? In a small group, discuss textual evidence that supports your responses.

---

[4] **soughing (sou´ĭng):** a soft moaning or whistling sound.

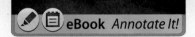

Support Inferences

RL 1

An **inference** is a conclusion based on facts. When analyzing literature, skilled readers make inferences drawn from the text. For instance, in the first paragraph of "The Metamorphosis," Franz Kafka writes that when Gregor Samsa woke up, "he found himself transformed in his bed into a horrible vermin." Based on this statement and the descriptive details that follow in the first paragraph, you might infer that Gregor actually was turned into an insect; or perhaps you might infer that he was just dreaming. As you read on, you'll make other inferences based on the evidence you encounter. You may also revise your earlier inferences and even discard them, based on further analysis of the text.

Analyzing the Text

RL 1, RL 2,
RL 3, RL 5,
RL 6, SL 1

Cite Text Evidence   Support your responses with evidence from the selection.

1. **Analyze** An author makes choices about how to structure and pace events to achieve a purpose. In lines 59–84, Gregor suddenly starts to worry about missing the train. From this point onward, how does Kafka manipulate time to create tension? Consider how the pacing creates a sense of urgency and panic.

2. **Infer** Kafka provides many details about how Gregor interacts with his parents. Based on these details, what can you infer about Gregor's relationship with his mother and father? Use text evidence to support your inferences.

3. **Summarize** What theme emerges in the story? Consider what Gregor's changing into an insect might symbolize. Summarize the plot to explain how the theme evolves through the responses of Gregor and others to his condition.

4. **Connect** Franz Kafka wrote this story in 1912 in what is now the Czech Republic. What insights into European culture in the early 1900s does the text provide? Cite evidence from the text to support your ideas.

PERFORMANCE TASK

Speaking Activity: Response to Literature What can you infer about the kind of person Gregor is based on how he responds to the change he has undergone?

- Make notes about the progression of Gregor's thoughts and actions in this selection. Use your notes to make inferences about Gregor's character, and jot down at least two adjectives that describe his personality.

- Use your notes to respond to this question in a group discussion: Does being changed into "a horrible vermin" really change Gregor? Why or why not? Write a summary of your group's answer.

Graphic Novel by Peter Kuper

AS YOU READ Pay attention to the text and graphic details that show what the main character is experiencing. Write down any questions you generate during reading.

When Gregor Samsa
awoke one morning from
disturbing dreams,
he found himself
transformed . . .

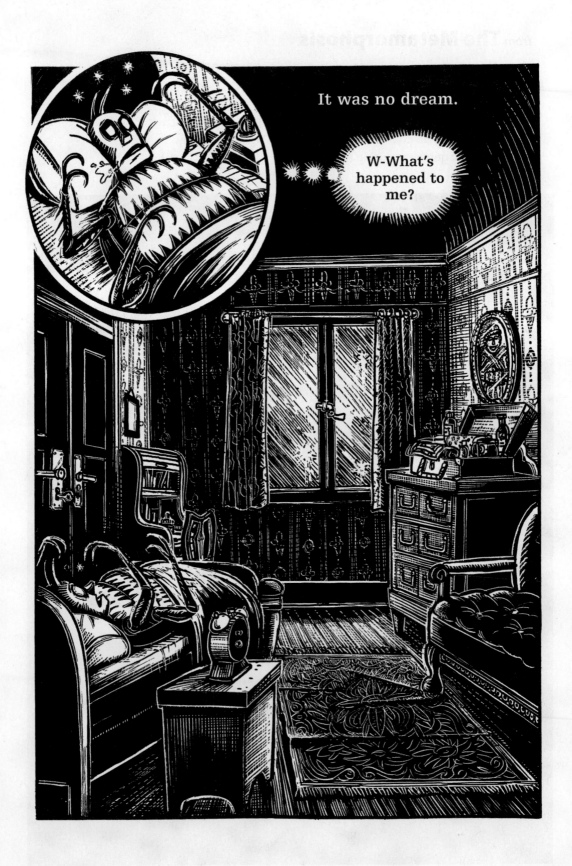

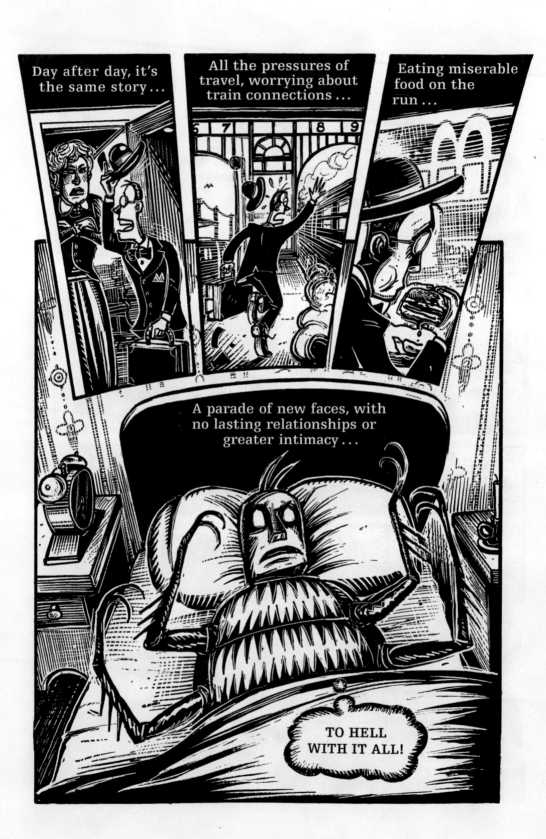

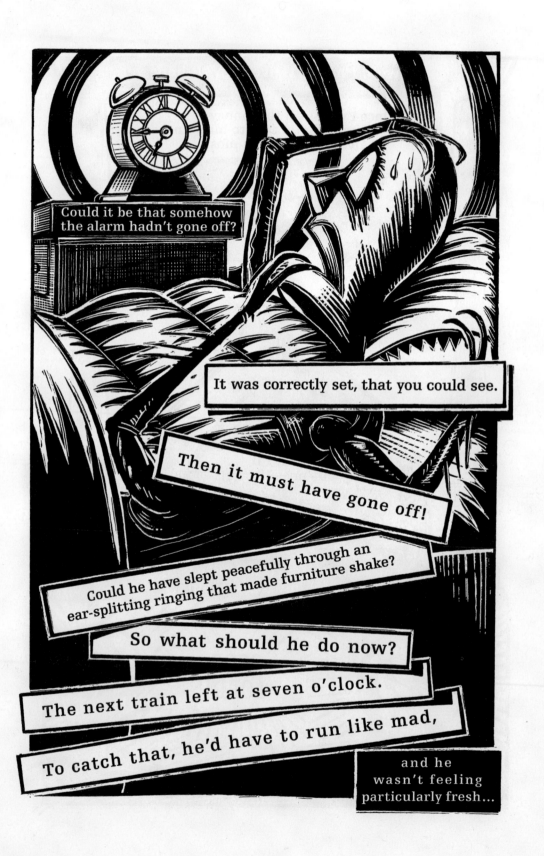

The change in Gregor's voice must have been muffled by the wooden door because his mother was reassured and shuffled off. However, their little exchange made his father and sister aware that Gregor had not, as they assumed, left for work.

Gregor, it's Grete, are you alright?

Do you need *anything*?

Please, Gregor, open the door.

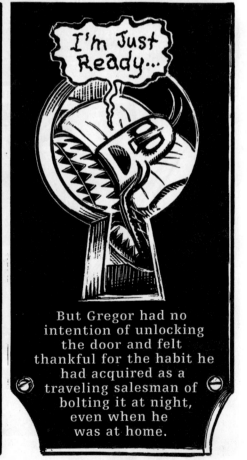

But Gregor had no intention of unlocking the door and felt thankful for the habit he had acquired as a traveling salesman of bolting it at night, even when he was at home.

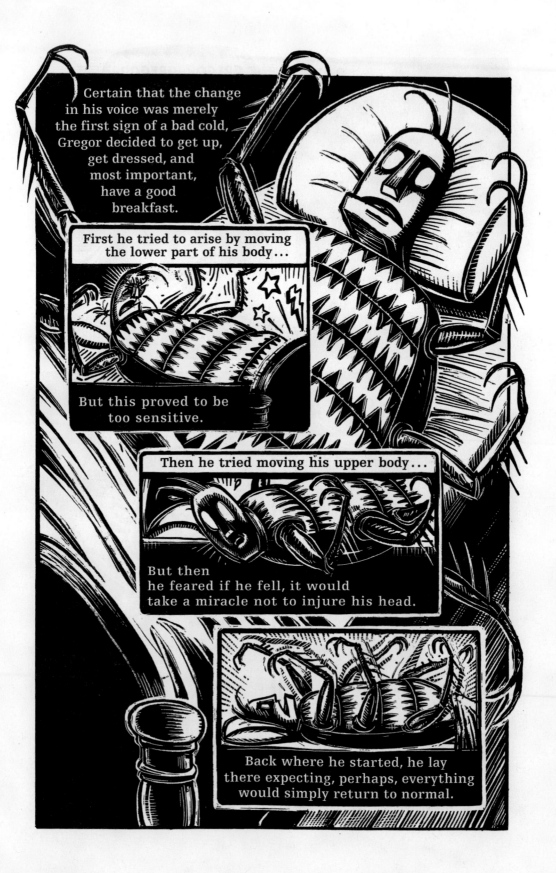

Certain that the change in his voice was merely the first sign of a bad cold, Gregor decided to get up, get dressed, and most important, have a good breakfast.

First he tried to arise by moving the lower part of his body...

But this proved to be too sensitive.

Then he tried moving his upper body...

But then he feared if he fell, it would take a miracle not to injure his head.

Back where he started, he lay there expecting, perhaps, everything would simply return to normal.

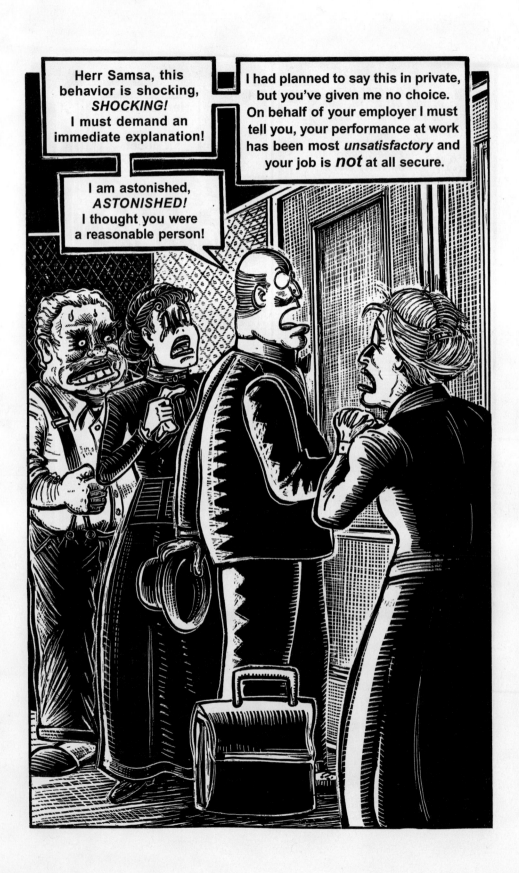

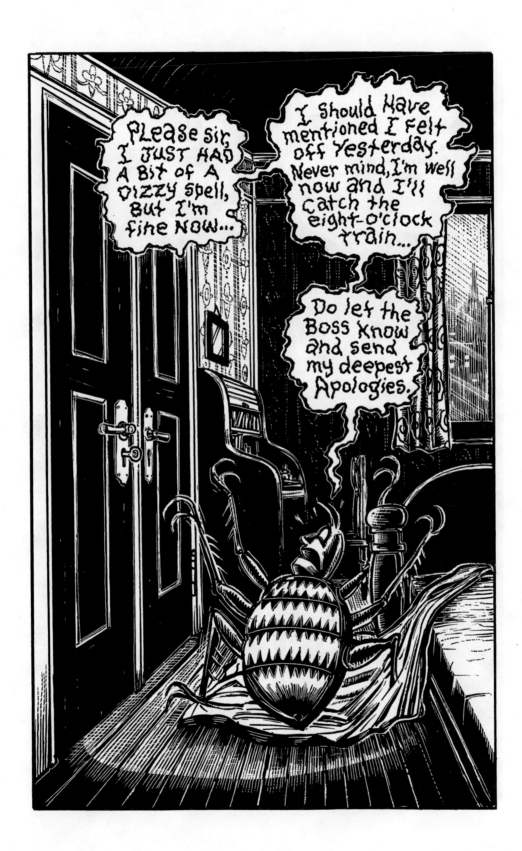

COLLABORATIVE DISCUSSION With a partner, discuss the text and graphic details that help you infer Gregor's state of mind. Cite specific textual and visual evidence from the story to support your ideas.

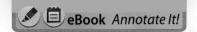

Analyze Representations in Different Mediums

RL 7

The graphic artist Peter Kuper and the writer Franz Kafka use the strengths of different **mediums**, or forms, to convey similar ideas. For instance, early in the graphic novel eight small panels show Gregor's struggles to get into a comfortable position. In his novella, Kafka conveys this scene in paragraph three, stating that Gregor "must have tried it a hundred times" ("it" being Gregor's attempts to find a comfortable position). The medium of writing allows us to understand Gregor's thoughts at this moment in ways that a visual medium could not. On the other hand, even Kafka's powers of description cannot give readers the clear visual image of Gregor's struggle that a few frames of Kuper's graphic novel can. As you compare these representations, keep in mind the strengths of both mediums.

Analyzing the Text

RL 1, RL 2, RL 5, RL 7, RL 9, SL 4

Cite Text Evidence   Support your responses with evidence from the selections.

1. **Compare** Reread paragraph five of Kafka's story, and then consider Kuper's depiction of Gregor's interaction with his boss. How does Kuper transform Gregor's thoughts about the boss into images? In your response, use evidence to support your ideas about the strengths of each medium.

2. **Evaluate** Sometimes, Kuper uses Kafka's exact words, but often he leaves out the words in the novella. Using details from both works, explain whether Kuper's use of language is effective in transforming the novella into a new work. Consider Kuper's graphic treatment of words in your explanation.

3. **Compare** Like Kafka, Kuper manipulates time to create tension. How are the graphic novel and story alike and different in their treatment of time? How does the idea of time figure into the story's theme in both works?

4. **Critique** The literary term *Kafkaesque* describes a distorted and oppressive sense of reality. Based on your careful reading of both works, is Kuper's graphic novel Kafkaesque? Use evidence from both works to support your ideas.

PERFORMANCE TASK

Speaking Activity: Informative Presentation How does the graphic novel expand on the ideas in Kafka's version of *The Metamorphosis*? Choose one page of the graphic novel to compare with the source text in a short speech.

- Identify the page of the graphic novel that is closest to or furthest from what you visualized as you read the novella. Complete a Venn diagram comparing the page you chose with the same part of the written story.

- In a speech, explain how Kuper interprets an idea from Kafka's story and evaluate how effectively the page you chose communicates Kafka's ideas. Show the page to facilitate your explanation.

Critical Vocabulary

vermin   **subordinate**   **plaintively**   **enunciate**

Practice and Apply Create a semantic map for each of the Critical Vocabulary words listed above. Use a dictionary or thesaurus as needed. The example is for a word appearing on line 164 of the novella.

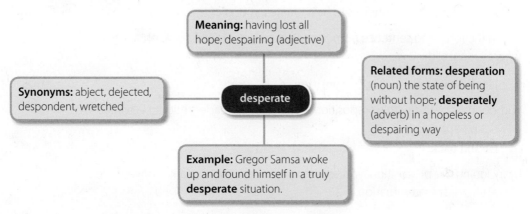

Meaning: having lost all hope; despairing (adjective)

Synonyms: abject, dejected, despondent, wretched

desperate

Related forms: desperation (noun) the state of being without hope; **desperately** (adverb) in a hopeless or despairing way

Example: Gregor Samsa woke up and found himself in a truly **desperate** situation.

Vocabulary Strategy: Verifying Word Meanings

When you encounter an unfamiliar word in your reading, you can often make an inference or educated guess about the word's meaning using context clues from the text. For example, in the first paragraph of the novella, the author uses the Critical Vocabulary word *vermin*. As you read, you can use context clues such as "stiff sections" and "many legs" to infer that *vermin* may refer to an insect. Since this word is so central to understanding Gregor's situation, you might want to verify that inferred meaning by reading further or by checking a dictionary.

Practice and Apply   Practice this strategy by choosing three unfamiliar words from "The Metamorphosis." Verify their meanings using both context clues from the story and a reference source. You may need to consult a college-level or bilingual dictionary to verify the meanings of advanced vocabulary or words from languages other than English. For each word, follow these steps:

1. Copy the sentence in which the word is used.

2. Using only the context of that sentence, write down what you think the word means in your own words. (Do not use a dictionary at this point.)

3. Return to the story and find context clues in the surrounding sentences that support your inferred meaning. List them under your definition. If you find clues that suggest the word may have a different meaning, list those as well. Then, revise your definition as needed.

4. Finally, use a dictionary to verify the meaning of the word. How similar was your definition to the dictionary definition?

Language and Style: Prepositional, Adjectival, and Adverbial Phrases

Using a variety of phrases in your writing helps convey ideas and hold readers' interest. For example, prepositional phrases show readers the connections between key words in a sentence, clarifying *what kind, how many,* or *which one.* They can also tell *where, when,* and *how* something took place. In "The Metamorphosis," Franz Kafka uses prepositional phrases to help create a mood of tension and despair.

In the following sentence from the selection, the prepositional phrase tells *where* Gregor slid:

He slid back <u>into his former position</u>.

Without the specificity this prepositional phrase adds, readers might be confused as to what is happening:

He slid back.

By including the prepositional phrase *into his former position*, Kafka conveys the character's desperate situation.

A prepositional phrase used to modify a noun is called an **adjectival phrase;** one that modifies a verb is called an **adverbial phrase:**

Type of Phrase	Example of Usage
Adjectival Phrase—is a prepositional phrase that modifies a noun or pronoun. In the example to the right, *in the graphic novel* is the adjectival phrase because it modifies the noun *depiction.*	Gregor Samsa's depiction *in the graphic novel* is very haunting.
Adverbial Phrase—is a prepositional phrase that modifies a verb, adjective, or adverb. In the example, *in the very first paragraph* is the adverbial phrase because it modifies the verb *revealed.*	Is Gregor Samsa's true character revealed *in the very first paragraph*?

Practice and Apply Revisit the speech you wrote comparing the novella with the graphic novel in this selection's Performance Task. Add or change at least three prepositional phrases. Be sure to include at least one adjectival phrase and one adverbial phrase. In a small group, present your revised speech and discuss how each added or revised phrase improved the specificity and variety of your sentences.

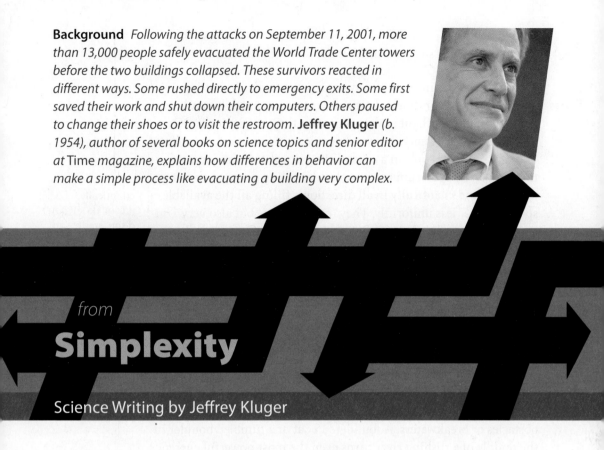

Background *Following the attacks on September 11, 2001, more than 13,000 people safely evacuated the World Trade Center towers before the two buildings collapsed. These survivors reacted in different ways. Some rushed directly to emergency exits. Some first saved their work and shut down their computers. Others paused to change their shoes or to visit the restroom.* **Jeffrey Kluger** *(b. 1954), author of several books on science topics and senior editor at* Time *magazine, explains how differences in behavior can make a simple process like evacuating a building very complex.*

from

Simplexity

Science Writing by Jeffrey Kluger

AS YOU READ Notice the role that human behavior plays when a large crowd exits a building.

The people who stayed behind in both towers on September 11, 2001—or waited too long before trying to leave—bore no responsibility for what happened to them that morning. They were, instead, twice victimized—once by the men who hijacked the planes and took so many lives; and once by the impossibly complex interplay of luck, guesswork, psychology, architecture, and more that is at play in any such mass movement of people. Fear plays a role, so does bravado, so does desperation. But so do ergonomics,[1] fluid dynamics, engineering, even physics—all combining to 10 determine which individuals get where they're going, which ones don't, and which survive the journey at all. Ultimately, we're misled by our most basic instincts—the belief that we know where the danger is and how best to respond to keep ourselves alive, when in fact we sometimes have no idea at all. It's the job of the people who think about such matters to tease all these things apart and put them back together in buildings and vehicles that keep their

---

[1] **ergonomics:** the science of maximizing workplace efficiency.

occupants alive. It's the job of those occupants to learn enough about the systems so that they have the sense to use them.

To scientists studying complex systems, evacuees[2] abandoning a building or city or disabled airplane are not so much humans engaged in mortal flight as data points on the complexity arc. On an ordinary day, twenty thousand people working in a skyscraper or half a million people in a coastal city occupy the same spot on the complexity spectrum as air molecules filling a room—moving randomly and **chaotically** in all directions, filling all the available space more or less uniformly. They're very active, but also very simple and disordered. Send the same people on a stampede down stairways or onto highways and things quickly grow overloaded and grind to a halt, jumping to the other end of the complexity arc—robust, unchanging, frozen in place, but every bit as simple as the ever-shifting air molecules. It's in the middle of the arc, where the molecules just begin to take some shape or the people in the tower just begin to move to the exits, that true complexity begins to emerge.

The best way to understand the elaborate manner in which people move en masse[3] may be to understand the equally complex way water does the same, particularly how it navigates around obstacles or breakwaters. A foundered boat or a tumbled boulder in the middle of a rushing river turns even the most powerful current chaotic, **reallocating** its energy into increased swirling and churning and decreased velocity. When people are fleeing a building, a similar kind of chaos can be a very good thing. Designers of interior spaces have found that a perfectly useless post positioned along the path to a fire exit may actually help people escape. Give evacuees storming toward a doorway a little something to avoid and you stagger their arrival slightly, allowing them to stream through the opening in a reasonably controlled flow, rather than colliding there at once and causing a pileup. The obstacle keeps you at the top of the complexity arc, preventing you from plunging headlong to the frozen end.

"You create a little **turbulence**," says Santa Fe Institute economist John Miller, who specializes in complex adaptive social systems. "By adding a little noise to the system you produce coherence in the flow."

The problem with the human-beings-as-water-particles idea is that it takes you only so far. Early fluid-based computer models that designers relied on to simulate crowd flow had a troubling habit of producing results that were simply too tidy. Put a single exit

chaotically
(kā-ŏt´ĭk-lē) *adv.*
disorderedly and
unpredictably.

reallocate
(rē-ăl´ə-kāt´) *v.*
to distribute or
apportion again;
reassign.

turbulence
(tûr´byə-ləns) *n.*
violent, disordered
movement.

---

[2] **evacuees:** people who have been relocated from a dangerous place.
[3] **en masse (ŏn măs´):** together as one.

in an office and the computerized evacuees would flow through
60 it at a particular rate of speed. Open a second exit somewhere else
and the people would respond appropriately, with half of them
choosing that new option and the flow at both doors adjusting itself
commensurately.[4] Put a breakwater somewhere along the route and
things smoothed out even more. Certainly, the programmers weren't
fools. They would correct for things like accessibility and **proximity**
of the exits—with more of the simulated evacuees choosing the
closer, more convenient egresses. But after that, the software assumed, the people would behave sensibly. This, of course, was
nonsense.

70   For one thing, people have different levels of decision-making
skills, with some inevitably behaving more rationally than others.
For another, all of us have a tendency to believe that the rest of
the group knows what it's doing, and thus will gravitate toward a
more popular exit simply because other people have chosen it, even
if the alternative is perfectly safe and much less congested. Every
additional person who chooses the more popular exit only makes
it likelier that the next person will select that one too. Finally,
information tends to get distributed unevenly, with some people
learning about an emergency first and acting before the others.

80 Once all of this was written into the fluid-based programs, the
simulations ran amok. "A fluid particle cannot experience fear or
pain," writes David Low, a civil engineer who studies evacuations
at Hariot-Watt University in Edinburgh, Scotland. "It cannot have
a preferred direction of motion, cannot make decisions, cannot
stumble or fall." Humans do all of those things and, in the process,
make a mess of most models.

    In response to such problems, evacuation software has gotten
a lot more sophisticated. Programs with such evocative names
as EGRESS, EESCAPE, and EXODUS take into consideration
90 everything from the nature of an emergency (fire, bomb scare,
blackout) to the season in which it occurs (cold weather causing
more problems since people have to collect their coats, which is not
only time-consuming but space-consuming once the bulkily clad
occupants of the building crowd into the stairwells) to the time of
day (fewer people being in the building at lunchtime, for example,
than at ten-thirty in the morning, meaning that the midday
evacuations will be quicker and smoother).

    Of course, computers can't model the existential terror that
comes along with any evacuation and programs like EGRESS are
100 thus limited by their very nature. One place those limitations show
themselves is in the evacuation stairway. Once frightened people

proximity
(prŏk-sĭm´ĭ-tē) *n.*
nearness.

---

[4] **commensurately:** in a corresponding or equivalent manner.

reach the stairways that should take them to safety, things ought to get easier. To complexity scientists, emergency stairways are nothing more than what are known as relaxation pathways, outlets that allow pressure or an imbalance to be relieved—in this case, the pressure of a mass of people trying to descend from higher floors to lower floors and then spill out of the building altogether. Given that, the only thing that ought to count in a stairway evacuation is pure speed; anything short of a stampede that will get the building emptied in a hurry is a good thing. But pure speed is hard to maintain.

110

Much has been made in the years since September 11 about the announcement in Tower Two that instructed workers to stay at their desks—something that undoubtedly contributed to some of the deaths that day even though that was precisely the correct thing to do as far as anyone at the moment knew. The improbability of one building suffering the kind of violence that was done to the towers that day—to say nothing of two—called not for a wholesale evacuation, but for a so-called sheltering in place, taking cover precisely where you are and thus staying safe from the chaos and debris on the street below. What's more, ordinary fires don't spread instantly across multiple floors and aren't fed by thousands of gallons of jet fuel. Fireproof doors and localized sprinklers are designed to keep people on unaffected floors safe so that they don't crowd the stairwells and slow the people who are in real danger.

120

Even in an unexceptional emergency, however, it doesn't take much for a smooth stream of downward-flowing evacuees to turn turbulent. For one thing, people from middle floors who enter the stairwell somewhere in mid-current can cause things to slow or stop. The delay flows back along the queue the same way a ripple **propagates** through water, or cars entering a highway briefly slow the ones closest to the on-ramp, causing a wave of tapped brake lights that may radiate miles back. Sequential evacuation is the best way to handle this problem, with people on lower floors leaving the building first and each higher floor following successively. But again, nobody pretends that people fearing for their lives would wait patiently at their desks until their floor was called, nor would it be wise in a situation like the September 11 attacks, when the towers themselves turned into ticking clocks, and people higher up needed every minute of evacuation time they could get before the buildings collapsed on top of them.

130

140

propagate
(prŏp´ə-gāt´) *v.* to reproduce or extend in quantity.

COLLABORATIVE DISCUSSION Were you surprised by the difficulties of planning a building evacuation? With a partner, discuss the many factors involved in creating a successful building evacuation plan. Cite specific textual evidence to support your ideas.

Analyze Author's Order: Cause and Effect

Physics and other fields of science seek to explain the causes and effects of events in the natural world. A **cause** is an event that leads another event to happen; the **effect** is the event that results from the cause. In *Simplexity*, Jeffrey Kluger describes the movement of people evacuating a building by drawing on scientific concepts. He breaks down complex scientific ideas into a series of simpler cause-and-effect relationships. Events are presented in the order in which they occur, and readers can infer that they are connected as causes and effects.

One way to analyze cause-and-effect organization in a piece of writing is to map out the events in a flow chart. Notice how an event, such as "Everyone heads for the stairway at once," is also the cause of the next event, thereby creating a chain of events.

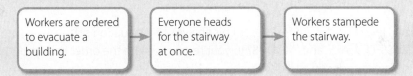

Workers are ordered to evacuate a building. → Everyone heads for the stairway at once. → Workers stampede the stairway.

Determine Technical Meanings

Science writing includes many **technical terms**—words with precise meanings in a particular field of study. Some of these terms may look familiar, but readers must determine their meanings as used in the text to understand exactly what the author means. For example, the word *particle* often means "speck" or "small bit of something." However, David Low's statement that "a fluid particle cannot experience fear or pain" (lines 81–82) uses the technical meaning of *particle*. In physics, a particle is a body, such as a water molecule, considered as a unit without regard to its internal structure.

When you encounter unfamiliar technical terms, try first to use context and other clues to determine their meanings. Sometimes, you may recognize a related word or word part. For instance, the author writes about "computer models that designers relied on to simulate crowd flow" (lines 56–57). The word *simulate* sounds a lot like *similar*, meaning "nearly the same or alike." The verb suffix *–ate* means "to act upon or become." The context discusses the use of computer models; we know that models represent images or ideas. Therefore, *simulate* means "to create a representation or model of."

If context alone won't help you determine a technical meaning, think about resources you can consult. Check the back of the book in which the word appears for a glossary of terms, or look online for a specialized dictionary devoted to the field of study. Note that a regular classroom dictionary may not include a word's technical meaning.

Analyzing the Text

RI 1, RI 3,
RI 4, RI 5, W 2

> **Cite Text Evidence**   Support your responses with evidence from the selection.

1. **Analyze** The author begins by referring to the destruction of the World Trade Center towers that occurred on September 11, 2001. What specific ideas does the author introduce to tie the events of September 11th to the scientific study of complex systems? Why might the author have decided to explain a scientific concept using a reference to a historic event?

2. **Infer** Using context clues in lines 19–34, determine the technical meaning of *complexity arc* as it is used in the text.

3. **Connect** In lines 35–50, how does the author develop his ideas about "the elaborate manner in which people move en masse"? Use evidence from the text to draw connections between the movement of people and the movement of water.

4. **Summarize** How does the author present his analysis of evacuation software such as EGRESS, EESCAPE, and EXODUS? In your response, note the order in which points are introduced and developed.

5. **Cause/Effect** Consider the problems that can cause "a smooth stream of downward-flowing evacuees to turn turbulent" (lines 126–128). Describe the causes and effects in this sequence of events.

6. **Analyze** The destruction of the World Trade Center towers happened when terrorists flew planes into the sides of the twin towers, setting off fiery explosions that eventually brought the towers down. Aside from his introduction, in what ways does the author keep the events of September 11th in the minds of readers throughout the article?

PERFORMANCE TASK

Writing Activity: Analysis   What does Kluger's analysis of responses during an evacuation tell you about human nature? Write an analysis using evidence from the text as well as your own experience.

- Reread *Simplexity*, making notes about how humans behave in crisis situations and why.
- Add to your notes your own thoughts about how you might react as well as evidence from other real-life events.

- Use your notes to draft a one-page analysis explaining your thesis about why people act as they do during a crisis.
- Organize your ideas in cause-and-effect order to make your points clear to readers.

Critical Vocabulary

chaotically   reallocate   turbulence   proximity   propagate

Practice and Apply Explain which Critical Vocabulary word listed above is most closely associated with each idea or situation.

1. Which word goes with whitewater rafting? Why?

2. Which word goes with students leaving the building on the last day of school? Why?

3. Which word goes with a next-door neighbor? Why?

4. Which word goes with farming? Why?

5. Which word goes with the movement of resources? Why?

Vocabulary Strategy: Figurative Meanings

In **figurative language**, words and phrases have meanings beyond the literal definitions of the words. In some cases, a word with a concrete meaning is used to describe an abstract idea or process. For example, the Critical Vocabulary word *turbulence* is defined in line 53 as "adding a little noise to the system." The most common meaning of *noise* is "sound." However, *noise* can be used to mean "a disturbance that interrupts a steady flow." This definition acts as a **metaphor**, a figure of speech that makes a comparison between two unlike things. Turbulence disrupts a calm flow of water in the same way that noise disrupts a radio broadcast.

Consider the effect of the metaphor in lines 138–141, in which the author refers to

> **a situation like the September 11 attacks, when the towers themselves turned into ticking clocks, and people higher up needed every minute of evacuation time they could get before the buildings collapsed on top of them.**

The towers did not literally turn into ticking clocks, but the metaphor conveys the urgency of the situation for the people in the buildings.

Practice and Apply Kluger uses an **extended metaphor**, one that continues through a long section of text, to compare people evacuating a building to water flowing in a stream. Trace the extended metaphor by following these steps.

1. Identify where the author introduces the metaphor. Where is the first mention of flowing water?

2. Review the text to find additional comparisons between people and water. Look for places where the author explains the similarities, and for places where he uses a term normally applied to water to describe a moving crowd of people.

3. Explain whether this extended metaphor effectively communicates the author's ideas. Does it help you understand the scientific concepts the author is presenting? Why?

Language and Style:
Transitional Words and Phrases

Transitional words and phrases connect ideas, making them easier to understand. Well-placed transitions act as stepping stones, guiding the reader from point to point, linking major sections of text from introduction to conclusion. The effect creates cohesion and clarifies the relationships among complex ideas and concepts. In *Simplexity*, Jeffrey Kluger uses transitional words and phrases to explain causes and effects in a complex process.

Note the underlined transitional words in this passage:

<u>Ultimately</u>, we're misled by our most basic instincts—the belief that we know where the danger is and how best to respond to keep ourselves alive, <u>when in fact</u> we <u>sometimes</u> have no idea at all.

Without transitions, the writing would be difficult to follow and less meaningful:

We're misled by our most basic instincts. We believe we know where the danger is and how best to respond to keep ourselves alive. We have no idea at all how to keep ourselves alive.

Notice how the transitions are used for different purposes: *ultimately* is used for emphasis; *when* and *sometimes* indicate time; *in fact* signals a contrast. Here are some other common transitions and their uses:

Transitions	
Word or Phrase	**Purpose**
again, and, also, equally, likewise, moreover, too, what's more	to show comparison
but, even so, however, in fact, not only, on the other hand, or, rather than, yet	to show contrast
after, before, during, finally, later, when, while	to show sequence or time
above, below, here, there, under	to show location
certainly, in fact, indeed, ultimately	to show emphasis
for example, in this case, like, such as, that is	to show examples

Practice and Apply Reread the selection, noting transitional words and phrases. Then, look back at the analysis you wrote for this selection's Performance Task. Revise it to add at least three transitional words or phrases that reflect your cause-and-effect order. Discuss with a partner how each added transition improves the meaning, flow, and cohesion of your work.

Background *Although individual circumstances differ, immigrants share the experience of adapting to a new and unfamiliar environment. They must learn new behaviors and languages while keeping alive the traditions and values of their original cultures. Poet* **Cathy Song** *was born in Honolulu in 1955. Her grandfather came to Hawaii from China; her grandmother arrived from Korea in an arranged marriage. Their experiences inform many of Song's poems.*

Magic Island

Poem by Cathy Song

AS YOU READ Look for clues that explain the meaning of the poem's title, "Magic Island." Write down any questions you generate during reading.

A collar of water
surrounds the park peninsula
at noon.
Voices are lost
5 in waves of wind
that catches a kite
and keeps it there
in the air above the trees.
If the day has one color,
10 it is this:
the blue immersion of horizons,
the sea taking the sky like a swimmer.

The picnickers have come
to rest their bicycles
15 in the sprawling shade.
Under each tree, a stillness
of small pleasures:
a boy, half in sunlight,
naps with his dog;
20 a woman of forty
squints up from her book
to bite into an apple.

It is a day an immigrant
and his family might remember,
25 the husband taking off his shirt
to sit like an Indian
before the hot grill.
He would not in his own language
call it work, to cook
30 the sticks of marinated meat
for his son circling a yarn
of joy around the chosen tree.
A bit of luck has made him generous.
At this moment in his life,
35 with the sun sifting through
the leaves in panes of light,
he can easily say he loves his wife.
She lifts an infant
onto her left shoulder
40 as if the child
were a treasured sack of rice.
He cannot see her happiness,
hidden in a thicket of blanket
and shining hair.
45 On the grass beside their straw mat,
a black umbrella,
blooming like an ancient flower,
betrays their recent arrival.
Suspicious of so much sunshine,
50 they keep expecting rain.

COLLABORATIVE DISCUSSION With a partner, discuss what clues point
to an explanation of the poem's title. Cite evidence from the text to
support your ideas.

Support Inferences About Theme

RL 1, RL 2

"Magic Island" uses language in powerful ways to create pictures in readers' minds and to convey meaning. By analyzing the language, you can infer themes that the poet wants to communicate. A **theme** is a message about life or people that emerges from details in the text.

This chart can guide your analysis of "Magic Island."

What Text Says Directly	**Inferences Drawn from Text**	**Theme**
Note what the characters in the poem do, say, and think. Look for **imagery**, or language that appeals to the senses. Use the imagery to form pictures in your mind of the poem's setting.	What inferences can you draw from details in the poem? Look for clues in the characters' actions that allow you to guess more about them. Interpret any **symbols**, or objects that have meaning beyond the literal.	What message about life is the poet trying to communicate? Review the details you have noted and the inferences you have drawn, and think about the deeper meaning they suggest.

Analyzing the Text

RL 1, RL 2, W 1

Cite Text Evidence   Support your responses with evidence from the selection.

1. **Analyze** Review lines 1–32. What images are the most striking? What **mood**, or feeling, do these images create?

2. **Interpret** Beginning in line 46, Song writes of "a black umbrella, / blooming like an ancient flower." What does the umbrella **symbolize**, or represent?

3. **Infer** Use your observations about the poem to summarize its meaning, or **theme**.

PERFORMANCE TASK

Writing Activity: Argument Consider the Chinese proverb, "When the wind of change blows, some build walls while others build windmills." Which does the family in this poem do? Explore your ideas in a written argument.

- Consider what "wind of change" has affected the family. Then make a two-column chart listing examples of their metaphorically building walls and windmills. Identify which column contains more or stronger examples.

- Write a paragraph in which you make your case for whether the family builds walls or windmills. Cite evidence from your chart to support your ideas.

Language and Style:
Noun Phrases and Verb Phrases

A **phrase** is a group of related words that functions in a sentence as a single part of speech. A **noun phrase** contains a noun and any words that modify it. A **verb phrase** contains a verb plus any words that modify or complement the verb. Noun and verb phrases help a writer convey specific meanings because the modifiers add richness and detail to the noun or verb at the heart of each phrase.

In "Magic Island," Cathy Song uses many noun and verb phrases to evoke mood and meaning. This chart shows some of the phrases used in the first two stanzas of "Magic Island."

Noun Phrases	Verb Phrases
"A collar of water"	"surrounds the park peninsula / at noon"
"the air above the trees"	"are lost / in waves of wind"
"the blue immersion of horizons"	"have come / to rest their bicycles / in the sprawling shade"
"a stillness / of small pleasures"	"naps with his dog"
"a woman of forty"	"squints up from her book / to bite into an apple"

Consider how lines 13–22 might read without the noun and verb phrases Song has crafted to include modifying details:

The picnickers have come.

Under each tree, a stillness:

a boy naps;

a woman squints up.

This simplified version gives the basic facts of the scene, but it provides few details to help readers imagine it. The description is abstract and vague rather than concrete and specific. In your own writing, think about when it is appropriate to elaborate on your nouns and verbs with modifiers that will show readers your exact meaning.

Practice and Apply Look back at the paragraph you wrote for this selection's Performance Task. Circle any noun phrases and underline any verb phrases you used. Revise your paragraph by adding more explicit details to existing phrases or by adding modifying words to build phrases around nouns and verbs. Discuss with a partner how your revisions improve the original paragraph.

MEDIA ANALYSIS

from
Rivers and Tides

Documentary Film by Thomas Riedelsheimer

AS YOU VIEW Pay attention to the settings shown in the film clip and how they affect your perception of the artist's work. Write down any questions you generate during viewing.

COLLABORATIVE DISCUSSION In a small group, discuss how the settings in the film clip interact with and become a part of Andy Goldsworthy's work. What changes within the settings are important to the art?

Analyze Development of Ideas

Rivers and Tides is a documentary film about the British artist Andy Goldsworthy. In this film, director Thomas Riedelsheimer documents the artist's process of creation.

Like a writer, a filmmaker works to develop ideas in a logical fashion. The **central idea** is the most important idea about a topic that a film conveys. **Supporting details** are the images and words that tell more about the central idea. A central idea will sometimes be shown or stated directly, but more often it will be implied by the supporting details. In order to appreciate and understand the central idea, the viewer needs to consider the order of and connections between images.

Filmmakers use a combination of elements to help them express a central idea.

- **Visual elements:** Film elements such as these help the filmmaker convey connections among ideas:
  camera shot—a single, continuous view taken by a camera
  camera angle—the angle at which the camera is positioned during the recording of a shot or image
  In *Rivers and Tides*, the filmmaker films the subject in different settings and then combines the images to show connections.

- **Sound elements:** Music, voice-over, and sound effects may be included in a film to give additional information and to set a mood or tone for a scene. For example, Andy Goldsworthy's monologue expresses what he thinks about his art pieces.

- **Special effects:** Special effects are manipulated video images. These can include
  speed—fast- or slow-motion sequences can heighten drama and create a tense or calm mood
  lighting—unusually bright or dim lighting can create a specific mood, and changes in lighting can communicate a shift in mood
  time-lapse—starting and stopping filming to connect images from one time period to the same images in another time period

- **Setting:** The locations in which a film is shot are its setting. In *Rivers and Tides*, the various settings are an integral part of how the filmmaker conveys the central idea.

- **Mood:** The mood is the atmosphere that the visual and sound elements in a film create for the viewer. Lighting, music, and sound effects all play a role in creating the mood. Mood helps support the central idea by reinforcing what the viewer is seeing.

- **Sequence:** A filmmaker presents images in a logical order. Sometimes this is a chronological order, but at other times, the images or scenes are shown in an order that helps the viewer relate the ideas being shown.

As you view the clip from *Rivers and Tides*, think about what central idea the director communicates through images, sounds, and **juxtaposition**, or side-by-side placement of key elements. If you were to summarize the clip for someone who had not seen it, what ideas and images would you emphasize? Developing an answer to that question is the beginning of media analysis.

Analyzing the Media

RI 1, RI 2, RI 3,
RI 5, SL 5

Cite Text Evidence   Support your responses with evidence from the selection.

1. **Connect** What visual elements does the filmmaker use in the clip to make a connection between the flow of the film and the rivers and tides of the title?

2. **Compare** What effect does the filmmaker's use of close-up shots of the artist's work and shots taken from farther away have on your understanding of the connections between the sculptures?

3. **Summarize** This film with director Thomas Riedelsheimer and Andy Goldsworthy evolved over a long period of time. What central idea about time does the film convey? Support your answer with descriptions of details from the film.

4. **Identify Patterns** How do the sound elements, such as music, background sounds, and voice-over, facilitate connections between the images in the film and the central idea? Cite specific evidence from the film.

5. **Analyze** What special effect does the film use to help the viewer link the sculptures to the idea of time and changes over time?

6. **Connect** Andy Goldsworthy sculpts in ice, stone, leaves, and other natural materials. He usually takes photographs of his sculptures because many of them are ephemeral and last for only a short period of time. He says this is his way to "talk" about his sculptures. What is the role of this film in bringing Goldsworthy's art to the public? How is that role different from the role of the photographs of Goldsworthy's sculptures?

7. **Synthesize** During the interview, Goldsworthy trails off when attempting to connect his art with major changes in people's lives. How would you complete his thought, based on images and ideas in the film as well as your own knowledge and experience?

PERFORMANCE TASK

Media Activity: Reflection What connections can you make between changes you see in nature or your community and the kinds of major life changes people experience? Share your ideas in a media presentation.

- Take photographs, make video recordings, or organize a collection of existing images of a meaningful change. (Be sure any images made by others are copyright free or allowed for classroom use.)

- Record an audio track to accompany your visuals that tells what change they show and how that change is a good metaphor for a specific life change—moving, changing schools, growing up, etc.

Participate in a Panel Discussion

This collection explores the concept of change and how people respond to it. Recall the anchor text *The Metamorphosis* (both versions) and the other texts you have read. Synthesize your ideas about them by making a generalization about the ways in which people adapt to a major change. Then make your case in a panel discussion, citing evidence from the texts to support your points.

An effective participant in a panel discussion

- makes a clear, logical, and well-defended generalization about the ways people adapt to change

- uses quotations and examples from *The Metamorphosis* and two other texts to illustrate his or her ideas

- synthesizes ideas from all three texts with his or her own experiences

- responds thoughtfully and politely to the ideas of others on the panel

- evaluates other panel members' contributions, including the use of valid reasoning and sound evidence

W 9a–b Draw evidence from literary or informational texts.

SL 1a–d Initiate and participate effectively in a range of collaborative discussions.

SL 3 Evaluate a speaker's point of view, reasoning, and use of evidence and rhetoric.

Visit hmhfyi.com to explore your topic and enhance your research.

PLAN ···

Get Organized Work with your classmates to prepare for the discussion.

- Join a small group and select one student to be the moderator for your discussion. The rest of your classmates will be the audience when you hold the discussion.

- Create a format for your discussion—a schedule that shows the order in which members of the panel will speak and for how many minutes. It will be the moderator's job to keep the discussion moving along on schedule.

- Set rules regarding the appropriate times for either the moderator or the audience to ask the panel members questions.

- Get together with your group and vote on which three texts from this collection, including a version of *The Metamorphosis,* you will use to discuss change and adaptation. Set a deadline by which everyone should have read and analyzed the chosen texts to keep your group on track.

Interactive Lessons
To help you prepare for your discussion, complete the following lesson:
- Preparing for Discussion

ACADEMIC VOCABULARY

As you participate in your panel discussion, try to use these words.

> *abstract*
> *evolve*
> *explicit*
> *facilitate*
> *infer*

Gather Evidence Work individually to analyze the texts from the collection, gathering evidence about how people adapt (or don't adapt) to major change. Consider both concrete, easy-to-see changes and abstract changes as you read. Note specific details, examples, or quotations that illustrate responses to change. Then, think about your own experiences. Ask yourself these questions as you take notes:

- What are some different ways in which people can respond to change? What works, and what doesn't?
- Why do some people adapt easily while others do not? Is it a result of individual personalities, does it depend on the type of change, or both?
- What **generalization**, or broad conclusion, can you make about people's responses to major changes?

Use the annotation tools in your eBook to find evidence from your chosen texts. Save each piece of evidence to *my*Notebook in a folder titled *Collection 3 Performance Task A*.

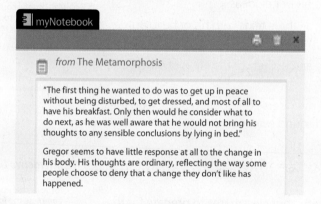

myNotebook

from The Metamorphosis

"The first thing he wanted to do was to get up in peace without being disturbed, to get dressed, and most of all to have his breakfast. Only then would he consider what to do next, as he was well aware that he would not bring his thoughts to any sensible conclusions by lying in bed."

Gregor seems to have little response at all to the change in his body. His thoughts are ordinary, reflecting the way some people choose to deny that a change they don't like has happened.

PRODUCE

Write your rough draft in *my*WriteSmart. Focus on getting your ideas down rather than perfecting your choice of language.

Plan and Practice Outline ideas and practice with a partner.

- State a clear generalization about the ways people respond to a major life change.
- Write several main ideas to discuss. Each idea should relate your generalization to a text or to your own experiences.
- Sort through the evidence you have collected and match each piece of evidence with the main idea it most clearly supports.
- Present your ideas to a partner. Your partner will play the role of moderator, asking questions about your ideas and examples. This will prepare you to "think on your feet" during the real discussion.

Reinforce Your Ideas Based on your practice session with your partner, make changes to your outline. Consider the following questions:

- Were you able to defend your generalization? If not, revise your generalization statement so that it better reflects your textual evidence and your ideas.

- Were you able to answer your partner's questions clearly and without hesitation? If not, you may need to reorganize your outline so that you can find the information you need quickly.

- Did your partner's questions help you see one of the texts in a new light? If so, add new evidence to your outline that you can share during the panel discussion.

Interactive Lessons
To help you respond appropriately, complete this lesson:
- Listening and Responding

PRESENT

Have the Discussion You are now ready to participate in a lively exchange of ideas. Have your outline and/or notes handy.

- The moderator will ask the first question and facilitate the discussion in the agreed-upon format.

- Use your outline to remind you of your main points, but don't just read from your paper.

- Listen closely to what all speakers say so that you can respond thoughtfully, summarizing points of agreement or disagreement when appropriate.

- Maintain a respectful tone toward your fellow panel members, even when you disagree with or challenge their ideas.

- In response to questions, be prepared to clarify your ideas, back them up with the evidence you have gathered, and make new connections between your ideas and those of other panelists.

PERFORMANCE TASK RUBRIC
PANEL DISCUSSION

	Ideas and Evidence	Organization	Language
4	• Panelist clearly states a generalization and supports it with strong, relevant ideas and well-chosen evidence from the texts and personal experience. • Panelist carefully evaluates others' evidence and reasoning and responds with insightful comments and questions. • Panelist concludes remarks in a way that synthesizes analysis of the texts and helps listeners understand the generalization.	• Panelist's remarks are based on a well-organized outline of supporting ideas and evidence. • Ideas are presented in a logical order with effective transitions to clearly link ideas. • Panelist concludes with a statement that reinforces the generalization and takes into account the ideas that have emerged from the discussion.	• Panelist adapts speech to the context of the discussion, using appropriately formal English to discuss literature and ideas. • Panelist quotes accurately from the texts to support ideas. • Panelist maintains a polite and thoughtful tone throughout the discussion.
3	• Panelist states a generalization and supports it with evidence from the texts and personal experience. • Panelist evaluates others' evidence and responds with appropriate comments and questions. • Panelist's concluding remark shows some synthesis of ideas and relates back to the generalization.	• Panelist's remarks are based on notes that identify supporting ideas and evidence. • Ideas are presented clearly and linked with transitions. • Panelist concludes with a statement that reinforces the generalization.	• Panelist mostly uses formal English to discuss literature and ideas. • Panelist usually quotes accurately from the texts to support ideas. • Panelist generally uses a polite and thoughtful tone.
2	• Panelist states a generalization and attempts to support it. • Panelist's response to others' comments shows limited evaluation of the evidence and reasoning. • Panelist's concluding remarks may simply repeat the generalization in a vague way.	• Panelist's remarks reflect notes but do not organize ideas and evidence well. • Ideas are presented in a disorganized way with few transitions. • Panelist concludes by restating the generalization.	• Panelist uses some informal English to discuss literature and ideas. • Panelist's quotations and examples sometimes do not accurately reflect the texts. • Panelist occasionally forgets to maintain a polite tone when responding to others' comments and questions.
1	• Panelist's generalization is unclear; ideas and evidence are not coherent. • Panelist does not evaluate others' evidence and reasoning. • Panelist does not provide a concluding remark.	• Panelist does not generate an outline or notes that organize ideas and evidence. • Ideas are presented in a disorganized way with no transitions. • Panelist's remarks lack a conclusion or summary.	• Panelist uses informal English and/or slang, resulting in ideas that are not clearly expressed. • Panelist's quotations and examples do not accurately reflect the texts. • Panelist does not maintain a polite tone when responding to others' comments and questions.

Write an Argument

This collection explores change and our response to it. Review the anchor selection *Rivers and Tides* and other collection texts. In each, is change viewed as mostly positive, mostly negative, or a combination of the two? Synthesize your ideas in an argumentative essay.

An effective argument

- includes a clear claim
- begins by engaging the reader with an interesting observation, quotation, or detail from one of the selections
- organizes central ideas logically, supporting and elaborating on the claim using quotations and examples from the texts
- uses transitions to create cohesion among sections of the text
- has a concluding section that follows logically from the body of the essay and expresses the writer's own viewpoint on change

W 1a–e Write arguments to support claims in an analysis of substantive topics or texts.
W 9a–b Draw evidence from literary or informational texts.

Visit hmhfyi.com to explore your topic and enhance your research.

PLAN

Analyze the Texts Watch the clip from *Rivers and Tides* again, making notes on ideas about change. Is Andy Goldsworthy's view of change positive, negative, or neutral? Decide what you can infer.

Use the annotation tools in your eBook to find evidence from two other texts in the collection. Save each piece of evidence to *my*Notebook, in a folder titled *Collection 3 Performance Task B*.

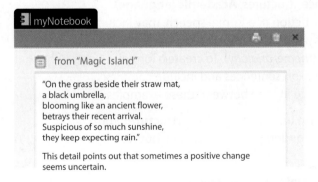

ACADEMIC VOCABULARY

As you share your ideas about perspectives on change, be sure to use these words.

> *abstract*
> *evolve*
> *explicit*
> *facilitate*
> *infer*

Clarify Your View Which text reflects your view of change? Or is your perspective not portrayed in this collection? Make notes of evidence to support why you agree or disagree with each text's view.

Get Organized Organize your details and evidence in an outline.

- Write a clear claim about how change is viewed in the video clip and in the texts you chose.

- Choose an organizational pattern for your essay. How you organize ideas may also depend on whether your claim focuses on a single view of change or if it presents a mixed perspective.

- Use your organizational pattern to sort the evidence you have gathered from the selections into a logical order.

- Choose an interesting quotation or idea to begin your argument.

- Write down some ideas for your conclusion that reflect your own perspective on change, including textual or personal evidence.

Interactive Lessons
To help you plan an effective structure, complete this lesson:
• Creating a Coherent Argument

PRODUCE

Draft Your Essay Follow your outline to draft your essay.

Interactive Lessons
To help you maintain an appropriate tone, complete this lesson:
• Formal Style

- Introduce your claim, the foundation for your entire argument. Be as explicit and clear as possible.

- Present your text evidence in logically ordered paragraphs. Explain how each piece of evidence supports each paragraph's central idea about the claim.

- Use transitions to link sections of the text and establish clear relationships among your claim, any counterclaims, reasons, and evidence.

- Write a conclusion that states your own perspective on change.

Language and Style: Formal Tone

To emphasize how seriously you take your claim, use academic language and formal sentence structures. **Academic language,** language used in school instruction or a formal speech, may include words that can apply to many situations (*develop, analyze*) or words that apply to a specific field (*theme, analogy*). To create a formal tone, avoid fragments and run-on sentences and include complex sentences. Notice the difference in tone between these examples:

Conversational language and informal sentence structure: You'd think that waking up like Gregor does would "bug" him, but weirdly it doesn't.

Academic language and formal sentence structure: Even more surprising than the fact that Gregor is transformed into "a horrible vermin" is his almost complete absence of a reaction to this change.

Review your draft, revising informal or conversational wording to make it more academic and formal.

Have your partner
or a group of peers
review your draft in
*my*WriteSmart. Ask
your reviewers to
note any reasons that
do not support the
claim or lack sufficient
evidence.

Improve Your Draft
Revise your draft to make sure it is clear, coherent, and engaging.

Questions	Tips	Revision Techniques
Does the introduction clearly state a claim and identify the texts discussed?	**Underline** the claim and **highlight** the titles and authors of collection texts.	**Revise** your introduction to more clearly state your claim, or **add** the titles and authors of the chosen texts.
Is the argument clearly structured around reasons and evidence?	**Note** the reason explored in each paragraph, and **highlight** the evidence that supports each reason.	**Add** evidence to support each analysis, and **revise** your analysis if warranted by the text evidence.
Do transitions effectively link the claim, reasons, and evidence?	**Underline** transitions and **note** any reason or evidence that is not introduced with a transition.	**Add** transitions to link ideas in the argument as needed.
Does the conclusion express a personal view of change?	**Underline** the concluding statement expressing an overall perspective.	**Add** a concluding statement about the nature of change if needed.
Is an appropriately formal tone used throughout the argument?	**Highlight** each academic word or phrase that contributes to a formal tone.	**Replace** informal word choices and sentence structures as needed.

PRESENT

Exchange Essays When your final draft is completed, exchange essays with a partner. Read your partner's essay and provide feedback.

- Which aspects of your partner's essay are particularly strong?
- Did any sections confuse you? If so, how could they be clarified?

Publish Online If your school has a website where you can post your writing, collaborate with your classmates to publish your collection of essays online. First, review your own essay and look for places to add links to other online sources that readers may find helpful. Then, as a group, create a front page that introduces the collection and invites readers to explore the individual essays. To allow for an exchange of ideas, consider setting up a blog in which readers can share their own perspectives on change and you can respond to them.

PERFORMANCE TASK RUBRIC
ARGUMENTATIVE ESSAY

	Ideas and Evidence	Organization	Language
4	• An eloquent introduction includes the titles and authors of the selections; the claim describes the view of change presented in three selections. • Specific, relevant details support the claim. • A satisfying concluding section synthesizes the ideas, summarizes the argument, and offers the writer's unique insight on change.	• Central ideas and supporting evidence are organized effectively and logically throughout the essay. • Varied transitions successfully show the relationships between ideas.	• The argument has an appropriately formal style and a knowledgeable, objective tone. • Language is precise and captures the writer's thoughts with originality. • Sentence beginnings, lengths, and structures vary and have a rhythmic flow. • Spelling, capitalization, and punctuation are correct. If handwritten, the argument is legible. • Grammar and usage are correct.
3	• The introduction identifies the titles and authors of the selections but could be more engaging; the claim is stated clearly. • One or two central ideas need more support. • The concluding section synthesizes most of the ideas and summarizes most of the argument, but it doesn't provide an original insight on change.	• The organization of central ideas and supporting evidence is mostly clear. • Transitions generally clarify the relationships between ideas.	• The style is usually formal, and the tone at times communicates confidence. • Most language is precise. • Sentence beginnings, lengths, and structures vary somewhat. • Some spelling, capitalization, and punctuation mistakes occur. If handwritten, the argument is mostly legible. • Some grammar and usage errors appear but do not interfere with the writer's message.
2	• The introduction identifies the titles and the authors of the selections; the claim only hints at the main idea of the argument. • Details support some central ideas but are often too general. • The concluding section gives an incomplete summary of the argument and merely restates the thesis.	• Most central ideas are organized logically, but many supporting details are out of place. • More transitions are needed throughout the essay to connect ideas.	• The style is informal in many places, and the tone reflects a superficial understanding of the selections. • Language is repetitive or vague at times. • Sentence structures barely vary, and some fragments or run-on sentences are present. • Spelling, capitalization, and punctuation are often incorrect. If handwritten, the argument may be partially illegible. • Grammar and usage are incorrect in many places.
1	• The appropriate elements of an introduction are missing. • Details and evidence are irrelevant or missing. • The argument lacks a concluding section.	• A logical organization is not used; ideas are presented randomly. • Transitions are not used, making the essay difficult to understand.	• The style and tone are inappropriate. • Language is inaccurate, repetitive, and vague. • Repetitive sentence structure, fragments, and run-on sentences make the writing difficult to follow. • Spelling, capitalization, and punctuation are incorrect throughout. If handwritten, the argument may be partially or mostly illegible. • Many grammatical and usage errors make ideas difficult to understand.

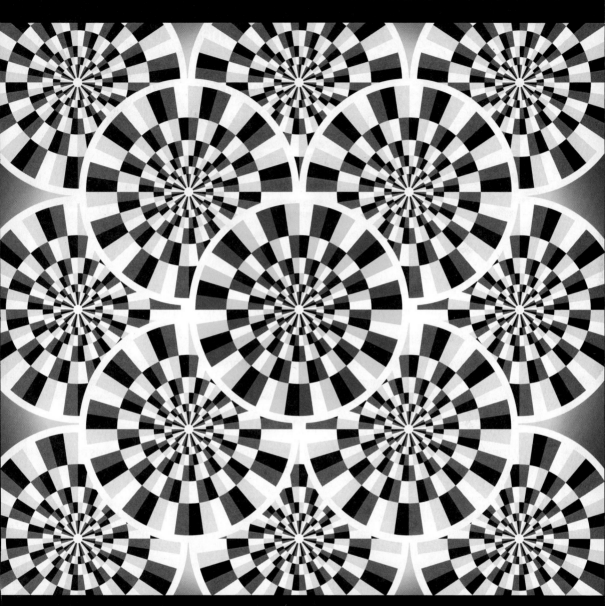

How We See Things

"The question is not what you look at, but what you see.**"**

—Henry David Thoreau

How We See Things

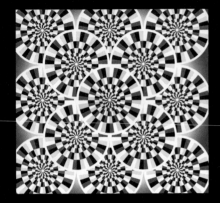

Our view of the world depends not only on our five senses but also on technology and surprising insights.

Stream to Start

hmhfyi.com

Channel One News®

COLLECTION

PERFORMANCE TASK Preview

At the end of this collection, you will have the opportunity to complete two tasks:

• Deliver a speech in response to the works in this collection.

• Write a narrative using techniques employed by authors in this collection.

ACADEMIC VOCABULARY

Study the words and their definitions in the chart below. You will use these words as you discuss and write about the texts in this collection.

Word	Definition	Related Forms
differentiate (dĭf´ə-rĕn´shē-āt´) v.	to distinguish or demonstrate the individual qualities of	differentiation, undifferentiated
incorporate (ĭn-kôr´pə-rāt´) v.	to absorb or make part of a whole	incorporation, incorporated
mode (mōd) n.	a way or means for expressing or doing something	modus operandi
orient (ôr´ē-ĕnt´) v.	to place or align in relation to something else	orientation, disoriented
perspective (pər-spĕk´tĭv) n.	a viewpoint from a particular position; an outlook or standpoint	perspectival, perspicacious

We grow accustomed to the Dark
Before I got my eye put out

Poems by Emily Dickinson

Emily Dickinson (1830–1886) *had only a handful of her poems published during her lifetime. Nevertheless, those poems and the many published after her death earned her a place as a leading nineteenth-century American poet. Dickinson was born and spent her life—except for one year spent at a nearby seminary—in Amherst, Massachusetts. She adored her stern and principled father, but had a complicated relationship with her mother. She was very close to her older brother, Austin, and her younger sister, Vinnie.*

As an adult, Dickinson was known for her reclusiveness. During one of her last journeys away from Amherst, she saw an ophthalmologist in Boston for aches in her eyes and sensitivity to light. Her poems "We grow accustomed to the Dark" and "Before I got my eye put out" use imagery related to sight and light.

After Dickinson's death, her sister carried out the poet's wishes, burning all of her letters from family and friends. However, she rescued a little box filled with poems. Since her late teens or early twenties, Emily Dickinson had been writing poetry—on scraps of paper, old recipes, and the backs of envelopes. Though she wrote 1,775 poems, Dickinson published only seven, anonymously, during her lifetime. The private poet left the world pondering her untold secrets.

We grow accustomed to the Dark

We grow accustomed to the Dark –
When Light is put away –
As when the Neighbor holds the Lamp
To witness her Goodbye –

5 A Moment – We uncertain step
For newness of the night –
Then – fit our Vision to the Dark –
And meet the Road – erect –

And so of larger – Darknesses –
10 Those Evenings of the Brain –
When not a Moon disclose a sign –
Or Star – come out – within –

The Bravest – grope a little –
And sometimes hit a Tree
15 Directly in the Forehead –
But as they learn to see –

Either the Darkness alters –
Or something in the sight
Adjusts itself to Midnight –
20 And Life steps almost straight.

Before I got my eye put out

Before I got my eye put out
I liked as well to see –
As other Creatures, that have Eyes
And know no other way –

5 But were it told to me – Today –
That I might have the sky
For mine – I tell you that my Heart
Would split, for size of me –

The Meadows – mine –
10 The Mountains – mine –
All Forests – Stintless¹ Stars –
As much of Noon as I could take
Between my finite eyes –

The Motions of the Dipping Birds –
15 The Morning's Amber Road –
For mine – to look at when I liked –
The News would strike me dead –

So safer – guess – with just my soul
Upon the Window pane –
20 Where other Creatures put their eyes –
Incautious – of the Sun –

COLLABORATIVE DISCUSSION Why are seeing and vision important in
these poems? With a partner, discuss the references you noted in both
poems to eyesight, seeing, or vision. Cite specific textual evidence from
the poems to support your ideas.

---

¹ **Stintless:** without limit or restraint.

Cite Evidence: Paraphrase and Summary

One way to approach reading and understanding poetry is to paraphrase or summarize parts of the poem as you read. A **paraphrase** is a restatement in your own words. A **summary** is a brief statement of the central ideas in a piece of writing. Notice the differences in the following examples.

"We grow accustomed to the Dark," Stanza 1	
Paraphrase—Our eyes adjust to the darkness when a light is taken away, as when someone we are visiting says goodbye and steps away from the door with the lamp.	**Summary**—We get used to the darkness when there is no light.

Although paraphrases and summaries do not incorporate all the detail or style of the original, they draw closely on the wording and ideas of the text. Thinking about details and imagery as you read will help you identify themes and summarize or paraphrase poems to check your understanding.

Analyze Author's Choices: Poetic Structure

When you first read a poem, you will notice its **structure**, or the way the words are arranged on the page. The main structural components of a poem are the length and placement of the **lines**, and the way the lines are placed into groups called **stanzas**. In "We grow accustomed to the Dark," Dickinson uses quatrains, or four-line stanzas. Other key structural elements of poetry include meter and rhyme.

Meter	Rhyme
• **Meter**, the rhythmic pattern in a line of poetry, is based on the number of syllables and the stresses on them. • Meter is classified by the number of **feet**—units of rhythm—in a line. A common foot is an iamb, which has an unstressed syllable followed by a stressed one. "Before I got my eye put out" is an example of iambic tetrameter because it has four iambs. • Meter can vary within a poem to create striking effects.	• **Rhyme** is the repetition of similar ending sounds in poetry as in *dark* and *lark*. • **Slant rhyme**, or **consonance**, is the repetition of end consonant sounds preceded by different vowels, as in *heart* and *hurt*. • **Assonance** is the repetition of similar vowel sounds followed by different consonant sounds, as in *grow, holds,* and *close*. • Rhyme can be used at the ends of lines or within lines.

 **eBook** *Annotate It!*

Analyzing the Text

RL 1, RL 2, RL 5,
RL 10, W 2, L 5

Cite Text Evidence   Support your responses with evidence from the selections.

1. **Interpret** Paraphrase stanza 2 of "We grow accustomed to the Dark." What is the central idea of this stanza?

2. **Infer** What does Dickinson mean beyond the literal meanings of the words when she says "We grow accustomed to the Dark"? With this interpretation in mind, consider the lines "And so of larger – Darknesses – / Those Evenings of the Brain – ": To what might these lines refer?

3. **Compare** Dickinson uses images of eyes and sight in both poems. Explain whether she uses these images for the same purpose in both poems.

4. **Analyze** Analyze the meter of "Before I got my eye put out." What pattern do most stanzas follow? What effect does the poet achieve by changing the meter?

5. **Identify Patterns** Review "Before I got my eye put out" and identify the number of lines in each stanza. Which stanza does not fit the pattern? What is the effect of this variation on Dickinson's meaning and tone?

6. **Synthesize** Write a summary of the conclusion the speaker comes to at the end of each poem. How and why do they differ? Cite lines from each poem to support your explanation.

PERFORMANCE TASK

Writing Activity: Essay Both of these poems are metaphorical—that is, they are not only about the literal loss of sight or physically stumbling in the darkness. Explore the metaphor of sight in Dickinson's poems by writing an analytical essay.

1. Identify what the speaker loses in "Before I got my eye put out" and explain the speaker's reaction to that loss. Would the speaker in "We grow accustomed to the Dark" react differently to the same loss?

2. In your essay, explain your interpretation of the attitude of each speaker toward sight.

3. Cite evidence from each poem to support your thesis, and use the conventions of standard English.

Language and Style: Writing Conventions

Emily Dickinson uses writing conventions such as capitalization and punctuation to achieve specific purposes.

Read the following line from "Before I got my eye put out."

As other Creatures, that have Eyes

Note that Dickinson capitalizes *Creatures* and *Eyes*. Dickinson often uses capitalization for emphasis. Scan this poem for other capitalized words. You'll find *Today, Meadows, Mountains, Forests, Stintless Stars, Noon, Motions, Dipping Birds, Morning's Amber Road, News, Window,* and *Sun.* In some cases, these words make something simple seem more important, while at other times the emphasis helps draw out patterns. Scan for capitalized words in "We grow accustomed to the Dark" and see what kinds of words you find.

In addition to capitalization, punctuation is another convention that Dickinson varies for effect. Look again at "Before I got my eye put out," and you'll see that there are very few periods or commas, but there are many dashes. Dashes are used in the place of commas, periods, parentheses, colons, and semicolons in her poems. Look at some of the reasons Dickinson uses dashes.

Use of Dashes	
Purpose	**Example**
Connect ideas	"The Meadows – mine – The Mountains – mine –"
Set off an idea as parenthetical	"But were it told to me – Today –"
Create a pause	"Adjusts itself to Midnight – And Life steps almost straight."
Create open-endedness	"Incautious – of the Sun –"

Dickinson often chooses not to use standard English conventions. These are not errors but rather careful choices that help set pace, emphasize ideas, and create meaning in her poems.

Practice and Apply Choose a stanza from either of Dickinson's poems. Rewrite the stanza using standard conventions of capitalization and punctuation. (Remember that some ideas continue into the next stanza, so you may need to rewrite more than your chosen stanza to come to the end of a sentence.) Compare your version to Dickinson's version. How does the use of standard conventions affect tone or meaning?

Neil deGrasse Tyson (b. 1958) *is an American astrophysicist and the director of the Hayden Planetarium at the American Museum of Natural History. But he is best known for helping to explain science to the public through his many books and television appearances. Tyson is the author of* The Pluto Files: The Rise and Fall of America's Favorite Planet *and* Death by Black Hole and Other Cosmic Quandaries. *In addition, he has hosted the television series* Cosmos: A Spacetime Odyssey *and the PBS miniseries* Origins *and* NOVA ScienceNOW.

Coming to Our Senses

Science Essay by Neil deGrasse Tyson

AS YOU READ Pay attention to the details the author provides about humans' five senses. Write down any questions you generate during reading.

> *Equipped with his five senses, man explores the universe around him and calls the adventure science.*
> —Edwin P. Hubble (1889–1953),
> *The Nature of Science*

Among our five senses, sight is the most special to us. Our eyes allow us to register information not only from across the room but also from across the universe. Without vision, the science of astronomy would never have been born and our capacity

10 to measure our place in the universe would have been hopelessly stunted. Think of bats. Whatever bat secrets get passed from one generation to the next, you can bet that none of them is based on the appearance of the night sky.

When thought of as an ensemble of experimental tools, our senses enjoy an astonishing **acuity** and range of sensitivity. Our ears can register the thunderous launch of the space shuttle, yet they can also hear a mosquito buzzing a foot away from our head. Our sense

acuity
(ə-kyo͞o´ĭ-tē) *n.* critical perceptiveness; awareness.

of touch allows us to feel the magnitude of a bowling ball dropped on our big toe, just as we can tell when a one-milligram bug crawls along our arm. Some people enjoy munching on habañero peppers while sensitive tongues can identify the presence of food flavors to the level of parts per million. And our eyes can register the bright sandy terrain on a sunny beach, yet these same eyes have no trouble spotting a lone match, freshly lit, hundreds of feet across a darkened auditorium.

But before we get carried away in praise of ourselves, note that what we gain in breadth we lose in precision: we register the world's **stimuli** in logarithmic[1] rather than linear increments. For example, if you increase the energy of a sound's volume by a factor of 10, your ears will judge this change to be rather small. Increase it by a factor of 2 and you will barely notice. The same holds for our capacity to measure light. If you have ever viewed a total solar eclipse you may have noticed that the Sun's disk must be at least 90 percent covered by the Moon before anybody comments that the sky has darkened. The stellar magnitude scale of brightness, the well-known acoustic decibel scale, and the seismic scale for earthquake severity[2] are each logarithmic, in part because of our biological **propensity** to see, hear, and feel the world that way.

What, if anything, lies beyond our senses? Does there exist a way of knowing that **transcends** our biological interfaces with the environment?

Consider that the human machine, while good at decoding the basics of our immediate environment—like when it's day or night or when a creature is about to eat us—has very little talent for decoding how the rest of nature works without the tools of science. If we want to know what's out there then we require detectors other than the ones we are born with. In nearly every case, the job of scientific apparatus is to transcend the breadth and depth of our senses.

Some people boast of having a sixth sense, where they profess to know or see things that others cannot. Fortune-tellers, mind readers, and mystics are at the top of the list of those who lay claim to mysterious powers. In doing so, they instill widespread fascination in others, especially book publishers and television producers. The questionable field of parapsychology[3] is founded

stimuli
(stĭm´yə-lī´) *n.* things that cause a response or reaction.

propensity
(prə-pĕn´sĭ-tē) *n.* a tendency to behave in a certain way.

transcend
(trăn-sĕnd´) *v.* to go beyond or rise above.

---

[1] **logarithmic:** capable of being raised by repeated multiplication of itself; exponential.

[2] **stellar magnitude scale . . . acoustic decibel scale . . . seismic scale:** systems of measurement for the brightness of starlight, the loudness of sounds, and the intensity of earthquakes.

[3] **parapsychology:** the study of unexplainable or supernatural mental phenomena.

on the expectation that at least some people actually harbor such talents. To me, the biggest mystery of them all is why so many fortune-telling psychics choose to work the phones on TV hotlines instead of becoming insanely wealthy trading futures contracts
60 on Wall Street.[4] And here's a news headline none of us has seen, "Psychic Wins the Lottery."

Quite independent of this mystery, the persistent failures of controlled, double-blind experiments to support the claims of parapsychology suggest that what's going on is nonsense rather than sixth sense.

"What, if anything, lies beyond our senses?"

On the other hand, modern science wields dozens of senses. And scientists do not claim these to be the expression of special powers, just special hardware. In the end, of course, the hardware converts the information gleaned from these extra senses into
70 simple tables, charts, diagrams, or images that our inborn senses can interpret. In the original *Star Trek* sci-fi series, the crew that beamed down from their starship to the uncharted planet always brought with them a tricorder—a handheld device that could analyze anything they encountered, living or inanimate, for its basic properties. As the tricorder was waved over the object in question, it made an audible spacey sound that was interpreted by the user.

Suppose a glowing blob of some unknown substance were parked right in front of us. Without some diagnostic tool like
80 a tricorder to help, we would be clueless to the blob's chemical or nuclear composition. Nor could we know whether it has an electromagnetic field, or whether it emits strongly in gamma rays, x-rays, ultraviolet, microwaves, or radio waves. Nor could we

---

[4] **trading futures contracts on Wall Street:** a form of speculative investment in which someone agrees to pay a fixed price for an item at a future date. The success of the investment is measured by the difference between the agreed-upon price and the actual market price on that future date.

determine the blob's cellular or crystalline structure. If the blob were far out in space, appearing as an unresolved point of light in the sky, our five senses would offer us no insight to its distance, velocity through space, or its rate of rotation. We further would have no capacity to see the spectrum of colors that compose its emitted light, nor could we know whether the light is polarized.

90   Without hardware to help our analysis, and without a particular urge to lick the stuff, all we can report back to the starship is, "Captain, it's a blob." Apologies to Edwin P. Hubble, the quote that opens this chapter, while poignant and poetic, should have instead been:

> *Equipped with our five senses, along with*
> *telescopes and microscopes and mass*
> *spectrometers and seismographs and*
> *magnetometers and particle accelerators*
> *and detectors across the electromagnetic*
100 *spectrum, we explore the universe around us*
> *and call the adventure science.*

Think of how much richer the world would appear to us and how much earlier the nature of the universe would have been discovered if we were born with high-precision, tunable eyeballs. Dial up the radio-wave part of the spectrum and the daytime sky becomes as dark as night. Dotting that sky would be bright and famous sources of radio waves, such as the center of the Milky Way, located behind some of the principal stars of the constellation Sagittarius. Tune into microwaves and the entire cosmos glows

110 with a remnant from the early universe, a wall of light set forth 380,000 years after the big bang. Tune into x-rays and you immediately spot the locations of black holes, with matter spiraling into them. Tune into gamma rays and see titanic explosions scattered throughout the universe at a rate of about one per day. Watch the effect of the explosion on the surrounding material as it heats up and glows in other bands of light.

If we were born with magnetic detectors, the compass would never have been invented because we wouldn't ever need one. Just tune into Earth's magnetic field lines and the direction of magnetic

120 north looms like Oz[5] beyond the horizon. If we had spectrum analyzers within our retinas, we would not have to wonder what we were breathing. We could just look at the register and know whether the air contained sufficient oxygen to sustain human life. And we would have learned thousands of years ago that the stars

---

[5] **Oz:** the magical city and destination for characters in L. Frank Baum's *The Wonderful Wizard of Oz.*

and nebulae in the Milky Way galaxy contain the same chemical elements found here on Earth.

And if we were born with big eyes and built-in Doppler motion detectors, we would have seen immediately, even as grunting troglodytes,[6] that the entire universe is expanding—with distant
130   galaxies all receding from us.

If our eyes had the resolution of high-performance microscopes, nobody would have ever blamed the plague and other sicknesses on divine wrath. The bacteria and viruses that made us sick would be in plain view as they crawled on our food or as they slid through open wounds in our skin. With simple experiments, we could easily tell which of these bugs were bad and which were good. And of course postoperative infection problems would have been identified and solved hundreds of years earlier.

If we could detect high-energy particles, we would spot
140   radioactive substances from great distances. No Geiger counters necessary. We could even watch radon gas seep through the basement floor of homes and not have to pay somebody to tell us about it.

The honing of our senses from birth through childhood allows us, as adults, to pass judgment on events and phenomena in our

---

[6] **troglodyte:** a primitive creature or a cave dweller.

lives, declaring whether they "make sense." Problem is, hardly any scientific discoveries of the past century flowed from the direct application of our five senses. They flowed instead from the direct application of sense-transcendent mathematics and hardware. This simple fact is entirely responsible for why, to the average person, relativity, particle physics, and 10-dimensional string theory make no sense. Include in the list black holes, wormholes, and the big bang. Actually, these ideas don't make much sense to scientists either, or at least not until we have explored the universe for a long time, with all the senses that are technologically available. What emerges, eventually, is a newer and higher level of "common sense" that enables a scientist to think creatively and to pass judgment in the unfamiliar underworld of the atom or in the mind-bending domain of higher-dimensional space. The twentieth-century German physicist Max Planck made a similar observation about the discovery of quantum mechanics:

> Modern Physics impresses us particularly
> with the truth of the old doctrine which
> teaches that there are realities existing apart
> from our sense-perceptions, and that there
> are problems and conflicts where these
> realities are of greater value for us than the
> richest treasures of the world of experience.
> (1931, p. 107)

Our five senses even interfere with sensible answers to stupid metaphysical questions like, "If a tree falls in the forest and nobody is around to hear it, does it make a sound?" My best answer is, "How do you know it fell?" But that just gets people angry. So I offer a senseless analogy, "Q: If you can't smell the carbon monoxide, then how do you know it's there? A: You drop dead." In modern times, if the sole measure of what's out there flows from your five senses then a **precarious** life awaits you.

Discovering new ways of knowing has always heralded new windows on the universe that tap into our growing list of nonbiological senses. Whenever this happens, a new level of majesty and complexity in the universe reveals itself to us, as though we were technologically evolving into supersentient beings, always coming to our senses.

precarious
(prĭ-kâr´ē-əs) *adj.*
unsafe or insecure.

COLLABORATIVE DISCUSSION What details does the author use to discuss humans' five senses? With a partner, discuss these details and how they make the essay more interesting.

Analyze Development of Ideas

The central idea of a nonfiction selection is usually developed through several key points, each of which is supported by details.

- The **central idea** is the main point the writer wants to make about the topic, or subject of the writing. In a nonfiction selection, a writer may state a central idea outright, but more often the reader needs to infer it by putting together key points and details presented in the selection. Think about the central idea to which all of the key points and details add up in "Coming to Our Senses."

- In developing a central idea, the author presents a series of **key points** in an order that helps expand the topic and draws connections between them. Like building a brick wall, where each layer of bricks acts as a support for the next layer, so an author builds an essay by laying down one key idea and then building on it with the next. In "Coming to Our Senses," the central idea emerges with the support of key points and details about the senses that humans use. In this way, the author moves readers from one idea to the next, shaping the support for his central ideas.

- While the key points create a kind of outline, **details and examples** complete those ideas, developing and refining each by answering *who, what, when, where, why*, and *how* questions to support the central idea. Details and examples make a nonfiction selection meaningful and interesting to readers.

- To understand a nonfiction selection, readers can create an objective summary of the text. A **summary** of the text explains the central idea and the key points, as well as the most important details. Use a graphic organizer like this one to help you identify the information that you need for a summary.

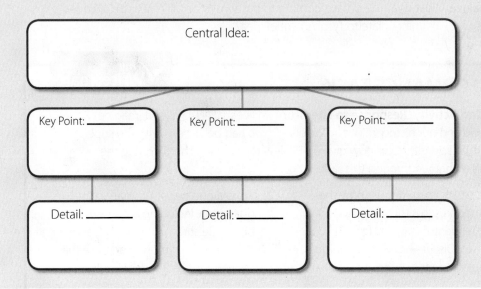

Central Idea:

Key Point: _____

Key Point: _____

Key Point: _____

Detail: _____

Detail: _____

Detail: _____

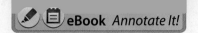

Analyzing the Text

RI 1, RI 2, RI 3,
RI 4, RI 5, RI 6,
RI 10, SL 1a

Cite Text Evidence   Support your responses with evidence from the selection.

1. **Identify** What is the central idea that the author develops throughout this essay? What key points support that central idea?

2. **Summarize** Why is using our five senses to understand the more complicated aspects of the world around us a problem, according to the author?

3. **Interpret** The author says, "we register the world's stimuli in logarithmic rather than linear increments." In your own words, explain what he means.

4. **Analyze** The author provides a brief explanation and discussion of parapsychology. Although it may seem like a digression, it serves his larger purpose. What function does this discussion serve?

5. **Synthesize** Why does the author begin the essay with a quotation by Edwin P. Hubble and then later suggest a revision of the quotation? How do the two versions of the quotation help shape and refine the essay's central idea?

6. **Interpret** Tyson writes, "In modern times, if the sole measure of what's out there flows from your five senses then a precarious life awaits you." Explain what he means by this statement.

7. **Evaluate** Toward the end of the essay, Tyson asserts that as we develop more scientific tools with which to see and understand the universe, "a new level of majesty and complexity in the universe reveals itself to us." What is the impact of the author's word choice on the tone of this passage? How does the author's word choice help you understand his perspective?

8. **Analyze** What does the phrase "coming to our senses" usually mean? How does this usual meaning relate to Tyson's central idea?

PERFORMANCE TASK

Speaking Activity: Response to Literature In lines 102–143, Tyson imagines how our world and our history might be different if we had been born with the super senses that scientific tools now give us. Review this section. Then, explore the author's technique through this task.

1. In a small group, discuss how the author presents this idea, inviting the reader to imagine life with super senses. Discuss how this technique helps shape the author's central idea.

2. Write a one-page summary of the discussion, including all relevant points. Be sure to organize ideas in a clear and coherent way and use the conventions of standard English.

Critical Vocabulary

acuity   stimuli   propensity   transcend   precarious

Practice and Apply Demonstrate an understanding of each Critical Vocabulary word by explaining your answer.

1. If you possessed **acuity** of vision, would you be more or less likely to need prescription glasses? Why?

2. Which of these **stimuli** is more likely to bring about a reaction from you: the sound of a ringing telephone or the smell escaping from a bakery? Why?

3. If you have a **propensity** for organization, is your closet messy or tidy? Explain.

4. If a singer's songs **transcend** musical genres, can you classify them as either country or rock? Why?

5. If your job was **precarious**, would you look for a new one? Explain.

Vocabulary Strategy: Using Reference Sources

The author of the essay incorporates pop culture, historical, and scientific references into the text. Though you may be able to discern the central idea without knowing what these references are, understanding them will enhance your comprehension. For example, if you didn't know the meaning of the Critical Vocabulary word *stimuli*, you would misunderstand the author's message about how we perceive the world through our senses.

To determine the meaning of an unknown word, name, or reference, consult general and specialized reference material, both print and digital. These may include college-level or bilingual dictionaries for defining specific words; encyclopedias for providing an explanation of places, events, and people; and a search engine for leading you to specialized online resources that will help identify more obscure references.

Practice and Apply Use print or digital resource materials to define or explain each reference from the essay.

1. Edwin P. Hubble

2. double-blind experiment

3. the *Star Trek* sci-fi series

4. Geiger counters

Language and Style: Parallel Structure

Parallel structure is the repetition of a pattern of words or phrases within a sentence or passage to signify that two or more events or ideas have the same level of importance. Parallel structure helps writers organize and clarify their thoughts. It can also affect the meaning and tone of a sentence or passage.

Read this sentence from the text:

Our eyes allow us to register information not only from across the room but also from across the universe.

The author repeats the words *across the,* giving equal weight to the eyes' ability to register information that originates from locations that are quite different. Consider that he could have written the sentence like this:

Our eyes allow us to register information from different locations.

This sentence does not emphasize the eyes' far-ranging abilities the way the first sentence does. It also lacks the strong rhythm that parallel structure creates.

Writers can use parallel structure not only within sentences but also within a passage. For example, Tyson begins two paragraphs similarly:

If we were born with magnetic detectors, . . .

And if we were born with big eyes and built-in Doppler motion detectors, . . .

By beginning the paragraphs as he does, the author emphasizes the conditional nature of his point ("*If* we were born with . . .") and gives both points equal weight and importance. The parallel structure also adds continuity to the passage, making the author's points easier to follow. In addition, the author's repetition is rhythmic, making it more memorable and enjoyable to read.

Practice and Apply Look back at the summary of the discussion you created in response to this selection's Performance Task. Revise the summary to add at least two examples of parallel structure within a sentence or between paragraphs. Then, discuss with a partner how each use of parallel structure improves your meaning or tone.

Julio Cortázar (1914–1984) *was an Argentine teacher, novelist, and short-story writer. A vocal opponent of the Argentinian government, Cortázar fled to Paris in 1951, where he remained until his death. He is best known for deftly weaving fantasy, hallucinations, and dreams into his fiction, as he does in "The Night Face Up." The Aztec sacrifice alluded to in this work was an important part of Aztec religious life. Human victims were usually prisoners of war or slaves; their sacrifice was thought to appease the gods and make them stronger.*

The Night Face Up

Short Story by Julio Cortázar   Translated by Paul Blackburn

AS YOU READ Notice the two separate stories that unfold at the same time. Write down any questions you generate during reading.

*And at certain periods they went out to hunt enemies; they called it the war of the blossom.**

Halfway down the long hotel vestibule,[1] he thought that probably he was going to be late, and hurried on into the street to get out his motorcycle from the corner where the next-door superintendent let him keep it. On the jewelry store at the corner he read that it was ten to nine; he had time to spare. The sun filtered through the tall downtown buildings, and he—because for himself, for just going along thinking, he did not have a name—he swung
10 onto the machine, savoring the idea of the ride. The motor whirred between his legs, and a cool wind whipped his pantslegs.

---

* The war of the blossom was the name the Aztecs gave to a ritual war in which they took prisoners for sacrifice. It is metaphysics to say that the gods see men as flowers, to be so uprooted, trampled, cut down. –Ed. [Cortázar's note]

[1] **vestibule:** a hall or entryway next to a building's exterior door.

He let the ministries[2] zip past (the pink, the white), and a series of stores on the main street, their windows flashing. Now he was beginning the most pleasant part of the run, the real ride: a long street bordered with trees, very little traffic, with spacious villas whose gardens rambled all the way down to the sidewalks, which were barely indicated by low hedges. A bit inattentive perhaps, but tooling along on the right side of the street, he allowed himself to be carried away by the freshness, by the weightless contraction of this hardly begun day. This involuntary relaxation, possibly, kept him from preventing the accident. When he saw that the woman standing on the corner had rushed into the crosswalk while he still had the green light, it was already somewhat too late for a simple solution. He braked hard with foot and hand, wrenching himself to the left; he heard the woman scream, and at the collision his vision went. It was like falling asleep all at once.

He came to abruptly. Four or five young men were getting him out from under the cycle. He felt the taste of salt and blood, one knee hurt, and when they hoisted him up he yelped, he couldn't bear the pressure on his right arm. Voices which did not seem to belong to the faces hanging above him encouraged him cheerfully with jokes and assurances. His single **solace** was to hear someone else confirm that the lights indeed had been in his favor. He asked about the woman, trying to keep down the nausea which was edging up into his throat. While they carried him face up to a nearby pharmacy, he learned that the cause of the accident had gotten only a few scrapes on the legs, "Nah, you barely got her at all, but when ya hit, the impact made the machine jump and flop on its side . . ." Opinions, recollections of other smashups, take it easy, work him in shoulders first, there, that's fine, and someone in a dust coat giving him a swallow of something soothing in the shadowy interior of the small local pharmacy.

Within five minutes the police ambulance arrived, and they lifted him onto a cushioned stretcher. It was a relief for him to be able to lie out flat. Completely **lucid,** but realizing that he was suffering the effects of a terrible shock, he gave his information to the officer riding in the ambulance with him. The arm almost didn't hurt; blood dripped down from a cut over the eyebrow all over his face. He licked his lips once or twice to drink it. He felt pretty good, it had been an accident, tough luck; stay quiet a few weeks, nothing worse. The guard said that the motorcycle didn't seem badly racked up, "Why should it," he replied. "It all landed on top of me." They both laughed, and when they got to the hospital, the guard shook his hand and wished him luck. Now the nausea

solace
(sŏl´ĭs) *n.* source of relief and comfort.

lucid
(lōō´sĭd) *adj.* thinking rationally and clearly.

---

[2] **ministries:** government offices.

was coming back little by little; meanwhile they were pushing him on a wheeled stretcher toward a pavilion further back, rolling along under trees full of birds, he shut his eyes and wished he were asleep or chloroformed.[3] But they kept him for a good while in a room with that hospital smell, filling out a form, getting his clothes off,
60 and dressing him in a stiff, grayish smock. They moved his arm carefully, it didn't hurt him. The nurses were constantly making wisecracks, and if it hadn't been for the stomach contractions he would have felt fine, almost happy.

They got him over to X-ray, and twenty minutes later, with the still-damp negative lying on his chest like a black tombstone, they pushed him into surgery. Someone tall and thin in white came over and began to look at the X-rays. A woman's hands were arranging his head, he felt that they were moving him from one stretcher to another. The man in white came over to him again, smiling,
70 something gleamed in his right hand. He patted his cheek and made a sign to someone stationed behind.

It was unusual as a dream because it was full of smells, and he never dreamt smells. First a marshy smell, there to the left of the trail the swamps began already, the quaking bogs from which no one ever returned. But the reek lifted, and instead there came a dark, fresh composite fragrance, like the night under which he moved, in flight from the Aztecs. And it was all so natural, he had to run from the Aztecs who had set out on their manhunt, and his sole chance was to find a place to hide in the deepest part of the
80 forest, taking care not to lose the narrow trail which only they, the Motecas, knew.

What tormented him the most was the odor, as though, notwithstanding the absolute acceptance of the dream, there was something which resisted that which was not habitual, which until that point had not participated in the game. "It smells of war," he thought, his hand going instinctively to the stone knife which was tucked at an angle into his girdle of woven wool. An unexpected sound made him crouch suddenly stock-still and shaking. To be afraid was nothing strange, there was plenty of fear in his dreams.
90 He waited, covered by the branches of a shrub and the starless night. Far off, probably on the other side of the big lake, they'd be lighting the bivouac[4] fires; that part of the sky had a reddish glare. The sound was not repeated. It had been like a broken limb. Maybe an animal that, like himself, was escaping from the smell of war. He stood erect slowly, sniffing the air. Not a sound could be heard, but the fear was still following, as was the smell, that cloying incense of the war of the blossom. He had to press forward, to stay out of the

---

[3] **chloroformed:** made unconscious by inhaling an anesthetic.

[4] **bivouac:** a temporary camp.

bogs and get to the heart of the forest. Groping uncertainly through
the dark, stooping every other moment to touch the packed earth
100 of the trail, he took a few steps. He would have liked to have broken
into a run, but the gurgling fens[5] lapped on either side of him. On
the path and in darkness, he took his bearings. Then he caught a
horrible blast of that foul smell he was most afraid of, and leaped
forward desperately.

"You're going to fall off the bed," said the patient next to him.
"Stop bouncing around, old buddy."

He opened his eyes and it was afternoon, the sun already
low in the oversized windows of the long ward. While trying to
smile at his neighbor, he detached himself almost physically from
110 the final scene of the nightmare. His arm, in a plaster cast, hung
suspended from an apparatus with weights and pulleys. He felt
thirsty, as though he'd been running for miles, but they didn't
want to give him much water, barely enough to moisten his lips
and make a mouthful. The fever was winning slowly and he would
have been able to sleep again, but he was enjoying the pleasure of
keeping awake, eyes half-closed, listening to the other patients'
conversation, answering a question from time to time. He saw a
little white pushcart come up beside the bed, a blond nurse rubbed
the front of his thigh with alcohol and stuck him with a fat needle
120 connected to a tube which ran up to a bottle filled with a milky,
opalescent liquid. A young intern arrived with some metal and
leather apparatus which he adjusted to fit onto the good arm to
check something or other. Night fell, and the fever went along
dragging him down softly to a state in which things seemed
embossed as through opera glasses,[6] they were real and soft and,
at the same time, vaguely distasteful; like sitting in a boring movie
and thinking that, well, still, it'd be worse out in the street, and
staying.

A cup of a marvelous golden broth came, smelling of leeks,
130 celery, and parsley. A small hunk of bread, more precious than
a whole banquet, found itself crumbling little by little. His arm
hardly hurt him at all, and only in the eyebrow where they'd
taken stitches a quick, hot pain sizzled occasionally. When the big
windows across the way turned to smudges of dark blue, he thought
it would not be difficult for him to sleep. Still on his back so a little
uncomfortable, running his tongue out over his hot, too-dry lips,
he tasted the broth still, and with a sigh of bliss, he let himself drift
off.

First there was a confusion, as of one drawing all his sensations,
140 for that moment blunted or muddled, into himself. He realized

---

[5] **fens:** wet, swampy land.

[6] **opera glasses:** small binoculars.

"He heard the cries and leaped up, knife in hand."

that he was running in pitch darkness, although, above, the sky criss-crossed with treetops was less black than the rest. "The trail," he thought, "I've gotten off the trail." His feet sank into a bed of leaves and mud, and then he couldn't take a step that the branches of shrubs did not whiplash against his ribs and legs. Out of breath, knowing despite the darkness and silence that he was surrounded, he crouched down to listen. Maybe the trail was very near, with the first daylight he would be able to see it again. Nothing now could help him to find it. The hand that had unconsciously gripped the haft of the dagger climbed like a fen scorpion up to his neck where the protecting amulet[7] hung. Barely moving his lips, he mumbled the supplication of the corn which brings about the **beneficent** moons, and the prayer to Her Very Highness, to the distributor of all Motecan possessions. At the same time he felt his ankles sinking deeper into the mud, and the waiting in the darkness of the obscure grove of live oak grew intolerable to him. The war of the blossom had started at the beginning of the moon and had been going on for three days and three nights now. If he managed to hide in the depths of the forest, getting off the trail further up past the marsh country, perhaps the warriors wouldn't follow his track. He thought of the many prisoners they'd already taken. But the number didn't count, only the **consecrated** period. The hunt would continue until the priests gave the sign to return. Everything had its number and its limit, and it was within the sacred period, and he on the other side from the hunters.

He heard the cries and leaped up, knife in hand. As if the sky were aflame on the horizon, he saw torches moving among the branches, very near him. The smell of war was unbearable, and when the first enemy jumped him, leaped at his throat, he felt an

150

160

beneficent
(bə-nĕf´ĭ-sənt) *adj.*
beneficial; producing good.

consecrate
(kŏn´sĭ-krāt´) *v.* to make or define as sacred.

---

[7] **amulet:** a charm or necklace believed to have protective powers.

170 almost-pleasure in sinking the stone blade flat to the haft into his chest. The lights were already around him, the happy cries. He managed to cut the air once or twice, then a rope snared him from behind.

"It's the fever," the man in the next bed said. "The same thing happened to me when they operated on my duodenum.[8] Take some water, you'll see, you'll sleep all right."

Laid next to the night from which he came back, the tepid shadow of the ward seemed delicious to him. A violet lamp kept watch high on the far wall like a guardian eye. You could hear
180 coughing, deep breathing, once in a while a conversation in whispers. Everything was pleasant and secure, without the chase, no . . . But he didn't want to go on thinking about the nightmare. There were lots of things to amuse himself with. He began to look at the cast on his arm, and the pulleys that held it so comfortably in the air. They'd left a bottle of mineral water on the night table beside him. He put the neck of the bottle to his mouth and drank it like a precious liqueur. He could now make out the different shapes in the ward, the thirty beds, the closets with glass doors. He guessed that his fever was down, his face felt cool. The cut
190 over the eyebrow barely hurt at all, like a recollection. He saw himself leaving the hotel again, wheeling out the cycle. Who'd have thought that it would end like this? He tried to fix the moment of the accident exactly, and it got him very angry to notice that there was a void there, an emptiness he could not manage to fill. Between the impact and the moment that they picked him up off the pavement, the passing out or what went on, there was nothing he could see. And at the same time he had the feeling that this void, this nothingness, had lasted an eternity. No, not even time, more as if, in this void, he had passed across something, or had run
200 back immense distances. The shock, the brutal dashing against the pavement. Anyway, he had felt an immense relief in coming out of the black pit while the people were lifting him off the ground. With pain in the broken arm, blood from the split eyebrow, contusion on the knee; with all that, a relief in returning to daylight, to the day, and to feel sustained and attended. That was weird. Someday he'd ask the doctor at the office about that. Now sleep began to take over again, to pull him slowly down. The pillow was so soft, and the coolness of the mineral water in his fevered throat. The violet light of the lamp up there was beginning to get dimmer and dimmer.
210 As he was sleeping on his back, the position in which he came to did not surprise him, but on the other hand the damp smell, the smell of oozing rock, blocked his throat and forced him to

---

[8] **duodenum** (doo′ə-dē′nəm): part of the small intestine.

understand. Open the eyes and look in all directions, hopeless. He was surrounded by an absolute darkness. Tried to get up and felt ropes pinning his wrists and ankles. He was staked to the ground on a floor of dank, icy stone slabs. The cold bit into his naked back, his legs. Dully, he tried to touch the amulet with his chin and found they had stripped him of it. Now he was lost, no prayer could save him from the final . . . From afar off, as though filtering through the rock of the dungeon, he heard the great kettledrums of the feast. They had carried him to the temple, he was in the underground cells of Teocalli[9] itself, awaiting his turn.

He heard a yell, a hoarse yell that rocked off the walls. Another yell, ending in a moan. It was he who was screaming in the darkness, he was screaming because he was alive, his whole body with that cry fended off what was coming, the inevitable end. He thought of his friends filling up the other dungeons, and of those already walking up the stairs of the sacrifice. He uttered another choked cry, he could barely open his mouth, his jaws were twisted back as if with a rope and a stick, and once in a while they would open slowly with an endless exertion, as if they were made of rubber. The creaking of the wooden latches jolted him like a whip. Rent, writhing, he fought to rid himself of the cords sinking into his flesh. His right arm, the strongest, strained until the pain became unbearable and he had to give up. He watched the double door open, and the smell of the torches reached him before the light did. Barely girdled by the ceremonial loincloths, the priests' acolytes[10] moved in his direction, looking at him with contempt. Lights reflected off the sweaty torsos and off the black hair dressed with feathers. The cords went slack, and in their place the grappling of hot hands, hard as bronze; he felt himself lifted, still face up, and jerked along by the four acolytes who carried him down the passageway. The torchbearers went ahead, indistinctly lighting up the corridor with its dripping walls and a ceiling so low that the acolytes had to duck their heads. Now they were taking him out, taking him out, it was the end. Face up, under a mile of living rock which, for a succession of moments, was lit up by a glimmer of torchlight. When the stars came out up there instead of the roof and the great terraced steps rose before him, on fire with cries and dances, it would be the end. The passage was never going to end, but now it was beginning to end, he would see suddenly the open sky full of stars, but not yet, they trundled him along endlessly in the reddish shadow, hauling him roughly along and he did not want that, but how to stop it if they had torn off the amulet, his real heart, the life-center.

9 **Teocalli (tē′ə-kăl′ē):** an ancient Mexican terraced pyramid and temple.
10 **acolytes:** people who assist in religious services.

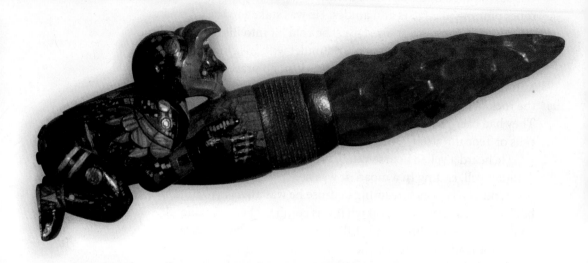

Aztec sacrificial knife

In a single jump he came out into the hospital night, to the high, gentle, bare ceiling, to the soft shadow wrapping him round. He thought he must have cried out, but his neighbors were peacefully snoring. The water in the bottle on the night table was somewhat bubbly, a **translucent** shape against the dark azure shadow of the windows. He panted, looking for some relief for his lungs, oblivion for those images still glued to his eyelids. Each time he shut his eyes he saw them take shape instantly, and he sat up, completely wrung out, but savoring at the same time the surety that now he was awake, that the night nurse would answer if he rang, that soon it would be daybreak, with the good, deep sleep he usually had at that hour, no images, no nothing . . . It was difficult to keep his eyes open, the drowsiness was more powerful than he. He made one last effort, he sketched a gesture toward the bottle of water with his good hand and did not manage to reach it, his fingers closed again on a black emptiness, and the passageway went on endlessly, rock after rock, with momentary ruddy flares, and face up he choked out a dull moan because the roof was about to end, it rose, was opening like a mouth of shadow, and the acolytes straightened up, and from on high a waning moon fell on a face whose eyes wanted not to see it, were closing and opening desperately, trying to pass to the other side, to find again the bare, protecting ceiling of the ward. And every time they opened, it was night and the moon, while they climbed the great terraced steps, his head hanging down backward now, and up at the top were the bonfires, red columns of perfumed smoke, and suddenly he saw the red stone, shiny with

translucent
(trăns-lōō′sənt) *adj.*
semi-transparent;
indistinct.

the blood dripping off it, and the spinning arcs cut by the feet of the victim whom they pulled off to throw him rolling down the north steps. With a last hope he shut his lids tightly, moaning to wake up. For a second he thought he had gotten there, because once more he was immobile in the bed, except that his head was hanging down off it, swinging. But he smelled death, and when he opened his eyes he saw the blood-soaked figure of the executioner-priest coming toward him with the stone knife in his hand. He managed to close his eyelids again, although he knew now he was not going to wake up, that he was awake, that the marvelous dream had been the other, absurd as all dreams are—a dream in which he was going through the strange avenues of an astonishing city, with green and red lights that burned without fire or smoke, on an enormous metal insect that whirred away between his legs. In the infinite lie of the dream, they had also picked him off the ground, someone had approached him also with a knife in his hand, approached him who was lying face up, face up with his eyes closed between the bonfires on the steps.

COLLABORATIVE DISCUSSION With a partner, discuss the ending of the story. Is it clear which of the two plots was "real"? Why or why not?

Cite Textual Evidence

RL 1

Readers must be able to cite **textual evidence**, or details from the text, to support an analysis of what the text says explicitly as well as their inferences about the text. To analyze what the text says explicitly, readers look at words and phrases and think about the author's meaning. To understand what is happening in "The Night Face Up," a reader must develop a clear picture of both worlds in which the main character finds himself—and be able to differentiate the two—based on the details Cortázar provides. When a story's setting or events are unfamiliar to you, take the time to note key details, and go back and re-read for evidence to make sure you understand what the author is communicating.

Analyze Author's Choices: Parallel Plots and Tension

RL 5

To communicate their ideas and to make a story exciting, writers make specific stylistic and structural choices. In "The Night Face Up," Cortázar uses **parallel plots** that develop alongside each other to create **tension,** a sense of anxious anticipation. The story moves back and forth between the plots. You can analyze the author's choices in this short story by examining both of these elements.

Parallel Plots	Tension
When two plots share equal time and importance in a story, they are called parallel plots. Parallel plots often counter each other in **tone** and in **pace**. For example, in "The Night Face Up," the author creates one plot that involves a man recuperating from an accident and another involving a manhunt by Aztec warriors. The two plots unwind at different paces, jumping from one plot to another, increasing the tension the reader feels. Each plot has its own tone, developed through specific word choices. To make parallel plots work effectively, the author includes a bridge or connector that orients each plot so that the narration flows smoothly from one plot line to the other. The two plots eventually converge in a final scene.	Tension or suspense in a story makes a reader want to keep reading to find out what will happen next. Cortázar creates tension through pacing, with progressively shorter amounts of time in the calm hospital setting as the story advances to its climax. The author adds to the tension with **foreshadowing**, or hints and clues as to what will happen later in the story. The first use of foreshadowing comes when the reader learns that the protagonist never dreams smells. The reader must determine what this fact foreshadows. The author then builds on this tension, using carefully chosen words and phrases to develop scenes as the narration switches back and forth between the parallel plots.

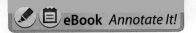
Analyzing the Text

RL 1, RL 2, RL 3,
RL 4, RL 5, RL 6,
RL 10, W 2

Cite Text Evidence   Support your responses with evidence from the selection.

1. **Analyze** Cortázar begins the narrative with the plot concerning the motorcycle accident rather than the one about the manhunt. Why is this choice an effective way to structure the story?

2. **Interpret** In lines 201–202, the author writes, "Anyway, he had felt an immense relief in coming out of the black pit while the people were lifting him off the ground." What does the black pit represent? How is the main character's relief ultimately ironic, or different from what was expected?

3. **Compare** In both plots, the author refers frequently to smells. Explain how the descriptions of smells differ in each plot. How do these differences affect the tone of each plot?

4. **Connect** The author, Julio Cortázar, is from Argentina. What details from the story might reflect his perspective as a South American writer?

5. **Analyze** The **protagonist**, or main character, is never named, but his reality and his ongoing dream make up the parallel plots of the story. How does the reader's perception of the protagonist change throughout the story? Cite text evidence to support your ideas.

6. **Identify Patterns** The author structures the story so that the parallel plots mirror each other. For example, the author describes a scene in which the protagonist is x-rayed, taken to surgery, and approached by a doctor. Where in the second plot does the author echo this scene? What is the effect of this mode of narration?

7. **Evaluate** The author mentions time frequently, beginning in the first paragraph. Look back at the story. How does the protagonist's perception of time change throughout the story? What effect does the author's treatment of time have on the story?

PERFORMANCE TASK

Writing Activity: Analysis A central message or idea that an author wants to communicate through a story is its **theme**. The theme is usually something universal about human nature or the human experience. Usually, the theme of a story is not explicitly stated; it is the reader's job to infer the theme through an analysis of characters, plot, setting, tone, and imagery. Think about "The Night Face Up." Write a one-page analysis of the story in which you consider the following points:

- the theme of the story
- how the characters, plot, imagery, tone, and setting help convey the theme

Support your thesis about the story's theme with evidence from the text, and write using the conventions of standard English.

Critical Vocabulary

solace   lucid   beneficent   consecrate   translucent

Practice and Apply Answer each question in a complete sentence that demonstrates your understanding of the meaning of each Critical Vocabulary word.

1. What **consecrated** place have you visited? Explain.

2. When have you ever sought **solace**? Why?

3. How can you tell someone is not completely **lucid**? Explain.

4. When did you behave in a **beneficent** manner? Explain.

5. Where might a **translucent** material be used in your home? Why?

Language and Style: Adverbial Clauses

Adverbial clauses modify verbs, adjectives, or adverbs. They help convey meaning by answering the questions *when, where, why, how,* or *to what degree*. They typically appear at the beginning or end of a sentence.

> This sentence from "The Night Face Up" contains an adverbial clause:
>
> <u>As if the sky were aflame on the horizon,</u> he saw torches moving among the branches, very near him.

The adverbial clause begins with a **subordinating conjunction**, *as if,* and includes a subject and a verb. The clause gives more information about the main verb *saw*. Cortázar incorporates adverbial clauses to add interest and variety to his writing.

> This chart shows some common subordinating conjunctions and the questions they answer about the main verb of the sentence.

Subordinating Conjunctions	Question They Answer
after, since, when, before, once, while	When?
where, wherever	Where?
because, since, so	Why?
as though, as if	How?
than	To what degree?

Practice and Apply Look back at the theme analysis you wrote for this selection's Performance Task. Revise your analysis to add at least two adverbial clauses. Try to use two different subordinating conjunctions in order to add variety to your writing.

from The Math Instinct

Math Essay by Keith Devlin

AS YOU READ Pay attention to the way the writer, an award-winning author of numerous popular mathematics books, explains the idea of an innate math instinct. Note any questions you generate during reading.

Where Am I and Where Am I Going?

Ahmed, who was the subject of a research paper published in 1981 by scholars R. Wehner and M. V. Srinivasan, lives in the Tunisian desert, on the northern edge of the Sahara. He has had no formal education, and everything he knows he has picked up by experience. Each day, Ahmed leaves his desert home and travels large distances in search of food. In his hunt, he heads first in one direction, then another, then another. He keeps going until he is successful, whereupon he does something very remarkable. Instead of retracing his steps—which may have been **obliterated**
10 by the wind blowing across the sands—he faces directly toward his home and sets off in a straight line, not stopping until he gets there, seemingly knowing in advance, to within a few paces, how far he has to go.

Ahmed has been unable to tell researchers how he performs this remarkable feat of navigation, nor how he acquired this ability. But the only known method is to use a technique known as "dead reckoning." Developed by the ancient mariners of long ago, the method was called "deductive reckoning" by British sailors, who abbreviated the name to "ded. reckoning," a term that in due course
20 acquired an incorrect spelling as "dead reckoning." In using this method, the traveler always moves in straight lines, with occasional sharp turns, keeping constant track of the direction in which he is heading, and keeping track too of his speed and the time that has elapsed since the last change of direction, or since setting off. From

obliterate
(ə-blĭtʹə-rāt´) *v.* erase completely.

knowledge of the speed and the time of travel, the traveler can calculate the exact distance covered in any straight segment of the journey. And by knowing the starting point and the exact direction of travel, it is possible to calculate the exact position at the end of each segment.

30   Dead reckoning requires the accurate use of arithmetic and trigonometry,[1] reliable ways to measure speed, time and direction, and good record-keeping. When seamen navigated by dead reckoning they used charts, tables, various measuring instruments, and a considerable amount of mathematics. (The main **impetus** to develop accurate clocks came from the needs of sailors who used dead reckoning to navigate vast tracts of featureless ocean.) Until the arrival of navigation by the Global Positioning System (GPS) in the mid 1970s, sailors and airline pilots used dead reckoning to navigate the globe, and in the 1960s and 1970s, NASA's Apollo
40   astronauts used dead reckoning to find their way to the moon and back.

impetus
(ĭm´pĭ-təs) *n.*
motivating force or incentive.

Yet Ahmed has none of the aids that mariners and lunar astronauts made use of. How does he do it? Clearly, this particular Tunisian is a remarkable individual. Remarkable indeed. For Ahmed measures little more than half a centimeter in length. He is not a person but an ant—a Tunisian desert ant, to be precise. Every day, this tiny creature wanders across the desert sands for a distance of up to fifty meters (165 feet) until it stumbles across the remains of a dead insect, whereupon it bites off a piece and takes
50   it directly back to its nest, a hole no more than one millimeter in diameter. How does he navigate?

Many kinds of ant find their way to their destination by following scents and chemical trails laid down by themselves or by other members of the colony. Not so the Tunisian desert ant. Observations carried out by Wehner and Srinivasan, the researchers mentioned above, leave little room for doubt. The only way Ahmed can perform this daily feat is by using dead reckoning.

Wehner and Srinivasan found that, if they moved one of these desert ants immediately after it had found its food, it would head
60   off in exactly the direction it *should* have taken to find its nest if it had not been moved, and, moreover, when it had covered the precise distance that should have brought it back home, it would stop and start a bewildered search for its nest. In other words, it knew the precise direction in which it should head in order to return home, and exactly how far in that direction it should travel, even though that straight-line path was nothing like the apparently random zigzag it had followed in its search for food.

---

[1] **trigonometry:** mathematical discipline that deals with the angles and sides of triangles.

"Just because something comes naturally or without conscious awareness does not mean it is trivial."

A recent study has shown that the desert ant measures distance by counting steps. It "knows" the length of an individual step, so it can calculate the distance traveled in any straight-line direction by multiplying that distance by the total number of steps.

Of course, no one is suggesting that this tiny creature is carrying out multiplications the way a human would, or that it finds its way by going through exactly the same mental processes that, say, Neil Armstrong did on his way to the moon in *Apollo 11*. Like all human navigators, the Apollo astronauts had to go to school to learn how to operate the relevant equipment and how to perform the necessary computations. The Tunisian desert ant simply does what comes naturally—it follows its instincts, which are the result of hundreds of thousands of years of evolution.

In terms of today's computer technology, evolution has provided Ahmed with a brain that amounts to a highly sophisticated, highly specific computer, honed over many generations to perform precisely the measurements and computations necessary to navigate by dead reckoning. Ahmed no more has to *think* about any of those measurements or computations than we have to think about the measurements and computations required to control our muscles in order to run or jump. In fact, in Ahmed's case, it is not at all clear that he is capable of anything we would normally call conscious mental activity.

But just because something comes naturally or without conscious awareness does not mean it is trivial. After all, almost fifty years of intensive research in computer science and engineering has failed to produce a robot that can walk as well as a toddler can manage a few days after taking its first faltering steps. Instead, what all that research has shown is how complicated are the mathematics and the engineering required to achieve that feat. Few adults ever master that level of consciously performed mathematics—let alone a small child that runs with perfect bodily control for the candy aisle in the supermarket. Rather, the ability to carry out the required computations for walking comes, as it were, hardwired in the human brain.

So too with the Tunisian desert ant. Its tiny brain might have a very limited **repertoire**. It may well be incapable of learning anything new, or of reflecting consciously on its own existence. But one thing it can do extremely well—indeed far better than the unaided human brain, as far as we know—is carry out the particular mathematical computation we call dead reckoning. That ability does not make the desert ant a "mathematician," of course, but that one computation is enough to ensure the desert ant's survival.

repertoire
(rĕp′ər-twär′) *n.* a set of skills, abilities or functions.

COLLABORATIVE DISCUSSION Discuss your response to learning that Ahmed is an ant. How does focusing on skills, not species, help the author to make a point about navigation?

Determine Meaning and Analyze Ideas

RI 4, RI 5

In an informational essay, a writer may explain an unknown concept to the audience by beginning with more familiar ideas. The new information a reader must take in may range from words and phrases to sentences to entire paragraphs.

Words and phrases	Watch for **technical meanings**, words and phrases specific to a particular field of study. In this essay, Devlin uses mathematical terms and measurements, but he introduces them with familiar examples. In some cases, a word familiar to you may be used with an unfamiliar technical meaning.
Sentences	The mental processes required to navigate by dead reckoning are complicated; Devlin expresses *how* complicated by using a sentence that makes a comparison with the Apollo astronauts.
Paragraphs	Devlin defines dead reckoning for readers not only through the example of Ahmed's movements but also through an entire paragraph discussing how sailors once used this technique.

Analyzing the Text

RI 2, RI 3, RI 5, W 7

Cite Text Evidence Support your responses with evidence from the selection.

1. **Evaluate** Why does Devlin structure his explanation as he does? Would the essay be more or less effective in explaining the concept of dead reckoning if you knew from the beginning that Ahmed is an ant? Explain.

2. **Analyze** How does Devlin's description of Ahmed's calculations help the reader differentiate between an instinctual act and an act of conscious mental activity as discussed in lines 85–90?

3. **Infer** What claim is Devlin supporting through his essay? Cite specific words and phrases in your explanation.

PERFORMANCE TASK

Writing Activity: Research Conduct research on the use of dead reckoning, and summarize your findings in a one-page essay.

1. Research how dead reckoning was used to navigate before the invention of GPS. How were sailors able to orient a ship correctly?

2. Compare the usefulness and accuracy of dead reckoning with GPS.

3. End with a conclusion that explains the pros and cons of each way of navigating.

4. List your sources at the end of the essay.

Critical Vocabulary

obliterate   impetus   repertoire

Practice and Apply For each Critical Vocabulary word, choose which of the two situations best fits the word's meaning, and explain why your choice is the best response.

1. **obliterate**
   a. erasing an incorrect answer on a test paper
   b. scribbling out a wrong answer and shredding the paper

2. **impetus**
   a. the push sending a go-cart downhill
   b. the preparations made for a race

3. **repertoire**
   a. a piano player's favorite songs
   b. all the songs a piano player knows

Vocabulary Strategy: Prefixes

The Critical Vocabulary word *impetus* contains the Latin prefix *im–*, which is a variation of the prefix *in–*. This prefix means "in, into, or within." It can also mean "not." Before the consonant *l*, *in–* is usually spelled *il–* and before *r* it is spelled *ir–*. With the consonants *b*, *m*, and *p*, the spelling changes to *im–* as in *impetus*. This prefix is used in many English words. To understand the meaning of words with the prefix *in–*, use your knowledge of the base word as well as your knowledge of the prefix.

in–	im–	il–	ir–
instinct	impervious	illegal	irrational
individual	implausible	illogical	irrefutable

Practice and Apply Use a dictionary or other resource to identify two additional words that use each version of the prefix shown in the chart—that is, two new words beginning with *in–*, two beginning with *im–*, and so on. For each word you identify, use the steps below.

1. Define the prefix and the base word separately.

2. Explain how the meanings of the prefix and base word combine to create the word's overall meaning.

3. Use the word in a sentence that accurately reflects its meaning.

Musée des Beaux Arts

MEDIA

Landscape with the Fall of Icarus

Poem by W. H. Auden   Painting by Pieter Breughel the Elder

Background *According to a Greek myth, King Minos imprisoned the architect and inventor Daedalus and his son Icarus on the isle of Crete. In order to escape, Daedalus built two pairs of wings with feathers and wax. Before fleeing the island, he warned his son to not fly too high, lest the warm sunlight melt the wax and destroy the wings. Once airborne, however, Icarus became exhilarated with the joy and freedom of flight. Higher and higher he flew, until the wax on his wings did indeed begin to soften. The feathers separated, and the young man fell and drowned in a part of the Aegean called the Icarian Sea.*

The story of Icarus shows the danger of upsetting the natural order, either through artifice or ambition. It has fascinated visual artists from ancient sculptors through Rubens and Matisse. Writers and poets, too, have expanded on the legend; the Roman poet Ovid published a particularly influential version in AD 8. Over the centuries, painters and poets have consistently informed and alluded to each others' work on the subject.

Ovid's tale inspired perhaps the best known Icarus painting, a work attributed to **Pieter Breughel the Elder** *(1525–1569). We know little about the life of the great Flemish painter, who became famous for his finely detailed, allegorical landscapes. Breughel began and ended his career in what is now Belgium, but he was greatly influenced by Italian art and spent several years painting in Italy.*

Breughel's Landscape with the Fall of Icarus *inspired a major 20th-century poet,* **W. H. Auden** *(1907–1973). Auden first viewed the painting in a Brussels museum in 1938, shortly before war broke out in Europe. In 1939 he moved from his native England to New York City. "Musée des Beaux Arts" appeared in 1940. Auden taught at universities and wrote plays, prose, music lyrics, and over a dozen books of poems. His poetry, which features keen observation and direct, accessible language, had a profound influence on a generation of modern poets.*

AS YOU READ Think about how the historical context in which Auden wrote the poem, just before World War II, might influence its theme. Write down any questions you generate during reading.

Musée des Beaux Arts
Poem by W. H. Auden

About suffering they were never wrong,
The Old Masters:[1] how well they understood
Its human position; how it takes place
While someone else is eating or opening a window or just
     walking dully along;
5 How, when the aged are reverently, passionately waiting
For the miraculous birth, there always must be
Children who did not specially want it to happen, skating
On a pond at the edge of the wood:
They never forgot
10 That even the dreadful martyrdom must run its course
Anyhow in a corner, some untidy spot
Where the dogs go on with their doggy life and the
     torturer's horse
Scratches its innocent behind on a tree.

In Breughel's *Icarus*, for instance: how everything turns away
15 Quite leisurely from the disaster; the ploughman may
Have heard the splash, the forsaken cry,
But for him it was not an important failure; the sun shone
As it had to on the white legs disappearing into the green
Water; and the expensive delicate ship that must have seen
20 Something amazing, a boy falling out of the sky,
Had somewhere to get to and sailed calmly on.

COLLABORATIVE DISCUSSION What did the "Old Masters" understand about suffering? With a partner, discuss Auden's own attitude toward their perspective. Cite specific evidence from the poem to support your ideas.

---

[1] **Old Masters:** Famous European painters of the Renaissance period.

MEDIA

AS YOU VIEW Consider the relationship between the painting's title and its composition. Write down any questions you generate while viewing it.

Landscape with the Fall of Icarus
Painting by Pieter Breughel the Elder

Landscape with the Fall of Icarus, c. 1558, by Pieter Breughel the Elder (1525–1569), oil on panel transferred onto canvas, 73 x 112 cm.

COLLABORATIVE DISCUSSION Which image in the painting do you think is most important? Discuss how and why the artist emphasized this part of the scene. Point out details from the painting that support your ideas.

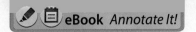

Analyze Representations in Different Mediums

RL 7

A **medium** is a vehicle for artistic expression, or a mode of communication. Examples include drama, music, text, and the visual arts. Artists working in different media often depict the same subject. Since each medium offers its own particular strengths and limitations, however, these artists often emphasize different aspects of the subject or scene. As a result, they may develop and address different themes within the same topic. For example, the visual art medium (painting) does not allow Breughel to represent the entire moral of the myth in his work.

Auden, for his part, emphasizes another aspect of the theme after viewing two paintings in the Musées Royaux des Beaux-Arts, a Brussels museum. (Auden's first stanza refers to Breughel's painting *The Census at Bethlehem.*) When considered together, the Icarus myth, the painting, and the poem provide a much broader range of meaning than each delivers on its own. When comparing representations of a subject in different mediums, you might ask yourself the following questions:

- What details are emphasized in each treatment?
- What details are present in one treatment but absent in the other?
- What is each artist's attitude toward the subject?

Analyzing the Text and Image

RL 2, RL 7, SL 4

Cite Text Evidence   Support your responses with evidence from the selections.

1. **Analyze** Describe how the two works incorporate the Icarus myth. Which parts of the story do they withhold, and which parts do they emphasize?

2. **Evaluate** Why does Icarus appear as a tiny pair of legs in a corner of the painting? Does he receive greater prominence in the poem? Explain.

3. **Synthesize** Auden interprets the scene as a human response to suffering. Do you agree or disagree with the poet's interpretation of the painting? Why?

PERFORMANCE TASK

Speaking Activity: Response to Literature Plan and deliver a short speech in which you compare Auden's poem with *Landscape with the Fall of Icarus.*

- Begin planning your comparison by making a Venn diagram in which you list key details from the painting and the poem.
- Draft a short speech in which you point out the details and ideas that appear in both works.

- Draft a conclusion in which you analyze the significance of these shared details.
- Deliver your speech. Be sure to quote from Auden's poem and point out details in the painting, using domain-specific vocabulary.

COLLECTION 4
PERFORMANCE TASK A

Present a Response to Literature

This collection explores how we perceive the world around us, from the use of our senses and instincts to scientific instruments. Review the Emily Dickinson poems and other collection texts. Synthesize your ideas about them by planning and presenting a response to literature.

SL 4 Present information, findings, and evidence.

W 9a–b Draw evidence from literary or informational texts.

An effective speech

- focuses the audience's attention on a clear thesis
- has a logically structured body including transitions
- provides evidence from the texts that illustrate the thesis
- concludes insightfully, logically following the speech's ideas
- demonstrates appropriate and clear use of language
- engages listeners through emphasis, volume, and gestures
- maintains a formal tone through the use of standard English

> PLAN

Analyze the Text Consider the quotation that begins this collection: "The question is not what you look at, but what you see." Identify how this idea is illustrated in two or more collection texts.

- Reread each of your chosen texts, taking notes on what the author describes.

- Record details and evidence from the texts that illustrate a difference between what the author or speaker looks at and what he or she sees. Save your evidence in a folder in *my*Notebook:

ACADEMIC VOCABULARY

As you share your ideas, be sure to incorporate these words.

differentiate
incorporate
mode
orient
perspective

State Your Thesis Next, draft a thesis statement about how your chosen texts support Thoreau's quotation. This statement will be the central idea of your speech.

Get Organized Make an outline to help you present ideas clearly, so your audience can easily follow the evidence for your claim.

- Draft your thesis statement, and refer to the quotation by Thoreau in your introduction. You might include an additional quotation or detail from one of your chosen texts to engage listeners.
- In the body section, list the central ideas that support your thesis and text evidence that supports each central idea.
- Conclude by restating your thesis and noting a thought-provoking idea.

PRODUCE

Write Your Speech Use your notes and outline to write a clearly organized speech that expresses your ideas. Remember to include

- an engaging introduction, a logically ordered body, and an interesting conclusion
- transitions between the main sections of your speech
- details, quotations, and text evidence to support your thesis
- language that creates an appropriately formal tone for a speech

Interactive Lessons
To incorporate text evidence into your draft, complete this lesson:
- Using Textual Evidence: Summarizing, Paraphrasing, and Quoting

Language and Style: Precise Language

If you've ever heard a speaker ramble on and on, you can appreciate the importance of condensing ideas. By using prepositional phrases and compound verbs, speakers can condense ideas while showing connections between them. A **prepositional phrase**—a preposition such as *about, by,* or *with* and its object—can provide context or detail to clarify ideas. A **compound verb**—two verbs linked by a conjunction such as *and* or *but*—can eliminate repetition. This sentence from "Coming to Our Senses" uses both techniques:

> What emerges, eventually, is a newer and higher level of "common sense" that enables a scientist to think creatively and to pass judgment in the unfamiliar underworld of the atom or in the mind-bending domain of higher-dimensional space.

Compare that concise and clear wording with the following rambling version, which lacks compound verbs and prepositional phrases:

> What emerges, eventually, is a newer and higher level of "common sense" that enables a scientist to think creatively. It also enables a scientist to pass judgment. The unfamiliar underworld of the atom is one area in which this might happen. Another is the mind-bending domain of higher-dimensional space.

Review your draft, looking for places where you can condense ideas by using prepositional phrases, compound verbs, or both.

Plan Your Presentation When you deliver your speech to your classmates, you will need to make it come alive with appropriate expression, volume, and gestures. Read over your draft, and mark places in the text where you might want to

- emphasize a word or detail
- pause to give the audience time to consider an important idea
- use gestures to convey meaning or emotion

REVISE

Have your partner or a group of peers review your draft in myWriteSmart.

Practice and Improve Practice your speech with a partner, incorporating the presentation techniques you marked on your draft.

Questions	Tips	Revision Techniques
Does the introduction state a thesis and link it to Thoreau's quotation?	**Underline** the thesis and **highlight** the connection made with Thoreau's quotation.	**Revise** to clearly state your thesis, or **add** a link between the thesis and the quotation.
Is the thesis supported by relevant text evidence?	**Note** the text from which each piece of evidence is drawn.	**Add** relevant evidence from collection texts to support your thesis.
Does the conclusion restate the thesis and state a thought-provoking idea?	**Underline** the restated thesis, and **highlight** any thought-provoking ideas.	**Add** a restatement of the thesis or a thought-provoking idea if needed.
Is an appropriately formal tone used throughout the speech?	**Highlight** each academic word or phrase that contributes to a formal tone.	**Replace** informal word choices and sentence structures as needed.

After you and your partner have presented your speeches, give each other feedback and revise your draft.

PRESENT

Make Your Speech Present your speech to the whole class. The audience should listen, take notes, and be prepared to ask questions.

- Introduce yourself and briefly state the topic of your speech.
- When you finish, ask for audience questions or comments.
- Afterward, take time to evaluate the strengths and weaknesses of your speech.

Interactive Lessons
To help you prepare to deliver your speech, complete this lesson:
- Giving a Presentation: Delivering Your Presentation

PERFORMANCE TASK RUBRIC
ORAL RESPONSE TO LITERATURE

	Ideas and Evidence	Organization	Language
4	• The speech begins memorably and engages the audience's attention. • A strong and interesting thesis is introduced at the start of the speech. • Information and supporting evidence are presented clearly, concisely, and logically so that the audience can follow the development of ideas.	• Central ideas and supporting evidence are presented in a logical and powerful way. • The speech maintains a consistent focus on the topic. • The speech ends with a satisfying and thought-provoking conclusion.	• The speech maintains a consistent and appropriately formal tone through the use of standard English. • The speech flows smoothly with the use of prepositional phrases and compound verbs. • The speaker is easy to understand and uses volume, pacing, and gestures appropriately.
3	• The speech starts in a way that engages the audience. • A thesis is introduced at the start of the speech. • Information and supporting evidence are presented clearly and logically, although some unnecessary information is included.	• Central ideas and supporting evidence are presented in a mostly logical way. • The speech stays focused on the topic, with a few minor lapses. • The speech ends with an appropriate conclusion.	• The speech mostly maintains a formal tone through the use of standard English. • The speech mostly flows smoothly with some prepositional phrases and at least one compound verb. • The speaker is generally easy to understand.
2	• The speech has a somewhat bland opening that may not engage the audience. • A thesis is hinted at but not made clear at the start of the speech. • Most information and supporting evidence are presented clearly, but there is some unnecessary information and some gaps in logic.	• Central ideas and some supporting evidence are presented, but the reasoning is often unclear. • The speech strays from the topic in several places. • The speech ends with a brief concluding statement but leaves some ideas unresolved.	• The speech has an inconsistent tone, sometimes using nonstandard or very informal English. • Several ideas in the speech could be condensed using prepositional phrases or compound verbs. • The speaker is sometimes difficult to understand and may rush or speak in a monotone.
1	• The speech opens in a way that does not engage the audience. • There is no thesis. • Information is not presented clearly and logically, and supporting evidence is lacking.	• Central ideas and supporting evidence are difficult for the audience to identify and understand. • The speech lacks focus throughout. • The speech ends abruptly.	• The speech has an overly informal tone, using nonstandard English and/or slang. • The speech is rambling and repetitive. • The speaker is often difficult to understand.

Write a Narrative

The texts in this collection focus on the sometimes surprising differences between how we see things and how they really are. Look back at the anchor text "Coming to Our Senses" and other texts from this collection, and think about the ways in which things are not as they may first appear in these texts. Use those surprising insights as the basis of a suspenseful or surprising narrative of your own.

W 3a–e Write narratives.
W 4 Produce clear and coherent writing.

An effective narrative

- begins by introducing a setting, a narrator, and a main character
- has an engaging plot with a central conflict
- uses a variety of narrative techniques to develop characters, plot, theme, and suspense or surprise
- includes sensory language and descriptive details
- ends with a logical and satisfying resolution to the conflict

> PLAN

Identify Narrative Techniques
Use the annotation tools in your eBook to identify narrative techniques in two texts from this collection, including "Coming to Our Senses." Save your notes to *my*Notebook in a folder titled *Collection 4 Performance Task B*. As you review the texts, ask yourself these questions:

- What point of view does each writer use? How does the point of view affect how or when information is revealed?
- How does the writer use dialogue and descriptive details to create suspense or reveal insights? How does the pacing allow for suspense or surprise?

ACADEMIC VOCABULARY

As you write your draft, try to use these words.

> differentiate
> incorporate
> mode
> orient
> perspective

myNotebook

"Coming to Our Senses"

"If our eyes had the resolution of high-performance microscopes, nobody would ever have blamed the plague and other sicknesses on divine wrath. The bacteria and viruses that made us sick would be in plain view as they crawled on our food or as they slid through open wounds in our skin."

Tyson uses narrative techniques, including descriptive details, to make a surprising claim.

Brainstorm Use a web diagram or other graphic organizer to generate ideas for your narrative.

- Think about an experience, event, or conflict you know about that involved an element of suspense or surprise.
- Use your imagination to create characters, setting, plot, conflict, and theme related to this experience or event.
- Remember that this may be a fictional account and that you can use ideas from real life to help you get started.

Get Organized Organize your notes. Combine the techniques you identified in the texts with your own ideas in an outline or a graphic organizer. Consider these points:

- How does the story begin? What can you do to engage readers and make them want to keep reading?
- What is the story's plot? What is the central conflict? Are there any other conflicts related to the central one?
- What is the sequence of events? How do they lead to a climax—a turning point or moment of greatest intensity? When is the moment of sudden insight?
- How does the story end? Is the conflict resolved? How?
- From which point of view will your narrative be told?
- What details will bring your setting and characters to life for readers?
- How will you create suspense or surprise?

PRODUCE

Draft Your Narrative Write a draft of your narrative, following your notes, outline, and graphic organizer.

- Begin by introducing the setting, the main character(s), and an experience or conflict that will be central to the plot.
- Describe a sequence of events surrounding the conflict. Pay attention to how you develop the element of surprise or suspense and the best moment to reveal a sudden insight.
- Use descriptive details, sensory language, and narrative techniques such as dialogue.
- Provide a satisfying ending that resolves the central conflict.

Interactive Lessons
To help you draft your narrative, complete the following lessons in Writing Narratives:
- Narrative Structure
- Narrative Techniques

Improve Your Draft Exchange drafts with a partner, evaluating each other's work using the following questions.

Interactive Lessons
To help you improve your draft, complete the following lesson:
• Writing as a Process: Revising and Editing

Questions	Tips	Revision Techniques
Does the narrative begin in an engaging way and introduce characters, setting, conflict, and point of view?	**Underline** the engaging opening and **highlight** clues about the characters, setting, conflict, or point of view.	**Revise** your introduction to begin with action or dialogue, and **add** details about the characters, setting, conflict, or narrator.
Do narrative techniques and precise language bring the story to life?	**Underline** dialogue, sensory details, and vivid verbs.	**Add** dialogue, sensory details, and vivid verbs where they are lacking.
Are suspense or surprise used effectively?	**Highlight** passages that build tension or reveal a surprise.	**Add** details that build tension. **Add** a surprising event.
Does the conclusion resolve the conflict in a logical way?	**Underline** the explanation of how the conflict is resolved.	**Add** dialogue or narration that logically resolves the conflict.

Language and Style: Modifying to Add Details

Writers of effective narratives use vivid details to make readers feel as if they are right there, experiencing the setting, characters, and events for themselves. As you revise, incorporate **adverbials** to express where, when, and how events in your narrative happen. Here are some examples from "The Night Face Up":

Adverbs: "He came to abruptly."

Adverb phrases: "He waited, covered by the branches of a shrub and the starless night."

Adverb clauses: "He felt thirsty, as though he'd been running for miles. . . ."

Prepositional phrases: "At the same time, he felt his ankles sinking deeper into the mud. . . ."

Review your draft, adding adverbials to help readers experience your narrative as you pictured it.

Stage a Reading When your final draft is completed, read your narrative to a small group. Use your voice and body language to present a lively reading. Be prepared to answer questions or respond to comments from your group members.

PERFORMANCE TASK RUBRIC
NARRATIVE

	Ideas and Evidence	Organization	Language
4	• The short story begins memorably; the exposition clearly introduces the setting and a main character and establishes the conflict in a unique way. • The writer regularly uses precise description and realistic dialogue to develop characters and events. • The plot is thoroughly developed; the story reveals a significant theme. • The story ends by resolving the conflict and tying up loose ends.	• The sequence of events is effective, clear, and logical. • The pace and organization keep the reader curious about the next plot event.	• The point of view is effective and consistent throughout the story. • Adverbials are used effectively to bring the story to life. • Sentence beginnings, lengths, and structures vary and have a rhythmic flow. • Spelling, capitalization, and punctuation are correct. If handwritten, the story is legible. • Grammar and usage are correct.
3	• The story introduces the setting, a main character, and a conflict, but it could be more engaging. • The writer often uses description and dialogue to develop characters and events. • The plot is adequately developed; the story suggests a theme. • The story resolves the conflict, but more details are needed to bring the plot to a satisfying conclusion.	• The sequence of events is mostly clear and logical. • The pace is usually effective.	• The point of view is mostly consistent. • A few adverbials add description. • Sentence beginnings, lengths, and structures mostly vary. • Some spelling, capitalization, and punctuation mistakes occur but are not distracting. If handwritten, the story is mostly legible. • Some minor grammatical and usage errors appear in the story.
2	• The story opening is uneventful; the exposition identifies a setting and a main character but only hints at a conflict. • The writer occasionally uses description and dialogue to develop characters and events. • The plot development is uneven in a few places; a theme is only hinted at. • The story resolves some parts of the conflict.	• The sequence of events is confusing in a few places. • The pace often lags.	• The point of view shifts in a few places. • One or two adverbials are used correctly. • Sentence structures vary somewhat. • Spelling, capitalization, and punctuation are often incorrect. If handwritten, the story may be partially illegible. • Grammar and usage are incorrect in many places.
1	• The short story is missing critical information about the setting and main character and doesn't set up a conflict. • The writer does not use description and dialogue to develop characters and events. • The plot is barely developed, and there is no recognizable theme. • The story lacks a clear resolution.	• There is no clear sequence of events, making it easy for the reader to lose interest in the plot. • The pace is ineffective.	• The story lacks a clear point of view. • Adverbials are absent or misused. • A repetitive sentence structure makes the writing monotonous. • Spelling, capitalization, and punctuation are incorrect throughout. If handwritten, the story may be partially or mostly illegible. • Many grammatical and usage errors change the meaning of the writer's ideas.

Absolute Power

Human ambition is timeless, and its fruits are fleeting.

Stream to Start

hmhfyi.com

Channel One News®

COLLECTION
PERFORMANCE TASK Preview

At the end of this collection, you will have an opportunity to complete this task:

• Write an analysis explaining how Macbeth's character contains a trait that all of us share.

ACADEMIC VOCABULARY

Study the words and their definitions in the chart below. You will use these words as you discuss and write about the texts in this collection.

Word	Definition	Related Forms
comprise (kəm-prīz´) *v.*	to consist or be made up of	comprising
incidence (ĭn´sĭ-dəns) *n.*	the occurrence or frequency of something	incident, coincidence
priority (prī-ôr´ĭ-tē) *n.*	something that is more important or considered more important than another thing	prioritize
thesis (thē´sĭs) *n.*	a statement or premise that is defended by an argument	hypothesis
ultimate (ŭl´tə-mĭt) *adj.*	concluding a process or progression; final	ultimately, ultimatum

Background *In September 2008, a large freshman class gathered on the campus of the Catholic University of America (CUA) in Washington, D.C., to begin their college careers. As happens every September, the university faculty greeted them in a convocation. That year, the highlight of the gathering was a speech delivered by English professor* **Michael Mack.** *Mack began "Why Read Shakespeare?" with a disclosure: as a Shakespeare scholar, he was hardly objective. Still, he noted, the value of reading Shakespeare must, from time to time, be articulated.*

Neither a borrower nor a lender be To be, or not to be—that is the question
you prick us, do we not bleed? Friends, Romans, countrymen, lend me your ears
ow is the winter of our discontent
What's in a name? That which we call a rose by any other name would smell as swee
Double, double toil and trouble; fire burn, and cauldron bubble.

from **Why Read Shakespeare?**

wards die many times before their deaths; the valiant never taste of death but once.
Et tu, Brute? Parting is such sweet sorrow O Romeo, Romeo! Wherefore art thou Romeo?
The lady doth protest too much, methinks

Argument by Michael Mack

AS YOU READ Note each reason Mack provides to support his central argument that people should read Shakespeare. Write down any questions you generate during reading.

myNotebook

As you read, mark up the text. Save your work to **myNotebook**.

- Highlight details
- Add notes and questions
- Add new words to **myWordList**

If college is a time for asking questions, it also is a time for broadening your interests. Why should Shakespeare be one of those interests that you seek to develop at CUA? The obvious argument to the contrary is that reading Shakespeare is hard work—and not particularly rewarding, at least the first time round. I would like to begin by addressing what I take to be a perfectly honest response to a first reading of Shakespeare, namely "I don't get it; is it really worth the effort?"

10   Let me try to explain by comparing Shakespeare to music. We all know that some kinds of music are easy on the ears. This is the ear candy that you like the very first time you hear it. And after you've heard it ten thousand times in twenty four hours, it turns into an ear worm that drives you crazy.

There also is music that you don't particularly like the first time you hear it. But, if you give it a chance, it grows on you. And you discover something new about it every time you listen. At a certain point, if you listen enough, you realize that what seemed random is really better described as "complex." What had been annoying now instead strikes you as appealingly edgy. And what initially seemed weird now looks strangely wonderful. This is the way Shakespeare works. He gives you a serious headache the first time you try to understand him—and the second. But if you stick with him, you can expect a breakthrough, and the excitement and satisfaction of being able to say, "I get it."

The first time you listen to a piece of complex music, you hear but don't hear. Why should it be any surprise, then, that the first time people read Shakespeare they don't get it? What would be surprising—and a genuine cause for concern—would be if someone read Shakespeare and thought they'd understood him.

This phenomenon of people having difficulty understanding Shakespeare is hardly new. It predates by centuries our **truncated** attention spans and our preference for the fast cuts of modern video. It is a problem that the editors of the First Folio[1] addressed in 1623, just seven years after the death of Shakespeare. The editors, John Heminge and Henry Condell, were two of Shakespeare's fellow players and shareholders in the Globe.[2] Addressing the "great variety of readers" of the volume, they wrote:

> Read him, therefore; and again and again.
> And if then you do not like him, surely
> you are in some manifest danger, not to
> understand him.

They did not expect readers to understand Shakespeare's works the first time they read them—and that's why they recommend rereading—"again and again." They recognize that Shakespeare is difficult, but they insist that he is worth the effort—and that if someone doesn't like Shakespeare, it's their fault, not his.

A Time for Exploring

The question Heminge and Condell don't answer—and the one I still haven't answered—is what you've understood when you've understood Shakespeare. When you get "it," what did you get?

I'd like to answer this by addressing in particular those who just don't see themselves as, well, the literary type. Some of you out there are thinking, "Reading Shakespeare—that's just not me: I'm just a normal guy, and the simple pleasures are good enough for me. Besides, what would my bowling buddies say?" I can hear others out there thinking, "I'm in a professional school, and I just want to get into my professional studies as quickly as

truncate
(trŭng´kāt´) *v.* make shorter.

---

[1] **First Folio:** the first published collection of Shakespeare's plays.
[2] **the Globe:** the London theater at which Shakespeare was based.

possible." Still others are thinking, "I much prefer something more scientific—I believe in studying "real" things: fiction is fun to read on summer break, but . . ."

60   In response to these serious-minded objections to reading Shakespeare, I would like to suggest that what you find in Shakespeare is as serious as the subject matter of your other courses. We think of biology and chemistry, history and politics, psychology and sociology as subjects that are focused on the real world. Well, as with these subjects, Shakespeare offers us a lens on the real world in which we live.

In Shakespeare's time, great books were thought of as mirrors. When you read a great book, the idea is, you are looking into a mirror—a pretty special mirror, one that reflects the world in a way

70   that allows us to see its true nature. What is more, as we hold the volume of Shakespeare in front of us, we see that it reflects not only the world around us, but also ourselves. What is it that we find in Shakespeare? Nothing less than ourselves and the world—certainly worthy subjects to study in college.

Indeed, some of Shakespeare's **contemporaries** justified the seriousness of literary fictions by pointing out that Christ Himself used them. Take the parable of the prodigal son:[3] in this fiction you learn about sin and forgiveness. And you also learn about yourself. You realize that the story is about you—you are the prodigal son.

80   The problem is that you are not only the prodigal son but also the resentful, self-righteous older brother. As you interpret the

contemporary
(kən-tĕmʹpə-rĕrʹē) *n.*
one living at the
same time as.

---

[3] **parable of the prodigal son:** a New Testament story about a father who celebrates the return of a son who has squandered his birthright.

> # What is it that we find in Shakespeare? Nothing less than ourselves and the world.

parable, you find that it interprets you—and in multiple ways. As you discover the true meaning of the parable you discover the truth about yourself.

In the case of *Macbeth*, we have a supreme reflection of ambition. But what makes the play terrifying is not that Macbeth looks like a fascist dictator[4]—a popular staging these days—but because he looks like us. If you don't see your own overreaching in the **phantasmagoric** restless ecstasy of Macbeth, you need to read
90 again. Either you don't understand the true nature of Macbeth's ambition or you don't know yourself. Or, quite possibly, both.

phantasmagoric
(făn-tăz´mə-gôr´ĭk)
adj. dreamlike or surreal.

What we see in these examples is a fairly complex interplay of life and literature. Literature teaches you about life, and the better you understand literature, the better you understand life. It also is true, though, that the more you know about life, the better equipped you are to understand what you find in literature. This two-way mirroring means that learning about literature and learning about life go hand in hand. And it means that finding beauty and meaning in Shakespeare is a sort of proving ground for
100 finding beauty and meaning in life.

Indeed, as you learn to read Shakespeare, you are learning to read the world. As you interpret Shakespeare's characters, you are practicing figuring out life's characters. Struggling with the complexities involved in interpreting Shakespeare is a superb preparation for struggling with the complexities of life. Shakespeare offers a world of **vicarious** experience—a virtual reality, a sort of

vicarious
(vī-kâr´ē-əs) *adj.*
seen through the imagined interpretations of another.

---

[4] **fascist dictator:** authoritarian ruler of an oppressive, nationalistic government.

flight simulator—that gives you a great advantage when it comes time to venture out into the real world.

So Shakespeare isn't just for literary types, he is for anyone who is interested in navigating the real world. . . .

There is Knowledge and there is Knowledge

As I conclude, I would like to remind you that college isn't just about your head, it's also about the heart. And, returning to Shakespeare, I can say that he can be particularly helpful in understanding the heart. Read Shakespeare and spare yourself a world of bad dates.

Shakespeare shows how the head and the heart need each other. One of the most important things for you to come to understand is your own emotional life. Why do you feel the way you do? Have other people felt this way before? What have they done about it, and how has it turned out?

By reading about the heart, your head and heart become more fully integrated. This integrity, when you understand what you feel and you hear with an understanding heart, is the mark of an educated person. . . .

So, again, "Why read Shakespeare?" I've proposed a link between getting to know Shakespeare and getting to know the world and ourselves. I encourage you to test out this hypothesis and to see if in becoming better at the art of reading Shakespeare, you become better at the art of living—to see if through reading Shakespeare you become someone better equipped to find happiness in life, someone who more highly values what is truly valuable in life.

COLLABORATIVE DISCUSSION With a partner, discuss the reasons that Mack gives for why people should read Shakespeare. Cite specific evidence from the text to support your ideas.

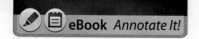
Analyze Argument and Rhetoric

RI 6,
RI 8

"Why Read Shakespeare?" is an **argument** in which the author attempts to persuade an audience to agree with his point of view. Michael Mack states a **claim,** or thesis, and supports it with valid reasoning and relevant evidence. He also makes these rhetorical choices, which appeal directly to his audience of college freshmen.

- The author directly addresses his audience's **potential concerns.** "Some of you out there are thinking, 'Reading Shakespeare—that's just not me: I'm just a normal guy, and the simple pleasures are good enough for me. Besides, what would my bowling buddies say?'" How might this question appeal to his audience?
- The author uses **comparisons** that his audience will relate to. He begins the speech by comparing Shakespeare to music. What assumption is the author making about his audience by using this comparison?
- The author appeals directly to the audience's **self-interest.** He explains that reading Shakespeare can ultimately help students understand matters of the heart: "Read Shakespeare and spare yourself a world of bad dates."

Analyzing the Text

RI 1, RI 4, RI 5,
RI 6, RI 8, W 1,
SL 4

Cite Text Evidence   Support your responses with evidence from the selection.

1. **Identify** Why did Shakespeare's contemporaries recommend rereading his works, and what might this information suggest to current readers?

2. **Infer** Mack uses the term "ear candy" in line 11. What does he mean by this term? How might the term appeal to his audience?

3. **Cite Evidence** What evidence does the author provide to support the claim that Shakespeare's works reflect the world and ourselves?

4. **Analyze** The author concludes the speech with a kind of challenge to his audience. Review lines 125–132, and then explain why he included this content.

PERFORMANCE TASK

Speaking Activity: Argument In his speech to college freshmen, Mack presents his opinion on the value of reading Shakespeare. Evaluate how successfully he appeals to his audience by writing and delivering a brief speech of your own.

- Present an argument about whether Mack succeeds in achieving the ultimate purpose of persuading his audience to read Shakespeare.

- Cite text evidence to discuss whether Mack's style and tone appeal to you as a student and whether you find the comparisons he makes relevant.

Critical Vocabulary

truncate   **contemporary**   **phantasmagoric**   **vicarious**

Practice and Apply Complete the sentences to demonstrate your understanding of each Critical Vocabulary word.

1. When it comes to Shakespeare, our **truncated** attention spans might make it difficult to . . .

2. A **contemporary** of Shakespeare's may have understood the language in his works because . . .

3. Many readers like the **phantasmagoric** scenes in Shakespeare's plays because . . .

4. We get a **vicarious** thrill out of reading fiction because . . .

Language and Style: Rhetorical Questions

Rhetorical questions are questions that do not require a reply. Writers use them to suggest that their arguments make the answers to the questions obvious or self-evident. In "Why Read Shakespeare?" Michael Mack uses rhetorical questions for three distinct purposes: to engage the audience, to introduce a topic, and to make a point. For example, note Mack's use of a rhetorical question in lines 26–27:

> **Why should it be any surprise, then, that the first time people read Shakespeare they don't get it?**

The author asks this question to appeal to the audience, to let them know that he understands their reluctance to read Shakespeare. He doesn't really expect an answer. Now look at this example from line 49:

> **When you get "it," what did you get?**

This question also does not require an answer. Instead, it introduces a topic in a way that allows the listener to follow the argument.

In this example (lines 72–74), Mack asks a rhetorical question and then immediately answers it:

> **What is it that we find in Shakespeare? Nothing less than ourselves and the world—certainly worthy subjects to study in college.**

Here, the author reasons aloud to state one of the points of his argument.

Practice and Apply Look back at the speech you wrote for this selection's Performance Task. Revise your speech to add at least two rhetorical questions. Present your revised speech to a partner and discuss the effectiveness of the rhetorical questions.

Shakespearean Drama

One reason Shakespeare's works have endured for over 400 years may be that his characters—figures from history and his imagination—transcend any particular time or place. Many of these characters are **archetypes**—familiar character types that appear over and over again in literature. The scheming characters and conspiracies at the heart of *The Tragedy of Macbeth* are as relevant today as they were in Shakespeare's time.

Characteristics of Shakespearean Tragedy

A **tragedy** is a drama in which a series of actions leads to the downfall of the main character, called the **tragic hero**. The plot builds to a **catastrophe**, or a disastrous final outcome, that usually involves the death of the hero and many others. To create suspense before this inevitable outcome and to help the audience understand the characters, Shakespeare used certain dramatic conventions, including dramatic irony, the soliloquy, and the aside.

Main Character	Dramatic Conventions
Tragic Hero • is of high social rank—a king, a prince, or a general • has a **tragic flaw**—an error in judgment or a character defect—that ultimately leads to his or her downfall • suffers complete ruin or death • faces his or her downfall with courage and dignity	**Dramatic Irony** • results when the audience knows more than one or more of the characters—for example, Duncan does not know that Macbeth is plotting against him, but the audience does • helps build suspense **Soliloquy** • is a speech given by a character alone on stage, used to reveal his or her private thoughts and feelings • may help the audience understand a character's motivation **Aside** • is a character's remark, either to the audience or to another character, that no one else on stage is supposed to hear • lets the audience in on a character's thoughts or secrets

The Language of Shakespeare

Shakespearean language can be challenging because of its unfamiliar vocabulary and sentence structure, but it shouldn't stop you from getting caught up in the intriguing plot that drives *Macbeth*. Here are some keys to reading Shakespeare's language:

Blank Verse Shakespeare's plays are **verse dramas,** in which most of the dialogue is written in the metrical patterns of poetry. Shakespeare wrote primarily in **blank verse,** or unrhymed lines of iambic pentameter. **Iambic pentameter** is a pattern of rhythm that has five unstressed syllables (ˇ), each followed by a stressed syllable (ʹ). Read this line aloud, noticing how the rhythm mimics that of everyday speech:

> ˇ ʹ   ˇ ʹ   ˇ ʹ ˇ ʹ   ˇ ʹ
> *So foul and fair a day I have not seen.*

Most of *Macbeth* is written in blank verse. In some places, however, Shakespeare broke the pattern to vary the rhythm, create dramatic tension, or distinguish low-ranking characters from those of higher rank.

Rhetorical Devices *Macbeth* is about power, ambition, and betrayal. The characters are constantly trying to persuade themselves, each other, and the audience of the rightness of their cause. As a result, the play is full of speeches that make masterful use of rhetorical devices, such as repetition, parallelism, and rhetorical questions.

Rhetorical Device	Example
REPETITION the use of words and phrases more than once to emphasize ideas	Thrice to thine, and thrice to mine And thrice again, to make up nine. —Act I, Scene 3, lines 35–36
PARALLELISM the repetition of grammatical structures to express ideas that are related or of equal importance	When the hurly-burly's done, When the battle's lost and won. —Act I, Scene 1, lines 3–4
RHETORICAL QUESTIONS the use of questions that require no answer to make the speaker's rightness seem self-evident	Do you not hope your children shall be kings When those that gave the Thane of Cawdor to me Promised no less to them? —Act I, Scene 3, lines 118–120

Reading Shakespearean Drama

Understanding Shakespearean drama can be challenging for modern readers. Use these strategies to help you appreciate and analyze *Macbeth*.

- Study the opening **cast of characters,** which in *Macbeth* will tell you the characters' ranks and how they are related to one another.

- Try to visualize the setting and action by using information in the **stage directions** and **dialogue**.

- Keep track of the characters, and think about what the words and actions reveal about their traits. Pay attention in particular to the actions and motivations of Macbeth and Lady Macbeth. At the end, consider how closely each fits the model of a **tragic hero**.

- Note examples of **foreshadowing,** and use each to predict events and better understand the characters' personalities.

- Use the **side notes** to understand unfamiliar words and expressions.

- Remember that the end of a line does not necessarily mean the end of a thought. Look closely at each line's punctuation, and try to figure out the meaning of the complete sentence or phrase.

- Paraphrase passages to help you understand characters' public personas as well as their private schemes. When you **paraphrase** a passage, you restate its key points in your own words.

Elizabethan Words to Know

Here are words that you will encounter often while reading *Macbeth*:

anon: soon	**naught:** nothing	**thither:** there
durst: dared	**nigh:** near	**'twixt:** between
ere: before	**perchance:** maybe	**whence:** where
fly: flee, run away	**prithee:** please	**wherefore:** why
hark: listen	**thence:** there	**whither:** where
hie: hurry	**thine:** your, yours	**withal:** also
issue: child, offspring		

The Tragedy of Macbeth

Drama by William Shakespeare

William Shakespeare *(1564–1616) was born in Stratford-upon-Avon to a fairly prosperous family. He attended the local grammar school, where he received a solid grounding in Latin and classical literature. When he was eighteen, he married Anne Hathaway. They had a daughter and then twins, a boy and a girl.*

Sometime around 1590, Shakespeare left Stratford for London. He found work as an actor and began what was to be a highly successful career as a playwright. He belonged to a theater company known as the Lord Chamberlain's Men, which performed for Queen Elizabeth I; this company also renovated a theater known as the Globe for their own performances. Shakespeare's success enabled him to buy a house for his family in Stratford. He lived in that house after his retirement in 1612 but continued to write until his death four years later at the age of fifty-two.

Shakespeare is recognized as the most influential writer in the English language. He mastered the sonnet form, making it his own with his highly original approach; he composed long narrative poems; and he left a dramatic legacy unsurpassed by any playwright before or since. Four centuries later, his plays continue to be performed on stage and made into films.

Shakespeare's plays are often grouped based on when they were written. In the early 1590s, he wrote history plays and comedies with plots derived from earlier stories. In the late 1590s, he wrote comedies, including A Midsummer Night's Dream, *in which he skillfully interwove complex plots to convey his themes. As the century ended, Shakespeare began exploring darker views of human nature in his work. Between 1600 and 1607, he wrote his greatest tragedies, including* Macbeth, Hamlet, *and* King Lear. *His later comedies, such as* The Tempest, *are often called tragicomedies, as they are tinged with sadness.*

After Shakespeare died, his plays were published in an edition known as the First Folio. *In the introduction, playwright Ben Jonson wrote that Shakespeare "was not of an age, but for all time."*

Background *It is believed that Shakespeare wrote* Macbeth *largely to please King James I. The Scottish-born king claimed to be descended from an 11th-century historical figure named Banquo. In* Macbeth, *the witches predict that Banquo will sire a long line of kings. James's interest in witchcraft—he wrote a book on the subject in 1597—may explain the prominence of the witches in the play. The play also addressed James's fears of assassination; he had survived several attempts on his life.*

THE TIME: The 11th century   **THE PLACE:** Scotland and England

CHARACTERS

Duncan, King of Scotland

His Sons

Malcolm
Donalbain

Noblemen of Scotland

Macbeth
Banquo
Macduff
Lennox
Ross
Menteith (měn-tēth´)
Angus
Caithness (kāth´nĭs)

Fleance (flā´əns), son to Banquo

Siward (syōō´ərd), earl of Northumberland, general of the English forces

Young Siward, his son

Seyton (sā´tən), an officer attending on Macbeth

Son, to Macduff

An English Doctor

A Scottish Doctor

A Porter

An Old Man

Three Murderers

Lady Macbeth

Lady Macduff

A Gentlewoman attending on Lady Macbeth

Hecate (hěk´ĭt), goddess of witchcraft

Three Witches

Apparitions

Lords, Officers, Soldiers, Messengers, and Attendants

AS YOU READ Notice the reactions of Macbeth and Banquo to the witches' words. Write down any questions you generate during reading.

ACT I

Scene 1 *An open place in Scotland.*

[*Thunder and lightning. Enter three* Witches.]

First Witch. When shall we three meet again?
In thunder, lightning, or in rain?

Second Witch. When the hurly-burly's done,
When the battle's lost and won.

5 **Third Witch.** That will be ere the set of sun.

First Witch. Where the place?

Second Witch.   Upon the heath.

Third Witch. There to meet with Macbeth.

First Witch. I come, Graymalkin.

Second Witch. Paddock calls.

Third Witch.   Anon.

10 **All.** Fair is foul, and foul is fair,
Hover through the fog and filthy air.

[*They exit.*]

Scene 2 *King Duncan's camp near the battlefield.*

[*Alarum within. Enter* King Duncan, Malcolm, Donalbain,
Lennox, *with* Attendants, *meeting a bleeding* Captain.]

Duncan. What bloody man is that? He can report,
As seemeth by his plight, of the revolt
The newest state.

Malcolm.   This is the sergeant
Who, like a good and hardy soldier, fought
5 'Gainst my captivity.—Hail, brave friend!
Say to the King the knowledge of the broil
As thou didst leave it.

Captain.   Doubtful it stood,
As two spent swimmers that do cling together
And choke their art. The merciless Macdonwald
10 (Worthy to be a rebel, for to that
The multiplying villainies of nature
Do swarm upon him) from the Western Isles
Of kerns and gallowglasses is supplied;

3 hurly-burly: turmoil; uproar.

8–9 Graymalkin ... Paddock: two demon helpers in the form of a cat and a toad; **Anon:** at once.

[Stage Direction] **Alarum within:** the sound of a trumpet offstage, a signal that soldiers should arm themselves.

5 'Gainst my captivity: to save me from capture.

6 broil: battle.

9–13 Macdonwald's evils (**multiplying villainies**) swarm like insects around him. His army consists of soldiers (**kerns and gallowglasses**) from the Hebrides (**Western Isles**).

And Fortune, on his damnèd quarrel smiling,
15   Showed like a rebel's whore. But all's too weak;
For brave Macbeth (well he deserves that name),
Disdaining Fortune, with his brandished steel,
Which smoked with bloody execution,
Like valor's minion, carved out his passage
20   Till he faced the slave;
Which ne'er shook hands, nor bade farewell to him,
Till he unseamed him from the nave to th' chops,
And fixed his head upon our battlements.

Duncan. O valiant cousin, worthy gentleman!

25   **Captain.** As whence the sun 'gins his reflection
Shipwracking storms and direful thunders break,
So from that spring whence comfort seemed to come
Discomfort swells. Mark, King of Scotland, mark:
No sooner justice had, with valor armed,
30   Compelled these skipping kerns to trust their heels,
But the Norweyan lord, surveying vantage,
With furbished arms and new supplies of men,
Began a fresh assault.

Duncan. Dismayed not this our captains, Macbeth and Banquo?

35   **Captain.** Yes, as sparrows eagles, or the hare the lion.
If I say sooth, I must report they were
As cannons overcharged with double cracks,
So they doubly redoubled strokes upon the foe.
Except they meant to bathe in reeking wounds
40   Or memorize another Golgotha,
I cannot tell—
But I am faint. My gashes cry for help.

Duncan. So well thy words become thee as thy wounds:
They smack of honor both.—Go, get him surgeons.

[*The* Captain *is led off by* Attendants.]
[*Enter* Ross *and* Angus.]
45   Who comes here?

Malcolm.   The worthy Thane of Ross.

Lennox. What a haste looks through his eyes!
So should he look that seems to speak things strange.

Ross. God save the King.

Duncan. Whence cam'st thou, worthy thane?

50   **Ross.** From Fife, great king,
Where the Norweyan banners flout the sky

19 valor's minion: the favorite of valor, meaning the bravest of all.

22 unseamed him . . . chops: split him open from the navel to the jaw.

25–28 As the rising sun is sometimes followed by storms, a new assault on Macbeth began.

36 sooth: the truth.

37 double cracks: a double load of ammunition.

39–40 The officer claims he cannot decide whether (**except**) Macbeth and Banquo wanted to bathe in blood or make the battlefield as famous as Golgotha, the site of Christ's crucifixion.

45 Thane: a Scottish noble.

49–59 Ross has arrived from Fife, where Norway's troops had invaded. There the king of Norway, with the Thane of Cawdor, met Macbeth (described as the husband of **Bellona,** the goddess of war). Macbeth, in heavy armor (**proof**), challenged the enemy.

And fan our people cold.
Norway himself, with terrible numbers,
Assisted by that most disloyal traitor,
55 The Thane of Cawdor, began a dismal conflict,
Till that Bellona's bridegroom, lapped in proof,
Confronted him with self-comparisons,
Point against point, rebellious arm 'gainst arm,
Curbing his lavish spirit. And to conclude,
60 The victory fell on us.

Duncan.   Great happiness!

Ross. That now Sweno,
The Norways' king, craves composition.
Nor would we deign him burial of his men
Till he disbursèd at Saint Colme's Inch
65 Ten thousand dollars to our general use.

Duncan. No more that Thane of Cawdor shall deceive
Our bosom interest. Go, pronounce his present death,
And with his former title greet Macbeth.

Ross. I'll see it done.

70 **Duncan.** What he hath lost, noble Macbeth hath won.

[*They exit.*]

Scene 3 *A bleak place near the battlefield.*

[*Thunder. Enter the three* Witches.]

First Witch. Where hast thou been, sister?

Second Witch. Killing swine.

Third Witch. Sister, where thou?

First Witch. A sailor's wife had chestnuts in her lap
5 And munched and munched and munched. "Give me," quoth I.
"Aroint thee, witch," the rump-fed runnion cries.
Her husband's to Aleppo gone, master o' th' *Tiger;*
But in a sieve I'll thither sail
And, like a rat without a tail,
10 I'll do, I'll do, and I'll do.

Second Witch. I'll give thee a wind.

First Witch. Th' art kind.

Third Witch. And I another.

First Witch. I myself have all the other,
15 And the very ports they blow,
All the quarters that they know

62 craves composition: wants a treaty.

63 deign: allow.

64 disbursèd at Saint Colme's Inch: paid at Saint Colme's Inch, an island in the North Sea.

66–67 deceive our bosom interest: betray our friendship; **present death:** immediate execution.

6 "Aroint thee, witch," . . . **runnion cries:** "Go away, witch!" the fatbottomed (**rump-fed**), ugly creature (**runnion**) cries.

7–8 The woman's husband, the master of a merchant ship (**th' Tiger**), has sailed to Aleppo. The witch will pursue him. Witches were thought to sail on strainers (**sieve**).

14–23 The witch controls the winds, covering all points of a compass (**shipman's card**). She will make the sailor sleepless, keeping his eyelids (**penthouse lid**) from closing. Thus, he will lead an accursed (**forbid**) life for weeks (**sev'nnights**), wasting away with fatigue.

I' th' shipman's card.
I'll drain him dry as hay.
Sleep shall neither night nor day

20 Hang upon his penthouse lid.
He shall live a man forbid.
Weary sev'nnights, nine times nine,
Shall he dwindle, peak, and pine.
Though his bark cannot be lost,

25 Yet it shall be tempest-tossed.
Look what I have.

Second Witch. Show me, show me.

First Witch. Here I have a pilot's thumb,
Wracked as homeward he did come.

[*Drum within*]

30 **Third Witch.** A drum, a drum!
Macbeth doth come.

All. [*Dancing in a circle*] The Weïrd Sisters, hand in hand,
Posters of the sea and land,
Thus do go about, about,

35 Thrice to thine, and thrice to mine
And thrice again, to make up nine.
Peace, the charm's wound up.

[*Enter* Macbeth *and* Banquo.]

Macbeth. So foul and fair a day I have not seen.

33 posters: quick riders.

36 Nine was considered a magical number by superstitious people.

Image Credits: ©Michael Shay/Taxi/Getty Images

Banquo. How far is 't called to Forres?—What are these,
40 So withered, and so wild in their attire,
That look not like th' inhabitants o' th' earth
And yet are on 't?—Live you? Or are you aught
That man may question? You seem to understand me
By each at once her choppy finger laying
45 Upon her skinny lips. You should be women,
And yet your beards forbid me to interpret
That you are so.

Macbeth.   Speak, if you can. What are you?

First Witch. All hail, Macbeth! Hail to thee, Thane of Glamis!

Second Witch. All hail, Macbeth! Hail to thee, Thane of Cawdor!

50 **Third Witch.** All hail, Macbeth, that shalt be king hereafter!

Banquo. Good sir, why do you start and seem to fear
Things that do sound so fair? I' th' name of truth,
Are you fantastical, or that indeed
Which outwardly you show? My noble partner
55 You greet with present grace and great prediction
Of noble having and of royal hope,
That he seems rapt withal. To me you speak not.
If you can look into the seeds of time
And say which grain will grow and which will not,
60 Speak, then, to me, who neither beg nor fear
Your favors nor your hate.

First Witch. Hail!

Second Witch. Hail!

Third Witch. Hail!

65 **First Witch.** Lesser than Macbeth and greater.

Second Witch. Not so happy, yet much happier.

Third Witch. Thou shalt get kings, though thou be none.
So all hail, Macbeth and Banquo!

First Witch. Banquo and Macbeth, all hail!

70 **Macbeth.** Stay, you imperfect speakers. Tell me more.
By Sinel's death I know I am Thane of Glamis.
But how of Cawdor? The Thane of Cawdor lives
A prosperous gentleman, and to be king
Stands not within the prospect of belief,
75 No more than to be Cawdor. Say from whence
You owe this strange intelligence or why

42–46 aught: anything;
choppy: chapped;
your beards: Beards on women identified them as witches.

53 are you fantastical: Are you (the witches) imaginary?

54–57 The witches' prophecies of noble possessions (**having**)—the lands and wealth of Cawdor—and kingship (**royal hope**) have left Macbeth dazed (**rapt withal**).

Upon this blasted heath you stop our way
With such prophetic greeting. Speak, I charge you.

[*Witches* vanish.]

Banquo. The earth hath bubbles, as the water has,
80 And these are of them. Whither are they vanished?

80 **whither:** where.

Macbeth. Into the air, and what seemed corporal melted,
As breath into the wind. Would they had stayed!

81 **corporal:** physical; real.

Banquo. Were such things here as we do speak about?
Or have we eaten on the insane root
85 That takes the reason prisoner?

84 **insane root:** A number of plants were believed to cause insanity when eaten.

Macbeth. Your children shall be kings.

Banquo.   You shall be king.

Macbeth. And Thane of Cawdor too. Went it not so?

Banquo. To th' selfsame tune and words.—Who's here?

[*Enter* Ross *and* Angus.]

Ross. The King hath happily received, Macbeth,
90 The news of thy success, and, when he reads
Thy personal venture in the rebels' fight,
His wonders and his praises do contend
Which should be thine or his. Silenced with that,
In viewing o'er the rest o' th' selfsame day
95 He finds thee in the stout Norweyan ranks,
Nothing afeard of what thyself didst make,
Strange images of death. As thick as hail
Came post with post, and every one did bear
Thy praises in his kingdom's great defense,
100 And poured them down before him.

92–93 King Duncan hesitates between awe (**wonders**) and gratitude (**praises**) and is, as a result, speechless.

96–97 Although Macbeth left many dead (**strange images of death**), he obviously did not fear death himself.

Angus.   We are sent
To give thee from our royal master thanks,
Only to herald thee into his sight,
Not pay thee.

Ross. And for an earnest of a greater honor,
105 He bade me, from him, call thee Thane of Cawdor,
In which addition, hail, most worthy thane,
For it is thine.

104 **earnest:** partial payment.

106 **addition:** title.

Banquo.   What, can the devil speak true?

Macbeth. The Thane of Cawdor lives. Why do you dress me
In borrowed robes?

Angus.   Who was the Thane lives yet,
110 But under heavy judgment bears that life

Which he deserves to lose. Whether he was combined
With those of Norway, or did line the rebel
With hidden help and vantage, or that with both
He labored in his country's wrack, I know not;
115 But treasons capital, confessed and proved,
Have overthrown him.

      Macbeth [*aside*].   Glamis and Thane of Cawdor!
The greatest is behind. [*To* Ross *and* Angus] Thanks for your pains.
[*Aside to* Banquo] Do you not hope your children shall be kings
When those that gave the Thane of Cawdor to me
120 Promised no less to them?

      Banquo.   That, trusted home,
Might yet enkindle you unto the crown,
Besides the Thane of Cawdor. But 'tis strange.
And oftentimes, to win us to our harm,
The instruments of darkness tell us truths,
125 Win us with honest trifles, to betray 's
In deepest consequence.—
Cousins, a word, I pray you.   [*They step aside.*]

      Macbeth [*aside*].   Two truths are told
As happy prologues to the swelling act
Of the imperial theme.—I thank you, gentlemen.
130 [*Aside*] This supernatural soliciting
Cannot be ill, cannot be good. If ill,
Why hath it given me earnest of success
Commencing in a truth? I am Thane of Cawdor.
If good, why do I yield to that suggestion
135 Whose horrid image doth unfix my hair
And make my seated heart knock at my ribs
Against the use of nature? Present fears
Are less than horrible imaginings.
My thought, whose murder yet is but fantastical,
140 Shakes so my single state of man
That function is smothered in surmise,
And nothing is but what is not.

      Banquo.   Look how our partner's rapt.

      Macbeth [*aside*]. If chance will have me king, why, chance may
      crown me
Without my stir.

      Banquo.   New honors come upon him,
145 Like our strange garments, cleave not to their mold
But with the aid of use.

111–116 Whether the former thane of Cawdor allied (**combined**) with the king of Norway or supported the traitor Macdonwald (**did line the rebel**), he is guilty of treasons that deserve the death penalty (**treasons capital**), having aimed at the country's ruin (**wrack**).

120 home: fully; completely.

121 enkindle you unto: inflame your ambitions.

123–126 Banquo warns that evil powers often offer little truths to tempt people. The witches may be lying about what matters most (**in deepest consequence**).

144 my stir: my doing anything.

Macbeth [*aside*].   Come what come may,
Time and the hour runs through the roughest day.

Banquo. Worthy Macbeth, we stay upon your leisure.

Macbeth. Give me your favor. My dull brain was wrought
150 With things forgotten. Kind gentlemen, your pains
Are registered where every day I turn
The leaf to read them. Let us toward the King.
[*Aside to* Banquo] Think upon what hath chanced, and
          at more time,
The interim having weighed it, let us speak
155 Our free hearts each to other.

Banquo.   Very gladly.

Macbeth. Till then, enough.—Come, friends.

[*They exit.*]

Scene 4 *A room in the king's palace at Forres.*

[*Flourish. Enter* King Duncan, Lennox, Malcolm, Donalbain,
and Attendants.]

Duncan. Is execution done on Cawdor? Are not
Those in commission yet returned?

Malcolm.   My liege,
They are not yet come back. But I have spoke
With one that saw him die, who did report
5 That very frankly he confessed his treasons,
Implored your Highness' pardon, and set forth
A deep repentance. Nothing in his life
Became him like the leaving it. He died
As one that had been studied in his death
10 To throw away the dearest thing he owed
As 'twere a careless trifle.

Duncan.   There's no art
To find the mind's construction in the face.
He was a gentleman on whom I built
An absolute trust.

[*Enter* Macbeth, Banquo, Ross, *and* Angus.]

                    O worthiest cousin,
15 The sin of my ingratitude even now
Was heavy on me. Thou art so far before
That swiftest wing of recompense is slow
To overtake thee. Would thou hadst less deserved,
That the proportion both of thanks and payment
20 Might have been mine! Only I have left to say,
More is thy due than more than all can pay.

**146–147 Come what
. . . roughest day:** The
future will arrive no
matter what.

148 stay: wait.

**150–152 your pains . . .
read them:** I will always
remember your efforts.
The metaphor refers
to keeping a diary and
reading it regularly.

153–155 Macbeth
wants to discuss the
prophecies later, after
he and Banquo have
had time to think about
them.

2 those in commission:
those who have the
responsibility for
Cawdor's execution.

6 set forth: showed.

**8–11 He died as . . .
trifle:** He died as if he
had rehearsed (**studied**)
the moment. Though
losing his life (**the
dearest thing he owed**),
he behaved with calm
dignity.

14–21 The king
feels that he cannot
repay (**recompense**)
Macbeth enough.
Macbeth's qualities and
accomplishments are
of greater value than
any thanks or payment
Duncan can give.

Macbeth. The service and the loyalty I owe
In doing it pays itself. Your Highness' part
Is to receive our duties, and our duties
25 Are to your throne and state children and servants,
Which do but what they should by doing everything
Safe toward your love and honor.

Duncan.   Welcome hither.
I have begun to plant thee and will labor
To make thee full of growing.—Noble Banquo,
30 That hast no less deserved nor must be known
No less to have done so, let me enfold thee
And hold thee to my heart.

Banquo.   There, if I grow,
The harvest is your own.

Duncan.   My plenteous joys,
Wanton in fullness, seek to hide themselves
35 In drops of sorrow.—Sons, kinsmen, thanes,
And you whose places are the nearest, know
We will establish our estate upon
Our eldest, Malcolm, whom we name hereafter
The Prince of Cumberland; which honor must
40 Not unaccompanied invest him only,
But signs of nobleness, like stars, shall shine
On all deservers.—From hence to Inverness,
And bind us further to you.

Macbeth. The rest is labor which is not used for you.
45 I'll be myself the harbinger and make joyful
The hearing of my wife with your approach.
So humbly take my leave.

Duncan.   My worthy Cawdor.

Macbeth [*aside*]. The Prince of Cumberland! That is a step
On which I must fall down or else o'erleap,
50 For in my way it lies. Stars, hide your fires;
Let not light see my black and deep desires.
The eye wink at the hand, yet let that be
Which the eye fears, when it is done, to see.

[*He exits.*]

Duncan. True, worthy Banquo. He is full so valiant,
55 And in his commendations I am fed:
It is a banquet to me.—Let's after him,
Whose care is gone before to bid us welcome.
It is a peerless kinsman.

[*Flourish. They exit.*]

28–29 The king plans to give more honors to Macbeth.

33–35 My plenteous . . . sorrow: The king is crying tears of joy.

39 Prince of Cumberland: the title given to the heir to the Scottish throne.

42 Inverness: site of Macbeth's castle, where the king has just invited himself, giving another honor to Macbeth.

45 harbinger: a representative sent before a royal party to make proper arrangements for its arrival.

Scene 5 *Macbeth's castle at Inverness.*

[*Enter* Lady Macbeth, *alone, with a letter.*]

Lady Macbeth. [*Reading the letter*] "They met me in the day of
success, and I have learned by the perfect'st report they have more
in them than mortal knowledge. When I burned in desire to
question them further, they made themselves air, into which they
5 vanished. Whiles I stood rapt in the wonder of it came missives
from the King, who all-hailed me 'Thane of Cawdor,' by which
title, before, these Weïrd Sisters saluted me and referred me to
the coming on of time with 'Hail, king that shalt be.' This have I
thought good to deliver thee, my dearest partner of greatness, that
10 thou might'st not lose the dues of rejoicing by being ignorant of
what greatness is promised thee. Lay it to thy heart, and farewell."
     Glamis thou art, and Cawdor, and shalt be
What thou art promised. Yet do I fear thy nature;
It is too full o' th' milk of human kindness
15 To catch the nearest way. Thou wouldst be great,
Art not without ambition, but without
The illness should attend it. What thou wouldst highly,
That wouldst thou holily; wouldst not play false
And yet wouldst wrongly win. Thou'd'st have, great Glamis,
20 That which cries "Thus thou must do," if thou have it,
And that which rather thou dost fear to do,
Than wishest should be undone. Hie thee hither,
That I may pour my spirits in thine ear
And chastise with the valor of my tongue
25 All that impedes thee from the golden round

13–18 Lady Macbeth
fears her husband is too
good (**too full o' th' milk
of human kindness**)
to seize the throne by
murder (**the nearest
way**). Lacking the
necessary wickedness
(**illness**), he wants to
gain power virtuously
(**holily**).

Which fate and metaphysical aid doth seem
To have thee crowned withal.

[*Enter* Messenger.]

What is your tidings?

Messenger. The King comes here tonight.

Lady Macbeth. Thou'rt mad to say it!
Is not thy master with him? who, were't so,
30 Would have informed for preparation.

Messenger. So please you, it is true. Our Thane is coming.
One of my fellows had the speed of him,
Who, almost dead for breath, had scarcely more
Than would make up his message.

32 had the speed of him: rode faster than he.

Lady Macbeth. Give him tending.
35 He brings great news.

[Messenger *exits*.]

The raven himself is hoarse
That croaks the fatal entrance of Duncan
Under my battlements. Come, you spirits
That tend on mortal thoughts, unsex me here,
And fill me from the crown to the toe top-full
40 Of direst cruelty. Make thick my blood.
Stop up th' access and passage to remorse,
That no compunctious visitings of nature
Shake my fell purpose, nor keep peace between
Th' effect and it. Come to my woman's breasts
45 And take my milk for gall, you murd'ring ministers,
Wherever in your sightless substances
You wait on nature's mischief. Come, thick night,
And pall thee in the dunnest smoke of hell,
That my keen knife see not the wound it makes,
50 Nor heaven peep through the blanket of the dark
To cry "Hold, hold!"

[*Enter* Macbeth.]

Great Glamis, worthy Cawdor,
Greater than both by the all-hail hereafter!
Thy letters have transported me beyond
This ignorant present, and I feel now
55 The future in the instant.

35 raven: The harsh cry of the raven, a bird symbolizing evil and misfortune, was supposed to indicate an approaching death.

37–51 Lady Macbeth calls on the spirits of evil to rid her of feminine weakness (**unsex me**) and to block out guilt. She wants no normal pangs of conscience (**compunctious visitings of nature**) to get in the way of her murderous plan. She asks that her mother's milk be turned to bile (**gall**) by the unseen evil forces (**murd'ring ministers, sightless substances**) that exist in nature. Furthermore, she asks that the night wrap (**pall**) itself in darkness as black as hell so that no one may see or stop the crime.

Macbeth. My dearest love,
Duncan comes here tonight.

Lady Macbeth. And when goes hence?

Macbeth. Tomorrow, as he purposes.

Lady Macbeth.   O, never
Shall sun that morrow see!
Your face, my thane, is as a book where men
60 May read strange matters. To beguile the time,
Look like the time. Bear welcome in your eye,
Your hand, your tongue. Look like th' innocent flower,
But be the serpent under 't. He that's coming
Must be provided for; and you shall put
65 This night's great business into my dispatch,
Which shall to all our nights and days to come
Give solely sovereign sway and masterdom.

Macbeth. We will speak further.

Lady Macbeth.   Only look up clear.
To alter favor ever is to fear.
70 Leave all the rest to me.

[*They exit.*]

Scene 6 *In front of Macbeth's castle.*

[*Hautboys and Torches. Enter* King Duncan, Malcolm,
Donalbain, Banquo, Lennox, Macduff, Ross, Angus, *and*
Attendants.]

Duncan. This castle hath a pleasant seat. The air
Nimbly and sweetly recommends itself
Unto our gentle senses.

Banquo.   This guest of summer,
The temple-haunting martlet, does approve,
5 By his loved mansionry, that the heaven's breath
Smells wooingly here. No jutty, frieze,
Buttress, nor coign of vantage, but this bird
Hath made his pendant bed and procreant cradle.
Where they most breed and haunt, I have observed,
10 The air is delicate.

[*Enter* Lady Macbeth.]

Duncan.   See, see, our honored hostess!—
The love that follows us sometime is our trouble,
Which still we thank as love. Herein I teach you
How you shall bid God 'ild us for your pains
And thank us for your trouble.

Lady Macbeth.   All our service,
15 In every point twice done and then done double,
Were poor and single business to contend

60–63 To beguile . . . under 't: To fool (**beguile**) everyone, act as expected at such a time.

65 my dispatch: my management.

67 give solely sovereign sway: bring absolute royal power.

69 To alter . . . fear: To change your expression (**favor**) is a sign of fear.

[Stage Direction] **hautboys:** oboes.

1 seat: location.

3–10 The martin (**martlet**) usually built its nest on a church (**temple**), where every projection (**jutty**), sculptured decoration (**frieze**), support (**buttress**), and convenient corner (**coign of vantage**) offered a good nesting site. Banquo sees the presence of the martin's hanging (**pendant**) nest, a breeding (**procreant**) place, as a sign of healthy air.

16 single business: weak service.

Against those honors deep and broad wherewith
Your Majesty loads our house. For those of old,
And the late dignities heaped up to them,
20 We rest your hermits.

Duncan.   Where's the Thane of Cawdor?
We coursed him at the heels and had a purpose
To be his purveyor; but he rides well,
And his great love (sharp as his spur) hath helped him
To his home before us. Fair and noble hostess,
25 We are your guest tonight.

Lady Macbeth.   Your servants ever
Have theirs, themselves, and what is theirs in compt
To make their audit at your Highness' pleasure,
Still to return your own.

Duncan.   Give me your hand.

[*Taking her hand*]

Conduct me to mine host. We love him highly
30 And shall continue our graces towards him.
By your leave, hostess.

[*They exit.*]

Scene 7 *A room in Macbeth's castle.*

[*Hautboys. Torches. Enter a* Sewer, *and divers* Servants *with dishes and service over the stage. Then enter* Macbeth.]

Macbeth. If it were done when 'tis done, then 'twere well
It were done quickly. If th' assassination
Could trammel up the consequence and catch
With his surcease success, that but this blow
5 Might be the be-all and the end-all here,
But here, upon this bank and shoal of time,
We'd jump the life to come. But in these cases
We still have judgment here, that we but teach
Bloody instructions, which, being taught, return
10 To plague th' inventor. This even-handed justice
Commends th' ingredience of our poisoned chalice
To our own lips. He's here in double trust:
First, as I am his kinsman and his subject,
Strong both against the deed; then, as his host,
15 Who should against his murderer shut the door,
Not bear the knife myself. Besides, this Duncan
Hath borne his faculties so meek, hath been
So clear in his great office, that his virtues
Will plead like angels, trumpet-tongued, against

20 we rest your hermits: we can only repay you with prayers. The rich hired hermits to pray for the dead.

21 coursed him at the heels: followed closely.

22 purveyor: one who makes advance arrangements for a royal visit.

25–28 Legally, Duncan owned everything in his kingdom. Lady Macbeth politely says that they hold his property in trust (**compt**), ready to return it (**make their audit**) whenever he wants.

[Stage Direction] **Sewer:** the steward, the servant in charge of arranging the banquet and tasting the king's food; **divers:** various.

1–10 If Duncan's murder would have no negative consequences and be successfully completed with his death (**surcease**), then Macbeth would risk eternal damnation. He knows, however, that terrible deeds (**bloody instructions**) often backfire.

20 The deep damnation of his taking-off;
And pity, like a naked newborn babe
Striding the blast, or heaven's cherubin horsed
Upon the sightless couriers of the air,
Shall blow the horrid deed in every eye,
25 That tears shall drown the wind. I have no spur
To prick the sides of my intent, but only
Vaulting ambition, which o'erleaps itself
And falls on th' other—

[*Enter* Lady Macbeth.]

How now? What news?

Lady Macbeth. He has almost supped. Why have you left the
chamber?

30 **Macbeth.** Hath he asked for me?

Lady Macbeth.   Know you not he has?

Macbeth. We will proceed no further in this business.
He hath honored me of late, and I have bought
Golden opinions from all sorts of people,
Which would be worn now in their newest gloss,
35 Not cast aside so soon.

Lady Macbeth.   Was the hope drunk
Wherein you dressed yourself? Hath it slept since?

**32–35 I have . . . so
soon:** The praises that
Macbeth has received
are, like new clothes,
to be worn, not quickly
thrown away.

35–38 Lady Macbeth
sarcastically suggests
that Macbeth's ambition
must have been drunk,
because it now seems
to have a hangover (**to
look so green and pale**).

And wakes it now, to look so green and pale
At what it did so freely? From this time
Such I account thy love. Art thou afeard
40 To be the same in thine own act and valor
As thou art in desire? Wouldst thou have that
Which thou esteem'st the ornament of life
And live a coward in thine own esteem,
Letting "I dare not" wait upon "I would,"
45 Like the poor cat i' th' adage?

Macbeth.   Prithee, peace.
I dare do all that may become a man.
Who dares do more is none.

Lady Macbeth.   What beast was't, then,
That made you break this enterprise to me?
When you durst do it, then you were a man;
50 And to be more than what you were, you would
Be so much more the man. Nor time nor place
Did then adhere, and yet you would make both.
They have made themselves, and that their fitness now
Does unmake you. I have given suck, and know
55 How tender 'tis to love the babe that milks me.
I would, while it was smiling in my face,
Have plucked my nipple from his boneless gums
And dashed the brains out, had I so sworn as you
Have done to this.

Macbeth.   If we should fail—

Lady Macbeth.   We fail?
60 But screw your courage to the sticking place
And we'll not fail. When Duncan is asleep
(Whereto the rather shall his day's hard journey
Soundly invite him), his two chamberlains
Will I with wine and wassail so convince
65 That memory, the warder of the brain,
Shall be a fume, and the receipt of reason
A limbeck only. When in swinish sleep
Their drenchèd natures lie as in a death,
What cannot you and I perform upon
70 Th' unguarded Duncan? What not put upon
His spongy officers, who shall bear the guilt
Of our great quell?

Macbeth.   Bring forth men-children only,
For thy undaunted mettle should compose
Nothing but males. Will it not be received,

39–45 Lady Macbeth criticizes Macbeth's weakened resolve and compares him to a cat in a proverb (**adage**) who wouldn't catch fish because it feared wet feet.

54 I have given suck: I have nursed a baby.

60 When each string of a guitar or lute is tightened to the peg (**sticking place**), the instrument is ready to be played.

65–67 Lady Macbeth will get the guards so drunk that their reason will become like a still (**limbeck**), producing confused thoughts.

72 quell: murder.

72–74 Bring forth . . . males: Your bold spirit (**undaunted mettle**) is better suited to raising males than females.

75 When we have marked with blood those sleepy two
Of his own chamber and used their very daggers,
That they have done 't?

Lady Macbeth. Who dares receive it other,
As we shall make our griefs and clamor roar
Upon his death?

Macbeth. I am settled and bend up
80 Each corporal agent to this terrible feat.
Away, and mock the time with fairest show.
False face must hide what the false heart doth know.

[*They exit.*]

79–82 Now that Macbeth has made up his mind, every part of his body (**each corporal agent**) is tightened like a bow. He and Lady Macbeth will deceive everyone (**mock the time**), hiding their evil plan with gracious faces.

COLLABORATIVE DISCUSSION With a partner, compare how Banquo and Macbeth each react to the witches' words. What might be the reason for Macbeth's reaction? Cite specific textual evidence from the play to support your ideas.

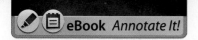
Analyzing the Text

RL 3, RL 4,
RL 5, W 2, L 5a

Cite Text Evidence   Support your responses with evidence from the selection.

1. **Analyze** What is the purpose of the first scene? Explain.

2. **Infer** Reread lines 16–23 of Scene 2. What impression of Macbeth is created by these details?

3. **Draw Conclusions** A **paradox** is an apparent contradiction that reveals a truth. The witches end the first scene with a paradox: "Fair is foul, and foul is fair." Explain the ways in which this contradiction is shown to be true in Act I.

4. **Predict** Review lines 2–14 in Scene 4. What does this description of the previous Thane of Cawdor's actions and ultimate fate **foreshadow**, or hint at, for Macbeth?

5. **Analyze** How is Macbeth's conflict intensified by the events in Scene 4? What lines from his aside in Scene 4 (lines 48–53) develop the audience's understanding of this conflict?

6. **Interpret** Reread Lady Macbeth's soliloquy, lines 35–51, in Scene 5. Why does she ask for the spirits to fill her with "direst cruelty" and "make thick my blood"? What does this speech reveal about her character?

7. **Analyze** Explain the dramatic irony of Duncan's reaction when he arrives at Macbeth's castle.

8. **Draw Conclusions** Review lines 28–32 in Scene 4 and Duncan's lines in Scene 6. How does Duncan's language in these passages convey his character? Explain.

PERFORMANCE TASK

Writing Activity: Analysis How are Macbeth and Lady Macbeth different? Use their major speeches in Scene 7 to contrast their characters.

- First, identify what lines 1–28 reveal about Macbeth as he lists the reasons they should not go ahead with the plan. What does he decide?

- Next, consider what is revealed about Lady Macbeth's character through her reaction to Macbeth's decision and her response in lines 47–59.
- Summarize their key differences in a paragraph.

AS YOU READ Look for details about how Macbeth conceals his plot. Write down any questions you generate during reading.

ACT II

Scene 1 *The court of Macbeth's castle.*

[*Enter* Banquo, *and* Fleance *with a torch before him.*]

Banquo. How goes the night, boy?

Fleance. The moon is down. I have not heard the clock.

Banquo. And she goes down at twelve.

Fleance. I take 't, 'tis later, sir.

Banquo. Hold, take my sword. [*Giving his sword to* Fleance]

There's husbandry in heaven;

5 Their candles are all out. Take thee that too.
A heavy summons lies like lead upon me,
And yet I would not sleep. Merciful powers,
Restrain in me the cursèd thoughts that nature
Gives way to in repose.

[*Enter* Macbeth, *and a* Servant *with a torch.*]

Give me my sword.—Who's there?

10 **Macbeth.** A friend.

Banquo. What, sir, not yet at rest? The King's abed.
He hath been in unusual pleasure, and
Sent forth great largess to your offices.
This diamond he greets your wife withal,
15 By the name of most kind hostess, and shut up
In measureless content. [*He gives* Macbeth *a diamond.*]

Macbeth. Being unprepared,
Our will became the servant to defect,
Which else should free have wrought.

Banquo. All's well.
I dreamt last night of the three Weïrd Sisters.
20 To you they have showed some truth.

Macbeth. I think not of them.
Yet, when we can entreat an hour to serve,
We would spend it in some words upon that business,
If you would grant the time.

Banquo. At your kind'st leisure.

Macbeth. If you shall cleave to my consent, when 'tis,
25 It shall make honor for you.

Banquo. So I lose none
In seeking to augment it, but still keep

4–5 The heavens show economy (**husbandry**) by keeping the lights (**candles**) out—it is a starless night.

6 heavy summons: desire for sleep.

13 largess to your offices: gifts to the servants' quarters.

15 shut up: went to bed.

21 can entreat an hour: both have the time.

24–28 Macbeth asks Banquo for his support (**cleave to my consent**), promising honors in return. Banquo is willing to increase (**augment**) his honor provided he can keep a clear conscience and remain loyal to the king (**keep my bosom . . . clear**).

My bosom franchised and allegiance clear,
I shall be counseled.

Macbeth.   Good repose the while.

Banquo. Thanks, sir. The like to you.

[Banquo *and* Fleance *exit.*]

30 **Macbeth.** Go bid thy mistress, when my drink is ready,
She strike upon the bell. Get thee to bed.

[Servant *exits.*]

Is this a dagger which I see before me,
The handle toward my hand? Come, let me clutch thee.
I have thee not, and yet I see thee still.
35 Art thou not, fatal vision, sensible
To feeling as to sight? or art thou but
A dagger of the mind, a false creation
Proceeding from the heat-oppressèd brain?
I see thee yet, in form as palpable
40 As this which now I draw. [*He draws his dagger.*]
Thou marshal'st me the way that I was going,
And such an instrument I was to use.
Mine eyes are made the fools o' th' other senses
Or else worth all the rest. I see thee still,
45 And, on thy blade and dudgeon, gouts of blood,
Which was not so before. There's no such thing.
It is the bloody business which informs
Thus to mine eyes. Now o'er the one-half world
Nature seems dead, and wicked dreams abuse
50 The curtained sleep. Witchcraft celebrates
Pale Hecate's off'rings, and withered murder,
Alarumed by his sentinel, the wolf,
Whose howl's his watch, thus with his stealthy pace,
With Tarquin's ravishing strides, towards his design
55 Moves like a ghost. Thou sure and firm-set earth,
Hear not my steps, which way they walk, for fear
Thy very stones prate of my whereabouts
And take the present horror from the time,
Which now suits with it. Whiles I threat, he lives.
60 Words to the heat of deeds too cold breath gives.

[*A bell rings.*]

I go, and it is done. The bell invites me.
Hear it not, Duncan, for it is a knell
That summons thee to heaven or to hell.

[*He exits.*]

32–42 Macbeth sees a dagger hanging in midair before him and questions whether it is real (**palpable**) or the illusion of a disturbed (**heat-oppressèd**) mind. The floating, imaginary dagger, which leads (**marshal'st**) him to Duncan's room, prompts him to draw his own dagger.

43–44 Either his eyes are mistaken (**fools**) or his other senses are.

45 He sees drops of blood on the blade and handle.

62 knell: funeral bell.

Scene 2 *Macbeth's castle.*

[*Enter* Lady Macbeth.]

Lady Macbeth. That which hath made them drunk hath made
    me bold.
What hath quenched them hath given me fire. Hark!—Peace.
It was the owl that shrieked, the fatal bellman,
Which gives the stern'st good-night. He is about it.

5 The doors are open, and the surfeited grooms
Do mock their charge with snores. I have drugged their possets,
That death and nature do contend about them
Whether they live or die.

Macbeth [*within*].   Who's there? what, ho!

Lady Macbeth. Alack, I am afraid they have awaked,
10 And 'tis not done. Th' attempt and not the deed
Confounds us. Hark!—I laid their daggers ready;
He could not miss 'em. Had he not resembled
My father as he slept, I had done 't.

[*Enter* Macbeth *with bloody daggers.*]

                      My husband?

Macbeth. I have done the deed. Didst thou not hear a noise?

15 **Lady Macbeth.** I heard the owl scream and the crickets cry.
Did not you speak?

Macbeth.   When?

Lady Macbeth.   Now.

Macbeth.   As I descended?

Lady Macbeth. Ay.

Macbeth.   Hark!—Who lies i' th' second chamber?

Lady Macbeth. Donalbain.

Macbeth.   This is a sorry sight.

Lady Macbeth. A foolish thought, to say a sorry sight.

20 **Macbeth.** There's one did laugh in 's sleep, and one cried
    "Murder!"
That they did wake each other. I stood and heard them.
But they did say their prayers and addressed them
Again to sleep.

Lady Macbeth. There are two lodged together.

Macbeth. One cried "God bless us" and "Amen" the other,
25 As they had seen me with these hangman's hands,

---

3 fatal bellman: town crier.

5 surfeited grooms: drunken servants.

6 possets: drinks.

11 confounds: destroys. If Duncan survives, they will be killed (as his attempted murderers).

25 As: as if. He imagines that the sleepers could see him.

List'ning their fear. I could not say "Amen"
When they did say "God bless us."

Lady Macbeth. Consider it not so deeply.

Macbeth. But wherefore could not I pronounce "Amen"?
30 I had most need of blessing, and "Amen"
Stuck in my throat.

Lady Macbeth.   These deeds must not be thought
After these ways; so, it will make us mad.

Macbeth. Methought I heard a voice cry "Sleep no more!
Macbeth does murder sleep"—the innocent sleep,
35 Sleep that knits up the raveled sleave of care,
The death of each day's life, sore labor's bath,
Balm of hurt minds, great nature's second course,
Chief nourisher in life's feast.

34–38 Sleep eases worries (**knits up the raveled sleave of care**), relieves the aches of physical work (**sore labor's bath**), soothes the anxious (**hurt minds**), and nourishes like food.

Lady Macbeth.   What do you mean?

Macbeth. Still it cried "Sleep no more!" to all the house.
40 "Glamis hath murdered sleep, and therefore Cawdor
Shall sleep no more. Macbeth shall sleep no more."

Lady Macbeth. Who was it that thus cried? Why, worthy thane,
You do unbend your noble strength to think
So brainsickly of things. Go get some water
45 And wash this filthy witness from your hand.—
Why did you bring these daggers from the place?

They must lie there. Go carry them and smear
The sleepy grooms with blood.

Macbeth.   I'll go no more.
I am afraid to think what I have done.
50 Look on 't again I dare not.

Lady Macbeth.   Infirm of purpose!
Give me the daggers. The sleeping and the dead
Are but as pictures. 'Tis the eye of childhood
That fears a painted devil. If he do bleed,
I'll gild the faces of the grooms withal,
55 For it must seem their guilt.

[*She exits with the daggers. Knock within.*]

Macbeth.   Whence is that knocking?
How is 't with me when every noise appalls me?
What hands are here? Ha, they pluck out mine eyes.
Will all great Neptune's ocean wash this blood
Clean from my hand? No, this my hand will rather
60 The multitudinous seas incarnadine,
Making the green one red.

[*Enter* Lady Macbeth.]

Lady Macbeth. My hands are of your color, but I shame
To wear a heart so white.   [*Knock*]

              I hear a knocking
At the south entry. Retire we to our chamber.
65 A little water clears us of this deed.
How easy is it, then! Your constancy
Hath left you unattended.   [*Knock*]

              Hark, more knocking.
Get on your nightgown, lest occasion call us
And show us to be watchers. Be not lost
70 So poorly in your thoughts.

Macbeth. To know my deed 'twere best not know myself.
                      [*Knock*]
Wake Duncan with thy knocking. I would thou couldst.

[*They exit.*]

Scene 3 *Within Macbeth's castle, near the gate.*

[*Knocking within. Enter a* Porter.]

Porter. Here's a knocking indeed! If a man were porter of hell
gate, he should have old turning the key. [*Knock*] Knock, knock,
knock! Who's there, i' th' name of Beelzebub? Here's a farmer
that hanged himself on th' expectation of plenty. Come in time!

54–55 She'll cover
(**gild**) the servants with
blood, blaming them for
the murder.

**59–61 this my hand...
one red:** The blood on
my hand will redden
(**incarnadine**) the seas.

**66–67 Your constancy
... unattended:** Your
courage has left you.

**68–69 lest...
watchers:** in case we
are called for and found
awake (**watchers**), which
would look suspicious.

71 To know...myself:
To come to terms with
what I have done, I must
lose my conscience.

2 old turning the key:
plenty of key turning.
Hell's porter would be
busy in such evil times.

3 Beelzebub: a devil.

5   Have napkins enough about you; here you'll sweat for 't. [*Knock*]
Knock, knock! Who's there, in th' other devil's name? Faith,
here's an equivocator that could swear in both the scales against
either scale, who committed treason enough for God's sake
yet could not equivocate to heaven. O, come in, equivocator.

10   [*Knock*] Knock, knock, knock! Who's there? Faith, here's an
English tailor come hither for stealing out of a French hose.
Come in, tailor. Here you may roast your goose. [*Knock*] Knock,
knock! Never at quiet. —What are you? —But this place is too
cold for hell. I'll devilporter it no further. I had thought to have

15   let in some of all professions that go the primrose way to th'
everlasting bonfire. [*Knock*] Anon, anon! [*The* Porter *opens the
door to* Macduff *and* Lennox.] I pray you, remember the porter.

Macduff. Was it so late, friend, ere you went to bed
That you do lie so late?

20   **Porter.** Faith, sir, we were carousing till the second cock, and
drink, sir, is a great provoker of three things.

Macduff. What three things does drink especially provoke?

Porter. Marry, sir, nose-painting, sleep, and urine. Lechery, sir, it
provokes and unprovokes. It provokes the desire, but it takes

25   away the performance. Therefore much drink may be said
to be an equivocator with lechery. It makes him, and it mars
him; it sets him on, and it takes him off; it persuades him and
disheartens him; makes him stand to and not stand to; in
conclusion, equivocates him in a sleep and, giving him the lie,

30   leaves him.

Macduff. I believe drink gave thee the lie last night.

Porter. That it did, sir, i' th' very throat on me; but I requited
him for his lie, and, I think, being too strong for him, though he
took up my legs sometime, yet I made a shift to cast him.

35   **Macduff.** Is thy master stirring?

[*Enter* Macbeth.]

Our knocking has awaked him. Here he comes.

[Porter *exits.*]

Lennox. Good morrow, noble sir.

Macbeth.   Good morrow, both.

Macduff. Is the King stirring, worthy thane?

Macbeth.   Not yet.

Macduff. He did command me to call timely on him.

40   I have almost slipped the hour.

3–11 The porter pretends he is welcoming a farmer who killed himself after his schemes to get rich (**expectation of plenty**) failed, a double talker (**equivocator**) who perjured himself yet couldn't talk his way into heaven, and a tailor who cheated his customers by skimping on material (**stealing out of a French hose**).

31–34 Alcohol is described as a wrestler thrown off (**cast**) by the porter, who thus paid him back (**requited him**) for disappointment in love. *Cast* also means "to vomit" and "to urinate."

39 timely: early.

40 slipped the hour: missed the time.

Macbeth.   I'll bring you to him.

Macduff. I know this is a joyful trouble to you,
But yet 'tis one.

Macbeth. The labor we delight in physics pain.
This is the door.

43 physics: cures.

Macduff.   I'll make so bold to call,
45 For 'tis my limited service. [Macduff *exits.*]

45 limited service:
appointed duty.

Lennox. Goes the King hence today?

Macbeth. He does. He did appoint so.

Lennox. The night has been unruly. Where we lay,
Our chimneys were blown down and, as they say,
50 Lamentings heard i' th' air, strange screams of death,
And prophesying, with accents terrible,
Of dire combustion and confused events
New hatched to th' woeful time. The obscure bird
Clamored the livelong night. Some say the earth
55 Was feverous and did shake.

Macbeth.   'Twas a rough night.

Lennox. My young remembrance cannot parallel
A fellow to it.

[*Enter* Macduff.]

Macduff.   O horror, horror, horror!
Tongue nor heart cannot conceive nor name thee!

Macbeth and Lennox. What's the matter?

60 **Macduff.** Confusion now hath made his masterpiece.
Most sacrilegious murder hath broke ope
The Lord's anointed temple and stole thence
The life o' th' building.

60–63 Macduff
mourns Duncan's death
as the destruction
(**confusion**) of order
and as sacrilegious,
violating all that is holy.
In Shakespeare's time
the king was believed
to be God's sacred
representative on earth.

Macbeth.   What is 't you say? The life?

Lennox. Mean you his majesty?

65 **Macduff.** Approach the chamber and destroy your sight
With a new Gorgon. Do not bid me speak.
See and then speak yourselves.

[Macbeth *and* Lennox *exit.*]
                         Awake, awake!
Ring the alarum bell.—Murder and treason!
Banquo and Donalbain, Malcolm, awake!
70 Shake off this downy sleep, death's counterfeit,
And look on death itself. Up, up, and see

66 new Gorgon:
Macduff compares the
shocking sight of the
corpse to a Gorgon.
In Greek mythology,
anyone who saw a
Gorgon turned to stone.

70 counterfeit:
imitation.

The great doom's image. Malcolm. Banquo.
As from your graves rise up and walk like sprites
To countenance this horror.—Ring the bell.

[*Bell rings.*]
[*Enter* Lady Macbeth.]

75 **Lady Macbeth.** What's the business,
That such a hideous trumpet calls to parley
The sleepers of the house? Speak, speak!

Macduff.   O gentle lady,
'Tis not for you to hear what I can speak.
The repetition in a woman's ear
80 Would murder as it fell.

[*Enter* Banquo.]

                         O Banquo, Banquo,
Our royal master's murdered.

Lady Macbeth.   Woe, alas!
What, in our house?

Banquo.   Too cruel anywhere. —
Dear Duff, I prithee, contradict thyself
And say it is not so.

[*Enter* Macbeth, Lennox, *and* Ross.]

85 **Macbeth.** Had I but died an hour before this chance,
I had lived a blessèd time; for from this instant
There's nothing serious in mortality.
All is but toys. Renown and grace is dead.
The wine of life is drawn, and the mere lees
90 Is left this vault to brag of.

[*Enter* Malcolm *and* Donalbain.]

Donalbain. What is amiss?

Macbeth.   You are, and do not know 't.
The spring, the head, the fountain of your blood
Is stopped; the very source of it is stopped.

Macduff. Your royal father's murdered.

Malcolm.   O, by whom?

95 **Lennox.** Those of his chamber, as it seemed, had done 't.
Their hands and faces were all badged with blood.
So were their daggers, which unwiped we found
Upon their pillows. They stared and were distracted.
No man's life was to be trusted with them.

72 great doom's image:
a picture like the Last
Judgment, the end of
the world.

73 sprites: spirits. The
spirits of the dead were
supposed to rise on
Judgment Day.

**76 trumpet calls to
parley:** She compares
the clanging bell to a
trumpet used to call
two sides of a battle to
negotiation.

**86–90 for from . . .
brag of:** From now
on, nothing matters
(**there's nothing
serious**) in human life
(**mortality**); even fame
and grace have been
made meaningless. The
good wine of life has
been removed (**drawn**),
leaving only the dregs
(**lees**).

96 badged: marked.

Macbeth. O, yet I do repent me of my fury,
That I did kill them.

Macduff.   Wherefore did you so?

Macbeth. Who can be wise, amazed, temp'rate, and furious,
Loyal, and neutral, in a moment? No man.
Th' expedition of my violent love
105   Outrun the pauser, reason. Here lay Duncan,
His silver skin laced with his golden blood,
And his gashed stabs looked like a breach in nature
For ruin's wasteful entrance; there the murderers,
Steeped in the colors of their trade, their daggers
110   Unmannerly breeched with gore. Who could refrain
That had a heart to love, and in that heart
Courage to make 's love known?

Lady Macbeth.   Help me hence, ho!

Macduff. Look to the lady.

Malcolm [*aside to* Donalbain]. Why do we hold our tongues,
That most may claim this argument for ours?

Donalbain [*aside to* Malcolm].
115   What should be spoken here, where our fate,
Hid in an auger hole, may rush and seize us?
Let's away. Our tears are not yet brewed.

Malcolm [*aside to* Donalbain].
Nor our strong sorrow upon the foot of motion.

Banquo. Look to the lady.

[Lady Macbeth *is assisted to leave.*]

120   And when we have our naked frailties hid,
That suffer in exposure, let us meet
And question this most bloody piece of work
To know it further. Fears and scruples shake us.
In the great hand of God I stand, and thence
125   Against the undivulged pretense I fight
Of treasonous malice.

Macduff.   And so do I.

All.   So all.

Macbeth. Let's briefly put on manly readiness
And meet i' th' hall together.

All.   Well contented.

[*All but* Malcolm *and* Donalbain *exit.*]

104–105 He claims his emotions overpowered his reason, which would have made him pause to think before he killed Duncan's servants.

107 breach: a military term to describe a break in defenses, such as a hole in a castle wall.

112 Lady Macbeth faints.

120–121 Banquo suggests that they all meet to discuss the murder after they have dressed (**our naked frailties hid**), since people are shivering in their nightclothes (**suffer in exposure**).

123–126 Though shaken by fears and doubts (**scruples**), he will fight against the secret plans (**undivulged pretense**) of the traitor.

Malcolm. What will you do? Let's not consort with them.
130 To show an unfelt sorrow is an office
Which the false man does easy. I'll to England.

Donalbain. To Ireland I. Our separated fortune
Shall keep us both the safer. Where we are,
There's daggers in men's smiles. The near in blood,
135 The nearer bloody.

Malcolm. This murderous shaft that's shot
Hath not yet lighted, and our safest way
Is to avoid the aim. Therefore to horse,
And let us not be dainty of leave-taking
But shift away. There's warrant in that theft
140 Which steals itself when there's no mercy left.

[They exit.]

Scene 4 *Outside Macbeth's castle.*

[Enter Ross *with an* Old Man.*]*

Old Man. Threescore and ten I can remember well,
Within the volume of which time I have seen
Hours dreadful and things strange, but this sore night
Hath trifled former knowings.

129–131 Malcolm does not want to join (**consort with**) the others because one of them may have plotted the murder.

139–140 There's . . . left: There's good reason (**warrant**) to steal away from a situation that promises no mercy.

1–4 Nothing the old man has seen in 70 years (**threescore and ten**) has been as strange and terrible (**sore**) as this night. It has made other times seem trivial (**hath trifled**) by comparison.

Ross.   Ha, good father,

5 Thou seest the heavens, as troubled with man's act,
Threaten his bloody stage. By th' clock 'tis day,
And yet dark night strangles the traveling lamp.
Is 't night's predominance or the day's shame
That darkness does the face of earth entomb
10 When living light should kiss it?

Old Man.   'Tis unnatural,
Even like the deed that's done. On Tuesday last
A falcon, tow'ring in her pride of place,
Was by a mousing owl hawked at and killed.

Ross. And Duncan's horses (a thing most strange and certain),
15 Beauteous and swift, the minions of their race,
Turned wild in nature, broke their stalls, flung out,
Contending 'gainst obedience, as they would
Make war with mankind.

Old Man.   'Tis said they eat each other.

Ross. They did so, to th' amazement of mine eyes
20 That looked upon 't.

[*Enter* Macduff.]

               Here comes the good Macduff.—
How goes the world, sir, now?

Macduff.   Why, see you not?

Ross. Is 't known who did this more than bloody deed?

Macduff. Those that Macbeth hath slain.

Ross.   Alas, the day,
What good could they pretend?

Macduff.   They were suborned.
25 Malcolm and Donalbain, the King's two sons,
Are stol'n away and fled, which puts upon them
Suspicion of the deed.

Ross.   'Gainst nature still!
Thriftless ambition, that will ravin up
Thine own lives' means. Then 'tis most like
30 The sovereignty will fall upon Macbeth.

Macduff. He is already named and gone to Scone
To be invested.

Ross.   Where is Duncan's body?

**6–10 By th' clock...
kiss it:** Though daytime,
an unnatural darkness
blots out the sun
(**strangles the traveling
lamp**).

12–13 The owl would
never be expected to
attack a high-flying
(**tow'ring**) falcon, much
less defeat one.

15 minions: best or
favorites.

**17 Contending
'gainst obedience:** The
well-trained horses
rebelliously fought
against all constraints.

24 What...pretend:
Ross wonders what
the servants could
have hoped to achieve
(**pretend**) by killing;
suborned: hired or
bribed.

27–29 He is horrified
by the thought that the
sons could act contrary
to nature (**'gainst
nature still**) because
of wasteful (**thriftless**)
ambition and greedily
destroy (**ravin up**) their
father, the source of
their own life (**thine
own lives' means**).

31–32 Macbeth went
to the traditional
site (**Scone**) where
Scotland's kings were
crowned.

Macduff. Carried to Colmekill,
The sacred storehouse of his predecessors
35 And guardian of their bones.

Ross.   Will you to Scone?

Macduff. No, cousin, I'll to Fife.

Ross.   Well, I will thither.

Macduff. Well, may you see things well done there. Adieu,
Lest our old robes sit easier than our new.

Ross. Farewell, father.

40 **Old Man.** God's benison go with you and with those
That would make good of bad and friends of foes.

[*All exit.*]

40–41 The old man gives his blessing (**benison**) to Macduff and all those who would bring peace to the troubled land.

COLLABORATIVE DISCUSSION How do Macbeth and Lady Macbeth conceal and carry out their plot? With a partner, discuss which parts of the plan go smoothly and which do not. Cite specific textual evidence from the play to support your ideas.

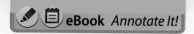

Analyzing the Text

RL 1, RL 2,
RL 3, RL 4,
RL 5, SL 1a

Cite Text Evidence   Support your responses with evidence from the selection.

1. **Analyze** Macbeth's active imagination contributes to his internal conflict. Explain what these passages from Act II reveal about this conflict.

   • the appearance of the dagger (Scene 1, lines 32–48)
   • the voice after the murder (Scene 2, lines 33–41)
   • his refusal to return to the room (Scene 2, lines 48–50)
   • his words after the discovery of Duncan's death (Scene 3, lines 85–90)

2. **Draw Conclusions** How does the porter's scene increase tension and suspense?

3. **Analyze** Explain the dramatic irony of lines 100–112 in Scene 3. Why is Macbeth's action significant?

4. **Identify Patterns** Throughout the play, **symbols**, or objects or ideas that stand for something other than themselves, are used to represent major ideas and themes. What is symbolized by the repeated incidences of images of blood, sleep, and darkness?

5. **Interpret** Explain how Donalbain's statement that "There's daggers in men's smiles" relates to the sons' decision to flee. How is their action interpreted by Duncan's nobles?

6. **Draw Conclusions** What do the images in lines 6–19 of Scene 4 suggest about the act of killing the king? What is foreshadowed about Macbeth's reign by the description in these lines?

7. **Infer** Explain Macduff's attitude toward Macbeth and his coronation. Use specific details from the text to support this inference.

8. **Cite Evidence** What is the mood or atmosphere of Act II? What images or details in characters' speeches help to create this mood?

PERFORMANCE TASK

Speaking Activity: Response to Literature Why does Lady Macbeth faint? Is it a distraction or is it real? Support your conclusion with evidence from the text.

• Jot down ideas about what Lady Macbeth does and says in Act II that might explain why she faints.

• In a small group, discuss these ideas and your interpretation of her action. Together, draw one or more conclusions about her motives.

• Summarize the group discussion and present your ideas to the class.

AS YOU READ Pay attention to the details that describe the condition of Scotland under Macbeth's rule. Write down any questions you generate during reading.

ACT III

Scene 1 *Macbeth's palace at Forres.*

[*Enter* Banquo.]

Banquo. Thou hast it now—King, Cawdor, Glamis, all
As the Weïrd Women promised, and I fear
Thou played'st most foully for 't. Yet it was said
It should not stand in thy posterity,
5 But that myself should be the root and father
Of many kings. If there come truth from them
(As upon thee, Macbeth, their speeches shine),
Why, by the verities on thee made good,
May they not be my oracles as well,
10 And set me up in hope? But hush, no more.

[*Sennet sounded. Enter* Macbeth *as King,* Lady Macbeth, Lennox, Ross, Lords, *and* Attendants.]

[Stage Direction] **Sennet sounded:** A trumpet is sounded.

Macbeth. Here's our chief guest.

Lady Macbeth.   If he had been forgotten,
It had been as a gap in our great feast
And all-thing unbecoming.

Macbeth. Tonight we hold a solemn supper, sir,
15 And I'll request your presence.

14–15 A king usually uses the royal pronoun *we.* Macbeth switches to *I* with Banquo.

Banquo.   Let your Highness
Command upon me, to the which my duties
Are with a most indissoluble tie
Forever knit.

15–18 Banquo says he is duty bound to serve the king.

Macbeth.   Ride you this afternoon?

Banquo. Ay, my good lord.

20 **Macbeth.** We should have else desired your good advice
(Which still hath been both grave and prosperous)
In this day's council, but we'll take tomorrow.
Is 't far you ride?

21 grave and prosperous: thoughtful and profitable.

Banquo. As far, my lord, as will fill up the time
25 'Twixt this and supper. Go not my horse the better,
I must become a borrower of the night
For a dark hour or twain.

25–27 If his horse goes no faster than usual, he'll be back an hour or two (**twain**) after dark.

Macbeth.   Fail not our feast.

Banquo. My lord, I will not.

Macbeth. We hear our bloody cousins are bestowed

30 In England and in Ireland, not confessing
Their cruel parricide, filling their hearers
With strange invention. But of that tomorrow,
When therewithal we shall have cause of state
Craving us jointly. Hie you to horse. Adieu,

35 Till you return at night. Goes Fleance with you?

Banquo. Ay, my good lord. Our time does call upon 's.

Macbeth. I wish your horses swift and sure of foot,
And so I do commend you to their backs.
Farewell.

[Banquo *exits*.]

40 Let every man be master of his time
Till seven at night. To make society
The sweeter welcome, we will keep ourself
Till suppertime alone. While then, God be with you.

[Lords *and all but* Macbeth *and a* Servant *exit*.]

Sirrah, a word with you. Attend those men

45 Our pleasure?

Servant. They are, my lord, without the palace gate.

Macbeth. Bring them before us.

[Servant *exits*.]

                    To be thus is nothing,
But to be safely thus. Our fears in Banquo
Stick deep, and in his royalty of nature

50 Reigns that which would be feared. 'Tis much he dares,
And to that dauntless temper of his mind
He hath a wisdom that doth guide his valor
To act in safety. There is none but he
Whose being I do fear; and under him

55 My genius is rebuked, as it is said
Mark Antony's was by Caesar. He chid the sisters
When first they put the name of king upon me
And bade them speak to him. Then, prophet-like,
They hailed him father to a line of kings.

60 Upon my head they placed a fruitless crown
And put a barren scepter in my grip,
Thence to be wrenched with an unlineal hand,
No son of mine succeeding. If 't be so,
For Banquo's issue have I filed my mind;

65 For them the gracious Duncan have I murdered,
Put rancors in the vessel of my peace

29 bloody cousins: murderous relatives (Malcolm and Donalbain); **bestowed:** settled.

32 strange invention: lies; stories they have invented.

33–34 when . . . jointly: when matters of state will require the attention of us both.

40 be master of his time: do what he wants.

43 while: until.

44–45 sirrah: a term of address to an inferior; **Attend . . . pleasure:** Are they waiting for me?

47–48 To be thus . . . safely thus: To be king is worthless unless my position as king is safe.

51 dauntless temper: fearless temperament.

55–56 Banquo's mere presence forces back (**rebukes**) Macbeth's ruling spirit (**genius**). In ancient Rome, Caesar, who became emperor, had the same effect on his rival, Mark Antony.

60–69 They gave me a childless (**fruitless, barren**) rule, which will be taken away by someone outside my family (**unlineal**). I have committed murder, poisoned (**filed**) my mind, and destroyed my soul (**eternal jewel**) only to benefit Banquo's heirs.

Only for them, and mine eternal jewel
Given to the common enemy of man
To make them kings, the seeds of Banquo kings.
70 Rather than so, come fate into the list,
And champion me to th' utterance.—Who's there?

[*Enter* Servant *and two* Murderers.]

[*To the* Servant] Now go to the door, and stay there till we call.

[Servant *exits.*]

Was it not yesterday we spoke together?

Murderers. It was, so please your Highness.

Macbeth.   Well then, now
75 Have you considered of my speeches? Know
That it was he, in the times past, which held you
So under fortune, which you thought had been
Our innocent self. This I made good to you
In our last conference, passed in probation with you
80 How you were borne in hand, how crossed, the instruments,
Who wrought with them, and all things else that might
To half a soul and to a notion crazed
Say "Thus did Banquo."

First Murderer.   You made it known to us.

Macbeth. I did so, and went further, which is now
85 Our point of second meeting. Do you find
Your patience so predominant in your nature
That you can let this go? Are you so gospeled
To pray for this good man and for his issue,
Whose heavy hand hath bowed you to the grave
90 And beggared yours forever?

First Murderer.   We are men, my liege.

Macbeth. Ay, in the catalogue you go for men,
As hounds and greyhounds, mongrels, spaniels, curs,
Shoughs, water-rugs, and demi-wolves are clept
All by the name of dogs. The valued file
95 Distinguishes the swift, the slow, the subtle,
The housekeeper, the hunter, every one
According to the gift which bounteous nature
Hath in him closed; whereby he does receive
Particular addition, from the bill
100 That writes them all alike. And so of men.
Now, if you have a station in the file,
Not i' th' worst rank of manhood, say 't,
And I will put that business in your bosoms

75–83 Macbeth
supposedly proved
(**passed in probation**)
Banquo's deception
(**how you were borne
in hand**), methods, and
allies. Even a half-wit
(**half a soul**) or a crazed
person would agree that
Banquo caused their
trouble.

87–90 He asks whether
they are so influenced
by the gospel's message
of forgiveness (**so
gospeled**) that they will
pray for Banquo and
his children despite his
harshness, which will
leave their own families
beggars.

91–100 The true
worth of a dog can
be measured only
by examining the
record (**valued file**)
of its special qualities
(**particular addition**).

103–107 Macbeth
will give them a secret
job (**business in your
bosoms**) that will
earn them his loyalty
(**grapples you to
the heart**) and love.
Banquo's death will
make this sick king
healthy.

Whose execution takes your enemy off,
105 Grapples you to the heart and love of us,
Who wear our health but sickly in his life,
Which in his death were perfect.

Second Murderer.   I am one, my liege,
Whom the vile blows and buffets of the world
Hath so incensed that I am reckless what
110 I do to spite the world.

First Murderer.   And I another
So weary with disasters, tugged with fortune,
That I would set my life on any chance,
To mend it or be rid on 't.

111 tugged with: knocked about by.

Macbeth.   Both of you
Know Banquo was your enemy.

Murderers.   True, my lord.

115 **Macbeth.** So is he mine, and in such bloody distance
That every minute of his being thrusts
Against my near'st of life. And though I could
With barefaced power sweep him from my sight
And bid my will avouch it, yet I must not,
120 For certain friends that are both his and mine,
Whose loves I may not drop, but wail his fall
Who I myself struck down. And thence it is
That I to your assistance do make love,

115–117 Banquo is near enough to draw blood, and like a menacing swordsman, his mere presence threatens (**thrusts against**) Macbeth's existence.

119 bid my will avouch it: justify it as my will.

Masking the business from the common eye
125 For sundry weighty reasons.

Second Murderer.   We shall, my lord,
Perform what you command us.

First Murderer.   Though our lives—

Macbeth. Your spirits shine through you. Within this hour at most
I will advise you where to plant yourselves,
Acquaint you with the perfect spy o' th' time,
130 The moment on 't, for 't must be done tonight
And something from the palace; always thought
That I require a clearness. And with him
(To leave no rubs nor botches in the work)
Fleance, his son, that keeps him company,
135 Whose absence is no less material to me
Than is his father's, must embrace the fate
Of that dark hour. Resolve yourselves apart.
I'll come to you anon.

Murderers.   We are resolved, my lord.

Macbeth. I'll call upon you straight. Abide within.

[*Murderers* exit.]

140 It is concluded. Banquo, thy soul's flight,
If it find heaven, must find it out tonight.

[*He exits.*]

Scene 2 *Macbeth's palace at Forres.*

[*Enter* Lady Macbeth *and a* Servant.]

Lady Macbeth. Is Banquo gone from court?

Servant. Ay, madam, but returns again tonight.

Lady Macbeth. Say to the King I would attend his leisure
For a few words.

Servant.   Madam, I will.

[*He exits.*]

Lady Macbeth.   Naught's had, all's spent,
5 Where our desire is got without content.
'Tis safer to be that which we destroy
Than by destruction dwell in doubtful joy.

[*Enter* Macbeth.]

How now, my lord? Why do you keep alone,
Of sorriest fancies your companions making,
10 Using those thoughts which should indeed have died

127 Your spirits shine through you: Your courage is evident.

131–132 something from . . . clearness: The murder must be done away from the palace so that I remain blameless (**I require a clearness**).

135 absence: death.

137 Resolve yourselves apart: Decide in private.

139 straight: soon.

4–7 Nothing (naught) has been gained; everything has been wasted (**spent**). It would be better to be dead like Duncan than to live in uncertain joy.

With them they think on? Things without all remedy
Should be without regard. What's done is done.

Macbeth. We have scorched the snake, not killed it.
She'll close and be herself whilst our poor malice
15 Remains in danger of her former tooth.
But let the frame of things disjoint, both the worlds suffer,
Ere we will eat our meal in fear, and sleep
In the affliction of these terrible dreams
That shake us nightly. Better be with the dead,
20 Whom we, to gain our peace, have sent to peace,
Than on the torture of the mind to lie
In restless ecstasy. Duncan is in his grave.
After life's fitful fever he sleeps well.
Treason has done his worst; nor steel nor poison,
25 Malice domestic, foreign levy, nothing
Can touch him further.

Lady Macbeth.   Come on, gentle my lord,
Sleek o'er your rugged looks. Be bright and jovial
Among your guests tonight.

Macbeth.   So shall I, love,
And so I pray be you. Let your remembrance
30 Apply to Banquo; present him eminence
Both with eye and tongue: unsafe the while that we
Must lave our honors in these flattering streams
And make our faces vizards to our hearts,
Disguising what they are.

Lady Macbeth.   You must leave this.

35 **Macbeth.** O, full of scorpions is my mind, dear wife!
Thou know'st that Banquo and his Fleance lives.

Lady Macbeth. But in them Nature's copy's not eterne.

Macbeth. There's comfort yet; they are assailable.
Then be thou jocund. Ere the bat hath flown
40 His cloistered flight, ere to black Hecate's summons
The shard-borne beetle with his drowsy hums
Hath rung night's yawning peal, there shall be done
A deed of dreadful note.

Lady Macbeth.   What's to be done?

Macbeth. Be innocent of the knowledge, dearest chuck,
45 Till thou applaud the deed.—Come, seeling night,
Scarf up the tender eye of pitiful day,
And with thy bloody and invisible hand
Cancel and tear to pieces that great bond

16–22 He would rather have the world fall apart (**the frame of things disjoint**) than be afflicted with such fears and nightmares. Death is preferable to life on the torture rack of mental anguish (**restless ecstasy**).

27 sleek: smooth.

30 present him eminence: pay special attention to him.

32 lave ... streams: wash (**lave**) our honor in streams of flattery—that is, falsify our feelings.

33 vizards: masks.

37 in them ... not eterne: Nature did not give them immortality.

39–43 jocund: cheerful; merry; **Ere the bat ... note:** Before nightfall, when the bats and beetles fly, something dreadful will happen.

44 chuck: chick (a term of affection).

45 seeling: blinding.

48 great bond: Banquo's life.

Which keeps me pale. Light thickens, and the crow
50 Makes wing to th' rooky wood.
Good things of day begin to droop and drowse,
Whiles night's black agents to their preys do rouse.—
Thou marvel'st at my words, but hold thee still.
Things bad begun make strong themselves by ill.
55 So prithee go with me.

[*They exit.*]

Scene 3 *A park near the palace.*

[*Enter three* Murderers.]

First Murderer. But who did bid thee join with us?

Third Murderer.   Macbeth.

Second Murderer [*to the* First Murderer].
He needs not our mistrust, since he delivers
Our offices and what we have to do
To the direction just.

First Murderer.   Then stand with us.—
5 The west yet glimmers with some streaks of day.
Now spurs the lated traveler apace
To gain the timely inn, and near approaches
The subject of our watch.

Third Murderer.   Hark, I hear horses.

Banquo [*within*]. Give us a light there, ho!

Second Murderer.   Then 'tis he. The rest
10 That are within the note of expectation
Already are i' th' court.

First Murderer.   His horses go about.

Third Murderer. Almost a mile; but he does usually
(So all men do) from hence to th' palace gate
Make it their walk.

[*Enter* Banquo *and* Fleance, *with a torch.*]

Second Murderer. A light, a light!

Third Murderer.   'Tis he.

15 **First Murderer.** Stand to 't.

Banquo. It will be rain tonight.

First Murderer.   Let it come down!

[*The three* Murderers *attack.*]

Banquo. O, treachery! Fly, good Fleance, fly, fly, fly!
Thou mayst revenge—O slave!

50 rooky: gloomy;
also, filled with rooks, or
crows.

54 Things brought
about through evil need
additional evil to make
them strong.

2–5 He needs . . . just:
Macbeth should not be
distrustful, since he gave
us the orders (**offices**)
and we plan to follow his
directions exactly.

6 lated: tardy; late.

9 Give us a light:
Banquo, nearing the
palace, calls for servants
to bring a light.

**9–11 Then 'tis
. . . court:** It must be
Banquo, since all the
other expected guests
are already in the palace.

15 Stand to 't: Be
prepared.

**18 Thou mayst
revenge:** You might live
to avenge my death.

[*He dies.* Fleance *exits.*]

Third Murderer. Who did strike out the light?

First Murderer.   Was 't not the way?

19 **Was 't not the way:** Isn't that what we were supposed to do?

20 **Third Murderer.** There's but one down. The son is fled.

Second Murderer. We have lost best half of our affair.

First Murderer. Well, let's away and say how much is done.

[*They exit.*]

Scene 4 *The hall in the palace.*

[*Banquet prepared. Enter* Macbeth, Lady Macbeth, Ross, Lennox, Lords, *and* Attendants.]

Macbeth. You know your own degrees; sit down. At first
And last, the hearty welcome.

1 **your own degrees:** where your rank entitles you to sit.

[*They sit.*]

Lords.   Thanks to your Majesty.

Macbeth. Ourself will mingle with society
And play the humble host.

5 Our hostess keeps her state, but in best time
We will require her welcome.

5 **keeps her state:** sits on her throne rather than at the banquet table.

Lady Macbeth. Pronounce it for me, sir, to all our friends,
For my heart speaks they are welcome.

[*Enter* First Murderer *to the door.*]

Macbeth. See, they encounter thee with their hearts' thanks.
10 Both sides are even. Here I'll sit i' th' midst.
Be large in mirth. Anon we'll drink a measure
The table round. [*Approaching the* Murderer] There's blood upon
    thy face.

11 **measure:** toast. Macbeth keeps talking to his wife and guests as he casually edges toward the door to speak privately with the murderer.

Murderer. 'Tis Banquo's then.

Macbeth. 'Tis better thee without than he within.
15 Is he dispatched?

15 **dispatched:** killed.

Murderer. My lord, his throat is cut. That I did for him.

Macbeth. Thou art the best o' th' cutthroats,
Yet he's good that did the like for Fleance.
If thou didst it, thou art the nonpareil.

19 **nonpareil:** best.

20 **Murderer.** Most royal sir, Fleance is 'scaped.

Macbeth [*aside*]. Then comes my fit again. I had else been
    perfect,
Whole as the marble, founded as the rock,
As broad and general as the casing air.

23 **casing:** surrounding.

But now I am cabined, cribbed, confined, bound in
25 To saucy doubts and fears.—But Banquo's safe?

Murderer. Ay, my good lord. Safe in a ditch he bides,
With twenty trenchèd gashes on his head,
The least a death to nature.

Macbeth.   Thanks for that.
There the grown serpent lies. The worm that's fled
30 Hath nature that in time will venom breed,
No teeth for th' present. Get thee gone. Tomorrow
We'll hear ourselves again.

[Murderer *exits*.]

Lady Macbeth.   My royal lord,
You do not give the cheer. The feast is sold
That is not often vouched, while 'tis a-making,
35 'Tis given with welcome. To feed were best at home;
From thence, the sauce to meat is ceremony;
Meeting were bare without it.

[*Enter the Ghost of* Banquo, *and sits in* Macbeth's *place*.]

Macbeth [*to* Lady Macbeth]. Sweet remembrancer!—
Now, good digestion wait on appetite
And health on both!

Lennox.   May't please your Highness sit.

40 **Macbeth.** Here had we now our country's honor roofed,
Were the graced person of our Banquo present,
Who may I rather challenge for unkindness
Than pity for mischance.

Ross.   His absence, sir,
Lays blame upon his promise. Please 't your Highness
45 To grace us with your royal company?

Macbeth. The table's full.

Lennox.   Here is a place reserved, sir.

Macbeth. Where?

Lennox. Here, my good lord. What is 't that moves your Highness?

Macbeth. Which of you have done this?

Lords.   What, my good lord?

50 **Macbeth** [*to the* Ghost]. Thou canst not say I did it. Never shake
Thy gory locks at me.

Ross. Gentlemen, rise. His Highness is not well.

29 worm: little serpent, that is, Fleance.

31 no teeth for th' present: too young to cause harm right now.

32 hear ourselves: talk together.

32–37 Macbeth must not forget his duties as host. A feast will be no different from a meal that one pays for unless the host gives his guests courteous attention (**ceremony**), the best part of any meal.

37 sweet remembrancer: a term of affection for his wife, who has reminded him of his duty.

40–43 The best people of Scotland would all be under Macbeth's roof if Banquo were present too. He hopes Banquo's absence is due to rudeness rather than to some accident (**mischance**).

46 Macbeth finally notices that Banquo's ghost is present and sitting in the king's chair.

Lady Macbeth. Sit, worthy friends. My lord is often thus
And hath been from his youth. Pray you, keep seat.
55 The fit is momentary; upon a thought
He will again be well. If much you note him
You shall offend him and extend his passion.
Feed and regard him not. [*Drawing* Macbeth *aside*] Are you a man?

Macbeth. Ay, and a bold one, that dare look on that
60 Which might appall the devil.

Lady Macbeth.   O, proper stuff !
This is the very painting of your fear.
This is the air-drawn dagger which you said
Led you to Duncan. O, these flaws and starts,
Impostors to true fear, would well become
65 A woman's story at a winter's fire,
Authorized by her grandam. Shame itself!
Why do you make such faces? When all's done,
You look but on a stool.

Macbeth. Prithee see there. Behold, look! [*To the* Ghost] Lo, how
     say you?
70 Why, what care I? If thou canst nod, speak too.—
If charnel houses and our graves must send
Those that we bury back, our monuments
Shall be the maws of kites.

[Ghost *exits*.]

Lady Macbeth.   What, quite unmanned in folly?

60–68 She dismisses his hallucination as utter nonsense (**proper stuff**). His outbursts (**flaws and starts**) are the product of imaginary fears (**impostors to true fear**) and are unmanly, the kind of behavior described in a woman's story.

71–73 If burial vaults (**charnel houses**) give back the dead, then we may as well throw our bodies to the birds (**kites**), whose stomachs (**maws**) will become our tombs (**monuments**).

Macbeth. If I stand here, I saw him.

Lady Macbeth.   Fie, for shame!

75 **Macbeth.** Blood hath been shed ere now, i' th' olden time,
Ere humane statute purged the gentle weal;
Ay, and since too, murders have been performed
Too terrible for the ear. The time has been
That, when the brains were out, the man would die,
80 And there an end. But now they rise again
With twenty mortal murders on their crowns
And push us from our stools. This is more strange
Than such a murder is.

Lady Macbeth.   My worthy lord,
Your noble friends do lack you.

Macbeth.   I do forget.—
85 Do not muse at me, my most worthy friends.
I have a strange infirmity, which is nothing
To those that know me. Come, love and health to all.
Then I'll sit down.—Give me some wine. Fill full.

[*Enter* Ghost.]

I drink to the general joy o' th' whole table
90 And to our dear friend Banquo, whom we miss.
Would he were here! To all and him we thirst,
And all to all.

Lords.   Our duties, and the pledge.

[*They raise their drinking cups.*]

Macbeth [*to the* Ghost]. Avaunt, and quit my sight! Let the earth
        hide thee.
Thy bones are marrowless; thy blood is cold;
95 Thou hast no speculation in those eyes
Which thou dost glare with.

Lady Macbeth.   Think of this, good peers,
But as a thing of custom. 'Tis no other;
Only it spoils the pleasure of the time.

Macbeth [*to the* Ghost]. What man dare, I dare.
100 Approach thou like the rugged Russian bear,
The armed rhinoceros, or th' Hyrcan tiger;
Take any shape but that, and my firm nerves
Shall never tremble. Or be alive again
And dare me to the desert with thy sword.
105 If trembling I inhabit then, protest me

75–78 Macbeth desperately tries to justify his murder of Banquo. Murder has been common from ancient times to the present, though laws (**humane statute**) have tried to rid civilized society (**gentle weal**) of violence.

85 muse: wonder.

93–96 avaunt: go away. Macbeth tells Banquo that he is only a ghost, with unreal bones, cold blood, and no consciousness (**speculation**).

99–104 Macbeth would be willing to face Banquo in any other form, even his living self.

105–106 If trembling . . . girl: If I still tremble, call me a girl's doll.

The baby of a girl. Hence, horrible shadow!
Unreal mock'ry, hence!

[Ghost *exits.*]
                              Why, so, being gone,
I am a man again.—Pray you sit still.

Lady Macbeth. You have displaced the mirth, broke the good
   meeting
110 With most admired disorder.

Macbeth.   Can such things be
And overcome us like a summer's cloud,
Without our special wonder? You make me strange
Even to the disposition that I owe,
When now I think you can behold such sights
115 And keep the natural ruby of your cheeks
When mine is blanched with fear.

Ross.   What sights, my lord?

Lady Macbeth. I pray you speak not. He grows worse and worse.
Question enrages him. At once, good night.
Stand not upon the order of your going,
120 But go at once.

Lennox.   Good night, and better health
Attend his Majesty.

Lady Macbeth.   A kind good night to all.

[Lords *and all but* Macbeth *and* Lady Macbeth *exit.*]

Macbeth. It will have blood, they say; blood will have blood.
Stones have been known to move, and trees to speak;
Augurs and understood relations have
125 By maggot pies and choughs and rooks brought forth
The secret'st man of blood.—What is the night?

Lady Macbeth. Almost at odds with morning, which is which.

Macbeth. How say'st thou that Macduff denies his person
At our great bidding?

Lady Macbeth.   Did you send to him, sir?

130 **Macbeth.** I hear it by the way; but I will send.
There's not a one of them but in his house
I keep a servant fee'd. I will tomorrow
(And betimes I will) to the Weïrd Sisters.
More shall they speak, for now I am bent to know
135 By the worst means the worst. For mine own good,
All causes shall give way. I am in blood

110 admired: astonishing.

110–116 Macbeth is bewildered by his wife's calm, which makes him seem a stranger to himself (**strange even to the disposition that I owe**): she has all the courage, while he is white (**blanched**) with fear.

119 Stand . . . going: Don't worry about the proper formalities of leaving.

122–126 Macbeth fears that Banquo's murder (**it**) will be revenged by his own murder. Stones, trees, or talking birds (**maggot pies and choughs and rooks**) may reveal the hidden knowledge (**augurs**) of his guilt.

128–129 How say'st . . . bidding: What do you think of Macduff's refusal to come?

131–132 Macbeth has paid (**fee'd**) household servants to spy on every noble, including Macduff.

133 betimes: early.

134 bent: determined.

135–140 Macbeth will do anything to protect himself. He will act on his unnatural (**strange**) thoughts without having examined (**scanned**) them.

Stepped in so far that, should I wade no more,
Returning were as tedious as go o'er.
Strange things I have in head, that will to hand,
140 Which must be acted ere they may be scanned.

Lady Macbeth. You lack the season of all natures, sleep.

Macbeth. Come, we'll to sleep. My strange and self-abuse
Is the initiate fear that wants hard use.
We are yet but young in deed.

[*They exit.*]

Scene 5 *A heath.*

[*Thunder. Enter the three* Witches, *meeting* Hecate.]

First Witch. Why, how now, Hecate? You look angerly.

Hecate. Have I not reason, beldams as you are,
Saucy and overbold, how did you dare
To trade and traffic with Macbeth
5 In riddles and affairs of death,
And I, the mistress of your charms,
The close contriver of all harms,
Was never called to bear my part
Or show the glory of our art?
10 And which is worse, all you have done
Hath been but for a wayward son,
Spiteful and wrathful, who, as others do,
Loves for his own ends, not for you.
But make amends now. Get you gone,
15 And at the pit of Acheron
Meet me i' th' morning. Thither he
Will come to know his destiny.
Your vessels and your spells provide,
Your charms and everything beside.
20 I am for th' air. This night I'll spend
Unto a dismal and a fatal end.
Great business must be wrought ere noon.
Upon the corner of the moon
There hangs a vap'rous drop profound.
25 I'll catch it ere it come to ground,
And that, distilled by magic sleights,
Shall raise such artificial sprites
As by the strength of their illusion
Shall draw him on to his confusion.
30 He shall spurn fate, scorn death, and bear
His hopes 'bove wisdom, grace, and fear.

141 season: preservative.

142–144 His vision of the ghost (**strange and self-abuse**) is only the result of a beginner's fear (**initiate fear**), to be cured with practice (**hard use**).

2 beldams: hags.

13 loves . . . you: cares only about his own goals, not about you.

15 Acheron: a river in hell, according to Greek mythology.

20–21 This . . . end: Tonight I'm working for a disastrous (**dismal**) and fatal end for Macbeth.

23–29 Hecate will obtain a magical drop from the moon, treat it with secret art, and so create spirits (**artificial sprites**) that will lead Macbeth to his destruction (**confusion**).

And you all know, security
Is mortals' chiefest enemy.

[*Music and a song*]

Hark! I am called. My little spirit, see,
35 Sits in a foggy cloud and stays for me.

[*Hecate exits.*]

[*Sing within "Come away, come away," etc.*]

First Witch. Come, let's make haste. She'll soon be back again.

[*They exit.*]

Scene 6 *The palace at Forres.*

[*Enter* Lennox *and another* Lord.]

Lennox. My former speeches have but hit your thoughts,
Which can interpret farther. Only I say
Things have been strangely borne. The gracious Duncan
Was pitied of Macbeth; marry, he was dead.
5 And the right valiant Banquo walked too late,
Whom you may say, if 't please you, Fleance killed,
For Fleance fled. Men must not walk too late.
Who cannot want the thought how monstrous
It was for Malcolm and for Donalbain
10 To kill their gracious father? Damnèd fact,
How it did grieve Macbeth! Did he not straight
In pious rage the two delinquents tear
That were the slaves of drink and thralls of sleep?
Was not that nobly done? Ay, and wisely, too,
15 For 'twould have angered any heart alive
To hear the men deny 't. So that I say
He has borne all things well. And I do think
That had he Duncan's sons under his key
(As, an 't please heaven, he shall not) they should find
20 What 'twere to kill a father. So should Fleance.
But peace. For from broad words, and 'cause he failed
His presence at the tyrant's feast, I hear
Macduff lives in disgrace. Sir, can you tell
Where he bestows himself?

Lord.   The son of Duncan
25 (From whom this tyrant holds the due of birth)
Lives in the English court and is received
Of the most pious Edward with such grace
That the malevolence of fortune nothing
Takes from his high respect. Thither Macduff
30 Is gone to pray the holy king upon his aid

34–35 Hecate has a demon helper (**my little spirit**), to which she is raised by pulley to "the heavens" of the stage.

1–3 Lennox and the other lord have shared suspicions of Macbeth.

6–7 Fleeing the scene of the crime must make Fleance guilty of his father's murder.

8–10 Everyone agrees on the horror of Duncan's murder by his sons.

12 pious: holy.

21 from broad words: because of his frank talk.

24 bestows himself: is staying.

25 Macbeth keeps Malcolm from his rightful throne.

27 Edward: Edward the Confessor, king of England from 1042 to 1066, a man known for his virtue and religion.

28–29 that . . . respect: Despite his bad fortune, Malcolm is treated respectfully by Edward.

29–37 Macduff wants the king to persuade the people of Northumberland and their earl, Siward, to join Malcolm's cause.

To wake Northumberland and warlike Siward
That, by the help of these (with Him above
To ratify the work), we may again
Give to our tables meat, sleep to our nights,
35 Free from our feasts and banquets bloody knives,
Do faithful homage, and receive free honors,
All which we pine for now. And this report
Hath so exasperate the King that he
Prepares for some attempt of war.

Lennox.   Sent he to Macduff?

40 **Lord.** He did, and with an absolute "Sir, not I,"
The cloudy messenger turns me his back
And hums, as who should say, "You'll rue the time
That clogs me with this answer."

Lennox.   And that well might
Advise him to a caution t' hold what distance
45 His wisdom can provide. Some holy angel
Fly to the court of England and unfold
His message ere he come, that a swift blessing
May soon return to this our suffering country
Under a hand accursed.

Lord.   I'll send my prayers with him.

[*They exit.*]

40–43 The messenger, fearing Macbeth's anger, was unhappy (**cloudy**) with Macduff's refusal to cooperate. Because Macduff burdens (**clogs**) him with bad news, he will not hurry back.

COLLABORATIVE DISCUSSION Are the people happy about Macbeth's rule? Why or why not? With a partner, discuss what is revealed about the way in which Macbeth governs. Cite specific textual evidence from the play to support your ideas.

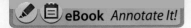
Analyzing the Text

RL 1, RL 3,
RL 4, RL 5, W 2

> *Cite Text Evidence* Support your responses with evidence from the selection.

1. **Infer** Reread lines 47–56 in Scene 1. Why does Macbeth fear Banquo and feel threatened by his "being"? What is suggested about Macbeth's character through his action of hiring murderers to carry out his plan?

2. **Analyze** What do these passages in Scene 2 suggest about the effect of Duncan's death on Macbeth, Lady Macbeth, and their relationship?

    - lines 4–7 ("Nought's had, all's spent . . . doubtful joy.")
    - lines 16–26 ("But let the frame of things disjoint . . . him further.")
    - lines 44–55 ("Be innocent of the knowledge . . . go with me.")

3. **Draw Conclusions** What does Fleance's escape suggest about Macbeth's luck?

4. **Analyze** What does Banquo's ghost in Scene 4 represent? Explain how the presence of the ghost affects Lady Macbeth's behavior, even though she cannot see it.

5. **Compare** Review lines 135–140 in Scene 4. In what way does this speech reveal a change in Macbeth's attitude from how he has felt in the past about his deeds?

6. **Draw Conclusions** Some critics believe that Scene 5 was not part of the original text but was added to the play later. What is the purpose of Scene 5?

7. **Analyze** Review Lennox's speech in lines 1–20 of Scene 6. What words and phrases in this speech convey an ironic tone?

8. **Predict** What possible plot developments are foreshadowed in Scene 6? Cite text evidence to support your prediction.

PERFORMANCE TASK

Writing Activity: Analysis How does dramatic irony intensify the impact of Act III?

- Create a three-column chart with these headings: *Lines; What characters do or say; What the audience knows*.
- With a partner, identify the two strongest instances of dramatic irony in Act III, and complete the chart with details from those instances.

- Using details from your chart, discuss in a paragraph or two the impact of dramatic irony on the audience's understanding of Macbeth's character.

AS YOU READ Pay attention to details that reveal Macbeth's willingness to embrace evil. Write down any questions you generate during reading.

ACT IV

Scene 1 *A cave. In the middle, a boiling cauldron.*

[*Thunder. Enter the three* Witches.]

First Witch. Thrice the brinded cat hath mewed.

Second Witch. Thrice, and once the hedge-pig whined.

Third Witch. Harpier cries "'Tis time, 'tis time!"

First Witch. Round about the cauldron go;
5　In the poisoned entrails throw.
　Toad, that under cold stone
　Days and nights has thirty-one
　Sweltered venom sleeping got,
　Boil thou first i' th' charmed pot.

[*The* Witches *circle the cauldron.*]

10　**All.** Double, double toil and trouble;
　Fire burn, and cauldron bubble.

Second Witch. Fillet of a fenny snake
　In the cauldron boil and bake.
　Eye of newt and toe of frog,
15　Wool of bat and tongue of dog,
　Adder's fork and blindworm's sting,
　Lizard's leg and howlet's wing,
　For a charm of powerful trouble,
　Like a hell-broth boil and bubble.

20　**All.** Double, double toil and trouble;
　Fire burn, and cauldron bubble.

Third Witch. Scale of dragon, tooth of wolf,
　Witch's mummy, maw and gulf
　Of the ravined salt-sea shark,
25　Root of hemlock digged i' th' dark,
　Liver of blaspheming Jew,
　Gall of goat and slips of yew
　Slivered in the moon's eclipse,
　Nose of Turk and Tartar's lips,
30　Finger of birth-strangled babe
　Ditch-delivered by a drab,
　Make the gruel thick and slab.
　Add thereto a tiger's chaudron
　For th' ingredient of our cauldron.

1–3 Magical signals and the call of the third witch's attending demon (**harpier**) tell the witches to begin.

4–34 The witches are stirring up a magical stew to bring trouble to humanity. Their recipe includes intestines (**entrails, chaudron**), a slice (**fillet**) of snake, eye of salamander (**newt**), snake tongue (**adder's fork**), a lizard (**blindworm**), a baby owl's (**howlet's**) wing, a shark's stomach and gullet (**maw and gulf**), the finger of a baby strangled by a prostitute (**drab**), and other gruesome ingredients. They stir their brew until it is thick and slimy (**slab**).

35 **All.** Double, double toil and trouble;
Fire burn, and cauldron bubble.

Second Witch. Cool it with a baboon's blood.
Then the charm is firm and good.

[*Enter* Hecate *and the other three* Witches.]

Hecate. O, well done! I commend your pains,
40 And everyone shall share i' th' gains.
And now about the cauldron sing
Like elves and fairies in a ring,
Enchanting all that you put in.

[*Music and a song: "Black Spirits," etc.* Hecate *exits.*]

Second Witch. By the pricking of my thumbs,
45 Something wicked this way comes.
Open, locks,
Whoever knocks.

[*Enter* Macbeth.]

Macbeth. How now, you secret, black, and midnight hags?
What is 't you do?

All.   A deed without a name.

50 **Macbeth.** I conjure you by that which you profess
(Howe'er you come to know it), answer me.
Though you untie the winds and let them fight
Against the churches, though the yeasty waves
Confound and swallow navigation up,
55 Though bladed corn be lodged and trees blown down,
Though castles topple on their warders' heads,
Though palaces and pyramids do slope
Their heads to their foundations, though the treasure
Of nature's germens tumble all together
60 Even till destruction sicken, answer me
To what I ask you.

First Witch.   Speak.

Second Witch.   Demand.

Third Witch.   We'll answer.

First Witch. Say if th' hadst rather hear it from our mouths
Or from our masters'.

Macbeth.   Call 'em. Let me see 'em.

First Witch. Pour in sow's blood that hath eaten
65 Her nine farrow; grease that's sweaten
From the murderers' gibbet throw
Into the flame.

50–61 Macbeth calls upon (**conjure**) the witches in the name of their dark magic (**that which you profess**). Though they unleash winds to topple churches and make foaming (**yeasty**) waves to destroy (**confound**) ships, though they flatten wheat (**corn**) fields, destroy buildings, and reduce nature's order to chaos by mixing all seeds (**germens**) together, he demands an answer to his question.

63 masters: the demons whom the witches serve.

65–66 farrow: newborn pigs; **grease . . . gibbet:** grease from a gallows where murderers were hung.

All.   Come high or low;
Thyself and office deftly show.

[*Thunder. First Apparition,* an Armed Head.]

Macbeth. Tell me, thou unknown power—

First Witch.   He knows thy thought.
70 Hear his speech but say thou naught.

First Apparition. Macbeth! Macbeth! Macbeth! Beware Macduff!
Beware the Thane of Fife! Dismiss me. Enough.

[*He descends.*]

Macbeth. Whate'er thou art, for thy good caution, thanks.
Thou hast harped my fear aright. But one word more—

75 **First Witch.** He will not be commanded. Here's another
More potent than the first.

[*Thunder. Second Apparition,* a Bloody Child.]

Second Apparition. Macbeth! Macbeth! Macbeth!—

Macbeth. Had I three ears, I'd hear thee.

Second Apparition. Be bloody, bold, and resolute. Laugh to scorn
80 The power of man, for none of woman born
Shall harm Macbeth.

[*He descends.*]

Macbeth. Then live, Macduff; what need I fear of thee?
But yet I'll make assurance double sure
And take a bond of fate. Thou shalt not live,
85 That I may tell pale-hearted fear it lies,
And sleep in spite of thunder.

[*Thunder. Third Apparition,* a Child Crowned, with a tree in his hand.]

                What is this
That rises like the issue of a king
And wears upon his baby brow the round
And top of sovereignty?

All.   Listen, but speak not to 't.

90 **Third Apparition.** Be lion-mettled, proud, and take no care
Who chafes, who frets, or where conspirers are.
Macbeth shall never vanquished be until
Great Birnam Wood to high Dunsinane Hill
Shall come against him.   [*He descends.*]

Macbeth.   That will never be.
95 Who can impress the forest, bid the tree

[Stage Direction] Each of the three apparitions holds a clue to Macbeth's future.

74 harped: guessed.

84 The murder of Macduff will give Macbeth a guarantee (**bond**) of his fate and put his fears to rest.

87 issue: child.

88–89 the round and top: the crown.

90–94 The third apparition tells Macbeth to take courage. He cannot be defeated unless Birnam Wood travels the 12-mile distance to Dunsinane Hill, where his castle is located.

95 impress: force into service.

Unfix his earthbound root? Sweet bodements, good!
Rebellious dead, rise never till the wood
Of Birnam rise, and our high-placed Macbeth
Shall live the lease of nature, pay his breath
100 To time and mortal custom. Yet my heart
Throbs to know one thing. Tell me, if your art
Can tell so much: shall Banquo's issue ever
Reign in this kingdom?

All.   Seek to know no more.

Macbeth. I will be satisfied. Deny me this,
105 And an eternal curse fall on you! Let me know!

[*Cauldron sinks. Hautboys.*]

Why sinks that cauldron? And what noise is this?

First Witch. Show.

Second Witch. Show.

Third Witch. Show.

110 **All.** Show his eyes, and grieve his heart.
Come like shadows; so depart.

[*A show of eight kings, the eighth king with a glass in his hand,
and* Banquo *last.*]

Macbeth. Thou art too like the spirit of Banquo. Down!
Thy crown does sear mine eyeballs. And thy hair,
Thou other gold-bound brow, is like the first.
115 A third is like the former.—Filthy hags,
Why do you show me this?—A fourth? Start, eyes!
What, will the line stretch out to th' crack of doom?
Another yet? A seventh? I'll see no more.
And yet the eighth appears who bears a glass
120 Which shows me many more, and some I see
That twofold balls and treble scepters carry.
Horrible sight! Now I see 'tis true,

96 bodements: prophecies.

97–100 Macbeth boasts that he will never again be troubled by ghosts (**rebellious dead**) and that he will live out his expected life span (**lease of nature**). He believes he will die (**pay his breath**) by natural causes (**mortal custom**).

[Stage Direction]
A show . . . : Macbeth next sees eight kings, the last carrying a mirror (**glass**). According to legend, Fleance escaped to England, where he founded the Stuart family, to which King James belonged.

112–124 All eight kings look like Banquo. The mirror shows a future with many more Banquo look-alikes as kings. The twofold balls and treble scepters foretell the union of Scotland and England in 1603, the year that James became king of both realms. Banquo, his hair matted (**boltered**) with blood, claims all the kings as his descendants.

For the blood-boltered Banquo smiles upon me
And points at them for his.

                       [*The* Apparitions *disappear.*]
                       What, is this so?

125 **First Witch.** Ay, sir, all this is so. But why
Stands Macbeth thus amazedly?
Come, sisters, cheer we up his sprites
And show the best of our delights.
I'll charm the air to give a sound
130 While you perform your antic round,
That this great king may kindly say
Our duties did his welcome pay.

[*Music. The* Witches *dance and vanish.*]

Macbeth. Where are they? Gone? Let this pernicious hour
Stand aye accursèd in the calendar!—
135 Come in, without there.

[*Enter* Lennox.]

Lennox.   What's your Grace's will?

Macbeth. Saw you the Weïrd Sisters?

Lennox.   No, my lord.

Macbeth. Came they not by you?

Lennox.   No, indeed, my lord.

Macbeth. Infected be the air whereon they ride,
And damned all those that trust them! I did hear
140 The galloping of horse. Who was 't came by?

Lennox. 'Tis two or three, my lord, that bring you word
Macduff is fled to England.

Macbeth.   Fled to England?

Lennox. Ay, my good lord.

Macbeth [*aside*]. Time, thou anticipat'st my dread exploits.
145 The flighty purpose never is o'ertook
Unless the deed go with it. From this moment
The very firstlings of my heart shall be
The firstlings of my hand. And even now,
To crown my thoughts with acts, be it thought and done:
150 The castle of Macduff I will surprise,
Seize upon Fife, give to th' edge o' th' sword
His wife, his babes, and all unfortunate souls
That trace him in his line. No boasting like a fool;
This deed I'll do before this purpose cool.

133 **pernicious:** evil.

134 **aye:** always.

135 After the witches
vanish, Macbeth hears
noises outside the cave
and calls out.

144–156 Frustrated in
his desire to kill Macduff,
Macbeth blames his own
hesitation, which gave
his enemy time to flee.
He concludes that one's
plans (**flighty purpose**)
are never achieved
(**o'ertook**) unless carried
out at once. From now
on, Macbeth promises,
he will act immediately
on his impulses
(**firstlings of my heart**)
and complete (**crown**)
his thoughts with
acts. He will surprise
Macduff's castle at Fife
and kill his wife and
children.

155 But no more sights!—Where are these gentlemen?
Come bring me where they are.

[*They exit.*]

Scene 2 *Macduff's castle at Fife.*

[*Enter* Lady Macduff, *her* Son, *and* Ross.]

Lady Macduff. What had he done to make him fly the land?

Ross. You must have patience, madam.

Lady Macduff.   He had none.
His flight was madness. When our actions do not,
Our fears do make us traitors.

Ross.   You know not
5 Whether it was his wisdom or his fear.

Lady Macduff. Wisdom? To leave his wife, to leave his babes,
His mansion and his titles in a place
From whence himself does fly? He loves us not;
He wants the natural touch; for the poor wren
10 (The most diminutive of birds) will fight,
Her young ones in her nest, against the owl.
All is the fear, and nothing is the love,
As little is the wisdom, where the flight
So runs against all reason.

Ross.   My dearest coz,
15 I pray you school yourself. But for your husband,
He is noble, wise, judicious, and best knows
The fits o' th' season. I dare not speak much further;
But cruel are the times when we are traitors
And do not know ourselves; when we hold rumor
20 From what we fear, yet know not what we fear,
But float upon a wild and violent sea
Each way and move—I take my leave of you.
Shall not be long but I'll be here again.
Things at the worst will cease or else climb upward
25 To what they were before.—My pretty cousin,
Blessing upon you.

Lady Macduff. Fathered he is, and yet he's fatherless.

Ross. I am so much a fool, should I stay longer
It would be my disgrace and your discomfort.
30 I take my leave at once.   [*Ross exits.*]

Lady Macduff.   Sirrah, your father's dead.
And what will you do now? How will you live?

3–4 Macduff's wife is worried that others will think her husband a traitor because his fears made him flee the country (**our fears do make us traitors**), though he was guilty of no wrongdoing

9 wants the natural touch: lacks the instinct to protect his family.

14 coz: cousin (a term used for any close relation).

15 school: control; **for:** as for.

17 fits o' th' season: disorders of the present time.

18–22 Ross laments the cruelty of the times that made Macduff flee. Fears make people believe (**hold**) rumors, though they do not know what to fear and drift aimlessly like ships tossed by a tempest.

28–30 Moved by pity for Macduff's family, Ross is near tears (**my disgrace**). He will leave before he embarrasses himself.

Son. As birds do, mother.

Lady Macduff. What, with worms and flies?

Son. With what I get, I mean; and so do they.

Lady Macduff. Poor bird, thou'dst never fear the net nor lime,
35 The pitfall nor the gin.

Son. Why should I, mother? Poor birds they are not set for.
My father is not dead, for all your saying.

Lady Macduff. Yes, he is dead. How wilt thou do for a father?

Son. Nay, how will you do for a husband?

40 **Lady Macduff.** Why, I can buy me twenty at any market.

Son. Then you'll buy 'em to sell again.

Lady Macduff. Thou speak'st with all thy wit,
And yet, i' faith, with wit enough for thee.

Son. Was my father a traitor, mother?

45 **Lady Macduff.** Ay, that he was.

Son. What is a traitor?

Lady Macduff. Why, one that swears and lies.

Son. And be all traitors that do so?

Lady Macduff. Every one that does so is a traitor and must be
hanged.

50 **Son.** And must they all be hanged that swear and lie?

32–35 The spirited son refuses to be defeated by their bleak situation. He will live as birds do, taking whatever comes his way. His mother responds in kind, calling attention to devices used to catch birds: nets, sticky birdlime (**lime**), snares (**pitfall**), and traps (**gin**).

40–43 Lady Macduff and her son affectionately joke about her ability to find a new husband. She expresses admiration for his intelligence (**with wit enough**).

Lady Macduff. Every one.

Son. Who must hang them?

Lady Macduff. Why, the honest men.

Son. Then the liars and swearers are fools, for there are liars and
55 swearers enough to beat the honest men and hang up them.

Lady Macduff. Now God help thee, poor monkey! But how wilt
thou do for a father?

Son. If he were dead, you'd weep for him. If you would not, it
were a good sign that I should quickly have a new father.

60 **Lady Macduff.** Poor prattler, how thou talk'st!

[*Enter a* Messenger.]

Messenger. Bless you, fair dame. I am not to you known,
Though in your state of honor I am perfect.
I doubt some danger does approach you nearly.
If you will take a homely man's advice,
65 Be not found here. Hence with your little ones!
To fright you thus methinks I am too savage;
To do worse to you were fell cruelty,
Which is too nigh your person. Heaven preserve you!
I dare abide no longer. [Messenger *exits.*]

Lady Macduff. Whither should I fly?
70 I have done no harm. But I remember now
I am in this earthly world, where to do harm
Is often laudable, to do good sometime
Accounted dangerous folly. Why then, alas,
Do I put up that womanly defense
75 To say I have done no harm?

[*Enter* Murderers.]

What are these faces?

Murderer. Where is your husband?

Lady Macduff. I hope in no place so unsanctified
Where such as thou mayst find him.

Murderer. He's a traitor.

Son. Thou liest, thou shag-eared villain!

Murderer. What, you egg!

[*Stabbing him*]
80 Young fry of treachery!

Son. He has killed me, mother.
Run away, I pray you,

54–60 Her son points out that traitors outnumber honest men in this troubled time. The mother's terms of affection, **monkey** and **prattler** (childish talker), suggest that his playfulness has won her over.

61–69 The messenger, who knows Lady Macduff is an honorable person (**in your state of honor I am perfect**), delivers a polite but desperate warning, urging her to flee immediately. While he apologizes for scaring her, he warns that she faces a deadly (**fell**) cruelty, one dangerously close (**too nigh**).

77 unsanctified: unholy.

79 shag-eared: long-haired.

80 young fry: small fish.

[Lady Macduff *exits, crying "Murder!" followed by the* Murderers *bearing the* Son's *body.*]

Scene 3 *England. Before King Edward's palace.*

[*Enter* Malcolm *and* Macduff.]

Malcolm. Let us seek out some desolate shade and there
Weep our sad bosoms empty.

Macduff.   Let us rather
Hold fast the mortal sword and, like good men,
Bestride our downfall'n birthdom. Each new morn
5 New widows howl, new orphans cry, new sorrows
Strike heaven on the face, that it resounds
As if it felt with Scotland, and yelled out
Like syllable of dolor.

Malcolm.   What I believe, I'll wail;
What know, believe; and what I can redress,
10 As I shall find the time to friend, I will.
What you have spoke, it may be so, perchance.
This tyrant, whose sole name blisters our tongues,
Was once thought honest. You have loved him well.
He hath not touched you yet. I am young, but something
15 You may deserve of him through me, and wisdom
To offer up a weak, poor, innocent lamb
T' appease an angry god.

Macduff. I am not treacherous.

Malcolm.   But Macbeth is.
A good and virtuous nature may recoil
20 In an imperial charge. But I shall crave your pardon.
That which you are, my thoughts cannot transpose.
Angels are bright still, though the brightest fell.
Though all things foul would wear the brows of grace,
Yet grace must still look so.

Macduff.   I have lost my hopes.

25 **Malcolm.** Perchance even there where I did find my doubts.
Why in that rawness left you wife and child,
Those precious motives, those strong knots of love,
Without leave-taking? I pray you,
Let not my jealousies be your dishonors,
30 But mine own safeties. You may be rightly just,
Whatever I shall think.

Macduff.   Bleed, bleed, poor country!
Great tyranny, lay thou thy basis sure,
For goodness dare not check thee. Wear thou thy wrongs;

1–8 Macduff advises that they grab a deadly (**mortal**) sword and defend their homeland (**birthdom**). The anguished cries of Macbeth's victims strike heaven and make the skies echo with cries of sorrow (**syllable of dolor**).

8–15 Malcolm will strike back only if the time is right (**as I shall find the time to friend**). Macduff may be sincere, but he may be deceiving Malcolm to gain a reward from Macbeth (**something you may deserve of him through me**).

18–24 Even a good person may fall (**recoil**) into wickedness because of a king's command (**imperial charge**). Suspicions cannot change (**transpose**) the nature (**that which you are**) of an innocent person. Virtue cannot be damaged even by those like Lucifer (**the brightest angel**), who can disguise themselves as virtuous (**wear the brows of grace**).

26 rawness: vulnerability.

29 jealousies: suspicions.

The title is affeered.—Fare thee well, lord.

35 I would not be the villain that thou think'st
For the whole space that's in the tyrant's grasp,
And the rich East to boot.

Malcolm.   Be not offended.
I speak not as in absolute fear of you.
I think our country sinks beneath the yoke.
40 It weeps, it bleeds, and each new day a gash
Is added to her wounds. I think withal
There would be hands uplifted in my right;
And here from gracious England have I offer
Of goodly thousands. But, for all this,
45 When I shall tread upon the tyrant's head
Or wear it on my sword, yet my poor country
Shall have more vices than it had before,
More suffer, and more sundry ways than ever,
By him that shall succeed.

Macduff.   What should he be?

50 **Malcolm.** It is myself I mean, in whom I know
All the particulars of vice so grafted
That, when they shall be opened, black Macbeth
Will seem as pure as snow, and the poor state
Esteem him as a lamb, being compared
55 With my confineless harms.

Macduff.   Not in the legions
Of horrid hell can come a devil more damned
In evils to top Macbeth.

Malcolm.   I grant him bloody,
Luxurious, avaricious, false, deceitful,
Sudden, malicious, smacking of every sin
60 That has a name. But there's no bottom, none,
In my voluptuousness. Your wives, your daughters,
Your matrons, and your maids could not fill up
The cistern of my lust, and my desire
All continent impediments would o'erbear
65 That did oppose my will. Better Macbeth
Than such an one to reign.

Macduff.   Boundless intemperance
In nature is a tyranny. It hath been
Th' untimely emptying of the happy throne
And fall of many kings. But fear not yet
70 To take upon you what is yours. You may
Convey your pleasures in a spacious plenty

34 affeered: confirmed.

46–49 yet my . . . succeed: To test Macduff's honor and loyalty, Malcolm begins a lengthy description of his own fictitious vices.

50–55 Malcolm says that his own vices are so plentiful and deeply planted (**grafted**) that Macbeth will seem innocent by comparison.

58 luxurious: lustful.

61 voluptuousness: lust.

63 cistern: large storage tank.

63–65 His lust is so great that it would overpower (**o'erbear**) all restraining obstacles (**continent impediments**).

66–76 Macduff describes uncontrolled desire (**boundless intemperance**) as a tyrant of human nature that has caused the early (**untimely**) downfall of many kings.

And yet seem cold—the time you may so hoodwink.
We have willing dames enough. There cannot be
That vulture in you to devour so many
75 As will to greatness dedicate themselves,
Finding it so inclined.

Malcolm.   With this there grows
In my most ill-composed affection such
A stanchless avarice that, were I king,
I should cut off the nobles for their lands,
80 Desire his jewels, and this other's house;
And my more-having would be as a sauce
To make me hunger more, that I should forge
Quarrels unjust against the good and loyal,
Destroying them for wealth.

Macduff.   This avarice
85 Sticks deeper, grows with more pernicious root
Than summer-seeming lust, and it hath been
The sword of our slain kings. Yet do not fear.
Scotland hath foisons to fill up your will
Of your mere own. All these are portable,
90 With other graces weighed.

Malcolm. But I have none. The king-becoming graces,
As justice, verity, temp'rance, stableness,
Bounty, perseverance, mercy, lowliness,
Devotion, patience, courage, fortitude,
95 I have no relish of them but abound
In the division of each several crime,
Acting it many ways. Nay, had I power, I should
Pour the sweet milk of concord into hell,
Uproar the universal peace, confound
100 All unity on earth.

Macduff.   O Scotland, Scotland!

Malcolm. If such a one be fit to govern, speak.
I am as I have spoken.

Macduff.   Fit to govern?
No, not to live.—O nation miserable,
With an untitled tyrant bloody-sceptered,
105 When shalt thou see thy wholesome days again,
Since that the truest issue of thy throne
By his own interdiction stands accursed
And does blaspheme his breed?—Thy royal father
Was a most sainted king. The queen that bore thee,
110 Oft'ner upon her knees than on her feet,

76–78 Malcolm adds insatiable greed (**stanchless avarice**) to the list of evils in his disposition (**affection**).

84–90 Macduff recognizes that greed is a deeper-rooted problem than lust, which passes as quickly as the summer (**summer-seeming**). But the king's property alone (**of your mere own**) offers plenty (**foisons**) to satisfy his desire. Malcolm's vices can be tolerated (**are portable**).

91–95 Malcolm lists the kingly virtues he lacks: truthfulness (**verity**), consistency (**stableness**), generosity (**bounty**), humility (**lowliness**), and religious devotion.

102–114 Macduff can see no relief for Scotland's suffering under a tyrant who has no right to the throne (**untitled**). The rightful heir (**truest issue**), Malcolm, bans himself from the throne (**by his own interdiction**) because of his evil. Malcolm's vices slander his parents (**blaspheme his breed**)—his saintly father and his mother who renounced the world (**died every day**) for her religion.

Died every day she lived. Fare thee well.
These evils thou repeat'st upon thyself
Have banished me from Scotland.—O my breast,
Thy hope ends here!

Malcolm.   Macduff, this noble passion,
115 Child of integrity, hath from my soul
Wiped the black scruples, reconciled my thoughts
To thy good truth and honor. Devilish Macbeth
By many of these trains hath sought to win me
Into his power, and modest wisdom plucks me
120 From overcredulous haste. But God above
Deal between thee and me, for even now
I put myself to thy direction and
Unspeak mine own detraction, here abjure
The taints and blames I laid upon myself
125 For strangers to my nature. I am yet
Unknown to woman, never was forsworn,
Scarcely have coveted what was mine own,
At no time broke my faith, would not betray
The devil to his fellow, and delight
130 No less in truth than life. My first false speaking
Was this upon myself. What I am truly
Is thine and my poor country's to command—
Whither indeed, before thy here-approach,
Old Siward with ten thousand warlike men,
135 Already at a point, was setting forth.

114–125 Macduff has finally convinced Malcolm of his honesty. Malcolm explains that his caution (**modest wisdom**) resulted from his fear of Macbeth's tricks. He takes back his accusations against himself (**unspeak mine own detraction**) and renounces (**abjure**) the evils he previously claimed.

133–137 Malcolm already has an army, 10,000 troops belonging to old Siward, the earl of Northumberland. Now that Macduff is an ally, he hopes the battle's result will match the justice of their cause (**warranted quarrel**).

Image Credits: ©AKG Images

Now we'll together, and the chance of goodness
Be like our warranted quarrel. Why are you silent?

Macduff. Such welcome and unwelcome things at once
'Tis hard to reconcile.

[*Enter a* Doctor.]

140 **Malcolm.** Well, more anon.—Comes the King forth, I pray you?

Doctor. Ay, sir. There are a crew of wretched souls
That stay his cure. Their malady convinces
The great assay of art, but at his touch
(Such sanctity hath heaven given his hand)
145 They presently amend.

Malcolm.   I thank you, doctor.

[Doctor *exits.*]

Macduff. What's the disease he means?

Malcolm.   'Tis called the evil:
A most miraculous work in this good king,
Which often since my here-remain in England
I have seen him do. How he solicits heaven
150 Himself best knows, but strangely visited people
All swoll'n and ulcerous, pitiful to the eye,
The mere despair of surgery, he cures,
Hanging a golden stamp about their necks
Put on with holy prayers; and, 'tis spoken,
155 To the succeeding royalty he leaves
The healing benediction. With this strange virtue,
He hath a heavenly gift of prophecy,
And sundry blessings hang about his throne
That speak him full of grace.

[*Enter* Ross.]

Macduff.   See who comes here.

160 **Malcolm.** My countryman, but yet I know him not.

Macduff. My ever-gentle cousin, welcome hither.

Malcolm. I know him now.—Good God betimes remove
The means that makes us strangers!

Ross.   Sir, amen.

Macduff. Stands Scotland where it did?

Ross.   Alas, poor country,
165 Almost afraid to know itself. It cannot
Be called our mother, but our grave, where nothing
But who knows nothing is once seen to smile;
Where sighs and groans and shrieks that rent the air

141–159 Edward the Confessor, king of England, could reportedly heal the disease of scrofula (**the evil**) by his saintly touch. The doctor describes people who cannot be helped by medicine's best efforts (**the great assay of art**) waiting for the touch of the king's hand. Edward has cured many victims of this disease. Each time, he hangs a gold coin around their neck and offers prayers, a healing ritual that he will teach to his royal descendants (**succeeding royalty**).

162–163 Good God ... strangers: May God remove Macbeth, who is the cause (**means**) of our being strangers.

Are made, not marked; where violent sorrow seems
170 A modern ecstasy. The dead man's knell
Is there scarce asked for who, and good men's lives
Expire before the flowers in their caps,
Dying or ere they sicken.

Macduff. O relation too nice and yet too true!

175 **Malcolm.** What's the newest grief?

Ross. That of an hour's age doth hiss the speaker.
Each minute teems a new one.

Macduff.   How does my wife?

Ross. Why, well.

Macduff.   And all my children?

Ross.   Well too.

Macduff. The tyrant has not battered at their peace?

180 **Ross.** No, they were well at peace when I did leave 'em.

Macduff. Be not a niggard of your speech. How goes 't?

Ross. When I came hither to transport the tidings
Which I have heavily borne, there ran a rumor
Of many worthy fellows that were out;
185 Which was to my belief witnessed the rather
For that I saw the tyrant's power afoot.
Now is the time of help. Your eye in Scotland
Would create soldiers, make our women fight
To doff their dire distresses.

Malcolm.   Be 't their comfort
190 We are coming thither. Gracious England hath
Lent us good Siward and ten thousand men;
An older and a better soldier none
That Christendom gives out.

Ross.   Would I could answer
This comfort with the like. But I have words
195 That would be howled out in the desert air,
Where hearing should not latch them.

Macduff.   What concern they—
The general cause, or is it a fee-grief
Due to some single breast?

Ross.   No mind that's honest
But in it shares some woe, though the main part
200 Pertains to you alone.

174 relation too nice: news that is too accurate.

176–177 If the news is more than an hour old, listeners hiss at the speaker for being outdated; every minute gives birth to a new grief.

180 well at peace: Ross knows about the murder of Macduff's wife and children, but the news is too terrible to report.

182–189 Ross mentions the rumors of nobles who are rebelling (**out**) against Macbeth. Ross believes the rumors because he saw Macbeth's troops on the march (**tyrant's power afoot**). The presence (**eye**) of Malcolm and Macduff in Scotland would help raise soldiers and remove (**doff**) Macbeth's evil (**dire distresses**).

195 would: should.

196 latch: catch.

197 fee-grief: private sorrow.

198–199 No mind ... woe: Every honorable (**honest**) person shares in this sorrow.

Macduff. If it be mine,
Keep it not from me. Quickly let me have it.

Ross. Let not your ears despise my tongue forever,
Which shall possess them with the heaviest sound
That ever yet they heard.

Macduff. Hum! I guess at it.

205 **Ross.** Your castle is surprised, your wife and babes
Savagely slaughtered. To relate the manner
Were on the quarry of these murdered deer
To add the death of you.

Malcolm. Merciful heaven!
What, man, ne'er pull your hat upon your brows.
210 Give sorrow words. The grief that does not speak
Whispers the o'erfraught heart and bids it break.

Macduff. My children too?

Ross. Wife, children, servants, all that could be found.

Macduff. And I must be from thence? My wife killed too?

215 **Ross.** I have said.

Malcolm. Be comforted.
Let's make us med'cines of our great revenge
To cure this deadly grief.

Macduff. He has no children. All my pretty ones?
220 Did you say "all"? O hell-kite! All?
What, all my pretty chickens and their dam
At one fell swoop?

Malcolm. Dispute it like a man.

Macduff. I shall do so,
But I must also feel it as a man.
225 I cannot but remember such things were
That were most precious to me. Did heaven look on
And would not take their part? Sinful Macduff,
They were all struck for thee! Naught that I am,
Not for their own demerits, but for mine,
230 Fell slaughter on their souls. Heaven rest them now.

Malcolm. Be this the whetstone of your sword. Let grief
Convert to anger. Blunt not the heart; enrage it.

Macduff. O, I could play the woman with mine eyes
And braggart with my tongue! But, gentle heavens,
235 Cut short all intermission! Front to front
Bring thou this fiend of Scotland and myself.

206–208 Ross won't add to Macduff's sorrow by telling him how his family was killed. He compares Macduff's dear ones to the piled bodies of killed deer (**quarry**).

210–211 The grief ... **break:** Silence will only push an overburdened heart to the breaking point.

219–222 He has no **children:** possibly a reference to Macbeth, who has no children to be killed for revenge. Macduff compares Macbeth to a bird of prey (**hell-kite**) who kills defenseless chickens and their mother.

228 naught: nothing.

231 whetstone: grindstone used for sharpening.

Within my sword's length set him. If he scape,
Heaven forgive him too.

Malcolm.　　　　　　　This tune goes manly.
Come, go we to the King. Our power is ready;
240　Our lack is nothing but our leave. Macbeth
Is ripe for shaking, and the powers above
Put on their instruments. Receive what cheer you may.
The night is long that never finds the day.

[*They exit.*]

239–243 Our troops are ready to attack, needing only the king's permission (**our lack is nothing but our leave**). Like a ripe fruit, Macbeth is ready to fall, and heavenly powers are preparing to assist us.

COLLABORATIVE DISCUSSION With a partner, discuss how Macbeth descends further into evil. Cite specific textual evidence from the play to support your ideas.

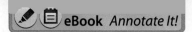

Analyzing the Text

RL 1, RL 3,
RL 5, SL 1a–d

Cite Text Evidence   Support your responses with evidence from the selection.

1. **Analyze** How does Macbeth interpret the prophecies pronounced by the first three apparitions? Explain how knowledge of the witches' intent affects the audience's perception of these prophecies.

2. **Infer** What is the purpose of the appearance and speech of the messenger in Scene 2? Who might have sent this messenger?

3. **Draw Conclusions** Lady Macduff and Malcolm both question Macduff's motives for fleeing Scotland. Think about the crimes Macbeth has already committed. Why might the nature of these crimes have led Macduff to believe his family would be safe at his castle?

4. **Infer** Why might Shakespeare have decided to show the murder of Lady Macduff and her children on stage? Explain how watching this scene rather than hearing about the event occurring offstage might affect the audience's view of Macbeth.

5. **Cite Evidence** What is Malcolm's initial attitude toward Macduff? What is shown about Malcolm through the way he assesses Macduff's sincerity?

6. **Interpret** Explain the dramatic irony of these lines in Scene 3:

   • lines 4–8 ("Each new morn . . .")
   • line 14 ("He hath not touched you yet.")
   • line 180 ("No, they were well at peace when I did leave 'em.")

7. **Analyze** Consider the description of Edward, the English king, in lines 146–159 of Scene 3. Why is this passage included in the play?

PERFORMANCE TASK

Speaking Activity: Debate Some directors omit much of the scene in which Malcolm tests Macduff. What would be lost or gained by omitting this part of the play?

• With a group, come to a consensus on the significance of that part of Scene 3. Create an outline that includes reasons and evidence to support your opinion.

• Present your argument in the form of a panel discussion or debate. Have other groups present their opposing arguments.

• Ask listening classmates to evaluate which argument is most compelling and why.

AS YOU READ Pay attention to whether the prophecies pronounced by the apparitions are fulfilled. Write down any questions you generate during reading.

ACT V

Scene 1 *Macbeth's castle at Dunsinane.*

[*Enter a* Doctor of Physic *and a* Waiting Gentlewoman.]

Doctor. I have two nights watched with you but can perceive no truth in your report. When was it she last walked?

Gentlewoman. Since his Majesty went into the field, I have seen her rise from her bed, throw her nightgown upon her,
5   unlock her closet, take forth paper, fold it, write upon' t, read it, afterwards seal it, and again return to bed; yet all this while in a most fast sleep.

Doctor. A great perturbation in nature, to receive at once the benefit of sleep and do the effects of watching. In this slumb'ry
10   agitation, besides her walking and other actual performances, what at any time have you heard her say?

Gentlewoman. That, sir, which I will not report after her.

Doctor. You may to me, and 'tis most meet you should.

Gentlewoman. Neither to you nor anyone, having no witness to
15   confirm my speech.

[*Enter* Lady Macbeth *with a taper.*]

Lo you, here she comes. This is her very guise and, upon my life, fast asleep. Observe her; stand close.

Doctor. How came she by that light?

Gentlewoman. Why, it stood by her. She has light by her
20   continually. 'Tis her command.

Doctor. You see her eyes are open.

Gentlewoman. Ay, but their sense are shut.

Doctor. What is it she does now? Look how she rubs her hands.

Gentlewoman. It is an accustomed action with her to seem thus
25   washing her hands. I have known her continue in this a quarter of an hour.

Lady Macbeth. Yet here's a spot.

Doctor. Hark, she speaks. I will set down what comes from her, to satisfy my remembrance the more strongly.

30   **Lady Macbeth.** Out, damned spot, out, I say! One. Two. Why then, 'tis time to do 't. Hell is murky. Fie, my lord, fie, a soldier and afeard? What need we fear who knows it, when none can

> **3 went into the field:** went to battle.

> **8–9 A great . . . of watching:** To behave as though awake (**watching**) while sleeping is a sign of a greatly troubled nature.

> **13 meet:** appropriate.

> **16 guise:** usual manner.

> **17 stand close:** hide yourself.

> **18 that light:** her candle.

call our power to account? Yet who would have thought the old man to have had so much blood in him?

35 **Doctor.** Do you mark that?

Lady Macbeth. The Thane of Fife had a wife. Where is she now? What, will these hands ne'er be clean? No more o' that, my lord, no more o' that. You mar all with this starting.

36–38 Lady Macbeth shows guilt about Macduff's wife. Then she addresses her husband, as if he were having another ghostly fit (**starting**).

Doctor. Go to, go to. You have known what you should not.

40 **Gentlewoman.** She has spoke what she should not, I am sure of that. Heaven knows what she has known.

Lady Macbeth. Here's the smell of the blood still. All the perfumes of Arabia will not sweeten this little hand. O, O, O!

Doctor. What a sigh is there! The heart is sorely charged.

44 **sorely charged:** heavily burdened.

45 **Gentlewoman.** I would not have such a heart in my bosom for the dignity of the whole body.

45–46 The gentlewoman says that she would not want Lady Macbeth's heavy heart in exchange for being queen.

Doctor. Well, well, well.

Gentlewoman. Pray God it be, sir.

Doctor. This disease is beyond my practice. Yet I have known
50 those which have walked in their sleep, who have died holily in their beds.

49 **practice:** skill.

Lady Macbeth. Wash your hands. Put on your nightgown. Look not so pale. I tell you yet again, Banquo's buried; he cannot come out on 's grave.

54 **on 's:** of his.

55 **Doctor.** Even so?

Lady Macbeth. To bed, to bed. There's knocking at the gate. Come, come, come, come. Give me your hand. What's done cannot be undone. To bed, to bed, to bed.

[Lady Macbeth *exits.*]

Doctor. Will she go now to bed?

60 **Gentlewoman.** Directly.

Doctor. Foul whisp'rings are abroad. Unnatural deeds
Do breed unnatural troubles. Infected minds
To their deaf pillows will discharge their secrets.
More needs she the divine than the physician.

61 **Foul whisp'rings are abroad:** Rumors of evil deeds are circulating.

64 She needs a priest more than a doctor.

65 God, God forgive us all. Look after her.
Remove from her the means of all annoyance
And still keep eyes upon her. So good night.
My mind she has mated, and amazed my sight.
I think but dare not speak.

66 **annoyance:** injury. The doctor may be worried about the possibility of Lady Macbeth's committing suicide.

Gentlewoman.   Good night, good doctor.

68 **mated:** astonished.

[*They exit.*]

Scene 2 *The country near Dunsinane.*

[*Drum and Colors. Enter* Menteith, Caithness, Angus, Lennox, *and* Soldiers.]

Menteith. The English power is near, led on by Malcolm,
His uncle Siward, and the good Macduff.
Revenges burn in them, for their dear causes
Would to the bleeding and the grim alarm
5 Excite the mortified man.

Angus.   Near Birnam Wood
Shall we well meet them. That way are they coming.

Caithness. Who knows if Donalbain be with his brother?

Lennox. For certain, sir, he is not. I have a file
Of all the gentry. There is Siward's son
10 And many unrough youths that even now
Protest their first of manhood.

Menteith.   What does the tyrant?

Caithness. Great Dunsinane he strongly fortifies.
Some say he's mad; others that lesser hate him
Do call it valiant fury. But for certain
15 He cannot buckle his distempered cause
Within the belt of rule.

Angus.   Now does he feel
His secret murders sticking on his hands.
Now minutely revolts upbraid his faith-breach.
Those he commands move only in command,
20 Nothing in love. Now does he feel his title
Hang loose about him, like a giant's robe
Upon a dwarfish thief.

Menteith.   Who, then, shall blame
His pestered senses to recoil and start
When all that is within him does condemn
25 Itself for being there?

Caithness.   Well, march we on
To give obedience where 'tis truly owed.
Meet we the med'cine of the sickly weal,
And with him pour we in our country's purge
Each drop of us.

Lennox.   Or so much as it needs
30 To dew the sovereign flower and drown the weeds.
Make we our march towards Birnam.

[*They exit marching.*]

3–5 for their dear … man: The cause of Malcolm and Macduff is so deeply felt that a dead (**mortified**) man would respond to their call to arms (**alarm**).

10–11 many … manhood: many soldiers who are too young to grow beards (**unrough**).

15–16 Like a man so swollen with disease (**distempered**) that he cannot buckle his belt, Macbeth cannot control his evil actions.

18 Every minute, revolts against Macbeth shame him for his treachery (**faith-breach**).

22–25 Macbeth's nerves, troubled by guilt, (**pestered senses**) have made him jumpy.

25–29 They give their loyalty to the only help (**med'cine**) for the sick country (**weal**). They are willing to sacrifice their last drop of blood to cleanse (**purge**) Scotland.

29–31 Lennox compares Malcolm to a flower that needs the blood of patriots to water (**dew**) it and drown out weeds like Macbeth.

Scene 3 *Dunsinane. A room in the castle.*

[*Enter* Macbeth, *the* Doctor, *and* Attendants.]

Macbeth. Bring me no more reports. Let them fly all.
Till Birnam Wood remove to Dunsinane
I cannot taint with fear. What's the boy Malcolm?
Was he not born of woman? The spirits that know
5 All mortal consequences have pronounced me thus:
"Fear not, Macbeth. No man that's born of woman
Shall e'er have power upon thee." Then fly, false thanes,
And mingle with the English epicures.
The mind I sway by and the heart I bear
10 Shall never sag with doubt nor shake with fear.

[*Enter* Servant.]

The devil damn thee black, thou cream-faced loon!
Where got'st thou that goose-look?

Servant. There is ten thousand—

Macbeth.   Geese, villain?

Servant.   Soldiers, sir.

Macbeth. Go prick thy face and over-red thy fear,
15 Thou lily-livered boy. What soldiers, patch?
Death of thy soul! Those linen cheeks of thine
Are counselors to fear. What soldiers, whey-face?

Servant. The English force, so please you.

Macbeth. Take thy face hence.

[*Servant exits.*]

                          Seyton!—I am sick at heart
20 When I behold—Seyton, I say!—This push
Will cheer me ever or disseat me now.
I have lived long enough. My way of life
Is fall'n into the sere, the yellow leaf,
And that which should accompany old age,
25 As honor, love, obedience, troops of friends,
I must not look to have, but in their stead
Curses, not loud but deep, mouth-honor, breath
Which the poor heart would fain deny and dare not.—
Seyton!

[*Enter* Seyton.]

30 **Seyton.** What's your gracious pleasure?

Macbeth.   What news more?

Seyton. All is confirmed, my lord, which was reported.

1 Macbeth wants no more news of thanes who have gone to Malcolm's side.

2–10 Macbeth will not be infected (**taint**) with fear, because the witches (**spirits**), who know all human events (**mortal consequences**), have convinced him that he is invincible. He mocks the self-indulgent English (**English epicures**), then swears that he will never lack confidence.

11 loon: stupid rascal.

12 goose-look: look of fear.

14–17 Macbeth suggests that the servant cut his face so that blood will hide his cowardice. He repeatedly insults the servant, calling him a coward (**lily-livered**) and a clown (**patch**) and making fun of his white complexion (**linen cheeks, whey-face**).

20–28 This push ... dare not: The upcoming battle will either make Macbeth secure (**cheer me ever**) or dethrone (**disseat**) him. He bitterly compares his life to a withered (**sere**) leaf. He cannot look forward to old age with friends and honor, but only to curses and empty flattery (**mouthhonor, breath**) from those too timid (**the poor heart**) to tell the truth.

Macbeth. I'll fight till from my bones my flesh be hacked.
Give me my armor.

Seyton. 'Tis not needed yet.

Macbeth. I'll put it on.
35 Send out more horses. Skirr the country round.
Hang those that talk of fear. Give me mine armor.—
How does your patient, doctor?

Doctor. Not so sick, my lord,
As she is troubled with thick-coming fancies
That keep her from her rest.

Macbeth. Cure her of that.
40 Canst thou not minister to a mind diseased,
Pluck from the memory a rooted sorrow,
Raze out the written troubles of the brain,
And with some sweet oblivious antidote
Cleanse the stuffed bosom of that perilous stuff
45 Which weighs upon the heart?

Doctor. Therein the patient
Must minister to himself.

Macbeth. Throw physic to the dogs, I'll none of it.—
Come, put mine armor on. Give me my staff.

[*Attendants* begin to arm him.]

Seyton, send out.—Doctor, the thanes fly from me.—
50 Come, sir, dispatch.—If thou couldst, doctor, cast
The water of my land, find her disease,
And purge it to a sound and pristine health,
I would applaud thee to the very echo
That should applaud again.—Pull 't off, I say.—
55 What rhubarb, senna, or what purgative drug
Would scour these English hence? Hear'st thou of them?

35 skirr: scour.

47–54 Macbeth has lost his faith in the ability of medicine (**physic**) to help his wife. He says that if the doctor could diagnose Scotland's disease (**cast . . . land**) and cure it, Macbeth would never stop praising him.

54 Pull 't off: Macbeth is referring to a piece of armor.

56 scour: purge; **them:** the English.

Doctor. Ay, my good lord. Your royal preparation
Makes us hear something.

Macbeth.   Bring it after me.—
I will not be afraid of death and bane
60   Till Birnam Forest come to Dunsinane.

58–60 Macbeth leaves for battle, telling Seyton to bring the armor.

Doctor [*aside*]. Were I from Dunsinane away and clear,
Profit again should hardly draw me here.

[*They exit.*]

Scene 4   *The country near Birnam Wood.*

[*Drum and Colors. Enter* Malcolm, Siward, Macduff, Siward's
son, Menteith, Caithness, Angus, *and* Soldiers, *marching.*]

Malcolm. Cousins, I hope the days are near at hand
That chambers will be safe.

Menteith.   We doubt it nothing.

Siward. What wood is this before us?

Menteith.   The wood of Birnam.

Malcolm. Let every soldier hew him down a bough
5   And bear 't before him. Thereby shall we shadow
The numbers of our host and make discovery
Err in report of us.

Soldiers.   It shall be done.

Siward. We learn no other but the confident tyrant
Keeps still in Dunsinane and will endure
10   Our setting down before 't.

10 setting down: siege.

Malcolm.   'Tis his main hope;
For, where there is advantage to be given,
Both more and less have given him the revolt,
And none serve with him but constrainèd things
Whose hearts are absent too.

10–14 Malcolm says that men of all ranks (**both more and less**) have abandoned Macbeth. Only weak men forced into service remain with him.

Macduff.   Let our just censures
15   Attend the true event, and put we on
Industrious soldiership.

14–16 Macduff warns against overconfidence and advises that they focus on fighting.

Siward.   The time approaches
That will with due decision make us know
What we shall say we have and what we owe.
Thoughts speculative their unsure hopes relate,
20   But certain issue strokes must arbitrate;
Towards which, advance the war.

16–21 Siward says that the approaching battle will decide whether their claims will match what they actually possess (**owe**). Now, their hopes and expectations are guesswork (**thoughts speculative**); only fighting (**strokes**) can settle (**arbitrate**) the issue.

[*They exit marching.*]

Scene 5 *Dunsinane. Within the castle.*

[*Enter* Macbeth, Seyton, *and* Soldiers, *with Drum and Colors.*]

Macbeth. Hang out our banners on the outward walls.
The cry is still "They come!" Our castle's strength
Will laugh a siege to scorn. Here let them lie
Till famine and the ague eat them up.

5　Were they not forced with those that should be ours,
We might have met them dareful, beard to beard,
And beat them backward home.

[*A cry within of women.*]

　　　　　　　　　　　　　　What is that noise?

Seyton. It is the cry of women, my good lord. [*He exits.*]

Macbeth. I have almost forgot the taste of fears.

10　The time has been my senses would have cooled
To hear a night-shriek, and my fell of hair
Would at a dismal treatise rouse and stir
As life were in 't. I have supped full with horrors.
Direness, familiar to my slaughterous thoughts,

15　Cannot once start me.

[*Enter* Seyton.]

　　　　　　　　　　　　　Wherefore was that cry?

Seyton. The Queen, my lord, is dead.

Macbeth. She should have died hereafter.
There would have been a time for such a word.
Tomorrow and tomorrow and tomorrow

20　Creeps in this petty pace from day to day
To the last syllable of recorded time,
And all our yesterdays have lighted fools
The way to dusty death. Out, out, brief candle!
Life's but a walking shadow, a poor player

25　That struts and frets his hour upon the stage
And then is heard no more. It is a tale
Told by an idiot, full of sound and fury,
Signifying nothing.

[*Enter a* Messenger.]

Thou com'st to use thy tongue: thy story quickly.

30　**Messenger.** Gracious my lord,
I should report that which I say I saw,
But know not how to do 't.

Macbeth.　　　　　　　　　Well, say, sir.

4 ague: fever.

5–7 Macbeth complains that the attackers have been reinforced (**forced**) by deserters (**those that should be ours**), which has forced him to wait at Dunsinane instead of seeking victory on the battlefield.

9–15 There was a time when a scream in the night would have frozen Macbeth in fear and a terrifying tale (**dismal treatise**) would have made the hair on his skin (**fell of hair**) stand on end. But since he has fed on horror (**direness**), it cannot stir (**start**) him anymore.

17–18 Macbeth wishes that his wife had died later (**hereafter**), when he would have had time to mourn her.

Messenger. As I did stand my watch upon the hill,
I looked toward Birnam, and anon methought
35 The wood began to move.

Macbeth.   Liar and slave!

Messenger. Let me endure your wrath, if 't be not so.
Within this three mile may you see it coming.
I say, a moving grove.

Macbeth.   If thou speak'st false,
Upon the next tree shall thou hang alive
40 Till famine cling thee. If thy speech be sooth,
I care not if thou dost for me as much.—
I pull in resolution and begin
To doubt th' equivocation of the fiend,
That lies like truth. "Fear not till Birnam Wood
45 Do come to Dunsinane," and now a wood
Comes toward Dunsinane. —Arm, arm, and out!—
If this which he avouches does appear,
There is nor flying hence nor tarrying here.
I 'gin to be aweary of the sun
50 And wish th' estate o' th' world were now undone.—
Ring the alarum bell! —Blow wind, come wrack,
At least we'll die with harness on our back.

[*They exit.*]

Scene 6 *Dunsinane. Before the castle.*

[*Drum and Colors. Enter* Malcolm, Siward, Macduff, *and their army, with boughs.*]

Malcolm. Now near enough. Your leafy screens throw down
And show like those you are. —You, worthy uncle,
Shall with my cousin, your right noble son,
Lead our first battle. Worthy Macduff and we
5 Shall take upon 's what else remains to do,
According to our order.

Siward.   Fare you well.
Do we but find the tyrant's power tonight,
Let us be beaten if we cannot fight.

Macduff. Make all our trumpets speak; give them all breath,
10 Those clamorous harbingers of blood and death.

[*They exit. Alarums continued.*]

38–52 The messenger's news has dampened Macbeth's determination (**resolution**); Macbeth begins to fear that the witches have tricked him (**to doubt th' equivocation of the fiend**). His fear that the messenger tells the truth (**avouches**) makes him decide to confront the enemy instead of staying in his castle. Weary of life, he nevertheless decides to face death and ruin (**wrack**) with his armor (**harness**) on.

1–6 Malcolm commands the troops to put down their branches (**leafy screens**) and gives the battle instructions.

7 power: forces.

10 harbingers: announcers.

Scene 7 *Another part of the battlefield.*

[*Enter* Macbeth.]

Macbeth. They have tied me to a stake. I cannot fly,
But, bear-like, I must fight the course. What's he
That was not born of woman? Such a one
Am I to fear, or none.

[*Enter* Young Siward.]

5   **Young Siward.** What is thy name?

Macbeth.   Thou'lt be afraid to hear it.

Young Siward. No, though thou call'st thyself a hotter name
Than any is in hell.

Macbeth.   My name's Macbeth.

Young Siward. The devil himself could not pronounce a title
More hateful to mine ear.

Macbeth.   No, nor more fearful.

10   **Young Siward.** Thou liest, abhorrèd tyrant. With my sword
I'll prove the lie thou speak'st.

[*They fight, and* Young Siward *is slain.*]

Macbeth.   Thou wast born of woman.
But swords I smile at, weapons laugh to scorn,
Brandished by man that's of a woman born. [*He exits.*]

[*Alarums. Enter* Macduff.]

Macduff. That way the noise is. Tyrant, show thy face!
15   If thou beest slain, and with no stroke of mine,
My wife and children's ghosts will haunt me still.
I cannot strike at wretched kerns, whose arms
Are hired to bear their staves. Either thou, Macbeth,
Or else my sword with an unbattered edge
20   I sheathe again undeeded. There thou shouldst be;
By this great clatter, one of greatest note
Seems bruited. Let me find him, Fortune,
And more I beg not.

[*He exits. Alarums.*]
[*Enter* Malcolm *and* Siward.]

Siward. This way, my lord. The castle's gently rendered.
25   The tyrant's people on both sides do fight,
The noble thanes do bravely in the war,
The day almost itself professes yours,
And little is to do.

1–4 Macbeth compares himself to a bear tied to a post (a reference to the sport of bearbaiting, in which a bear was tied to a stake and attacked by dogs).

14–20 Macduff hopes to find Macbeth before someone else has the chance to kill him. Macduff does not want to fight the miserable hired soldiers (**kerns**), who are armed only with spears (**staves**). If he can't fight Macbeth, Macduff will leave his sword unused (**undeeded**).

22 bruited: rumored or heard.

24 gently rendered: surrendered without a fight.

27 You have almost won the day.

28–29 During the battle many of Macbeth's men deserted to Malcolm's army.

Malcolm.   We have met with foes
That strike beside us.

Siward.   Enter, sir, the castle.

[*They exit. Alarum.*]

Scene 8 *Another part of the battlefield.*

[*Enter* Macbeth.]

Macbeth. Why should I play the Roman fool and die
On mine own sword? Whiles I see lives, the gashes
Do better upon them.

[*Enter* Macduff.]

Macduff.   Turn, hellhound, turn!

Macbeth. Of all men else I have avoided thee.
5 But get thee back. My soul is too much charged
With blood of thine already.

Macduff.   I have no words;
My voice is in my sword, thou bloodier villain
Than terms can give thee out.

[*Fight. Alarum.*]

Macbeth.   Thou losest labor.
As easy mayst thou the intrenchant air
10 With thy keen sword impress as make me bleed.
Let fall thy blade on vulnerable crests;
I bear a charmèd life, which must not yield
To one of woman born.

Macduff.   Despair thy charm,
And let the angel whom thou still hast served
15 Tell thee Macduff was from his mother's womb
Untimely ripped.

Macbeth. Accursèd be that tongue that tells me so,
For it hath cowed my better part of man!
And be these juggling fiends no more believed
20 That palter with us in a double sense,
That keep the word of promise to our ear
And break it to our hope. I'll not fight with thee.

Macduff. Then yield thee, coward,
And live to be the show and gaze o' th' time.
25 We'll have thee, as our rarer monsters are,
Painted upon a pole, and underwrit
"Here may you see the tyrant."

1–3 Macbeth refuses to commit suicide in the style of a defeated Roman general.

4–6 Macbeth does not want to fight Macduff, having already killed so many members of Macduff's family.

8–13 Macbeth says that Macduff is wasting his effort. Trying to wound Macbeth is as useless as trying to wound the invulnerable (**intrenchant**) air. Macduff should strike at the helmets (**crests**) of more vulnerable foes.

15–16 Macduff ... **untimely ripped:** Macduff was a premature baby delivered by cesarean section, an operation that removes the child directly from the mother's womb.

18 cowed: made fearful.

19–22 The cheating witches (**juggling fiends**) have tricked him (**palter with us**) with words that have double meanings.

23–27 Macduff tells Macbeth to surrender and become a public spectacle (**the show and gaze o' th' time**), with his picture displayed (**painted upon a pole**) as if he were in a circus sideshow.

Macbeth.   I will not yield
To kiss the ground before young Malcolm's feet
And to be baited with the rabble's curse.
30 Though Birnam Wood be come to Dunsinane
And thou opposed, being of no woman born,
Yet I will try the last. Before my body
I throw my warlike shield. Lay on, Macduff,
And damned be him that first cries "Hold! Enough!"

[*They exit fighting. Alarums.*]
[*They enter fighting, and* Macbeth *is slain.* Macduff *exits carrying off* Macbeth's *body. Retreat and flourish. Enter, with Drum and Colors,* Malcolm, Siward, Ross, Thanes, *and* Soldiers.]

35 **Malcolm.** I would the friends we miss were safe arrived.

Siward. Some must go off; and yet by these I see
So great a day as this is cheaply bought.

Malcolm. Macduff is missing, and your noble son.

Ross. Your son, my lord, has paid a soldier's debt.
40 He only lived but till he was a man,
The which no sooner had his prowess confirmed
In the unshrinking station where he fought,
But like a man he died.

Siward.   Then he is dead?

Ross. Ay, and brought off the field. Your cause of sorrow
45 Must not be measured by his worth, for then
It hath no end.

[Stage Direction] **Retreat . . . :** The first trumpet call (**retreat**) signals the battle's end. The next one (**flourish**) announces Malcolm's entrance.

36–37 Though some must die (**go off**) in battle, Siward can see that their side does not have many casualties.

Image Credits: ©David Muscroft/Superstock/Glow Images

Siward.   Had he his hurts before?

Ross. Ay, on the front.

Siward.   Why then, God's soldier be he!
Had I as many sons as I have hairs,
I would not wish them to a fairer death;
50 And so his knell is knolled.

Malcolm. He's worth more sorrow, and that I'll spend for him.

Siward. He's worth no more.
They say he parted well and paid his score,
And so, God be with him. Here comes newer comfort.

[*Enter* Macduff *with* Macbeth's *head*.]

55 **Macduff.** Hail, King! for so thou art. Behold where stands
Th' usurper's cursèd head. The time is free.
I see thee compassed with thy kingdom's pearl,
That speak my salutation in their minds,
Whose voices I desire aloud with mine.
60 Hail, King of Scotland!

All.   Hail, King of Scotland!

[*Flourish*]

Malcolm. We shall not spend a large expense of time
Before we reckon with your several loves
And make us even with you. My thanes and kinsmen,
Henceforth be earls, the first that ever Scotland
65 In such an honor named. What's more to do,
Which would be planted newly with the time,
As calling home our exiled friends abroad
That fled the snares of watchful tyranny,
Producing forth the cruel ministers
70 Of this dead butcher and his fiend-like queen
(Who, as 'tis thought, by self and violent hands,
Took off her life)—this, and what needful else
That calls upon us, by the grace of grace,
We will perform in measure, time, and place.
75 So thanks to all at once and to each one,
Whom we invite to see us crowned at Scone.

[*Flourish. All exit*.]

46 hurts before: wounds in the front of his body, which indicate he died facing his enemy.

50 knell is knolled: Young Siward's death bell has already rung.

[Stage Direction] Macduff is probably carrying Macbeth's head on a pole.

56–57 The time . . . pearl: Macduff declares that the age (**time**) is now freed from tyranny. He sees Malcolm surrounded by Scotland's noblest men (**thy kingdom's pearl**).

61–76 Malcolm promises that he will quickly reward his nobles according to the devotion (**several loves**) they have shown. He gives the thanes new titles (**henceforth be earls**) and declares his intention, as a sign of the new age (**planted newly with the time**), to welcome back the exiles who fled Macbeth's tyranny and his cruel agents (**ministers**).

COLLABORATIVE DISCUSSION With a partner, discuss how each prophecy is fulfilled in spite of its seeming impossibility. Cite specific textual evidence from the play to support your ideas.

Analyze Character and Theme

The **theme** of a work of literature is the insight about life and human nature that the writer wants to communicate. Theme is conveyed through the writer's development of elements such as character and plot.

In his play, Shakespeare presents several themes. These ideas are brought out by the actions, thoughts, and feelings of the characters, particularly those of Macbeth.

Macbeth is a multi-dimensional, complex character who changes as a result of the decisions he makes and the way he reacts to conflict. Consider these key aspects of the interplay between character and theme together with examples from the play:

How the character changes over time	Early in Act I: Macbeth, loyal to Duncan, wins a great victory for the king.
	Later in Act I: Macbeth considers murdering the king based on the words of the witches and Lady Macbeth.
	Act II: Hoping the violence will end there, Macbeth murders the king and his guards.
	Act III: Macbeth has Banquo killed on the basis of mere suspicions, but he also begins to show signs of a guilty conscience.
How the character interacts with others	Once the first prophecy is fulfilled, Macbeth unquestioningly believes all the witches say, and seeks their advice.
	Macbeth solves conflicts, both real and imagined, by murdering anyone who might oppose him.
How the character advances the plot	Macbeth's decision to have Macduff's family murdered leads to his own death at Macduff's hands.

Through Macbeth's conflict, his subsequent actions, his thoughts, and his feelings, Shakespeare conveys profound lessons about the consequences of a person's decisions. Each poor decision Macbeth makes paves the way for the next, until by Act III he says "I am in blood / Stepped in so far that, should I wade no more, / Returning were as tedious as go o'er." Consider what theme is expressed through Macbeth's character and fate.

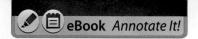

Analyzing the Text

Cite Text Evidence   Support your responses with evidence from the selection.

1. **Analyze** Using these passages as a guide, explain how Macbeth's attempt to resolve his conflict changes him. What message does Shakespeare convey through his change?

    - Act I, Scene 3, lines 130–142; Scene 7, lines 31–35
    - Act II, Scene 2, lines 56–61
    - Act III, Scene 4, lines 93–96; lines 122–126
    - Act V, Scene 3, lines 19–28; Scene 5, lines 9–15

2. **Evaluate** Explain how Lady Macbeth's actions in Act V, Scene 1, draw meaning from the images of blood, darkness, and sleep that have run through the play. Does her deterioration redeem her character in the eyes of the audience? Why or why not?

3. **Analyze** In what ways do Macbeth's strengths contribute to his downfall? Cite examples from the entire play to support your ideas.

4. **Cite Evidence** What moment might be called the climax, or highest point of tension, in Act V? What is clear to the audience and to Macbeth at this point?

5. **Identify Patterns** The witches are sometimes seen as representing fate, or destiny. Do they merely reveal what will happen, or do they manipulate events?

6. **Analyze** In Shakespeare's tragedies, often the main character is given a chance to say something significant about his life just before he dies. What speech might function as Macbeth's farewell, even though it doesn't occur in Act V, Scene 8? Defend your choice with evidence from the text.

7. **Compare** Review Malcolm's last speech in Act V, Scene 8. How are his words an echo of Duncan's language earlier in the play? How does this speech thematically and structurally unify the play?

PERFORMANCE TASK

Writing Activity: Argument Is Macbeth a tragic hero? Refer to the introductory essay on Shakespearean Drama, and explore your ideas in an essay.

- Review the definition of a tragic hero. Decide which of the characteristics Macbeth embodies. Find details in the text to support your thesis.

- Organize your ideas logically. Write an essay in which you defend your view of Macbeth.
- Use the conventions of standard written English in your essay.

Language and Style: Inverted Sentence Structure

A key aspect of Shakespeare's style is his use of inverted sentence structure. In an **inverted sentence**, the normal word order is reversed. Some examples of inverted structure include: all or part of the predicate comes before the subject; a subject comes between a helping verb and a main verb; a direct object precedes a verb, and a prepositional phrase comes before the noun or verb it modifies. Shakespeare includes many of these inverted sentence structures in his play.

Read these lines from *The Tragedy of Macbeth:*

Come, go we to the King. (Act IV, Scene 3, line 239)

The castle of Macduff I will surprise. (Act IV, Scene 1, line 150)

Notice that in the first example the verb *go* precedes the subject *we*. In the second example, the direct object *the castle* and its modifier *of Macduff* appear before both the subject *I* and the verb phrase *will surprise*. Shakespeare could have written the lines this way:

Come, we go to the King.

I will surprise the castle of Macduff.

Instead, Shakespeare chose to use inverted structures for poetic effect.

Writers also use inverted sentence structures to add variety to their writing or to emphasize a word or an idea.

Practice and Apply Working independently, identify the part that is inverted in each of Shakespeare's sentences below. Rewrite each sentence without the inversion. Then, working with a partner, write five original sentences on topics of your choice that use the same inverted structures found in Shakespeare's sentences.

1. O, full of scorpions is my mind, dear wife! (Act III, Scene 2, line 35)

2. I'll fight till from my bones my flesh be hacked. (Act V, Scene 3, line 32)

3. Retire we to our chamber. (Act II, Scene 2, line 64)

4. For them the gracious Duncan have I murdered. (Act III, Scene 1, line 65)

5. Then comes my fit again. (Act III, Scene 4, line 21)

Background *In 1997, the BBC (British Broadcasting Corporation) produced a new version of Shakespeare's Scottish play—Macbeth on the Estate. Award-winning director Penny Woolcock reset the play as a modern crime drama and filmed it in the Ladywood Estate, a low-income housing development in Birmingham, England. Action was set in the estate's apartments, courtyards, and roofs, but the production retained Shakespeare's powerful language. Residents from the estate worked on the film and participated as actors. Reviews were polarized, with some critics preferring a more traditional approach and others embracing this affirmation of Shakespeare's universality.*

MEDIA ANALYSIS

from

Macbeth on the Estate

Film directed by Penny Woolcock

AS YOU VIEW Consider how the modern setting creates a certain mood or tone. Write down any questions you have during viewing.

COLLABORATIVE DISCUSSION In a small group, discuss how the modern setting adds to the mood of the production. What atmosphere, or feeling, is conveyed? Cite specific images to support your ideas.

Image Credits: (t) ©MJ Kim/Getty Images; (c) (b) ©BBC Motion Gallery

Analyze Representations

The "Tomorrow and tomorrow and tomorrow" speech—Macbeth's reaction to Lady Macbeth's death amid his preparations for war—is one of Shakespeare's most famous scenes. Every actor or director attempting this scene brings a unique approach to it, comprising a personal reading of Shakespeare's words and a particular message or feeling he or she wants to communicate through the speech. Consider what this production emphasizes in the scene as well as what it omits from the original play. In addition, think about how the director uses the medium of film in concert with Shakespeare's words.

- **Setting/Sets:** How do background noise, buildings, and other features of the location affect the tone and theme of the scene?
- **Film shots and angles:** What is the effect of multiple shots of the bystanders from various angles?
- **Actors:** Why might the director have chosen to surround Lady Macbeth's body with bystanders when the play did not?

Analyzing the Media

Cite Text Evidence   Support your responses with evidence from the selection.

1. **Analyze** How do the choices made by the director of *Macbeth on the Estate* help convey tone? Cite specific images and staging to support your answer.

2. **Compare** Which passages of Shakespeare's original text are omitted from this production of the scene? Explain how leaving out these lines affects the pacing and theme of the scene.

3. **Evaluate** How do the actors' use of emphasis and expression add meaning to this scene and help clarify your understanding? Cite specific lines.

PERFORMANCE TASK

Speaking Activity: Argument How effective was this modern resetting of *Macbeth* in expressing key themes of Shakespeare's play? Discuss your thesis in a short speech, using domain-specific vocabulary.

- Review the clip, making notes of themes that emerge through the modern setting. Cite specific details from the film in your notes.
- Compare those themes to major themes of the play.

- Draft a statement expressing your overall evaluation of the modern production's effectiveness.
- Present your evaluation in a short speech in which you support your claim with specific, relevant evidence from both the film and the play.

Background *For many of his historical plays such as* Macbeth, *Shakespeare relied on the* Chronicles, *first published in 1577, as his main source. Raphael Holinshed is credited as the* Chronicles' *sole author, but many other writers contributed to this work. Although Shakespeare's* Macbeth *resembles the "historical" Macbeth in the* Chronicles, *most scholars do not consider the* Chronicles *to be a reliable document. In fact, the "real" Macbeth (c. 1005–1057) was a Scottish king whom those same scholars consider a just ruler, not a tragic hero.*

from
Holinshed's Chronicles
History by Raphael Holinshed

AS YOU READ Pay attention to the details on which Shakespeare drew to create his tragic hero. Write down any questions you generate during reading.

Duncan's Murder

It fortuned, as Macbeth and Banquo journeyed toward Forres, where the King then lay, they went sporting by the way together without other company save only themselves, passing through the woods and fields, when suddenly, in midst of a laund,[1] there met them three women in strange and wild apparel, resembling creatures of elder world; whom when they attentively beheld, wondering much at the sight, the first of them spoke and said, "All hail, Macbeth, Thane of Glamis!" (for he had lately entered into that dignity and office by the death of his father Sinel). The second of them said, "Hail, Macbeth, Thane of Cawdor!" But the third said, "All hail, Macbeth, that hereafter shalt be King of Scotland!"

Then Banquo. "What manner of women," saith he, "are you, that seem so little favorable unto me, whereas to my fellow here, besides high offices, ye assign also the kingdom, appointing forth

---
[1] **laund:** a clearing in the forest.

nothing for me at all?" "Yes," saith the first of them, "we promise greater benefits unto thee than unto him, for he shall reign indeed, but with an unlucky end; neither shall he leave any issue behind him to succeed in his place, where contrarily thou indeed shalt not reign at all, but of thee those shall be born which shall govern the
20 Scottish kingdom by long order of continual descent." Herewith the foresaid women vanished immediately out of their sight. . . . Shortly after, the Thane of Cawdor being condemned at Forres of treason against the King committed, his lands, livings, and offices were given of the King's liberality to Macbeth. . . .

    Shortly after it chanced that King Duncan, having two sons by his wife (which was the daughter of Siward Earl of Northumberland), he made the elder of them (called Malcolm) Prince of Cumberland, as it were thereby to appoint him his successor in the kingdom immediately after his decease. Macbeth,
30 sore troubled herewith, for that he saw by this means his hope sore hindered . . . he began to take counsel how he might **usurp** the kingdom by force, having a just quarrel[2] so to do (as he took the matter), for that Duncan did what in him lay to defraud him of all manner of title and claim which he might, in time to come, pretend[3] unto the crown.

    The words of the three Weird Sisters also (of whom before ye have heard) greatly encouraged him hereunto; but specially his wife lay sore upon him to attempt the thing, as she that was very ambitious, burning in unquenchable desire to bear the name of a

usurp
(yo͞o-sûrp´) *v.* to take control of illegally.

---

[2] **quarrel:** reason or cause.
[3] **pretend:** lay claim.

40 queen. At length, therefore, communicating his purposed intent
with his trusty friends, amongst whom Banquo was the chiefest,
upon confidence of their promised aid he slew the King at Inverness
or (as some say) at Bothgowanan, in the sixth year of his reign.

Banquo's Murder

This was but a counterfeit zeal of equity[4] showed by him, partly
against his natural inclination, to purchase thereby the favor of
the people. Shortly after, he began to show what he was, instead of
equity practicing cruelty. For the prick of conscience (as it chanceth
ever in tyrants and such as attain to any estate by unrighteous
means) caused him ever to fear lest he should be served of the same
50 cup as he had ministered to his **predecessor**. The words also of
the three Weird Sisters would not out of his mind, which as they
promised him the kingdom, so likewise did they promise it at the
same time unto the posterity of Banquo. He willed therefore the
same Banquo, with his son named Fleance, to come to a supper that
he had prepared for them; which was indeed, as he had devised,
present death at the hands of certain murderers whom he hired
to execute that deed, appointing them to meet with the same
Banquo and his son without the palace, as they returned to their
lodgings, and there to slay them, so that he would not have his
60 house slandered but that in time to come he might clear himself
if anything were laid to his charge upon any suspicion that might
arise.

    It chanced by the benefit of the dark night that, though the
father were slain, yet the son, by the help of almighty God reserving
him to better fortune, escaped that danger; and afterward, having
some inkling (by the **admonition** of some friends which he had
in the court) how his life was sought no less than his father's, who
was slain not by chance-medley[5] (as by the handling of the matter
Macbeth would have had it to appear) but even upon a prepensed[6]
70 device, whereupon to avoid further peril he fled into Wales.

predecessor
(prĕd´ĭ-sĕs´ər) *n.* the
person who held a
position prior to the
current holder.

admonition
(ăd´mə-nĭsh´ən) *n.* a
warning.

COLLABORATIVE DISCUSSION In a small group, discuss similarities and
differences between this excerpt from the *Chronicles* and Shakespeare's
Macbeth. Support your ideas with evidence from both texts.

---

4 **counterfeit zeal of equity:** a false show of fairness.
5 **chance-medley:** accident.
6 **prepensed:** intentional.

 **eBook** *Annotate It!*

Analyze Source Material

RI 1, RL 9

When reading a historical text, you will encounter unfamiliar words and sentence structures that require you to slow down and make sure you understand the author's explicit meaning. Use footnote definitions of challenging words, and try to paraphrase, or restate in your own words, any sentences that don't at first make sense to you. Once you understand the basic information being conveyed, then you can evaluate the historical significance of the text.

As you read the excerpt from the *Chronicles*, you should have noticed ways in which Shakespeare drew upon and transformed this source material to create his character of Macbeth. For example, lines 1–10 from the Holinshed text describe how Macbeth and Banquo came upon "three women in strange and wild apparel, resembling creatures of elder world." In Act I, Scene 3 of *Macbeth*, Shakespeare expands on Holinshed's description of this encounter, bringing it to life.

Analyzing the Text

RI 1, RI 2, RI 3, RI 6, RL 9, SL 1

Cite Text Evidence   Support your responses with evidence from the selection.

1. **Interpret** Direct quotations comprise much of the content of lines 1–20. Is the use of direct quotations effective in supporting the author's purpose in this text? Explain.

2. **Compare** In both the play and the history, Macbeth can be viewed as a flawed, tragic hero. What are the similarities and differences in how each text conveys Macbeth's motivations for killing Duncan and Banquo? Which author is more successful in conveying Macbeth's motivations, and why? Cite textual evidence to support your answer.

3. **Evaluate** Based on your understanding of Shakespeare's context for writing *Macbeth*, how and why did he transform the character from the *Chronicles* to suit his purpose? Consider his priority, and cite evidence from both works.

PERFORMANCE TASK

Speaking Activity: Response to Literature In a small group, discuss *Macbeth* and the *Chronicles*:

- What events and characters are similar? What differences did you notice?
- What does each work reveal about that author's point of view toward Macbeth?

- What might account for differences between the two views of Macbeth?
- Take notes and cite evidence from each text to support your ideas. Then, write a paragraph summarizing your discussion.

Critical Vocabulary

usurp   predecessor   admonition

Practice and Apply   For each Critical Vocabulary word, choose which of the two situations best fits the word's meaning, and explain why your choice is correct.

1. usurp
   a. a player taking over as team captain when the captain is sick
   b. a coach appointing a temporary team captain

2. predecessor
   a. an earlier president
   b. the newly-elected president

3. admonition
   a. a gentle reminder
   b. a stern warning

Vocabulary Strategy: Archaic Language

Many words and phrases in the *Chronicles* are **archaic**, rarely used because they belong to an earlier period of history. Determining their meanings is essential to understanding ideas and events in the text. Here are three strategies you can use:

- Use general and specialized **reference material,** both print and digital. These may include dictionaries for defining specific words; encyclopedias for providing an explanation of places, events, and people; and a search engine for finding specialized online resources to define more obscure references. For high-level words or words from languages other than English, you may need to consult a college-level or bilingual dictionary.
- Consult the **footnotes.** For example, in the *Chronicles*, you can use the footnote for *laund* to learn that it means "an open space or clearing in a forest."
- **Recast** sentences containing an archaic word or phrase. First, use context clues to determine the general meaning of the sentence. Then, rewrite the sentence in your own words while retaining the archaic word or phrase. Try changing the position of the archaic word or phrase in your sentence to test how this affects the general meaning of the sentence.

Practice and Apply   Use print or digital resource materials to define or explain each archaic word or phrase from the *Chronicles*.

creatures of elder world (line 6)	livings (line 23)
beheld (line 6)	hereunto (line 37)
Thane (line 8)	chanceth (line 47)
saith (line 12)	laid to his charge (line 61)

Language and Style: Absolute Phrases

To add information and variety to sentences, writers often use absolute phrases. An **absolute phrase** consists of a noun and a participle (a verb form ending in *–ed* or *–ing* that acts as an adjective), and is always set off with commas. Absolute phrases may also contain the participle's object and any modifiers. Because absolute phrases describe the entire main clause of the sentence, they function as modifiers.

Look at this example of an absolute phrase from Holinshed's *Chronicles*:

> Shortly after, <u>the Thane of Cawdor being condemned at Forres of treason against the King committed</u>, his lands, livings, and offices were given of the King's liberality to Macbeth. . . .

Because this sentence contains archaic language, it may be challenging to understand. However, by identifying the absolute phrase and determining its meaning, readers can comprehend the entire sentence and its significance. In this sentence, the absolute phrase explains why Macbeth gained the "lands, livings, and offices" of the Thane of Cawdor—because the Thane, or lord, was convicted of being disloyal to the King. This incidence of treason thus allowed the second witch's prophecy for Macbeth to be fulfilled.

This chart shows two other examples of absolute phrases.

Absolute Phrase	What It Modifies
<u>Its wheels squealing</u>, the horse-drawn carriage took the corner too fast.	The noun *wheels* is modified by the participle *squealing* and the modifier *Its*. This absolute phrase modifies, or describes, the rest of the sentence, *the horse-drawn carriage took the corner too fast*.
Macbeth thought only about the witches' prophecies, <u>his mind captured by these wild creatures</u>.	The noun *mind* is modified by the participle *captured* and the additional modifiers *his* and *by these wild creatures*. This absolute phrase modifies the rest of the sentence, *Macbeth thought only about the witches' prophecies*.

Practice and Apply Work with a partner to write three sentences that include absolute phrases comparing Holinshed's *Chronicles* with Shakespeare's *Macbeth*. Choose your most effective sentence to share with the class.

Background *English murder mysteries follow a predictable framework and typically contain these elements that help readers predict the conclusion: a dead body; an intelligent detective; an isolated setting; a group of suspects; clues, some of which are misleading; a surprise twist; a capture; and an explanation of how the crime was committed.*

James Thurber (1894–1961) *was an American humor writer and cartoonist. He began his career as a journalist and went on to write essays, short stories, fables, fairy tales, picture books, and plays. In 1997, the Thurber Prize for American Humor was created in his honor.*

The
Macbeth
Murder Mystery

Short Story by James Thurber

AS YOU READ Look for evidence of how James Thurber uses humor to transform Shakespeare's dramatic tragedy *Macbeth* into a murder mystery. Write down any questions you generate during reading.

"It was a stupid mistake to make," said the American woman I had met at my hotel in the English lake country, "but it was on the counter with the other Penguin books—the little sixpenny[1] ones, you know, with the paper covers—and I supposed of course it was a detective story. All the others were detective stories. I'd read all the others, so I bought this one without really looking at it carefully. You can imagine how mad I was when I found out it was Shakespeare." I murmured something sympathetically. "I don't see why the Penguin-books people had to get out Shakespeare's plays 10 in the same size and everything as the detective stories," went on my companion. "I think they have different-colored jackets," I said. "Well, I didn't notice that," she said. "Anyway, I got real comfy in bed that night and all ready to read a good mystery story and here I had 'The Tragedy of Macbeth'—a book for high-school students.

---

[1] **sixpenny:** a former British monetary unit that is equal to six pennies.

Like 'Ivanhoe.'" "Or 'Lorna Doone,'"[2] I said. "Exactly," said the
American lady. "And I was just crazy for a good Agatha Christie,
or something. Hercule Poirot[3] is my favorite detective." "Is he the
rabbity one?" I asked. "Oh, no," said my crime-fiction expert. "He's
the Belgian one. You're thinking of Mr. Pinkerton, the one that
20   helps Inspector Bull.[4] He's good, too."

Over her second cup of tea my companion began to tell the plot
of a detective story that had fooled her completely—it seems it was
the old family doctor all the time. But I cut in on her. "Tell me," I
said. "Did you read 'Macbeth'?" "I had to read it," she said. "There
wasn't a scrap of anything else to read in the whole room." "Did you
like it?" I asked. "No, I did not," she said, **decisively**. "In the first
place, I don't think for a moment that Macbeth did it." I looked at
her blankly. "Did what?" I asked. "I don't think for a moment that
he killed the King," she said. "I don't think the Macbeth woman
30   was mixed up in it, either. You suspect them the most, of course,
but those are the ones that are never guilty—or shouldn't be,
anyway." "I'm afraid," I began, "that I—" "But don't you see?" said
the American lady. "It would spoil everything if you could figure
out right away who did it. Shakespeare was too smart for that. I've
read that people never have figured out 'Hamlet,' so it isn't likely
Shakespeare would have made 'Macbeth' as simple as it seems." I
thought this over while I filled my pipe. "Who do you suspect?"
I asked, suddenly. "Macduff," she said, promptly. "Good God!" I
whispered, softly.
40   "Oh, Macduff did it, all right," said the murder specialist.
"Hercule Poirot would have got him easily." "How did you figure
it out?" I demanded. "Well," she said, "I didn't right away. At first I
suspected Banquo. And then, of course, he was the second person
killed. That was good right in there, that part. The person you
suspect of the first murder should always be the second victim."
"Is that so?" I murmured. "Oh, yes," said my informant. "They
have to keep surprising you. Well after the second murder I
didn't know who the killer was for a while." "How about Malcolm
and Donalbain, the King's sons?" I asked. "As I remember it,
50   they fled right after the first murder. That looks suspicious."
"Too suspicious," said the American lady. "Much too suspicious.
When they flee, they're never guilty. You can count on that." "I

decisively
(dĭ-sī´sĭv-lē) *adv.* in
a firm and resolute
manner.

---

[2] **Ivanhoe . . . Lorna Doone:** historical romance novels set in England and
written in the 1800s by Sir Walter Scott and Richard Doddridge Blackmore,
respectively.

[3] **Agatha Christie . . . Hercule Poirot:** Agatha Christie is a British author of
crime novels, short stories, and plays; Hercule Poirot is a Belgian detective
character who appears in many of her works.

[4] **Mr. Pinkerton . . . Inspector Bull:** series characters in American David
Frome's (pseudonym for Zenith Jones Brown) mystery novels.

"I don't think for a moment that Macbeth did it."

believe," I said, "I'll have a brandy," and I summoned the waiter. My companion leaned toward me, her eyes bright, her teacup quivering. "Do you know who discovered Duncan's body?" she demanded. I said I was sorry, but I had forgotten. "Macduff discovers it," she said, slipping into the historical present. "Then he comes running downstairs and shouts, 'Confusion has broke open the Lord's anointed temple' and '**Sacrilegious** murder has made his

60 masterpiece' and on and on like that." The good lady tapped me on the knee. "All that stuff was rehearsed," she said. "You wouldn't say a lot of stuff like that, off-hand, would you—if you had found a body?" She fixed me with a glittering eye. "I—" I began. "You're right!" she said. "You wouldn't! Unless you had practiced it in advance. 'My God, there's a body in here!' is what an innocent man would say." She sat back with a confident glare.

I thought for a while. "But what do you make of the Third Murderer?" I asked. "You know, the Third Murderer has puzzled 'Macbeth' scholars for three hundred years." "That's because

70 they never thought of Macduff," said the American lady. "It was Macduff, I'm certain. You couldn't have one of the victims murdered by two ordinary thugs—the murderer always has to be somebody important." "But what about the banquet scene?" I asked, after a moment. "How do you account for Macbeth's guilty actions there, when Banquo's ghost came in and sat in his chair?" The lady leaned forward and tapped me on the knee again. "There wasn't any ghost," she said. "A big, strong man like that doesn't go around seeing ghosts—especially in a brightly lighted banquet hall with dozens of people around. Macbeth was shielding somebody!" "Who

80 was he shielding?" I asked. "Mrs. Macbeth, of course," she said. "He

sacrilegious
(săk´rə-lĭj´əs) *adj.* grossly irreverent toward what is sacred.

thought she did it and he was going to take the rap himself. The husband always does that when the wife is suspected." "But what," I demanded, "about the sleepwalking scene, then?" "The same thing, only the other way around," said my companion. "That time she was shielding him. She wasn't asleep at all. Do you remember where it says, 'Enter Lady Macbeth with a taper'?" "Yes," I said. "Well, people who walk in their sleep never carry lights!" said my fellow-traveler. "They have second sight. Did you ever hear of a sleepwalker carrying a light?" "No," I said, "I never did." "Well,

90   then, she wasn't asleep. She was acting guilty to shield Macbeth." "I think," I said, "I'll have another brandy," and I called the waiter. When he brought it, I drank it rapidly and rose to go. "I believe," I said, "that you have got hold of something. Would you lend me that 'Macbeth'? I'd like to look it over tonight. I don't feel, somehow, as if I'd ever really read it." "I'll get it for you," she said. "But you'll find that I am right."

I read the play over carefully that night, and the next morning, after breakfast, I sought out the American woman. She was on the putting green, and I came up behind her silently and took her arm.

100   She gave an exclamation. "Could I see you alone?" I asked, in a low voice. She nodded cautiously and followed me to a **secluded** spot. "You've found out something?" she breathed. "I've found out," I said triumphantly, "the name of the murderer!" "You mean it wasn't Macduff?" she said. "Macduff is as innocent of those murders," I said, "as Macbeth and the Macbeth woman." I opened the copy of the play, which I had with me, and turned to Act II, Scene 2. "Here," I said, "you will see where Lady Macbeth says, 'I laid their daggers ready. He could not miss 'em. Had he not resembled my father as he slept, I had done it.' Do you see?" "No," said the American woman,

110   bluntly, "I don't." "But it's simple!" I exclaimed. "I wonder I didn't see it years ago. The reason Duncan resembled Lady Macbeth's father as he slept is that it actually was her father!" "Good God!" breathed my companion, softly. "Lady Macbeth's father killed the King," I said, "and hearing someone coming, thrust the body under the bed and crawled into the bed himself." "But," said the lady, "you can't have a murderer who only appears in the story once. You can't have that." "I know that," I said, and I turned to Act II, Scene 4. "It says here, 'Enter Ross with an old Man.' Now, that old man is never identified and it is my **contention** that he was old Mr. Macbeth,

120   whose ambition it was to make his daughter Queen. There you have your motive." "But even then," cried the American lady, "he's still a minor character!" "Not," I said, gleefully, "when you realize that he was also one of the weird sisters in disguise!" "You mean one of the three witches?" "Precisely," I said. "Listen to this speech of

secluded
(sĭ-klōō′dĭd) *adj.*
hidden from view.

contention
(kən-tĕn′shən) *n.* an assertion put forward in argument.

the old man's. 'On Tuesday last, a falcon towering in her pride of place, was by a mousing owl hawk'd at and kill'd.' Who does that sound like?" "It sounds like the way the three witches talk," said my companion, reluctantly. "Precisely!" I said again. "Well, said the American woman, "maybe you're right, but—" "I'm sure I am," I said. "And do you know what I'm going to do now?" "No," she said. "What?" "Buy a copy of 'Hamlet,'" I said, "and solve that!" My companion's eyes brightened. "Then," she said, "you don't think Hamlet did it?" "I am," I said, "absolutely positive he didn't." "But who," she demanded, "do you suspect?" I looked at her **cryptically**. "Everybody," I said, and disappeared into a small grove of trees as silently as I had come.

130

cryptically
(krĭp´tĭk-lē) *adv.*
in a secretive or
mysterious manner.

COLLABORATIVE DISCUSSION With a partner, discuss the characteristics of murder mysteries you've read or seen. Which characteristics does Thurber use to classify *Macbeth* as a murder mystery? In your discussion, cite evidence from the text.

Analyze How an Author Draws on Shakespeare

The works of William Shakespeare have influenced many authors over the centuries. Shakespeare's plays contain insights on human nature that are timeless. For example, his tragedy *Macbeth* is known for themes of uncontrolled ambition, betrayal, and corrupting power, themes shared by many literary works. Not only are Shakespeare's themes familiar, but his characters and conflicts are as well. When an author refers to a Shakespearean character, such as Lady Macbeth, or to a situation, such as King Duncan's murder, that reference makes a connection with the audience and deepens our understanding of the author's work.

In "The Macbeth Murder Mystery," James Thurber draws upon Shakespeare's *Macbeth* to create a **satire**, a literary work that ridicules a vice or folly found in society. Satirists use humor in their works to cause people to change how they think or what their priorities are. Readers of Thurber's short story will be familiar with the references to *Macbeth*, but the unexpected way Thurber's characters transform the tragedy into a formulaic British murder mystery allows him to comment on how people approach literature. As you analyze "The Macbeth Murder Mystery," consider these questions:

> **To which elements of Shakespeare's play does Thurber refer in his story?**

> **How are the play's elements transformed in the short story?**

> **What effect do these changes have on the characters? on the reader?**

> **What issue does Thurber ridicule in his story?**

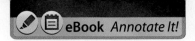

Analyzing the Text

RL 1, RL 4, RL 9, W 3

Cite Text Evidence   Support your responses with evidence from the selection.

1. **Connect** Writers use **satire** to ridicule follies or foolish ideas commonly held in a society. What does Thurber ridicule in his satire? What point does he make regarding the expectations of reading different types of literature?

2. **Draw Conclusions** The American woman explains why some characters in the play are not guilty of Macbeth's murder. What reasons does she provide to prove that Malcolm, Donalbain, Macbeth, and Lady Macbeth are innocent? Does she have an understanding of Shakespeare's play? Explain your answer.

3. **Interpret** In lines 94–95, the narrator says of Shakespeare's play, "I don't feel, somehow, as if I'd ever really read it." In what way is this statement ironic? How does this incidence of irony add to Thurber's satire?

4. **Compare** In the last paragraph, the narrator presents his solution to *Macbeth*'s murder mystery. How does his version of Duncan's murder differ from Shakespeare's? Explain how the characters are recast and the events of the play are changed.

5. **Analyze** Thurber is known for his humor and wit. How does he convey humor in this story? Cite details from the text to support your response.

PERFORMANCE TASK

Writing Activity: Narrative In this story, characters misinterpret a dramatic tragedy as a murder mystery. How does the understanding of literary genres shape the interpretation of a story? Can characteristics of one genre be applied to another for a different interpretation? Explore these ideas by transforming one type of story into another.

1. With a partner, choose a familiar fable or fairy tale. Note the elements that make the story you chose a fable or fairy tale.

2. Think about the conflict or characters in the story. In what different genre might the conflict or characters appear? List the elements of the new genre. Genres you might consider include romance, science fiction, mystery, and comedy.

3. Rewrite your story so that it maintains the same events but contains the characteristics of the new genre. For example, a fairy tale can be rewritten as a science fiction story by eliminating the magical elements and by changing the setting.

4. Exchange your story with another pair and try to identify the fairy tale or fable your classmates used as their source.

The Macbeth Murder Mystery **307**

Critical Vocabulary

decisively   sacrilegious   secluded   contention   cryptically

Practice and Apply   Explain which Critical Vocabulary word is most closely associated with each idea or situation.

1. Which Critical Vocabulary word goes with a disagreement? Why?

2. Which Critical Vocabulary word goes with a mysterious note? Why?

3. Which Critical Vocabulary word goes with a judge's ruling? Why?

4. Which Critical Vocabulary word goes with swearing in anger? Why?

5. Which Critical Vocabulary word goes with a secret hideout? Why?

Vocabulary Strategy: Words from Latin

A word's **etymology** shows the ultimate origin and historical development of that word. Many English words are derived from Latin ones. For example, the Critical Vocabulary word *sacrilegious* comes from the Latin word *sacer*, which means "holy." *Sacrilegious* contains the root or basic word part *sacr–*. Understanding a word's etymology will help you grasp the word's meaning. In addition, knowing the meaning of roots will help you define other words with similar roots.

Practice and Apply   Follow these steps to complete the activity:

1. Use a dictionary to look up the etymology of each word in the chart, and write the meaning of its Latin root.

2. Identify two additional words that contain the same Latin root.

3. Write three sentences for each root, one using the word from the selection and two others using the additional related words you identified.

Word	Root
suspected (line 43)	*spec–*
certain (line 71)	*cert–*
exclamation (line 100)	*clam–*
motive (line 121)	*mot–*

5 P.M., Tuesday, August 23, 2005

Poem by Patricia Smith

Background *A hurricane develops in stages. At any point, the storm may either fall apart or become more organized and intense, progressing to the next stage. In the first stage, a tropical disturbance occurs, in which loosely-organized, heavy rain clouds develop. The storm system draws moisture from the warm, humid air on the ocean's surface. This warm air rises and cooler air moves down to replace it, creating a swirling pattern of winds, a tropical depression. If the winds reach 39 to 73 miles per hour, the depression becomes a tropical storm. At 74 miles per hour, the storm becomes a hurricane.*

On August 23, 2005, a tropical depression formed off the southern coast of the United States. It would develop over the next few days into Hurricane Katrina, first sweeping over the east coast of Florida and then homing in on Mississippi and Louisiana, where it made a second landfall on August 29. One of the most powerful and devastating hurricanes to ever hit U.S. soil, Katrina's massive winds and torrential rainfall created a storm surge of more than 25 feet, breaching a crucial levee and plunging most of the city of New Orleans under water. The hurricane was responsible for at least 1,800 deaths, and it forever changed the Gulf Coast and its inhabitants.

Patricia Smith (b. 1955) *is an award-winning poet, performance artist, and four-time National Poetry Slam champion. She is known for using personas—first-person voices that range from gang members to monsters of Greek mythology—to expose uncomfortable truths about situations that most people don't want to face. Her work evokes such themes as self-destruction, betrayal, and vindictiveness, highlighting the spiritual and political impact of the subjects she explores. This poem appears in her book* Blood Dazzler, *a collection that traces the environmental and human costs of Hurricane Katrina. The book earned Smith a National Book Award nomination in 2008.*

5 P.M., Tuesday, August 23, 2005

*"Data from an Air Force reserve unit reconnaissance aircraft . . . along
with observations from the Bahamas and nearby ships . . . indicate the
broad low pressure area over the southeastern Bahamas has become
organized enough to be classified as tropical depression twelve."*

5   —NATIONAL HURRICANE CENTER

A muted thread of gray light, hovering ocean,
becomes throat, pulls in wriggle, anemone, kelp,[1]
widens with the want of it. I become
a mouth, thrashing hair, an overdone eye. How dare
10 the water belittle my thirst, treat me as just
another
small
disturbance,

try to feed me
15 from the bottom of its hand?

I will require praise,
unbridled winds to define my body,
a crime behind my teeth
because

20 every woman begins as weather,
sips slow thunder, knows her hips. Every woman
harbors a chaos, can
wait for it, straddling a fever.

For now,
25 I console myself with small furies,
those dips in my dawning system. I pull in
a bored breath. The brine[2] shivers.

COLLABORATIVE DISCUSSION How would you describe the poem's
speaker? With a partner, discuss how the poet creates a vivid character as
the voice of the poem. Cite specific lines to support your ideas.

---

[1] **anemone, kelp:** sea anemones are brightly colored, tentacled sea creatures; kelp
is a kind of seaweed.
[2] **brine:** salt water or sea water.

Support Inferences About Word Choice

Poetry packs a lot of meaning into a small space, so poets must choose and arrange their words carefully. Using **figurative language**, or words that communicate meaning beyond the literal interpretation, is one way a poet can add an extra dimension to the text. One example is a **metaphor**, a figure of speech that implies a comparison between two unlike things that share a key characteristic. An **extended metaphor** is developed at length, often continuing across several stanzas or throughout the poem.

Another figure of speech often used by poets is **personification**, in which human qualities are given to a nonhuman subject. Like a metaphor, personification makes a comparison between two things that are dissimilar in order to shed new light on one or both of them.

Poets also choose words for their **connotative** meanings, or the feelings associated with them. By interpreting the figurative and connotative language in a poem, readers can infer the speaker's **tone**, or attitude toward the subject, which often reveals the poet's meaning.

Consider the questions in the chart to help you analyze the poem.

Words from Text	Analysis
A muted thread of gray light, hovering ocean, becomes throat . . .	**This image sets the scene for what is to come.** • What is the "thread of gray light"? • In what way is a developing hurricane like a throat?
. . . How dare the water belittle my thirst, treat me as just another small disturbance . . .	**These lines develop the character of the poem's speaker.** • From whose point of view is this poem presented? • What effect does the use of single words on each line create?
every woman begins as weather, . . . Every woman harbors a chaos . . .	**These lines develop a comparison.** • Is it literally true that "every woman begins as weather"? • What is being compared in these lines?
For now, I console myself with small furies, . . . I pull in a bored breath. The brine shivers.	**The poem ends on a suspenseful note.** • What is the speaker's tone in these lines? • Why does the brine shiver?

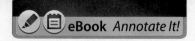

Analyzing the Text

RL 1, RL 2,
RL 4, RL 5, SL 6

Cite Text Evidence   Support your responses with evidence from the selection.

1. **Draw Conclusions** Why does the poet begin this poem with a quotation from the National Hurricane Center? What does this information convey to the reader?

2. **Cite Evidence** What nonhuman subject is personified in the poem? Identify specific words and phrases that give the subject human qualities.

3. **Analyze** Describe the speaker's tone in this poem. What words and phrases does the poet use to establish this tone?

4. **Interpret** What words and phrases from the poem have especially strong connotative meanings? What feelings do they convey?

5. **Analyze** Read the first two stanzas aloud, keeping in mind the voice and personality of the speaker. How do the short lines at the end of this passage affect tone and meaning?

6. **Infer** What ultimate **theme**, or deeper message about life, does the poet convey through the personification and imagery in the poem?

PERFORMANCE TASK

Speaking Activity: Poetry Recitation Patricia Smith is a National Poetry Slam Champion, and this poem is meant to be spoken. Work with a small group to adapt the poem for a male voice and practice reading it aloud.

1. Discuss what words and phrases in the poem stand out and what figurative and connotative meanings they have. How should those words be spoken? Ominously? Angrily?

2. Think about how the poem could have instead personified the hurricane as male. Discuss what words and phrases could be substituted to adapt this poem for a male voice.

3. Take turns reading the poem aloud, emphasizing key words and phrases. Read both versions, demonstrating both female and male voices.

4. Write a brief summary of what you learned by reading the poem aloud and by adapting the language to suit a male speaker.

5. Finally, memorize and recite your adaptation, using your voice and body language, to contribute to a class poetry slam.

Write an Informative Essay

This collection focuses on human ambition and our eternal quest for power. In his speech "Why Read Shakespeare?" Michael Mack argues that if you don't see yourself in Macbeth's ambition, you're either misreading the play or misreading yourself. Review the texts in this collection, including the anchor, Shakespeare's *Macbeth*. Then write an informative essay that explains how one aspect of Macbeth's character represents a universal human trait.

W 2a–f Write informative/ explanatory texts.
W 9a–b Draw evidence from literary or informational texts to support analysis.

An effective informative essay

- includes a clear thesis about the universality of one of Macbeth's key personality traits

- engages readers with an interesting observation, quotation, or detail

- organizes central ideas in a logically structured body that clearly develops the thesis

- uses domain-specific vocabulary and logical transitions to clarify and connect ideas

- includes evidence from the texts to illustrate central ideas

- has a concluding section that follows logically from the body of the essay and sums up the central ideas of the analysis

Visit hmhfyi.com to explore your topic and enhance your research.

PLAN

myNotebook

Analyze the Texts Review *Macbeth* and other collection texts.

- Take notes on Macbeth's character traits. Which of his traits are revealed in other texts in this collection and in people today?

- Choose other texts that provide strong support for your thesis.

- Write down important details, examples, and relevant quotations from all of your chosen texts that support your thesis.

Use the annotation tools in your eBook to find evidence that supports your ideas. Save each piece of evidence to your notebook.

Mentor Text Here is an example of how Michael Mack supports a thesis using text evidence in "Why Read Shakespeare?"

" Take the parable of the prodigal son: in this fiction you learn about sin and forgiveness. And you also learn about yourself. You realize that the story is about you—you are the prodigal son. The problem is that you are not only the prodigal son but also the resentful, self-righteous older brother. "

ACADEMIC VOCABULARY

As you share your ideas about ambition, be sure to use these words.

comprise
incidence
priority
thesis
ultimate

Get Organized Prioritize your ideas in a graphic organizer.

- Write a thesis statement about how your chosen trait is a human quality that all people exhibit.

- Decide which organizational pattern you will use to develop your essay. Be sure your key ideas and support are presented in a logical order that flows from one to the next.

- Use your organizational pattern to sort the evidence you have gathered from the selections. A hierarchy diagram can help you organize ideas and evidence for the body of your essay.

Interactive Lessons
To help you choose an effective order, complete the following lesson:
• Writing Informative Texts: Organizing Ideas

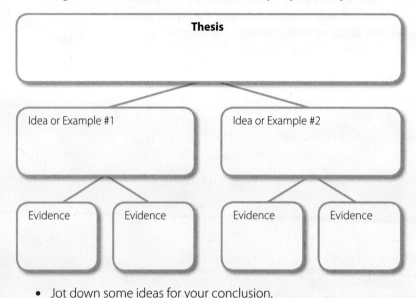

- Jot down some ideas for your conclusion.

PRODUCE

Draft Your Essay Write a draft of your essay, following your graphic organizer. Remember that essay writing requires formal language and a respectful tone.

Write your rough draft in *my*WriteSmart. Focus on getting your ideas down, rather than perfecting your choice of language.

- Introduce a clear and concise thesis statement, and begin with an interesting quotation or detail.

- Present your details, quotations, and examples from the selections in logically ordered paragraphs. Each paragraph should have a central idea related to your thesis with relevant evidence to support it. Be sure to use precise language, including domain-specific terms, to make your ideas clear for readers.

- Use transitions to connect the main sections of your essay and to clarify the relationships among your ideas.

- Write a conclusion that summarizes your analysis and presents a final synthesis of your central ideas.

Language and Style: Create Cohesion

Your essay draws from multiple texts to develop a complex idea, so make sure readers can follow your line of reasoning. Transitional words and phrases can make ideas and evidence **cohesive**, or logically connected. Notice how Michael Mack links ideas with transitions of varying lengths:

> "In response to these serious-minded objections to reading Shakespeare, I would like to suggest that what you find in Shakespeare is as serious as the subject matter of your other courses."

> "What is more, as we hold the volume of Shakespeare in front of us, we see that it reflects not only the world around us, but also ourselves."

Review your draft, adding a variety of transitions to link ideas and create cohesion.

REVISE

Exchange Essays Share your essay with a partner. As you read your partner's essay, consider these questions:

Questions	Tips	Revision Techniques
Does the introduction engage readers and state a clear thesis?	**Underline** the thesis statement and **highlight** an engaging idea in the introduction.	**Add** a thesis statement, and **add** an attention-getting detail to the introduction.
Are ideas organized logically and linked with transitions?	**Note** the idea explored in each paragraph. **Underline** transitional words and phrases.	**Reorder** evidence to center each paragraph on one idea. **Add** transitions to link ideas.
Does text evidence support the ideas in each paragraph?	**Highlight** text evidence in each paragraph.	**Add** evidence from more than one text to each paragraph.
Does the conclusion effectively summarize ideas?	**Underline** the restated thesis or summary of ideas in the conclusion.	**Add** a restatement of the thesis or summary of the essay's ideas.
Is the style appropriately formal, including domain-specific vocabulary?	**Note** slang or informal word choices. **Highlight** domain-specific terms.	**Replace** informal language. **Add** literary, psychological, or academic language.

Share feedback with your partner, and use it to strengthen your essay.

myWriteSmart

Have your partner or a group of peers review your draft in *my*WriteSmart. Ask your reviewers to note any evidence that does not support the thesis.

Interactive Lessons

To help you use an appropriate tone, complete the following lesson:
- Writing Informative Texts: Precise Language and Vocabulary

PRESENT

Share Your Work Read your final draft to a small group. The audience should listen, take notes, and comment or ask questions.

PERFORMANCE TASK RUBRIC
INFORMATIVE ESSAY

	Ideas and Evidence	Organization	Language
4	• An eloquent introduction includes titles and authors of selections; a clear thesis statement describes the view of the chosen trait presented in the texts. • Specific, relevant details support the central ideas. • A satisfying conclusion synthesizes the ideas and summarizes the analysis.	• Central ideas and supporting evidence are organized effectively and logically throughout the essay. • Varied transitions successfully show the relationships between ideas.	• The analysis uses an appropriately formal style and a knowledgeable, objective tone. • Language is precise and captures the writer's thoughts with originality. • Sentence beginnings, lengths, and structures vary and flow well. • Spelling, capitalization, and punctuation are correct. • Grammar and usage are correct.
3	• The introduction identifies selection titles and authors but could be more engaging; the thesis statement identifies the chosen trait but may be cursory. • Most central ideas are adequately supported. • The concluding section synthesizes most of the ideas and summarizes most of the analysis.	• The organization of central ideas and supporting evidence is usually easy to follow. • Transitions generally clarify the relationships between ideas.	• The style is generally formal, and the tone usually communicates confidence. • Most language is precise. • Sentence beginnings, lengths, and structures vary somewhat. • A few spelling, capitalization, and punctuation mistakes occur. • Some grammatical and usage errors occur but do not interfere with understanding.
2	• The introduction identifies the selections; the thesis statement only hints at the main idea of the analysis. • Details support some central ideas but are often too general. • The concluding section gives an incomplete summary of the analysis and merely restates the thesis.	• Most central ideas are organized logically, but supporting details may be out of place. • More transitions are needed throughout the essay to connect ideas.	• The style is often informal, and the tone reflects a superficial understanding of the texts. • Language is repetitive or vague at times. • Sentence structures barely vary, and some fragments or run-on sentences are present. • Spelling, capitalization, and punctuation are often incorrect. • Grammar and usage are incorrect in many places, sometimes making the writer's ideas unclear.
1	• The appropriate elements of an introduction are missing. • Details and evidence are irrelevant or missing. • The analysis lacks a concluding section.	• A logical organization is not used; ideas are presented randomly. • Transitions are not used, making the essay difficult to understand.	• Style and tone are inappropriate. • Language is inaccurate, repetitive, and vague. • Repetitive sentence structure, fragments, and run-on sentences make the writing difficult to follow. • Numerous errors in spelling, capitalization, or punctuation occur. • Many grammar and usage errors interfere with the writer's ideas.

Hard-Won Liberty

"There is no easy walk to freedom anywhere."

—Nelson Mandela

Hard-Won Liberty

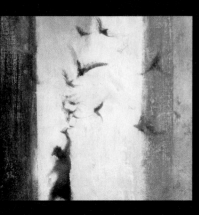

This collection travels around the world to explore how people win their freedom from oppression.

Stream to Start

hmhfyi.com

Channel One News®

COLLECTION
PERFORMANCE TASK Preview

At the end of this collection, you will have the opportunity to complete this task:

• Deliver an argument that answers this question: What constitutes true freedom?

ACADEMIC VOCABULARY

Study the words and their definitions in the chart below. You will use these words as you discuss and write about the texts in this collection.

Word	Definition	Related Forms
comprehensive (kŏm´prĭ-hĕn´sĭv) *adj.*	complete or of sufficient scope to include all aspects	comprehensively, comprehension
equivalent (ĭ-kwĭv´ə-lənt) *adj.*	equal to or similar	equivalence, equivalently
incentive (ĭn-sĕn´tĭv) *n.*	an inducement or motivation to do something	disincentive, incentivize
innovate (ĭn´ə-vāt´) *v.*	to change or develop through new or original methods, processes, or ideas	innovation, innovator, innovative
media (mē´dē-ə) *n.*	a means or vehicle for communication	medium

Martin Luther King Jr. (1929–1968) *led a nonviolent protest in 1963 against lunch counter segregation in Birmingham, Alabama. He was jailed along with many of his supporters. While in jail, King wrote this letter in response to the local clergy. As a Baptist minister and a leader of the civil rights movement, King helped to organize the 1963 March on Washington, where he delivered his "I Have a Dream" speech. His leadership was crucial in passing the Civil Rights Act of 1964. In the same year, he received the Nobel Peace Prize. King was assassinated in 1968.*

Letter from Birmingham Jail

Argument by Martin Luther King Jr.

AS YOU READ Pay attention to what King hoped to achieve in Birmingham. Write down any questions you generate during reading.

As you read, save new words to *my*WordList.

April 16, 1963
My Dear Fellow Clergymen:

While confined here in the Birmingham city jail, I came across your recent statement calling my present activities "unwise and untimely." Seldom do I pause to answer criticism of my work and ideas. If I sought to answer all the criticisms that cross my desk, my secretaries would have little time for anything other than such correspondence in the course of the day, and I would have no time for constructive work. But since I feel that you are men of genuine
10 good will and that your criticisms are sincerely set forth, I want to try to answer your statement in what I hope will be patient and reasonable terms.

I think I should indicate why I am here in Birmingham, since you have been influenced by the view which argues against "outsiders coming in." I have the honor of serving as president of the Southern Christian Leadership Conference, an organization operating in every southern state, with headquarters in Atlanta, Georgia. We have some eighty-five affiliated organizations across the South, and one of them is the Alabama Christian Movement for

20 Human Rights. Frequently we share staff, educational and financial resources with our affiliates. Several months ago the affiliate here in Birmingham asked us to be on call to engage in a nonviolent direct-action program if such were deemed necessary. We readily consented, and when the hour came we lived up to our promise. So I, along with several members of my staff, am here because I was invited here. I am here because I have organizational ties here.

But more basically, I am in Birmingham because injustice is here. Just as the prophets of the eighth century B.C. left their villages and carried their "thus saith the Lord" far beyond the

30 boundaries of their home towns, and just as the Apostle Paul left his village of Tarsus and carried the gospel of Jesus Christ to the far corners of the Greco-Roman world, so am I compelled to carry the gospel of freedom beyond my own home town. Like Paul, I must constantly respond to the Macedonian call for aid.[1]

Moreover, I am **cognizant** of the interrelatedness of all communities and states. I cannot sit idly by in Atlanta and not be concerned about what happens in Birmingham. Injustice anywhere is a threat to justice everywhere. We are caught in an inescapable network of mutuality, tied in a single garment of destiny. Whatever

40 affects one directly, affects all indirectly. Never again can we afford to live with the narrow, provincial "outside agitator" idea. Anyone who lives inside the United States can never be considered an outsider anywhere within its bounds.

You deplore the demonstrations taking place in Birmingham. But your statement, I am sorry to say, fails to express a similar concern for the conditions that brought about the demonstrations. I am sure that none of you would want to rest content with the superficial kind of social analysis that deals merely with effects and does not grapple with underlying causes. It is unfortunate that

50 demonstrations are taking place in Birmingham, but it is even more unfortunate that the city's white power structure left the Negro community with no alternative.

In any nonviolent campaign there are four basic steps: collection of the facts to determine whether injustices exist; negotiation; self-purification; and direct action. We have gone through all these steps in Birmingham. There can be no gainsaying the fact that racial injustice engulfs this community. Birmingham is probably the most thoroughly segregated city in the United States. Its ugly record of brutality is widely known. Negroes have

cognizant
(kŏg′nĭ-zənt) *adj.*
aware or conscious of.

---

[1] **Macedonian call for aid:** according to the Bible (Acts 16), the apostle Paul received a vision calling him to preach in Macedonia, an area north of Greece.

60 experienced grossly unjust treatment in the courts. There have been more unsolved bombings of Negro homes and churches in Birmingham than in any other city in the nation. These are the hard, brutal facts of the case. On the basis of these conditions, Negro leaders sought to negotiate with the city fathers. But the latter consistently refused to engage in good-faith negotiation.

Then, last September, came the opportunity to talk with leaders of Birmingham's economic community. In the course of the negotiations, certain promises were made by the merchants—for example, to remove the stores' humiliating racial signs.[2] On the
70 basis of these promises, the Reverend Fred Shuttlesworth and the leaders of the Alabama Christian Movement for Human Rights agreed to a **moratorium** on all demonstrations. As the weeks and months went by, we realized that we were the victims of a broken promise. A few signs, briefly removed, returned; the others remained.

moratorium (môr´ə-tôr´ē-əm) *n.* a temporary suspension or agreed-upon delay.

As in so many past experiences, our hopes had been blasted, and the shadow of deep disappointment settled upon us. We had no alternative except to prepare for direct action, whereby we would present our very bodies as a means of laying our case before
80 the conscience of the local and the national community. Mindful of the difficulties involved, we decided to undertake a process of self-purification. We began a series of workshops on nonviolence, and we repeatedly asked ourselves: "Are you able to accept blows without **retaliating**?" "Are you able to endure the ordeal of jail?" We decided to schedule our direct-action program for the Easter season, realizing that except for Christmas, this is the main shopping period of the year. Knowing that a strong economic-withdrawal program[3] would be the by-product of direct action, we felt that this would be the best time to bring pressure to bear on the
90 merchants for the needed change.

retaliate (rĭ-tăl´ē-āt´) *v.* to respond in kind to having been acted upon, often with harmful intent.

Then it occurred to us that Birmingham's mayoralty election was coming up in March, and we speedily decided to postpone action until after election day. When we discovered that the Commissioner of Public Safety, Eugene "Bull" Connor, had piled up enough votes to be in the run-off, we decided again to postpone action until the day after the run-off so that the demonstrations could not be used to cloud the issues. Like many others, we waited to see Mr. Connor defeated, and to this end we endured postponement after postponement. Having aided in this
100 community need, we felt that our direct-action program could be delayed no longer.

---

[2] **racial signs:** signs that marked segregated areas of buildings and other facilities.
[3] **economic withdrawal program:** boycott.

You may well ask: "Why direct action? Why sit-ins, marches and so forth? Isn't negotiation a better path?" You are quite right in calling for negotiation. Indeed, this is the very purpose of direct action. Nonviolent direct action seeks to create such a crisis and foster such a tension that a community which has constantly refused to negotiate is forced to confront the issue. It seeks so to dramatize the issue that it can no longer be ignored. My citing the creation of tension as part of the work of the nonviolent-resister

110 may sound rather shocking. But I must confess that I am not afraid of the word "tension." I have earnestly opposed violent tension, but there is a type of constructive, nonviolent tension which is necessary for growth. Just as Socrates[4] felt that it was necessary to create a tension in the mind so that individuals could rise from the bondage of myths and half-truths to the unfettered realm of creative analysis and objective appraisal, so must we see the need for nonviolent gadflies to create the kind of tension in society that will help men rise from the dark depths of prejudice and racism to the majestic heights of understanding and brotherhood.

120 The purpose of our direct-action program is to create a situation so crisis-packed that it will inevitably open the door to negotiation. I therefore concur with you in your call for negotiation. Too long has our beloved Southland been bogged down in a tragic effort to live in monologue rather than dialogue.

One of the basic points in your statement is that the action that I and my associates have taken in Birmingham is untimely. Some have asked: "Why didn't you give the new city administration time to act?" The only answer that I can give to this query is that the new Birmingham administration must be prodded about as much

130 as the outgoing one, before it will act. . . . My friends, I must say to you that we have not made a single gain in civil rights without determined legal and nonviolent pressure. Lamentably, it is an historical fact that privileged groups seldom give up their privileges voluntarily. Individuals may see the moral light and voluntarily give up their unjust posture; but, as Reinhold Niebuhr[5] has reminded us, groups tend to be more immoral than individuals.

We know through painful experience that freedom is never voluntarily given by the oppressor; it must be demanded by the oppressed. Frankly, I have yet to engage in a direct-action campaign

140 that was "well timed" in the view of those who have not suffered unduly from the disease of segregation. For years now I have heard the word "Wait!" It rings in the ear of every Negro with piercing

---

[4] **Socrates:** (c. 470–399 BC) Greek philosopher and major influence in the development of Western thought.

[5] **Reinhold Niebuhr:** (1892–1971) American theologian whose writings address moral and social problems.

Martin Luther King Jr. (seated at left of table) speaks at a news conference in Birmingham, AL, in May of 1963.

familiarity. This "Wait" has almost always meant "Never." We must come to see, with one of our distinguished jurists, that "justice too long delayed is justice denied."

We have waited for more than 340 years for our constitutional and God-given rights. The nations of Asia and Africa are moving with jetlike speed toward gaining political independence, but we still creep at horse-and-buggy pace toward gaining a cup of coffee
150 at a lunch counter. Perhaps it is easy for those who have never felt the stinging darts of segregation to say, "Wait." But when you have seen vicious mobs lynch your mothers and fathers at will and drown your sisters and brothers at whim; when you have seen hate-filled policemen curse, kick and even kill your black brothers and sisters; when you see the vast majority of your twenty million Negro brothers smothering in an airtight cage of poverty in the midst of an affluent society; when you suddenly find your tongue twisted and your speech stammering as you seek to explain to your six-year-old daughter why she can't go to the public amusement
160 park that has just been advertised on television, and see tears

welling up in her eyes when she is told that Funtown is closed to colored children, and see ominous clouds of inferiority beginning to form in her little mental sky, and see her beginning to distort her personality by developing an unconscious bitterness toward white people; when you have to concoct an answer for a five-year-old son who is asking: "Daddy, why do white people treat colored people so mean?"; when you take a cross-country drive and find it necessary to sleep night after night in the uncomfortable corners of your automobile because no motel will accept you; when you are
170 humiliated day in and day out by nagging signs reading "white" and "colored"; when your first name becomes "nigger," your middle name becomes "boy" (however old you are) and your last name becomes "John," and your wife and mother are never given the respected title "Mrs."; when you are harried by day and haunted by night by the fact that you are a Negro, living constantly at tiptoe stance, never quite knowing what to expect next, and are plagued with inner fears and outer resentments; when you are forever fighting a degenerating sense of "nobodiness"—then you will understand why we find it difficult to wait. There comes a
180 time when the cup of endurance runs over, and men are no longer willing to be plunged into the abyss of despair. I hope, sirs, you can understand our legitimate and unavoidable impatience.

You express a great deal of anxiety over our willingness to break laws. This is certainly a legitimate concern. Since we so diligently urge people to obey the Supreme Court's decision of 1954 outlawing segregation in the public schools,[6] at first glance it may seem rather paradoxical for us consciously to break laws. One may well ask: "How can you advocate breaking some laws and obeying others?" The answer lies in the fact that there are two types of laws:
190 just and unjust. I would be the first to advocate obeying just laws. One has not only a legal but a moral responsibility to obey just laws. Conversely, one has a moral responsibility to disobey unjust laws. I would agree with St. Augustine[7] that "an unjust law is no law at all."

Now, what is the difference between the two? How does one determine whether a law is just or unjust? A just law is a man-made code that squares with the moral law or the law of God. An unjust law is a code that is out of harmony with the moral law. To put it in the terms of St. Thomas Aquinas:[8] An unjust law is a
200 human law that is not rooted in eternal law and natural law. Any

---

[6] **Supreme Court . . . public schools:** The U.S. Supreme Court's decision in the case *Brown* v. *Board of Education of Topeka, Kansas.*

[7] **St. Augustine:** North African bishop (AD 354–430) regarded as a founder of Christianity.

[8] **St. Thomas Aquinas:** noted philosopher and theologian (1225–1274).

law that uplifts human personality is just. Any law that degrades human personality is unjust. All segregation statutes are unjust because segregation distorts the soul and damages the personality. It gives the segregator a false sense of superiority and the segregated a false sense of inferiority. Segregation, to use the terminology of the Jewish philosopher Martin Buber,[9] substitutes an "I-it" relationship for an "I-thou" relationship and ends up relegating persons to the status of things. Hence segregation is not only politically, economically and sociologically unsound, it is morally wrong and sinful. Paul Tillich[10] has said that sin is separation. Is not segregation an existential expression of man's tragic separation, his awful estrangement, his terrible sinfulness? Thus it is that I can urge men to obey the 1954 decision of the Supreme Court, for it is morally right; and I can urge them to disobey segregation ordinances, for they are morally wrong.

Let us consider a more concrete example of just and unjust laws. An unjust law is a code that a numerical or power majority group compels a minority group to obey but does not make binding on itself. This is *difference* made legal. By the same token, a just law is a code that a majority compels a minority to follow and that it is willing to follow itself. This is *sameness* made legal.

Let me give another explanation. A law is unjust if it is inflicted on a minority that, as a result of being denied the right to vote, had no part in enacting or devising the law. Who can say that the legislature of Alabama which set up that state's segregation laws was democratically elected? Throughout Alabama all sorts of devious methods are used to prevent Negroes from becoming registered voters, and there are some counties in which, even though Negroes constitute a majority of the population, not a single Negro is registered. Can any law enacted under such circumstances be considered democratically structured?

Sometimes a law is just on its face and unjust in its application. For instance, I have been arrested on a charge of parading without a permit. Now, there is nothing wrong in having an ordinance which requires a permit for a parade. But such an ordinance becomes unjust when it is used to maintain segregation and to deny citizens the First-Amendment privilege of peaceful assembly and protest.

I hope you are able to see the distinction I am trying to point out. In no sense do I advocate evading or defying the law, as would the rabid segregationist. That would lead to anarchy. One who breaks an unjust law must do so openly, lovingly, and with

---

[9] **Martin Buber:** influential philosopher (1878–1965) with a great impact on Jewish and Christian theology.
[10] **Paul Tillich:** (1886–1965) influential German-American philosopher and Christian theologian.

a willingness to accept the penalty. I submit that an individual who breaks a law that conscience tells him is unjust, and who willingly accepts the penalty of imprisonment in order to arouse the conscience of the community over its injustice, is in reality expressing the highest respect for law.

Of course, there is nothing new about this kind of civil disobedience. It was evidenced sublimely in the refusal of Shadrach, Meshach and Abednego to obey the laws of Nebuchadnezzar,[11] on the ground that a higher moral law was at stake. It was practiced superbly by the early Christians, who were willing to face hungry lions and the excruciating pain of chopping blocks rather than submit to certain unjust laws of the Roman Empire. To a degree, academic freedom is a reality today because Socrates practiced civil disobedience. In our own nation, the Boston Tea Party[12] represented a massive act of civil disobedience.

We should never forget that everything Adolf Hitler did in Germany was "legal" and everything the Hungarian freedom fighters[13] did in Hungary was "illegal." It was "illegal" to aid and comfort a Jew in Hitler's Germany. Even so, I am sure that, had I lived in Germany at the time, I would have aided and comforted my Jewish brothers. If today I lived in a Communist country where certain principles dear to the Christian faith are suppressed, I would openly advocate disobeying that country's antireligious laws.

I must make two honest confessions to you, my Christian and Jewish brothers. First, I must confess that over the past few years I have been gravely disappointed with the white moderate. I have almost reached the regrettable conclusion that the Negro's great stumbling block in his stride toward freedom is not the White Citizen's Counciler or the Ku Klux Klanner,[14] but the white moderate, who is more devoted to "order" than to justice; who prefers a negative peace which is the absence of tension to a positive peace which is the presence of justice; who constantly says: "I agree with you in the goal you seek, but I cannot agree with your methods of direct action"; who paternalistically believes he can set the timetable for another man's freedom; who lives by a mythical concept of time and who constantly advises the Negro to wait for a "more convenient season." Shallow understanding from people of good will is more frustrating than absolute misunderstanding from

---

[11] **refusal ... Nebuchadnezzar:** Biblical account of three Hebrews condemned for refusing to worship an idol as required by the King of Babylon. The three were miraculously protected from the flames into which they were thrown.

[12] **Boston Tea Party:** a 1773 protest against the British Tea Act in which American colonists dumped 342 chests of tea into Boston Harbor.

[13] **Hungarian freedom fighters:** participants in the 1956 revolt against Hungary's Soviet-backed government.

[14] **White ... Klanner:** members of white-supremacist groups.

Image Credits: (t) ©Bettmann/Corbis (b) ©Michael Ochs Archives/Getty Images

280　people of ill will. Lukewarm acceptance is much more bewildering than outright rejection.

　　I had hoped that the white moderate would understand that law and order exist for the purpose of establishing justice and that when they fail in this purpose they become the dangerously structured dams that block the flow of social progress. I had hoped that the white moderate would understand that the present tension in the South is a necessary phase of the transition from an obnoxious negative peace, in which the Negro passively accepted his unjust plight, to a substantive and positive peace, in which all men will

290　respect the dignity and worth of human personality. Actually, we who engage in nonviolent direct action are not the creators of tension. We merely bring to the surface the hidden tension that is already alive. We bring it out in the open, where it can be seen and dealt with. Like a boil that can never be cured so long as it is covered up but must be opened with all its ugliness to the natural medicines of air and light, injustice must be exposed, with all the tension its exposure creates, to the light of human conscience and the air of national opinion before it can be cured.

In your statement you assert that our actions, even though peaceful, must be condemned because they **precipitate** violence. But is this a logical assertion? Isn't this like condemning a robbed man because his possession of money precipitated the evil act of robbery? Isn't this like condemning Socrates because his unswerving commitment to truth and his philosophical inquiries precipitated the act by the misguided populace in which they made him drink hemlock? Isn't this like condemning Jesus because his unique God-consciousness and never-ceasing devotion to God's will precipitated the evil act of crucifixion? We must come to see that, as the federal courts have consistently affirmed, it is wrong to urge an individual to cease his efforts to gain his basic constitutional rights because the quest may precipitate violence. Society must protect the robbed and punish the robber.

I had also hoped that the white moderate would reject the myth concerning time in relation to the struggle for freedom. I have just received a letter from a white brother in Texas. He writes: "All Christians know that the colored people will receive equal rights eventually, but it is possible that you are in too great a religious hurry. It has taken Christianity almost two thousand years to accomplish what it has. The teachings of Christ take time to come to earth." Such an attitude stems from a tragic misconception of time, from the strangely irrational notion that there is something in the very flow of time that will inevitably cure all ills. Actually, time itself is neutral; it can be used either destructively or constructively. More and more I feel that the people of ill will have used time much more effectively than have the people of good will. We will have to repent in this generation not merely for the hateful words and actions of the bad people but for the appalling silence of the good people. Human progress never rolls in on wheels of inevitability; it comes through the tireless efforts of men willing to be coworkers with God, and without this hard work, time itself becomes an ally of the forces of social stagnation. We must use time creatively, in the knowledge that the time is always ripe to do right. Now is the time to make real the promise of democracy and transform our pending national elegy into a creative psalm[15] of brotherhood. Now is the time to lift our national policy from the quicksand of racial injustice to the solid rock of human dignity.

You speak of our activity in Birmingham as extreme. At first I was rather disappointed that fellow clergymen would see my nonviolent efforts as those of an extremist. I began thinking

precipitate
(prǐ-sǐp´ǐ-tāt´) *v.* to cause something to happen rapidly or unexpectedly.

---

[15] **elegy . . . psalm:** an elegy is a lament for the dead; a psalm is a song of praise.

340 about the fact that I stand in the middle of two opposing forces
in the Negro community. One is a force of **complacency**, made
up in part of Negroes who, as a result of long years of oppression,
are so drained of self-respect and a sense of "somebodiness" that
they have adjusted to segregation; and in part of a few middle-
class Negroes who, because of a degree of academic and economic
security and because in some ways they profit by segregation, have
become insensitive to the problems of the masses. The other force
is one of bitterness and hatred, and it comes perilously close to
advocating violence. It is expressed in the various black nationalist
350 groups that are springing up across the nation, the largest and best
known being Elijah Muhammad's Muslim movement.[16] Nourished
by the Negro's frustration over the continued existence of racial
discrimination, this movement is made up of people who have lost
faith in America, who have absolutely repudiated Christianity, and
who have concluded that the white man is an incorrigible "devil."

I have tried to stand between these two forces, saying that we
need emulate neither the "do-nothingism" of the complacent nor
the hatred and despair of the black nationalist. For there is the
more excellent way of love and nonviolent protest. I am grateful to
360 God that, through the influence of the Negro church, the way of
nonviolence became an integral part of our struggle.

If this philosophy had not emerged, by now many streets of the
South would, I am convinced, be flowing with blood. . . .

Oppressed people cannot remain oppressed forever. The
yearning for freedom eventually **manifests** itself, and that is
what has happened to the American Negro. Something within
has reminded him of his birthright of freedom, and something
without has reminded him that it can be gained. Consciously or
unconsciously, he has been caught up by the *Zeitgeist*,[17] and with
370 his black brothers of Africa and his brown and yellow brothers of
Asia, South America and the Caribbean, the United States Negro
is moving with a sense of great urgency toward the promised land
of racial justice. If one recognizes this vital urge that has engulfed
the Negro community, one should readily understand why public
demonstrations are taking place. The Negro has many pent-up
resentments and latent frustrations, and he must release them. So
let him march; let him make prayer pilgrimages to the city hall; let
him go on freedom rides—and try to understand why he must do
so. If his repressed emotions are not released in nonviolent ways,

complacency
(kəm-plā´sən-sē) *n.*
contented self-
satisfaction.

manifest
(măn´ə-fĕst´) *v.* to
show or reveal.

---

[16] **black nationalist . . . Elijah Muhammad's Muslim movement:** groups
that proposed economic and social independence for African American
communities, including the Nation of Islam, founded in 1930 and led by Elijah
Muhammad (1897–1975) from 1934 until his death.

[17] *Zeitgeist* **(tsīt´gīst´):** German for "the spirit of the time," referring to the
attitudes and beliefs of most people living during a period.

380 they will seek expression through violence; this is not a threat but a fact of history. So I have not said to my people: "Get rid of your discontent." Rather, I have tried to say that this normal and healthy discontent can be channeled into the creative outlet of nonviolent direct action. And now this approach is being termed extremist.

But though I was initially disappointed at being categorized as an extremist, as I continued to think about the matter I gradually gained a measure of satisfaction from the label. Was not Jesus an extremist for love: "Love your enemies, bless them that curse you, do good to them that hate you, and pray for them

390 which despitefully use you, and persecute you." Was not Amos[18] an extremist for justice: "Let justice roll down like waters and righteousness like an ever-flowing stream." Was not Paul an extremist for the Christian gospel: "I bear in my body the marks of the Lord Jesus." Was not Martin Luther[19] an extremist: "Here I stand; I cannot do otherwise, so help me God." And John Bunyan:[20] "I will stay in jail to the end of my days before I make a butchery of my conscience." And Abraham Lincoln: "This nation cannot survive half slave and half free." And Thomas Jefferson: "We hold these truths to be self-evident, that all men are created equal . . ."

400 So the question is not whether we will be extremists, but what kind of extremists we will be. Will we be extremists for hate or for love? Will we be extremists for the preservation of injustice or for the extension of justice? In that dramatic scene on Calvary's hill[21] three men were crucified. We must never forget that all three were crucified for the same crime—the crime of extremism. Two were extremists for immorality, and thus fell below their environment. The other, Jesus Christ, was an extremist for love, truth and goodness, and thereby rose above his environment. Perhaps the South, the nation and the world are in dire need of creative

410 extremists.

I had hoped that the white moderate would see this need. Perhaps I was too optimistic; perhaps I expected too much. I suppose I should have realized that few members of the oppressor race can understand the deep groans and passionate yearnings of the oppressed race, and still fewer have the vision to see that injustice must be rooted out by strong, persistent and determined action. I am thankful, however, that some of our white brothers in the South have grasped the meaning of this social revolution and

---

[18] **Amos:** Hebrew prophet whose words are recorded in the Old Testament book bearing his name.

[19] **Martin Luther:** (1483-1546) German monk who launched the Protestant Reformation.

[20] **John Bunyan:** (1628-1688) English preacher and writer, author of *The Pilgrim's Progress.*

[21] **Calvary's hill:** the site of Jesus' crucifixion.

"WILL WE BE EXTREMISTS FOR HATE OR FOR LOVE?"

committed themselves to it. They are still all too few in quantity,
but they are big in quality. Some—such as Ralph McGill, Lillian
Smith, Harry Golden, James McBride Dabbs, Ann Braden and
Sarah Patton Boyle—have written about our struggle in eloquent
and prophetic terms. Others have marched with us down nameless
streets of the South. They have languished in filthy, roach-infested
jails, suffering the abuse and brutality of policemen who view them
as "dirty nigger-lovers." Unlike so many of their moderate brothers
and sisters, they have recognized the urgency of the moment and
sensed the need for powerful "action" antidotes to combat the
disease of segregation.

Let me take note of my other major disappointment. I have
been so greatly disappointed with the white church and its
leadership. Of course, there are some notable exceptions. I am not
unmindful of the fact that each of you has taken some significant
stands on this issue. I commend you, Reverend Stallings, for your
Christian stand on this past Sunday, in welcoming Negroes to your
worship service on a nonsegregated basis. I commend the Catholic
leaders of this state for integrating Spring Hill College several years
ago.

But despite these notable exceptions, I must honestly reiterate
that I have been disappointed with the church. I do not say this as
one of those negative critics who can always find something wrong
with the church. I say this as a minister of the gospel, who loves the
church; who was nurtured in its bosom; who has been sustained by
its spiritual blessings and who will remain true to it as long as the
cord of life shall lengthen.

When I was suddenly catapulted into the leadership of the bus protest in Montgomery, Alabama,[22] a few years ago, I felt we would be supported by the white church. I felt that the white ministers, priests and rabbis of the South would be among our strongest 450 allies. Instead, some have been outright opponents, refusing to understand the freedom movement and misrepresenting its leaders; all too many others have been more cautious than courageous and have remained silent behind the anesthetizing security of stained glass windows.

In spite of my shattered dreams, I came to Birmingham with the hope that the white religious leadership of this community would see the justice of our cause and, with deep moral concern, would serve as the channel through which our just grievances could reach the power structure. I had hoped that each of you would 460 understand. But again I have been disappointed.

I have heard numerous southern religious leaders admonish their worshipers to comply with a desegregation decision because it is the law, but I have longed to hear white ministers declare: "Follow this decree because integration is morally right and because the Negro is your brother." In the midst of blatant injustices inflicted upon the Negro, I have watched white churchmen stand on the sideline and mouth pious irrelevancies and sanctimonious trivialities. In the midst of a mighty struggle to rid our nation of racial and economic injustice, I have heard many ministers 470 say: "Those are social issues, with which the gospel has no real concern." And I have watched many churches commit themselves to a completely otherworldly religion which makes a strange, un-Biblical distinction between body and soul, between the sacred and the secular.

I have traveled the length and breadth of Alabama, Mississippi and all the other southern states. On sweltering summer days and crisp autumn mornings I have looked at the South's beautiful churches with their lofty spires pointing heavenward. I have beheld the impressive outlines of her massive religious-education 480 buildings. Over and over I have found myself asking: "What kind of people worship here? Who is their God? Where were their voices when the lips of Governor Barnett dripped with words of interposition and nullification? Where were they when Governor Wallace[23] gave a clarion call for defiance and hatred? Where were their voices of support when bruised and weary Negro men and

---

[22]**bus protest in Montgomery, Alabama:** the 1955–1956 boycott that ended segregated seating in Montgomery's transportation system.
[23]**Gov. Barnett . . . Gov. Wallace:** Ross Barnett (1898–1987) and George Wallace (1919–1998), segregationist governors of Mississippi and Alabama, respectively, during the 1960s.

women decided to rise from the dark dungeons of complacency to the bright hills of creative protest?"

Yes, these questions are still in my mind. In deep disappointment I have wept over the laxity of the church. But be assured that my tears have been tears of love. There can be no deep disappointment where there is not deep love. Yes, I love the church. How could I do otherwise? I am in the rather unique position of being the son, the grandson and the great-grandson of preachers. Yes, I see the church as the body of Christ. But, oh! How we have blemished and scarred that body through social neglect and through fear of being nonconformists.

There was a time when the church was very powerful—in the time when the early Christians rejoiced at being deemed worthy to suffer for what they believed. In those days the church was not merely a thermometer that recorded the ideas and principles of popular opinion; it was a thermostat that transformed the **mores** of society. Whenever the early Christians entered a town, the people in power became disturbed and immediately sought to convict the Christians for being "disturbers of the peace" and "outside agitators." But the Christians pressed on, in the conviction that they were "a colony of heaven," called to obey God rather than man. Small in number, they were big in commitment. They were too God-intoxicated to be "astronomically intimidated." By their effort and example they brought an end to such ancient evils as infanticide and gladiatorial contests.[24]

Things are different now. So often the contemporary church is a weak, ineffectual voice with an uncertain sound. So often it is an archdefender of the status quo. Far from being disturbed by the presence of the church, the power structure of the average community is consoled by the church's silent—and often even vocal—sanction of things as they are.

But the judgment of God is upon the church as never before. If today's church does not recapture the sacrificial spirit of the early church, it will lose its authenticity, forfeit the loyalty of millions, and be dismissed as an irrelevant social club with no meaning for the twentieth century. Every day I meet young people whose disappointment with the church has turned into outright disgust.

Perhaps I have once again been too optimistic. Is organized religion too inextricably bound to the status quo to save our nation and the world? Perhaps I must turn my faith to the inner spiritual church, the church within the church, as the true *ekklesia*[25] and

mores
(môr´āz´) *n.*
established customs and conventions.

---

[24]**ancient evils . . . contests:** despicable past practices of killing unwanted babies and of forcing men to fight to the death for sport.

[25]*ekklesia* (ĭ-klē´zē-ə): a Greek term meaning "an assembly of people for worship," often translated into English as "church."

the hope of the world. But again I am thankful to God that some noble souls from the ranks of organized religion have broken loose from the paralyzing chains of conformity and joined us as active partners in the struggle for freedom. They have left their secure congregations and walked the streets of Albany, Georgia, with us. They have gone down the highways of the South on tortuous rides for freedom. Yes, they have gone to jail with us. Some have been dismissed from their churches, have lost the support of their bishops and fellow ministers. But they have acted in the faith that right defeated is stronger than evil triumphant. Their witness has been the spiritual salt that has preserved the true meaning of the gospel in these troubled times. They have carved a tunnel of hope through the dark mountain of disappointment.

I hope the church as a whole will meet the challenge of this decisive hour. But even if the church does not come to the aid of justice, I have no despair about the future. I have no fear about the outcome of our struggle in Birmingham, even if our motives are at present misunderstood. We will reach the goal of freedom in Birmingham and all over the nation, because the goal of America is freedom. Abused and scorned though we may be, our destiny is tied up with America's destiny. Before the pilgrims landed at Plymouth, we were here. Before the pen of Jefferson etched the majestic words of the Declaration of Independence across the pages of history, we were here. For more than two centuries our forebears labored in this country without wages; they made cotton king; they built the homes of their masters while suffering gross injustice and shameful humiliation—and yet out of a bottomless vitality they continued to thrive and develop. If the inexpressible cruelties of slavery could not stop us, the opposition we now face will surely fail. We will win our freedom because the sacred heritage of our nation and the eternal will of God are embodied in our echoing demands.

Before closing I feel impelled to mention one other point in your statement that has troubled me profoundly. You warmly commended the Birmingham police force for keeping "order" and "preventing violence." I doubt that you would have so warmly commended the police force if you had seen its dogs sinking their teeth into unarmed, nonviolent Negroes. I doubt that you would so quickly commend the policemen if you were to observe their ugly and inhumane treatment of Negroes here in the city jail; if you were to watch them push and curse old Negro women and young Negro girls; if you were to see them slap and kick old Negro men and young boys; if you were to observe them, as they did on two occasions, refuse to give us food because we wanted to sing our grace together. I cannot join you in your praise of the Birmingham police department.

It is true that the police have exercised a degree of discipline in handling the demonstrators. In this sense they have conducted themselves rather "nonviolently" in public. But for what purpose? To preserve the evil system of segregation. Over the past few years I have consistently preached that nonviolence demands that the means we use must be as pure as the ends we seek. I have tried to make clear that it is wrong to use immoral means to attain moral ends. But now I must affirm that it is just as wrong, or perhaps even more so, to use moral means to preserve immoral ends. Perhaps Mr. Connor and his policemen have been rather nonviolent in public, as was Chief Pritchett in Albany, Georgia, but they have used the moral means of nonviolence to maintain the immoral end of racial injustice. As T. S. Eliot has said: "The last temptation is the greatest treason: To do the right deed for the wrong reason."

I wish you had commended the Negro sit-inners and demonstrators of Birmingham for their sublime courage, their willingness to suffer and their amazing discipline in the midst of great **provocation**. One day the South will recognize its real heroes. They will be the James Merediths,[26] with the noble sense of purpose that enables them to face jeering and hostile mobs, and with the agonizing loneliness that characterizes the life of the pioneer.

provocation
(prŏv′ə-kā′shən) *n.*
an action intended to elicit an angered response.

---

[26]**James Merediths:** people like James Meredith, who endured violent opposition from whites to become the first African American to attend the University of Mississippi.

They will be old, oppressed, battered Negro women, symbolized
in a seventy-two-year-old woman in Montgomery, Alabama, who
rose up with a sense of dignity and with her people decided not to
ride segregated buses, and who responded with ungrammatical
profundity to one who inquired about her weariness: "My feets is
tired, but my soul is at rest." They will be the young high school
and college students, the young ministers of the gospel and a host
600 of their elders, courageously and nonviolently sitting in at lunch
counters and willingly going to jail for conscience' sake. One day
the South will know that when these disinherited children of God
sat down at lunch counters, they were in reality standing up for
what is best in the American dream and for the most sacred values
in our Judaeo-Christian heritage, thereby bringing our nation
back to those great wells of democracy which were dug deep by the
founding fathers in their formulation of the Constitution and the
Declaration of Independence.

Never before have I written so long a letter. I'm afraid it is much
610 too long to take your precious time. I can assure you that it would
have been much shorter if I had been writing from a comfortable
desk, but what else can one do when he is alone in a narrow jail cell
other than write long letters, think long thoughts and pray long
prayers?

If I have said anything in this letter that overstates the truth
and indicates an unreasonable impatience, I beg you to forgive me.
If I have said anything that understates the truth and indicates my
having a patience that allows me to settle for anything less than
brotherhood, I beg God to forgive me.

620 I hope this letter finds you strong in the faith. I also hope
that circumstances will soon make it possible for me to meet each
of you, not as an integrationist or a civil-rights leader but as a
fellow clergyman and a Christian brother. Let us all hope that the
dark clouds of racial prejudice will soon pass away and the deep
fog of misunderstanding will be lifted from our fear-drenched
communities, and in some not too distant tomorrow the radiant
stars of love and brotherhood will shine over our great nation with
all their scintillating beauty.

Yours for the cause of Peace and Brotherhood,
Martin Luther King, Jr.

COLLABORATIVE DISCUSSION What parts of King's argument do you
find most compelling? Discuss your reaction to the letter with a partner.
Cite specific evidence from the text to support your ideas.

Analyze Argument in a Seminal Document

When you analyze an argument, you must identify the **claims**, or the writer's positions on the issue or problem. You also need to examine and evaluate the reasons and evidence used to support the claims, while also looking at the counterarguments provided to address opposing views. For example, in "Letter from Birmingham Jail," note the different types of reasons King provides to justify his presence in Birmingham and consider questions that might help you assess the validity of his reasoning and the relevance and sufficiency of his evidence.

Organizational Reasons	Religious/Historical Reasons	Moral Reasons
"I am here because I have organizational ties here." • What facts does King provide to contest the idea that he is an outsider?	"Just as the prophets . . . so am I compelled to carry the gospel of freedom beyond my own home town." • How does this reasoning appeal to the shared beliefs of King's audience?	"I cannot sit idly by in Atlanta and not be concerned about what happens in Birmingham." • Is this a valid statement? What evidence supports this reasoning?

Although King's letter was addressed to his "Fellow Clergymen," it was disseminated by the media to the public. To better comprehend why this letter, a seminal U.S. document, had such an impact on the civil rights cause, think about the **themes**, or the underlying messages, that King wants his audience to understand. As you explore the themes and consider the impact of King's letter, consider these questions:

- A **universal theme** is a message that can be found throughout the literature of all time periods. What universal themes does King explore in his letter? What makes these themes universal?
- An **allusion** is an indirect reference to a famous person, place, event, or literary work. King uses allusions to help connect the civil rights movement to other historical and religious figures and events. In what ways do allusions add power to King's letter? How might they help promote his cause? How might they influence other groups of people?

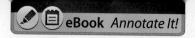
Analyzing the Text

RI 1, RI 2, RI 8,
RI 9, W 9b,
W 10

Cite Text Evidence   Support your responses with evidence from the selection.

1. **Summarize** Based on details in the letter, what do you know about King's position and the events that prompted him to write this letter? What claim is he supporting in this argument?

2. **Analyze** How does King define just and unjust laws? To what opposing view is he providing a counterargument? Consider how defining certain laws as unjust provides an incentive for his readers to support his actions.

3. **Cite Evidence** Provide three examples of allusions that King uses to support his reasoning about his claim. How does this type of evidence strengthen his argument?

4. **Summarize** According to King, what are the four basic steps in a nonviolent campaign, and how did King's organization follow these steps in Birmingham?

5. **Interpret** What does King mean when he says "Shallow understanding from people of good will is more frustrating than absolute misunderstanding from people of ill will"?

6. **Draw Conclusions** King says that "This 'Wait' has almost always meant 'Never.'" To what does he refer, and how does he defend his position?

7. **Analyze** Discuss whether King uses valid reasoning when he states that "Injustice anywhere is a threat to justice everywhere." What evidence does he provide to support this idea?

PERFORMANCE TASK

Writing Activity: Comparison Seminal U.S. texts often center on the themes of rights and freedom. Compare the ideas in King's letter with those in President Franklin Roosevelt's seminal "Four Freedoms" speech (See page R22).

1. As you read Roosevelt's speech and reread King's letter, make notes about how they both address related themes and equivalent concepts.

2. Write an essay in which you explain how the two documents explore people's fundamental human rights and what the two authors want done to end the injustice.

Critical Vocabulary

cognizant	moratorium	retaliate	precipitate
complacency	manifest	mores	provocation

Practice and Apply Use your understanding of the Critical Vocabulary words to answer the following questions. Then, explain your answers to a partner.

1. Which might cause someone to **retaliate**: Losing a point in a game because of a foul or getting a well-deserved award?

2. Which might cause a brief **moratorium** on road building, a bad storm or potholes?

3. If I am **cognizant** of your plans, do I know about them or have I forgotten them?

4. If a movie reflected a society's **mores**, would it show traditional or unconventional practices?

5. If a motive for a crime begins to **manifest** itself, will it be easier or harder to prove the suspect's guilt?

6. What might be a **provocation** for war, breaking a treaty or signing one?

7. If you show **complacency** toward a bossy friend, how do you respond to his or her demands?

8. If my actions **precipitate** an accident, do I cause the accident or prevent it?

Vocabulary Strategy: Context Clues

A word's **context,** the words and sentences that surround it, often gives clues to its meaning. Context can also add shades of meaning to a word. Consider how context shapes the meaning of the word *tension* in King's letter:

Definition	Context Clues
tension: a strained relationship	"Nonviolent direct action seeks to . . . foster such a **tension** that a community . . . is forced to confront the issue.";"I have earnestly opposed violent **tension**, but there is a type of constructive, nonviolent **tension** which is necessary for growth";"Just as Socrates felt that it was necessary to create a **tension** in the mind . . . so must we . . . create the kind of **tension** in society that will help men rise from the dark depths of prejudice."

As you can see from the context, King's use of the word *tension* describes a powerful force, one that can be positive rather than violent or hostile. Think about how replacing it with an equivalent word, such as *conflict*, might change King's intended meaning.

Practice and Apply Use context clues to define the words *moderate* (lines 266–280), *condemned/condemning* (lines 299–311), and *extremist* (lines 385–410). Verify your preliminary definition of each word in a dictionary. Then, in a small group, discuss how King adds nuances to each word's meaning in the context of his letter.

Language and Style:
Repetition and Parallelism

Repetition is a technique in which a sound, word, or phrase is repeated for emphasis or unity. **Parallelism** is the use of similar grammatical forms to express ideas that are related or equal in importance. King skillfully uses repetition and parallelism to make his message resonate with his audience. Consider the following examples and their effects:

Example	Effects
"**when you** have seen vicious mobs . . . **when you** have seen hate-filled policemen . . . **when you** see the vast majority of your twenty million Negro brothers smothering . . . **when you** suddenly find your tongue twisted . . . **when you** have to concoct an answer . . . **when you** take a cross-country drive . . . **when you** are humiliated . . . **when you** are harried by day and haunted by night . . . **when you** are forever fighting . . . —**then you** will understand why we find it difficult to wait.""	Starting each subordinate clause with the words *when you* and then varying the parallel structure to *then you* emphasizes and dramatizes King's point that African Americans have waited long enough for their constitutional and God-given rights.
"the white moderate, **who** is more devoted to 'order' than to justice; **who** prefers a negative peace . . . **who** constantly says . . . **who** paternalistically believes . . . **who** lives by a mythical concept of time and **who** constantly advises the Negro to wait."	The relative pronoun *who* draws attention to the reasons King is frustrated with the white moderate.
"**Was not** Jesus an **extremist** for love . . . **Was not** Amos an **extremist** for justice . . . **Was not** Paul an **extremist** for the Christian gospel . . . **Was not** Martin Luther an **extremist** . . . **And** John Bunyan . . . **And** Abraham Lincoln . . . **And** Thomas Jefferson . . . So the question is not whether **we will be extremists**, but what kind of **extremists we will be. Will we be extremists** for hate or for love? **Will we be extremists** for the preservation of injustice or for the extension of justice?"	The repetition of the words *extremist* and *and* and the parallel structures created by the verbal phrase *was not* and the clause *we will be/will we be* link King's approach to that of other religious and historical figures.

Practice and Apply Locate other examples of repetition and parallel structure in King's letter and consider their effects. Then, look back at the essay you wrote for this selection's Performance Task. Revise your essay to include two examples each of repetition and parallelism. Discuss with a partner the effects of your revisions.

Background *In December 2010, angry protests erupted against the authoritarian government in the north African nation of Tunisia. Within a month, protesters brought down the government. Days later, on January 25, 2011 ("Jan25"), protests spread to Egypt. There, mass demonstrations similar to those in Tunisia were held, through the work of organizers including* **Wael Ghonim** *(b. 1980), a high-tech executive and administrator of the Facebook page "We are all Khaled Said." Thousands of people massed daily in Cairo's Tahrir Square, eventually forcing Egypt's president of thirty years to step down. The unrest spread to other nations and became known as the Arab Spring.*

from

Revolution 2.0

Memoir by Wael Ghonim

AS YOU READ Identify how the author organizes information and think about the kinds of information the author includes in the document. Write down any questions you generate during reading.

I continued to rally supporters on the page. I shared writings, images, and designs made by the page members that promised a victorious Jan25. I tried to induce confidence and belief that youth would be capable of leading change. I also highlighted the government's frightened reactions.

    I decided to compile all the information relevant to Jan25 in a document that was easy to print and to distribute online. It summarized the reasons for protesting and for choosing this day and these locations. It also described the unified chants that had been chosen and provided phone numbers for activists responsible for supporting arrested protesters and for redirecting demonstrators to other locations if the protests at any one place were obstructed. I uploaded the file to Google Docs, where more than 50,000 people accessed it. Its content was also **disseminated** through various online forums, political websites, Facebook pages, and Twitter accounts.

10

disseminate
(dĭ-sĕm´ə-nāt´) *v.* to spread or circulate widely.

Everything You Need to Know about Jan25

Important note: Please visit the page regularly for frequent updates.

Who Are We?

The call for protests on Jan25 began from the Facebook page
"Kullena Khaled Said," a page created to support the case of
20 Khaled Said, who was beaten and tortured to death on the street
in Alexandria in June of 2010. The call was spontaneous and not
planned by any political or popular force. After the invitation
spread, and because of events in Tunisia, many Egyptians were
encouraged to participate and spread the word. The Facebook
page is not influenced by any political party, group, movement, or
organization. It is independent and does not support any person or
specific **ideology**. It belongs to all Egyptians who wish to defend
their rights. The page is managed through its member volunteers,
and this is the secret to its success.

ideology
(ī´dē-ŏl´ə-jē) *n.* a
system of doctrines
or beliefs.

Why Protest?

30 Egypt is going through one of the worst periods in its history on all
fronts. Despite the reports propagated by the government that aim
to polish its image, reality is unfortunately different. Our collective
participation on Jan25 is the beginning of the end—the end of
silence, acceptance, and submission to all that is happening in our
country, and the beginning of a new page of coming forward and
demanding our rights. Jan25 is not a revolution in the sense of a
coup,[1] but rather a revolution against our government to let them
know that we have taken interest in one another's problems and
that we shall reclaim all our rights and will not be silent anymore.

40   There are 30 million Egyptians suffering from depression,
including 1.5 million with severe depression. There were more than
100,000 suicide attempts in 2009, resulting in the deaths of 5,000
people. There are 48 million poor citizens in Egypt, including 2.5
million who live in extreme poverty. 12 million Egyptians have
no shelter, including 1.5 million who live in cemeteries. Habitual
corruption has led to graft[2] totaling more than 39 billion pounds[3]
during one year alone. And Egypt ranks 115th out of 139 nations
in the Corruption Perceptions Index. More than three million
young Egyptians are unemployed; the unemployment rate among

50 youth has surpassed 30 percent. Egypt also came in last place
among 139 countries in terms of hiring transparency. We have
the highest rate of newborn deaths in the world: 50 of every 1,000
newborn Egyptians die. Half of Egypt's children are anemic, and
eight million Egyptians are infected with hepatitis C. More than
100,000 citizens suffer from cancer every year because of water
pollution. Our rate of ambulance cars to citizens is 1:35,000. Egypt's
emergency law has caused the death of many Egyptians as the result
of torture and also facilitated the arrests of thousands without
official warrants. Security forces' involvement in monitoring

60 politicians and blocking their activism has led to shameless rigging
of parliamentary elections, producing a people's assembly that was
more than 90 percent controlled by the ruling party . . .

Why Jan25?

In 1952, using simple rifles, our forefathers in the police force
fought the British army's tanks. Fifty became martyrs, and more
than 100 were taken as prisoners. They were heroic and offered
a model of sacrificing one's life for one's homeland. Now, more

---

[1] **coup:** a sudden, unlawful seizure of government power.

[2] **graft:** illegal or unethical exchanges of money.

[3] **pounds:** the main unit of Egyptian currency.

than 50 years later, we suffer from a police force that has become a machine for torturing and humiliating Egyptians. We chose this day specifically because it represents the fusion of the police and
70 the people. We hope that decent and honest officers will join our ranks on Jan25 because our cause is one with theirs. Jan25 is a national holiday, which should allow all Egyptians to participate without hurting their productivity on any level.

What Are Our Demands?

Demand One: Addressing the poverty problem before it explodes by respecting the judiciary's verdict to increase the minimum wage fairly, particularly in health care and education, in order to improve the services offered to the people. Also, to issue unemployment benefits that reach up to 500 Egyptian pounds, for a limited period, for every university graduate unable to find a job.

80 Demand Two: **Annulling** the emergency law, which has led to the control of Egypt by the security apparatus and has allowed the illegal arrest of political opposition members without cause. We demand that attorneys general take charge of police stations to stop the routine torture practices that take place there. We also demand implementation of the judiciary's verdicts by the government.

annul
(ə-nŭl´) *v.* render or declare invalid.

Demand Three: Firing Minister of Interior Habib el-Adly. His loose security measures have led to terrorist attacks as well as the spread of crime at the hands of police officers and other Ministry of Interior forces.

90 Demand Four: Placing a two-term limit on the presidency. Absolute power corrupts, and no advanced nation allows a president to stay in power for decades. It is our right to choose our president, and it is our right not to have a president monopolize power until his death.

Of course Egyptians have many further demands in areas such as health and education. We begin by moving together, pressuring the government, and achieving one demand at a time. This is our role as a people: to direct the government, hold it accountable, and determine its priorities.

Time and Place of Protests

100 It is very important to realize that the point of the protests is to mobilize all people to our side. Everyone is frustrated and dissatisfied with the nation's condition. We must encourage them to participate. This is why we must organize marches in all working-class neighborhoods. And people must move together in numbers of more than ten until they reach the protest destination. And by the way, the locations are not just the ones mentioned here. There are other locations that have not been announced where protests

will be organized in different governorates.[4] The important thing
is for you to come out and express your anger in whatever way
110 you can.

   Greater Cairo: Shubra Roundabout, Matariyya Square, Cairo
University, the Arab League Street

   Alexandria: Al-Manshiyya Square, Mahatet Masr Square

   Important note: Other groups are organizing protests
and marches in popular neighborhoods all over Cairo, Giza,
Alexandria, and many other cities across Egypt. If you are in a
working-class neighborhood, come out on Jan25 and join them . . .

Protesting Guidelines

1. The protests are peaceful. We are peace advocates and not
    advocates of violence. We are demanding our rights and
120   must uphold the rights of others. We will not respond to
    any provocation from security forces and lose control.
    This is what they want us to do. One of the security forces'
    main goals is to portray the protesters as thugs who want
    to destroy our country. We must discipline ourselves and
    refrain from foolishness or any violations of the law, and
    we must not endanger any person's life or cause harm to
    any public or private property. If you see someone behaving
    violently, please circle around this person and take him out
    of the protest.

130 2. Please be at the protest location promptly at the determined
    time. Delays will hinder our efforts and risk the failure of
    the protest. Being present at the same time makes it easy to
    start the protest and makes it hard for the security forces to
    prevent it.

3. When leaving your house, do not carry anything you don't
    need, such as membership cards or licenses or credit cards.
    Carry only your personal ID and a sum of money sufficient
    for an emergency. Please don't bring your watch or anything
    easily breakable. The ideal attire would be sportswear or
140   jeans along with a jacket to keep warm in case the protest
    runs long or develops into a sit-in. Please bring a large bottle
    of water, because there is always a shortage of water inside
    the protest.

4. Please carry the Egyptian flag and refrain from carrying any
    signs of a political party, movement, group, organization,
    or religious sect. Jan25 is for all Egyptians. We are all

---

[4] **governorates:** the 27 political districts of Egypt, each headed by a governor.

demanding equal rights and social justice and do not want to be **divisive**.

divisive
(dĭ-vī´sĭv) *adj.*
causing division or disagreement.

5. If you are not an experienced protester, leave the front lines for experienced protesters to lead the march in order to avoid conflicting decisions.

6. The chants are unified and agreed upon. Please refrain from all profanity and do not enter into quarrels with security force members. Central Security is not your enemy. They are guards who have been forced to spend their compulsory military service in this capacity, and if they disobeyed the orders they would be punished badly. Try as much as possible to target your anger at the real enemy.

7. Try as much as possible not to disturb traffic. We are not out to punish the citizens but to demand our rights. Try not to interrupt traffic flow deliberately. It is understandable that when tens of thousands of people take to the streets, traffic flow will be affected. This is not what we are referring to.

8. Do not come out alone. It is very important not to come out alone, because friends come in handy in situations like these. Please be with someone and talk someone into coming out together, just like we take to the stadiums when there is a match to watch.

Unified Chants

The unified chants are one of the most important protest ideas. We are all out for the sake of Egypt, and we must unite and act as one. We will all stick to the chants together and will focus on the issues of unemployment and poverty. These are the issues that concern all Egyptians. These are the chants that have been agreed upon:

- Long live Egypt . . . Long live Egypt
- Bread . . . Freedom . . . Human dignity
- Dear freedom, where are you? . . . Emergency law is keeping us away from you
- We will not fear, we will not bow . . . Like we've done for so long
- Beloved people of Tunisia . . . The revolution sun will not set
- We shall sacrifice our blood and lives for you, dear Egypt
- Raise your voice up high . . . With injustice we will not comply
- Alert the people and rock the universe . . . We will not let our homeland go
- Minimum wage now . . . before all the Egyptians revolt

- It's my right to find work and live . . . The petty income is not enough
- Let's make it happen, Egyptians, wake your spirit . . . The gates of liberty are open
- Let's go, people, transcend the fear . . . Let the whole world know
- A people with the civilization and glory of years . . . Will not bow until Judgment Day

♡ 1,977 likes   ◯ 1,527 comments   506,871 | views

COLLABORATIVE DISCUSSION With a partner, discuss how the organization of the document makes it easy or difficult for someone participating in the protests to use. Cite specific textual evidence to support your ideas.

Analyze Evidence and Author's Ideas

RI 1, RI 5

The excerpt from *Revolution 2.0* is in part a **functional document**, a text that provides directions for performing a task. Functional documents can include schedules or directions for installing software. They are written with clear, concise language and organized to help readers quickly acquire information needed to achieve a goal. Effective functional documents have these text features and characteristics:

- Clear **headings** that enable readers to locate information easily. How do the headings in the selection help direct readers' attention?
- A clear and logical **structure** or organization. For example, notice where the author places the unified chants in the document. Why is this location logical?
- Clear, concise **language.** Note that each demand the author provides begins with a verb, for example, "annulling the emergency law." Why might writing the demands in such a way be effective?

Analyzing the Text

RI 1, RI 3, RI 4, RI 5, RI 6, W 7, W 8, SL 2, SL 4

Cite Text Evidence   Support your responses with evidence from the selection.

1. **Analyze** The author begins by introducing the organizers of the demonstrations. Why is this an effective way to begin the document?

2. **Interpret** Note the wording of the Protesting Guidelines. What word choices create a tone of reason and control? How might this tone affect readers?

3. **Cite Evidence** The author cites several statistics in the section "Why Protest?" What are some of these statistics, and what is their function in the document?

4. **Interpret** How are key ideas refined with clear and concise language in the section "What Are Our Demands?" What purpose does this section serve?

5. **Evaluate** Based on this excerpt, why might the use of social media have been effective in inspiring young Egyptians to take action?

PERFORMANCE TASK

Speaking Activity: Research Much has happened in Egypt since the events mentioned in this excerpt. Choose one section of the text, and give a short informative presentation about current developments having to do with the section you chose.

1. Research current developments regarding one subtopic, for example difficulties Egyptians face. Note your sources and find photos or other media to support your ideas.

2. In a speech, use domain-specific vocabulary to compare ideas in your chosen section of the text with information from your research. Conclude with your view of whether or not progress has been achieved.

Critical Vocabulary

disseminate	**ideology**	**annul**	**divisive**

Practice and Apply Answer each question to demonstrate your understanding of the Critical Vocabulary words.

1. How might a discussion about pets become **divisive?**

2. What is a rule you would like to **annul?**

3. What is the most effective way to **disseminate** information about a class party?

4. How might a political candidate's **ideology** affect his or her actions once elected?

Vocabulary Strategy: Domain-specific Words

Reading and writing about a specific field, such as social studies or science, will require knowledge of **domain-specific words.** For example, if you were to read a science book about geology, you would need to be familiar with terms like *mantle, inner core,* and *magma.* Likewise, the author of *Revolution 2.0* uses words that are specific to politics. For example, the Critical Vocabulary word *ideology* is used to discuss how an Egyptian Facebook page is independent of influence from a specific group or set of ideas.

To help you determine the meaning of domain-specific words and phrases in a passage, use these strategies:

- Think about what you just read and **paraphrase** it.

- Think about the **context** of the passage. For example, in the section "What Are Our Demands?" the term *judiciary* is used in the context of fairness and verdicts. Those are clues to the word's meaning.

- Make an initial **guess** at the word's meaning. For example, you might guess that *judiciary* means "justice."

- Determine whether your guess makes sense in the context of the passage. If not, think of **alternatives.** What alternatives can you think of as meanings for the word *judiciary?*

- If you cannot determine the meaning of the word by its context, look up the word in a dictionary, glossary, or specialized **reference** book.

Practice and Apply Work with a partner to complete these activities.

1. Find these domain-specific words and phrases in the text: *hiring transparency* (line 51), *warrants* (line 59), *parliamentary* (line 61), and *security apparatus* (line 81). Reread the section in which each term appears, and write a definition of the word or phrase based on your understanding of its context.

2. Compare your definition to the definition found in a college-level dictionary, digital reference source, or specialized reference book.

Language and Style: Colons

Authors use punctuation not only to help them construct meaning in a text but also to help them organize ideas. In *Revolution 2.0*, the author uses colons for several purposes. A colon acts as a signal to readers to be alert because something important will follow. In a text that provides directions for action, the use of colons is particularly effective. Colons allow the writer to organize the information, to make it clear and concise, and to add emphasis where necessary.

Read this sentence from the selection:

This is our role as a people: to direct the government, hold it accountable, and determine its priorities.

The author could instead have written the sentence this way:

Our role as a people is to direct the government, to hold it accountable, and to determine its priorities.

While the revised example makes sense, it may not catch the reader's attention. By using a colon to prepare readers for something important, the author adds emphasis to his statement.

In addition to using colons for emphasis, Ghonim also uses colons in these ways:

Purpose	Example
to introduce lists	Greater Cairo: Shubra Roundabout, Matariyya Square, Cairo University, the Arab League Street
to concisely present key ideas	Demand One: Addressing the poverty problem . . .
to draw attention to the most important points for action	Important note: Please visit the page regularly for frequent updates.

Practice and Apply Work with a partner to complete the following steps.

1. First, discuss your response to the selection, considering the role of social media in Egypt's revolution.

2. Next, collaborate with your partner to draft a paragraph that conveys the ideas you discussed.

3. Finally, revise the paragraph to include a list introduced by a colon, two or more key ideas introduced by colons, and one important point introduced by a colon.

from
Letter to Viceroy, Lord Irwin

MEDIA

from **Gandhi: The Rise to Fame**

Argument by Mohandas K. Gandhi

Documentary Film by BBC

Background *The Salt March, also known as the Salt Satyagraha, took place in India in 1930. The March protested the living conditions endured by the Indian people, including a high tax on salt and a prohibition against producing salt independently. Mohandas Gandhi, already a prominent leader in the Indian independence movement, wrote this letter on March 2, 1930. The British colonial government refused Gandhi's demands. Beginning on March 12, a group of Indians marched over 200 miles to the sea to protest the salt tax. On April 5, Gandhi arrived at the sea and then on April 6 broke the law by picking up handfuls of salt—essentially producing salt without paying the tax. This action sparked a national campaign of nonviolent protest that eventually led to Indian independence from Britain in 1947.*

Mohandas K. Gandhi (1869–1948), *often called by the title "Mahatma" ("Great Soul"), was one of the people who spearheaded the Indian drive for independence from British rule. His leadership helped the Indian people achieve independence through non-cooperation with unfair laws imposed by the British. His actions also inspired leaders of the American civil rights movement, such as Martin Luther King Jr., to follow his example on the path to achieving their goals.*

from Letter to Viceroy, Lord Irwin

Argument by Mohandas K. Gandhi

AS YOU READ Identify ways in which Gandhi appeals to his audience, an important British official. Write down any questions you generate during reading.

Dear Friend,

Before embarking on Civil Disobedience and taking the risk I have dreaded to take all these years, I would fain[1] approach you and find a way out. My personal faith is absolutely clear. I cannot intentionally hurt any thing that lives, much less fellow-human beings even though they may do the greatest wrong to me and mine. *Whilst therefore I hold the British rule to be a curse, I do not intend to harm a single Englishman or any legitimate interest he may have in India.*

I must not be misunderstood. Though I hold the British rule 10 in India to be a curse, I do not therefore consider Englishmen in general to be worse than any other people on earth. I have the privilege of claiming many Englishmen as dearest friends. Indeed much that I have learnt of the evil of British rule is due to the writings of frank and courageous Englishmen who have not hesitated to tell the **unpalatable** truth about that rule.

And why do I regard the British rule as a curse?

It has impoverished the dumb millions by a system of progressive exploitation and by a ruinously expensive military and civil administration which the country can never afford.

20 It has reduced us politically to serfdom.[2] It has sapped the foundations of our culture, and, by the policy of disarmament,[3] it has degraded us spiritually. Lacking inward strength, we have been reduced by all but universal disarmament to a state bordering on cowardly helplessness.

. . . If India is to live as a nation, if the slow death by starvation of her people is to stop, some remedy must be found for immediate relief. The proposed conference is certainly not the remedy. It is not a matter of carrying conviction by argument. The matter resolves itself into one of matching forces. Conviction or no conviction 30 Great Britain would defend her Indian commerce and interest by all the forces at her command. India must consequently evolve

unpalatable
(ŭn-păl´ə-tə-bəl) *adj.*
unpleasant or unacceptable.

---

[1] **fain:** with pleasure.
[2] **serfdom:** the lowest class of a feudal system, which held people in bondage.
[3] **disarmament:** the reduction or elimination of weapons.

> # "My ambition is no less than to convert the British people through non-violence and thus make them see the wrong they have done to India."

force enough to free herself from that embrace of death. It is common cause that, however disorganized and for the time being insignificant it may be, the party of violence is gaining ground and making itself felt. Its end is the same as mine. But I am convinced that it cannot bring the desired relief to the dumb millions. And the conviction is growing deeper and deeper in me that nothing but **unadulterated** non-violence can check the organized violence of the British Government. Many think that non-violence is not an active

40 force. It is my purpose to set in motion that force as well against the organized violent force of the British rule as the unorganized violent force of the growing party of violence. To sit still would be to give rein to both the forces above mentioned. Having an unquestioning and immovable faith in the efficacy of non-violence as I know it, it would be sinful on my part to wait any longer. . . .

I know that in embarking on non-violence, I shall be running what might fairly be termed a mad risk, but the victories of truth have never been won without risks, often of the gravest character. Conversion of a nation that has consciously or unconsciously

50 preyed upon another far more numerous, far more ancient and no less cultured than itself is worth any amount of risk.

I have deliberately used the word conversion. For my ambition is no less than to convert the British people through non-violence and thus make them see the wrong they have done to India. I do not seek to harm your people. I want to serve them even as I

unadulterated
(ŭn´ə-dŭl´tə-rā´tĭd)
adj. pure and untainted.

Gandhi (fourth from left) walks with his followers during the 1930 Salt March.

want to serve my own. I believe that I have always served them. I served them up to 1919 blindly. But when my eyes were opened, and I conceived non-cooperation the object still was to serve them. I employed the same weapon that I have in all **humility**

60 successfully used against the dearest members of my family. If I have equal love for your people with mine, it will not long remain hidden. It will be acknowledged by them even as the members of my family acknowledged it after they had tried me for several years. If the people join me as I expect they will, the sufferings they will undergo, unless the British nation sooner retraces its steps, will be enough to melt the stoniest hearts.

The plan through civil disobedience will be to combat such evils as I have sampled out.

If we want to sever the British connection it is because of such

70 evils. When they are removed the path becomes easy. Then the way to friendly negotiation will be open. If the British commerce with India is purified of greed, you will have no difficulty in recognizing our independence. I respectfully invite you then to pave the way for an immediate removal of those evils and thus open a way for a real conference between equals, interested only in promoting the common good of mankind through voluntary fellowship and in arranging terms of mutual help and commerce suited to both. You have unnecessarily laid stress upon the communal problems that unhappily affect this land. Important though they undoubtedly

80 are for the consideration of any scheme of government, they have

humility
(hyōō-mĭl´ĭ-tē) *n.* modesty; lack of superiority over others.

little bearing on the greater problems which are above communities and which affect them all equally. *But if you cannot see your way to deal with these evils and my letter makes no appeal to your heart, on the 11th day of this month, I shall proceed with such co-workers of the Ashram[4] as I can take to disregard the provisions of the Salt laws.* I regard this tax to be the most **iniquitous** of all from the poor man's standpoint. As the Independence Movement is essentially for the poorest in the land, the beginning will be made with this evil. The wonder is, that we have submitted to the cruel monopoly[5]

90 for so long. It is, I know, open to you to frustrate my design by arresting me. I hope that there will be tens of thousands ready in a disciplined manner to take up the work after me, and in the act of disobeying the Salt Act to lay themselves open to the penalties of a law that should never have disfigured the Statute-book.

I have no desire to cause you unnecessary embarrassment or any at all so far as I can help. If you think that there is any substance in my letter, and if you will care to discuss matters with me, and if to that end you would like me to postpone publication of this letter, I shall gladly refrain on receipt of a telegram to that

100 effect soon after this reaches you. You will however do me the favor not to deflect me from my course unless you can see your way to conform to the substance of this letter.

This letter is not in any way intended as a threat, but is a simple and sacred duty **peremptory** on a civil resister. Therefore I am having it specially delivered by a young English friend, who believes in the Indian cause and is a full believer in non-violence and whom Providence[6] seems to have sent to me as it were for the very purpose.

> I remain,
> Your Sincere friend,
>
> *M·K·Gandhi*
>
> M.K. Gandhi

iniquitous
(ĭ-nĭk´wĭ-təs) *adj.*
wicked, evil.

peremptory
(pə-rĕmp´tə-rē) *adj.*
imperative; required;
not able to be denied.

COLLABORATIVE DISCUSSION How does Gandhi appeal to his audience? Cite specific words, phrases, and examples from the text.

---

[4] **Ashram:** a secluded residence of a Hindu religious leader and followers.
[5] **monopoly:** the complete and exclusive control of a product or service.
[6] **Providence:** God or a supernatural power.

Analyze Argument and Rhetoric

A formal argument sets forth a specific claim and supports it with valid reasoning and relevant evidence. In his letter, Gandhi crafted his argument and rhetoric to appeal to his specific audience, the Viceroy of India. In doing this, Gandhi hoped that his argument would sway the Viceroy to improve the living conditions of the Indian people. As you analyze the argument and rhetoric of the letter, consider these elements and questions:

Elements to Consider	Questions to Ask about the Text
The **claim**—the central point of the argument—should be specific and reasonable.	How does Gandhi use the rhetorical question in line 16 to help define his claim?
Reasons that support a claim must be **valid**—both accurate and logical. No matter how appealing a reason may be, readers should ask themselves how it supports the writer's position and whether it is really true.	What is Gandhi's point of view about the English people? How does he use the distinction he makes between the English people and British rule to contribute to the power of his argument?
Evidence that is **relevant** must be used to elaborate on reasons. In other words, the evidence must be clearly linked to the reason and be sufficient, or comprehensive enough to provide solid support. Irrelevant or insufficient evidence weakens a writer's argument.	Why does Gandhi state in lines 64–66 that the suffering of the Indian people will be "enough to melt the stoniest hearts"?
Rhetoric is what a writer uses to effectively communicate ideas to an audience. A writer can construct a strong argument by establishing credibility and using an appropriate tone. Rhetoric can include emotionally charged words and appeals as well as memorable phrasing. The use of rhetoric can determine whether readers accept or reject an argument.	How do Gandhi's use of language and the style of the letter give the Viceroy an incentive to consider the power and persuasiveness of Gandhi's argument?

Analyzing the Text

RI 1, RI 3, RI 4,
RI 5, RI 6, RI 8,
W 2, W 9

Cite Text Evidence   Support your responses with evidence from the selection.

1. **Cause/Effect** Identify positive statements Gandhi makes about the English (or British) people. What effect might these statements have on his reader? Why?

2. **Analyze** Identify Gandhi's central claim in this letter. What key reasons does he provide to support this claim?

3. **Evaluate** Notice how Gandhi structures this argument. Why is this order of ideas effective?

4. **Draw Conclusions** Identify the places where Gandhi uses the word *curse* and where he uses the word *conversion*. Why are these word choices significant, and how do they affect his tone?

5. **Analyze** What similarities and differences does Gandhi point out between his movement and the "party of violence"? Why is it important for Gandhi to include in the letter a discussion of why the two movements are not equivalent?

6. **Infer** Identify Gandhi's purpose, or reason for writing this letter. What specific goals does he hope to achieve?

PERFORMANCE TASK

Writing Activity: Analysis Overall, how would you evaluate the strength of Gandhi's argument?

- Write a one-paragraph analysis of his claims, reasons, evidence, and rhetoric, providing examples from the text of the letter.

- Then, discuss in a second paragraph why you think this argument failed to persuade the Viceroy to change the conditions imposed on the Indian people or even to respond to Gandhi.

Critical Vocabulary

unpalatable   **unadulterated**   **humility**   **iniquitous**   **peremptory**

Practice and Apply For each Critical Vocabulary word, choose which of the two situations best fits the word's meaning. Explain why your choice is the best response.

1. **unpalatable**
   a. a sandwich covered with mold
   b. a sandwich too large to eat

2. **unadulterated**
   a. a sterile beaker of distilled water
   b. a precise mixture of water and iodine

3. **humility**
   a. a race winner pumping his fist in the air
   b. a race winner thanking his coach

4. **iniquitous**
   a. a hungry person stealing an apple
   b. a career criminal robbing people's homes

5. **peremptory**
   a. a passport carried by a traveler to China
   b. a map of Beijing bought by a tourist

Vocabulary Strategy: Denotations and Connotations

To persuade his audience, Gandhi uses words with strong **connotations**, or associated meanings and emotions. For example, he uses the Critical Vocabulary word *iniquitous*, which has a negative connotation of something that is not only wrong but also immoral. How would the meaning of the sentence change if the word *unjust* were used instead? *Unjust* has a **denotation,** or dictionary meaning , similar to that of *iniquitous*, but it carries a less immoral connotation. As you read an argument, consider the rhetorical effect of words with strong connotations.

Practice and Apply Analyze the nuances presented by each pair of words with similar denotations. Note that the boldfaced words are from the letter. Use each word in a sentence, and then explain the connotation of each word.

feared/**dreaded** (line 2)   unpleasant/**unpalatable** (line 15)

weakened/**degraded** (line 22)   hunger/**starvation** (line 25)

silent/**dumb** (line 36)   wrong/**sinful** (line 45)

from Gandhi: The Rise to Fame

Documentary Film by BBC

Background *In 2009, the British Broadcasting Corporation (BBC) aired a three-part documentary series on the life and legacy of Mohandas Gandhi. In it, British-born journalist Mishal Husain retraces Gandhi's steps, interviews those who knew him personally, and provides context for historical footage and photos. Husain's heritage is Pakistani, but her grandfather served in the Indian army before partition, the division of the former British colony into the independent nations of India and Pakistan.*

AS YOU VIEW Identify points of comparison between the letter and film. Write down any questions you generate during viewing.

COLLABORATIVE DISCUSSION With a partner, discuss common elements in the letter and film clip, supporting your ideas with evidence from both.

Analyze Accounts in Different Mediums

RI 7

The narrator of this documentary, Mishal Husain, discusses Gandhi's rise to fame from his beginnings as a lawyer through his emergence as a powerful figure in Indian politics. Factual information about important people and events can be presented in a variety of media, including written biographies, documentary films, and multimedia websites. Each medium has particular strengths and weaknesses. In addition, each person who creates an account in any medium does so from a certain point of view and with a certain purpose. This person's purpose may even drive the choice of medium—for example, video would be the best choice of medium for someone who wanted to emphasize a political leader's speaking skills and personality. To get the most comprehensive picture of a person or event, choose a variety of media sources, and think about the kinds of information that are included, omitted, and emphasized in each account.

Analyzing Text and Media

RI 1, RI 2, RI 3, RI 4, RI 6, RI 7, RI 8, SL 1

Cite Text Evidence   Support your responses with evidence from the selections.

1. **Interpret** Describe the narrator's tone and word choice, providing examples from the video. What can you infer from those word choices about the purpose of this documentary?

2. **Evaluate** In this film, the history of Gandhi's rise to fame is documented in chronological order with the use of present-day narration and commentary interspersed with some supporting archival images. Why is this an effective way to organize a biography but not an argument?

3. **Compare** Which arguments or ideas are apparent in both the letter and the film?

4. **Synthesize** What ideas and events are emphasized in the film? How do the film and letter work together to create a fuller picture of Gandhi than either could alone?

PERFORMANCE TASK

Speaking Activity: Debate Which communicates Gandhi's ideas more effectively, the letter or the film? Decide by participating in a debate.

- Form teams of two to three students each, with half defending the letter as more effective and half defending the film clip. Each team should gather evidence from both the letter and the film to support its position.

- Follow the rules for debating on page R14. Afterward, write a brief evaluation of which side presented a more compelling argument.

Background *The protagonist of "The Briefcase" is a political prisoner in an unnamed country, a man who has been arrested for associating with the wrong people. Political prisoners are detained, imprisoned, and sometimes executed, without benefit of trial or jury, due to political associations or beliefs that conflict with those of the people in power. Such detentions happen all over the world under regimes that hold absolute power over the people and the press. In this story, author* **Rebecca Makkai** *(b. 1978) innovates the universality of political imprisonment through the use of basic astronomy.*

The
Briefcase

Short Story by Rebecca Makkai

AS YOU READ Pay attention to details that reveal something about the chef's character. Write down any questions you generate during reading.

He thought how strange that a political prisoner, marched through town in a line, chained to the man behind and chained to the man ahead, should take comfort in the fact that all this had happened before. He thought of other chains of men on other islands of the Earth, and he thought how since there have been men there have been prisoners. He thought of mankind as a line of miserable monkeys chained at the wrist, dragging each other back into the ground.

In the early morning of December first the sun was finally warming
10 them all, enough that they could walk faster. With his left hand, he adjusted the loop of steel that cuffed his right hand to the line of doomed men. His hand was starved, his wrist was thin, his body was cold: the cuff slipped off. In one beat of the heart he looked back to the man behind him and forward to the man limping ahead, and knew that neither saw his naked, red wrist; each saw

only his own mother weeping in a kitchen, his own love on a bed in white sheets and sunlight.

He walked in step with them to the end of the block.

Before the war this man had been a chef, and his one crime was feeding the people who sat at his tables in small clouds of smoke and talked politics. He served them the wine that fueled their underground newspaper, their aborted revolution. And after the night his restaurant disappeared in fire, he had run and hidden and gone without food — he who had roasted ducks until the meat jumped from the bone, he who had evaporated three bottles of wine into one pot of cream soup, he who had peeled the skin from small pumpkins with a twist of his hand.

And here was his hand, twisted free of the chain, and here he was running and crawling, until he was through a doorway. It was a building of empty classrooms — part of the university he had never attended. He watched from the bottom corner of a second-story window as the young soldiers stopped the line, counted 199 men, shouted to each other, shouted at the men in the panicked voices of children who barely filled the shoulders of their uniforms. One soldier, a bigger one, a louder one, stopped a man walking by. A man in a suit, with a briefcase, a beard — some sort of professor. The soldiers stripped him of his coat, his shirt, his leather case, cuffed him to the chain. They marched again. And as soon as they were past — no, not that soon; many minutes later, when he had the stomach — the chef ran down to the street and collected the man's briefcase, coat and shirt.

In the alley, the chef sat against a wall and buttoned the professor's shirt over his own ribs. When he opened the briefcase, papers flew out, a thousand doves **flailing** against the walls of the alley. The chef ran after them all, stopped them with his feet and arms, herded them back into the case. Pages of numbers, of arrows and notes and hand-drawn star maps. Here were business cards: a professor of physics. Envelopes showed his name and address — information that might have been useful in some other lifetime, one where the chef could ring the bell of this man's house and explain to his wife about empty chains, empty wrists, empty classrooms. Here were graded papers, a fall syllabus, the typed draft of an exam. The question at the end, a good one: "Using modern astronomical data, construct, to the best of your ability, a proof that the sun actually revolves around the Earth."

flail
(flāl) *v.* to thrash or wave about wildly.

The chef knew nothing of physics. He understood chemistry only insofar as it related to the baking time of bread at various elevations or the evaporation rate of alcohol. His knowledge of biology was limited to the deboning of chickens and the behavior

60 of *Saccharomyces cerevisiae*, common bread yeast. And what did he know at all of moving bodies and gravity? He knew this: he had moved from his line of men, creating a vacuum — one that had sucked the good professor in to fill the void.

The chef sat on his bed in the widow K——'s basement and felt, in the cool leather of the briefcase, a second vacuum: here was a vacated life. Here were salary receipts, travel records, train tickets, a small address book. And these belonged to a man whose name was not blackened like his own, a man whose life was not hunted. If he wanted to live through the next year, the chef would have to

70 learn this life and fill it — and oddly, this felt not like a robbery but an apology, a way to put the world back in balance. The professor would not die, because he himself would become the professor, and he would live.

Surely he could not teach at the university; surely he could not slip into the man's bed unnoticed. But what was in this leather case, it seemed, had been left for him to use. These addresses of friends; this card of identification; this riddle about the **inversion** of the universe.

inversion
(ĭn-vûr'zhən) *n.*
reversal or upside-down placement.

Five cities east, he now gave his name as the professor's, and grew

80 out his beard so it would match the photograph on the card he now carried in his pocket. The two men did not, anymore, look entirely dissimilar. To the first name in the address book, the chef had written a typed letter: "Am in trouble and have fled the city. Tell my dear wife I am safe, but for her safety do not tell her where I am. If you are able to help a poor old man, send money to the following post box . . . I hope to remain your friend, Professor T——."

He had to write this about the wife; how could he ask these men for money if she held a funeral? And what of it, if she kept her

90 happiness another few months, another year?

The next twenty-six letters were similar in nature, and money arrived now in brown envelopes and white ones. The bills came wrapped in notes — (Was his life in danger? Did he have his health?) — and with the money he paid another widow for another basement, and he bought weak cigarettes. He sat on café chairs and drew pictures of the universe, showed stars and planets looping each other in light. He felt, perhaps, that if he used the other papers in the briefcase, he must also make use of the question. Or perhaps he felt that if he could answer it, he could put the universe back

100 together. Or perhaps it was something to fill his empty days.

He wrote in his small notebook: "The light of my cigarette is a fire like the sun. From where I sit, all the universe is **equidistant**

equidistant
(ē'kwĭ-dĭs'tənt) *adj.* at equal distance from.

from my cigarette. Ergo,[1] my cigarette is the center of the universe.
My cigarette is on Earth. Ergo, the Earth is the center of the
universe. If all heavenly bodies move, they must therefore move in
relation to the Earth, and in relation to my cigarette."

His hand ached. These words were the most he had written
since school, which had ended for him at age sixteen. He had
been a smart boy, even talented in languages and mathematics,
110 but his mother knew these were no way to make a living. He was
not blessed, like the professor, with years of scholarship and quiet
offices and leather books. He was blessed instead with chicken
stocks and herbs and sherry. Thirty years had passed since his last
day of school, and his hand was accustomed now to wooden spoon,
mandoline, peeling knife, rolling pin.

Today, his hands smelled of ink, when for thirty years they had
smelled of leeks. They were the hands of the professor; ergo, he was
now the professor.

He had written to friends A through L, and now he saved the rest
120 and wrote instead to students. Here in the briefcase's outermost
pocket were class rosters from the past two years; letters addressed
to those young men care of the university were sure to reach them.
The amounts they sent were smaller, the notes that accompanied
them more inquisitive. What exactly had **transpired**? Could they
come to the city and meet him?

transpire
(trăn-spīr´) *v.* to
happen or occur.

The post box, of course, was in a different city than the one
where he stayed. He arrived at the post office just before closing,

---

[1] **Ergo (ûr´gō):** the Latin equivalent of "therefore."

and came only once every two or three weeks. He always looked through the window first to check that the lobby was empty. If it was not, he would leave and come again another day. Surely one of these days, a friend of the professor would be waiting there for him. He prepared a story, that he was the honored professor's assistant, that he could not reveal the man's location but would certainly pass on your kindest regards, sir.

If the Earth moved, all it would take for a man to travel its distance would be a strong balloon. Rise twenty feet above, and wait for the Earth to turn under you; you would be home again in a day. But this was not true, and a man could not escape his spot on the Earth but to run along the surface. Ergo, the Earth was still. Ergo, the sun was the moving body of the two.

No, he did not believe it. He wanted only to know who this professor was, this man who would teach his students the laws of the universe, then ask them to prove as true what was false.

On the wall of the café: plate-sized canvas, delicate oils of an apple, half-peeled. Signed, below, by a girl he had known in school. The price was more than a month of groceries, and so he did not buy it, but for weeks he read his news under the apple and drank his coffee. Staining his fingers in cheap black ink were the signal fires of the world, the distress sirens, the dispatches from the trenches and hospitals and abattoirs[2] of the war; but here, on the wall, a sign from another world. He had known this girl as well as any other: had spoken with her every day, but had not made love to her; had gone to her home one winter holiday, but knew nothing of her life since then. And here, a clue, perfect and round and unfathomable. After all this time: apple.

After he finished the news, he worked at the proof and saw in the coil of green-edged skin some model of spiraling, of expansion. The stars were at one time part of the Earth, until the hand of God peeled them away, leaving us in the dark. They do not revolve around us: they escape in widening circles. The Milky Way is the edge of this peel.

Outside the café window, a beggar screeched his bow against a defeated violin. A different kind of case, open on the ground, this one collecting the pennies of the more compassionate passers-by. The café owner shooed him away, and the chef sighed in guilty relief that he would not have to pass, on the way out, his double.

After eight months in the new city, the chef stopped buying his newspapers on the street by the café and began instead to read the year-old news the widow gave him for his fires. Here, fourteen

---

[2] **abattoirs** (ăb´ə-twärs´): slaughterhouses.

170 months ago: Minister P—— of the Interior predicts war. One day
he found that in a box near the widow's furnace were papers three,
four, five years old. Pages were missing, edges eaten. He took his
fragments of yellowed paper to the café and read the beginnings
and ends of opinions and letters. He read reports from what used to
be his country's borders.

When he had finished the last paper of the box, he began to
read the widow's history books. The Americas, before Columbus;
the oceans, before the British; the Romans, before their fall.

History was safer than the news, because there was no question
180 of how it would end.

He took a lover in the city and told her he was a professor of
physics. He showed her the stars in the sky and explained that they
circled the Earth, along with the sun.

That's not true at all, she said. You tease because you think I'm
just a silly girl.

No, he said and touched her neck, You are the only one who
might understand. The universe has been folded inside out.

A full year had passed, and he paid the widow in coins. He wrote to
friends M through Z. I have been in hiding for a year, he wrote. Tell
190 my dear wife I have my health. May time and history forgive us all.

A year had passed, but so had many years passed for many
men. And after all what was a year, if the Earth did not circle the
sun?

The Earth does not circle the sun, he wrote. Ergo: The years do
not pass. The Earth, being stationary, does not erase the past nor
escape towards the future. Rather, the years pile on like blankets,
existing at once. The year is 1848; the year is 1789; the year is 1956.

If the Earth hangs still in space, does it spin? If the Earth were
to spin, the space I occupy I will therefore vacate in an instant. This
200 city will leave its spot, and the city to the west will usurp its place.
Ergo, this city is all cities at all times. This is Kabul; this is Dresden;
this is Johannesburg.[3]

I run by standing still.

At the post office, he collects his envelopes of money. He has
learned from the notes of concerned colleagues and students and
friends that the professor suffered from infections of the inner ear
that often threw off his balance. He has learned of the professor's
wife, A——, whose father died the year they married. He has
learned that he has a young son. Rather, the professor has a son.

---

[3] **Kabul ... Dresden ... Johannesburg:** cities in Afghanistan, Germany, and
South Africa, respectively.

At each visit to the post office, he fears he will forget the combination. It is an old lock, and complicated: F1, clockwise to B3, back to A6, forward again to J3. He must shake the little latch before it opens. More than forgetting, perhaps what he fears is that he will be denied access — that the little box will one day recognize him behind his thick and convincing beard, will decide he has no right of entry.

One night, asleep with his head on his lover's leg, he dreams that a letter has arrived from the professor himself. They freed me at the end of the march, it says, and I crawled my way home. My hands are bloody and my knees are worn through, and I want my briefcase back.

In his dream, the chef takes the case and runs west. If the professor takes it back, there will be no name left for the chef, no place on the Earth. The moment his fingers leave the leather loop of the handle, he will fall off the planet.

He sits in a wooden chair on the lawn behind the widow's house. Inside, he hears her washing dishes. In exchange for the room, he cooks all her meals. It is March, and the cold makes the hairs rise from his arms, but the sun warms the arm beneath them. He thinks, The tragedy of a moving sun is that it leaves us each day. Hence the Aztec sacrifices, the ancient rites of the eclipse. If the sun so willingly leaves us, each morning it returns is a stay of execution, an undeserved gift.

Whereas: If it is we who turn, how can we so **flagrantly** leave behind that which has warmed us and given us light? If we are moving, then each turn is a turn away. Each revolution a revolt.

flagrantly
(flā´grənt-lē) *adv.*
in a blatantly or conspicuously offensive manner.

The money comes less often, and even old friends who used to write monthly now send only rare, apologetic notes, a few small bills. Things are more difficult now, their letters say. No one understood when he first ran away, but now it is clear: After they finished with the artists, the journalists, the fighters, they came for the professors. How wise he was, to leave when he did. Some letters come back unopened, with a black stamp.

Life is harder here, too. Half the shops are closed. His lover has left him. The little café is filled with soldiers. The beggar with the violin has disappeared, and the chef fears him dead.

One afternoon, he enters the post office two minutes before closing. The lobby is empty but for the postman and his broom.

The mailbox is empty as well, and he turns to leave but hears the voice of the postman behind him. You are the good Professor T——, no? I have something for you in the back.

Yes, he says, I am the professor. And it feels as if this is true, and he will have no guilt over the professor's signature when the box is brought out. He is even wearing the professor's shirt, as loose again over his hungry ribs as it was the day he slipped it on in the alley.

From behind the counter, the postman brings no box, but a woman in a long gray dress, a white handkerchief in her fingers.

She moves towards him, looks at his hands and his shoes and his face. Forgive me for coming, she says, and the postman pulls the cover down over his window and vanishes. She says, No one would tell me anything, only that my husband had his health. And then a student gave me the number of the box and the name of the city.

He begins to say, You are the widow. But why would he say this? What proof is there that the professor is dead? Only that it must be; that it follows logically.

She says, I don't understand what has happened.

He begins to say, I am the good professor's assistant, madam — but then what next? She would ask questions he has no way to answer.

I don't understand, she says again.

All he can say is, This is his shirt. He holds out an arm so she can see the gaping sleeve.

She says, What have you done with him? She has a calm voice and wet, brown eyes. He feels he has seen her before, in the streets of the old city. Perhaps he served her a meal, a bottle of wine. Perhaps, in another lifetime, she was the center of his universe.

This is his beard, he says.

She begins to cry into the handkerchief. She says, Then he is dead. He sees now from the quiet of her voice that she must have known this long ago. She has come here only to confirm.

He feels the floor of the post office move beneath him, and he tries to turn his eyes from her, to ground his gaze in something solid: postbox, ceiling tile, window. He finds he cannot turn away. She is a force of gravity in her long gray dress.

No, he says. No, no, no, no, no, I am right here.

No, he does not believe it, but he knows that if he had time, he could prove it. And he must, because he is the only piece of the professor left alive. The woman does not see how she is murdering her husband, right here in the post office lobby. He whispers to her: Let me go home with you. I'll be a father to your son, and I'll warm your bed, and I'll keep you safe.

He wraps his hands around her small, cold wrists, but she pulls loose. She might be the most beautiful woman he has ever seen.

As if from far away, he hears her call to the postmaster to send for the police.

His head is light, and he feels he might float away from the post office forever. It is an act of will not to fly off, but to hold tight to

the Earth and wait. If the police aren't too busy to come, he feels
300 confident he can prove to them that he is the professor. He has the
papers, after all — and in the **havoc** of war, what else will they have
the time to look for?

She is backing away from him on steady feet, and he feels it like
a peeling off of skin.

If not the police, perhaps he'll convince a city judge. The
witnesses who would denounce him are mostly gone or killed,
and the others would fear to come before the law. If the city judge
will not listen, he can prove it to the high court. One day he might
convince the professor's own child. He feels certain that somewhere
310 down the line, someone will believe him.

havoc
(hăv´ək) *n.*
destructive disorder
or chaos.

COLLABORATIVE DISCUSSION With a partner, discuss your impression
of the chef. Explain whether you think he is resourceful or simply
dishonest. Cite specific evidence from the story to support your ideas.

Analyze Character and Theme

Characters are the people who experience the events in a story. Like real people, they display certain qualities and develop and change over time. Readers come to understand characters through their thoughts, actions, dialogue, and interactions with others. Their **motivations,** or reasons for doing what they do, advance the plot of a story and reveal its theme.

In this story, only the character of the chef is fully developed, and we learn much about him through his interactions with and observations of other minor characters. For example, consider the beggar outside the café. What does the chef think about the beggar? What does this reveal about his character?

Theme is the central idea of a story or the insight about life that the author wants to convey. Themes may be universal, such as "Crime does not pay" or "Love conquers all," or they may be more specific to the story. An author might state a theme directly, but most often readers must infer theme, relying on character development and unfolding events to make an educated guess about what message the author wants to convey.

Use these key elements to analyze the chef's character and determine the theme of the story:

The Character's Actions	Think about the chef's actions in the story. What does his assumption of the professor's identity tell you about him?
The Character's Interactions with Others	The chef interacts with others through letters. He also interacts with his landlady, his lover, the post office clerk, and the professor's wife. What does each interaction reveal about his character?
The Character's Thoughts	Throughout the story, the chef is preoccupied with answering the professor's astronomy question. Here are some examples of his thoughts about it. Given his situation, are these thoughts about more than astronomy? • "My cigarette is on Earth. Ergo, the Earth is the center of the universe. If all heavenly bodies move, they must therefore move in relation to the Earth, and in relation to my cigarette." • ". . . a man could not escape his spot on the Earth but to run along the surface. Ergo, the Earth was still. Ergo, the sun was the moving body of the two." • "The Earth does not circle the sun, he wrote. Ergo: The years do not pass. The Earth, being stationary, does not erase the past nor escape towards the future."

 **eBook** *Annotate It!*

Analyzing the Text

RL 1, RL 2,
RL 3, RL 4,
RL 5, W 4

Cite Text Evidence   Support your responses with evidence from the selection.

1. **Cite Evidence** What evidence does the author provide that the chef, even after a year in hiding, fears discovery?

2. **Infer** When the chef first opens the professor's briefcase, the author writes that "papers flew out, a thousand doves flailing against the walls of the alley" (lines 43–44). What might the author want to achieve by comparing the professor's papers to doves? What tone does this image create?

3. **Summarize** How does the chef justify the theft of the professor's briefcase and identity?

4. **Analyze** The author compresses a long period of time into a few pages. Instead of providing a comprehensive summary of events in the chef's life during this year, she looks closely at specific moments in time, reminding the reader that eight months, and then a year, have passed. How does this pacing create tension in the story?

5. **Interpret** In what way is the beggar outside the café the chef's "double" (line 166)? Why does the chef not want to walk past him?

6. **Interpret** After eight months, the chef prefers to read old newspapers and history books rather than the daily news. What does this choice reveal about the chef's character? How has he changed?

7. **Analyze** Throughout the story, the author comes back to the astronomy question again and again. What connection can be made between this riddle and the chef's predicament? What incentive does he have to solve the riddle?

8. **Draw Conclusions** Does the chef ever begin to believe his own lie? Cite evidence from the story to support your answer.

PERFORMANCE TASK

Writing Activity: Personal Letter Assume the identity of the chef. Write a letter to the professor's son in which you attempt to convince him that you could serve as the boy's father.

1. Gather details from the story that support the chef's idea that he has become the professor.

2. Write a brief letter to the son based on the evidence you have gathered from the text. Address the son using a voice and logic suited to the chef's character, and mention events and relationships of which the chef would be aware.

Critical Vocabulary

flail	inversion	equidistant
transpire	flagrantly	havoc

Practice and Apply Answer each question to demonstrate your understanding of the Critical Vocabulary words.

1. The war had created **havoc** in the chef's country. What might you assume everyday life was like for people?

2. The guards **flagrantly** disregarded the law in seizing the professor. How concerned were they that others would find out the professor had been unlawfully arrested?

3. If the chef believes that all things in the universe are **equidistant** from him, is the sun farther from the chef than the moon? Explain your response.

4. The professor's wife tracked down the chef to determine what had **transpired.** What did she hope to find out?

5. When the chef reads the professor's test question, he interprets it as an **inversion** of the universe. Explain why.

6. If the professor's arms were **flailing** when he was seized, did he meekly obey or resist arrest?

Language and Style: Semicolons

Writers use semicolons for three main purposes: to link two independent clauses, to link an independent clause with another clause that begins with a conjunctive adverb (such as *therefore, meanwhile, also,* or *however*), and to separate items in a list when the items already contain commas. Makkai uses semicolons to provide structure and organization in her writing, but she also uses them to influence meaning. Read this sentence from the story:

> Surely he could not teach at the university; surely he could not slip into the man's bed unnoticed.

The author could have separated the two independent clauses with a period, but the two thoughts are closely connected, and Makkai wanted to convey that idea to her readers. Now, read this sentence from the story:

> They were the hands of the professor; ergo, he was now the professor.

In this example, the semicolon links two thoughts, and a conjunctive adverb (*ergo*) shows that the second thought results from the first.

Practice and Apply Look back at the letter you wrote for this selection's Performance Task. Revise your letter to link two independent clauses with semicolons. Then, discuss with a partner how using semicolons helps clarify the meaning of your letter.

Jimmy Santiago Baca (b. 1952) *was born in Santa Fe, New Mexico. Abandoned by his parents, Baca had a difficult childhood. In his early twenties, he was arrested and subsequently spent over five years in prison. Though locked up, Baca realized the liberating power of language when he began to read and write poetry. Baca has since written several volumes of poetry, essays, memoirs, and a screenplay. "Cloudy Day" first appeared in* Immigrants in Our Own Land, *Baca's first book of poetry, which was based on his time in prison.*

Cloudy Day

Poem by Jimmy Santiago Baca

AS YOU READ Notice the details that tell you about the author of this autobiographical poem. Write down any questions you generate during reading.

It is windy today. A wall of wind crashes against,
windows clunk against, iron frames
as wind swings past broken glass
and seethes, like a frightened cat
5 in empty spaces of the cellblock.

In the exercise yard
we sat huddled in our prison jackets,
on our haunches[1] against the fence,
and the wind carried our words
10 over the fence,
while the vigilant guard on the tower
held his cap at the sudden gust.

---

[1] **haunches:** the hips and thighs.

I could see the main tower from where I sat,
and the wind in my face
15   gave me the feeling I could grasp
the tower like a cornstalk,
and snap it from its roots of rock.

The wind plays it like a flute,
this hollow shoot of rock.
20   The brim girded[2] with barbwire
with a guard sitting there also,
listening intently to the sounds
as clouds cover the sun.

I thought of the day I was coming to prison,
25   in the back seat of a police car,
hands and ankles chained, the policeman pointed,
      "See that big water tank? The big
      silver one out there, sticking up?
      That's the prison."

30   And here I am, I cannot believe it.
Sometimes it is such a dream, a dream,
where I stand up in the face of the wind,
like now, it blows at my jacket,
and my eyelids flick a little bit,
35   while I stare disbelieving. . . .

The third day of spring,
and four years later, I can tell you,
how a man can endure, how a man
can become so cruel, how he can die
40   or become so cold. I can tell you this,
I have seen it every day, every day,
and still I am strong enough to love you,
love myself and feel good;
even as the earth shakes and trembles,
45   and I have not a thing to my name,
I feel as if I have everything, everything.

COLLABORATIVE DISCUSSION With a partner, discuss your impression of the poem's speaker. Explain what incentive Baca might have had to write a poem about his imprisonment. Cite specific evidence from the text to support your ideas.

---

[2] **girded:** encircled, surrounded.

RL 2, RL 4

Analyze Theme and Tone

Tone is a writer's attitude toward his or her subject and audience. Writers convey tone through word choice and details. Sometimes, the tone of a work shifts as the author's attitude toward the subject matter changes to create a comprehensive view of the subject. For example, Baca creates an image of crouching, fearful animals early in this poem. Think about the tone this image implies. Then, consider how Baca uses language in the last stanza to express a very different tone.

A selection's tone contributes to its **theme**, or the underlying message the author wants to convey. Use these questions to analyze tone and theme in "Cloudy Day":

- How does the poet feel about his subject matter at the poem's beginning?
- How does the poet feel about his subject matter at the end of the poem?
- What does the shift in tone say about the speaker? What does it say about the nature of people?

RL 1, RL 2,
RL 3, RL 4,
RL 5, SL 1a

Analyzing the Text

> **Cite Text Evidence**   Support your responses with evidence from the selection.

1. **Infer** What words in lines 1–5 have strong connotations? How do these connotations affect the tone of the poem?

2. **Cite Evidence** What evidence does the poet provide in lines 13–17 about how the speaker feels? How do these lines contrast with the first two stanzas of the poem?

3. **Analyze** Lines 24–29 contain a flashback to four years earlier when the author arrived in prison. What purpose does the flashback serve?

4. **Interpret** How do the speaker's descriptions of and feelings about the wind change as the poem progresses? How does this shift show a change in the tone of the poem?

5. **Evaluate** What theme emerges by the end of the poem? How does Baca use contrasts to help build this theme?

PERFORMANCE TASK

Speaking Activity: Response to Literature Consider the poet's use of imagery and repetition.

1. Make a list of details from the poem that appeal to any of your five senses, and label them as expressing either confinement or freedom. Also, list examples of repeated phrases or ideas in the poem, and label them the same way.

2. Bring your notes to a group discussion, and use them to analyze the themes of the poem.

3. At the end of the discussion, write a summary of how the discussion extended or challenged your ideas about the poem's theme.

Language and Style: Prepositional Phrases

Prepositions are words that show relationships between a noun or pronoun and another word in the sentence. The words *in, against,* and *over* are examples of prepositions. Prepositions are used in a phrase called a **prepositional phrase,** which includes the preposition plus a noun object. In his poem "Cloudy Day," Baca uses prepositional phrases to add detail and to create imagery. He also uses them to create rhythm and tone by employing prepositional phrases with parallel structure.

Reread lines 7–10 from the poem:

we sat huddled in our prison jackets,
on our haunches against the fence,
and the wind carried our words
over the fence,

The author could instead have written the lines this way:

we sat huddled
and the wind carried our words

This example lacks the detail of the first. Without the detail, the tone of the poem is more difficult to convey. This example also lacks rhythm. In lines 7–10, the author uses two prepositional phrases of equivalent lengths that end with the words *the fence.* The result is a parallel structure that creates rhythm and makes the poem more enjoyable to read.

Here are some other common prepositions:

Common Prepositions	
Preposition	Example from the Poem
in	in the exercise yard
of	of the cellblock
to	to the sounds
at	at my jacket
from	from where I sat

Practice and Apply Write a short poem on the topic of your choice. Use several prepositional phrases to add detail as well as rhythm through parallel structure. Use a rhyming dictionary as needed if you plan to make your poem rhyme.

COLLECTION **6**
PERFORMANCE TASK

Present an Argument

This collection explores the struggle for freedom experienced around the world and ways in which people fight to overcome oppression. Look back at the texts in this collection, including the anchor text, "Letter from Birmingham Jail," and consider this question: What constitutes true freedom? Synthesize your ideas about the texts by writing and delivering an argument about the meaning of freedom.

W 1a–e Write arguments to support claims in an analysis.
W 9a–b Draw evidence from literary or informational texts.

An effective argument

- makes a persuasive claim about what constitutes freedom
- develops the claim with valid reasons and relevant text evidence
- anticipates and addresses counterclaims
- uses transitions to link reasons and textual evidence to the claim
- includes a logically structured body
- has a satisfying conclusion that effectively summarizes the claim
- demonstrates appropriate, clear use of language, maintaining a formal tone through the use of standard academic English

Visit hmhfyi.com to explore your topic and enhance your research.

PLAN

Make a Claim Consider the texts in this collection and each writer's views regarding oppression and what constitutes true freedom. Does the meaning of freedom vary from person to person and culture to culture, or is it more universal? Write a claim that states your position on the meaning of freedom. You will need to provide sufficient evidence from the texts to support your position.

Gather Evidence Use the annotation tools in your eBook to find evidence from your chosen texts. Save each piece of evidence to *my*Notebook, in a folder titled *Collection 6 Performance Task*.

ACADEMIC VOCABULARY

As you build your argument about freedom, be sure to use these words.

comprehensive
equivalent
incentive
innovate
media

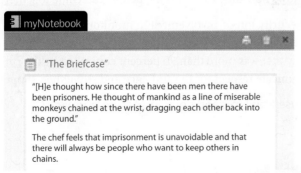

Structure Your Argument We may not all possess the persuasive gifts of King and Gandhi, but following the structure of their arguments is a start. Notice that both writers

- begin with a clear statement of the claim
- directly address the audience's opposing views
- clearly organize reasons and relevant evidence
- progress logically from one reason to the next
- place the strongest reasons near the beginning and end
- conclude by reiterating the claim and making a personal appeal

As you outline your argument, try to follow this powerful structure.

Interactive Lessons
To help you plan your argument, complete the following lessons from Writing an Argument:
• Building Effective Support
• Creating a Coherent Argument

> **PRODUCE**

✓ my WriteSmart

Write your rough draft in *my*WriteSmart. Focus on getting your ideas down, rather than perfecting your choice of language.

Draft Your Essay Use your outline to guide your first draft, and remember to consider your purpose and audience. Be sure to

- present ideas in a memorable way that will appeal to your audience
- explain how text evidence supports your ideas
- include transitions to connect your reasons, evidence, and claim
- use formal language, including domain-specific terms, and a respectful tone appropriate for an academic context
- write a conclusion that summarizes your position; you might also include a powerful quotation or a call to action

Language and Style: Academic and Domain-Specific Language

An effective argument is specific and takes its subject and audience seriously. To achieve this goal in your argument, incorporate general **academic language**—words and phrases used in school and formal speaking—as well as **domain-specific terms** that apply to the subject you are discussing. Here are some examples from *Revolution 2.0:*

general academic language "We chose this day specifically because it represents the fusion of the police and the people." Contrast this language with "We picked this day on purpose because it shows how the police and the people can come together."

domain-specific terms "Security forces' involvement in monitoring politicians and blocking their activism has led to shameless rigging of parliamentary elections, producing a people's assembly that was more than 90 percent controlled by the ruling party." Political terms communicate respect for the audience and strengthen support.

Reread your draft, revising to use academic and domain-specific language.

Have your partner or a group of peers review your draft in *my*WriteSmart. Ask your reviewers to note any reasons that do not support the claim or that lack sufficient evidence.

Refine Your Argument To make sure your argument is as clear and persuasive as possible, revise your draft using the questions, tips, and revision techniques below.

Questions	Tips	Revision Techniques
Does the introduction create interest and confidently state a claim?	**Underline** the claim and **highlight** the attention-getting opening.	**Add** a clear claim, and **add** a relevant attention-getting quotation or detail.
Are reasons organized logically and linked with transitions?	**Note** the reason explored in each body paragraph. **Underline** transitional words and phrases.	**Reorder** reasons and evidence in a logical sequence. **Add** transitions to link reasons and evidence.
Does evidence from multiple texts support each reason?	**Highlight** the text evidence that supports each reason.	**Add** relevant evidence to support each reason.
Are opposing views addressed effectively?	**Underline** opposing views and sentences that address or refute those views.	**Add** an opposing view or **revise** to refute an opposing view with valid reasons.
Is the style appropriately formal, including domain-specific terms?	**Highlight** domain-specific terms and academic vocabulary throughout the essay.	**Add** domain-specific terms or general academic language to clarify ideas.

State Your Case Rehearse your speech several times to ensure a convincing delivery. Keep these tips in mind:

- Speak loudly enough that listeners in the back of the room can easily understand you, and vary your volume as appropriate to emphasize key points.
- Speak clearly, paying special attention to pronouncing domain-specific vocabulary precisely.
- Make eye contact with members of your audience, moving your gaze around the room as you speak.

Interactive Lessons

For help with your presentation, use the following lessons from Giving a Presentation:
· Knowing Your Audience
· Style in Presentation

PERFORMANCE TASK RUBRIC
ARGUMENTATIVE SPEECH

	Ideas and Evidence	Organization	Language
4	• The introduction is memorable and persuasive; the claim clearly states a position on the topic. • Valid reasons and relevant evidence from the texts convincingly support the claim. • Counterclaims are anticipated and effectively addressed with counterarguments. • The concluding section effectively summarizes the claim.	• The reasons and textual evidence are organized consistently and logically throughout the argument. • Varied transitions logically connect reasons and textual evidence to the speaker's claim.	• The writing reflects a formal style and an objective, controlled tone. • Academic and domain-specific language clearly express ideas. • The speaker uses appropriate volume and correct pronunciation. • Grammar and usage are correct.
3	• The introduction states a clear position on an issue. • Most reasons and evidence from the texts support the speaker's claim. • Counterclaims are anticipated, but the counterarguments need to be developed more. • The concluding section restates the claim.	• The organization of reasons and textual evidence is generally clear. • Transitions usually connect reasons and textual evidence to the speaker's claim.	• The style is mostly formal, but the tone is occasionally subjective. • Some academic or domain-specific terms are used. • The speaker is mostly audible and pronounces most words correctly. • Grammatical and usage errors occur but do not interfere with the speaker's message.
2	• The introduction is ordinary; the claim identifies an issue, but the speaker's position is not clearly stated. • The reasons and evidence from the texts are not always logical or relevant. • Counterclaims are anticipated but not addressed logically. • The concluding section includes an incomplete summary of the claim.	• The organization of reasons and textual evidence is logical in some places, but it often doesn't follow a pattern. • Many more transitions are needed to connect reasons and textual evidence to the speaker's position.	• The style is informal in many places, and the tone is often dismissive of other viewpoints. • One or two academic or domain-specific terms are used. • The speaker is difficult to hear at times, and several words are mispronounced. • Grammar and usage are incorrect in many places, causing some confusion.
1	• The introduction is missing. • Significant supporting reasons and evidence from the texts are missing. • Counterclaims are not addressed. • The concluding section is missing.	• An organizational strategy is not evident; reasons and evidence are presented randomly. • Transitions are not used, making the argument difficult to understand.	• The style is inappropriate, and the tone is disrespectful. • Academic and domain-specific terms are absent or misused. • The speaker is mostly inaudible and mispronounces many words. • Many grammatical and usage errors change the meaning of the speaker's ideas.

Writing Arguments

Many of the Performance Tasks in this book ask you to craft an argument in which you support your ideas with text evidence. Any argument you write should include the following sections and characteristics.

Introduce Your Claim

Clearly state your **claim**—the point your argument makes. As needed, provide context or background information to help readers understand your position. Note the most common opposing views as a way to distinguish and clarify your ideas. From the very beginning, make it clear for readers why your claim is strong; consider providing an overview of your reasons or a quotation that emphasizes your view in your introduction.

EXAMPLES

Vague claim: We need more lunch choices.	**Precise claim:** Our school district should allow fast-food restaurants to offer nutritious menu items in the school cafeteria.
Not distinguished from opposing view: There are plenty of people who consider fast food bad.	**Distinguished from opposing view:** While some people consider all fast food unhealthful, the facts say differently.
Confusing relationship of ideas: Teens need more choices. Fast food is enjoyed by people of all ages.	**Clear relationship of ideas:** Access to healthful fast-food lunch choices will improve student morale and provide revenue to the school.

Develop Your Claim

The body of your argument must provide strong, logical reasons for your claim and must support those reasons with relevant evidence. A **reason** tells why your claim is valid; **evidence** provides specific examples that illustrate a reason. In the process of developing your claim, you should also refute **counterclaims**, or opposing views, with equally strong reasons

and evidence. To demonstrate that you have thoroughly considered your view, provide a well-rounded look at both the strengths and limitations of both your claim and opposing claims. The goal is not to undercut your argument but rather to answer your readers' potential objections to it. Be sure, too, to consider how much your audience may already know about your topic in order to avoid boring or confusing your readers.

EXAMPLES

Claim lacking reasons: Fast-food menu items would be a good thing.	**Claim developed by reasons:** Among the benefits of offering fast-food menu choices are a potential increase in student morale and increased cafeteria revenue for the school.
Omission of limitations: The people opposed to this idea do not eat lunch at our school.	**Fair discussion of limitations:** We should not dismiss nutritional concerns. Plans for offering fast-food options should investigate healthful possibilities.
Inattention to audience's knowledge: Information about minimum daily nutritional requirements, chemical additives, and cholesterol-increasing foods is a critical aspect of the plan.	**Awareness of audience's knowledge:** Readers unfamiliar with fast-food menu options may be surprised to learn that many fast-food restaurants now offer nutritionally balanced, low-fat items.

Link Ideas

Even the strongest reasons and evidence will fail to sway readers if it is unclear how the reasons relate to the central claim of an argument. Make the connections clear for your readers, using not only transitional words and phrases, but also clauses and even entire sentences as bridges between ideas you have already discussed and ideas you are introducing.

EXAMPLES

Transitional word linking claim and reason: Students who buy their lunch from the cafeteria bring hundreds of dollars into the school each day. Consequently, well-chosen offerings of fast-food items would be an important source of revenue for the school.

Transitional phrase linking reason and evidence: Providing fast-food menu items would improve student morale. In fact, the school district's chief dietitian comments that "more healthful options would address students' complaints about boring lunches."

Transitional clause linking claim and counterclaim: The benefits of offering these menu options are clear. Those opposed to the plan, though, would say otherwise: They feel that there is too much potential for school-sponsored poor nutrition.

Use Appropriate Style and Tone

An effective argument is most often written in a direct and formal style. The style and tone you choose in an argument should not be an afterthought; the way you express your argument can either drive home your ideas or detract from them. Even as you argue in favor of your viewpoint, take care to remain objective in tone. Avoid using loaded language when discussing opposing claims.

EXAMPLES

Informal style: Offering fast-food menu options will be way cool.	**Formal style:** Because expanding the lunch menu provides a range of benefits, it is logical for the school district to approve the plan.
Biased tone: It doesn't make any sense to be against this plan.	**Objective tone:** Arguments opposing this plan have been refuted by evidence from many sources.
Inattention to conventions: We need to make this dream a reality!	**Attention to conventions:** This proposal, which will greatly benefit our school, deserves school district attention.

Conclude Your Argument

Your conclusion may range from a sentence to a full paragraph, but it must wrap up your argument in a satisfying way; a conclusion that sounds tacked-on helps your argument no more than providing no conclusion at all. A strong conclusion is a logical extension of the argument you have presented. It carries forth your ideas through an inference, question, quotation, or challenge.

EXAMPLES

Inference: Building lifelong healthful eating habits begins at school.

Question: Who doesn't want to have the choice of carefully selected fast-food menu items?

Quotation: As the sophomore class president points out, "The school district and cafeteria manager can promote student engagement and improve morale by providing new lunch menu choices."

Challenge: Menu options of this type make the difference between an average school cafeteria and a truly responsive one.

Writing Informative Essays

Many of the Performance Tasks in this book ask you to write informational or explanatory texts in which you present a topic and examine it thoughtfully, through a well-organized analysis of relevant content. Any informative or explanatory text that you create should include the following parts and features.

Introduce Your Topic

Develop a strong **thesis statement.** That is, clearly state your topic and the organizational framework through which you will connect or distinguish elements of your topic. For example, you might state that your text will compare ideas, examine causes and effects, or explore a problem and its solutions.

EXAMPLE

Topic: *Urban Sprawl*
Sample Thesis Statements
Compare-contrast: The statistics on suburban growth currently and two decades ago reveal the extent of urban sprawl in our community.
Cause-effect: A problem now for more than 50 years, urban sprawl affects the health of both cities and rural areas.
Problem-solution: Our city faces a growing problem with urban sprawl, but through strategic city planning we can manage the issue.

Clarifying the organizational framework up front will help you organize the body of your text, suggest headings you can use to guide your readers, and help you identify graphics that you may need to clarify information. For example, if you analyze causes and effects of urban sprawl, you might create a chart like the one shown to guide your writing. Each row will constitute a separate paragraph.

Overall cause: urban sprawl	Overall effects: • damages city's economic and human resources • endangers farmland
Cause: suburbs grow	**Effects:** • population loss in city • loss of jobs in city • brain drain from city
Cause: brain drain from city	**Effect:** decline in school quality in city
Cause: redirection of resources to suburbs	**Effect:** decline in urban centers

Develop Your Topic

In the body of your essay, flesh out the organizational framework you established in your introduction with strong supporting paragraphs. Include only support directly relevant to your topic. Don't rely only on a single source, and make sure the sources you do use are reputable and current. The following table illustrates types of support you might use to develop aspects of your topic. It also shows how transitions link text sections, create cohesion, and clarify the relationships among ideas.

Types of Support	Uses of Transitions
Statistics: One effect of urban sprawl is the loss of farmland; for example, 332,800 acres of farmland in Texas were lost to suburban development between 1992 and 1997.	*One effect* signals the shift from the introduction to the body text in a cause-and-effect essay. *For example* introduces the statistical support for the effect being cited.
Concrete details: Cities also experience a "brain drain"; consequently, the quality of city schools declines.	*Consequently* transitions the reader from a cause to its effect in a cause-and-effect essay.
Facts and examples: Turn to legislation in the city of Portland, Oregon, if you want to see "smart growth" that preserves farmland and expands downtown housing options.	The entire transitional sentence introduces the part of a cause-and-effect essay that summarizes the positive effects of urban sprawl.

You can't always include all of the information you'd like to in a short essay, but you can plan to point readers directly to useful **multimedia links** either in the body or at the end of your essay.

Use Appropriate Style and Tone

Use formal English to establish your credibility as a source of information. To project authority, use the language of the domain, or field, that you are writing about. However, be sure to define unfamiliar terms to avoid using jargon your audience may not know. Provide extended definitions when your audience is likely to have limited knowledge of the topic.

Using quotations from reputable sources can also give your text authority; be sure to credit the source of quoted material. In general, keep the tone objective, avoiding slang or biased expressions.

Informal, jargon-filled, biased language: Portland, Oregon, a very cool city out there on the edge of the continent, has put a cap on exploding suburbs.

Extended definition in formal style and objective tone: One good example of an urban area that has applied the ideas of smart growth is Portland, Oregon; the city has curbed urban sprawl through legislation, community activism, and efficient city growth.

Conclude Your Essay

Wrap up your essay with a concluding statement or section that sums up or extends the information in your essay.

EXAMPLES

Articulate implications: Urban sprawl threatens cities and rural areas, robbing urban communities of population and resources and gobbling up farmland for development.

Emphasize significance: With the country's population increasing, the loss of prime farmland to strip malls and apartment complexes is a serious problem that will affect our nation's economy for decades to come.

Writing Narratives

When you are writing a fictional tale, an autobiographical incident, or a firsthand biography, you write in the narrative mode. That means telling a story with a beginning, a climax, and a conclusion. Though there are important differences between fictional and nonfiction narratives, you will use similar processes to develop them.

Identify a Problem, Situation, or Observation

For a nonfiction narrative, dig into your memory bank for a problem you dealt with or an observation you've made about your life. For fiction, try to invent a problem or situation that can unfold in interesting ways.

EXAMPLES

Problem (nonfiction)	Last year I wanted to overcome my fear of public speaking.
Situation (fiction)	A high-school tennis player is anxious about asking a classmate for a date.

Establish a Point of View

Decide who will tell your story. If you are writing a reflective essay about an important experience or person in your own life, you will be the narrator of the events you relate. If you are writing a work of fiction, you can choose to create a first-person narrator or tell the story from the third-person point of view. In that case, the narrator can focus on one character or reveal the thoughts and feelings of all the characters. The examples below show the differences between a first- and third-person narrator.

First-person narrator (nonfiction example)	Standing up to give a speech to my classmates shouldn't have made my hands shake and my stomach turn somersaults, but it did last year.
Third-person narrator (fiction example)	After English class, Carlos asked Peter if he had asked Maggie out on a date yet. It was all Peter could do to respond calmly. He really wanted to blurt out—to scream out—that everyone should just let him ask her out when he was good and ready.

Gather Details

To make real or imaginary experiences come alive on the page, you will need to use narrative techniques like description and dialogue. The questions in the left column in the chart below can help you search your memory or imagination for the details that will form the basis of your narrative. You don't have to respond in full sentences, but try to capture the sights, sounds, and feelings that bring your narrative to life.

Who, What, When, Where?	Narrative Techniques
People: Who are the people or characters involved in the experience? What did they look like? What did they do? What did they say?	**Description:** Peter's friend Carlos, also on the tennis team and friend to Peter since Carlos transferred to the high school least year. **Dialogue:** Carlos said, "You should just ask her out, Peter. If you don't, someone else probably will." Peter replied sharply, "I'm just waiting for the right moment, okay?"
Experience: What led up to or caused the event? What is the main event in the experience? What happened as a result of the event?	**Description:** Peter liked Maggie but was too shy to ask her out on a date. He had a jumpy feeling in his stomach, tight muscles, and insomnia. He was grumpy and short-tempered, so his mother suggested he try a yoga class at school. He resisted trying new things like yoga. After falling asleep in class and being stopped by the hall monitor, Peter ended up in the gym, where the yoga class was just beginning. And there was Maggie, right next to the spot where he placed his yoga mat. She smiled at him.

continued

Who, What, When, Where?	Narrative Techniques
Places: When and where did the events take place? What were the sights, sounds, and smells of this place?	**Description:** Spring of ninth grade: It was the first year of high school and everyone felt both confident and insecure at the same time. Spring meant tennis tournaments on brisk, sunny days and first thoughts about the dances that would end the year.

Sequence Events

Before you begin writing, list the key events of the experience or story in **chronological,** or time, order. Place a star next to the point of highest tension—for example, the point at which a key decision determines the outcome of events. In fiction, this point is called the **climax,** but a gripping nonfiction narrative will also have a climactic event.

To build **suspense**—the uncertainty a reader feels about what will happen next—you'll want to think about the pacing or rhythm of your narrative. Consider disrupting the chronological order of events by beginning at the end, then going back in time to earlier events. Or, interrupt the forward progression or flow of events with a **flashback,** which takes the reader to an earlier point in the narrative.

Another way to build suspense is with multiple plot lines. For example, in the fictional narrative, Peter's anxiety about asking Maggie for a date involves a second plot line in which he has to overcome his hesitancy about trying something new and taking yoga. Both plot lines intersect when Peter goes to yoga class, and as a result ends up next to Maggie, who smiles at him.

Use Vivid Language

As you revise, make an effort to use vivid language. Use precise words and phrases to describe feelings and actions. Use telling details to show, rather than directly state, what a character is like. Use **sensory language** that lets readers see, feel, hear, smell, and taste what you or your characters experienced.

First Draft	Revision
Peter could barely stay awake in class.	Peter floated in a half-wakeful state through his next four classes. [telling details]
Peter went down to the kitchen.	The stairs groaned tiredly under Peter's steps. He also groaned tiredly as he plopped down at the kitchen table. [precise words and phrases]
He had no appetite at lunch.	At lunch, Peter found his stomach was too knotted to let him eat. [sensory details]

Conclude Your Story

At the conclusion of the narrative, you or your narrator will reflect on the meaning of the events. The conclusion should follow logically from the climactic moment of the narrative. The narrator of a personal narrative usually reflects on the significance of the experience—the lessons learned or the legacy left. A fictional narrative will end with the resolution of the conflict described over the course of the story.

EXAMPLE

Peter breathed in. He dared to look around. Maggie was right next to him. He choked a little and coughed. She glanced over and smiled warmly. Peter smiled back and took his first deep breath in days. Maybe yoga wasn't such a bad idea after all.

Conducting Research

W 2a–f, W 7, W 8, L 3a

Some Performance Tasks in this book will require you to complete research projects related to the texts you've read in the collections. Whether the topic is stated in a Performance Task or is one you generate, the following information will guide you through your research project.

Focus Your Research and Formulate a Question

Some topics for a research project can be effectively covered in three pages; others require an entire book for a thorough treatment. Begin by developing a topic that is neither too narrow nor too broad for the time frame of the assignment. Also, check your school and local libraries and databases to help you determine how to choose your topic. If there's too little information, you'll need to broaden your focus; if there's too much, you'll need to limit it.

With a topic in hand, formulate a research question; it will keep you on track as you conduct your research. A good research question cannot be answered in a single word and should be open-ended. It should require investigation. You can also develop related research questions to explore your topic in more depth.

EXAMPLES

Possible topics about Julius Caesar, the Roman emperor	• Famous assassinations in history—too broad • Popularity of soothsayers in Roman times—too narrow • Historical figures—fact or fiction?
Possible research question	What was the real Julius Caesar like?
Related questions	• How much of *Julius Caesar*, Shakespeare's play, is based on historical fact? • How did historians of Caesar's time describe him?

Locate and Evaluate Sources

To find answers to your research question, you'll need to investigate primary and secondary sources, whether in print or digital formats. **Primary sources** contain original, firsthand information, such as diaries, autobiographies, interviews, speeches, and eyewitness accounts. **Secondary sources** provide other people's versions of primary sources in encyclopedias, newspaper and magazine articles, biographies, and documentaries.

Your search for sources begins at the library and on the World Wide Web. Use **advanced search features** to help you find things quickly. For example, add a minus sign (-) before a word that should not appear in your results or use an asterisk (*) in place of unknown words. List the name of and location of each possible source, adding comments about its potential usefulness. Assessing, or evaluating, your sources is an important step in the research process. Your goal is to use sources that are **credible,** or reliable and trustworthy.

Criteria for Assessing Sources	
Relevance: It covers the target aspect of my topic.	• How will the source be useful in answering my specific research question?
Accuracy: It includes information that can be verified by more than one authoritative source.	• Is the information up-to-date? Are the facts accurate? How can I verify them? • What qualifies the author to write about this topic? Is he or she an authority?
Objectivity: It presents multiple viewpoints on the topic.	• What, if any, biases can I detect? Does the writer favor one view of the topic?

Incorporate and Cite Source Material

When you draft your research project, you'll need to include material from your sources. This material can be direct quotations, summaries, or paraphrases of the original source material. Two well-known style manuals provide information on how to cite a range of print and digital sources: the *MLA Handbook for Writers of Research Papers* (published by the Modern Language Association) and Kate L. Turabian's *A Manual for Writers of Research Papers, Theses, and Dissertations* (published by The University of Chicago Press). Both style manuals provide a wealth of information about conducting, formatting, drafting, and presenting your research, including guidelines for citing sources within the text (called parenthetical citations) and preparing the list of Works Cited, as well as correct use of the mechanics of writing. Your teacher will indicate which style manual you should use. The following examples use the format in the *MLA Handbook*.

EXAMPLES

Direct quotation [The writer is citing the description given by Roman historian Suetonius.]	In his biographical text *The Lives of the Caesars,* the Roman historian Suetonius describes Caesar as "tall of stature, with a fair complexion, shapely limbs, a somewhat full face, and keen black eyes" (Suetonius 45).
Summary [The writer is summarizing the conclusion in an article about Roman government.]	Rome's republican government was made up of consuls, praetors, a senate, and people's assemblies. The position of dictator was temporary and only used during emergencies (36).
Paraphrase [The writer is paraphrasing, or stating in his own words, material from an article about the nature of Rome's government during Caesar's time.]	During Caesar's time, Rome was a republic. Two consuls with equal authority were the leaders. Senators suggested laws, and general assemblies voted on whether to approve the suggestions. The position of dictator was used only when there were serious outbreaks of lawlessness (Cross, *Bestriding* 21).

Any material from sources must be completely documented, or you will commit **plagiarism,** the unauthorized use of someone else's words or ideas. Plagiarism is not honest. As you take notes for your research project, be sure to keep complete information about your sources so that you can cite them correctly in the body of your paper. This applies to all sources, whether print or digital. Having complete information will also enable you to prepare the list of Works Cited. The list of Works Cited, which concludes your research project, provides author, title, and publication information for both print and digital sources. The following section shows the *MLA Handbook's* Works Cited citation formats for a variety of sources.

MLA Citation Guidelines

Today, you can find free Web sites that generate ready-made citations for research papers, using the information you provide. Although using such sites can save you some time, always check your citations carefully before you turn in your final paper. If you are following MLA style, use these guidelines to evaluate and finalize your work.

Books

One author

Schanzer, Ernest. *The Problem Plays of Shakespeare.* New York: Schocken, 1965.

Two authors or editors

McIver, Bruce, and Ruth Stevenson, eds. *Teaching Shakespeare: Critics in the Classroom.* Newark: U of Delaware Press, 1994. Print.

Three authors

Bennett, Josephine W., Oscar Cargill, and Vernon Hall, Jr., eds. *Studies in the English Renaissance Drama.* New York: New York UP, 1959. Print.

Four or more authors

The abbreviation et al. means "and others." Use et al. instead of listing all the authors.

Wells, Stanley, et al. *The Complete Works of William Shakespeare.* New York: Oxford UP, 1986. Print.

No author given

Elizabethan Literature. New York: Capital, 1957. Print.

An author and a translator

Suetonius. *Lives of the Caesars.* Trans. Catherine Edwards. New York: Oxford UP, 2000. Print.

An author, a translator, and an editor

Moretti, Salvatore. *Essays on Julius Caesar.* Trans. Jonathan Walsh. Ed. Louis Kind. New York: Devonshire, 1962. Print.

Parts of Books

An introduction, a preface, a foreword, or an afterword written by someone other than the author(s) of a work

Heminge, John, and Henry Condell. Preface. *Dramatic Works of Shakespeare.* Edinburgh: William Peterson, 1883. Print.

A poem, a short story, an essay, or a chapter in a collection of works by one author

Roe, John. " 'Character' in Plutarch and Shakespeare: Brutus, Julius Caesar, and Mark Antony." *Shakespeare and the Classics.* Ed. Charles Martindale and A. B. Taylor. New York: Cambridge, 2004. Print.

A novel or a play in an anthology

Shakespeare, William. *The Tragedy of Julius Caesar.* Ed. John Jowett. *William
   Shakespeare: The Complete Works.* Ed. Stanley Wells and Gary Taylor. Compact
   ed. Oxford: Clarendon, 1988. 599–626. Print.

Magazines, Newspapers, and Encyclopedias

An article in a newspaper

Weber, Bruce. "Power Play: "Friends, Generals and Captains of Industry, Lend Me
   Your Ears."" *New York Times* 31 Jan. 2005: B1+. Print.

An article in a magazine

Tynan, William. "Cleopatra." *Time* 24 May 1999: 37–38. Print.

An article in an encyclopedia

"Julius Caesar." *Encyclopaedia Britannica.* 2004 ed. Print.

Miscellaneous Print and Nonprint Sources

An interview

Covington, Nigel. Personal Interview. 1 Feb. 2011.

A video recording

Julius Caesar. Lions Gate, 2000. DVD.

Electronic Publications

A CD-ROM

"Antony, Mark." *Britannica Student Encyclopedia.* 2004 ed. Chicago: Encyclopaedia
   Britannica, 2004. CD-ROM.

A document from an Internet site

Entries for online sources should contain as much of the information shown as available.

Author or compiler   Title or description of document

Vernon, Jennifer. | "Ides of March Marked Murder of Julius Caesar."

Title of Internet site   Site sponsor   Date of Internet site

National Geographic News. | Natl. Geographic Soc. | 12 Mar. 2004.

Medium of publication   Date of access

Web. | 18 May 2011.

Participating in a Collaborative Discussion

Often, class activities, including the Performance Tasks in this book, will require you to work collaboratively with classmates. Whether your group will analyze a work of literature or try to solve a community problem, use the following guidelines to ensure a productive discussion.

Prepare for the Discussion

A productive discussion is one in which all the participants bring useful information and ideas to share. If your group will discuss a short story the class read, first reread and annotate a copy of the story. Your annotations will help you quickly locate evidence to support your points. Participants in a discussion about an important issue should first research the issue and bring notes or information sources that will help guide the group. If you disagree with a point made by another group member, your case will be stronger if you back it up with specific evidence from your sources.

EXAMPLES

Disagreeing without evidence: I don't think Shakespeare is relevant today because nobody talks like that.

Providing evidence for disagreement: I disagree about Shakespeare's relevance because his language is so hard for modern kids to understand. For example, in *Macbeth*, Banquo tells the witches, "My noble partner / You greet with present grace and great prediction / Of noble having and of royal hope, / That he seems rapt withal." Who can figure that out? Maybe if it said, "My friend here is so stunned about what you've said— that he's been promoted and will one day be king—that he seems like he's in a trance," kids today would find it relevant. An idea that's this simple shouldn't be so complicated to unravel.

Set Ground Rules

The rules your group needs will depend on what your group is expected to accomplish. A discussion of themes in a poem will be unlikely to produce a single consensus; however, a discussion aimed at developing a solution to a problem should result in one strong proposal that all group members support. Answer the following questions to set ground rules that fit your group's purpose:

- What will this group produce? A range of ideas, a single decision, a plan of action, or something else?
- How much time is available? How much of that time should be allotted to each part of our discussion (presenting ideas, summarizing or voting on final ideas, creating a product such as a written analysis or speech)?
- What roles need to be assigned within the group? Do we need a leader, a note-taker, a timekeeper, or other specific roles?
- What is the best way to synthesize our group's ideas? Should we take a vote, list group members as "for" or "against" in a chart, or use some other method to reach consensus or sum up the results of the discussion?

Move the Discussion Forward

Everyone in the group should be actively involved in synthesizing ideas. To make sure this happens, ask questions that draw out ideas, especially from less-talkative members of the group. If an idea or statement is confusing, try to paraphrase it, or ask the speaker to explain more about it. If you disagree with a statement, say so politely and explain in detail why you disagree.

SAMPLE DISCUSSION

JACK: How about you, Ella? Do you think Shakespeare is relevant to today's teenagers? The rest of us say he is.	*Question draws out quiet member*
ELLA: Well, I don't know. I see how people refer to Shakespeare all the time in movies and commercials and things, but he talks so much about rich, important people with servants and power. That doesn't have anything to do with me or my friends.	*Response relates discussion to larger ideas*
DANTE: But don't people in power have some of the same problems regular people do? I mean, everybody wants love and respect, right?	*Question challenges Ella's conclusion*
ELLA: Sure, but then why not have Macbeth be a regular guy scheming to get the woman he loves or his boss's approval or something? Why does everybody have to be royalty?	*Response elaborates on ideas*
VIVIAN: So you mean that people's struggles are different depending on their class? I can see that, but Shakespeare's plays were really popular with the common people in his time, so it seems like people can identify with his characters despite their differences.	*Paraphrases idea and challenges it further based on evidence*

Respond to Ideas

In a diverse group, everyone may have a different perspective on the topic of discussion, and that's a good thing. Consider what everyone has to say, and don't resist changing your view if other group members provide convincing evidence for theirs. If, instead, you feel more strongly than ever about your view, don't hesitate to say so and provide reasons related to what those with opposing views have said. Before wrapping up the discussion, try to sum up the points on which your group agrees and disagrees.

SAMPLE DISCUSSION

VIVIAN: OK, we just have a few more minutes. What does everybody think? Do we want to take a vote?	*Vivian and Jack try to summarize points of agreement.*
JACK: Sure. I think the three positions are YES, NO, and YES, BUT. . . . Does that sound right?	
DANTE: Yeah, let's make a chart of these. I still say YES, Shakespeare is relevant today. No BUT about it, because realistic characters are at the core.	*Dante maintains his position.*
ELLA: And I say YES, BUT. You've convinced me that he talks about some universal experiences and emotions, but I still think that the status of the characters and the difficulty of the language present a big barrier for a lot of readers today.	*Ella and Jack qualify their views based on what they have heard.*
JACK: That makes sense. I'm changing my position from solid YES to YES, BUT. I don't think the status is such a big deal because people can always imagine themselves being rich and powerful, but his language is really challenging.	
VIVIAN: I'm with Dante. I think the characters outweigh any barriers. Modern interpretations and movies of Shakespeare's plays will always be popular.	*Vivian supports her position by making a new connection.*

Debating an Issue

The selection and collection Performance Tasks in this book will direct you to engage in debates about issues relating to the selections you are reading. Use the guidelines that follow to have a productive and balanced argument about both sides of an issue.

The Structure of a Formal Debate

A debate is a balanced argument discussing opposing sides of an issue. In a debate, two teams compete to win the support of the audience. In a **formal debate,** two teams, each with three members, present their arguments on a given proposition or policy statement. One team argues for the proposition or statement and the other team argues against it. Each debater must consider the proposition closely and must research both sides of it. To argue convincingly either for or against a proposition, a debater must be familiar with both sides of the issue.

Plan the Debate

The purpose of a debate is to allow participants and audience members to consider both sides of an issue. Use these planning suggestions to hold a balanced and productive debate:

- **Identify Debate Teams** Form groups of six members based on the issues that the Performance Tasks include. Three members of the team will argue for the **affirmative** side of the issue—that is, they support the issue. The other three members will argue for the **negative** side of the issue—that is, they do not support the issue.
- **Appoint a Moderator** The moderator will present the topic and goals of the debate, keep track of the time, and introduce and thank the participants.
- **Research and Prepare Notes** Search the texts you've read as well as print and online sources for valid reasons and evidence to support your team's claim. As with a written argument, be sure to anticipate possible

opposing claims and compile evidence to counter those claims. You will use notes from your research during the debate.
- **Assign Debate Roles** One team member will introduce the team's claim and supporting evidence. Another team member will respond to questions and opposing claims in an exchange with a member of the opposing team. The last member will present a strong closing argument.

Hold the Debate

A formal debate is not a shouting match—rather, a well-run debate is an excellent forum for participants to express their viewpoints, build on others' ideas, and have a thoughtful, well-reasoned exchange of ideas. The moderator will begin by stating the topic or issue and introducing the participants. Participants should follow the moderator's instructions concerning whose turn it is to speak and how much time each speaker has.

FORMAL DEBATE FORMAT

SPEAKER	ROLE	TIME
Affirmative Speaker 1	Present the claim and supporting evidence for the affirmative ("pro") side of the argument.	5 minutes
Negative Speaker 1	Ask probing questions that will prompt the other team to address flaws in the argument.	3 minutes

continued

SPEAKER	ROLE	TIME
Affirmative Speaker 2	Respond to the questions posed by the opposing team and counter any concerns.	3 minutes
Negative Speaker 2	Present the claim and supporting evidence for the negative ("con") side of the argument.	5 minutes
Affirmative Speaker 3	Summarize the claim and evidence for the affirmative side and explain why your reasoning is more valid.	3 minutes
Negative Speaker 3	Summarize the claim and evidence for the negative side and explain why your reasoning is more valid.	3 minutes

Evaluate the Debate

Use the following guidelines to evaluate a team in a debate:

- Did the team prove that a significant problem does or does not exist? How thorough was the team's analysis of the problem?
- How did the team convince you that the proposition is or is not the best solution to the problem?
- How effectively did the team present reasons and evidence, including evidence from texts, to support the proposition?
- How effectively did the team **rebut,** or respond to, arguments made by the opposing team?
- Did the speakers maintain eye contact and speak at an appropriate rate and volume?
- Did the speakers observe proper debate etiquette—that is, did they follow the moderator's instructions, stay within their allotted time limits, and treat their opponents respectfully?

Reading Arguments

An argument expresses a position on an issue or problem and supports it with reasons and evidence. Being able to analyze and evaluate arguments will help you distinguish between claims you should accept and those you should not.

Analyzing an Argument

A sound argument should appeal to reason. However, arguments are often used in texts that contain other types of persuasive devices. An argument includes the following elements:

- A **claim** is the writer's position on an issue or central idea.
- **Support** is any material that serves to prove a claim. In an argument, support usually consists of reasons and evidence.
- **Reasons** are declarations made to justify an action, a decision, or a belief—for example, "The reason I think we'll be late is that we can't get to the appointment in five minutes."
- **Evidence** is the specific references, quotations, facts, examples, and opinions that support a claim. Evidence may also consist of statistics, reports of personal experience, or the views of experts.
- A **counterargument** or counterclaim is an argument against a position. A good argument anticipates the opposition's objections and provides counterarguments to disprove or answer them.

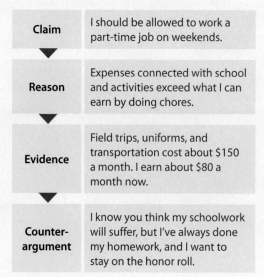

Claim	I should be allowed to work a part-time job on weekends.
Reason	Expenses connected with school and activities exceed what I can earn by doing chores.
Evidence	Field trips, uniforms, and transportation cost about $150 a month. I earn about $80 a month now.
Counter-argument	I know you think my schoolwork will suffer, but I've always done my homework, and I want to stay on the honor roll.

Practice and Apply

Read the following editorial, and identify the claim, reason, evidence, and counterargument.

Extracurricular Sports Should Satisfy State Physical Education Requirement

Track, football, soccer, baseball, basketball, and other sports attract dedicated student athletes who often practice every day after school and then participate in weekend games. Should these students be forced to give up an elective class period to take a required physical education class? In order to meet the state's physical education (P.E.) course requirements, that is exactly what Whitman High School asks them to do. I believe that this policy doesn't make any sense. Instead, the Montgomery County public schools should exempt student athletes from taking P.E. classes.

First of all, participating in an extracurricular sport meets the objectives of the state's course requirements. Those objectives are to promote fitness and improve athletic skill, according to the Whitman course catalog. Involvement in either a varsity or a club sport for one season already makes a student fit and athletically skilled.

A second reason to change the policy is that the physical education requirement forces students to give up an elective class period. High school students can generally choose only eight elective courses from dozens of class offerings. By eliminating the P.E. requirement for student athletes, the county would give students more freedom in selecting their courses.

Finally, exposing students to different sports is one goal of the P.E. requirement, but this objective alone is not important enough to

continued

require students to take P.E. class. Students seldom take P.E. class as seriously as they would an extracurricular sport, so students do not always appreciate sports they sample in P.E. class.

Varsity and club sports require a great deal of time and effort from athletes. The county should recognize that team sports encourage physical activity more effectively than P.E. class. It is more important for student athletes to become well-rounded academically by taking electives than to take P.E. class.

Recognizing Persuasive Techniques

Arguments typically rely on more than just the logical appeal of an argument to be convincing. They also depend on **persuasive techniques**—devices that can sway you to adopt a position or take an action.

This chart explains several ways a writer may attempt to sway you to adopt his or her position. Learn to recognize these techniques, and you are less likely to be influenced by them.

Persuasive Technique	Example
Appeals by Association	
Bandwagon appeal Suggests that a person should believe or do something because "everyone else" does	Be where it's at—shop the Magnificent Mall.
Testimonial Relies on endorsements from well-known people or satisfied customers	Golf champion Links Lorimer uses Gofar clubs. Shouldn't you?
Snob appeal Taps into people's desire to be special or part of an elite group	Dine at the elite Plaza Inn, where you will be treated like royalty.
Transfer Links a product, candidate, or cause to a positive emotion or idea	One spray of Woodsy air freshener and you'll find inner peace.
Appeal to loyalty Relies on people's affiliation with a particular group	Support the Tatum Tigers by wearing the new Win-Team windbreaker.

Emotional Appeals	
Appeals to pity, fear, or vanity Use strong feelings, rather than facts, to persuade	Don't these abandoned animals deserve a chance? Adopt a pet today.
Word Choice	
Glittering generality Makes a generalization that includes a word or phrase with positive connotations, such as *freedom* or *honor*, to promote a product or idea.	Hop on a Swiftee moped and experience pure freedom.

Practice and Apply

Identify the persuasive techniques used in this model.

The True Holiday Spirit

The holiday season is almost upon us, and caring people everywhere are opening their hearts and wallets to those who are less fortunate. Charity and community service show democracy in action, and Mayor Adam Miner's actions are setting a good example for village residents. For the last three years, he has volunteered once a week at the local Meals for the Many program. Busing tables, serving soup, and helping wash dishes has made him aware of how fortunate he is and how important it is to share that good fortune. In his Thanksgiving address last week, he urged citizens, "Make this holiday—and all the days that follow—a time of true giving. Join your friends and neighbors in serving others today."

Analyzing Logic and Reasoning

When you evaluate an argument, you need to look closely at the writer's logic and reasoning. To do this, it is helpful to identify the type of reasoning the writer is using.

The Inductive Mode of Reasoning

When a writer leads from specific evidence to a general principle or generalization, that writer is using **inductive reasoning**. Here is an example of inductive reasoning:

Specific Facts

Fact 1: Fewer than 100 Arizona agave century plants remain in existence.

Fact 2: Over the last three generations, there has been a 50 percent reduction in the number of African elephants.

Fact 3: Only 50 Hawaiian crows are left in the world.

Generalization

Extinction is a problem facing many classes of living things.

Strategies for Determining the Soundness of Inductive Arguments

Ask yourself the following questions to evaluate an inductive argument:

- **Is the evidence valid and sufficient support for the conclusion?** Inaccurate facts lead to inaccurate conclusions.
- **Does the conclusion follow logically from the evidence?** From the facts listed in the previous example, the conclusion that extinction is a problem facing *all* living things would be too broad a generalization.
- **Is the evidence drawn from a large enough sample?** Even though there are only three facts listed above, the sample is large enough to support the claim. If you wanted to support the conclusion that extinction is a problem facing all classes of living things, the sample would not be large enough.

The Deductive Mode of Reasoning

When a writer arrives at a conclusion by applying a general principle to a specific situation, the writer is using **deductive reasoning**. Here's an example:

Regular exercise improves academic performance.	General principle or premise
▼	
Stefan has started a running program.	Specific situation
▼	
Stefan's grades may improve.	Specific conclusion

Strategies for Determining the Soundness of Deductive Arguments

Ask yourself the following questions to evaluate a deductive argument:

- **Is the general principle stated, or is it implied?** Note that writers often use deductive reasoning in an argument without stating the general principle. They just assume that readers will recognize and agree with the principle. You may want to identify the general principle for yourself.
- **Is the general principle sound?** Don't just assume the general principle is sound. Ask yourself whether it is really true.
- **Is the conclusion valid?** To be valid, a conclusion in a deductive argument must follow logically from the general principle and the specific situation.

This chart shows two conclusions drawn from the same general principle:

All government offices were closed last Monday.	
Accurate Deduction	**Inaccurate Deduction**
West Post Office is a government office; therefore, West Post Office was closed last Monday.	Soon-Lin's Spa was closed last Monday; therefore, Soon-Lin's Spa is a government office.

Soon-Lin might have closed her spa because there would be fewer customers in town when government offices were closed—or for another reason entirely.

Identify the mode of reasoning used in the following paragraph.

A large part of the U.S. population is overweight or obese. There are various weight-loss plans to follow. Fads come and go, but a definite way to lose weight is through a combination of diet and exercise. Because she wants to feel better and have more energy to play with her nephews, Consuelo recently decided to lose some weight. She has cut back on sugary and fatty foods and goes to the gym twice a week. Soon she'll be able to keep up with her nephews no matter how fast they run.

Identifying Faulty Reasoning

Sometimes an argument at first appears to make sense but isn't valid because it is based on a fallacy. A **fallacy** is an error in logic. Learn to recognize these common rhetorical and logical fallacies:

Type of Fallacy	Definition	Example
Circular reasoning	Supporting a statement by simply repeating it in different words	Wearing a bicycle helmet should be required because **cyclists should use protective headgear.**
Either/or fallacy	A statement that suggests that there are only two choices available in a situation that really offers more than two options	**Either** you eat a balanced diet, **or** you'll die before you're 50.
Oversimplification	An explanation of a complex situation or problem as if it were much simpler than it is	Shared interests lead to a **successful relationship.**
Overgeneralization	A generalization that is too broad. You can often recognize overgeneralizations by the use of words such as *all, everyone, every time, anything, no one,* and *none.*	**Everyone** wants to go to college.
Stereotyping	A dangerous type of overgeneralization. Stereotypes are broad statements about people on the basis of their gender, ethnicity, race, or political, social, professional, or religious group.	**Teenagers** just don't care about future generations.
Personal attack or name-calling	An attempt to discredit an idea by attacking the person or group associated with it. Candidates often engage in name-calling during political campaigns.	**Mr. Edmonds drives a beat-up car and never mows his lawn,** so you shouldn't take music lessons from him.
Evading the issue	Refuting an objection with arguments and evidence that do not address its central point	I know I didn't clean up my room, **but that gave me more time to study and improve my grades.**

Type of Fallacy	Definition	Example
Non sequitur	A statement that uses irrelevant "proof" to support a claim. A non sequitur is sometimes used to win an argument by diverting the reader's attention to proof that can't be challenged.	I'll probably flunk the driving test. **I was late for school today.**
False causation	The mistake of assuming that because one event occurred after another event in time, the first event caused the second one to occur	Marc wore his new goggles in the swim meet and **as a result won with his best time ever.**
False analogy	A comparison that doesn't hold up because of a critical difference between the two subjects	I bet my little brother will be a great skier when he grows up **because he loves playing on the slide.**
Hasty generalization	A conclusion drawn from too little evidence or from evidence that is biased	**I got sick after eating at the pizzeria,** so Italian food must be bad for me.
Commonly held opinions	An argument that is deemed correct just because everyone else supposedly thinks it is correct	**Everyone knows** that cats make better pets than dogs.
Appeal to pity	An argument that uses pity to make you feel sorry for someone	I couldn't finish my homework **because my dog was sick.**

Practice and Apply

Look for examples of logical fallacies in the following argument. Identify each one and explain why you identified it as such.

Everyone agrees that running is the best form of exercise. All you need is a good pair of shoes and you're ready to hit the road. I've run a mile twice this week, so I should know. As a result, I've slept better and my tone on the clarinet has improved. When you run, your heart beats faster because your pulse rate increases. That means that your cells get more oxygen, which is the second most common gas in the earth's atmosphere. You also get to enjoy the beauty of the world around you as you build up your stamina. So if you don't want to be a hopeless couch potato, get going and run for your life!

Evaluating Arguments

Learning how to evaluate arguments and identify bias will help you become more selective when doing research and also help you improve your own reasoning and arguing skills. **Bias** is an inclination for or against a particular opinion or viewpoint. A writer may reveal a strongly positive or negative opinion on an issue by presenting only one way of looking at it or by heavily weighting the evidence on one side of the argument. Additionally, the presence of either of the following is often a sign of bias:

Loaded language consists of words with strongly positive or negative connotations that are intended to influence a reader's attitude.

EXAMPLE:
People who mistreat animals are subhuman and deserve to be locked up for life. (*Subhuman* and *locked up* have negative connotations.)

Propaganda is any form of communication that is so distorted that it conveys false or misleading information. Some politicians create and distribute propaganda. Many logical fallacies, such as name-calling, the either/or fallacy, and false causation, are often used in propaganda. The following example shows an oversimplification. The writer uses one fact to support a particular point of view but omits another fact that does not support that viewpoint.

EXAMPLE:

Since we moved to the city, our gas and electric bills have gone down. (The writer does not include the fact that the move occurred in the spring, when the demand for heat or air conditioning is low anyway.)

Strategies for Evaluating Evidence

It is important to have a set of standards by which you can evaluate persuasive texts. Use the questions below to help you critically assess facts and opinions that are presented as evidence.

- **Are the facts presented verifiable?** Facts can be proved by eyewitness accounts, authoritative sources such as encyclopedias and almanacs, experts, or research.
- **Are the opinions presented well-informed?** Any opinions offered should be supported by facts, be based on research or eyewitness accounts, or be the opinions of experts on the topic.
- **Is the evidence thorough?** Thorough evidence leaves no reasonable questions unanswered. If a choice is offered, background for making the choice should be provided. Any shifts in perspective in arguments should be explained and supported.
- **Is the evidence biased?** Be alert to evidence that contains loaded language and other signs of bias.
- **Is the evidence authoritative?** The people, groups, or organizations that provided the evidence should have credentials that verify their credibility.
- **Is it important that the evidence be current?** Where timeliness is crucial, as in the areas of medicine and technology, the evidence should reflect the latest developments in the areas.

Practice and Apply

Read the argument below. Identify facts, opinions, and elements of bias.

Are you tired of listening to people talking on their cell phones? I think those disgusting machines should be banned. Using the dumb things while driving or riding a bicycle distracts the user and creates a serious hazard. The phones also give off energy frequencies that can cause cancer. Cell phone users in a German study, for example, were three times more likely to develop eye cancer than people in the control group. Another study done in Sweden showed that people who used cell phones for ten years or more increased their risk of brain cancer by 77 percent. Although other researchers found no connection between cell phones and cancer, those studies stink. People should wise up and stop harming themselves and bothering everybody else.

Strategies for Determining a Strong Argument

To decide whether an argument is strong, make sure that all or most of the following statements are true:

- The argument presents a claim or thesis.
- The claim is connected to its support by a general principle that most readers would readily agree with.

  > Valid general principle: *It is the job of a school to provide a well-rounded physical education program.*

  > Invalid general principle: *It is the job of a school to produce healthy, physically fit people.*

- The reasons make sense.
- The reasons are presented in a logical and effective order.
- The claim and all reasons are adequately supported by sound evidence.
- The evidence is adequate, accurate, and appropriate.
- The logic is sound. There are no instances of faulty reasoning.

Use the preceding criteria to evaluate the strength of the following excerpt from a seminal speech by President Franklin Roosevelt, often called the "Four Freedoms" speech:

In the future days, which we seek to make secure, we look forward to a world founded upon four essential human freedoms.

The first is freedom of speech and expression—everywhere in the world.

The second is freedom of every person to worship God in his own way—everywhere in the world.

The third is freedom from want, which, translated into world terms, means economic understandings which will secure to every nation a healthy peacetime life for its inhabitants—everywhere in the world.

The fourth is freedom from fear, which, translated into world terms, means a world-wide reduction of armaments to such a point and in such a thorough fashion that no nation will be in a position to commit an act of physical aggression against any neighbor—anywhere in the world.

That is no vision of a distant millennium. It is a definite basis for a kind of world attainable in our own time and generation. That kind of world is the very antithesis of the so-called "new order" of tyranny which the dictators seek to create with the crash of a bomb.

To that new order we oppose the greater conception—the moral order. A good society is able to face schemes of world domination and foreign revolutions alike without fear.

Since the beginning of our American history we have been engaged in change, in a perpetual, peaceful revolution, a revolution which goes on steadily, quietly, adjusting itself to changing conditions without the concentration camp or the quicklime in the ditch. The world order which we seek is the cooperation of free countries, working together in a friendly, civilized society.

This nation has placed its destiny in the hands and heads and hearts of its millions of free men and women, and its faith in freedom under the guidance of God. Freedom means the supremacy of human rights everywhere. Our support goes to those who struggle to gain those rights and keep them. Our strength is our unity of purpose.

To that high concept there can be no end save victory.

Grammar

Writing that has many mistakes can confuse or even annoy a reader. For example, a business letter with a punctuation error might lead to miscommunication and delay a reply, or an essay that includes a sentence fragment might earn its writer a lower grade. Paying attention to grammar, punctuation, and capitalization rules can make your writing clearer and easier to read.

Quick Reference: Parts of Speech

Part of Speech	Function	Examples
Noun	names a person, a place, a thing, an idea, a quality, or an action	
Common	serves as a general name, or a name common to an entire group	boat, anchor, water, sky
Proper	names a specific person, place, or thing	Nile River, Acapulco, Swahili
Singular	refers to a single person, place, thing, or idea	map, berry, deer, mouse
Plural	refers to more than one person, place, thing, or idea	maps, berries, deer, mice
Concrete	names something that can be perceived by the senses	stone, crate, wall, knife
Abstract	names something that cannot be perceived by the senses	courage, caution, tyranny, importance
Compound	expresses a single idea through a combination of two or more words	toothbrush, sister-in-law, South Carolina
Collective	refers to a group of people or things	herd, family, team, staff
Possessive	shows who or what owns something	Kenya's, Les's, women's, waitresses'
Pronoun	takes the place of a noun or another pronoun	
Personal	refers to the person making a statement, the person(s) being addressed, or the person(s) or thing(s) the statement is about	I, me, my, mine, we, us, our, ours, you, your, yours, she, he, it, her, him, hers, his, its, they, them, their, theirs
Reflexive	follows a verb or preposition and refers to a preceding noun or pronoun	myself, yourself, herself, himself, itself, ourselves, yourselves, themselves
Intensive	emphasizes a noun or another pronoun	(same as reflexives)
Demonstrative	points to one or more specific persons or things	this, that, these, those

continued

Part of Speech	Function	Examples
Interrogative	signals a question	who, whom, whose, which, what
Indefinite	refers to one or more persons or things not specifically mentioned	both, all, most, many, anyone, everybody, several, none, some
Relative	introduces an adjective clause by relating it to a word in the clause	who, whom, whose, which, that
Reciprocal	expresses a mutual action or relationship	each other, one another
Verb	expresses an action, a condition, or a state of being	
Action	tells what the subject does or did, physically or mentally	run, reaches, listened, consider, decides, dreamed
Linking	connects the subject to something that identifies or describes it	am, is, are, was, were, sound, taste, appear, feel, become, remain, seem
Auxiliary	precedes the main verb in a verb phrase	be, have, do, can, could, will, would, may, might
Transitive	directs the action toward someone or something; always has an object	Mom **broke** the plate.
Intransitive	does not direct the action toward someone or something; does not have an object	The plate **broke**.
Adjective	modifies a noun or pronoun	**frightened** man, **two** epics, **enough** time
Adverb	modifies a verb, an adjective, or another adverb	walked **fast, really** funny, **far** away
Preposition	relates one word to another word	at, by, for, from, in, of, on, to, with
Conjunction	joins words or word groups	
Coordinating	joins words or word groups used the same way	and, but, or, for, so, yet, nor
Correlative	used as a pair to join words or word groups used the same way	both . . . and, either . . . or, neither . . . nor
Subordinating	introduces a clause that cannot stand by itself as a complete sentence	although, after, as, before, because, when, if, unless
Interjection	expresses emotion	whew, yikes, uh-oh

Quick Reference: The Sentence and Its Parts

The diagrams that follow will give you a brief review of the essentials of a sentence and some of its parts.

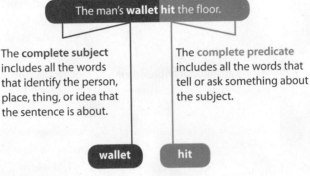

The man's **wallet hit** the floor.

The **complete subject** includes all the words that identify the person, place, thing, or idea that the sentence is about.

The **complete predicate** includes all the words that tell or ask something about the subject.

wallet

hit

The **simple subject** tells exactly whom or what the sentence is about. It may be one word or a group of words, but it does not include modifiers.

The **simple predicate**, or **verb**, tells what the subject does or is. It may be one word or several, but it does not include modifiers.

Every word in a sentence is part of a complete subject or a complete predicate.

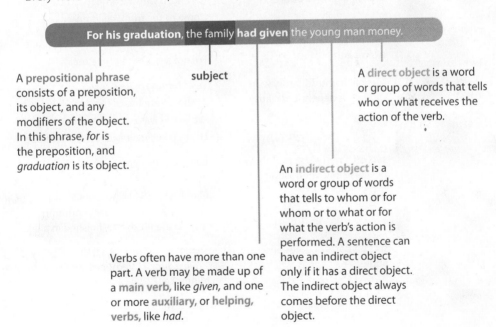

For his graduation, the family **had given** the young man money.

A prepositional phrase consists of a preposition, its object, and any modifiers of the object. In this phrase, *for* is the preposition, and *graduation* is its object.

subject

A **direct object** is a word or group of words that tells who or what receives the action of the verb.

An **indirect object** is a word or group of words that tells to whom or for whom or to what or for what the verb's action is performed. A sentence can have an indirect object only if it has a direct object. The indirect object always comes before the direct object.

Verbs often have more than one part. A verb may be made up of a **main verb**, like *given*, and one or more **auxiliary**, or **helping**, **verbs**, like *had*.

Quick Reference: Punctuation

Part of Speech	Function	Examples
End Marks period, question mark, exclamation point	ends a sentence	The games begin today. Who is your favorite contestant? What a play Jamie made!
period	follows an initial or abbreviation **Exception:** postal abbreviations of states	Prof. Ted Bakerman, D. H. Lawrence, p.m., oz., ft., Blvd., St. , NE (Nebraska), NV (Nevada)

period	follows a number or letter in an outline	I. Volcanoes
		  A. Central-vent
		    1. Shield

Comma	separates parts of a compound sentence	I have never disliked poetry, but now I really love it.
	separates items in a series	She is brave, loyal, and kind.
	separates adjectives of equal rank that modify the same noun	The slow, easy route is best.
	sets off a term of address	O Wind, if winter comes . . . Come to the front, children.
	sets off a parenthetical expression	Hard workers, as you know, don't quit. I'm not a quitter, believe me.
	sets off an introductory word, phrase, or dependent clause	Yes, I forgot my key. At the beginning of the day, I feel fresh. While she was out, I was here. Having finished my chores, I went out.
	sets off a nonrestrictive phrase or clause and contrasting expressions	Ed Pawn, the captain of the chess team, won. Marla, who was sick, finished last. The two leading runners, sprinting toward the finish line, finished in a tie.
	sets off parts of dates and addresses	Send it by August 18, 2010, to Cherry Jubilee, Inc., 21 Vernona St., Oakland, Minnesota.
	follows the salutation and closing of a letter	Dear Jim, Sincerely yours,
	separates words to avoid confusion	By noon, time had run out. What the minister does, does matter. While cooking, Jim burned his hand.
Semicolon	separates items that contain commas in a series	We invited my sister, Jan; her boyfriend, Don; my uncle Jack; and Mary Dodd.

continued

Part of Speech	Function	Examples
	separates parts of a compound sentence that are not joined by a coordinating conjunction	The last shall be first; the first shall be last. I read the Bible; however, I have not memorized it.
	separates parts of a compound sentence when the parts contain commas	After I ran out of money, I called my parents; but only my sister was home, unfortunately.
Colon	introduces a list	Those we wrote were the following: Dana, John, and Will.
	introduces a long quotation	Susan B. Anthony said: "Woman must not depend upon the protection of man...."
	follows the salutation of a business letter	To Whom It May Concern: Dear Ms. Costa:
	separates certain numbers	1:28 p.m. Genesis 2:5
Dash	indicates an abrupt break in thought and adds emphasis to parenthetical information	I was thinking of my mother—who is arriving tomorrow—just as you walked in.
Parentheses	enclose less-important material	Throughout her life (though some might think otherwise), she worked hard. The temperature on this July day (would you believe it?) is 65 degrees!
Hyphen	joins parts of a compound adjective before a noun	She lives in a first-floor apartment.
	joins part of a compound with *all-*, *ex-*, *self-*, or *-elect*	The president-elect is well respected.
	joins part of a compound number (to ninety-nine)	Today I turn twenty-one.
	joins part of a fraction	My cup is one-third full.
	joins a prefix to a word beginning with a capital letter	Is this a pre–Bronze Age artifact? Caesar had a bad day in mid-March.
	indicates that a word is divided at the end of a line	Finding the right title has been a challenge for the committee.
Apostrophe	used with *s* to form the possessive of a noun or an indefinite pronoun	my friend's book, my friends' books, anyone's guess, somebody else's problem
	replaces one or more omitted letters in a contraction or numbers in a date	don't (omitted *o*), he'd (omitted *woul*), the class of '99 (omitted *19*)

continued

Part of Speech	Function	Examples
	used with *s* to form the plural of a letter	I had two A's on my report card.
Quotation Marks	set off a speaker's exact words	Sara said, "I'm finally ready." "I'm ready," Sara said, "finally." Did Sara say, "I'm ready"? Sara said, "I'm ready!"
	set off the title of a story, an article, a short poem, an essay, a song, or a chapter	We read Hansberry's "On Summer" and Alvarez's "Exile."
	indicate sarcasm or irony	Oh, she's an "expert," all right.
Ellipses	replace material omitted from a quotation	"Neither slavery nor involuntary servitude . . . shall exist within the United States. . . ."
Italics	indicate the title of a book, a play, a magazine, a long poem, an opera, a film or a TV series, or the name of a ship	*The Mists of Avalon, Julius Caesar, Newsweek, Paradise Lost, La Bohème, Twilight, Glee, USS John F. Kennedy*

Quick Reference: Capitalization

Category	Examples
People and Titles	
Names and initials of people	Alice Walker, E. B. White
Titles used before or in place of names	Professor Holmes, Senator Long
Deities and members of religious groups	Jesus, Allah, Buddha, Zeus, Baptists, Roman Catholics
Names of ethnic and national groups	Hispanics, Jews, African Americans
Geographical Names	
Cities, states, countries, continents	Charleston, Nevada, France, Asia
Regions, bodies of water, mountains	the Midwest, Lake Michigan, Mount Everest
Geographic features, parks	Continental Divide, Everglades, Yellowstone
Streets and roads, planets	361 South Twenty-third Street, Miller Avenue, Jupiter, Saturn
Organizations, Events, Etc.	
Companies, organizations, teams	Monsanto, the Elks, Chicago Bulls
Buildings, bridges, monuments	the Alamo, Golden Gate Bridge, Lincoln Memorial
Documents, awards	the Constitution, World Cup

continued

Category	Examples
Special named events	Super Bowl, World Series
Government bodies, historical periods and events	the Supreme Court, Congress, the Middle Ages, Boston Tea Party
Days and months, holidays	Tuesday, October, Thanksgiving, Valentine's Day
Specific cars, boats, trains, planes	Cadillac, Titanic, Orient Express
Proper Adjectives	
Adjectives formed from proper nouns	Doppler effect, Mexican music, Elizabethan age, Midwestern town
First Words and the Pronoun *I*	
First word in a sentence or quotation	This is it. He said, "Let's go."
First word of sentence in parentheses that is not within another sentence	The spelling rules are covered in another section. (Consult that section for more information.)
First words in the salutation and closing of a letter	Dear Madam, Very truly yours,
First word in each line of most poetry Personal pronoun *I*	Then am I A happy fly If I live Or if I die.
First word, last word, and all important words in a title	*A Tale of Two Cities*, "The World Is Too Much with Us"

Grammar Handbook

1 Nouns

A **noun** is a word used to name a person, a place, a thing, an idea, a quality, or an action. Nouns can be classified in several ways.

1.1 COMMON NOUNS

Common nouns are general names, common to entire groups.

1.2 PROPER NOUNS

Proper nouns name specific, one-of-a-kind things.

Common	Proper
motor, tree, time, children	Bradbury, Eastern Standard Time, Maine

1.3 SINGULAR AND PLURAL NOUNS

A noun may take a singular or a plural form, depending on whether it names a single person, place, thing, or idea or more than one. Make sure you use appropriate spellings when forming plurals.

Singular	Plural
rocket, sky, life	rockets, skies, lives

1.4 POSSESSIVE NOUNS

A **possessive noun** shows who or what owns something.

2 Pronouns

A **pronoun** is a word that is used in place of a noun or another pronoun. The word or word group to which the pronoun refers is called its **antecedent.**

2.1 PERSONAL PRONOUNS

Personal pronouns change their form to express person, number, gender, and case. The forms of these pronouns are shown in the following chart.

	Nominative	Objective	Possessive
Singular			
First Person	I	me	my, mine
Second Person	you	you	your, yours
Third Person	she, he, it	her, him, it	her, hers, his, its
Plural			
First Person	we	us	our, ours
Second Person	you	you	your, yours
Third Person	they	them	their, theirs

2.2 AGREEMENT WITH ANTECEDENT

Pronouns should agree with their antecedents in number, gender, and person.

If an antecedent is singular, use a singular pronoun.

EXAMPLE: *Malcolm waved as he boarded the bus to the airport.*

If an antecedent is plural, use a plural pronoun.

EXAMPLES:
Malcolm and Hal shared a sandwich as they waited to board the plane.
Delores and Arnetta rode their bikes to the park.

The gender of a pronoun must be the same as the gender of its antecedent.

EXAMPLES:

William will give his performance tonight.
Marla played her trumpet.

The person of the pronoun must be the same as the person of its antecedent. As the chart in Section 2.1 shows, a pronoun can be in first-, second-, or third-person form.

EXAMPLE: *You classical music fans still have time to buy your tickets.*

Rewrite each sentence so that the under-lined pronoun agrees with its antecedent.

1. "The Lottery" tells about a small town and his strange custom.
2. Mr. Summers keeps the box so the villagers can use them each year.
3. Each of the men draws for their family.
4. The people of the town take its chances in the drawing.
5. After the other slips are shown, Tessie is forced to reveal theirs.

2.3 PRONOUN CASE

Personal pronouns change form to show how they function in sentences. Different functions are shown by different **cases: nominative, objective,** and **possessive.** For examples, see Section 2.1.

A **nominative pronoun** is used as a subject or a predicate nominative in a sentence.

An **objective pronoun** is used as a direct object, an indirect object, or the object of a preposition.

SUBJECT OBJECT OBJECT OF PREPOSITION

She *brought him to us.*

A **possessive pronoun** shows ownership. The pronouns *mine, yours, hers, his, its, ours,* and *theirs* can be used in place of nouns.

EXAMPLE: *This horse is mine.*

The pronouns *my, your, her, his, its, our,* and *their* are used before nouns.

EXAMPLE: *This is my book.*

WATCH OUT! Don't confuse the possessive pronouns *its* and *their* with the contractions *it's* and *they're.*

TIP To decide which pronoun to use in a comparison, such as "He runs faster than (*I* or *me*)," fill in the missing word(s): *He runs faster than I do.*

Replace the underlined words in each sentence with an appropriate pronoun, and identify the pronoun as a nominative, an objective, or a possessive pronoun.

1. Shakespeare was the most famous playwright who ever lived.
2. *Macbeth* is one of Shakespeare's most powerful tragedies.
3. Macbeth and Lady Macbeth are two of the main characters.
4. Macbeth causes the murders of Duncan and Banquo.
5. Duncan's sons are the rightful heirs to the throne.

2.4 REFLEXIVE AND INTENSIVE PRONOUNS

These pronouns are formed by adding –*self* or –*selves* to certain personal pronouns. Their forms are the same, and they differ only in how they are used.

A **reflexive pronoun** follows a verb or preposition and reflects back on an earlier noun or pronoun.

EXAMPLES:
He likes himself too much.
Kiyoko treated herself to dessert.

Intensive pronouns intensify or emphasize the nouns or pronouns to which they refer.

EXAMPLES:
The merchants themselves enjoyed sampling the foods.
You did it yourself.

WATCH OUT! Avoid using *hisself* or *theirselves.* Standard English does not include these forms.

NONSTANDARD: *The children sang theirselves to sleep.*

STANDARD: *The children sang themselves to sleep.*

2.5 RECIPROCAL PRONOUNS

Reciprocal pronouns express mutual actions or relationships between the members they represent. Reciprocal pronouns also take the possessive forms **each other's** and **one another's.**

EXAMPLES:

The children exchanged gifts with one another.

Sean and Julie laughed at each other's jokes.

2.6 DEMONSTRATIVE PRONOUNS

Demonstrative pronouns point out things and persons near and far.

	Singular	Plural
Near	this	these
Far	that	those

2.7 INDEFINITE PRONOUNS

Indefinite pronouns do not refer to specific persons or things and usually have no antecedents. The chart shows some commonly used indefinite pronouns.

Singular	Plural	Singular or Plural	
another	both	all	most
anybody	few	any	none
no one	many	more	some
neither	several		

TIP Indefinite pronouns that end in *–one, –body,* or *–thing* are always singular.

INCORRECT: *Everyone brought their clarinet.*

CORRECT: *Everyone brought his or her clarinet.*

If the indefinite pronoun might refer to either a male or a female, *his or her* may be used, or the sentence may be rewritten.

EXAMPLES:

Did everybody play his or her part well?
Did all the students play their parts well?

2.8 INTERROGATIVE PRONOUNS

An **interrogative pronoun** tells a reader or listener that a question is coming. The interrogative pronouns are *who, whom, whose, which,* and *what.*

EXAMPLES:

Who wrote that song?
From whom did you get the answer?

TIP *Who* is used as a subject; *whom,* as an object. To decide which pronoun you need to use in a question, change the question to a statement.

QUESTION: *(Who/Whom) are you speaking to?*

STATEMENT: *You are speaking to (?).*

Since the verb has a subject (*you*), the needed word must be the object form, *whom.*

EXAMPLE: *Whom are you speaking to?*

WATCH OUT! A special problem arises when you use an interrupter, such as *do you think,* within a question.

EXAMPLE: *(Who/Whom) do you think is the better singer?*

If you eliminate the interrupter, it is clear that the word you need is *who.*

2.9 RELATIVE PRONOUNS

Relative pronouns relate, or connect, adjective clauses to the words they modify in sentences. The noun or pronoun that a relative clause modifies is the antecedent of the relative pronoun.

Here are the relative pronouns and their uses:

Replaces	Subject	Object	Possessive
Person	who	whom	whose
Thing	which	which	whose
Thing/Person	that	that	whose

Often short sentences with related ideas can be combined by using a relative pronoun to create a more effective sentence.

SHORT SENTENCE: *Joan Aiken decided to become a writer at an early age.*

RELATED SENTENCE: *Joan Aiken's father was a poet.*

COMBINED SENTENCE: *Joan Aiken, whose father was a poet, decided to become a writer at an early age.*

Practice and Apply

Write the correct form of each incorrect pronoun.

1. Whom has read "By the Waters of Babylon"?
2. Stephen Vincent Benét, which is a famous American author, wrote the story.
3. In "By the Waters of Babylon," him who touches the metal in the Dead Places must be a priest or son of a priest.
4. The narrator's father hisself is a priest.
5. When the narrator sees a heap of broken stones, he cautiously approaches them stones.

2.10 PRONOUN REFERENCE PROBLEMS

The referent of a pronoun should always be clear. Avoid problems by rewriting sentences.

An **indefinite reference** occurs when the pronoun *it, you,* or *they* does not clearly refer to a specific antecedent.

UNCLEAR: *In the article, it claims that the new Pink Blur CD is terrific.*

CLEAR: *The article claims that the new Pink Blur CD is terrific.*

A **general reference** occurs when the pronoun *it, this, that, which,* or *such* is used to refer to a general idea rather than a specific antecedent.

UNCLEAR: *Trudy practices the guitar every day. This has improved her playing.*

CLEAR: *Trudy practices the guitar every day. Practicing has improved her playing.*

Ambiguous means "having more than one possible meaning." An **ambiguous reference** occurs when a pronoun could refer to two or more antecedents.

UNCLEAR: *Jeb talked to Max while he listened to music.*

CLEAR: *While Jeb listened to music, he talked to Max.*

Practice and Apply

Rewrite the following sentences to correct indefinite, ambiguous, and general pronoun references.

1. In the story "To Build A Fire," it tells about a man trying to survive in extremely cold conditions.
2. The man almost steps in a trap. This makes him use the dog to test the trail's safety.
3. An old-timer in the story tells the miner that running will make his feet freeze faster.
4. Snow from a tree falls and puts out the man's fire. This makes him panic.

3 Verbs

A **verb** is a word that expresses an action, a condition, or a state of being.

3.1 ACTION VERBS

Action verbs express mental or physical activity.

EXAMPLE: *You hit the target.*

3.2 LINKING VERBS

Linking verbs join subjects with words or phrases that rename or describe them.

EXAMPLE: *She is our queen.*

3.3 PRINCIPAL PARTS

Action and linking verbs typically have four principal parts, which are used to form verb tenses. The principal parts are the **present,** the **present participle,** the **past,** and the **past participle.**

Action verbs and some linking verbs also fall into two categories: regular and irregular. A **regular verb** is a verb that forms its past and past participle by adding *–ed* or *–d* to the present form.

Present	Present Participle	Past	Past Participle
perform	(is) performing	performed	(has) performed
hope	(is) hoping	hoped	(has) hoped
stop	(is) stopping	stopped	(has) stopped
marry	(is) marrying	married	(has) married

An **irregular verb** forms its past and past participle in some other way besides adding −ed or −d to the present form.

Present	Present Participle	Past	Past Participle
bring	(is) bringing	brought	(has) brought
swim	(is) swimming	swam	(has) swum
steal	(is) stealing	stole	(has) stolen
grow	(is) growing	grew	(has) grown

3.4 VERB TENSE

The **tense** of a verb indicates the time of the action or state of being. An action or state of being can occur in the present, the past, or the future. There are six tenses, each expressing a different range of time.

The **present tense** expresses an action or state that is happening at the present time, occurs regularly, or is constant or generally true. Use the present part.

NOW: *This soup tastes delicious.*

REGULAR: *I make vegetable soup often.*

GENERAL: *Crops require sun, rain, and rich soil.*

The **past tense** expresses an action that began and ended in the past. Use the past part.

EXAMPLE: *The diver bought a shark cage.*

The **future tense** expresses an action or state that will occur. Use *shall* or *will* with the present part.

EXAMPLE: *The shark will destroy this cage.*

The **present perfect tense** expresses an action or state that (1) was completed at an indefinite time in the past or (2) began in the past and continues into the present. Use *have* or *has* with the past participle.

EXAMPLE: *The diver has used shark cages before.*

The **past perfect tense** expresses an action in the past that came before another action in the past. Use *had* with the past participle.

EXAMPLE: *He had looked everywhere for a cage.*

The **future perfect tense** expresses an action in the future that will be completed before another action in the future. Use *shall have* or *will have* with the past participle.

EXAMPLE: *Before the day ends, the shark will have destroyed three cages.*

TIP A past-tense form of an irregular verb is not used with an auxiliary verb, but a past-participle main irregular verb is always used with an auxiliary verb.

INCORRECT: *I have saw her somewhere before.*

CORRECT: *I have seen her somewhere before.*

INCORRECT: *I seen her somewhere before.*

3.5 PROGRESSIVE FORMS

The progressive forms of the six tenses show ongoing actions. Use forms of *be* with the present participles of verbs.

PRESENT PROGRESSIVE: *We are dancing.*

PAST PROGRESSIVE: *We were dancing yesterday.*

FUTURE PROGRESSIVE: *We will be dancing on Friday.*

PRESENT PERFECT PROGRESSIVE: *We have been dancing once a week.*

PAST PERFECT PROGRESSIVE: *We had been dancing for a long time.*

FUTURE PERFECT PROGRESSIVE: *We will have been dancing as partners for six months next week.*

WATCH OUT! Do not shift from tense to tense needlessly. Watch out for these special cases.

- In most compound sentences and in sentences with compound predicates, keep the tenses the same.

  INCORRECT: *I keyed in the password, but I get an error message.*

  CORRECT: *I keyed in the password, but I got an error message.*

- If one past action happened before another, do shift tenses.

  INCORRECT: *They wished they started earlier.*

  CORRECT: *They wished they had started earlier.*

Practice and Apply

Rewrite each sentence, using a form of the verb in parentheses. Identify each form that you use.

1. In his stories, Franz Kafka (show) the struggles of people against faceless bureacracy.
2. Kafka (write) "The Metamorphosis."
3. In the story, Gregor (know) both of his parents' concerns well.
4. The chief clerk (visit) the house.
5. Struggling with difficulties, Gregor (unlock) the door.
6. The story (reflect) how Gregor approaches even bizarre events by focusing on work.

Rewrite each sentence to correct an error in tense.

7. Gregor wants to communicate with his family and tried to talk to them through the door.
8. The clerk is angry and gave Gregor a stern warning.
9. Gregor's parents and sister had not knew what happened to him.
10. Gregor's mother have fainted at the sight of him.

3.6 ACTIVE AND PASSIVE VOICE

The voice of a verb tells whether its subject performs or receives the action expressed by the verb. When the subject performs the action, the verb is in the **active voice.** When the subject is the receiver of the action, the verb is in the **passive voice.**

Compare these two sentences:

ACTIVE: *Her sunglasses hid her face.*

PASSIVE: *Her face was hidden by her sunglasses.*

To form the passive voice, use a form of *be* with the past participle of the verb.

WATCH OUT! Use the passive voice sparingly. It can make writing awkward and less direct.

AWKWARD: *She was given the handmade quilts by her mother.*

BETTER: *Her mother gave her the handmade quilts.*

There are occasions when you will choose to use the passive voice because

- you want to emphasize the receiver: *The king was shot.*
- the doer is unknown: *My books were stolen.*
- the doer is unimportant: *French is spoken here.*

4 Modifiers

Modifiers are words or groups of words that change or limit the meanings of other words. Adjectives and adverbs are common modifiers.

4.1 ADJECTIVES

Adjectives modify nouns and pronouns by telling which one, what kind, how many, or how much.

WHICH ONE: *this, that, these, those*

EXAMPLE: *These tomatoes have grown quickly.*

WHAT KIND: *tiny, impressive, bold, rotten*

EXAMPLE: *The bold officer stood in front of the crowd.*

HOW MANY: *some, few, ten, none, both, each*

EXAMPLE: *Some diners had sweet potatoes.*

HOW MUCH: *more, less, enough, plenty*

EXAMPLE: *There was enough chicken to serve everyone.*

4.2 PREDICATE ADJECTIVES

Most adjectives come before the nouns they modify, as in the preceding examples. A **predicate adjective,** however, follows a linking verb and describes the subject.

EXAMPLE: *My friends are very intelligent.*

Be especially careful to use adjectives (not adverbs) after such linking verbs as *look, feel, grow, taste,* and *smell.*

EXAMPLE: *The weather grows cold.*

4.3 ADVERBS

Adverbs modify verbs, adjectives, and other adverbs by telling where, when, how, or to what extent.

WHERE: *The children played outside.*

WHEN: *The author spoke yesterday.*

HOW: *We walked slowly behind the leader.*

TO WHAT EXTENT: *He worked very hard.*

Adverbs may occur in many places in sentences, both before and after the words they modify.

EXAMPLES:

Suddenly the wind shifted.

The wind suddenly shifted.

The wind shifted suddenly.

4.4 ADJECTIVE OR ADVERB?

Many adverbs are formed by adding –*ly* to adjectives.

EXAMPLES:

sweet, sweetly; gentle, gently

However, –*ly* added to a noun will usually yield an adjective.

EXAMPLES:

friend, friendly; woman, womanly

4.5 COMPARISON OF MODIFIERS

Modifiers can be used to compare two or more things. The form of a modifier shows the degree of comparison. Both adjectives and adverbs have **comparative** and **superlative** forms.

The **comparative form** is used to compare two things, groups, or actions.

EXAMPLES:

His emperor's chariots are faster than mine.

Brutus' speech was more effective than Cassius' speech.

The **superlative form** is used to compare more than two things, groups, or actions.

EXAMPLES:

The emperor's chariots are the fastest.

Antony's speech was the most effective of all.

4.6 REGULAR COMPARISONS

Most one-syllable and some two-syllable adjectives and adverbs have comparatives and superlatives formed by adding –*er* and –*est.* All three-syllable and most two-syllable modifiers have comparatives and superlatives formed with *more* or *most.*

Modifier	Comparative	Superlative
tall	taller	tallest
kind	kinder	kindest
droopy	droopier	droopiest
expensive	more expensive	most expensive
wasteful	more wasteful	most wasteful

WATCH OUT! Note that spelling changes must sometimes be made to form the comparatives and superlatives of modifiers.

EXAMPLES:

friendly, friendlier (Change *y* to *i* and add the ending.)

sad, sadder (Double the final consonant and add the ending.)

4.7 IRREGULAR COMPARISONS

Some commonly used modifiers have irregular comparative and superlative forms. They are listed in the following chart:

Modifier	Comparative	Superlative
good	better	best
bad	worse	worst
far	farther *or* further	farthest *or* furthest
little	less *or* lesser	least
many	more	most
well	better	best
much	more	most

4.8 PROBLEMS WITH MODIFIERS

Study the tips that follow to avoid common mistakes:

Farther and Further Use *farther* for distances; use *further* for everything else.

Double Comparisons Make a comparison by using *–er/–est* or by using *more/most*. Using *–er* with *more* or using *–est* with *most* is incorrect.

INCORRECT: *I like her more better than she likes me.*

CORRECT: *I like her better than she likes me.*

Illogical Comparisons An illogical or confusing comparison results when two unrelated things are compared or when something is compared with itself. The word *other* or the word *else* should be used when comparing an individual member to the rest of a group.

ILLOGICAL: *The narrator was more curious about the war than any student in his class.* (implies that the narrator isn't a student in the class)

LOGICAL: *The narrator was more curious about the war than any other student in his class.* (identifies that the narrator is a student)

Bad vs. **Badly** *Bad,* as an adjective, is used before a noun or after a linking verb. *Badly,* always an adverb, never modifies a noun. Be sure to use the right form after a linking verb.

INCORRECT: *Ed felt badly after his team lost.*

CORRECT: *Ed felt bad after his team lost.*

Good vs. **Well** *Good,* as an adjective, is used before a noun or after a linking verb. *Well* is often an adverb meaning "expertly" or "properly." *Well* can also be used as an adjective after a linking verb when it means "in good health."

INCORRECT: *Helen writes very good.*

CORRECT: *Helen writes very well.*

CORRECT: *Yesterday I felt bad; today I feel well.*

Double Negatives If you add a negative word to a sentence that is already negative, the result will be an error known as a double negative. When using *not* or *–n't* with a verb, use *any–* words, such as *anybody* or *anything,* rather than *no–* words, such as *nobody* or *nothing,* later in the sentence.

INCORRECT: *I don't have no money.*

CORRECT: *I don't have any money.*

Using *hardly, barely,* or *scarcely* after a negative word is also incorrect.

INCORRECT: *They couldn't barely see two feet ahead.*

CORRECT: *They could barely see two feet ahead.*

Misplaced Modifiers Sometimes a modifier is placed so far away from the word it modifies that the intended meaning of the sentence is unclear. Prepositional phrases and participial phrases are often misplaced. Place modifiers as close as possible to the words they modify.

MISPLACED: *The ranger explained how to find ducks in her office.* (The ducks were not in the ranger's office.)

CLEARER: *In her office, the ranger explained how to find ducks.*

Dangling Modifiers Sometimes a modifier doesn't appear to modify any word in a sentence. Most dangling modifiers are participial phrases or infinitive phrases.

DANGLING: *Coming home with groceries, our parrot said, "Hello!"*

CLEARER: *Coming home with groceries, we heard our parrot say, "Hello!"*

Practice and Apply

Choose the correct word or words from each pair in parentheses.

1. The play *Julius Caesar* is about the death of the (powerfulest, most powerful) emperor of Roman times.
2. The emperor didn't pay (no, any) attention to the soothsayer who warned him about the ides of March.
3. Caesar (could, couldn't) hardly know what lay in store for him.
4. He thought Brutus loved him (well, good).

Practice and Apply

Rewrite each sentence that contains a misplaced or dangling modifier. Write "correct" if the sentence is written correctly.

1. Soldiers marched toward Macbeth's castle hidden by trees.
2. Angry at the witches, his many mistakes became clear to Macbeth.
3. Weary of struggling for power, Macbeth called for his armor.
4. Reckless ambition is a key theme in *Macbeth,* striving for success at any cost.

5   The Sentence and Its Parts

A **sentence** is a group of words used to express a complete thought. A complete sentence has a subject and a predicate.

5.1 KINDS OF SENTENCES

There are four basic types of sentences:

Type	Definition	Example
Declarative	states a fact, a wish, an intent, or a feeling	I read White's essay last night.
Interrogative	asks a question	Did you like the essay?
Imperative	gives a command or direction	Read this paragraph aloud.
Exclamatory	expresses strong feeling or excitement	I wish I had thought of that!

5.2 COMPOUND SUBJECTS AND PREDICATES

A compound subject consists of two or more subjects that share the same verb. They are typically joined by the coordinating conjunction *and* or *or*.

EXAMPLE: *Ray and Joe write about families.*

A compound predicate consists of two or more predicates that share the same subject. They too are typically joined by a coordinating conjunction, usually *and, but,* or *or*.

EXAMPLE: *The father in the poem "Those Winter Sundays" got up early and dressed in the dark.*

5.3 COMPLEMENTS

A **complement** is a word or group of words that completes the meaning of the sentence. Some sentences contain only a subject and a verb. Most sentences, however, require additional words placed after the verb to complete the meaning of the sentence. There are three kinds of complements: direct objects, indirect objects, and subject complements.

Direct objects are words or word groups that receive the action of action verbs. A direct object answers the question *what* or *whom.*

> EXAMPLES:
> *The students asked many questions.* (Asked what?)
>
> *The teacher quickly answered the students.* (Answered whom?)

Indirect objects tell to whom or what or for whom or what the actions of verbs are performed. Indirect objects come before direct objects. In the examples that follow, the indirect objects are highlighted.

> EXAMPLES:
> *My sister usually gave her friends good advice.* (Gave to whom?)
>
> *Her brother sent the store a heavy package.* (Sent to what?)

Subject complements come after linking verbs and identify or describe the subjects. A subject complement that names or identifies a subject is called a **predicate nominative.** Predicate nominatives include **predicate nouns** and **predicate pronouns.**

> EXAMPLES:
> *My friends are very hard workers.*
>
> *The best writer in the class is she.*

A subject complement that describes a subject is called a **predicate adjective.**

> EXAMPLE: *The pianist appeared very energetic.*

6 Phrases

A **phrase** is a group of related words that does not contain a subject and a predicate but functions in a sentence as a single part of speech.

6.1 NOUN PHRASE

A **noun phrase** includes a noun and the modifiers that distinguish it. Modifiers might come before or after the noun.

> EXAMPLES:
> *The world-class pianist received many accolades after her performance.*

The pianist who played at Carnegie Hall was famous for tackling challenging pieces.

In these examples, the noun *pianist* is modified by *world-class* and *who played at Carnegie Hall.* The noun and its modifiers form the noun phrase.

> ### Practice and Apply
>
> Add a modifier to at least one noun in each sentence to create a noun phrase.
> 1. The song was a hit.
> 2. My teacher gives a pop quiz every week.
> 3. A fence borders the edge of campus.
> 4. The museum was inspiring.
> 5. The restaurant is known for its cuisine.

6.2 VERB PHRASES

A **verb phrase** consists of at least one main verb and one or more helping verbs. A helping verb (also called an auxiliary verb) helps the main verb express action or state of being.

Besides all forms of the verb *be,* some common helping verbs are *can, could, did, do, does, had, have, may, might, must, shall, should, will,* and *would.*

> EXAMPLE: *The veterinarian should consider an expansion of his practice.*

Sometimes the parts of a verb phrase are interrupted by other parts of speech.

> EXAMPLE: *The veterinarian had recently been considering an expansion of his practice.*

The word *not* is an adverb. It is never part of a verb phrase, even when it is joined to a verb as the contraction *–n't.*

> EXAMPLES:
> *The dog should not have bitten the boy.*
>
> *The dog shouldn't have bitten the boy.*

6.3 PREPOSITIONAL PHRASES

A **prepositional phrase** is a phrase that consists of a preposition, its object, and any modifiers of the object. Prepositional phrases that modify nouns or pronouns are called **adjective phrases.** Prepositional phrases that modify verbs, adjectives, or adverbs are **adverb phrases.**

> ADJECTIVE PHRASE: *The central character of the story is a villain.*

> ADVERB PHRASE: *He reveals his nature in the first scene.*

Remember that adjectives modify nouns by telling which one, what kind, how much, or how many. Adverbs modify verbs, adjectives, and other adverbs by telling where, when, how, or to what extent. The same is true of prepositional phrases that act as adjective phrases or adverb phrases.

6.4 APPOSITIVES AND APPOSITIVE PHRASES

An **appositive** is a noun or pronoun that identifies or renames another noun or pronoun. An **appositive phrase** includes an appositive and modifiers of it.

An appositive can be either **essential** or **nonessential.** An **essential appositive** provides information that is needed to identify what is referred to by the preceding noun or pronoun.

> EXAMPLE: *This poem was written by author Walt Whitman.*

A **nonessential appositive** adds extra information about a noun or pronoun whose meaning is already clear. Nonessential appositives and appositive phrases are set off with commas.

> EXAMPLE: *He wrote this poem, a sad remembrance of war, about an artilleryman.*

7 Verbals and Verbal Phrases

A **verbal** is a verb form that is used as a noun, an adjective, or an adverb. A **verbal phrase** consists of a verbal along with its modifiers and complements. There are three kinds of verbals: **infinitives, participles,** and **gerunds.**

7.1 INFINITIVES AND INFINITIVE PHRASES

An **infinitive** is a verb form that usually begins with *to* and functions as a noun, an adjective, or an adverb. An **infinitive phrase** consists of an infinitive plus its modifiers and complements. The examples that follow show several uses of infinitive phrases.

> NOUN: *To know her is my only desire.* (subject)

> *I'm planning to walk with you.* (direct object)

> *Her goal was to promote women's rights.* (predicate nominative)

> ADJECTIVE: *We saw his need to be loved.* (adjective modifying *need*)

> ADVERB: *She wrote to voice her opinions.* (adverb modifying *wrote*)

Because *to,* the sign of the infinitive, precedes infinitives, it is usually easy to recognize them. However, sometimes *to* may be omitted.

> **EXAMPLE:** *Let no one dare [to] enter this shrine.*

7.2 PARTICIPLES AND PARTICIPIAL PHRASES

A **participle** is a verb form that functions as an adjective. Like adjectives, participles modify nouns and pronouns. Most participles are present-participle forms, ending in *–ing,* or past-participle forms ending in *–ed* or *–en.* In these examples, the participles are highlighted.

> **MODIFYING A NOUN:** *The smiling man ate another dumpling.*

> **MODIFYING A PRONOUN:** *Ignored, she slipped out of the room unnoticed.*

Participial phrases are participles with all their modifiers and complements.

> **MODIFYING A NOUN:** *Visiting gardens, butterflies flit among the flowers.*

> **MODIFYING A PRONOUN:** *Driven by instinct, they use the flowers as meal stops.*

Practice and Apply

Identify the participial phrases and participles that are used as adjectives in the following sentences, and indicate the word each phrase modifies.

1. Aided by good weather and clear skies, the sailors sailed into port a day early.
2. Searching through old clothes in a trunk, Ricardo found a map showing the location of buried treasure.
3. I would love to see it blooming: it must be quite a sight!
4. The cat hissed at the dog barking in the yard next door.
5. Waxing his car in the driveway, Joe overheard a bit of song from an open window nearby.

7.3 DANGLING AND MISPLACED PARTICIPLES

A participle or participial phrase should be placed as close as possible to the word that it modifies. Otherwise the meaning of the sentence may not be clear.

> **MISPLACED:** *The boys were looking for squirrels searching the trees.*

> **CLEARER:** *The boys searching the trees were looking for squirrels.*

A participle or participial phrase that does not clearly modify anything in a sentence is called a **dangling participle.** A dangling participle causes confusion because it appears to modify a word that it cannot sensibly modify. Correct a dangling participle by providing a word for the participle to modify.

> **DANGLING:** *Running like the wind,* my hat fell off. (The hat wasn't running.)

> **CLEARER:** *Running like the wind,* I lost my hat.

7.4 GERUNDS AND GERUND PHRASES

A **gerund** is a verb form ending in *–ing* that functions as a noun. A gerund may perform any function that a noun performs.

> **SUBJECT:** *Running is my favorite pastime.*

> **DIRECT OBJECT:** *I truly love running.*

> **INDIRECT OBJECT:** *You should give running a try.*

> **SUBJECT COMPLEMENT:** *My deepest passion is running.*

> **OBJECT OF PREPOSITION:** *Her love of running keeps her strong.*

Gerund phrases are gerunds with all their modifiers and complements.

> **SUBJECT:** *Wishing on a star never got me far.*

> **OBJECT OF PREPOSITION:** *I will finish before leaving the office.*

> **APPOSITIVE:** *Her avocation, flying airplanes, finally led to full-time employment.*

7.5 ABSOLUTE PHRASES

An **absolute phrase** is a noun or pronoun, its participle, and any modifiers. It modifies an entire clause, rather than just one word.

EXAMPLE: *The backyard filling with lightning bugs, the children shouted with delight.*

In this example, *The backyard filling with lightning bugs* is an absolute phrase that modifies the sentence *the children shouted with delight.* The noun *backyard* is modified by the participle *filling* and by the prepositional phrase *with lightning bugs.* Notice that a comma separates the absolute phrase from the sentence.

Practice and Apply

Add an absolute phrase to modify each sentence.

1. Dexter waited for his date to arrive.
2. The road never seemed to end.
3. Maria prepared a feast.
4. The sun set beyond the sparkling lake.
5. The test was more difficult than we expected.

Practice and Apply

Rewrite each sentence, adding the type of phrase shown in parentheses.

1. Last year, Katrina and her family moved to St. Louis. (participial phrase)
2. At a highway rest stop, her pet cat escaped. (appositive phrase)
3. The family searched desperately. (infinitive phrase)
4. They had to keep going. (gerund phrase)
5. Katrina's cat tracked them all the way to their new home. (absolute phrase)

8 Clauses

A **clause** is a group of words that contains a subject and a verb. There are two kinds of clauses: independent clauses and subordinate clauses.

8.1 INDEPENDENT AND SUBORDINATE CLAUSES

An **independent clause** can stand alone as a sentence, as the word *independent* suggests.

INDEPENDENT CLAUSE: *Emily Dickinson did not wish her poems to be published.*

A sentence may contain more than one independent clause.

EXAMPLE: *Emily Dickinson did not wish her poems to be published, but seven were published during her lifetime.*

In the preceding example, the coordinating conjunction *but* joins two independent clauses.

Two independent clauses can also be joined with a **conjunctive adverb,** such as *consequently, finally, furthermore, however, moreover,* or *nevertheless.* To separate the two independent clauses, a semicolon is often used before the conjunctive adverb.

EXAMPLE: *The painter decided to take up sculpture; however, his studio was not big enough for large projects.*

A **subordinate clause ,** or **dependent clause,** cannot stand alone as a sentence. It is subordinate to, or dependent on, an independent clause.

EXAMPLE: *Emily Dickinson did not wish her poems to be published, although she shared them with friends.*

The highlighted clause cannot stand by itself.

Identify each italicized clause in the following sentences as independent or subordinate (dependent). Explain your responses.

1. I heard that one of the guests *who spoke at the ceremony* was Barbara Jordan.
2. *Whenever I think of Barbara Jordan*, I imagine her as she looks in a picture taken at my mother's college graduation in 1986.
3. According to my mother, *Jordan spoke eloquently about the importance of values in our society*.
4. *When Jordan began her public service career in 1966*, she became the first African American woman to serve in the Texas legislature.
5. Two years after the speech, *Jordan decided that she would retire from national politics*.

8.2 ADJECTIVE CLAUSES

An **adjective clause,** or **relative clause,** is a subordinate clause used as an adjective. It usually follows the noun or pronoun it modifies.

EXAMPLE: *Robert Frost wrote about birch tree branches that boys swing on.*

Adjective clauses are typically introduced by the relative pronoun *who, whom, whose, which,* or *that.*

EXAMPLES:
One song that we like became our theme song. Emily Dickinson, whose poems have touched many, lived a very quiet life.

An adjective clause can be either essential or nonessential. An **essential adjective clause** provides information that is necessary to identify the preceding noun or pronoun.

EXAMPLE: *The candidate whom we selected promised to serve us well.*

A **nonessential adjective clause** adds additional information about a noun or pronoun whose meaning is already clear.

Nonessential clauses are set off with commas.

EXAMPLE: *Brookhaven National Laboratory, which employs Mr. Davis, is in Upton, New York.*

TIP The relative pronouns *whom, which,* and *that* may sometimes be omitted when they are objects in adjective clauses.

EXAMPLE: *Frost is a writer [whom] millions enjoy.*

Revise the following sentences by substituting an adjective clause (relative clause) for each italicized adjective. Add specific details to make your sentences interesting.

1. As I ran on the track, a *large* dog approached me.
2. The *international* artist received many awards.
3. The four students discussed the *annual* tournament.
4. After the party, the caterer made himself a *delicious* cup of tea.
5. Angela and her classmates excitedly entered the *old* theater.

8.3 ADVERB CLAUSES

An **adverb clause** is a subordinate clause that is used to modify a verb, an adjective, or an adverb. It is introduced by a subordinating conjunction.

Adverb clauses typically occur at the beginning or end of sentences.

MODIFYING A VERB: *When we need you, we will call.*

MODIFYING AN ADVERB: *I'll stay here where there is shelter from the rain.*

MODIFYING AN ADJECTIVE: *Roman felt as good as he had ever felt.*

Identify the adverb clause and subordinating conjuction in each of the following sentences.

1. While the others worked inside the house, Ruth, Lou, and I worked in the yard.
2. Because the house had been vacant for so long, the lawn and gardens were overgrown.
3. The grass in the front looked as if it hadn't been cut in months.
4. Ruth began mowing the lawn while Lou and I weeded the flower beds.
5. We decided to borrow some tools since the weeds were extremely thick.

8.4 NOUN CLAUSES

A **noun clause** is a subordinate clause that is used as a noun. A noun clause may be used as a subject, a direct object, an indirect object, a predicate nominative, or the object of a preposition. Noun clauses are introduced either by pronouns, such as *that, what, who, whoever, which,* and *whose,* or by subordinating conjunctions, such as *how, when, where, why,* and *whether.*

TIP Because the same words may introduce adjective and noun clauses, you need to consider how a clause functions within its sentence. To determine whether a clause is a noun clause, try substituting *something* or *someone* for the clause. If you can do it, it is probably a noun clause.

EXAMPLES: *I know whose woods these are.* ("I know *something.*" The clause is a noun clause, direct object of the verb *know.*) *Give a copy to whoever wants one.* ("Give a copy to *someone.*" The clause is a noun clause, object of the preposition *to.*)

Identify the noun clause in each sentence. Then, tell how each clause is used: as a subject, a predicate nominative, a direct object, an indirect object, or an object of a preposition.

1. Mr. Perkins, the band director, announced that we would play at half time this week.
2. Mr. Perkins did not tell us, however, what we would be playing during the half-time show.
3. What we can never predict is whether he will choose a familiar march or a show tune.
4. He always gives whoever is asked to play each selection a chance to express an opinion about it.
5. He is genuinely interested in what we think of his sometimes unusual choices.

Add descriptive details to each sentence by writing the type of clause indicated in parentheses.

1. Ms. Nguyen is a scientist. (adjective clause)
2. She has invented many things. (adjective clause)
3. She works. (adverb clause)
4. She does her best thinking at night. (adverb clause)
5. She should invent a better backpack. (adjective clause)

9 The Structure of Sentences

When classified by their structure, there are four kinds of sentences: simple, compound, complex, and compound-complex.

9.1 SIMPLE SENTENCES

A **simple sentence** is a sentence that has one independent clause and no subordinate clauses.

The fact that such a sentence is called simple does not mean that it is uncomplicated. Various parts of simple sentences may be compound, and simple sentences may contain grammatical structures such as appositive and verbal phrases.

> EXAMPLES:
> *Mark Twain, an unsuccessful gold miner, wrote many successful satires and tall tales.* (appositive and compound direct object)
> *Pablo Neruda, drawn to writing poetry at an early age, won celebrity at age 20.* (participial and gerund phrases)

9.2 COMPOUND SENTENCES

A **compound sentence** consists of two or more independent clauses. The clauses in compound sentences are joined with commas and coordinating conjunctions (*and, but, or, nor, yet, for, so*) or with semicolons. Like simple sentences, compound sentences do not contain any subordinate clauses.

> EXAMPLES:
> *I enjoyed Bradbury's story "The Utterly Perfect Murder," and I want to read more of his stories.*
> *Amy Lowell's poem "The Taxi" has powerful images; however, it does not use the word "taxi" anywhere in it.*

WATCH OUT! Do not confuse compound sentences with simple sentences that have compound parts.

> EXAMPLE: *A subcommittee drafted a document and immediately presented it to the entire group.* (Here *and* joins parts of a compound predicate, not a compound sentence.)

9.3 COMPLEX SENTENCES

A **complex sentence** consists of one independent clause and one or more subordinate clauses. Each subordinate clause can be used as a noun or as a modifier. If it is used as a modifier, a subordinate clause usually modifies a word in the independent clause, and the independent clause can stand alone. However, when a subordinate clause is a noun clause, it is a part of the independent clause; the two cannot be separated.

> MODIFIER: *One should not complain unless one has a better solution.*
> NOUN CLAUSE: *We sketched pictures of whomever we wished.* (The noun clause is the object of the preposition *of* and cannot be separated from the rest of the sentence.)

9.4 COMPOUND-COMPLEX SENTENCES

A **compound-complex sentence** contains two or more independent clauses and one or more subordinate clauses. Compound-complex sentences are both compound and complex. If you start with a compound sentence, all you need to do to form a compound-complex sentence is add a subordinate clause.

> COMPOUND: *All the students knew the answer, yet they were too shy to volunteer.*
> COMPOUND-COMPLEX: *All the students knew the answer that their teacher expected, yet they were too shy to volunteer.*

9.5 PARALLEL STRUCTURE

When you write sentences, make sure that coordinate parts are equivalent, or **parallel,** in structure.

> NOT PARALLEL: *Erin loved basketball and to play hockey.* (*Basketball* is a noun; *to play hockey* is a phrase.)
> PARALLEL: *Erin loved basketball and hockey.* (*Basketball* and *hockey* are both nouns.)
> NOT PARALLEL: *He wanted to rent an apartment, a new car, and traveling around the country.* (*To rent* is an infinitive, *car* is a noun, and *traveling* is a gerund.)
> PARALLEL: *He wanted to rent an apartment, to drive a new car, and to travel around the country.* (*To rent, to drive,* and *to travel* are all infinitives.)

10 Writing Complete Sentences

Remember, a sentence is a group of words that expresses a complete thought. In formal writing, try to avoid both sentence fragments and run-on sentences.

10.1 CORRECTING FRAGMENTS

A **sentence fragment** is a group of words that is only part of a sentence. It does not express a complete thought and may be confusing to a reader or listener. A sentence fragment may be lacking a subject, a predicate, or both.

FRAGMENT: *Waited for the boat to arrive.* (no subject)

CORRECTED: *We waited for the boat to arrive.*

FRAGMENT: *People of various races, ages, and creeds.* (no predicate)

CORRECTED: *People of various races, ages, and creeds gathered together.*

FRAGMENT: *Near the old cottage.* (neither subject nor predicate)

CORRECTED: *The burial ground is near the old cottage.*

In your writing, fragments may be a result of haste or incorrect punctuation. Sometimes fixing a fragment will be a matter of attaching it to a preceding or following sentence.

FRAGMENT: *We saw the two girls. Waiting for the bus to arrive.*

CORRECTED: *We saw the two girls waiting for the bus to arrive.*

10.2 CORRECTING RUN-ON SENTENCES

A **run-on sentence** is made up of two or more sentences written as though they were one. Some run-ons have no punctuation within them. Others may have only commas where conjunctions or stronger punctuation marks are necessary. Use your judgment in correcting run-on sentences, as you have choices. You can make a run-on two sentences if the thoughts are not closely connected. If the thoughts are closely related, you can keep the run-on as one sentence by adding a semicolon or a conjunction.

RUN-ON: *We found a place for the picnic by a small pond it was three miles from the village.*

MAKE TWO SENTENCES: *We found a place for the picnic by a small pond. It was three miles from the village.*

RUN-ON: *We found a place for the picnic by a small pond it was perfect.*

USE A SEMICOLON: *We found a place for the picnic by a small pond near the village; it was perfect.*

ADD A CONJUNCTION: *We found a place for the picnic by a small pond, and it was perfect.*

WATCH OUT! When you form compound sentences, make sure you use appropriate punctuation: use a comma before a coordinating conjunction, and use a semicolon when there is no coordinating conjunction. A very common mistake is to use a comma alone instead of a comma and a conjunction. This error is called a **comma splice.**

INCORRECT: *He finished the apprenticeship, he left the village.*

CORRECT: *He finished the apprenticeship, and he left the village.*

11 Subject-Verb Agreement

The subject and verb in a clause must agree in number. Agreement means that if the subject is singular, the verb is also singular, and if the subject is plural, the verb is also plural.

11.1 BASIC AGREEMENT

Fortunately, agreement between subjects and verbs in English is usually simple. Most verbs show the difference between singular and plural only in the third person of the present tense. In the present tense, the third-person plural form does not change, but the third-person singular form ends in *–s.*

Present-Tense Verb Forms	
Singular	**Plural**
I jog	we jog
you jog	you jog
she, he, it jogs	they jog

11.2 AGREEMENT WITH *BE*

The verb *be* presents special problems in agreement, because this verb does not follow the usual verb patterns.

Forms of *Be*			
Present Tense		**Past Tense**	
Singular	**Plural**	**Singular**	**Plural**
I am	we are	I was	we were
you are	you are	you were	you were
she, he, it is	they are	she, he, it was	they were

11.3 WORDS BETWEEN SUBJECT AND VERB

A verb agrees only with its subject. When words come between a subject and a verb, ignore them when considering proper agreement. Identify the subject, and make sure the verb agrees with it.

> EXAMPLES: *A story in the newspapers tells about the 1890s.*
>
> *Dad as well as Mom reads the paper daily*

11.4 AGREEMENT WITH COMPOUND SUBJECTS

Use plural verbs with most compound subjects joined by the word *and*.

> EXAMPLE: *My father and his friends play chess every day.*

To confirm that you need a plural verb, you could substitute the plural pronoun *they* for *my father and his friends*.

If a compound subject is thought of as a unit, use a singular verb. Test this by substituting the singular pronoun *it*.

> EXAMPLE: *Peanut butter and jelly [it] is my brother's favorite sandwich.*

Use a singular verb with a compound subject that is preceded by *each, every,* or *many a*.

> EXAMPLE: *Each novel and short story seems grounded in personal experience.*

When the parts of a compound subject are joined by *or, nor,* or the correlative conjunctions *either . . . or* or *neither . . . nor,* make the verb agree with the noun or pronoun nearest the verb.

> EXAMPLES:
> *Cookies or ice cream is my favorite dessert.*
>
> *Either Cheryl or her friends are being invited.*
>
> *Neither ice storms nor snow is predicted today.*

11.5 PERSONAL PRONOUNS AS SUBJECTS

When using a personal pronoun as a subject, make sure to match it with the correct form of the verb *be*. (See the chart in Section 11.2.) Note especially that the pronoun *you* takes the forms *are* and *were*, regardless of whether it is singular or plural.

WATCH OUT! *You is* and *you was* are nonstandard forms and should be avoided in writing and speaking. *We was* and *they was* are also forms to be avoided.

> INCORRECT: *You was helping me.*
>
> CORRECT: *You were helping me.*
>
> INCORRECT: *They was hoping for this.*
>
> CORRECT: *They were hoping for this.*

11.6 INDEFINITE PRONOUNS AS SUBJECTS

Some indefinite pronouns are always singular; some are always plural.

Singular Indefinite Pronouns			
another	either	neither	one
anybody	everbody	nobody	somebody
anyone	everyone	no one	someone
anything	everything	nothing	something
each	much		

EXAMPLES:

Each of the first-time writers *was given an award*.

Somebody in the bedroom upstairs *is sleeping*.

Plural Indefinite Pronouns			
both	few	many	several

EXAMPLES:

Many of the books in our library *are* not in circulation.
Few have been *returned* recently.

Still other indefinite pronouns may be either singular or plural, depending on the context.

Singular or Plural Indefinite Pronouns		
all	more	none
any	most	some

The number of the indefinite pronoun *any* or *none* often depends on the intended meaning.

EXAMPLES:

Any of these topics *has* potential for a good article. (any one topic)
Any of these topics *have* potential for good articles. (all of the many topics)

The indefinite pronouns *all*, *some*, *more*, *most*, and *none* are singular when they refer to quantities or parts of things. They are plural when they refer to numbers of individual things. Context will usually give you a clue.

EXAMPLES:

All of the flour *is* gone. (referring to a quantity)
All of the flowers *are* gone. (referring to individual items)

11.7 INVERTED SENTENCES

Problems in agreement often occur in inverted sentences beginning with *here* or *there*; in questions beginning with *how, when, why, where,* or *what*; and in inverted sentences beginning with phrases. Identify the subject—wherever it is— before deciding on the verb.

EXAMPLES:

There clearly *are* far too many *cooks* in this kitchen.

What *is* the correct *ingredient* for this stew?
Far from the embroiled cooks *stands* the *master chef*.

Practice and Apply

1. Most scholars (think, thinks) the author of *Le Morte d'Arthur* is Sir Thomas Malory.
2. (Is, Are) the author Syr Thomas Maleore, knight, the same as Sir Thomas Malory?
3. Sir Thomas himself, who lived during the Middle Ages, (was, were) a knight.
4. There (is, are) many knights and ladies in the tales of King Arthur.
5. One of the greatest prose works in the English language, *Le Morte d'Arthur* (was, were) based on French versions that were told earlier.
6. Many legends of King Arthur (was, were) also preserved in Wales.
7. Nearly everyone reading these tales (enjoy, enjoys) the adventures of the knights and ladies.
8. Several times Malory (was, were) put in prison.
9. He spent the last three years of his life in prison; he wrote *Le Morte d'Arthur* while he (was, were) there.
10. These tales featuring King Arthur (was, were) published after Malory's death.

11.8 SENTENCES WITH PREDICATE NOMINATIVES

When a predicate nominative serves as a complement in a sentence, use a verb that agrees with the subject, not the complement.

EXAMPLES:

The tales of King Arthur are a great work of literature. (*Tales* is the subject and it takes the plural verb *are*.)
A great work of literature is the tales of King Arthur. (The subject is the singular noun *work*.)

11.9 *DON'T* AND *DOESN'T* AS AUXILIARY VERBS

The auxiliary verb *doesn't* is used with singular subjects and with the personal pronouns *she, he,* and *it*. The auxiliary verb *don't* is used with plural subjects and with the personal pronouns *I, we, you,* and *they*.

SINGULAR:

She doesn't want to be without her cane.

Doesn't the school provide help?

PLURAL:

They don't know what it's like to be hungry.

Bees don't like these flowers by the door.

11.10 COLLECTIVE NOUNS AS SUBJECTS

Collective nouns are singular nouns that name groups of persons or things. *Team,* for example, is the collective name of a group of individuals. A collective noun takes a singular verb when the group acts as a single unit. It takes a plural verb when the members of the group act separately.

EXAMPLES:

Our team usually wins. (The team as a whole wins.)

Our team vote differently on most issues. (The individual members vote.)

11.11 RELATIVE PRONOUNS AS SUBJECTS

When the relative pronoun *who, which,* or *that* is used as a subject in an adjective clause, the verb in the clause must agree in number with the antecedent of the pronoun.

SINGULAR: *Have you selected **one** of the poems that **is** meaningful to you?*

The antecedent of the relative pronoun *that* is the singular *one;* therefore, *that* is singular and must take the singular verb *is.*

PLURAL: *The younger **redwoods, which grow** in a circle around an older tree, are also very tall.*

The antecedent of the relative pronoun *which* is the plural *redwoods.* Therefore, *which* is plural, and it takes the plural verb *grow.*

Vocabulary and Spelling

One key to becoming an independent reader is to develop a toolkit of vocabulary strategies. By learning and practicing the strategies, you'll know what to do when you encounter unfamiliar words while reading. You'll also know how to refine the words you use for different situations—personal, school, and work.

Good spelling is important for communicating your ideas in writing. Learning basic spelling rules and checking your spelling in a dictionary will help you spell words you may not use frequently.

1 Using Context Clues

A word's **context** includes the words, sentences, and paragraphs surrounding it. A word's context can give you important clues about its meaning and help you distinguish between its denotative and connotative meanings.

1.1 GENERAL CONTEXT

Sometimes you need to infer the meaning of an unfamiliar word by reading all the information in a passage.

On extremely hot days, Mariah languidly tends her garden. First she strolls to the yard to water her plants. Then she relaxes under a shady tree.

You can figure out from the context that *languidly* means "in a slow and unenergetic way."

1.2 SPECIFIC CONTEXT CLUES

Sometimes writers help you understand the meanings of words by providing specific clues of the kinds in the chart.

Specific Context Clues		
Type of Clue	**Key Words/Phrases**	**Example**
Definition or **restatement** of the meaning of the word	or, which is, that is, in other words, also known as, also called	A lichen is an example of *symbiosis*, **a relationship in which two species benefit from living closely together.**
Example following an unfamiliar word	such as, like, as if, for example, especially, including	*Prokaryotes*, which **include bacteria,** are among the oldest forms of animal life.
Comparison with a more familiar word or concept	like, also, similarly, in the same way, as, likewise	**Like** his **practical-joker** brother, Abe was a *prankster*.
Contrast with a familiar word or experience	unlike, but, however, although, on the other hand, on the contrary	Most organisms **need oxygen to survive, but** many types of bacteria are *anaerobic*.
Cause-and-effect relationship in which one term is familiar	because, since, when, consequently, as a result, therefore	**Because** they have a system of *membranes*, fish can use their **skin and gill tissue** to adjust to different conditions.

1.3 IDIOMS, SLANG, AND FIGURATIVE LANGUAGE

An **idiom** is an expression whose overall meaning is different from the meaning of the individual words. **Slang** is informal language in which made-up words and ordinary words are used to mean something different from their meanings in formal English. **Figurative language** is language that communicates meaning beyond the literal meaning of words. Use context clues to figure out the meanings of idioms, slang, and figurative language.

> *Trying to find the ring was like looking for a needle in a haystack.* (idiom; conveys idea of "difficulty")
> *When Brenda couldn't find her ring right away, she went ballistic.* (slang; means "became angry")
> *Mr. Gray has had the same car for over 20 years. Now it is just a rusty tin can.* (figurative language; rusty tin can symbolizes the age and condition of the car)

2 Analyzing Word Structure

Many words can be broken into smaller parts. These word parts include base words, roots, prefixes, and suffixes.

2.1 BASE WORDS

A **base word** is a word part that by itself is also a word. Other words or word parts can be added to base words to form new words.

2.2 ROOTS

A **root** is a word part that contains the core meaning of the word. Many English words contain roots that come from older languages such as Greek, Latin, Old English (Anglo-Saxon), and Norse. Knowing the meaning of the word's root can help you determine the word's meaning.

Root	Meaning	Example
anthrop (Greek)	human being	anthropology
hydr (Greek)	water	dehydrate
quer, quest (Latin)	ask, seek	question
pend, pens (Latin)	hang	pendulum
hēadfod (Old English)	head, top	headfirst

2.3 PREFIXES

A **prefix** is a word part attached to the beginning of a word. Most prefixes come from Greek, Latin, or Old English.

Prefix	Meaning	Example
anti–	opposed to	antisocial
de–	down, away from	degrade
sub–	under	submarine

2.4 SUFFIXES

A **suffix** is a word part that appears at the end of a root or base word to form a new word. Some suffixes do not change word meaning. These suffixes are

- added to nouns to change the number of persons or objects
- added to verbs to change the tense
- added to modifiers to change the degree of comparison

Suffixes	Meaning	Example
–s, –es	to change the number of a noun	trunk + s = trunks
–d, –ed, –ing	to change verb tense	sprinkle + d = sprinkled
–er, –est	to change the degree of comparison in modifiers	cold + er = colder icy + est = iciest

Other suffixes can be added to a root or base to change the word's meaning. These suffixes can also determine a word's part of speech.

Suffix	Meaning	Example
–ic	characterized by	sarcastic
–ion	process of	capitalization
–ness	condition of	uneasiness

Strategies for Understanding Unfamiliar Words

- Look for any prefixes or suffixes. Remove them to isolate the base word or the root.
- See if you recognize any elements— prefix, suffix, root, or base —of the word. You may be able to guess its meaning by analyzing one or two elements.
- Consider the way the word is used in the sentence. Use the context and the word parts to make a logical guess about the word's meaning.
- Consult a dictionary to see whether you are correct.

3 Understanding Word Origins

3.1 ETYMOLOGIES

Etymologies show the origin and historical development of a word. When you study a word's history and origin, you can find out when, where, and how the word came to be.

co•ma (kō´mə) *n., pl.* **-mas** A state of deep, often prolonged unconsciousness, usually the result of injury, disease, or poison, in which an individual is incapable of sensing or responding to external stimuli and internal needs. [Greek *kōma*, deep sleep.]

gar•lic (gär´lĭk) *n.* **1.** An onionlike plant of southern Europe having a bulb that breaks into separate cloves with a strong distinctive odor and flavor. **2.** The bulb of this plant. [Middle English, from Old English *gārlēac: gār*, spear + *lēac*, leek.]

vin•dic•tive (vĭn-dĭk´tĭv) *adj.*
1. Disposed to seek revenge; revengeful.
2. Marked by or resulting from a desire to hurt; spiteful. (From Latin *vindicta*, vengeance, from *vindex, vindic-*, surety, avenger.]

3.2 WORD FAMILIES

Words that have the same root make up a word family and have related meanings. The chart shows a common Greek and a common Latin root. Notice how the meanings of the example words are related to the meanings of their roots.

Latin Root	*spect:* "see"
English	**inspect** look at carefully **respect** look at with esteem **spectator** someone who watches an event

Greek Root	*phil:* "love"
English	**philharmonic** devoted to music **philosophy** love and pursuit of wisdom **philanthropy** love of humankind

3.3 WORDS FROM CLASSICAL MYTHOLOGY

The English language includes many words from classical mythology. You can use your knowledge of Greek, Roman, and Norse myths to understand the origins and meanings of these words. For example, *herculean task* refers to the mythological hero Hercules. Thus *herculean task* probably means "a job that is large or difficult." The chart shows a few common words from mythology.

Greek	Roman	Norse
nemesis	insomnia	Thursday
atlas	fury	berserk
Adonis	Saturday	rune
mentor	January	valkyrie

Look up the etymology of each word in the chart and locate the myth associated with it. Use the information from the myth to explain the origin and meaning of each word.

3.4 FOREIGN WORDS

The English language includes words from diverse languages such as French, Dutch, Spanish, Italian, and Chinese. Many of these words retained their original spellings from the source language.

French	Dutch	Spanish	Italian
mirage	cookie	tornado	studio
vague	snoop	bronco	ravioli
beau	hook	salsa	opera

4 Synonyms and Antonyms

4.1 SYNONYMS

A **synonym** is a word with a meaning similar to that of another word. You can find synonyms in a thesaurus or a dictionary. In a dictionary, synonyms are often given as part of the definition of a word. These word pairs are synonyms:

dry/arid   enthralled/fascinated
gaunt/thin   vigorous/strong

4.2 ANTONYMS

An **antonym** is a word with a meaning opposite that of another word. The following word pairs are antonyms:

friend/enemy   absurd/logical
courteous/rude   languid/energetic

5 Denotation and Connotation

5.1 DENOTATION

A word's dictionary meaning is called its **denotation**. For example, the denotation of the word *rascal* is "an unethical, dishonest person."

5.2 CONNOTATION

The images or feelings you connect to a word add a finer shade of meaning, called **connotation.** The connation of a word goes beyond its basic dictionary definition. Writers use connotations of words to communicate positive or negative feelings.

Positive	Neutral	Negative
save	store	hoard
fragrance	smell	stench
display	show	flaunt

Make sure you understand the denotation and connotation of a word when you read it or use it in your writing.

6 Analogies

An **analogy** is a comparison between two things that are similar in some way or share a clear relationship. Analogies are sometimes used in writing when unfamiliar subjects or ideas are explained in terms of familiar ones. Analogies often appear on tests as well, usually in a format like this:

TERRIER : DOG ::   A) rat : fish
                   B) kitten : cat
                   C) trout : fish
                   D) fish : trout
                   E) poodle : collie

Follow these steps to determine the correct answer:

- Read the part in capital letters as "terrier is to dog as. . . . "
- Read the answer choices as "rat is to fish," "kitten is to cat," and so on.
- Ask yourself how the words *terrier* and *dog* are related. (A terrier is a type of dog.)
- Ask yourself which of the choices shows the same relationship. (A kitten is a young cat, but not a specific breed of cat. Therefore, the answer is C.)

7 Homonyms and Homophones

7.1 HOMONYMS

Homonyms are words that have the same spelling but have different origins and meanings.

> I don't want to bore you with a story about how I had to bore through the living room wall.

Bore can mean "to cause a person to lose interest," but an identically spelled word means "to drill a hole."

> My dog likes to bark while it scratches the bark on the tree in the backyard.

Bark can mean "to make the sound of a dog." However, another identically spelled word means "the outer covering of a tree." Each word has a different meaning and its own dictionary entry.

Sometimes only one of the meanings of a homonym may be familiar to you. Use context clues to help you figure out the meaning of an unfamiliar word.

7.2 HOMOPHONES

Homophones are words that sound alike but have different meanings and spellings. The following homophones are frequently misused:

it's/its	they're/their/there
to/too/two	stationary/stationery

Many misused homophones are pronouns and contractions. Whenever you are unsure whether to write *your* or *you're* and *who's* or *whose*, ask yourself whether you mean *you are* and *who is/has*. If you do, write the contraction. For other homophones, such as *scent* and *sent,* use the meaning of the word to help you decide which one to use.

8 Words with Multiple Meanings

Over time, some words have acquired additional meanings that are based on the original meaning.

EXAMPLES: *I was in a hurry, so I jammed my clothes into the suitcase. Unfortunately, I jammed my finger in the process.*

These two uses of *jam* have different meanings, but they have the same origin. You will find all the meanings of this word listed in one entry in the dictionary.

9 Specialized Vocabulary

Specialized vocabulary is special terms suited to a particular field, or domain, of study or work. For example, science, mathematics, and history all have their own domain-specific technical or specialized vocabularies. To figure out specialized terms, you can use context clues and reference sources, such as dictionaries on specific subjects, atlases, or manuals.

10 Using Reference Sources

10.1 DICTIONARIES

A **general dictionary** will tell you not only a word's definitions but also its pronunciation, parts of speech, and history and origin. A **specialized dictionary** focuses on terms related to a particular field of study or work. Use a dictionary to check the spelling of any word you are unsure of in your English class and other classes as well.

10.2 THESAURI

A **thesaurus** is a dictionary of synonyms. A thesaurus can be especially helpful when you find yourself using the same modifiers over and over again.

10.3 SYNONYM FINDERS

A **synonym finder** is often included in wordprocessing software. It enables you to highlight a word and be shown a display of its synonyms.

10.4 GLOSSARIES

A **glossary** is a list of specialized terms and their definitions. It is often found in the back of a book and sometimes includes pronunciations. Many textbooks contain glossaries. In fact, this textbook has three glossaries: the **Glossary of Literary and Informational Terms**, the **Glossary of Academic Vocabulary**, and the **Glossary of Critical Vocabulary**. Use these glossaries to help you understand how terms are used in this textbook.

11 Spelling Rules

11.1 WORDS ENDING IN A SILENT E

Before adding a suffix beginning with a vowel or *y* to a word ending in a silent *e*, drop the *e* (with some exceptions).

> amaze + -ing = amazing
> love + -able = lovable
> create + -ed = created
> nerve + -ous = nervous

Sample exceptions: *change + -able = changeable; courage + -ous = courageous*

When adding a suffix beginning with a consonant to a word ending in a silent **e**, keep the **e** (with some exceptions).

> late + -ly = lately
> spite + -ful = spiteful
> noise + -less = noiseless
> state + -ment = statement

Sample exceptions: *truly, ninth, wholly, awful*

When a suffix beginning with *a* or *o* is added to a word with a final silent *e*, the final *e* is usually retained if it is preceded by a soft *c* or a soft *g*.

> bridge + -able = bridgeable
> peace + -able = peaceable
> outrage + -ous = outrageous
> advantage + -ous = advantageous

When a suffix beginning with a vowel is added to words ending in *ee* or *oe*, the final, silent *e* is retained.

> agree + -ing = agreeing free + -ing = freeing
> shoe + -ing = shoeing   see + -ing = seeing

11.2 WORDS ENDING IN Y

Before adding most suffixes to a word that ends in *y* preceded by a consonant, change the *y* to *i*.

> easy + -est = easiest
> crazy + -est = craziest
> silly + -ness = silliness
> marry + -age = marriage

Sample exceptions: *dryness, shyness, slyness.*

However, when you add *-ing*, the *y* does not change.

> empty + -ed = emptied but
> empty + -ing = emptying

When you add a suffix to a word that ends in *y* preceded by a vowel, the *y* usually does not change.

> play + -er = player
> employ + -ed = employed
> coy + -ness = coyness
> pay + -able = payable

11.3 WORDS ENDING IN A CONSONANT

In one-syllable words that end in one consonant preceded by one short vowel, double the final consonant before adding a suffix beginning with a vowel, such as *–ed* or *–ing*. These are sometimes called 1+1+1 words.

> dip + -ed = dipped   set + -ing = setting
> slim + -est = slimmest   fit + -er = fitter

The rule does not apply to words of one syllable that end in a consonant preceded by two vowels.

> feel + -ing = feeling   peel + -ed = peeled
> reap + -ed = reaped   loot + -ed = looted

In words of more than one syllable, double the final consonant when the accent is on the last syllable. The accent remains on the same syllable once the suffix is added, as in the following examples:

be•gin´ + -ing = be•gin´ ning = beginning

per•mit´ + -ed = per•mit´ ted = permitted

In some words with more than one syllable, though the accent remains on the same syllable when a suffix is added, the final consonant is nevertheless not doubled, as in the following examples:

tra´vel + er = tra´vel•er = traveler

mar´ket + er = mar´ket•er = marketer

In the following examples the accent does not remain on the same syllable; thus the final consonant is not doubled.

re•fer´ + -ence = ref´er•ence = reference

con•fer´ + -ence = con´fer•ence = conference

11.4 PREFIXES AND SUFFIXES

When adding a prefix to a word, do not change the spelling of the base word. When a prefix creates a double letter, keep both letters.

dis- + approve = disapprove

re- + build = rebuild

ir- + regular = irregular

mis- + spell = misspell

anti- + trust = antitrust

il- + logical = illogical

When adding –ly to a word ending in l, keep both l's. When adding –ness to a word ending in n, keep both n's.

careful + -ly = carefully

sudden + -ness = suddenness

final + -ly = finally

thin + -ness = thinness

11.5 FORMING PLURAL NOUNS

To form the plural of most nouns, just add –s.

prizes   dreams   circles   stations

For most singular nouns ending in o, add –s.

solos.   halos   studios   photos   pianos

For a few nouns ending in o, add –es.

heroes   tomatoes   potatoes   echoes

When the singular noun ends in s, sh, ch, x, or z, add –es.

waitresses   brushes   ditches   axes   buzzes

When a singular noun ends in y with a consonant before it, change the y to i and add –es.

army—armies   candy—candies

baby—babies   diary—diaries

ferry—ferries   conspiracy—conspiracies

When a vowel (a, e, i, o, u) comes before the y, just add –s.

boy—boys   way—ways

array—arrays   alloy—alloys

weekday—weekdays   jockey—jockeys

For most nouns ending in f or fe, change the f to v and add –es or –s.

life—lives   calf—calves   knife—knives

thief—thieves shelf—shelves loaf—loaves

However, for some nouns ending in f, add –s to make the plural.

roofs   chiefs   reefs   beliefs

Some nouns have the same form for both singular and plural.

deer   sheep   moose   salmon   trout

For some nouns, the plural is formed in a special way.

man—men   goose—geese

ox—oxen   woman—women

mouse—mice   child—children

For a compound noun written as one word, form the plural by changing the last word in the compound to its plural form.

stepchild—stepchildren   firefly—fireflies

If a compound noun is written as a hyphenated word or as two separate words, change the most important word to the plural form.

brother-in-law—brothers-in-law

life jacket—life jackets

11.6 FORMING POSSESSIVES

If a noun is singular, add 's.

mother—my mother's car

Ross—Ross's desk

Exception: The s after the apostrophe is dropped after *Jesus', Moses',* and certain names in classical mythology *(Zeus').* These possessive forms can thus be pronounced easily.

If a noun is plural and ends with s, just add an apostrophe.

parents—my parents' car

the Santinis—the Santinis' house

If a noun is plural but does not end in s, add 's.

people—the people's choice

women—the women's coats

11.7 SPECIAL SPELLING PROBLEMS

Only one English word ends in *–sede: supersede.* Three words end in *–ceed: exceed, proceed,* and *succeed.* All other verbs ending in the sound "seed" (except for the verb *seed*) are spelled with *–cede.*

concede   precede   recede   secede

In words with *ie* or *ei,* when the sound is long *e* (as in *she*), the word is spelled *ie* except after *c* (with some exceptions).

i before *e*	thief	relieve	field
	piece	grieve	pier
except after *c*	conceit	perceive	ceiling
	receive	receipt	
Exceptions:	either	neither	weird
	leisure	seize	

12 Commonly Confused Words

Words	Definitions	Examples
accept/except	The verb *accept* means "to receive or believe"; *except* is usually a preposition meaning "excluding."	**Except** for some of the more extraordinary events, I can **accept** that the *Odyssey* recounts a real journey.
advice/advise	*Advise* is a verb; *advice* is a noun naming that which an *adviser* gives.	I **advise** you to take that job. Whom should I ask for **advice**?
affect/effect	As a verb, *affect* means "to influence." *Effect* as a verb means "to cause." If you want a noun, you will almost always want *effect*.	Did Circe's wine **affect** Odysseus' mind? It did **effect** a change in Odysseus' men. In fact, it had an **effect** on everyone else who drank it.
all ready/already	*All ready* is an adjective meaning "fully ready." *Already* is an adverb meaning "before or by this time."	He was **all ready** to go at noon. I have **already** seen that movie.
allusion/illusion	An *allusion* is an indirect reference to something. An *illusion* is a false picture or idea.	There are many **allusions** to the works of Homer in English literature. The world's apparent flatness is an **illusion**.
among/between	*Between* is used when you are speaking of only two things. *Among* is used for three or more.	**Between** *Hamlet* and *King Lear*, I prefer the latter. Emily Dickinson is **among** my favorite poets.
bring/take	*Bring* is used to denote motion toward a speaker or place. *Take* is used to denote motion away from such a person or place.	**Bring** the books over here, and I will **take** them to the library.

Words	Definitions	Examples
fewer/less	*Fewer* refers to the number of separate, countable units. *Less* refers to bulk quantity.	We have **less** literature and **fewer** selections in this year's curriculum.
leave/let	*Leave* means "to allow something to remain behind." *Let* means "to permit."	The librarian will **leave** some books on display but will not **let** us borrow any.
lie/lay	*Lie* means "to rest or recline." It does not take an object. *Lay* always takes an object.	Rover loves to **lie** in the sun. We always **lay** some bones next to him.
loose/lose	*Loose* (lo͞os) means "free, not restrained"; *lose* (lo͞oz) means "to misplace or fail to find."	Who turned the horses **loose**? I hope we won't **lose** any of them.
precede/proceed	*Precede* means "to go or come before." Use *proceed* for other meanings.	Emily Dickinson's poetry **precedes** that of Alice Walker. You may **proceed** to the next section of the test.
than/then	Use *than* in making comparisons; use *then* on all other occasions.	Who can say whether Amy Lowell is a better poet **than** Denise Levertov? I will read Lowell first, and **then** I will read Levertov.
their/there/they're	*Their* means "belonging to them." *There* means "in that place." *They're* is the contraction for "they are."	**There** is a movie playing at 9 p.m. **They're** going to see it with me. Sakara and Jessica drove away in **their** car after the movie.
two/too/to	*Two* is the number. *Too* is an adverb meaning "also" or "very." Use *to* before a verb or as a preposition.	Meg had **to** go **to** town, **too**. We had **too** much reading **to** do. **Two** chapters is **too** many.

Glossary of Literary and Informational Terms

Act An act is a major division within a play, similar to a chapter in a book. Each act may be further divided into smaller sections, called scenes. Plays can have as many as five acts, or as few as one.

Allegory An allegory is a work with two levels of meaning—a literal one and a symbolic one. In such a work, most of the characters, objects, settings, and events represent abstract qualities. Personification is often used in traditional allegories. As in a fable or a parable, the purpose of an allegory may be to convey truths about life, to teach religious or moral lessons, or to criticize social institutions.

Alliteration Alliteration is the repetition of consonant sounds at the beginning of words. Note the repetition of the *d* sound in this line: The <u>d</u>aredevil <u>d</u>ove into the <u>d</u>eep sea.

See also Consonance.

Allusion An allusion is an indirect reference to a famous person, place, event, or literary work.

Almanac *See* Reference Works.

Analogy An analogy is a point-by-point comparison between two things that are alike in some respect. Often, writers use analogies in nonfiction to explain unfamiliar subjects or ideas in terms of familiar ones.

See also Extended Metaphor; Metaphor; Simile.

Antagonist An antagonist is a principal character or force in opposition to a **protagonist**, or main character. The antagonist is usually another character but sometimes can be a force of nature, a set of circumstances, some aspect of society, or a force within the protagonist.

Archetype An archetype is a pattern in literature that is found in a variety of works from different cultures throughout the ages. An archetype can be a plot, a character, an image, or a setting. For example, the association of death and rebirth with winter and spring is an archetype common to many cultures.

Argument An argument is speech or writing that presents a claim about an issue or problem and supports it with reasons and evidence. An argument often takes into account other points of view, anticipating and answering objections that opponents of the position might raise.

See also Claim; Counterargument; Evidence.

Argumentative Essay *See* Essay.

Aside In drama, an aside is a short speech directed to the audience, or another character, that is not heard by the other characters on stage.

See also Soliloquy.

Assonance Assonance is the repetition of vowel sounds within nonrhyming words. An example of assonance is the repetition of the *u* sound in the following line: I made my <u>u</u>sual man<u>eu</u>ver on my snowboard.

Assumption An assumption is an opinion or belief that is taken for granted. It can be about a specific situation, a person, or the world in general. Assumptions are often unstated.

Author's Message An author's message is the main idea or theme of a particular work.

See also Main Idea; Theme

Author's Perspective An author's perspective, or point of view, is a unique combination of ideas, values, feelings, and beliefs that influences the way the writer looks at a topic. **Tone**, or attitude, often reveals an author's perspective.

See also Author's Purpose; Tone.

Author's Position An author's position is his or her opinion on an issue or topic.

See also Claim.

Author's Purpose A writer usually writes for one or more of these purposes: to express thoughts or feelings, to inform or explain, to persuade, to entertain.

See also Author's Perspective.

Autobiography An autobiography is a writer's account of his or her own life. In almost every case, it is told from the first-person point of view. Generally, an autobiography focuses on the most significant events and people in the writer's life over a period of time. Shorter autobiographical narratives include **journals, diaries,** and **letters.** An **autobiographical essay**, another type of short autobiographical work, focuses on a single person or event in the writer's life.

See also Memoir.

Ballad A ballad is a type of narrative poem that tells a story and was originally meant to be sung or recited. Because it tells a story, a ballad has a setting, a plot, and characters. **Traditional ballads** are written in four-line stanzas with regular rhythm and rhyme. **Folk ballads** were composed orally and handed down by word of mouth. These ballads usually tell about ordinary people who have unusual adventures or perform daring deeds. A **literary ballad** is a poem written by a poet in imitation of the form and content of a folk ballad.

Bias Bias is an inclination toward a particular judgment on a topic or issue. A writer often reveals a strongly positive or strongly negative opinion by presenting only one way of looking at an issue or by heavily weighting the evidence. Words with intensely positive or negative connotations are often a signal of a writer's bias.

Bibliography A bibliography is a list of books and other materials related to the topic of a text. Bibliographies can be good sources of works for further study on a subject.

See also Works Consulted.

Biography A biography is the true account of a person's life, written by another person. As such, a biography is usually told from a third-person point of view. The writer of a biography usually researches his or her subject in order to present accurate information. The best biographers strive for honesty and balance in their accounts of their subjects' lives.

Blank Verse Blank verse is unrhymed poetry written in **iambic pentameter.** That is, each line of blank verse has five pairs of syllables. In most pairs, an unstressed syllable is followed by a stressed syllable. The most versatile of poetic forms, blank verse imitates the natural rhythms of English speech. Much of Shakespeare's drama is in blank verse.

See also Iambic Pentameter.

Business Correspondence Business correspondence includes all written business communications, such as business letters, e-mails, and memos. In general, business correspondence is brief, to the point, clear, courteous, and professional.

Cast of Characters In the script of a play, a cast of characters is a list of all the characters in the play, usually in order of appearance. It may include a brief description of each character.

Cause and Effect A cause is an event or action that directly results in another event or action. An effect is the direct or logical outcome of an event or action. Basic **cause-and-effect relationships** include a single cause with a single effect, one cause with multiple effects, multiple causes with a single effect, and a chain of causes and effects. The concept of cause and effect also provides a way of organizing a piece of writing. It helps a writer show the relationships between events or ideas.

Central Idea *See* Main Idea; Theme.

Character Characters are the individuals who participate in the action of a literary work. Like real people, characters display certain qualities, or **character traits;** they develop and change over time; and they usually have **motivations,** or reasons, for their behaviors. Complex characters can have multiple or conflicting motivations.

Main characters: Main characters are the most important characters in literary works. Generally, the plot of a short story focuses on one main character, but a novel may have several main characters.

Minor characters: The less prominent characters in a literary work are known as minor characters. Minor characters support the plot. The story is not centered on them, but they help carry out the action of the story and help the reader learn more about the main character.

Dynamic character: A dynamic character is one who undergoes important changes as a plot unfolds. The changes occur because of his or her actions and experiences in the story. The change is usually internal and may be good or bad. Main characters are usually, though not always, dynamic.

Static character: A static character is one who remains the same throughout a story. The character may experience events and have interactions with other characters, but he or she is not changed because of them.

Round character: A round character is one who is complex and highly developed, having a variety of traits and different sides to his or her personality. Some of the traits may create conflict in the character. Round characters tend to display strengths, weaknesses, and a full range of emotions. The writer provides enough detail for the reader to understand their feelings and emotions.

Flat character: A flat character is one who is not highly developed. A flat character is one-sided: he or she usually has one outstanding trait, characteristic, or role. Flat characters exist mainly to advance the plot, and they display only the traits needed for their limited roles. Minor characters are usually flat characters.

See also Characterization.

Characterization The way a writer creates and develops characters' personalities is known as characterization. There are four basic methods of characterization:

- The writer may make direct comments about a character's personality or nature through the voice of the narrator.
- The writer may describe the character's physical appearance.
- The writer may present the character's own thoughts, speech, and actions.
- The writer may present thoughts, speech, and actions of other characters in response to a character.

See also Character.

Chorus In early Greek tragedy, the chorus commented on the actions of the characters in a drama. In some Elizabethan plays, such as Shakespeare's *Romeo and Juliet,* the role of the chorus is taken by a single actor who serves as a narrator and speaks the lines in the **prologue** (and sometimes in an **epilogue**). The chorus serves to foreshadow or summarize events.

Chronological Order Chronological order is the arrangement of events in their order of occurrence. This type of organization is used in both fictional narratives and in historical writing, biography, and autobiography.

Citation Writers of reports and arguments that include quotations or research information document their sources using a citation method such as footnotes or endnotes.

See also Works Cited.

Claim In an argument, a claim is the writer's position on an issue or problem. Although an argument focuses on supporting one claim, a writer may make more than one claim in a work.

See also Argument; Thesis Statement.

Clarify Clarifying is a reading strategy that helps a reader to understand or make clear what he or she is reading. Readers usually clarify by rereading, reading aloud, or discussing.

Classification Classification is a pattern of organization in which objects, ideas, or information is presented in groups, or classes, based on common characteristics.

Cliché A cliché is an overused expression. "Better late than never" and "hard as nails" are common examples. Good writers generally avoid clichés unless they are using them in dialogue to indicate something about characters' personalities.

Climax In a plot, the climax is the point of maximum interest or tension. Usually the climax is a turning point in the story, which occurs after the reader has understood the **conflict** and become emotionally involved with the characters. The climax sometimes, but not always, points to the **resolution** of the conflict.

See also Plot.

Comedy A comedy is a dramatic work that is light and often humorous in tone, usually ending happily with a peaceful resolution of the main conflict. A comedy differs from a farce by having a more believable plot, more realistic characters, and less boisterous behavior.

Comic Relief Comic relief consists of humorous scenes, incidents, or speeches that are included in a serious drama to provide a reduction in emotional intensity. Because comic relief breaks the tension, it allows an audience to prepare emotionally for events to come. Shakespeare often uses this device in his tragedies.

Compare and Contrast To compare and contrast is to identify similarities and differences in two or more subjects. Compare-and-contrast organization can be used to structure a piece of writing, serving as a framework for analyzing the similarities and differences in two or more subjects.

Complex Character *See* Character.

Complication A complication is an additional factor or problem introduced into the rising action of a story to make the conflict more difficult. Often, a plot complication makes it seem as though the main character is getting farther away from the thing he or she wants.

Conclusion A conclusion is a statement of belief based on evidence, experience, and reasoning. A **valid conclusion** is a conclusion that logically follows from the facts or statements upon which it is based. A **deductive conclusion** is one that follows from a particular generalization or premise. An **inductive conclusion** is a broad conclusion or generalization that is reached by arguing from specific facts and examples.

Conflict A conflict is a struggle between opposing forces. Almost every story has a main conflict—a conflict that is the story's focus. An **external conflict** involves a character pitted against an outside force, such as nature, a physical obstacle, or another character. An **internal conflict** is one that occurs within a character.

See also Plot.

Connect Connecting is a reader's process of relating the content of a text to his or her own knowledge and experience.

Connotation A connotation is an attitude or a feeling associated with a word, in contrast to the word's **denotation,** which is its literal, or dictionary, meaning. The connotations of a word may be positive or negative. For example, *enthusiastic* has positive associations, while *rowdy* has negative ones. Connotations of words can have an important influence on style and meaning and are particularly important in poetry.

Consonance Consonance is the repetition of consonant sounds within and at the end of words, as in "lonely afternoon." Consonance is unlike rhyme in that the vowel sounds preceding or following the repeated consonant sounds differ. Consonance is often used together with **alliteration, assonance,** and **rhyme** to create a musical quality, to emphasize certain words, or to unify a poem.

See also Alliteration.

Consumer Documents Consumer documents are printed materials that accompany products and services. They are intended for the buyers or users of the products or services and usually provide information about use, care, operation, or assembly. Some common consumer documents are applications, contracts, warranties, manuals, instructions, package inserts, labels, brochures, and schedules.

Context Clues When you encounter an unfamiliar word, you can often use context clues as aids for understanding. Context clues are the words and phrases surrounding the word that provide hints about the word's meaning.

Controlling Idea *See* Main Idea.

Counterargument A counterargument is an argument made to answer an opposing argument, or **counterclaim.** A good argument anticipates opposing viewpoints and provides counterarguments to refute (disprove) or answer them.

Counterclaim *See* Counterargument.

Couplet A couplet is a rhymed pair of lines. A couplet may be written in any rhythmic pattern, for example:

> Follow your heart's desire
> And good things may transpire.

See also Stanza.

Credibility Credibility refers to the believability or trustworthiness of a source and the information it contains.

Critical Essay *See* Essay.

Critical Review A critical review is an evaluation or critique by a reviewer or critic. Different types of reviews include film reviews, book reviews, music reviews, and art-show reviews.

Critique *See* Critical Review.

Database A database is a collection of information that can be quickly and easily accessed and searched and from which information can be easily retrieved. It is frequently presented in an electronic format.

Debate A debate is basically an argument— but a very structured one that requires a good deal of preparation. In academic settings, debate usually refers to a formal argumentation contest in which two opposing teams defend and attack a proposition.

See also Argument.

Deductive Reasoning Deductive reasoning is a way of thinking that begins with a generalization, presents a specific situation, and then advances with facts and evidence to a logical conclusion. The following passage has a deductive argument embedded in it: "All students in the drama class must attend the play on Thursday. Since Ava is in the class, she had better show up." This deductive argument can be broken down as follows: generalization— all students in the drama class must attend the play on Thursday; specific situation—Ava is a student in the drama class; conclusion—Ava must attend the play.

Denotation *See* Connotation.

Dénouement *See* Falling Action.

Dialect A dialect is a form of language that is spoken in a particular geographic area or by a particular social or ethnic group. A group's dialect is reflected in its pronunciations, vocabulary, expressions, and grammatical structures. Writers use dialects to capture the flavors of locales and to bring characters to life, re-creating the way they actually speak.

Dialogue Dialogue is written conversation between two or more characters. Writers use dialogue to bring characters to life and to give readers insights into the characters' qualities, traits, and reactions to other characters. Realistic, well-paced dialogue also advances the plot of a narrative. In fiction, dialogue is usually set off with quotation marks. In drama, stories are told primarily through dialogue. Playwrights use stage directions to indicate how they intend the dialogue to be interpreted by actors.

Diary A diary is a daily record of a writer's thoughts, experiences, and feelings. As such, it is a type of autobiographical writing. The terms *diary* and *journal* are often used synonymously.

Diction A writer's or speaker's choice of words and way of arranging the words in sentences is called diction. Diction can be broadly characterized as formal or informal. It can also be described as technical or common, abstract or concrete, and literal or figurative. A writer for a science journal would use a more formal, more technical, and possibly more abstract diction than would a writer for the science section of a local newspaper.

See also Style.

Dictionary *See* Reference Works.

Domain-Specific Vocabulary Domain-specific vocabulary includes terms and expressions used in a particular field, or domain. For example, the terms in this glossary are from the domain of language arts.

Drama Drama is literature in which plots and characters are developed through dialogue and action; in other words, it is literature in play form. Drama is meant to be performed. Stage plays, radio plays, movies, and television programs are types of drama. Most plays are divided into acts, with each act having an emotional peak, or climax. Certain modern plays have only one act. Most plays contain stage directions, which describe settings, lighting, sound effects, the movements and emotions of actors, and the ways in which dialogue should be spoken.

Dramatic Irony *See* Irony.

Dramatic Monologue A dramatic monologue is a lyric poem in which a speaker addresses a silent or absent listener in a moment of high intensity or deep emotion, as if engaged in private conversation. The speaker proceeds without interruption or argument, and the effect on the reader is that of hearing just one side of a conversation. This technique allows the poet to focus on the feelings, personality, and motivations of the speaker.

See also Lyric Poetry; Soliloquy.

Draw Conclusions To draw a conclusion is to make a judgment or arrive at a belief based on evidence, experience, and reasoning.

Dynamic Character *See* Character.

Editorial An editorial is an opinion piece that usually appears on the editorial page of a newspaper or as part of a news broadcast. The editorial section of a newspaper presents opinions rather than objective news reports.

See also Op-Ed Piece.

Either/Or Fallacy An either/or fallacy is a statement that suggests there are only two possible ways to view a situation or only two options to choose from. In doing so, it falsely frames a dilemma, giving the impression that no options exist but the two presented—for example, "Either we stop the construction of a new airport, or the surrounding suburbs will become ghost towns."

Elegy An elegy is an extended meditative poem in which the speaker reflects on death—often in tribute to a person who has died recently—or on an equally serious subject. Most elegies are written in formal, dignified language and are serious in tone.

Emotional Appeals Emotional appeals are messages that persuade by evoking strong feelings—such as fear, pity, or vanity—instead of using facts and evidence. An **appeal to fear** is a message that taps into people's fear of losing their safety or security. An **appeal to pity** taps into people's sympathy and compassion for others to build support for an idea, cause, or proposed action. An **appeal to vanity** attempts to persuade by tapping into people's desire to feel good about themselves.

Encyclopedia *See* Reference Works.

Epic An epic is a long narrative poem on a serious subject, presented in an elevated or formal style. It traces the adventures of a great hero whose actions reflect the ideals and values of a nation or race. Epics address universal concerns, such as good and evil, life and death, and sin and redemption. The *Odyssey* is an epic.

Epic Hero An epic hero is a larger-than-life figure who embodies the ideals of a nation or race. Epic heroes take part in dangerous adventures and accomplish great deeds. Many undertake long, difficult journeys and display great courage and superhuman strength.

Epic Simile An epic simile (also called a Homeric simile) is a long, elaborate comparison that often continues for a number of lines. Homer uses epic similes in the *Odyssey*.

See also Simile.

Epilogue An epilogue is a short addition at the end of a literary work, often dealing with the future of the characters. The concluding speech by Prince Escalus in *Romeo and Juliet* serves as an epilogue.

Epithet An epithet is a brief phrase that points out traits associated with a particular person or thing. In the *Odyssey*, Odysseus is often called "the master strategist."

Essay An essay is a short work of nonfiction that deals with a single subject. Some essays are **formal**—that is, tightly structured and written in an impersonal style. Others are **informal**, with a looser structure and a more personal style. Generally, an **informative** or **expository essay** presents or explains information and ideas. A **personal essay** is typically an informal essay in which the writer expresses his or her thoughts and feelings about a subject, focusing on the meaning of events and issues in his or her own life. In a **reflective essay**, the author makes a connection between a personal observation or experience and a universal idea, such as love, courage, or freedom. A **critical essay** evaluates a situation, a course of action, or a work of art. In an **argumentative** or **persuasive essay**, the author attempts to convince readers to adopt a certain viewpoint or to take a particular stand.

Evaluate To evaluate is to examine something carefully and judge its value or worth. Evaluating is an important skill for gaining insight into what you read. A reader can evaluate the actions of a particular character, for example, or can form an opinion about the value of an entire work.

Evidence Evidence is the specific pieces of information that support a claim. Evidence can take the form of facts, quotations, examples, statistics, or personal experiences, among others.

Exposition Exposition is the first stage of a plot in a typical story. The exposition provides important background information and introduces the setting and the important characters. The conflict the characters face may also be introduced in the exposition, or it may be introduced later, in the rising action.

See also Plot.

Expository Essay *See* Essay.

Extended Metaphor An extended metaphor is a figure of speech that compares two essentially unlike things at some length and in several ways. It does not contain the word *like* or *as*.

See also Metaphor.

External Conflict *See* Conflict.

Fable A fable is a brief tale told to illustrate a moral or teach a lesson. Often the moral of a fable appears in a distinct and memorable statement near the tale's beginning or end.

See also Moral.

Fact versus Opinion A fact is a statement that can be proved or verified. An opinion, on the other hand, is a statement that cannot be proved because it expresses a person's beliefs, feelings, or thoughts.

See also Inference; Generalization.

Fallacy A fallacy is an error in reasoning. Typically, a fallacy is based on an incorrect inference or a misuse of evidence. Some common logical fallacies are circular reasoning, either/or fallacy, oversimplification, overgeneralization, and stereotyping.

See also Either/Or Fallacy, Logical Appeal, Overgeneralization.

Falling Action In a plot, the falling action follows the climax and shows the results of the important action that happened at the climax. Tension eases as the falling action begins; however, the final outcome of the story is not yet fully worked out at this stage. Events in the falling action lead to the **resolution**, or **dénouement**, of the plot.

See also Climax; Plot.

Fantasy Fantasy is a type of fiction that is highly imaginative and portrays events, settings, or characters that are unrealistic. The setting might be a nonexistent world, the plot might involve magic or the supernatural, and the characters might employ superhuman powers.

Farce Farce is a type of exaggerated comedy that features an absurd plot, ridiculous situations, and humorous dialogue. The main purpose of a farce is to keep an audience laughing. The characters are usually stereotypes, or simplified examples of individual traits or qualities. Comic devices typically used in farces include mistaken identity, deception, physical comedy, wordplay—such as puns and double meanings—and exaggeration.

Faulty Reasoning *See* Fallacy.

Feature Article A feature article is a main article in a newspaper or a cover story in a magazine. A feature article is focused more on entertaining than informing. Features are lighter or more general than hard news and tend to be about human interest or lifestyles.

Fiction Fiction is prose writing that consists of imaginary elements. Although fiction can be inspired by actual events and real people, it usually springs from writers' imaginations. The basic elements of fiction are plot, character, setting, and theme. The novel and short story are forms of fiction.

See also Character; Novel; Plot; Setting; Short Story; Theme.

Figurative Language Figurative language is language that communicates meanings beyond the literal meanings of words. In figurative language, words are often used to symbolize ideas and concepts they would not otherwise be associated with. Writers use figurative language to create effects, emphasize ideas, and evoke emotions. Simile, metaphor, extended metaphor, hyperbole, and personification are examples of figurative language.

See also Hyperbole; Metaphor; Personification; Simile.

Figure of Speech *See* Figurative Language; Hyperbole; Metaphor; Personification; Simile; Understatement.

First-Person Point of View *See* Point of View.

Flashback A flashback is an account of a conversation, an episode, or an event that happened before the beginning of a story. Often, a flashback interrupts the chronological flow of a story to give the reader information needed to understand a character's present situation. Flashbacks also help create such effects as mystery, tension, or surprise.

Foil A foil is a character who provides a striking contrast to another character. By using a foil, a writer can call attention to certain traits possessed by a main character or simply enhance a character by contrast. In Shakespeare's *Romeo and Juliet*, Mercutio serves as a foil to Romeo.

Foreshadowing Foreshadowing is a writer's use of hints or clues to suggest events that will occur later in a story. The hints and clues might be included in a character's dialogue or behavior, or they might be included in details of description. Foreshadowing creates suspense, mystery, and surprise, and makes readers eager to find out what will happen.

Form Form refers to principles of arrangement in a poem—the ways in which lines are organized. Form in poetry includes the length of lines, the placement of lines, and the grouping of lines into stanzas.

See also Stanza.

Frame Story A frame story exists when a story is told within a narrative setting, or "frame"; it creates a story within a story. This storytelling technique has been used for over one thousand years and was employed in famous works such as *One Thousand and One Arabian Nights* and Geoffrey Chaucer's *The Canterbury Tales*.

Free Verse Free verse is poetry that does not contain regular patterns of rhythm or rhyme. The lines in free verse often flow more naturally than do rhymed, metrical lines and thus achieve a rhythm more like that of everyday speech. Although free verse lacks conventional meter, it may contain various rhythmic and sound effects, such as repetitions of syllables or words. Free verse can be used for a variety of subjects.

See also Meter; Rhyme.

Functional Documents *See* Consumer Documents; Public Documents; Workplace Documents.

Generalization A generalization is a broad statement about a class or category of people, ideas, or things, based on a study of only some of its members.

See also Overgeneralization.

Genre The term *genre* refers to a category in which a work of literature is classified. The major genres in literature are fiction, nonfiction, poetry, and drama.

Government Publications Government publications are documents produced by government organizations. Pamphlets, brochures, and reports are just some of the many forms these publications may take. Government publications can be reliable resources for a wide variety of topics.

Graphic Aid A graphic aid is a text feature that is printed, handwritten, or drawn. Charts, diagrams, graphs, photographs, maps, and captions can all be graphic aids.

Graphic Organizer A graphic organizer is a "word picture"—a visual illustration of a verbal statement—that helps a reader understand a text. Charts, tables, webs, and diagrams can all be graphic organizers. Graphic organizers and graphic aids can look the same. For example, a table in a science article will not be constructed differently from a table used as a graphic organizer. However, graphic organizers and graphic aids do differ in how they are used. Graphic aids are the visual representations that people encounter when they read informational texts. Graphic organizers are visuals that people construct to help them understand texts or organize information.

Haiku Haiku is a form of Japanese poetry in which 17 syllables are arranged in three lines of 5, 7, and 5 syllables each. The rules of haiku are strict. In addition to the syllabic count, the poet must create a clear picture that will evoke a strong emotional response in the reader. Nature is a particularly important source of inspiration for Japanese haiku poets, and details from nature are often the subjects of their poems.

Hero A hero is a main character or protagonist in a story. In older literary works, heroes tend to be better than ordinary humans. They are typically courageous, strong, honorable, and intelligent. They are protectors of society who hold back the forces of evil and fight to make the world a better place. In modern literature, a hero may simply be the most important character in a story. Such a hero is often an ordinary person with ordinary problems.

Historical Documents Historical documents are writings that have played a significant role in human events or are themselves records of such events. The Declaration of Independence, for example, is a historical document.

Historical Fiction A short story or novel can be classified as historical fiction when the settings and details of the plot include real places and real events of historical importance. Historical figures may appear as major or minor characters. In historical fiction, the setting generally influences the plot in important ways.

Horror Fiction Horror fiction contains strange, mysterious, violent, and often supernatural events that create suspense and terror in the reader. Edgar Allan Poe and Stephen King are famous authors of horror fiction.

How-To Writing A how-to book or article is written to explain how to do something— usually an activity, a sport, or a household project.

Humor In literature, there are three basic types of humor, all of which may involve exaggeration or irony. **Humor of situation** arises out of the plot of a work. It usually involves exaggerated events or situational irony, which arises when something happens that is different from what was expected. **Humor of character** is often based on exaggerated personalities or on

characters' failure to recognize their own flaws, a form of dramatic irony. **Humor of language** may include sarcasm, exaggeration, puns, or verbal irony, in which what is said is not what is meant.

See also Irony.

Hyperbole Hyperbole is a figure of speech in which the truth is exaggerated for emphasis or humorous effect.

Iambic Pentameter Iambic pentameter is a metrical pattern of five feet, or units, each of which is made up of two syllables, the first unstressed and the second stressed. Iambic pentameter is the most common meter used in English poetry; it is the meter used in blank verse and in the sonnet. Shakespeare used iambic pentameter in his plays.

See also Blank Verse; Sonnet.

Idiom An idiom is a common figure of speech whose meaning is different from the literal meaning of its words. For example, the phrase "raining cats and dogs" does not literally mean that cats and dogs are falling from the sky; the expression means "raining heavily."

Imagery Imagery consists of descriptive words and phrases that re-create sensory experiences for the reader. Imagery usually appeals to one or more of the five senses— sight, hearing, smell, taste, and touch—to help the reader imagine exactly what is being described.

Implied Controlling Idea An implied controlling idea is one that is suggested by details rather than stated explicitly.

See also Main Idea.

Implied Main Idea *See* Main Idea.

Index The index of a book is an alphabetized list of important topics and details covered in the book and the page numbers on which they can be found. An index can be used to quickly find specific information about a topic.

Inductive Reasoning Inductive reasoning is the process of logically reasoning from specific observations, examples, and facts to arrive at a general conclusion or principle.

Inference An inference is a logical assumption that is based on observed facts and one's own knowledge and experience.

Informational Nonfiction Informational nonfiction is writing that provides factual information. It often explains ideas or teaches processes. Examples include news reports, science textbooks, software instructions, and lab reports.

Informative Essay *See* Essay.

Internal Conflict *See* Conflict.

Internet The Internet is a global, interconnected system of computer networks that allows for communication through e-mail, listservers, and the World Wide Web. The Internet connects computers and computer users throughout the world.

Interview An interview is a conversation conducted by a writer or reporter in which facts or statements are elicited from another person, recorded, and then broadcast or published.

Irony Irony is a special kind of contrast between appearance and reality—usually one in which reality is the opposite of what it seems. One type of irony is **situational irony,** a contrast between what a reader or character expects and what actually exists or happens. Another type of irony is **dramatic irony,** in which the reader or viewer knows something that a character does not know. **Verbal irony** exists when someone knowingly exaggerates or says one thing and means another.

Journal A journal is a periodical publication issued by a legal, medical, or other professional organization. Alternatively, the term may be used to refer to a diary or daily record.

See also Diary.

Legend A legend is a story handed down from the past, especially one that is popularly believed to be based on historical events. Though legends often incorporate supernatural or magical elements, they claim to be the story of a real human being and are often set in a particular time and place. These characteristics separate a legend from a myth.

See also Myth.

Limited Point of View *See* Point of View.

Line The line is the core unit of a poem. In poetry, line length is an essential element of the poem's meaning and rhythm. **Line breaks,** where a line of poetry ends, may coincide with grammatical units. However, a line break may also occur in the middle of a grammatical or syntactical unit, creating a meaningful pause or emphasis. Poets use a variety of line breaks to manipulate sense, grammar, and syntax and thereby create a wide range of effects.

Literary Criticism *See* Text Criticism.

Literary Nonfiction Literary nonfiction is nonfiction that is recognized as being of artistic value or that is about literature. Autobiographies, biographies, essays, and eloquent speeches typically fall into this category.

Loaded Language Loaded language consists of words with strongly positive or negative connotations intended to influence a reader's or listener's attitude.

Logical Appeal A logical appeal relies on logic and facts, appealing to people's reasoning or intellect rather than to their values or emotions. Flawed logical appeals—that is, errors in reasoning—are considered logical fallacies.

See also Fallacy.

Logical Argument A logical argument is an argument in which the logical relationship between the support and the claim is sound.

Lyric Poetry A lyric poem is a short poem in which a single speaker expresses personal thoughts and feelings. Most poems other than dramatic and narrative poems are lyric poems. In ancient Greece, lyric poetry was meant to be sung. Modern lyrics are usually not intended for singing, but they are characterized by strong melodic rhythms. Lyric poetry has a variety of forms and covers many subjects, from love and death to everyday experiences.

Magical Realism Magical realism is a literary genre that combines fantastic or magical events with realistic occurrences in a matter-of-fact way to delight or surprise the reader. A famous example of magical realism is Gabriel García Márquez's novel *One Hundred Years of Solitude*.

Main Idea A main idea, or controlling idea, is the most important idea or impression about a topic that a writer or speaker conveys. It can be the central idea of an entire work or of just a paragraph. Often, the main idea of a paragraph is expressed in a topic sentence. However, a main idea may just be implied, or suggested, by details. A main idea and supporting details can serve as a basic pattern of organization in a piece of writing, with the central idea about a topic being supported by details.

Make Inferences *See* Inference.

Memoir A memoir is a form of autobiographical writing in which a writer shares his or her personal experiences and observations of significant events or people. Often informal or even intimate in tone, memoirs usually give readers insight into the impact of historical events on people's lives.

See also Autobiography.

Metaphor A metaphor is a figure of speech that makes a comparison between two things that are basically unlike but have something in common. Unlike similes, metaphors do not contain the word *like* or *as*.

See also Extended Metaphor; Figurative Language; Simile.

Meter Meter is a regular pattern of stressed and unstressed syllables in a poem. The meter of a poem emphasizes the musical quality of the language. Each unit of meter, known as a **foot**, consists of one stressed syllable and one or two unstressed syllables. In representations of meter, a stressed syllable is indicated by the symbol ´; an unstressed syllable, by the symbol ˘. The four basic types of metrical feet are the **iamb**, an unstressed syllable followed by a stressed syllable (˘ ´); the **trochee**, a stressed syllable followed by an unstressed syllable (´ ˘); the **anapest**, two unstressed syllables followed by a stressed syllable (˘ ˘ ´); and the **dactyl**, a stressed syllable followed by two unstressed syllables (´ ˘ ˘).

See also Rhythm.

Mise en Scène *Mise en scène* is a term from the French that refers to the various physical aspects of a dramatic presentation, such as lighting, costumes, scenery, makeup, and props.

Monitor Monitoring is the strategy of checking your comprehension as you are reading and modifying the strategies you are using to suit your needs. Monitoring may include some or all of the following strategies: questioning, clarifying, visualizing, predicting, connecting, and rereading.

Mood In a literary work, mood is the feeling or atmosphere that a writer creates for the reader. Descriptive words, imagery, and figurative language contribute to the mood of a work, as do the sound and rhythm of the language used.

See also Tone.

Moral A moral is a lesson taught in a literary work, such as a fable. For example, the moral "Do not count your chickens before they are hatched" teaches that one should not count on one's fortunes or blessings until they appear.

See also Fable.

Motivation *See* Character.

Myth A myth is a traditional story, usually concerning some superhuman being or unlikely event, that was once widely believed to be true. Frequently, myths were attempts to explain natural phenomena, such as solar and lunar eclipses or the cycle of the seasons. For some peoples, myths were both a kind of science and a religion. In addition, myths served as literature and entertainment, just as they do for modern-day audiences.

Greek mythology forms much of the background in Homer's *Odyssey*. For example, the myth of the judgment of Paris describes events that led to the Trojan War. The goddesses Athena, Hera, and Aphrodite asked a mortal—Paris—to decide which of them was the most beautiful. Paris chose Aphrodite and was rewarded by her with Helen, wife of the Greek king Menelaus.

Narrative Nonfiction Narrative nonfiction is writing that reads much like fiction, except that the characters, setting, and plot are real rather than imaginary. Its purpose is usually to entertain or to express opinions or feelings. Narrative nonfiction includes, but is not limited to, autobiographies, biographies, memoirs, diaries, and journals.

Narrative Poetry Narrative poetry tells a story or recounts events. Like a short story or a novel, a narrative poem has the following elements: plot, characters, setting, and theme.

Narrator The narrator of a story is the character or voice that relates the story's events to the reader.

See also Persona; Point of View.

News Article A news article is a piece of writing that reports on a recent event. In newspapers, news articles are usually written concisely and report the latest news, presenting the most important facts first and then more detailed information. In magazines, news articles are usually more elaborate than those in newspapers because they are written to provide both information and analysis. Also, news articles in magazines do not necessarily present the most important facts first.

Nonfiction Nonfiction is writing that tells about real people, places, and events. Unlike fiction, nonfiction is mainly written to convey factual information, although writers of nonfiction shape information in accordance with their own purposes and attitudes. Nonfiction can be a good source of information, but readers frequently have to examine it carefully in order to detect biases, notice gaps in the information provided, and identify errors in logic. Nonfiction includes a diverse range of writing—newspaper articles, letters, essays, biographies, movie reviews, speeches, true-life adventure stories, advertising, and more.

Novel A novel is an extended work of fiction. Like a short story, a novel is essentially the product of a writer's imagination. Because a novel is considerably longer than a short story, a novelist can develop a wider range of characters and a more complex plot.

Novella A novella is a work of fiction that is longer than a short story but shorter than a novel. A novella differs from a novel in that it concentrates on a limited cast of characters, a relatively short time span, and a single chain of events. The novella is an attempt to combine the compression of the short story with the development of the novel.

Ode An ode is a complex lyric poem that develops a serious and dignified theme. Odes appeal to both the imagination and the intellect, and many commemorate events or praise people or elements of nature.

Omniscient Point of View *See* Point of View.

Onomatopoeia Onomatopoeia is the use of words whose sounds echo their meanings, such as *buzz, whisper, gargle,* and *murmur.* Onomatopoeia as a literary technique goes beyond the use of simple echoic words, however. Skilled writers, especially poets, choose words whose sounds intensify images and suggest meanings.

Op-Ed Piece An op-ed piece is an opinion piece that usually appears opposite ("op") the editorial page of a newspaper. Unlike editorials, op-ed pieces are written and submitted by named writers.

Organization *See* Pattern of Organization.

Overgeneralization An overgeneralization is a generalization that is too broad. You can often recognize overgeneralizations by the appearance of words and phrases such as *all, everyone, every time, any, anything, no one,* and *none.* Consider, for example, this statement: "None of the sanitation workers in our city really care about keeping the environment clean." In all probability, there are many exceptions; the writer can't possibly know the feelings of every sanitation worker in the city.

Overview An overview is a short summary of a story, a speech, or an essay. It orients the reader by providing a preview of the text to come.

Oxymoron An oxymoron is a special kind of concise paradox that brings together two contradictory terms. "Deafening silence" and "original copy" are examples of oxymorons.

Paradox A paradox is a seemingly contradictory or absurd statement that may nonetheless suggest an important truth.

Parallelism Parallelism is the use of similar grammatical constructions to express ideas that are related or equal in importance. Martin Luther King Jr. uses parallelism in his "Letter from Birmingham Jail."

Parallel Plot   A parallel plot is a narrative structure in which two stories of equal importance are told simultaneously. The story moves back and forth between the two plots.

Paraphrase   Paraphrasing is the restating of information in one's own words.

See also Summarize.

Parody   A parody is an imitation of another work, a genre, or a writer's style, usually for the purpose of poking fun. It may serve as an element of a larger work or be a complete work in itself. The purpose of parody may be to ridicule through broad humor, using such techniques as exaggeration or inappropriate subject matter. Such techniques may even provide insights into the original work.

Pastoral   A pastoral is a poem presenting shepherds in rural settings, usually in an idealized way. The language and form of a pastoral tends to be formal. English Renaissance poets used the pastoral to convey emotions and ideas, particularly about love.

Pattern of Organization   A pattern of organization is an arrangement of ideas and information. Such a pattern may organize an entire composition or a section of a longer work. The most common patterns of organization are: cause-and-effect, chronological, compare-and-contrast, classification, deductive, inductive, order of importance, problem-solution, sequential, and spatial.

See also Cause and Effect; Chronological Order; Classification; Compare and Contrast; Problem-Solution Order; Sequential Order.

Periodical   A periodical is a publication that is issued at regular intervals of more than one day. For example, a periodical may be a weekly, monthly, or quarterly journal or magazine. Newspapers and other daily publications generally are not classified as periodicals.

Persona   A persona is a voice that a writer assumes in a particular work. A persona is like a mask worn by the writer, separating his or her identity from that of the speaker or the narrator. It is the persona's voice—not the writer's— that narrates a story or speaks in a poem.

See also Narrator; Speaker.

Personal Essay   *See* Essay.

Personification   Personification is a figure of speech in which human qualities are given to an object, animal, or idea, for example: The night wind sings an eerie song.

See also Figurative Language.

Persuasion   Persuasion is the art of swaying others' feelings, beliefs, or actions. Persuasion normally appeals to both the intellect and the emotions of readers. **Persuasive techniques** are the methods used to influence others to adopt certain opinions or beliefs or to act in certain ways. Types of persuasive techniques include emotional appeals, logical appeals, and loaded language. When used properly, persuasive techniques can add depth to writing that's meant to persuade. Persuasive techniques can, however, be misused to cloud factual information, disguise poor reasoning, or unfairly exploit people's emotions in order to shape their opinions.

See also Emotional Appeals; Loaded Language; Logical Appeal.

Persuasive Essay   *See* Essay.

Play   *See* Drama.

Plot   The sequence of events in a story is called the plot. A plot focuses on a central **conflict** or problem faced by the main character. The actions that the characters take to resolve the conflict build toward a climax. In general, it is not long after this point that the conflict is resolved and the story ends. A plot typically develops in five stages: exposition, rising action, climax, falling action, and resolution.

See also Climax; Exposition; Falling Action; Rising Action.

Poetry   Poetry is a type of literature in which words are carefully chosen and arranged to create certain effects. Poets use a variety of sound devices, imagery, and figurative language to express emotions and ideas.

See also Alliteration; Assonance; Ballad; Free Verse; Imagery; Meter; Rhyme; Rhythm; Stanza.

Point of View Point of view refers to the method of narration used in a short story, novel, narrative poem, or work of nonfiction. In a work told from a **first-person** point of view, the narrator is a character in the story. In a work told from a **third-person** point of view, the narrative voice is outside the action, not one of the characters. If a story is told from a **third-person omniscient,** or all-knowing, point of view, the narrator sees into the minds of all the characters. If events are related from a **third-person limited** point of view, the narrator tells what only one character thinks, feels, and observes.

See also Narrator.

Predict Predicting is a reading strategy that involves using text clues to make a reasonable guess about what will happen next in a story.

Primary Source *See* Sources.

Prior Knowledge Prior knowledge is the knowledge a reader already possesses about a topic. This information might come from personal experiences, expert accounts, books, films, or other sources.

Problem-Solution Order Problem-solution order is a pattern of organization in which a problem is stated and analyzed and then one or more solutions are proposed and examined. Writers use words and phrases such as *propose, conclude, reason for, problem, answer,* and *solution* to connect ideas and details when writing about problems and solutions.

Procedural Texts Procedural texts are functional texts that were created to communicate instructions, rules, processes, or other detailed, step-by-step information.

See also Consumer Documents; Public Documents; Workplace Documents.

Prologue A prologue is an introductory scene in a drama. Some Elizabethan plays include prologues that comment on the theme or moral point that will be revealed in the play. The prologue is a feature of all Greek drama.

Prop The word *prop*, originally an abbreviation of the word *property*, refers to any physical object that is used in a drama.

Propaganda Propaganda is a form of communication that may use distorted, false, or misleading information. It usually refers to manipulative political discourse.

Prose Generally, prose refers to all forms of written or spoken expression that are not in verse. The term, therefore, may be used to describe very different forms of writing—short stories as well as essays, for example.

Protagonist A protagonist is the main character in a work of literature—the character involved in the story's central conflict. Usually, the protagonist changes after the central conflict reaches a climax. He or she may be a hero and is usually the one with whom the audience tends to identify.

Public Documents Public documents are documents that were written for the public to provide information that is of public interest or concern. They include government documents, speeches, signs, and rules and regulations.

See also Government Publications.

Pun A pun is a joke that comes from a play on words. It can make use of a word's multiple meanings or of a word's sound.

Quatrain A quatrain is a four-line stanza, or group of lines, in poetry. The most common stanza in English poetry, the quatrain can have a variety of meters and rhyme schemes.

Realistic Fiction Realistic fiction is fiction that is a truthful imitation of ordinary life.

Recitation A recitation is an expressive oral presentation of a speech or work of literature, usually delivered from memory.

Recurring Theme *See* Theme.

Reference Works General reference works compile facts and background information on a wide range of subjects. More specific reference works contain in-depth information on a single subject. Reliable reference works have been reviewed by experts. Common reference works include: encyclopedias, college-level and high-school dictionaries, bilingual dictionaries, rhyming dictionaries, thesauri, almanacs, atlases, chronologies, biographical dictionaries, and directories.

Reflective Essay *See* Essay.

Refrain A refrain is one or more lines repeated in each stanza of a poem.

See also Stanza.

Repetition Repetition is a technique in which a sound, word, phrase, or line is repeated for emphasis or unity. Repetition often helps to reinforce meaning and create an appealing rhythm. The term includes specific devices associated with both prose and poetry, such as alliteration and parallelism.

See also Alliteration; Parallelism; Sound Devices.

Resolution *See* Falling Action.

Review *See* Critical Review.

Rhetorical Devices Rhetorical devices are techniques writers use to enhance their arguments and communicate more effectively. Rhetorical devices include analogy, parallelism, rhetorical questions, and repetition.

See also Analogy; Repetition; Rhetorical Questions.

Rhetorical Questions Rhetorical questions are those that do not require a reply. Writers use them to suggest that their arguments make the answer obvious or self-evident.

Rhyme Rhyme is the occurrence of similar or identical sounds at the end of two or more words, such as *suite, heat,* and *complete*. Rhyme that occurs within a single line of poetry is **internal rhyme.** Rhyme that occurs at the ends of lines of poetry is called **end rhyme.** End rhyme that is not exact but approximate is called **slant rhyme,** or **off rhyme.** Notice this slant rhyme using the words *care* and *dear:*

> You act like you don't care,
> But I know you do, my dear.

Rhyme Scheme A rhyme scheme is a pattern of end rhymes in a poem. A rhyme scheme is noted by assigning a letter of the alphabet, beginning with *a*, to each line. Lines that rhyme are given the same letter.

Rhythm Rhythm is a pattern of stressed and unstressed syllables in a line of poetry. Poets use rhythm to bring out the musical quality of language, to emphasize ideas, to create moods, to unify works, and to heighten emotional responses. Devices such as alliteration, rhyme, assonance, consonance, and parallelism often contribute to creating rhythm.

See also Meter.

Rising Action Rising action is the stage in a plot in which the conflict develops and story events build toward a climax. During this stage, complications arise that make the conflict more intense. Tension grows as the characters struggle to resolve the conflict.

See also Plot.

Romance A romance refers to any imaginative story concerned with noble heroes, chivalric codes of honor, passionate love, daring deeds, and supernatural events. Writers of romances tend to idealize their heroes as well as the eras in which the heroes live. Medieval romances include stories of kings, knights, and ladies who are motivated by love, religious faith, or simply a desire for adventure.

Sarcasm Sarcasm is a kind of particularly cutting irony. Generally, sarcasm is the taunting use of praise to mean its opposite—that is, to insult someone or something.

Satire Satire is a literary technique in which ideas, customs, behaviors, or institutions are ridiculed for the purpose of improving society. Satire may be gently witty, mildly abrasive, or bitterly critical, and it often involves the use of irony and exaggeration to force readers to see something in a critical light.

Scanning Scanning is the process of searching through writing for a particular fact or piece of information. When you scan, your eyes sweep across a page, looking for key words that may lead you to the information you want.

Scansion Scansion is the notation of stressed and unstressed syllables in poetry. A stressed syllable is indicated by the symbol ´; an unstressed syllable, by the symbol ˘. Using scansion can help you determine the rhythm and meter of a poem.

See also Meter.

Scene In drama, the action is often divided into acts and scenes. Each scene presents an episode of the play's plot and typically occurs at a single place and time.

See also Act.

Scenery Scenery is a painted backdrop or other structures used to create the setting for a play.

Science Fiction Science fiction is fiction in which a writer explores unexpected possibilities of the past or the future, using known scientific data and theories as well as his or her creative imagination. Most science fiction writers create believable worlds, although some create fantasy worlds that have familiar elements.

See also Fantasy.

Screenplay A screenplay is a play written for film.

See also Teleplay.

Script The text of a play, film, or broadcast is called a script.

Secondary Source *See* Sources.

Sensory Details Sensory details are words and phrases that appeal to the reader's senses of sight, hearing, touch, smell, and taste. For example, the sensory detail "a fine film of rain" appeals to the senses of sight and touch. Sensory details stimulate the reader to create images in his or her mind.

See also Imagery.

Sequential Order A pattern of organization that shows the order in which events or actions occur is called sequential order. Writers typically use this pattern of organization to explain steps or stages in a process.

Setting Setting is the time and place of the action of a story.

See also Fiction.

Setting a Purpose The process of establishing specific reasons for reading a text is called setting a purpose.

Short Story A short story is a work of fiction that centers on a single idea and can be read in one sitting. Generally, a short story has one main conflict that involves the characters, keeps the story moving, and stimulates readers' interest.

See also Fiction.

Sidebar A sidebar is additional information set in a box alongside or within a news or feature article. Popular magazines often make use of sidebar information.

Signal Words Signal words are words and phrases that indicate what is to come in a text. Readers can use signal words to discover a text's pattern of organization and to analyze the relationships among the ideas in the text.

Simile A simile is a figure of speech that makes a comparison between two unlike things, using the word *like* or *as*, for example:

Her blue-eyed stare was like ice.

See also Epic Simile; Figurative Language; Metaphor.

Situational Irony *See* Irony.

Soliloquy In drama, a soliloquy is a speech in which a character speaks his or her thoughts aloud. Generally, the character is on the stage alone, not speaking to other characters and perhaps not even consciously addressing an audience. At the beginning of Act One, Scene 7, of *Macbeth*, Macbeth considers his plans in a long soliloquy. Shakespeare makes use of soliloquies in many of his plays.

See also Aside; Dramatic Monologue.

Sonnet A sonnet is a lyric poem of 14 lines, commonly written in **iambic pentameter**. Sonnets are often classified as Petrarchan or Shakespearean. The Shakespearean, or Elizabethan, sonnet consists of three quatrains, or four-line units, and a final couplet. The typical rhyme scheme is *abab cdcd efef gg*.

See also Iambic Pentameter; Rhyme Scheme.

Sound Devices Sound devices, or uses of words for their auditory effect, can convey meaning and mood or unify a work. Some common sound devices are alliteration, assonance, consonance, meter, onomatopoeia, repetition, rhyme, and rhythm.

See also Alliteration; Assonance; Consonance; Meter; Onomatopoeia; Repetition; Rhyme; Rhythm.

Sources A source is anything that supplies information. **Primary sources** are materials written by people who were present at events, either as participants or as observers. Letters, diaries, autobiographies, speeches, and photographs are primary sources. **Secondary sources** are records of events that were created sometime after the events occurred; the writers were not directly involved or were not present when the events took place. Encyclopedias, textbooks, biographies, most newspaper and magazine articles, and books and articles that interpret or review research are secondary sources.

Spatial Order Spatial order is a pattern of organization that highlights the physical positions or relationships of details or objects. This pattern of organization is typically found in descriptive writing. Writers use words and phrases such as *on the left, to the right, here, over there, above, below, beyond, nearby,* and *in the distance* to indicate the arrangement of details.

Speaker In poetry the speaker is the voice that "talks" to the reader, similar to the narrator in fiction. The speaker is not necessarily the poet.

See also Persona.

Speech A speech is a talk or public address. The purpose of a speech may be to entertain, to explain, to present a claim, to inspire, or any combination of these aims. "I Have a Dream" by Martin Luther King Jr. was written and delivered in order to inspire an audience.

Stage Directions A play typically includes instructions called stage directions, which are usually printed in italic type. They serve as a guide to directors, set and lighting designers, performers, and readers. When stage directions appear within passages of dialogue, parentheses are usually used to set them off from the words spoken by characters.

Stanza A stanza is a group of two or more lines that form a unit in a poem. A stanza is comparable to a paragraph in prose. Each stanza may have the same number of lines, or the number of lines may vary.

See also Couplet; Form; Poetry; Quatrain.

Static Character *See* Character.

Stereotype In literature, a simplified or stock character who conforms to a fixed pattern or is defined by a single trait is known as a stereotype. Such a character does not usually demonstrate the complexity of a real person. Familiar stereotypes in popular literature include the absentminded professor and the busybody.

Stereotyping Stereotyping is a type of overgeneralization. Stereotypes are broad statements made about people on the basis of their gender, ethnicity, race, or political, social, professional, or religious group.

Stream of Consciousness Stream of consciousness is a literary technique developed by modern writers, in which thoughts, feelings, moods, perceptions, and memories are presented as they randomly flow through a character's mind.

Structure Structure is the way in which the parts of a work of literature are put together. In poetry, structure involves the arrangement of words and lines to produce a desired effect. A common structural unit in poetry is the stanza, of which there are numerous types. In prose, structure is the arrangement of larger units or parts of a work. Paragraphs, for example, are basic units in prose, as are chapters in novels and acts in plays. The structure of a poem, short story, novel, play, or nonfictional work usually emphasizes certain important aspects of content.

See also Act; Stanza.

Style Style is the particular way in which a work of literature is written—not *what* is said but *how* it is said. It is the writer's unique way of communicating ideas. Many elements contribute to style, including word choice, sentence structure and length, tone, figurative language, and point of view. A literary style may be described in a variety of ways, such as formal, informal, journalistic, conversational, wordy, ornate, poetic, or dynamic.

Summarize To summarize is to briefly retell, or encapsulate, the main ideas of a piece of writing in one's own words.

See also Paraphrase.

Support Support is any material that serves to prove a claim. In an argument, support typically consists of reasons and evidence. In persuasive texts and speeches, however, support may include appeals to the needs and values of the audience.

Supporting Detail *See* Main Idea.

Surprise Ending A surprise ending is an unexpected plot twist at the end of a story. The surprise may be a sudden turn in the action or a piece of information that gives a different perspective to the entire story.

Suspense Suspense is the excitement or tension that readers feel as they wait to find out how a story ends or a conflict is resolved. Writers create suspense by raising questions in readers' minds about what might happen next. The use of **foreshadowing** and **flashback** are two ways in which writers create suspense.

See also Foreshadowing; Flashback.

Symbol A symbol is a person, a place, an object, or an activity that stands for something beyond itself. For example, a flag is a colored piece of cloth that stands for a country. A white dove is a bird that represents peace.

Synthesize To synthesize information is to take individual pieces of information and combine them with other pieces of information and with prior knowledge or experience to gain a better understanding of a subject or to create a new product or idea.

Tall Tale A tall tale is a humorously exaggerated story about impossible events, often involving the supernatural abilities of the main character. Stories about folk heroes such as Pecos Bill and Paul Bunyan are typical tall tales.

Teleplay A teleplay is a play written for television. In a teleplay, scenes can change quickly and dramatically. The camera can focus the viewer's attention on specific actions. The camera directions in teleplays are much like the stage directions in stage plays.

Text Criticism Text criticism is writing in which literary works, including their various elements, are analyzed, interpreted, evaluated, or compared.

Text Features Text features are design elements that indicate the organizational structure of a text and help make the key ideas and supporting information understandable. Text features include headers, captions, boldface type, italic type, bulleted or numbered lists, sidebars, and graphic aids such as charts, tables, timelines, illustrations, and photographs.

Theme A theme, or central idea, is an underlying message about life or human nature that a writer wants the reader to understand. In most cases, themes are not stated directly but must be inferred. A theme may imply how a person should live but should not be confused with a **moral.**

Recurring themes are themes found in a variety of works. For example, authors from varying backgrounds might convey similar themes having to do with the importance of family values. **Universal themes** are themes that are found throughout the literature of all time periods. For example, the *Odyssey* contains a universal theme relating to the hero's search for truth, goodness, and honor.

See also Moral.

Thesaurus *See* Reference Works.

Thesis Statement In an argument, a thesis statement is an expression of the claim that the writer or speaker is trying to support. In an essay, a thesis statement is an expression, in one or two sentences, of the main idea or purpose of the piece of writing.

See also Claim.

Third-Person Point of View *See* Point of View.

Tone Tone is the attitude a writer takes toward a subject. Unlike mood, which is intended to shape the reader's emotional response, tone reflects the feelings of the writer. A writer communicates tone through choice of words and details. Tone may often be described by a single word, such as *serious, humorous, formal, informal, somber, sarcastic, playful, ironic, bitter,* or *objective*.

See also Author's Perspective; Mood.

Topic Sentence The topic sentence of a paragraph states the paragraph's central idea. All other sentences in the paragraph provide supporting details.

Tragedy A tragedy is a dramatic work that presents the downfall of a dignified character (**tragic hero**) or characters who are involved in historically or socially significant events. The events in a tragic plot are set in motion by a decision that is often an error in judgment (**tragic flaw**) on the part of the hero. Succeeding events are linked in a cause-and-effect relationship and lead inevitably to a disastrous conclusion, usually death. Shakespeare's *Macbeth* is a tragedy.

Tragic Flaw *See* Tragedy.

Tragic Hero *See* Tragedy.

Traits *See* Character.

Turning Point *See* Climax.

Understatement Understatement is a technique of creating emphasis by saying less than is actually or literally true. It is the opposite of **hyperbole**, or exaggeration. One of the primary devices of irony, understatement can be used to develop a humorous effect, to create satire, or to achieve a restrained tone.

See also Hyperbole; Irony.

Universal Theme *See* Theme.

Verbal Irony *See* Irony.

Visualize Visualizing is the process of forming a mental picture based on written or spoken information.

Voice Voice is a writer's unique use of language that allows a reader to "hear" a human personality in the writer's work. Elements of style that contribute to a writer's voice include sentence structure, diction, and tone. Voice can reveal much about the author's personality, beliefs, and attitudes.

Website A website is a collection of "pages" on the World Wide Web that is usually devoted to one specific subject. Pages are linked together and are accessed by clicking hyperlinks or menus, which send the user from page to page within the site. Websites are created by companies, organizations, educational institutions, branches of the government, the military, and individuals.

Word Choice *See* Diction.

Workplace Documents Workplace documents are materials that are produced or used within a work setting, usually to aid in the functioning of the workplace. They include job applications, office memos, training manuals, job descriptions, and sales reports. Many functional workplace documents include helpful text features, such as graphics, headers, and captions.

Works Cited A list of works cited lists names of all the works a writer has referred to in his or her text. This list often includes not only books and articles but also nonprint sources.

Works Consulted A list of works consulted names all the works a writer consulted in order to create his or her text. It is not limited just to those works cited in the text.

See also Bibliography.

Using the Glossaries

The following glossaries list the Academic Vocabulary and Critical Vocabulary words found in this book in alphabetical order. Use these glossaries just as you would a dictionary—to determine the meanings, parts of speech, pronunciation, and syllabication of words. (Some technical, foreign, and more obscure words in this book are not listed here but are defined for you in the footnotes that accompany many of the selections.)

Many words in the English language have more than one meaning. These glossaries give the meanings that apply to the words as they are used in this book. Words closely related in form and meaning are listed together in one entry (for instance, *consumption* and *consume*), and the definition is given for the first form.

The following abbreviations are used to identify parts of speech of words:

adj. adjective *adv.* adverb *n.* noun *v.* verb

Each word's pronunciation is given in parentheses. A guide to the pronunciation symbols appears in the Pronunciation Key below. The stress marks in the Pronunciation Key are used to indicate the force given to each syllable in a word. They can also help you determine where words are divided into syllables.

For more information about the words in these glossaries or for information about words not listed here, consult a dictionary.

Pronunciation Key

Symbol	Examples	Symbol	Examples	Symbol	Examples
ă	pat	m	mum	ûr	urge, term, firm, word, heard
ā	pay	n	no, sudden* (sud'n)	**Symbol**	**Examples**
ä	father	ng	thing	v	valve
âr	care	ŏ	pot	w	with
b	bib	ō	toe	y	yes
ch	church	ô	caught, paw	z	zebra, xylem
d	deed, milled	ôr	core	zh	vision, pleasure, garage
ĕ	pet	oi	noise	ə	about, item, edible, gallop, circus
ē	bee	o͝o	took		
f	fife, phase, rough	o͝or	lure	ər	butter
g	gag	o͞o	boot		
h	hat	ou	out		
hw	which	p	pop	**Sounds in Foreign Words**	
ĭ	pit	r	roar	KH	*German* ich, ach; *Scottish* loch
ī	pie, by	s	sauce	N (bôn)	*French,* bon fin
îr	pier	sh	ship, dish	œ	*French* feu, oeuf; *German* schön
j	judge	t	tight, stopped	ü	*French* tu; *German* über
k	kick, cat, pique	th	thin		
l	lid, needle* (nēd'l)	th	this		
		ŭ	cut		

* In English the consonants *l* and *n* often constitute complete syllables by themselves.

Stress Marks

The relevant emphasis with which the syllables of a word or phrase are spoken, called stress, is indicated in three different ways. The strongest, or primary, stress is marked with a bold mark ('). An intermediate, or secondary, level of stress is marked with a similar but lighter mark ('). The weakest stress is unmarked. Words of one syllable show no stress mark.

Glossary of Academic Vocabulary

abstract (ăb-străkt´) *adj.* apart from physical existence; theoretical rather than concrete.

advocate (ăd´və-kāt´) *v.* to argue for or plead in favor of.

comprehensive (kŏm´prĭ-hĕn´sĭv) *adj.* complete or of sufficient scope to include all aspects.

comprise (kəm-prīz´) *v.* to consist or be made up of.

differentiate (dĭf´ə-rĕn´shē-āt´) *v.* to distinguish or demonstrate the individual qualities of.

discrete (dĭ-skrēt´) *adj.* made up of separate or distinct things or parts.

discriminate (dĭ-skrĭm´ə-nāt´) *v.* to note clear differences; to separate into categories.

diverse (dĭ-vûrs´) *adj.* made up of elements that are different from each other.

domain (dō-mān´) *n.* a sphere of activity.

enhance (ĕn-hăns´) *v.* to make better, or add to the value or effectiveness.

equivalent (ĭ-kwĭv´ə-lənt) *adj.* equal to or similar.

evolve (ĭ-vŏlv´) *v.* to change or develop gradually over time.

explicit (ĭk-splĭs´ĭt) *adj.* clearly stated or expressed.

facilitate (fə-sĭl´ĭ-tāt´) *v.* to make something easier.

incentive (ĭn-sĕn´tĭv) *n.* an inducement or motivation to do something.

incidence (ĭn´sĭ-dəns) *n.* the occurrence or frequency of something.

incorporate (ĭn-kôr´pə-rāt´) *v.* to absorb or make part of a whole.

infer (ĭn-fûr´) *v.* to deduce from evidence or reason.

inhibit (ĭn-hĭb´ĭt) *v.* to hold back or prevent from acting.

innovate (ĭn´ə-vāt) *v.* to change or develop through new or original methods, processes, or ideas.

intervene (ĭn´ tər-vēn´) *v.* to come between two things, persons, or events.

media (mē´dē-ə) *n.* a means or vehicle for communication.

mode (mōd) *n.* a way or means for expressing or doing something.

orient (ôr´ē-ĕnt´) *v.* to place or align in relation to something else.

perspective (pər-spĕk´tĭv) *n.* a viewpoint from a particular position ; an outlook or standpoint.

priority (prī-ôr´ĭ-tē) *n.* something that is more important or considered more important than another thing.

rational (răsh´ə-nəl) *adj.* based on logic or sound reasoning.

scope (skōp) *n.* the size or extent of the activity or subject that is involved.

thesis (thē´sĭs) *n.* a statement or premise that is defended by an argument.

ultimate (ŭl´tə-mĭt) *adj.* concluding a process or progression; final.

Glossary of Critical Vocabulary

acuity (ə-kyōō′ ĭ-tē) *n.* critical perceptiveness; awareness.

admonition (ăd′mə-nĭsh′ən) *n.* a warning.

annul (ə-nŭl′) *v.* to render or declare invalid.

beleaguered (bĭ-lē′gərd) *adj.* troubled with many problems.

benefaction (bĕn′ə-făk′shən) *n.* a gift or assistance.

beneficent (bə-nĕf′ ĭ-sənt) *adj.* beneficial; producing good.

botanical (bə-tăn′ ĭ-kəl) *adj.* related to plants.

chaotically (kā-ŏt′ĭk-lē) *adv.* disorderedly and unpredictably.

clime (klīm) *n.* climate area.

cognizant (kŏg′nĭ-zənt) *adj.* aware or conscious of.

complacency (kəm-plā′sən-sē) *n.* contented self-satisfaction.

compulsion (kəm-pŭl′shən) *n.* forced obligation.

consecrate (kŏn′sĭ-krāt′) *v.* to make or define as sacred.

consensus (kən-sĕn′səs) *n.* agreement.

contemporary (kən-tĕm′pə-rĕr′ē) *n.* one living at the same time as.

contention (kən-tĕn′shən) *n.* an assertion put forward in argument.

cryptically (krĭp′tĭk-lē) *adv.* in a secretive or mysterious manner.

decisively (dĭ-sī′sĭv-lē) *adv.* in a firm and resolute manner.

defiantly (dĭ-fī′ənt-lē) *adv.* boldly, rebelliously.

denizen (dĕn′ ĭ-zən) *n.* a resident.

disseminate (dĭ-sĕm′ə-nāt′) *v.* to spread or circulate widely.

dissenter (dĭ-sĕn′tər) *n.* one who disagrees or refuses to accept.

divisive (dĭ-vī′sĭv) *adj.* causing division or disagreement.

dogma (dôg′mə) *n.* principles or beliefs that an authority insists are true.

enunciate (ĭ-nŭn′sē-āt′) *v.* to articulate or pronounce clearly.

ephemeral (ĭ-fĕm′ər-əl) *n.* a short-lived plant.

equidistant (ē′kwĭ-dĭs′tənt) *adj.* at equal distance from.

flagrantly (flā′grənt-lē) *adv.* in a blatantly or conspicuously offensive manner.

flail (flāl) *v.* to thrash or wave about wildly.

fluent (flōō′ənt) *adj.* able to express oneself clearly and easily.

havoc (hăv′ək) *n.* destructive disorder or chaos.

humility (hyōō-mĭl′ ĭ-tē) *n.* modesty; lack of superiority over others.

ideology (ī′dē-ŏl′ə-jē) *n.* a system of doctrines or beliefs.

impetus (ĭm′pĭ-təs) *n.* motivating force or incentive.

implicit (ĭm-plĭs′ ĭt) *adj.* understood, but not expressed.

incendiary (ĭn-sĕn′dē-ĕr′ē) *adj.* intended to cause fire; flammable.

iniquitous (ĭ-nĭk′wĭ-təs) *adj.* wicked, evil.

inversion (ĭn-vûr′zhən) *n.* reversal or upside-down placement.

loathe (lōth) *v.* to hate or despise.

lucid (lōō′sĭd) *adj.* thinking rationally and clearly.

manifest (măn′ə-fĕst′) *v.* to show or reveal.

moratorium (môr′ə-tôr′ē-əm) *n.* a temporary suspension or agreed-upon delay.

mores (môr′āz′) *n.* established customs and conventions.

obliterate (ə-blĭt′ə-rāt′) *v.* erase completely.

orthodoxy (ôr′thə-dŏk′sē) *n.* traditionally accepted codes and customs.

peremptory (pə-rĕmp'tə-rē) *adj.* imperative; required; not able to be denied.

perfunctory (pər-fŭngk'tə-rē) *adj.* done mechanically and without enthusiasm.

petulantly (pĕch'ə-lənt-lē) *adv.* in a grouchy or bad-tempered way.

phantasmagoric (făn-tăz'mə-gôr'ĭk) *adj.* dreamlike or surreal.

plaintively (plān'tĭv-lē) *adv.* sadly or wistfully.

poignant (poin'yənt) *adj.* emotionally moving or stimulating.

pollinate (pŏl'ə-nāt') *v.* to fertilize.

precarious (prĭ-kâr'ē-əs) *adj.* unsafe or insecure.

precipitate (prĭ-sĭp'ĭ-tāt') *v.* to cause something to happen rapidly or unexpectedly.

precipitous (prĭ-sĭp'ĭ-təs) *adj.* sudden and rapid.

predecessor (prĕd'ĭ-sĕs'ər) *n.* the person who held a position prior to the current holder.

profusely (prə-fyōōs'lē) *adv.* plentifully, in a freely available way.

prognosticate (prŏg-nŏs'tĭ-kāt') *v.* to forecast or predict.

propagate (prŏp'ə-gāt') *v.* to reproduce or extend in quantity.

propensity (prə-pĕn'sĭ-tē) *n.* a tendency to behave in a certain way.

provocation (prŏv'ə-kā'shən) *n.* an action intended to elicit an angered response.

proximity (prŏk-sĭm'ĭ-tē) *n.* nearness.

reaffirmation (rē'ăf-ər-mā'shən) *n.* the act of verifying or endorsing again.

reallocate (rē-ăl'ə-kāt') *v.* to distribute or apportion again; reassign.

repertoire (rĕp'ər-twär') *n.* a set of skills, abilities, or functions.

resilience (rĭ-zĭl'yəns) *n.* ability to return to a normal state after a change or an injury.

retaliate (rĭ-tăl'ē-āt') *v.* to respond in kind to having been acted upon, often with harmful intent.

sacrilegious (săk'rə-lĭj'əs) *adj.* grossly irreverent toward what is sacred.

sanctity (săngk'tĭ-tē) *n.* sacredness or ultimate importance.

sate (sāt) *v.* to fully feed or satisfy an appetite.

secluded (sĭ-klōō'dĭd) *adj.* hidden from view.

solace (sŏl'ĭs) *n.* source of relief and comfort.

stimuli (stĭm'yə-lī') *n.* things that cause a response or reaction.

subordinate (sə-bôr'dn-ĭt) *n.* a person of a lesser rank or under another's authority.

subtleties (sŭt'l-tēz) *n.* fine details or nuances.

transcend (trăn-sĕnd') *v.* to go beyond or rise above.

translucent (trăns-lōō'sənt) *adj.* semi-transparent; indistinct.

transpire (trăn-spīr') *v.* to happen or occur.

truncate (trŭng'kāt) *v.* to make shorter.

turbulence (tûr'byə-ləns) *n.* violent, disordered movement.

unadulterated (ŭn'ə-dŭl'tə-rā'tĭd) *adj.* pure and untainted.

unpalatable (ŭn-păl'ə-tə-bəl) *adj.* unpleasant or unacceptable.

usurp (yōō-sûrp') *v.* to take control of illegally.

vermin (vûr'mĭn) *n.* creatures that are considered destructive, annoying, or repulsive; pests.

vicarious (vī-kâr'ē-əs) *adj.* seen through the imagined interpretations of another.

wizened (wĭz'ənd) *adj.* shrunken and wrinkled.

Index of Skills

A

absolute phrases, 300, R42
abstract nouns, R23
academic language, 378
Academic Vocabulary, 2, 41, 45, 50, 83, 87, 92, 145, 149, 154, 193, 197, 202, 313, 318, 377. *See also* Glossary of Academic Vocabulary
accept/except, R57
act (in play), R59
action verbs, R24, R33
active voice, R35
activities
    media activity, 144
    speaking activity, 10, 14, 40, 82, 106, 126, 168, 192, 208, 244, 277, 294, 298, 312, 348, 360, 375
    writing activity, 17, 22, 36, 134, 139, 159, 181, 187, 231, 260, 291, 338, 357, 371
adjective clauses, 70, R43
adjective phrases, 128, R40
adjectives, R24, R35–R36
    vs. adverbs, R36
    comparatives, R36–R37
    predicate, R36
    proper, R29
    superlatives, R36–R37
adverbial clauses, 182, 199, R43–R44
adverbial phrases, 128, 199, R40
adverbs, R24, R36
    vs. adjectives, R36
    comparatives, R36–R37
    conjunctive, R42
    relative, 70
    superlatives, R36–R37
advice/advise, R57
A&E® (Arts and Entertainment), 171, 213
affect/effect, R57
affirmative side, in debates, R14
affixes. *See* prefixes; suffixes
allegory, R59
alliteration, R59
all ready/already, R57
allusion, 337, R59
allusion/illusion, R57
ambiguous references, R33
among/between, R57
analogies, R53, R59. *See also* metaphors; similes
    false, R20
analysis
    writing activity, 22, 68, 134, 181, 231, 260, 357

analytical essays
    draft of, 46, 314–315
    elements of effective, 45, 313
    exchanging with partner, 47, 315
    organization, 46, 314
    Performance Task Evaluation Rubric, 48, 316
    planning, 313–314
    reading aloud, 315
    revising, 47, 315
    writing, 22, 45–48, 134, 159, 181, 313–316, 338
analyzing
    arguments, 208, 337, R16–R17
    author's choices, 35, 75, 158, 180, 181
    author's claim, 67, 337
    characters, 290, 370
    characters' motivations, 9, 370
    claims, 67, 337, 356, 357
    development of ideas, 142–143
    evidence, 208, 356
    film, 13, 141, 142, 293
    ideas, 167, 187, 348
    images, 126, 192
    impact of word choice, 12, 21, 35, 56, 311
    media, 13, 14, 141, 144, 294, 360
    order, 14, 133, 143
    poetry, 40, 60, 82, 139, 159, 192, 312, 375
    point of view, 9, 14, 356, 360
    representations, 294
    representations in different mediums, 126, 192, 360
    rhetoric, to advance author's point of view, 67, 68, 208, 356
    seminal documents, 17, 337
    Shakespearean drama, 244, 260, 277
    Shakespearean references, 306
    source material, 298
    structure, 14, 75, 133, 143, 158, 180, 348
    text, 41, 45, 192, 313, 360
    theme, 10, 181, 290, 337, 370, 375
    tone, 12, 21, 35, 55, 60, 68, 180, 311, 375
Analyzing Text and Media, 360
Analyzing the Media, 14, 144, 294
Analyzing the Text, 10, 17, 22, 36, 40, 56, 60, 68, 76, 82, 88, 106, 126, 134, 139, 159, 168, 181, 187, 193, 208, 231, 244, 260, 277, 291, 298, 307, 312, 313, 338, 348, 357, 371, 375
anapest, R69

Annotate It!, 10, 17, 22, 36, 40, 56, 60, 68, 76, 82, 106, 126, 134, 139, 159, 168, 181, 187, 192, 208, 231, 244, 260, 277, 291, 298, 307, 312, 338, 348, 357, 371, 375
antagonist, R59
antecedent, R30
    pronoun agreement with, R30–R31
antonyms, R53
apostrophe, R27
appeals
    by association, R17
    bandwagon, R17
    emotional, R17, R64
    logical, R68
    to loyalty, R17
    to pity, fear, or vanity, R17, R20, R64
    to self-interest, 208
appositive phrases, R40
appositives, R40
archetypes, R59
argumentative essays, 149–152, R64. *See also* arguments
arguments, R59
    analyzing, 208, 337, 356, R16–17
    assessing validity of, 22, 67, 208, 356
    claims, 67, 337, 377, R2
    clarifying own view for, 149
    conclusions to, 150, 378–379, R3
    counterarguments, 337, R2, R16
    deductive, R18–R19
    delivering, 377–340
    draft of, 150, 378–379
    elements of effective, 149, 377
    evaluating, 22, 68, 208, 337, 356, 357, R20–R22
    evidence in, 17, 68, 208, 356
    examples, 61–66, 203–207, 319–336, 351–355, R22
    exchanging with partner, 151, 379
    false statements and fallacious reasoning in, 22, R19–R20
    gathering evidence for, 378
    inductive, R18
    linking ideas in, R3
    logical, R68
    logic and reasoning in, R17–R19
    organization for, 150, 378
    Performance Task Evaluation Rubric, 152, 380
    planning, 149–150, 377–378
    presenting, 151, 379
    publishing online, 151
    reading, R16–R22
    recognizing persuasive techniques, R17

formal tone, 12, 150, R3
fragments, sentence, R46
frame story, R66
free verse, R66
functional documents, 348
further/farther, R37
future perfect progressive tense, R34
future perfect tense, R34
future progressive tense, R34
future tense, R34
fyi, 2, 50, 154, 202, 318

G

general dictionary, R54
generalizations, R66
  glittering generalities, R17
  hasty, R20
  making, 42
  overgeneralization, R19, R70
general references, R33
genre, R66
gerund phrases, R41
gerunds, R41
glittering generalities, R17
glossaries, 57, 77, R55
Glossary of Academic Vocabulary, R79
Glossary of Critical Vocabulary, R80–R81
Glossary of Literary and Informational Terms, R59–R77
good vs. *well*, R37
grammar
  capitalization, 160, R28–R29
  handbook, R30–R49
  parts of speech, R23–R24
  punctuation, 78, 160, 372, R26–R28
  sentence parts, R25
  sentences, R25
graphic aids, R66
graphic novels, 107–125
graphic organizers, R66
  charts, 139
  flow charts, 133
  hierarchy diagrams, 167, 314
  semantic maps, 127
  web diagrams, 55, 198
graphics, in informative text, R4
Greek words, R52
group discussions, 198, R12–R13

H

haiku, R66–R67
hasty generalization, R20
headings, 348, R4
helping verbs, R25
heroes, R67
  epic, R64
  tragic, 210, 212, R76
hierarchy diagrams, 314
historical documents, R67

historical fiction, R67
historical text, 295–298
HISTORY®, 39, 137, 309, 319
homonyms, R54
homophones, R54
horror fiction, R67
how-to writing, R67
humor, R67
hyperbole, R67, R77
hyphens, R27

I

I, R29
iamb, R69
iambic pentameter, 211, R60, R67
ideas
  analyzing, 187, 348
  central, 55, 56, 142, 144, 167, 168, 370, R16
  connecting, 46
  development of, analyzing, 142–143, 167
  implied controlling, R67
  linking, in arguments, 150, 378, R3
  main, 55, R68–R69
identifying
  bias, R20
  central idea, 168
  narrative techniques, 197–198
  patterns, 144, 159, 181, 244, 291
idioms, R51, R67
illogical comparisons, R37
illusion/allusion, R57
imagery, 139, R67
images, analyzing, 192
imperative sentences, R38
implied controlling idea, R67
indefinite pronouns, R24, R32, R47–R48
indefinite references, R33
independent clauses, 24, R42–R43
index, R67
indirect objects, R25, R39
inductive conclusion, R62
inductive reasoning, R18, R67
inferences, R67
  about author's purpose, 68, 357
  about character, 10
  about poetry, 159
  about Shakespearean drama, 231, 244, 260, 277
  about text, 22, 36, 82, 106, 187, 208, 371, 375
  about theme, 40, 81, 139, 312
  about word choice, 311
  about word meanings, 127, 134
  making, 21, 81, 106, 139
  supporting, 40, 81, 106, 139, 311
infinitive phrases, R40–R41
infinitives, R40–R41

informal essays, R64
informal tone, 12, R3
informational nonfiction, R67–R68
informational texts, 51–54, 61–66, 129–132, 161–166, 183–186, 341–347
informative essays, 22, 45–48, 83–86, 134, 159, 181, 187, 313–316, 338, R4–R5, R64. *See also* analytical essays
informative presentations, 76, 126, 348
intensive pronouns, R23, R31
Interactive Lessons, 41, 42, 43, 45, 46, 47, 83, 87, 88, 89, 145, 147, 149, 150, 193, 194, 195, 197, 199, 313, 314, 315, 377, 378, 379
interjections, R24
internal conflict, R62
internal rhyme, R73
Internet, R68
Internet documents, citing, R11
interpreting
  media, 14, 294
  poetry, 139, 159, 375
  Shakespearean drama, 231, 277
  symbols, 82, 139
  text, 76, 168, 181, 338, 348, 371
  video, 360
interrogative pronouns, R24, R32
interrogative sentences, R38
interviews, R68
  citing, R11
intransitive verbs, R24
introductions, writing, 46, 84, 314, 378, 379
inverted sentences, 292, R48
irony, 307, R68
  dramatic, 210, R68
  sarcasm, 228, R73
  situational, 35, R67, R68
  use of, 36, 307
  verbal, 307, R68
irregular verbs, R34
italics, R28

J

jargon, R5
journal, R68
juxtaposition, 14, 143

K

key points, 167

L

language
  archaic, 299
  biased, R5, R20
  comparing word choices, 21
  connotative, 55, 311
  denotation and connotation, 37
  domain-specific, 55, 133, 349

verbal irony, 307, R68
verbal phrases, R40–R42
verbals, R40–R42
verb phrases, 140, R39–R40
verbs, R24, R33–R34
　action, R24, R33
　active voice, R35
　auxiliary, R24, R25, R49
　compound, 194
　gerunds, R41
　helping, R25
　intransitive, R24
　irregular, R34
　linking, R24, R33
　main, R24
　participles, R41
　passive voice, R35
　principal parts, R33–R34
　progressive forms, R34–R35
　regular, R33–R34
　subject-verb agreement, R46–R49
　tenses, R34–R35
　transitive, R24
verse dramas, 211
video recordings, citing, R11
visual elements, of film, 142
visualizing, R77
vivid language, R7
vocabulary
　Academic Vocabulary, 2, 41, 45, 50,
　　83, 87, 92, 145, 149, 154, 193,
　　197, 202, 313, 318, 377
　commonly confused words,
　　R57–R58
　Critical Vocabulary, 11, 23, 37, 57,
　　69, 77, 127, 135, 169, 182, 188,
　　209, 299, 308, 339, 349, 358, 372
　domain-specific, 192, 348, 378
　specialized, R54
　strategies for understanding,
　　R50–R57

Vocabulary Strategy
　archaic language, 299
　context clues, 11, 339, R50–R51
　denotation and connotation, 37,
　　358
　domain-specific words, 349
　figurative meanings, 135
　Latin words, 23, 308
　patterns of word changes, 69
　prefixes, 188
　scientific terms, 57
　using reference sources, 77, 169
　verifying word meanings, 127
voice, R77

W

web diagrams, 55, 198
websites, 83, R77
word choice
　analyzing impact of, 21, 35
　evaluating, 168
　inferences about, supporting, 311
　meaning and, 55
　tone and, 12, 21, 55, 311
word families, R52
word meanings
　affixes and root words, 69
　denotation and connotation, 37,
　　358, R53, R62
　determining, 55, 77, 169, 339, 349
　figurative, 55, 75, 135
　inferences about, 127, 134
　technical meanings, 133
　verifying, 127
word origins, R52–R53
workplace documents, R77
works cited, R9, R10, R77
works consulted, R77
writer. See author

writing
　analytical essays, 22, 45–48, 134,
　　159, 181, 313–316, 338
　arguments, 36, 139, 149–152, 291,
　　377–380, R2–R3
　complete sentences, R46
　drafts, 46, 84, 150, 199, 314–315,
　　378–379
　essays, 45–48, 149–152, 313–316,
　　377–380, R2–R7
　informative essays, 22, 45–48,
　　83–86, 134, 159, 181, 187,
　　313–316, 338, R4–R5
　narratives, 197–200, 307, R6–R7
　outlines, for panel discussion, 146
　research reports, 83–86
　short story, 197–200
　speeches, 42, 194
　summaries, 147
　using technology in, 45–48, 83–86,
　　149–152, 197–200, 313–316,
　　377–380
writing activity
　analysis, 22, 68, 134, 159, 181, 231,
　　260, 357
　argument, 139, 291
　comparison, 17, 60, 338
　essay, 22, 134, 159, 181, 187, 338
　letter, 36
　narrative, 307
　personal letter, 371
　research, 187

Index of Titles and Authors

Acknowledgments

Excerpt from "All Together Now" by Barbara Jordan from *Sesame Street Parents Magazine,* September 1994. Text copyright © 1994 by Barbara Jordan. Reprinted by permission of the Sesame Workshop. All Rights Reserved.

"American Burying Beetle" from *Hope for Animals and Their World* by Jane Goodall with Thane Maynard and Gail Hudson. Text copyright © 2009 by Jane Goodall and Thane Maynard. Reprinted by permission of Hachette Publishing, Inc.

Excerpt from "American Flag Stands for Tolerance" by Ronald J. Allen, from *Chicago Tribune*, June 30, 1989. Text copyright © 1989 by Ronald J. Allen. Reprinted by permission of Ronald J. Allen.

Excerpt from *The American Heritage Dictionary of the English Language, Fifth Edition.* Text copyright © 2011 by Houghton Mifflin Harcourt. Adapted and reprinted by permission of Houghton Mifflin Harcourt Publishing Company.

"The Briefcase" by Rebecca Makkai from *The New England Review*, Vol. 29, No. 2, 2008. Text copyright © 2008 by Rebecca Makkai. Reprinted by permission of Rebecca Makkai and Aragi Inc.

"Called Out" from *Small Wonder: Essays* by Barbara Kingsolver. Text copyright © 2002 by Barbara Kingsolver. Reprinted by permission of HarperCollins Publishers and The Frances Goldin Literary Agency.

"Carry" from *The Book of Medicines* by Linda Hogan. Text copyright © 1993 by Linda Hogan. Reprinted by permission of The Permissions Company on behalf of Coffee House Press.

"Cloudy Day" from *Immigrants in Our Own Land* by Jimmy Santiago Baca. Text copyright © 1979 by Jimmy Santiago Baca. Reprinted by permission of New Directions Publishing Corporation.

"Coming to Our Senses" from *Natural History,* March 2001. Text copyright © 2001 by Natural History Magazine, Inc. Reprinted by permission of Natural History Magazine, Inc.

"5 p.m., Tuesday, August 23, 2005" from *Blood Dazzler* by Patricia Smith. Text copyright © 2008 by Patricia Smith. Reprinted by permission of The Permissions Company on behalf of Coffee House Press.

Excerpt from "Letter from Birmingham Jail" by Martin Luther King, Jr. Text copyright © 1963 by Martin Luther King, Jr. Text copyright renewed © 1991 by Coretta Scott King. Reprinted by permission of Writers House on behalf of the Heirs to the Estate of Martin Luther King, Jr.

"Letter to Viceroy, Lord Irwin" from *Famous Letters of Mahatma Gandhi* by Mohandas Gandhi and edited by R.L. Khipple. Text copyright © 1947 by Mohandas Gandhi. Reprinted by permission of Navajivan Trust.

"The Lottery" from *The Lottery and Other Stories* by Shirley Jackson. Text copyright © 1948, 1949 by Shirley Jackson. Text copyright renewed © 1976, 1977 by Laurence Hyman, Barry Hyman, Mrs. Sarah Webster and Mrs. Joanne Schnurer. Reprinted by permission of A.M. Heath & Co. Ltd. and Farrar, Straus & Giroux, LLC.

"The Macbeth Murder Mystery" from *My World and Welcome to It* by James Thurber. Text copyright © 2008 by Rosemary A. Thurber. Originally published in *The New Yorker,* October 2, 1937. Reprinted by permission of Rosemary A. Thurber and The Barbara Hogenson Agency, Inc. All rights reserved.

"Magic Island" by Cathy Song from *Making Waves: An Anthology of Writings By and About Asian American Women* edited by Asian Women United of California. Text copyright © 1989 by Asian Women United of California. Reprinted by permission of Copyright Clearance Center on behalf of Beacon Press.

Excerpt from *The Math Instinct* by Keith Devlin. Text copyright © 2005 by Keith Devlin. Reprinted by permission of Perseus Books.

Excerpt from *The Metamorphosis* by Peter Kuper. Copyright © 2003 by Peter Kuper. Adapted from the classic novel by Franz Kafka. Reprinted by permission of Crown Publishers, a division of Random House, Inc. Any third party use of this material, outside of this publication, is prohibited. Interested parties must apply directly to Random House, Inc. for permission.

Excerpt from "Metamorphosis" from *Metamorphosis and The Trial* by Franz Kafka, translated by David Wyllie. Text copyright © 2007 by David Wyllie. Reprinted by permission of David Wyllie.

"Musée des Beaux Arts" from *Collected Poems of W. H. Auden* by W. H. Auden. Text copyright © 1940, renewed © 1968 by W. H. Auden. Reprinted by permission of Curtis Brown, Ltd. and Random House, Inc. Any third party use of this material, outside of this publication, is prohibited. Interested parties must apply directly to Random House, Inc. for permission.

"My Life as a Bat" from *Good Bones and Simple Murders* by Margaret Atwood. Text copyright © 1983 by O. W. Toad, Ltd. Reprinted by permission of Doubleday, a division of Random House, Inc., McClelland & Stewart, Phoebe Larmore Agency on behalf of Margaret Atwood, and Virago, an imprint of Little, Brown Book Group. Any third party use of this material, outside of this publication, is prohibited. Interested parties must apply directly to Random House, Inc. for permission.

"The Night Face Up" from *End of the Game and Other Stories.* Originally published in Spanish as "La noche boca arriba" by Julio Cortázar, translated by Paul Blackburn. Translation copyright © 1963 by Random House, Inc. Text copyright © by the Heirs of Julio Cortázar. Reprinted by permission of Random House, Inc. and Agencia Literaria Carmen Balcells S.A. Any third party use of this material, outside of this publication, is prohibited. Interested parties must apply directly to Random House, Inc. for permission.

Excerpt from "Presidential Address to the ANC Transvaal Congress, 9/21/53," also known as the "No easy walk to freedom" speech, by Nelson Mandela, quoting Jawaharlal Nehru. Text copyright © 1953 by Nelson Mandela. Reprinted by permission of the Nelson Mandela Foundation.

Excerpt from *Revolution 2.0* by Wael Ghonim. Text copyright © 2012 by Wael Ghonim. Reprinted by permission of Houghton Mifflin Harcourt Publishing Company and HarperCollins Publishers Ltd.

Excerpt from *Simplexity* by Jeffrey Kluger. Text copyright © 2008 by Jeffrey Kluger. Reprinted by permission of Hyperion, an imprint of Buena Vista Books, Inc. All rights reserved.

"We grow accustomed to the Dark" by Emily Dickinson from *The Poems of Emily Dickinson* by Thomas H. Johnson, ed. Text copyright © 1951, 1955, 1979, 1983 by the President and Fellows of Harvard College. Reprinted by permission of Harvard University Press and the Trustees of Amherst College.

"What, of This Goldfish, Would You Wish?" from *Suddenly, A Knock on the Door* by Etgar Keret, translated by Miriam Shlesinger, Sondra Siverstein and Nathan Englander. Text copyright © 2010 by Etgar Keret. Translation text copyright © 2012 by Etgar Keret. Reprinted by permission of Farrar, Straus and Giroux, LLC, Random House Australia and The Random House Group Limited.

Excerpt from "Why Read Shakespeare?: A Real Question and the Search for a Good Answer" by Michael Mack. Text copyright © 2008 by Michael Mack. Reprinted by permission of Michael Mack.

"Without Title" from *Iron Woman* by Diane Glancy. Text copyright © 1990 by Diane Glancy. Reprinted by permission of The Permissions Company on behalf of New Rivers Press.